Experimental Methodology

TENTH EDITION

Larry B. Christensen
University of South Alabama

Boston | New York | San Francisco

Mexico City | Montreal | Toronto | London | Madrid | Munich | Paris

Hong Kong | Singapore | Tokyo | Cape Town | Sydney

Editor-in-Chief: Susan Hartman
Series Editorial Assistant: Therese Felser
Executive Marketing Manager, Psychology: Karen Natale
Production Editor: Won McIntosh
Editorial Production Service: Publishers' Design and Production Services, Inc.
Composition Buyer: Linda Cox
Manufacturing Buyer: JoAnne Sweeney
Electronic Composition: Publishers' Design and Production Services, Inc.
Interior Design: Lisa Devenish
Cover Administrator: Kristina Mose-Libon

For related titles and support materials, visit our online catalog at www.ablongman.com.

Between the time website information is gathered and then published, it is not unusual for some sites to have closed. Also, the transcription of URLs can result in typographical errors. The publisher would appreciate notification where these errors occur so that they may be corrected in subsequent editions.

Library of Congress Cataloging-in-Publication Data

Christensen, Larry B.
    Experimental methodology / Larry B. Christensen.—10th ed. p. cm.
        ISBN 0-205-48473-5 (alk. paper)
        1. Psychology, Experimental—Textbooks. 2. Psychology—Experiments—Textbooks.
    3. Experimental design. I. Title.
    BF181.C48 2006
    150.72'4—dc22

                                                                    2006043234

Printed in the United States of America
10 9 8 7 6 5 4 3 2 1   RRD-VA   10 09 08 07 06

■ Contents

CHAPTER 2   Nonexperimental Research Approaches | 37

CHAPTER 8 Construct and External Validity in Experimental Research | 231

CHAPTER 9 Control Techniques | 261

■ Preface

Over the last three decades that I have been writing this research methods book I have been guided by two underlying goals. The first is to write a book that conveys an understanding of the research methods that psychologists use to obtain information about behavior. In striving to accomplish this goal I have attempted to keep up with current methodological advancements and methodological trends used by psychologists in answering their research questions. For example, since the publication of the last edition of this textbook, psychologists have increasingly made use of the Internet to solicit research participants and to conduct their research studies. This increased use of the Internet is a trend that I think will gain increasing use because of the advantages it affords the researcher. This is just one example of changes in the methodology used by researchers that has been included in this edition of *Experimental Methodology* in an effort to ensure that the content of the book is current.

The second guiding goal that I have used is to present information in a way that is understandable to students. I have attempted to achieve this goal by not only presenting the material in as simple and straightforward a manner as possible, but to illustrate each point and concept with examples, typically taken from the psychological literature. It is my firm belief that the principles of psychological research are most effectively understood when they are placed in the context of actual research studies. In this way students can not only see how the research concept or principle is used but will also see that psychologists make use of these principles when they conduct their research studies.

Overview and Organization of the Textbook

Experimental Methodology is written at the undergraduate level and is intended to be used in the undergraduate research methods course. While the title suggests that the book focuses on the experimental method, this is only partially true. While the primary emphasis of the book is on the experimental approach to research, I fully recognize that psychologists use nonexperimental as well as experimental approaches in the conduct of their studies. I have, therefore, devoted one rather long chapter to nonexperimental research approaches so that students will get an exposure to both types of research approaches. In addition to instructing students in experimental and nonexperimental research approaches, I have also tried to confer to them some appreciation of the nature of this beast we call science. The first chapter of the textbook is devoted to a discussion of science and the nature and characteristics of scientific research. From this discussion students should realize that science is not a stable, unchanging entity, but something that has evolved over the years, although slowly. It is also something that is the subject of philosophical debate.

Following the discussion of the nature of science is a discussion of nonexperimental approaches prior to conducting research. The remainder of the book focuses on the experimental approach to conducting research. This discussion is organized to follow the basic steps involved in the research process with the emphasis on experimental research. The chapters of the book take the student through the process of identifying a research problem and then designing a valid research study that will provide an answer to this research problem. True experimental research designs are discussed as well as quasi-experimental designs and single-case designs to give students knowledge of the various approaches that can be used in designing a research study and to illustrate that in some situations true experimental designs cannot be used. The necessity of conducting ethical human and animal research is emphasized in the ethics chapter. The next chapters of the textbook focus on collection and analysis of the data that will be used to provide an answer to the research problem. The final chapter of the book discusses the communication of the research study in the form of a research report.

Pedagogical Features

In each chapter I have incorporated a number of pedagogical features that are designed to improve the student's comprehension of the material presented. Each chapter begins with a concept map revealing the ideas that will be discussed in the chapter. A vignette, taken from events reported in magazines and newspapers, is presented not only to enhance interest in the material, but also to demonstrate the connection and value that exists between everyday life and good psychological research. This is followed by a chapter preview that identifies the goals of the chapter. Each chapter highlights the important terms and concepts and includes marginal definitions to maximize the probability that students will acquire the appropriate definition of these terms and concepts. Study questions are spaced throughout the chapters to enhance learning and the retention of the material read. Each chapter ends with a summary of the chapter material as well as a list of key concepts and terms and a list of relevant Internet sites that discuss the issues covered in the chapter. A short practice test appears at the end of the chapter that should allow the student to test his or her knowledge of the concepts covered. These are followed by challenge exercises that should give the students concrete exposure to and experience with performing some of the activities required in the conduct of an actual experiment.

In addition to the pedagogical aids in the textbook, there is an Internet companion site maintained by Allyn & Bacon. This Internet site contains a longer practice test, flash cards focusing on the key terms and concepts, a list of related Internet sites, and answers to the study questions in each chapter.

New to the Tenth Edition

Reviewers represent my most important barometer of changes that need to be made and I consider their comments very seriously. In the tenth edition of *Experimental Methodology* I have made a number of these changes. In addition to reviewer comments, there are some changes that need to be made to ensure that the material in the book is current. The changes that were made are as follows:

1. The discussion of science has been expanded and changed to reflect the historical and evolving nature of science, including a discussion of logical positivism, naturalism, and Feyerabend's anarchists theory of science.

2. I have included a discussion of pseudoscience to emphasize the difference between pseudoscience and science.

3. Additional challenge questions have been added in several chapters.

4. The opening vignettes in several chapters have been changed to reflect current events that illustrate and relate to psychological research methods.

5. Some of the related Internet sites have been deleted and new ones added. The deleted sites are ones that no longer exist and the new ones that are added are ones that appear to be ones that may exist for several years.

6. A discussion of Internet experiments has been added as this type of experimentation is being used by an increasing number of psychologists.

7. I have included a discussion of attempts by some legislators to influence science.

8. The discussion of the ethical issues surrounding confidentiality, anonymity, and privacy has been expanded.

9. The ethical issues involved in conducting research over the Internet are discussed in the ethics chapter.

10. Ethical issues involved in the preparation of the research report are discussed in the ethics chapter.

11. I have added a discussion of experimental reliability and experimental validity as well as a discussion of the relationship between reliability and validity.

12. A discussion of obtaining human participants from the Internet has been added as well as collecting data over the Internet and debriefing participants.

13. A section on computing and interpreting correlation coefficients has been added to the hypothesis testing chapter.

14. The errors that existed in the format of the sample research article have been corrected.

Acknowledgments

The tenth edition of *Experimental Methodology* is, as were the previous editions, a product of the excellent input I have received from many colleagues and students. Although I have not been able to incorporate all the suggestions given to me, I can assure everyone that each suggestion was carefully considered and weighted and I thank you for them. Without this continuous high-quality input, the textbook would not be as well received as it is. I encourage both faculty and students to continue to provide me with their candid comments—both positive and negative—as well as with suggestions for alterations and additions of any material I may have omitted. I will take each suggestion seriously and will do my best to include your suggestions in the next edition. You can send your comments to me at the Department of Psychology, University of South Alabama, Mobile, AL 36688, or e-mail me at lchriste@usouthal.edu.

Special thanks go to David Alfano, Community College of Rhode Island; Wendy Heath, Rider University; Constance Jones, California State University, Fresno; and Angelina MacKewn, University of Tennessee, Martin, who have reviewed and provided valuable input to the current edition of *Experimental Methodology*.

Finally, I thank the staff at Allyn & Bacon for their continued support and careful handling of the current edition. Special thanks go to my editor, Susan Hartman, and her assistant Therese Felser.

1

Introduction to Scientific Research

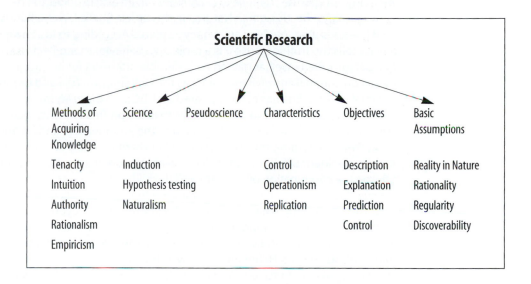

Scientific Research

Methods of Acquiring Knowledge	Science	Pseudoscience	Characteristics	Objectives	Basic Assumptions
Tenacity	Induction		Control	Description	Reality in Nature
Intuition	Hypothesis testing		Operationism	Explanation	Rationality
Authority	Naturalism		Replication	Prediction	Regularity
Rationalism				Control	Discoverability
Empiricism					

On July 5, 1998, the *Los Angeles Daily News* ran an article under the headline "Handwriting Analyst Reads Human Nature." In this article Sheila Lowe, a handwriting analyst for 31 years, stated that "you are what you write." According to Ms. Lowe, handwriting always tells the truth because it is a projective behavior that reflects all the experiences of a person's life. Lowe has gained considerable attention for her comments to the media on criminal and civil trials such as the O. J. Simpson trial and the JonBenet Ramsey murder case. She has even appeared on NBC's *Unsolved Mysteries*. She states that when she analyzes handwriting she tries to focus on small details, such as how Ts are crossed, as well as the larger picture such as the arrangement and balance on the page and whether anything stands out. From a handwriting analysis of individuals such as former president Bill Clinton and Elvis Presley, she drew the following conclusions. "Bill Clinton is a combination of strength and flexibility. He can stand firm and build a consensus." Elvis Presley's handwriting indicated that he was in ill health and depressed.

Is there anything to handwriting analysis? Are you what you write, as claimed by Ms. Lowe? It would be wonderful if we could tell what a person was like just from analyzing a sample of an individual's handwriting. There are, however, many skeptics of handwriting analysis. Handwriting analysis has typically been scorned by scientists as something akin to fortune-telling and palm reading. In spite of this, some individuals and companies are turning to individuals such as Ms. Lowe to assist them in identifying desirable employees and in providing guidance in child rearing. Law enforcement agencies have employed her to assist in background investigations, as have individuals involved in romantic entanglements. Ms. Lowe has even sold a computer program that analyzes handwriting because of the tremendous demand for her services.

There seems to be little question that there is an interest in handwriting analysis by different groups of individuals in areas of the country such as southern California. The important question is whether handwriting analysis really does provide a window into the personality of an individual. Obviously many individuals think it does because they use it in making some very important decisions. But how do we know for sure? In order to determine if handwriting analysis can provide an accurate assessment of the personality of an individual, we must conduct a scientific study. You may wonder how something that seems as subjective as handwriting analysis can be scientifically investigated. Few people understand the nature of a scientific investigation or the need to conduct such an investigation in a situation like this. This lack of understanding may be because scientists are usually conceptualized as people in white coats who work in a laboratory, conducting experiments on complex theories that are far beyond the comprehension of the average individual. Handwriting analysis is something that most people have at least heard of, even if they don't understand how it is done. Actually studying the validity of something like handwriting analysis seems very mysterious. This is probably because the actual process by which scientists uncover the mysteries of the universe totally eludes most people. It is as if the research process were encompassed in a shroud of secrecy and could be revealed only to the scientist. Research, however, is not a mysterious phenomenon. Rather, it is a very logical and rigorous method for attempting to gather facts.

Chapter Preview

In this opening chapter, I introduce you to the way that knowledge is accumulated in psychology. This is a very important chapter because much of what is passed off as psychological knowledge comes from individuals' own convictions and beliefs and is promoted in the media through self-help books, tapes, and weekend workshops. Although the information transmitted in these sources is interesting, it frequently involves telling people what they want to hear or what they can relate to rather than what is correct. In every psychology course we offer, we want to give you the most accurate information possible. This means that the information transmitted in each course must be acquired in an unbiased way. The only way in which this can be done is to conduct good research. In this chapter, I introduce you to the various ways in which knowledge is acquired and show you that scientific research is the most unbiased way of acquiring information. Then I discuss the characteristics and objectives of research as well as the basic assumptions we must make to engage in the research enterprise. I end the chapter with a discussion of some of the characteristics that scientists need to possess.

Introduction

In our daily lives, we continually encounter problems and questions relating to behavior. For example, one person may have a tremendous fear of taking tests. Others may have problems with alcoholism or drug abuse or problems in their marriage. People who encounter such problems typically want to eliminate them, but often lack the knowledge or ability to handle the problems themselves. Consequently, they seek out professionals, such as psychologists, to help them to remediate such difficulties.

Other people may enlist the assistance of professionals in understanding the behavior of others. For example, salespeople differ greatly in their ability to sell merchandise. One car salesperson may be capable of selling twice as many cars as another salesperson can. If the sales manager could discover why such differences in ability exist, he or she might be able to develop either better training programs or more effective criteria for selecting the sales force.

In an attempt to gain information about behavior, people turn to the field of psychology. As you should know by now, a great deal of information about the behavior of organisms has been accumulated. We have knowledge that enables us to treat disorders such as test anxiety. Similarly, we have identified many of the variables influencing persuasion and aggression. Although we know a great deal about behavior, there is still much to be learned. For example, we have an inadequate understanding of childhood autism and of leadership ability. In order to learn more about such behaviors, we must engage in scientific research because this is the only way in which we can fill the gaps in our knowledge. However, the ability to understand and engage in the research process does not come easily; it is definitely not an ability that comes from taking introductory or abnormal psychology. These content courses give little insight into the way in which psychological facts and data are acquired. They state implicitly or explicitly that such facts and data have been acquired from scientific research, but the nature of the scientific research process itself remains elusive.

In order to learn about the scientific research process, one needs more direct instruction. The course in which you are now enrolled is aimed at providing you with information about the way in which the scientific research process is conducted. Some students may object that such a course is not necessary for their education because they have no intention of becoming research psychologists. But, as Table 1.1 reveals, there are a number of very good reasons for all students to take a research methods course. One reason identified in Table 1.1 is to help us become more informed and critical consumers of information. We are all continually bombarded by the results of scientific research, and we need tools to determine which research outcomes are conclusive. For example, saccharin has been demonstrated to cause cancer in laboratory animals, yet there are many people who consume saccharin and do not contract cancer. You as a consumer must be able to resolve these discrepancies in order to decide whether or not you are going to eat foods containing saccharin.

Similarly, television commercials often present what appears to be a scientific test in order to convince us of the superiority of one product over another. Several years ago the manufacturers of Schlitz beer were concerned with the decline in the sales of their product. In an effort to reverse this decline, the company conducted a live "Challenge" on television in which devotees of another brand were challenged to see if they could distinguish their preferred brand from Schlitz. This live demonstration consistently showed that about 50 percent of these beer drinkers chose Schlitz over their preferred brand as the better tasting beer. On the surface, this challenge seems to reveal that Schlitz is an excellent beer because so many people chose it. If you had

TABLE 1.1
Reasons for Taking a Research Methods Course

- Learn how to conduct psychological research
- Provides the foundation for topic specific courses such as abnormal, social cognitive, biopsychology, and developmental psychology
- Can be a more informed and critical consumer of information
- Helps develop critical and analytical thinking
- Provides the information needed to critically read a research article
- Necessary for admission into most graduate programs in psychology

some knowledge of research design and statistics, however, you would be able to see that this contest did not prove anything about the superiority of Schlitz over other beers because the challenge was conducted on live television, in the midst of a lot of noise and commotion. Such distractions would minimize a person's ability to distinguish one beer from another. If there were enough distractions that people could not distinguish one beer from another, they would probably select one beer about the same number of times as the other. This is exactly what happened, because Schlitz and the other brand were *each* picked by about 50 percent of the people. From this example, you can see that an understanding of the scientific research process induces a way of thinking that will enable you to evaluate critically the information with which you are confronted. Given that our society is constantly becoming more complex and we are having to rely more and more on scientific evidence, our ability to evaluate the evidence intelligently becomes increasingly important.

Methods of Acquiring Knowledge

There are many procedures by which we obtain information about a given phenomenon or situation. We acquire a great deal of information from the events we experience as we go through life. Experts also provide us with much information. Helmstadter (1970) has posited that there are at least six approaches to acquiring knowledge, only one of which involves science. In order to enable you to gain an appreciation of the rigor and accuracy that is achieved by science, we will begin by taking a look at the five unscientific approaches to acquiring knowledge and then look at the scientific approach to acquiring knowledge. You should be able to see that each successive approach represents a more acceptable means of acquiring knowledge.

This does not mean that these unscientific approaches have no place in science. Although they do not contribute to the accumulation of scientific knowledge, they are used in the scientific process. When discussing each of these approaches I also discuss how they are used when the scientific approach is implemented.

Tenacity

Tenacity
A method of acquiring knowledge based on superstition or habit

Mere exposure
The development of a positive attitude toward something as a function of increased familiarity with it

The first approach can be labeled **tenacity,** defined in *Webster's Third New International Dictionary* as "the quality or state of holding fast." This approach to acquiring knowledge seems to boil down to the acquisition and persistence of superstitions, because superstitions represent beliefs that are reacted to as if they were fact. Habit, or what might be labeled the principle of longevity, also illustrates tenacity at work. Habit leads us to continue believing something we have always believed.

The principle of longevity can be seen in statements such as "You can't teach an old dog new tricks." In general, the more frequently we are exposed to such statements, the more we tend to believe them. Social psychologists have identified a similar process operating in attitude formation; they call it **mere exposure**. The more we are exposed to something or the more familiar it becomes, the more we like it.

Politicians are very aware of this principle and discuss it in terms of name recognition. When running for office, a politician will plaster his or her name all over town, repeatedly exposing the public to it without ever mentioning campaign issues. This repeated exposure can engender in voters a more positive attitude toward the politician and a belief that he or she is the best candidate for the position.

Although tenacity is a method of acquiring knowledge, it has two problems that diminish its value. First, knowledge that is acquired through mere exposure may be inaccurate. Everyone has heard that old dogs can't learn new tricks, but in fact the elderly can and do learn. They may be more resistant, but they learn. Second, tenacity does not provide a mechanism for correcting erroneous superstitions and habits in the face of evidence to the contrary.

Tenacity does, however, permeate scientific research when a scientist persists in believing in an idea, a hypothesis, or the results of research in the face of criticism from colleagues. Garcia's (1981) research on conditioned taste aversion, for example, was severely criticized initially as being incompetently conducted and was rejected for publication. However, Garcia believed in his ideas and the quality of his research. His tenacity eventually led to the publication of his research and the demonstration of conditioned taste aversion as a robust psychological phenomenon.

Tenacity also operates in science when a favorite theory is maintained in the face of conflicting evidence or in the absence of much scientific evidence. Freud's psychoanalytic theory, for example, is taught in virtually every introductory psychology course. However, there is little scientific evidence supporting such concepts as the superego or the id.

Intuition

Intuition
An approach to acquiring knowledge that is not based on reasoning or inferring

Intuition is the second approach to acquiring knowledge. *Webster's Third New International Dictionary* defines intuition as "the act or process of coming to direct knowledge or certainty without reasoning or inferring." Such psychics as Edgar Cayce seem to have derived their knowledge from intuition. The predictions and descriptions made by psychics are not based on any known reasoning or inferring process; therefore, such knowledge must be intuitive.

The problem with the intuitive approach is that it does not provide a mechanism for separating accurate from inaccurate knowledge. This does not mean that knowledge acquired from psychics is undesirable or inappropriate—only that it is not scientific.

The use of intuition in science is probably seen most readily in the process of forming hypotheses. Although most scientific hypotheses are derived from prior research, some hypotheses arise from hunches. You may, for example, think that women are better at assessing the quality of a relationship than are men. This belief may have been derived from things others told you, your own experience, or any of a variety of other factors. Somehow you put together prior experience and other sources of information to arrive at this belief. If someone asked you why you held this belief, you probably could not identify the relevant factors—you might instead say it was based on your intuition. From a scientific perspective, this intuition could be molded into a hypothesis and tested. A scientific research study could be designed to determine whether women are better at assessing the quality of a relationship than are men.

Authority

Authority
A basis for acceptance of information because it is acquired from a highly respected source

Authority as an approach to acquiring knowledge represents an acceptance of information or facts stated by another because that person is a highly respected source. For example, on July 4, 1936, the Central Committee of the Communist Party of the Soviet Union issued a "Decree Against Pedology" (Woodworth and Sheehan, 1964), which, among other things, outlawed the use of standardized tests in schools. Because no one had the right to question such a decree, the need to eliminate standardized tests had to be accepted as fact. The problem with the authority approach is that the information or facts stated by the authority may be inaccurate.

If the authority approach dictates that we accept whatever is decreed, how can this approach be used in science? In the beginning stages of the research process, when the problem is being identified and the hypothesis is being formed, a scientist may consult someone who is considered "the" authority in the area to assess the probability that the hypothesis is one that is testable and addresses an important research question. Virtually every area of endeavor has a leading proponent who is considered the authority or expert on a given topic. This is the person who has the most information on a given topic.

Although authority plays an integral part in the development of hypotheses, it is not without its problems. A person who is perceived as an authority can be incorrect. For example, Key (1980) has been a major proponent of the claim that advertisers resort to "subliminal advertising" to influence public buying and has been perceived by some as being the authority on this topic. He has stated, for instance, that implicitly sexual associations in advertisements enhance memorability. Fortunately, such claims by authority figures are subject to assessment by research studies. The claims made by Key (1980) are readily testable and were tested by Vokey and Read (1985) in their study of subliminal messages. Vokey and Read demonstrated that Key's claims were unfounded.

Authority is also used in the design stage of a study. If you are unsure of how to design a study to test a specific variable, you may call someone who is considered an authority in the area and get his or her input. Similarly, if you have collected data on a given topic and you are not sure how to interpret the data or how they fit with the other data in the field, you may consult with someone who is considered an authority in the area and obtain input. As you can see, the authority approach is used in research. However, an authority is more of an expert whose facts and information are subject to testing using the scientific process.

Rationalism

Rationalism
The acquisition of knowledge through reasoning

A fourth approach to gaining knowledge is **rationalism**. This approach uses reasoning to arrive at knowledge and assumes that valid knowledge is acquired if the correct reasoning process is used. During the sixteenth century, rationalism was assumed to be the dominant mode by which one could arrive at truth. In fact, it was believed that knowledge derived from reason was just as valid as, and often superior to, knowledge gained from observation. The following anecdote represents an extreme example of the rationalistic approach to acquiring knowledge.

In the year of our Lord 1432, there arose a grievous quarrel among the brethren over the number of teeth in the mouth of a horse. For thirteen days the disputation raged without ceasing. All the ancient books and chronicles were fetched out, and wonderful and ponderous erudition, such as was never before heard of in this region, was made manifest. At the beginning of the fourteenth day, a youthful friar of goodly bearing asked his learned superiors for permission to add a word, and straightway, to the wonderment of the disputants, whose deep wisdom he sore vexed, he beseeched them to unbend in a manner coarse and unheard-of, and to look in the open mouth of a horse and find answer to their questionings. At this, their dignity being grievously hurt, they waxed exceedingly wroth; and joining in a mighty uproar, they flew upon him and smote his hip and thigh, and cast him out forthwith. For, said they, surely Satan hath tempted this bold neophyte to declare unholy and unheard-of ways of finding truth contrary to all the teachings of the fathers. After many days of grievous strife the dove of peace sat on the assembly, and they as one man, declaring the problem to be an everlasting mystery because of the grievous dearth of historical and theological evidence thereof, so ordered the same writ down. (Francis Bacon, quoted in Mees, 1934, p. 17)

This quotation should clearly illustrate the danger of relying solely on rationalism for acquiring knowledge. Rationalism, or reasoning, does not necessarily reflect reality and frequently does not provide accurate information. For example, it is not unusual for two well-meaning and honest individuals to use rationalism to reach different conclusions. Undoubtedly both conclusions are not correct—possibly neither is correct.

This does not mean that science does not use reasoning or rationalism. In fact, reasoning is a vital element in the scientific process, but the two are not synonymous. Scientists make use of the reasoning process not only to derive hypotheses but also to identify the manner in which these hypotheses are to be tested.

Empiricism

Empiricism
The acquisition of knowledge through experience

The fifth and final unscientific approach to gaining knowledge is through **empiricism**. This approach says, "If I have experienced something, then it is valid and true." Therefore, any facts that concur with experience are accepted, and those that do not are rejected. This is exactly the approach that was used by the members of religious groups who stated that satanic messages were included on some records. These individuals had played the records backwards and had heard messages such as "Oh Satan, move in our voices." Because these individuals had actually listened to the records and heard the messages, this information seemed to be irrefutable.

Although this approach is very appealing and has much to recommend it, several dangers exist if it is used alone. Our perceptions are affected by a number of variables. Research has demonstrated that such variables as past experiences and our motivations at the time of perceiving can drastically alter what we see. Research has also revealed that our memory for events does not remain constant. Not only do we tend to forget things, but at times an actual distortion of memory may take place. Stratton's classic experiment on the inversion of the retinal image epitomizes the alteration that can take place in our experience of the world. Stratton (1897) designed a set of lenses, or glasses, that would turn the world upside down. Anyone who put on the glasses saw objects on the left when they were really on the right, and vice versa. Likewise, objects that were above the observer appeared to be below. Consequently, once a person put on the glasses, the world appeared totally opposite to reality. When Stratton first put these glasses on, his movements were very confused and uncoordinated because objects were not as they appeared. He had to remind himself that if he saw something on his right it was really on his left. He had to use a trial-and-error process whenever he reached for something. After about three days, however, something astonishing happened. His movements became more skilled, and his confusion began to disappear. By the eighth day, the world no longer appeared upside down. Rather, the world appeared normal, and objects that were actually above him now appeared to be above him. Similarly, objects on the right appeared on the right and objects on the left appeared on the left. Somehow, the brain had compensated for the distortion produced by the glasses. After eight days of wearing the glasses, Stratton took them off. Up to now, Stratton's brain had been compensating for the distortion produced by the glasses, a distortion that no longer existed once he took the glasses off. But his brain was still compensating, so the world again appeared reversed. It took about another eight days for his brain to compensate for the absence of the distortion previously produced by the glasses and for him once again to see the world right side up. This experiment dramatically illustrates that the things we see are not necessarily true.

Empiricism is probably the most obvious approach that is used in science. Science is based on observation, and empiricism refers to the observation of a given phenomenon. The scientific studies investigating the satanic messages that supposedly existed when certain records were played backwards made use of the same empirical observations as did the unscientific approach. Greenwald (mentioned in Vokey & Read, 1985), for example, played records backwards and asked people to hear for themselves the satanic messages that appeared on the records. In doing so, Greenwald relied on empiricism to convince the listeners that satanic messages were actually on the records. Scientific studies such as those conducted by Vokey and Read (1985) and Thorne and Himelstein (1984) make use of the same type of data. These studies also ask people to identify what they hear on records played backwards. The difference is the degree of objectivity that is imposed on the observation. Greenwald proposed to the listeners that the source of the messages was Satan or an evil-minded producer, thereby generating an expectation of the type of message that might exist on the records. In science, researchers avoid setting up such an expectation unless the purpose of the study is to test such an expectation. Vokey and Read (1985), for example, used religious material as well as a meaningless passage and asked subjects to try to identify messages. These research participants were not, however, informed of the probable source of the message. Interestingly, Vokey and Read discovered that messages were identified in both meaningless and religious passages played backwards and subjects found that some of these messages had satanic suggestions.

Empiricism is a vital element in science, but in science empiricism refers to the collection of unbiased data, not to personal experience of an event.

STUDY QUESTION 1.1 | **Explain each of the nonscientific approaches to acquiring knowledge and how these methods are used in science.**

Science

The word *science* has its origins in the Latin verb scire, meaning "to know." You have just seen that there are many ways of "knowing"—tenacity, intuition, authority, and empiricism. These are, however, nonscientific ways of knowing or acquiring knowledge. **Science** is just another way of acquiring knowledge. However, scientific knowledge seems to somehow be better than knowledge acquired in a nonscientific way. There is the general belief that there is something special about the knowledge acquired through science and its methods. To claim that information is based on science conveys some kind of special merit or special kind of reliability. This is because scientific knowledge tends to be devoid of personal beliefs, perceptions, biases, values, attitudes, and emotions. This is accomplished by empirically testing ideas and beliefs according to specific testing procedures that are open to public inspection. The knowledge attained is dependable because it is based on objectively observed evidence.

One might think that there is only one method by which scientific knowledge is acquired. While this is a logical thought, Proctor and Capaldi (2001) have pointed out that different scientific methods have been popular at different points in time. The different scientific methods include induction, hypothesis testing, and naturalism.

Science
A way of acquiring knowledge that is not tied to one universal method that is invariant across time

Induction

Induction is a reasoning process that involves going from the specific to the general. For example, if you see a child hitting and kicking other children you may infer that the child is aggressive or angry. This inference of the general state of aggression or anger from the observation of the specific instances of hitting and kicking involves inductive reasoning because you are taking the specific observations and inferring a general state. Induction was the scientific method used from the late seventeenth century to about the middle of the nineteenth century (Proctor & Capaldi, 2001). It was during this time that scientific advances were made by careful observation of phenomena with the intent to arrive at correct generalizations. Both Francis Bacon and Isaac Newton advocated this approach. Newton, for example, has stated that "principles deduced from phenomena and made general by induction, *represent* (italics mine) the highest evidence that a proposition can have . . ." (Thayer, 1953, p. 6).

While induction is not the primary scientific method used today, it is still used in science. For example, Latané (1981) observed that people do not exert as much effort in a group as they do when working alone and inferred that this represented the construct of social loafing. When Latané made this generalization of social loafing from the specific observation that less effort was expended in a group, he was engaged in inductive reasoning. Inductive reasoning is, therefore, an integral part of science. It is not, however, the only reasoning process used in science. Deductive reasoning is also used in science.

Deductive reasoning refers to going from the general to the specific. For example, Levine (2000) predicted that a person who views the group's task as important and does not expect others to contribute adequately to the group's performance will work harder. Here Levine was going from the general proposition of social loafing and

Induction
A reasoning process that involves going from the specific to the general

Deductive reasoning
A reasoning process that involves going from the general to the specific

deducing a specific set of events that would reduce social loafing. Specifically, Levine deduced that viewing the group's task as important and not expecting others to contribute adequately would cause a person to work harder or counter the social loafing effect.

Science, therefore, makes use of both inductive and deductive thinking. However, neither of these approaches represents the only or primary approach to science.

Hypothesis Testing

Hypothesis testing

The process of testing a predicted relationship or hypothesis by making observations and then comparing the observed facts with the hypothesis or predicted relationship

Hypothesis testing refers to a process by which an investigator formulates a hypothesis to explain some phenomenon that has been observed and then compares the hypothesis with the facts. Around 1850, induction was considered to be inadequate for the task of creating good scientific theories. Scientists and philosophers suggested hypothesis testing should be added to induction as the appropriate scientific method (Proctor & Capaldi, 2001). According to Whewell (1967), "The process of scientific discovery is cautious and rigorous, not by abstaining from hypothesis, but by rigorously comparing hypothesis with facts, and by resolutely rejecting all which the comparison does not confirm" (p. 468). According to this approach, scientific activity involves the testing of hypotheses derived from theory or experience. Whewell (1967) suggested that science should focus on the confirmation of predictions derived from theory and experience.

While individuals such as Proctor and Capaldi (2001) state that the era of hypothesis testing extended to about 1960, hypothesis testing has been, and still is, an important component of scientific activity in psychology. For example, Fuller, Luck, McMahon and Gold (2005) investigated cognitive impairments in schizophrenic patients. They hypothesized that schizophrenics working memory representation would be abnormally fragile, making them prone to being disrupted by distracting stimuli. They then designed a study to collect data that would test the validity of this hypothesis.

Hypothesis testing as a scientific methodology has been associated with a logical positivist position. This connection between hypothesis testing and logical positivism was the outgrowth of a group of scholars at the University of Vienna with a scientific background and a philosophical bent. This group became known as the Vienna Circle and espoused a logical positivism philosophical position (Miller, 1999). One of the central views of the Vienna Circle was that a statement is meaningful only when it is verifiable by observation. The philosophical approach of this group of scientists/philosophers came to be known as **logical positivism**. Logical positivists, therefore, believed that an important aspect of science was the confirmation of hypotheses by objective observation, or hypothesis testing.

Logical positivism

A philosophical approach that advocated hypothesis testing as an important method of science

Hypothesis testing is an inductive approach to science because it advocates taking a very specific observation and using that observation to confirm some more general hypothesis. An example of this would be hypothesizing that one engages in social loafing or expends less effort when working in a group than when working individually. If you then observed that several people did in fact expend less effort when working in a group you would take this as evidence confirming the hypothesized social loafing theory.

While logical positivism had it supporters, it was also criticized. One of the most severe critics was Karl Popper. Popper (1968) argued that the truth of any theory can never be completely verified and that science should be oriented toward attempting to falsify hypotheses. **Falsification** is a deductive approach to science because the focus of attention is on the hypothesis that is derived from a theory and whether this hypothesis is confirmed or refuted. Although Popper advocated a falsification approach to science, the inductive approach of hypothesis testing has dominated.

Naturalism

Since the 1960s we have entered a methodological era in science that has evolved from a movement in the philosophy of science called naturalism (Callebaut, 1993; Proctor and Capaldi, 2001). **Naturalism** takes the position that science should be studied and evaluated empirically in the same way as any of the specific sciences, such as chemistry or psychology. The issue of the methodology of science should evolve from this study of science. This position advocates that we will have a more adequate account of science if we attempt to understand the theoretical framework in which scientific activity takes place. If you look at the history of science, you can see that scientific advances exhibit a structure that is not captured by hypothesis testing or induction. Since about 1960 several different scientific theoretical frameworks has been suggested.

Kuhn and Paradigms   Kuhn (1962) conducted a historical analysis of science and concluded that science reflects two types of activities, normal science and revolutionary science. **Normal science**, according to Kuhn, is governed by a single paradigm, or a set of concepts, values, perceptions, and practices shared by a community that forms a particular view of reality. A **paradigm**, therefore, is a framework of thought or beliefs by which you interpret reality. **Revolutionary science** occurs when one paradigm is replaced by another paradigm. Replacement of one paradigm with another is, therefore, a significant event because the belief system that governs the view of reality is changed. This time is characterized by a brief period of chaos because the fundamental beliefs that previously supported science are jettisoned and replaced by a new set of beliefs.

Lakatos and Research Programs   Lakatos (1970) took an approach similar to that of Kuhn by attempting to portray scientific activity as taking place within a framework. Kuhn labeled this framework a paradigm whereas Lakatos coined the phrase "**research program**" to represent this framework. According to Lakatos, a research program involves a succession of theories that are linked by a set of fundamental principles. These fundamental principles represent the defining characteristics of a research program. For example, one of the fundamental principles of the Copernican program was that the earth and the planets orbit a stationary sun.

Falsification
A deductive approach to science that focuses on whether a hypothesis is falsified or confirmed

Naturalism
A philosophical position stating that science should be studied and empirically evaluated in the same way as any specific scientific field

Normal science
A period in which scientific activity that is governed and directed by a single paradigm

Paradigm
A framework of thought or beliefs by which reality is interpreted

Revolutionary science
A period in which scientific activity is characterized by the replacement of one paradigm with another

Research program
A succession of theories that are linked by a set of fundamental principles that represent the defining characteristics of the research program

One of the developments within the field of psychology of learning provides an example of what Kuhn would have called paradigms or Lakatos would have called a research program. In the early 1930s a "mechanistic" paradigm or research program had developed in the psychology of learning. The basic set of concepts and beliefs or the fundamental principles of this mechanistic view was that learning is achieved through the conditioning and extinction of specific stimulus-response pairs. The organism is reactive in that learning occurs as a result of the application of an external force known as a reinforcer.

A competing paradigm that existed at this time was an "organismic" paradigm or research program. The basic set of concepts and beliefs or the fundamental principles of the organismic view was that learning is achieved through the testing of rules or hypotheses and that the organism is reactive. Change or learning occurs by some internal transformation such as would be advocated by Gestalt theory, information processing or cognitive psychology (Gholson and Barker, 1985). Piaget's theory of child development would represent an example of the organismic view. Other paradigms, research programs or research traditions (Laudan, 1977) in psychology include associationism, behaviorism, and cognitive psychology.

Feyerabend's Anarchists Theory of Science   Feyerabend was a philosopher of science who looked at the various methodological approaches to science that had been advocated and was not surprised to see that each had been criticized and was lacking in one or more areas. For example, the hypothesis testing approach advocated by the logical positivists floundered because the facts upon which hypotheses are tested are not as straightforward and free of error as appears on the surface. This is a point that will be discussed in detail later. Falsificationism does not fare much better because it is difficult to identify the cause of the faulty prediction. Is it because the theory is false or because some component of the experiment was faulty that led to the faulty observation? Kuhn and Lakatos attempted to solve these problems by focusing on the theoretical framework in which scientists work. However, Kuhn's paradigm approach did not provide a mechanism by which a change from one paradigm to another would occur. Lakatos tried to avoid this trap, but in doing so, his criterion for characterizing science was so lax that just about anything could be included as science (Chalmers, 1999).

As a result of these failures to identify the distinguishing characteristic of science, Feyerabend (1975) argued that there is no such thing as the method of science. According to him, science does not possess features that result in the production of knowledge that is superior to other forms of knowledge. Feyerabend took the position that the single unchanging principle of scientific method is that "anything goes." He felt that the high regard we have for science is dangerous and can play a repressive role similar to that portrayed by Christianity in the seventeenth century. Feyerabend placed a high value on individual freedom and believed that by removing the scientist from methodological constraints increased their freedom to choose between science and other forms of knowledge. When we adopt this free society approach, science will not be given preference over other forms of knowledge.

What Is Science?

So just what is science? To state that there is a universal, ahistorical method of science that can be applied to all sciences regardless of whether the field is physics, psychology, or creation science seems to be ridiculous. The idea that there is a universal and ahistorical method seems to be highly implausible. Science just does not seem to run according to a set of fixed and universal rules and to attempt to do so would seem to be detrimental to science because it would neglect the complex character of science and make it less adaptable and more dogmatic. There just does not seem to be a specific method that is capable of directing the development of scientific knowledge of all kinds in the past, present, and future. Given this situation, Feyerabend seems to have a legitimate case against method if method is understood as universal, unchanging method. However, a case against method does not mean that there is no method. Rather, as Chalmers (1999) has pointed out, there are methods and standards in science that can vary from science to science and can, within a science, be changed—and changed for the better. Science, therefore, is not a single universal method that is applied in all fields of study. Rather, at a specific stage in the development of a field, "a science will consist of some specific aims to arrive at knowledge of some specific kind, methods for arriving at those aims together with the standards for judging the extent to which they have been met, and specific facts and theories that represent the current state of play as far as the realization of the aim is concerned" (Chalmers, 1999, p. 168).

If there is no universal scientific method, but a variety of methods and standards that can vary from science to science, where does that leave us with regard to scientific knowledge? Current philosophers of science seek a relatively secure basis for science in experimentation or what Robert Ackermann (1989) calls "the new experimentalism." According to this approach, experimentation can have a life of its own independent of theory, and scientific progress is seen as the steady buildup of experimental knowledge (Chalmers, 1999) or knowledge acquired from experimentation. The experimental evidence is valid only if it is free from error. Earlier in this section I stated that knowledge acquired from scientific research tends to be devoid of personal beliefs, perceptions, biases, values, attitudes, and emotions. It is this attempt to make observations that are absent of opinion, bias, and prejudice that makes scientific knowledge, or knowledge acquired from experimentation, error free. Therefore, according to at least some current philosophers of science, scientific knowledge is knowledge derived from experiments that are free from error and not bound to any theoretical assumptions. It is this type of experimentation that is the focus of attention in this textbook.

STUDY QUESTION 1.2

- **What is science and how have the methods of science changed over time?**
- **What is the difference between induction and deduction?**
- **What is naturalism as an approach to science?**
- **What are the similarities between Kuhn's and Lakatos's approach to science?**
- **Why has Feyerabend argued that there is no such thing as a method of science?**
- **How do we, at the present time, acquire scientific knowledge?**

Pseudoscience

I have just talked about science and pointed out that it is one of the ways of acquiring knowledge. Scientific knowledge has a special status because this type of knowledge conveys a degree of reliability and validity that supersedes other ways of acquiring knowledge. Pseudoscience also refers to a body of knowledge. However, pseudoscience represents knowledge that purports to be scientific or supported by science but is based on methods that violate the basic assumptions of science. **Pseudoscience**, therefore, represents a body of knowledge that masquerades as science in an attempt to gain legitimacy.

In the recent past there has been an increase in pseudoscientific practices or beliefs. Just look at Table 1.2 and you can see that in the twenty-two years from 1976 to 1998 there has been a substantial increase in the percentage of people who believe in a variety of nonscientific practices such as astrology (Shermer, 1999). During this same time period a relatively large number of pseudoscientific or otherwise questionable areas of psychology have made their appearance or flourished (Lilienfeld, Lohr, & Morier, 2001). These include phenomena such as extrasensory perception (ESP), biorhythms, subliminal self-help, and suggestive therapeutic techniques such as hypnosis and guided imagery for recovering purported memories of child abuse and alien abductions.

Why should we be concerned with pseudoscientific beliefs? Why not just let anyone who wants to believe in pseudoscientific claims continue to believe in them? Perhaps the biggest problem with accepting pseudoscientific claims is that it can contribute to the uncritical acceptance of unsubstantiated assertions both within and outside the field of psychology. Within the field of psychology a number of largely unvalidated treatments for trauma, such as thought field therapy (Lilienfeld, 1998), have appeared. There is a burgeoning industry of self-help books for just about any type of psychological disorder. Similarly, there have been assertions outside the field of psychology for such things as unidentified flying objects, the Loch Ness monster, or alien visitations. This uncritical acceptance of pseudoscientific beliefs makes individuals

TABLE 1.2
Survey of Beliefs in a Variety of Nonscientific Practices and Bodies of Knowledge

Area	Year 1976	1998	Increase
Spiritualism	12%	52%	40%
Faith healing	10%	45%	35%
Astrology	17%	37%	20%
UFOs	24%	30%	6%
Reincarnation	9%	25%	16%
Fortune telling	4%	14%	10%

vulnerable to inadequately validated treatments. It also contributes to an inability to critically evaluate scientific assertions such as global warming.

Just what makes some beliefs scientific and others pseudoscientific? The difference between scientific and pseudoscientific beliefs is one of degree rather than kind. There is no absolute and clear separation of scientific from pseudoscientific claims. Although the boundary between scientific and pseudoscientific beliefs is not clear-cut, this does not mean that a distinction does not exist between the two. Lilienfeld, Lynn, and Lohr (2003) have identified a number of indicators or warning signs that indicate that a discipline or field is crossing the dividing line between science and pseudoscience.

Overuse of ad hoc Hypotheses to Escape Refutation

Pseudosciences are characterized by making statements that can never be falsified. They do this by the use of ad hoc hypotheses to explain away negative findings or findings that go against core beliefs. For example, consider a supposedly novel treatment, eye movement desensitization and reprocessing therapy (EMDR; Shapiro, 1995), for psychological trauma. This therapy requires a person who has experienced trauma to imagine the trauma and the physical sensations associated with it. While maintaining an image of the trauma, the therapist has the client visually track the therapist's finger as it moves from one side of the client's visual field to the other side. At the same time the client is asked to express any negative thoughts about the trauma experienced and to create more positive thoughts about the trauma. This is referred to as "reprocessing," which is added to the desensitization that accompanies imaging the trauma. Healing is supposed to occur after the eye movements and other features of the clinical protocol unlock the pathological condition.

This therapeutic technique is supposedly in use by many clinicians and the EMDR Institute is said to have trained over 30,000 mental health clinicians (Lilienfeld et al., 2003). Research studies, however, have revealed that the eye movements incorporated into EMDR are not effective and what is effective about the treatment is not new. If EMDR represented a scientifically validated treatment, the proponents would accept the research and admit that the eye movements do nothing and eliminate this part of the treatment. However they do not. Instead, some proponents of EMDR have come up with an ad hoc modification of the treatment stating that eye movements are not necessary for EMDR to be effective. This ad hoc hypothesis states that EMDR is a complex method that combines many different modalities and eye movement is just one (Lilienfeld et al., 2003). However, if eye movements are not necessary, what components are? Without specifying the necessary features of the treatment, a variety of ad hoc hypotheses can be used to explain away disconfirmatory evidence. The use of such ad hoc hypotheses is one indication of a pseudoscientific treatment.

Emphasis on Confirmation Rather Than Refutation

The difference between science and pseudoscience is that science tends to bend over backwards to prove its hypotheses wrong. Pseudoscience, on the other hand, bends over backwards to confirm their beliefs. In an effort to avoid refutation of their beliefs, pseudosciences frequently reinterpret negative findings as support for their claims (Bunge, 1967). For example, individuals who believe in extrasensory perception (ESP) have sometimes taken instances of a failure to demonstrate ESP as evidence of ESP. Something that they call "psi missing" (Lilienfeld et al., 2003).

Absence of Self-Correction

One of the hallmarks of science is that hypotheses can be proven wrong. When they are, science documents the inaccurate hypotheses and drops them from further pursuit. For example, in the 1970s Feingold (1975) formulated the hypothesis that synthetic food additives such as preservatives and food colors were the cause of many cases of hyperactivity. This hypothesis was subjected to several scientific studies to assess the validity of this hypothesis. These studies, reviewed by Kavale and Forness (1983), revealed that the food additive hypothesis was false except, perhaps, for a very small percentage of children. As a result of these studies, the food additive hypothesis has been dropped and there are very few individuals who believe food additives are a primary contributor to hyperactivity.

Pseudoscience does not subject its claims to such rigorous testing. Rather, pseudoscience tends to be characterized by stagnation and a failure to attempt to verify or refute its claims. All one has to do is look at the field of astrology. This is a field that has changed little in the past 2,500 years (Hines, 1988).

Reversed Burden of Proof

The proponents of pseudoscientific claims typically place the onus of proof on critics. For example, someone who believes in facilitated communication for treating infantile autism would mandate that a critic of this treatment prove that it is ineffective. Proponents of unidentified flying objects (UFOs) have insisted that skeptics of UFOs provide an explanation of any report of an unusual event in the sky and demonstrate that these instances are *not* UFOs. Science, on the other hand, seeks to confirm any claims that are made. If the existence of UFOs represented a scientific claim, the person making the claim would strive to prove that such events existed.

Overreliance on Testimonials and Anecdotal Evidence

Pseudoscientific claims rely excessively on testimonials and anecdotal evidence to confirm their assertions. For example, a number of years ago Roger Williams (1959) advocated that nutritional therapy held great promise for the treatment of a variety of disorders such as alcoholism and various mental disorders. In his book *Alcoholism: A Nutritional Approach* (Williams, 1959), Williams presented the following evidence of the power of nutritional therapy. "A woman patient thought her neighbors were conspiring to kill her; she often had imaginary violent encounters with various vicious animals—not only could she see them; she could feel their attacks. Eventually she became unmanageable and paid no attention whatever to conversation or to the doctor's instructions. She was given a nutritional supplement and in forty-eight hours was completely cured of her mental derangement" (p. 78). This represents anecdotal evidence and was used by Williams to support the thesis that nutritional supplements not only can cure mental disease but a nutritional deficiency is the cause of the mental disorder.

Science regards such testimonials, at best, as hypotheses to be studied and either confirmed or refuted. They definitely do not represent confirmatory evidence. Pseudoscience, however, makes use of such testimonials and anecdotes as confirmatory evidence in support of their hypotheses. This does not mean that testimonials and anecdotal evidence are not used and are not useful in science. As Gilovich (1991) has pointed out, testimonials and anecdotal evidence provide necessary evidence for a claim but almost never provide sufficient evidence. For example, if a new drug for depression is effective, you should certainly expect the individuals taking the drug to report an improvement in mood. However, such anecdotal evidence does not provide adequate evidence for the effectiveness of the drug because many other variables, such as a placebo effect, could also have provided the improvement in mood. It is only when the influence of such other variables have been ruled out that science claims that the drug is effective.

Use of Obscurantist Language

Obscurantist language refers to language that seems to have the primary function of confusing instead of clarifying. Much of this language is sprinkled with scientific-sounding terms to try to give the appearance of respectability and scientific rigor to the claim that is being made. For example, Shapiro (1995), in attempting to explain the efficacy of EMDR, stated that ". . . valences of the neural receptors of the respective neuro networks, which separately store various information plateaus and levels of adaptive information, are represented by the letters Z through A. It is hypothesized that the high-valence target network (Z) cannot link up with the more adaptive information, which is stored in networks with a lower valence. That is, the synaptic potential is different for each level of affect held in the various neuro networks. . . . The theory is that when the processing system is catalyzed in EMDR, the valence of the receptors is shifted downward so that they are capable of linking with the receptors of the neuro networks with progressively lower valences . . ." (pp. 317–318).

Absence of "Connectivity" with Other Disciplines

Pseudoscientific claims are often characterized by an absence of any connection to other disciplines. Many pseudoscientific bodies of knowledge construct entirely new theories and paradigms that are essentially void of supporting evidence and do not build on current scientific knowledge. Consider, for example, the fields of astrology, chiropractic medicine, homeopathy, parapsychology, telekinesis, or telepathy. Each of these fields has a body of knowledge with its theories and practices. However, the primary theories and knowledge base is unique to that field. Astrology, for example, assumes that you can predict human behavior from the position of the planets, sun, and moon. This is a theoretical assumption that is totally unique to astrology. Similarly, parapsychology makes the assumption that mental processes can cause certain things to happen such as the transfer of thoughts or the movement of objects, and to perceive things that are beyond the human senses. No other field of psychology makes such an assumption. Also, to assume that mental processes can produce such effects violates almost everything we currently know about physical signals.

STUDY QUESTION 1.3

- **What is pseudoscience?**
- **Why should we be concerned with pseudoscientific beliefs?**
- **What are the characteristics that distinguish pseudoscience from science?**

Advantage of Scientific Research

The scientific method has been contrasted with five other methods of acquiring knowledge, and it has been stated that the scientific method is the preferred method. If you closely scrutinize the six methods of acquiring knowledge, you should be able to see why. Science relies on data obtained through systematic empirical observation. Scientific research specifies that we obtain our observations through a particular systematic logic of inquiry. This logic is established in order to allow us to obtain **objective observations**. In other words, scientific research enables us to make observations that are as independent of opinion, bias, and prejudice as we can make them. Such is not the case with the other five methods. Empiricism, although based on experience, does not provide a means for eliminating the possibility that our experience is biased in some manner. Similarly, rationalism, intuition, authority, and tenacity do not preclude the existence of prejudice. In order for us to uncover the basic laws of behavior, we must acquire data that are devoid of such bias, and the only way we can do so is through the scientific research.

| Objective observation
Observation that is
independent of
opinion or bias

Scientific research is also better than the other methods of attaining knowledge because it enables us to establish the superiority of one belief over another. For example, two people may experience different results from taking a vitamin supplement. One person may suddenly become more energetic, whereas another may feel no difference at all. Based on their experiences, the two people would hold different beliefs regarding the vitamin supplement. Which belief is correct? Or are they both correct? Only through scientific research can we ultimately weed out fact from fiction.

STUDY QUESTION 1.4

Why is scientific knowledge considered to be "better" than knowledge acquired from other methods?

Characteristics of Scientific Research

Science is considered to be superior to other methods of acquiring knowledge because it allows us to obtain knowledge that is free of bias and opinion. In order to produce such objective knowledge, the process must possess certain characteristics that, although necessary to science, are not limited to the realm of science. We now look at the three most important characteristics of scientific research: control, operationalism, and replication.

Control

Perhaps the single most important element in scientific research, *control* refers to eliminating the influence of any extraneous variable that could affect observations. Control is important because it enables scientists to identify the causes of their observations. Experiments are conducted in an attempt to answer certain questions, such as why something happens, what causes some event, or under what conditions an event occurs. In order to provide unambiguous answers to such questions, experimenters must use control. Marx and Hillix (1973, p. 8) present an example of how control is necessary in answering a practical question.

> A farmer with both hounds and chickens might find that at least one of his four dogs is sucking eggs. If it were impractical to keep his dogs locked away from the chicken house permanently, he would want to find the culprit so that it could be sold to a friend who has no chickens, or to an enemy who does. The experiment could be run in just two nights by locking up one pair of hounds the first night and observing whether eggs were broken; if so, one additional dog would be locked up the second night, and the results observed. If none were broken, the two dogs originally released would be locked up with one of the others, and the results observed. Whatever the outcome, the guilty dog would be isolated. A careful farmer would, of course, check negative results by giving the guilty party a positive opportunity to demonstrate his presumed skill, and he would check positive results by making sure that only one dog was an egg sucker.[1]

In this example, the farmer, in the final analysis, controlled for the simultaneous influence of all dogs by releasing only one dog at a time in order to isolate the egg sucker. To answer questions in psychology, we also must eliminate the simultaneous influence of many variables in order to isolate the cause of an effect. Controlled inquiry is an absolutely essential process in scientific research because without it the cause of an effect could not be isolated. The observed effect could be due to any one or a combination of the uncontrolled variables. The following historical example shows the necessity of control in arriving at causative relationships.

In 1938 Norman Maier presented a paper at a meeting of the American Association for the Advancement of Science. In this paper (Maier, 1973), he illustrated a technique for producing abnormal behavior in rats by giving them a discrimination problem that had no solution. Shortly thereafter, other investigators examined the procedure used by Maier and became interested in one of its components. Maier had found that the rats, when confronted with the insoluble problem, normally refused to jump off the testing platform. To induce jumping behavior, experimenters directed

---

[1]From *Systems and Theories in Psychology* by M. H. Marx and W. A. Hillix. Copyright © 1973 by McGraw-Hill, Inc. Used by permission of McGraw-Hill Co.

a blast of hot air at an animal. Shortly thereafter, Morgan and Morgan (1939) duplicated Maier's results by simply exposing rats to the high-pitched tones of the hot air blast that Maier had used to make his rats leave the jumping stand. The significant point made in the Morgan and Morgan study was that conflict and elaborate discrimination training were not necessary to generate the abnormal behavior. This led to a controversy regarding the role of frustration in fixation that lasted for a number of years (Maier, 1949).

The important point for our purposes is that the potential effect of the auditory stimulus was not controlled. Therefore, one could not conclude from Maier's 1938 study that the insoluble discrimination problem produced the abnormal behavior because the noise also could have been the culprit. Exercise of control over such variables is essential.

Operationalism

The principle of operational definition was originally set forth by Bridgman (1927). Bridgman argued that science must be specific and precise and that concepts must be defined by the steps or operations used to measure them. Length, for example, would be defined as nothing more than the set of operations by which it was measured. If length was measured with a ruler or tape measure graded in terms of inches, length would be defined as a specific number of inches. If length was measured with a ruler or tape measure graded in terms of centimeters, length would be defined as a specific number of centimeters. This type of definition came to be known as an **operational definition**.

Operational definition The definition of concepts by the operations used to attain or measure them

Operational definitions were initially embraced by research psychologists because it seemed to provide the desired level of specificity and precision. However, using a strict operational definition of psychological concepts didn't last long because of the limitations it imposed.

One of the early criticisms of operational definitions was that their demands were too strict. If everything had to be defined operationally, one could never begin the investigation of a problem. Critics were concerned that it would be virtually impossible to formulate a problem concerning the functional relationships among events. Instead of stating a relationship between hunger and selective perception, one would have to talk about the relationship between number of hours of food deprivation and inaccurate description of ambiguous stimuli presented tachistoscopically—that is, for very brief time intervals.

Another criticism was that each operational definition completely specified the meaning of the term. Any change in the set of operations would specify a new concept, which would lead to a multiplicity of concepts. Such a notion suggests that there is no overlap among the operations—that, for example, there is no relationship among three different operational measures (responses to a questionnaire, galvanic skin response [GSR] readings, and amount of urination and defecation by rats in an open-field situation) of a concept such as anxiety or that they are not concerned with the same thing. Campbell (1988) has also criticized operational definitions on the grounds that any set of operations will always be incomplete and that there will always be some feature of the construct that is not specified. For example, aggression has been defined in different research studies as honking of horns, hitting a BoBo doll, delivering electric shocks to another, and the force with which a pad is hit. However, none of these behaviors represents a complete definition of aggression.

These criticisms do not mean that **operationalism**, or representing constructs by a specific set of operations, should not be used. Rather, Campbell (1988) encourages the use of operationalism to identify the features used to represent a construct because using these features promotes precision and communication. Consider, for example, the construct of hunger. What is meant by hunger? Stating that hunger refers to being starved is imprecise and can be interpreted differently by different individuals. However, stating that hunger refers to not having eaten for eight hours communicates a clear idea. Now others know what you mean by hunger. Setting down a specific set of operations forces one to identify the specific exemplifications of the construct and minimizes ambiguity.

Now consider a more difficult construct of "good car salesperson." How would you operationalize a good car salesperson or what empirical referents would you use to characterize this construct? As Figure 1.1 reveals, these empirical referents might consist of selling many cars, pointing out a car's good features, helping the customer to find financing, and complimenting the customer on an excellent choice. Once such behaviors have been identified, meaning can be communicated with minimal ambiguity and maximum precision.

Although operationalism is necessary to communicate the way in which a construct is represented in a research study, seldom, if ever, does an operationalization of a construct completely represent the construct being investigated. For example, intelligence could be represented by the score a person makes on an intelligence test. Although this score may be a representation of a person's intelligence, it would be foolish to assume that it was a completely accurate representation. Any test score is a function of many things such as the accuracy of the test, extraneous noises, and whether the test taker has had sufficient rest. Every operation is affected by factors that bear no relation to the construct being measured (Campbell, 1988).

The important point to remember is that there are many different ways of operationally representing a construct and that each operationalization represents only a portion of the construct. The most accurate representation of a construct involves measuring it in several different ways. As more and more measures of the same

Operationalism
Representing contructs by a specific set of operations

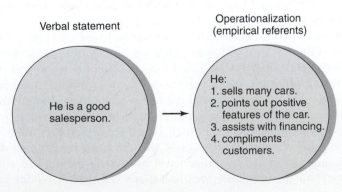

FIGURE 1.1
Example of an operationalization of a good car salesperson.

Verbal statement

He is a good salesperson.

Operationalization (empirical referents)

He:
1. sells many cars.
2. points out positive features of the car.
3. assists with financing.
4. compliments customers.

construct are included, the probability of obtaining a more complete representation of the construct increases. The use of multiple measures of a construct is called **multiple operationalism**. One of the advantages of using several different operationalizations of a construct is that confidence in the result is increased if all operationalizations produce the same result.

Multiple Operationalism
Using multiple measures of a construct

Replication

Replication
The reproduction of the results of a study

A third requirement of scientific research is that the observations made must be replicable. **Replication** refers to the reproduction of the results obtained from a study. In other words, the data obtained in an experiment must be reliable—the same results must be found if the study is repeated. The need for scientific research to have such a requirement is quite obvious because the goal of research is to obtain knowledge about the world. If observations are not repeatable, our descriptions and explanations are unreliable and therefore useless.

Reproducibility of observations can be investigated by making intergroup, intersubject, or intrasubject observations. Intergroup observations involve attempting to duplicate the results on another group of individuals; intersubject observations involve assessing the reliability of observations on other individuals; and intrasubject observations involve attempting to duplicate the results with the same person on different occasions.

Whenever we use one or more of these procedures to obtain evidence of the replicability of our results, we will obtain one of two possible outcomes. We will either replicate or fail to replicate the results of a previous study. If we replicate the results of a previous study, it gives us additional assurance that the results are reliable. Failure to replicate the results of a previous study, however, can be interpreted in several ways, because there are several possible reasons why it might occur. The first and most obvious possibility is that the results of the prior study were due entirely to chance, which means that the phenomenon that was previously identified did not really exist. If the phenomenon did not exist, it obviously cannot be reproduced in a replication study. The second reason that one may not be able to replicate the results of a study is more subtle. The replication experiment might have altered some seemingly nonsignificant element of the experiment, and this element in turn may have produced an altered response on the part of the research participants. For example, Gardner (1978) found that research participant's performance in the presence of environmental noise could be altered by either telling or not telling the participants that they were free to discontinue participation in the study at any time. Most investigators would not consider such a minor alteration to have a significant impact on the individuals. However, psychological experiments can be affected by seemingly minor influences, and thus such apparently minor influences can be the cause of a failure to replicate. Consequently, whenever you conduct a replication experiment, you must remember that the experiment is just that—a replication. Therefore, you must conduct the experiment in exactly the same manner as it was previously performed. Even if you replicate every detail exactly, however, there is one element that in many instances cannot be replicated. That element is the experimenter—unless, of course, you are the one who conducted both the original and the replication experiment. More commonly, however, the replication is conducted by a different experimenter at a different location using different participants. These differences must be taken into consideration when interpreting a failure to replicate.

Although replication is accepted as a characteristic of scientific research, Campbell and Jackson (1979) have pointed out that an inconsistency exists between the acceptance of this characteristic and researchers' behavioral commitment to replication research. Few researchers are conducting replication research, primarily because it is difficult to publish such studies. Also, it seems as though most researchers believe that well-designed and well-controlled studies can be replicated and, therefore, that replication research is not as important as original research. The one exception is in the field of parapsychology, where numerous replication studies are conducted because it is very difficult to attain replication. Lack of commitment to conducting replication studies does not, however, diminish the role of replication as one of the salient characteristics of scientific research. Only through replication can we have any confidence that the results of our studies are valid and reliable.

STUDY QUESTION 1.5 | **List and define the characteristics of scientific research. Then explain why each is a characteristic of the research process.**

Objectives of Scientific Research

Ultimately, the objective of scientific research is to understand the world in which we live. This goal pervades all scientific disciplines, but to say that the objective of scientific research is understanding is rather nebulous. Ordinary people as well as scientists demand understanding. There is, however, a difference between the level of understanding referred to by the scientist and that referred to by the ordinary person. Understanding on the part of the nonscientist usually consists of the ability to provide some explanation, however crude, for the occurrence of a phenomenon. Most people, for example, do not totally understand the operation of the internal combustion engine. Some are satisfied with knowing that it requires turning a key in the ignition switch and simultaneously depressing the accelerator. Others are not satisfied until they acquire additional information. For the ordinary person, understanding—or knowing the reasons—ceases when curiosity rests.

Scientific research demands a detailed examination of a phenomenon. Only when a phenomenon is accurately described and explained—and therefore predictable and in most cases capable of being controlled—will a scientist say that it is understood. Consequently, scientific understanding requires four specific objectives: description, explanation, prediction, and control.

Description

Description
The portrayal of a situation or phenomenon

The first objective, **description**, requires one to portray the phenomenon accurately, to identify the variables that exist, and then to determine the degree to which they exist. For example, Piaget's theory of child development arose from his detailed observations and descriptions of his own child. Any new area of study usually begins with the descriptive process because it identifies the variables that exist. Only after we have some knowledge of which variables exist can we begin to explain why they exist. For example, we would not be able to explain the existence of separation anxiety (an infant's crying and visual searching behavior when the mother departs) if we had not first identified this behavior. Scientific knowledge typically begins with description.

Explanation

Explanation
Determination of the cause of a given phenomenon

The second objective is the **explanation** of the phenomenon, and this requires knowledge of why the phenomenon exists or what causes it. Therefore, we must be able to identify the antecedent conditions that result in the occurrence of the phenomenon. Assume that the behavior connoting separation anxiety existed when an infant was handled by few adults other than its parents and that it did not exist when the infant was handled by and left with many adults other than parents. We would conclude that one of the antecedent conditions of this behavior was frequency of handling by adults other than the parents. Note that frequency was only *one* of the antecedents. Scientists are cautious and conservative individuals, recognizing that most phenomena are multidetermined and that new evidence may necessitate replacing an old explanation with a better one. As the research process proceeds, we acquire more and more knowledge concerning the causes of phenomena. With this increasing knowledge comes the ability to predict and possibly control what happens.

Prediction

Prediction
The ability to anticipate the occurrence of an event

Prediction refers to the ability to anticipate an event prior to its actual occurrence. We can, for example, predict very accurately when an eclipse will occur. Making this kind of accurate prediction requires knowledge of the antecedent conditions that produce such a phenomenon. It requires knowledge of the movement of the moon and Earth and of the fact that Earth, the moon, and the sun must be in a particular relationship for an eclipse to occur. If we knew the combination of variables that resulted in academic success, we could then predict accurately who would succeed academically. To the extent that we cannot accurately predict a phenomenon, we have a gap in our understanding of it.

Control

Control
(1) A comparison group; (2) elimination of the influence of extraneous variables; or (3) manipulation of antecedent conditions to produce a change in behavior

Control refers to the manipulation of the *conditions that determine a phenomenon.* Control, in this sense, means knowledge of the causes or antecedent conditions of a phenomenon. When the antecedent conditions are known, they can be manipulated so as to produce the desired phenomenon. Psychologists, therefore, indirectly influence behavior by directly controlling the variables that, in turn, influence behavior.

Once psychologists understand the conditions that produce a behavior, the behavior can be controlled by either allowing or not allowing the conditions to exist. Consider the hypothesis that frustration leads to aggression. If we knew that this hypothesis were completely correct, we could control aggressive behavior by allowing or not allowing a person to become frustrated. Control, then, refers to the manipulation of conditions that produce a phenomenon, not of the phenomenon itself.

At this point, it seems appropriate to provide some additional insight into the concept of control. So far, control has been discussed in two slightly different ways. In the discussion of the characteristics of scientific research, control was referred to in terms of holding constant or eliminating the influence of extraneous variables in an experiment. In the present discussion, control refers to the antecedent conditions determining a behavior. Boring (1954) noted that the word *control* has three meanings. First, control refers to a check or verification in terms of a comparison. Second, it refers to a restraint—keeping conditions constant or eliminating the influence of extraneous conditions from the experiment. Third, control refers to guidance or direction in the sense of producing an exact change or a specific behavior. The second and third meanings identified by Boring are those used in this book so far. Because all of these meanings will be used at various times, it would be to your advantage to memorize them.

STUDY QUESTION 1.6 **List and define the objectives of research. Then explain why each is an objective of the research process.**

Basic Assumptions Underlying Scientific Research

In order for scientists to have confidence in the capacity of scientific research to achieve a solution to questions and problems, they must accept one basic axiom about the nature of the objects, events, and things with which they work. Scientists must believe that there is uniformity in nature; otherwise, there can be no scientific research. Skinner (1953, p. 13), for example, stated that science is "a search for order, for uniformities, for lawful relations among the events in nature." If there were no uniformity in nature, there could be no understanding, explanation, or knowledge about nature. Without uniformity, we could not develop theories, laws, or facts. Implicit in the assumption of uniformity is the notion of **determinism**—the belief that there are causes, or determinants, of behavior. In our efforts to uncover the uniform laws of behavior, we attempt to identify the variables that are linked together. We construct experiments that attempt to identify the effects produced by given events; in this way, we try to establish the determinants of events. Once we have determined the events that produce a given behavior or set of behaviors, we have uncovered the uniformity of nature.

Determinism
The belief that behavior is caused by specific events

Although a belief in the uniformity of nature is the basic assumption underlying scientific research, several axioms must exist to enable the scientist to uncover the deterministic relationships inherent in this uniformity. These axioms refer to the reality, rationality, regularity, and discoverability of events in nature.

Reality in Nature

One of the assumptions that we all make as we go through our daily lives is that the things we see, hear, feel, and taste are real and have substance. We assume that other

Reality in nature
The assumption that the things we see, hear, feel, and taste are real and have substance

people, objects, or events like marriage or divorce are not just creations of our imagination. This **reality in nature** represents an assumption underlying scientific research. This does not mean that creations of our imagination don't exist. Remember that Stratton (1897) devised a pair of glasses that turned the world upside down. After wearing them for eight days Stratton found that the world had righted itself somehow and no longer appeared upside down. This suggests that regardless of how the world really appears, we want to see it a particular way and our mind will eventually create that image. Scientific Research, however, represents an investigation of the uniformity of nature and not our own perceptions of it. This means that the research process makes the assumption that there is an underlying reality and attempts to uncover this reality.

Rationality

Rationality
The assumption that there is a rational basis for the events that occur in nature and they can be understood through the use of logical thinking

For the scientific study of behavior to be successful, the events that occur in nature must be rational. This means that there must be some rational basis for their existence and that the events must be understood through use of logical thinking. This requirement of **rationality** logically follows from the basic assumption of the uniformity of nature. For uniformity and determinism to exist in nature, there must be some logical and rational basis for the existence of all events. For example, a depressed person's ruminations and negative outlook on life may seem unreasonable and illogical to friends and relatives. However, the scientist studying depression focuses on these negative cognitions (in addition to other events), attempts to understand them through logic and rationality, and derives experiments to verify the logical and rational basis of depression.

Regularity

Regularity
The assumption that events in nature follow the same laws and occur the same way at all times and places

Regularity refers to the fact that events in nature follow the same laws and occur the same way at all times and places. Depressed people, for example, consistently view the world, themselves, and the future very pessimistically. Without this regularity it would be impossible to identify any underlying causes of behavior because a lack of regularity would suggest that there is little uniformity in nature. If there is uniformity in nature, there must be regularity. If regularity exists, then we can conduct studies to identify these regularities and in this way uncover the uniformity of nature.

Discoverability

Discoverability
The assumption that it is possible to discover the uniformities that exist in nature

Scientists believe not only that there is uniformity in nature but also that there is **discoverability**—that is, it is possible to discover this uniformity. This does not mean that the task of discovering the uniformities that exist in nature will be simple. Nature is very reluctant to reveal its secrets. It takes little imagination to provide examples of the difficulty in discovering the relationships that nature holds. Scientists have been working on discovering the cause and cure for cancer for decades. Although significant progress has been made, we still do not know the exact cause of all forms of cancer or the contributors to the development of cancer. Similarly, a complete cure for cancer still does not exist. An intensive effort is also taking place within the scientific community to identify a cure for AIDS. However, scientists have yet to uncover nature's secrets in this arena.

The intensive effort that has existed to uncover the cause of such diseases as cancer and AIDS or, within the field of psychology, such disorders as schizophrenia, depression, or numerous other behavioral aberrations, reveals one of the basic processes of research. The research process is similar to putting a puzzle together. When putting a puzzle together you have all the pieces in front of you and then try to put them together to get the overall picture. Scientific research includes the difficult task of first discovering the pieces of the puzzle. Each study conducted on a given problem has the potential of uncovering a piece of the puzzle. Only when each of these pieces has been discovered is it possible for someone to put them together to enable us to see the total picture. Consequently, discoverability incorporates two components. The first is discovery of the pieces of the puzzle, and the second is putting the pieces together or discovery of the nature of the total picture.

The Role of Theory in Scientific Research

Use of the research process in making objective observations is absolutely essential to the accumulation of a highly reliable set of facts. Accumulating such a body of facts, however, is not sufficient to answer many of the riddles of human nature. For example, research has revealed that individuals who are paid less than someone else for doing the same job get angry and upset. Similarly, couples break up if one of them always demands his or her way. Employees who are paid more than they think is appropriate for a job will tend to work harder and perhaps do more than is absolutely necessary to get the job done. Once facts such as these have been accumulated through the use of the research process, they must somehow be integrated and summarized to provide a more adequate explanation of behavior. This is one of the roles theory plays in the scientific enterprise. Equity theory, for example, summarized and integrated a large portion of the data related to the notion of fairness and justice to provide a more adequate explanation of interpersonal interactions. Theories are not created just to summarize and integrate existing data, however. A good theory must also suggest new hypotheses that are capable of being tested empirically. Consequently, a theory must have the capacity to guide research as well as to summarize the results of previous research. This means that there is a constant interaction between theory and empirical observation, as illustrated in Figure 1.2. From this figure you can see that theory is originally based on empirical observations obtained from research; once the theory has been generated, it must direct future research. The outcome of the future research then feeds back and determines the usefulness of the theory. If the predictions of the theory are confirmed by subsequent research evidence exists that the theory is useful in accounting for a given phenomenon. If the predictions are refuted by subsequent research, the theory has been demonstrated to be inaccurate and must either be revised so as to account for the experimental data or be thrown out.

FIGURE 1.2
Illustration of the relationship between theory and research.

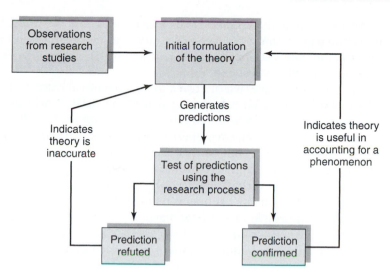

From this discussion you can see that theory generation is a valuable part of the scientific enterprise. Theory is a valued activity within the field of science because it integrates and summarizes facts obtained from research studies and thus allows us to arrive at a more adequate explanation of a given phenomenon. Another reason theory is valued within the scientific enterprise is because it suggests research studies that might otherwise be overlooked.

STUDY QUESTION 1.7

- **List the basic assumptions of scientific research and explain why these assumptions have to exist.**
- **Explain the role theory plays in scientific research.**

The Role of the Scientist in Research

One very significant component in research is the scientist—the individual who employs the scientific approach and who ultimately makes science possible. Is the scientist just any person, or does he or she possess special characteristics? As might be expected, certain characteristics are necessary. A scientist is any individual who rigorously employs the scientific research process in the pursuit of knowledge. Nature's secrets are revealed reluctantly, however. The scientist must actively search and probe nature to uncover orderly relationships, so he or she must be curious, patient, objective, and tolerant of change.

Curiosity

The scientist's goal is the pursuit of knowledge, the uncovering of the laws of nature. Scientists attempt to answer questions: What? When? Why? How? Under what conditions? With what restriction? These questions are the starting point of scientific investigation, and they continue to be asked throughout the study. To ask these questions, the scientist must be inquisitive, must exhibit curiosity, and must never think that the ultimate solution has been reached. If these questions ever cease, then so does the scientific process.

Garcia, for example, was involved in radiobiological research for about a decade. This research convinced him that several of the classical principles of conditioning had some specific limitations. One of these limitations, he felt, was that unconditioned stimuli had a selective effect on what was learned. He then proceeded to demonstrate this limitation (Garcia, 1981). Such an example illustrates that the scientist must maintain an open mind, never becoming rigid in orientation or in method of experimentation. Such rigidity could cause him or her to become blinded and incapable of capitalizing on, or even seeing, unusual events. This relates to Skinner's "fifth unformalized principle of scientific practice . . . serendipity—the art of finding one thing while looking for another" (1956, p. 227). If they weren't inquisitive and open to new and different phenomena, scientists would never make the accidental discoveries that periodically occur.

Patience

The reluctance of nature to reveal secrets is seen in the slow progress made in scientific inquiry. When individuals read or hear of significant advances in some field of scientific inquiry, they marvel at the scientists' ability and think of the excitement and pleasure that must have surrounded the discovery. Although moments of excitement and pleasure do occur, most people do not realize the many months or years of tedious, painstaking work that go into such an achievement. Many failures usually precede a success, so the scientist must be extremely patient and must be satisfied with rewards that are few and far between. Note the many years of effort that have gone into cancer research; many advances have been made, but a cure is still not available.

Objectivity

One of the prerequisites of the research process is objectivity. Ideally, the scientist's personal wishes and attitudes should not affect his or her observations. Realistically, however, perfect objectivity cannot be attained, as scientists are only human. No matter how severe the attempt to eliminate bias, the scientist still has certain desires that may influence the research being conducted. Rosenthal (1966) has repeatedly demonstrated that experimenter expectancies can influence the results of experiments. In addition to expectancies, gender is also a variable that seems to be capable of influencing scientific inquiry.

Idealistically and theoretically, the gender of the scientist should have no bearing on the knowledge base that is acquired from scientific research, because objectivity is one of the prerequisites of good research. Despite this prerequisite training, it is impossible for any scientist to be totally objective. Attitudes, values, and opinions influence observations and interpretations of these observations. In recent years, some female scientists have pointed out that the domination of the field of science by males has created a biased knowledge base. Matlin (1993) and Unger and Crawford (1992) as well as others have pointed out that a gender bias can enter the research process at virtually any stage, from the selection of the research question and formulation of the research design to the communication of the findings.

Change

Scientific investigation necessitates change. The scientist is always devising new methods and new techniques for investigating phenomena. This process typically results in change. When a particular approach to a problem fails, a new approach must be devised, which also necessitates change. When change no longer exists, the scientific process ceases because we then continue to rely on and accept old facts and old ways of doing things. If we are no longer asking questions, we are assuming that we have solved all the problems. Change does not necessitate abandoning all past facts and methods; it merely means the scientist must be critical of the past and constantly alert to facts or techniques that may represent an improvement.

Despite the need for the scientist to accept change as part of the research process, it seems that new ideas are resisted if they do not somehow fit in with current knowledge. Polanyi (1963), for example, relayed his own experience of the reaction to his theory of the absorption (adhesion) of gases on solids following its publication in 1914. He was chastised by Albert Einstein for showing a "total disregard" for what was then known about the structure of matter. Polanyi, however, was later proved to be correct. Garcia (1981) experienced a similar reaction to his research on taste aversion. Some of his manuscripts were returned with caustic and gratuitous personal insults. Garcia noted that in one instance a reviewer stated that his "manuscript would not have been acceptable as a learning paper in [the reviewer's] learning class." However, as Garcia also pointed out, these comments typically surfaced when he and his colleagues sent in their first paper on a given research topic; the next research manuscript they submitted on the same topic, designed to answer the same research question, was typically accepted. Such a phenomenon seems to illustrate that greater familiarity with a point of view increases the probability of its acceptance, as long as the research is conducted competently.

STUDY QUESTION 1.8 | **What are the characteristics a person has to have to be a good scientist, and why are these characteristics necessary?**

Summary

There are at least six different approaches to acquiring knowledge. Five of these approaches—tenacity, intuition, authority, rationalism, and empiricism—are considered to be unscientific. Tenacity, or the state of holding fast, represents knowledge acquired through superstition. Intuition refers to knowledge acquired in the absence of any reasoning or inferring. Authority represents knowledge acquired from a highly respected source of information. Rationalism refers to the acquisition of knowledge through correct reasoning. Empiricism represents the acquisition of knowledge from experience.

The sixth and best approach to acquiring knowledge is science. While scientific knowledge is viewed as the most reliable because it tends to be void of bias, the scientific methods used have changed over time. From the seventeenth century to about the middle of the nineteenth century induction was the primary scientific method in use. From about 1850 to about 1960 hypothesis testing was the primary scientific method in use due to the influence of a philosophical group of scientists/philosophers known as logical positivists. During the time that logical positivism flourished, critics such as Popper existed who argued for a falsification approach to science because the truth of any theory can never be completely verified.

Since 1960 we have entered a methodological era of naturalism that says we should study science and evaluate it empirically. From this position Kuhn stated that science reflects two types of activities, normal science and revolutionary science. Lakatos took a similar approach portraying science as taking place within a framework he called a research program. Feyerabend looked at the various methodological approaches to science and found all to be lacking in one or more areas, so he argued that there is no such thing as a method of science and that scientific knowledge should not be held in greater esteem than any other form of knowledge.

All this suggests that there is not a universal, ahistorical method of science. However, there are methods and standards in science that can vary from science to science and can change for the better. Current philosophers of science state that the secure basis for scientific knowledge lies in experimentation where scientific progress is seen as the steady buildup of experimental knowledge.

Pseudoscience refers to a body of knowledge that masquerades as science in an attempt to gain legitimacy. The recent past has seen an increase in pseudoscientific beliefs and practices. This is a concern because it can lead to the uncritical acceptance of unsubstantiated claims and can make individuals vulnerable to inadequate treatments and the inability to critically evaluate legitimate scientific assertions. While the difference between science and pseudoscience is one of degree, there are indicators of when a claim or practice is crossing over into pseudoscience. These indicators include (1) overuse of ad hoc hypotheses to escape refutation, (2) emphasis on confirmation rather than on refutation, (3) absence of self-correction, (4) reversed burden of proof, (5) overreliance on testimonials and anecdotal evidence, (6) use of obscurantist language, and (7) absence of connectivity with other disciplines.

Scientific research has certain characteristics. *Control* is the most important characteristic because it enables the scientist to identify causation; without control, it would be impossible to identify the cause of a given effect. A second characteristic of scientific research is *operationalism,* which refers to the fact that terms must be defined by the steps or operations used to measure them. Defining terms operationally is necessary to eliminate confusion in meaning and communication. The third characteristic of scientific research is *replication*. The scientific observations that are made must be repeatable. If these characteristics are not satisfied, the results of an investigation are useless because they are not reliable.

Scientific research has certain objectives that it strives to achieve in attempting to reach the ultimate goal of providing us with an understanding of the world in which we live. The first objective is *description,* or portraying an accurate picture of the phenomenon under study. The second objective is *explanation,* or determining why a phenomenon exists or what causes it. The third objective is *prediction,* or the anticipation of an event prior to its occurrence. The fourth and last objective is *control,* in the sense of being able to manipulate the antecedent conditions that determine the occurrence of a given phenomenon. In order to pursue these goals, the scientist must believe that there is uniformity in nature.

Once knowledge has been gained from scientific research, it must somehow be integrated and summarized. This is the role that theory plays in the scientific process. Theory should not only assume the role of integrating and summarizing scientific facts, but also suggest new ideas and additional research studies. Consequently, there is always a constant interaction between theory and the scientific process.

In attempting to gain knowledge from scientific research, the scientist must engage in experimentation. Any individual who rigorously conducts scientific research is a scientist. Nature is reluctant to reveal its secrets, however, so the successful scientist must be curious enough to ask questions and patient enough to gain the answers. The scientist must also be objective so as not to bias the data and must accept change in the form of new techniques and facts. Unfortunately, a gender bias can influence the research process at any stage from formulation of the research question to the interpretation of the data.

Key Terms and Concepts

Tenacity	Research program
Mere exposure	Pseudoscience
Intuition	Objective observation
Authority	Operational definition
Rationalism	Operationalism
Empiricism	Multiple operationalism
Science	Replication
Induction	Description
Deductive reasoning	Explanation
Hypothesis testing	Prediction
Logical positivism	Control
Falsification	Determinism
Naturalism	Reality in nature
Normal science	Rationality
Paradigm	Regularity
Revolutionary science	Discoverability

Related Internet Sites

www.pbs.org/wgbh/aso/databank/humbeh.html
This Internet site gives a short summary of the training and scientific contributions made by eleven scientists who figure very prominently in the history of psychology. This site also gives a brief discussion of a number of discoveries made by scientists from the early 1900s to 1993 that have significantly impacted the field of psychology.

http://quasar.as.utexas.edu/BillInfo/Quack.html
This Internet site discusses a number of flaws that characterize bogus theories.

http://psychology.wadsworth.com/workshops/workshops.html
This Internet site gives a link to a workshop in statistics and research methods. For Chapter 1, go to this Internet site and click on the Web page link corresponding to the workshop titled Research Methods Workshops. Then click on the "What Is Science?" Link.

www.chem1.com/acad/sci/pseudosci.html
This Internet site discusses pseudoscience and how to recognize it.

Practice Test

Five multiple choice questions are included at the end of each chapter to enable you to test your knowledge of the chapter material. If you would like a more extensive assessment of your mastery, you can go to the Allyn and Bacon Web site accompanying this textbook where you will find additional review questions. Prior to taking these sample tests, you should study the chapter. When you think you know the material, take the practice test to get some feedback regarding the extent to which you have mastered the material.

The answers to these questions can be found in Appendix A.

1. Empiricism is a vital element in scientific studies. As an important element in science, empiricism refers to what?
   a. Unbiased observations
   b. A person's personal experience of an event
   c. Mere exposure
   d. The observations and experience of individuals in positions of authority

2. Scientific activities have included
   a. Induction
   b. Hypothesis testing
   c. Paradigms
   d. Research programs
   e. All of the above

3. Professor Albert was conducting an experiment investigating the influence of status on a person's persuasive influence. In this study he manipulated status using dress. A high-status person was dressed in an expensive business suit and carried a briefcase. The low-status person was dressed in faded jeans and torn shirt. The differing dress of the high- and low-status person was used to
   a. Control for the influence of extraneous variables
   b. Operationalize the construct of status

   c. Enable him to replicate the results of his study

   d. Control for the type of dress the participants wore

4. If you conducted a study in which you wanted to determine why help is not given to people who obviously need it, you would have conducted a study with which of the following objectives?

   a. Description

   b. Explanation

   c. Prediction

   d. Control

5. The scientist, in order to have confidence in the scientific research process, must believe in several axioms. Which of the following is *not* one of these axioms?

   a. There is an underlying reality in nature.

   b. There is a rational basis for the existence of nature's events.

   c. The uniformity in nature is not only difficult but probably impossible to discover.

   d. Events follow the same laws and occur in the same way at all times and places.

Challenge Exercises

In addition to the review questions, each chapter ends with challenge exercises. These exercises will encourage you to think about the concepts discussed in the chapter to give you an opportunity to apply what you have learned.

1. Many people have a strong belief in the existence of God and believe that God has a personal influence on their life. You have read that there are at least six different ways of acquiring knowledge. Consider each of these sources of information and explain how each of these sources of information may or may not contribute to a person's belief in the existence of God and/or the personal influence God has on his or her life.

2. Psychology makes use of many concepts when explaining behavior and when conducting research. Consider each of the following concepts and identify a set of operations that will be representative of each concept.

   a. Depression

   b. Aggression

   c. Child abuse

   d. Attitude

   e. Leadership

3. Women have been taking the hormone estrogen for decades to eliminate many of the symptoms of menopause, such as the hot flashes that accompany this stage of life. In the latter half of 2002, the media reported that medical research had found that this hormone replacement therapy increased the risk of uterine cancer. Consider the three characteristics of science and discuss how you might apply them in assessing this reported research.

4. The medical community has repeatedly expressed concern about the fact that the average weight among Americans is increasing. The concern focuses on the health risks of people who are overweight. Think about each of the objectives of science and apply each of these objectives to this concern of the medical community

5. What would happen to the science of psychology if none of the assumptions underlying science existed? What would happen in our daily lives if these assumptions did not exist?

6. Identify an area that would be considered to be pseudoscientific such as astrology, palm reading, on ESP. Find evidence for claims made by these fields and explain why this evidence is pseudoscientific.

7. Are the following fields scientific or pseudoscientific?
   a. Chiropractic medicine
   b. Faith Healing
   c. Homeopathy
   d. Acupuncture
   e. Parapsychology

2 Nonexperimental Research Approaches

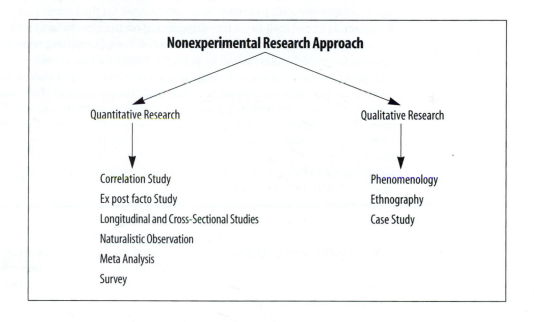

Nonexperimental Research Approach

Quantitative Research

- Correlation Study
- Ex post facto Study
- Longitudinal and Cross-Sectional Studies
- Naturalistic Observation
- Meta Analysis
- Survey

Qualitative Research

- Phenomenology
- Ethnography
- Case Study

On July 7, 2005, Michael Henning, a 39-year-old banker, was reading the morning paper while making his morning commute to work on the London underground transit system. At about 8:50 A.M., a bomb exploded on the train he was riding on, blinding him with a yellow light and throwing him to the floor. Everything went pitch black and Henning felt blood on his face as he at least realized that he was alive. A few seconds later, about two miles away, a second blast occurred as another train with several hundred passengers descended into a 12-foot-wide tunnel deep into the heart of London. The train cars were immediately plunged into darkness and the air was filled with acrid smoke. Breathing became difficult and passengers began to shout, cry, and bang on windows. After ten or fifteen minutes had passed the passengers realized no immediate help was on the way so they slowly climbed out of the train and moved down the dark tunnel into Russell Square Station. As they walked down the tunnel they passed people mutilated from the blast.

In central London, a double-decker bus was diverted away from the second bombing causing the driver to take several detours. One of the passengers on the bus appeared agitated at the detours and kept reaching into his knapsack, fiddling with something. Police suspect that this olive-skinned man was trying to reset the timer on the bomb contained in the knapsack. At 9:47 A.M., nearly an hour after the London tube (subway) bombings, the bus exploded. Metal, glass, and body parts blew up and out of the rear of the bus.

Following the explosions many questions were asked. Why did the bombings occur, who was responsible, what was the motive for blowing up the subway trains and bus, and why would someone do this? The bombings appeared to be timed to coincide with the meeting of the leaders of the world's greatest industrial nations, known as the G8, in an attempt to undermine the conference. But who would commit such a heinous crime and what would be the impact on Londoners and the economy of Britain? British Prime Minister Tony Blair stated that "we are simply not going to be terrorized by terror in this way" (Terror, 2005). Later he said that such terrorist's acts would not change the way of life of the British people. However, such events do have an impact on individuals' lives. While it is impossible to identify all the effects of such events, it is possible to provide a descriptive account of the events and how they have impacted and altered individuals' lives.

Chapter Preview

In this chapter I introduce you to a number of nonexperimental research approaches. The primary function of the nonexperimental research approaches is to provide a descriptive account of events such as the one illustrated by the tragedy of the London bombings discussed in the opening vignette. In this chapter, you will learn that the nonexperimental research approaches can be dichotomized into quantitative and qualitative research approaches. Then I introduce you to the more common quantitative research approaches including correlational, ex post facto, longitudinal and cross-sectional survey, naturalistic observations, and meta analysis studies. From there, I discuss three types of qualitative research approaches: phenomenology, ethnography, and case studies.

Introduction

Experimental research
Research that attempts to identify cause-and-effect relationships

Descriptive research
Research that attempts to describe some phenomenon, event, or situation

Quantitative research study
A research study that collects numerical data

Numerical data
Data that consists of numbers

Qualitative research study
A research study that collects non-numerical data

Non-numerical data
Data that consists of pictures, words, statements, clothing, written records or documents, or a description of behavior

The various approaches to conducting psychological research traditionally have been categorized as experimental or descriptive. This categorization was based on the goals of the various research approaches. **Experimental research** attempts to identify cause-and-effect relationships by conducting controlled psychological experiments. **Descriptive research** focuses on describing some phenomenon, event, or situation. Consequently, the experimental/descriptive dichotomy was a very useful way of presenting the various types of research approaches used in psychology.

More recently, another way of dichotomizing research approaches has appeared in the psychological literature. This approach is the quantitative/qualitative dichotomy, which is a dichotomy that is based on the type of data collected in a study. A **quantitative research study** is one that collects some type of **numerical data** to answer a given research question. For example, a study that collects information such as a person's ratings of attractiveness, the number of times a child hits another child, the number of times a rat presses a bar, or the score a person makes on a personality test is a quantitative study.

A **qualitative research study** is a study that collects some type of **non-numerical** data to answer a research question. Non-numerical data consist of data such as the statements made by a person during an interview, written records, pictures, clothing, or observed behavior. A number of individuals, for example, Creswell (1998) and Patton (1990), feel that research that collects only quantitative data often provides an incomplete analysis or picture of the phenomenon, event, or situation being investigated and that the addition of qualitative data provides an added level of understanding.

To illustrate this point, consider the study (cited in Patton, 1990, pp. 15–19) that evaluated the outcome and effectiveness of a literacy center. This study revealed that the participants in the center's program achieved substantial achievement test gains. However, this study also revealed that there was also a tremendous amount of variation in achievement across the participants, which led to the conclusion that the center did not attract a typical student. Rather, the students come in at very different levels, with very different goals, and make very different gains. To develop an understanding of the meaning of the individual variation and the meaning that the program had for the participants, the investigators collected qualitative data by interviewing the participants.

These interviews, for example, revealed that one participant, a sixty-five-year-old African American grandmother, who had never learned to read, acquired the ability to read. This allowed her to read the Bible, fill out a job application, fill out forms at the doctor's office, and do the little things most of us take for granted. The program allowed another participant to receive her GED and enter college. Before this time, she was always scared that someone would discover that she was not a high school graduate and fire her or would not accept her because she had not graduated. This type of qualitative data added to the quantitative data by providing individual information and meaning that added to the understanding of the value of the program.

The argument that adding qualitative data to psychological studies is beneficial has apparently been very compelling because during the last decade we have witnessed an increase in research that makes use of this type of data. For example, a burgeoning literature has developed in organizational management, social psychology, aging, education, and family studies (Denzin & Lincoln, 1994; Gilgun, Daly, & Handel, 1992; Gubrium & Sankar, 1993; Silverman, 1993) that focuses on the collection and analysis of qualitative data. In this chapter, I discuss several qualitative and nonexperimental quantitative research approaches. The rest of the book focuses on the quantitative experimental research approach because this is the research approach used by most psychologists.

STUDY QUESTION 2.1 | **Distinguish between experimental and descriptive research and between quantitative and qualitative research.**

Nonexperimental Quantitative Research

Nonexperimental quantitative research
A descriptive type of research study that collects quantitative data to describe the variables of interest

The primary characteristic of **nonexperimental quantitative research** is that it is a descriptive type of research in which the goal is to attempt to provide an accurate description or picture of a particular situation or phenomenon. A more advanced and sophisticated use of these approaches does attempt to identify causal relationships. However, the most frequent use of these approaches is to attempt to identify variables that exist in a given situation and, at times, to describe the relationship that exists between these variables. Therefore, the descriptive approach is widely used and is of great importance. We can see the outcome of the descriptive approach whenever the results of Gallup polls or other surveys are reported. Helmstadter (1970, p. 65) has even gone so far as to say that the "descriptive approaches are the most widely used . . . research methods."

When initially investigating a new area, scientists frequently use the nonexperimental descriptive type of quantitative research to identify existing factors and relationships among them. Such knowledge is used to formulate hypotheses to be subjected to experimental investigation. Also, the descriptive method is frequently used to describe the status of a situation once a solution, suggested by experimental analysis, has been put into effect. Here the descriptive approach can provide input regarding the effectiveness of the proposed solution, as well as hypotheses about how a more effective solution could be reached. Thus, the nonexperimental descriptive type of quantitative research is useful in both the initial and the final stages of investigation into an area.

Correlational Study

Correlational study
A study that seeks to describe the degree of relationship that exists between two measured variables

In its simplest form, a **correlational study** consists of measuring two variables and then determining the degree of relationship that exists between them. Consequently, a correlational study can be incorporated into other quantitative research approaches. A relatively old study commonly cited in introductory and developmental texts is the study by Conrad and Jones (1940) of the relationship between the IQ scores of parents and those of their offspring. To accomplish the goals of this study, Conrad and Jones measured the IQs of the parents and correlated them with their children's IQs. In this way, a descriptive index was obtained that accurately and quantitatively portrayed the relationship between these two variables. As you can see, correlational studies do not make any attempt to manipulate the variables of concern, but simply measure them in their natural state.

The correlational approach enables us to accomplish the goal of prediction. If a reliable relationship is found between two variables, we not only have described the relationship between these two variables but also have gained the ability to predict one variable from a knowledge of the other variable. Sears, Whiting, Nowlis, and Sears (1953), for example, found that there is a positive relationship between severity of weaning and later psychological adjustment problems. Knowledge of this relationship enables one to predict a child's psychological adjustment when one knows only the severity with which the child was weaned.

The weakness of the correlational approach is apparent in the Sears et al. study. Given the study's results, some individuals would say that severity of weaning was the agent causing later psychological maladjustment. But, because of the so-called third variable problem, such an inference is not justified. The *third variable problem* refers to the fact that two variables may be correlated not because they are causally related but because some third variable caused both of them. As Figure 2.1 illustrates, the degree of severity with which a child is weaned and that child's later psychological adjustment may both be influenced by the parents' child-rearing skills. If the parents are unskilled, they may both wean their child in a severe manner and inflict verbal or physical abuse, leading the child to become psychologically maladjusted later. If the parents are skilled at child rearing, weaning may take place with little or no trauma and the child may have a healthy relationship with his or her parents, leading to stable psychological adjustment. In such a situation, although a correlation exists between severity of weaning and later psychological adjustment, these variables are not causally related. Rather, both are caused by an underlying third variable: the parents' parenting skills.

To further emphasize the third variable problem, let us look at a correlational study conducted by Orlebeke, Knol, and Verhulst (1999). As you probably know, smoking is bad for your health. Studies have revealed that smoking during pregnancy

FIGURE 2.1
Illustration of the third
variable problem in
correlation.

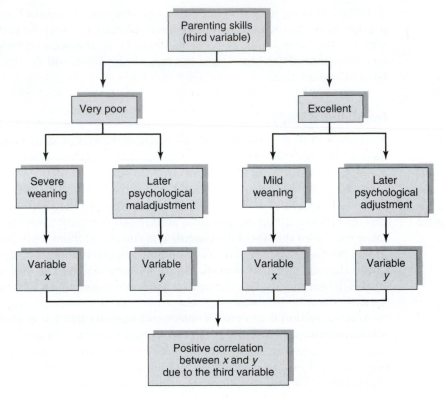

FIGURE 2.1
Illustration of the third
variable problem in
correlation.

affects infant mortality rates and the emotional and intellectual development of the child. Some of this effect is due to the low birth weight of the infant, but other effects are due to maternal smoking. Maternal smoking causes a decrease in blood flow through the placenta to the fetus. It also reduces the intrauterine partial pressure of oxygen and carbon monoxide, which produces a decrease in the oxygen supply to the fetus.

Orlebeke et al. (1999) reasoned that the toxic effects of the constituents of tobacco smoke are also transported to the unborn child. This assumption has been supported by a number of animal studies indicating that brain neurochemicals are altered when the pregnant female ingests nicotine. This alteration in brain neurochemicals has behavioral implications and suggests that children born to mothers who smoke should have an increased incidence of behavior problems. Observations have indeed supported this assumption. Children born to mothers who smoke have more behavior problems, especially hyperactivity, poor language development, and delayed general cognitive development. However, these observations are confounded by the fact that smoking mothers also tend to bottle-feed their children, thus depriving them of some of the "contact comfort" they may derive from being breast fed. Orlebeke et al. (1999) hypothesized that a relationship existed between maternal smoking and problem behavior independent of whether the child was bottle or breast-fed.

To test this hypothesis, Orlebeke et al. (1999) correlated parents' ratings of problem behaviors in their two- to three-year-old children with the extent to which the mother had smoked during pregnancy, controlling for effects such as birth weight and amount of breast-feeding. These investigators found a positive correlation between maternal smoking and a child's problem behavior, particularly in aggressive and over-active behavior. In other words, the more the mother smoked during pregnancy, the greater the degree of problem behavior observed in the child.

Does this prove that maternal smoking causes child behavior problems? Certainly not. It is possible that such a relationship exists. However, such a correlational analysis does not provide evidence of such a causal relationship. All this study did was describe the relationship that existed between the two variables of maternal smoking and child behavior problems, both of which could have been caused by some third variable. For example, there may have been considerable marital stress in the home that contributed to an increase in smoking by the expectant mother and poor parenting by both the mother and father, which in turn led to the behavior problems in the child. There are some rather complex correlational procedures that do give evidence of causation; the two-variable case just discussed does not.

The fallacy of assuming causation is not inherent in the correlational study but is merely a tendency on the part of the people who use the study results. If the purpose of an investigation is to describe the degree of relationship that exists between variables, then this approach is the appropriate one to use.

Ex Post Facto Study

Ex post facto study
A study comparing the effects of two or more variables where the variables being manipulated are not under the experimenter's control

Individual difference variable
A trait, characteristic, or experience on which individuals differ.

An **ex post facto study** is a study in which the variable or variables of interest to the investigator are not subject to direct manipulation but must be chosen after the fact. The variables investigated in an ex post facto study are, therefore, **individual difference variables** or variables on which individuals naturally differ. These variables could be some trait, characteristic, or some experience, as illustrated in Table 2.1. For example, individuals could differ in level of depression, weight, or having experienced an earthquake. When an investigator conducts an ex post facto study, he or she begins with two or more groups of research participants that already differ on

TABLE 2.1
Examples of Individual Difference Variables

Trait	Characteristic	Experience
Intelligence	Height	Death of a love one
Depression	Weight	Earthquake
Extraversion	Ethnic group	Winning the lottery
Submissiveness	Political affiliation	Divorce
Anxiety	Hair color	Hurricane

FIGURE 2.2

Mean depression scores for rape victims and control subjects.

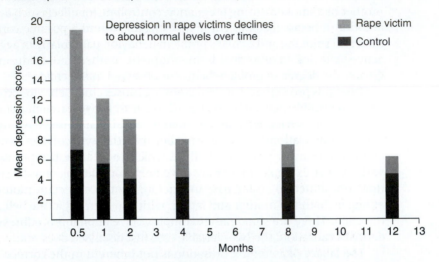

(Based on data from "Victims of Rape: Repeated Assessment of Depressive Symptoms" by B. M. Atkeson, K. S. Calhoun, P. A. Resick, and E. M. Ellis, 1982, *Journal of Consulting and Clinical Psychology, 50,* pp. 96–102.)

one of the individual difference variables and then records their behavior to determine whether they respond differently in a common situation. These and other characteristics of ex post facto research are illustrated by a study by Atkeson, Calhoun, Resick, and Ellis (1982), who investigated the incidence, severity, and duration of the depressive symptoms of rape victims. Using several measures of depression, these researchers compared rape victims over time with a group of females who had not been raped. As Figure 2.2 illustrates, the results show that rape victims initially exhibited quite a bit of depression but that their depression declined to an approximately normal level over time.

If you look at Figure 2.3, you can see that the Atkeson et al. study has the appearance of a field experiment by virtue of the fact that the experience of being raped was varied and then the consequence of having been raped was assessed across time. Consequently, the investigation compared the degree of depression experienced by rape victims with that of control, or nonraped, females. However, the nature of the

FIGURE 2.3

Graphic illustration of the design of the Atkeson et al. (1982) study.

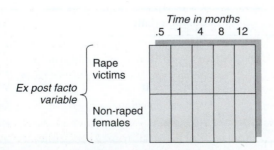

manipulation of the experience of rape determines the ex post facto nature of the study. The experimenters did not have control over who was and who was not raped. Instead, the females came to the study with their prior differential experiences and, therefore, *assigned themselves* to one of the two groups. The variable of interest was out of the experimenter's control, which is the distinguishing characteristic of an ex post facto study. The process of self-selection that determines the ex post facto nature of the research also is responsible for its weakness. Participants who make up the different groups because of some individual difference, characteristic, or experience may also possess other characteristics extraneous to the research problem. It may be one of these other characteristics and not the variable supposedly being manipulated in the study that produced the observed difference. Atkeson et al. recognized this limitation of the study and, instead of concluding that the experience of being raped was the causative factor of the observed differences, discussed the possible contribution of other factors (such as repeated assessment of degree of depression, the participants' knowledge of the fact that they were in a psychological study, the stress on the poorer victims created by living in an area with a high crime rate, and the age of the research participants). As can be seen from this example, ex post facto studies resemble correlational studies in that both types of studies have third variable problems which limits the ability to infer causality. Causality cannot be inferred in correlational studies because the correlation between the two variables may be due to some third variable. Similarly, causation cannot be inferred in ex post facto studies because the difference observed in the behavior of the various groups of participants may be due to some variable other than the one that was varied.

Longitudinal Study and Cross-Sectional Study

Longitudinal and cross-sectional studies investigate changes that take place over time. The approaches used by these two basic techniques are somewhat different, however. The **longitudinal study** involves choosing a single group of participants and measuring them repeatedly at selected time intervals to note changes that occur over time in the specified characteristics. For example, Gathercole and Willis (1992) measured a group of children's phonological memory and their vocabulary knowledge at four, five, six, and eight years of age to determine if the relationship between these two variables changed as the children got older. On the other hand, a **cross-sectional study** identifies representative samples of individuals that differ on some characteristic, such as age, gender, ethnic group, or religion, and measures these different samples of individuals on the same variable or variable often at one point in time. Wagner, Torgesen, Laughon, Simmons, and Rashotte (1993) took this approach in their study of the nature and development of young children's phonological processing abilities. They randomly selected a group of ninety-five kindergarten and eighty-nine second-grade students from three elementary schools and administered a number of phonological tasks to both groups to determine whether phonological processing abilities differ among these two age groups.

Although the longitudinal and cross-sectional research approaches are frequently used in developmental research, this type of study is not confined to this specific area. For example, Moskowitz and Wrubel (2005) took a longitudinal approach to gaining

Longitudinal study
A study that repeatedly measures the same characteristics in a single sample of individuals at selected time intervals

Cross-sectional study
A study that measures the same variable in representative samples of individuals that differ on some characteristics, such as age levels, often at one point in time

a more in depth understanding of the meaning of having contracted HIV. To accomplish the purpose of this study, Moskowitz and Wrubel identified fifty-seven gay men testing positive for HIV and then conducted bimonthly interviews over the course of two years to identify how these individuals appraise their HIV changes over time. Andersen, Franckowiak, Christmas, Walston, and Crespo (2001) took a cross-sectional approach to assess the relationship between not participating in leisure time physical activity and body weight among older U.S. adults. To accomplish the goal of the study these investigators surveyed a national representative cross-section of the U.S. population (e.g., Hispanic Americans, African Americans, Caucasian Americans) of individuals aged sixty and older regarding their weight and participation in leisure time activity.

The longitudinal and cross-sectional approaches to developmental research have frequently been used in the past, and there has been much discussion about the relative advantages and disadvantages of each technique. One significant point is that these two techniques have not always generated similar results. The classic example of this discrepancy in results is in data regarding the development of intelligence during adulthood. As seen in Figure 2.4, cross-sectional studies have suggested that adult intelligence begins to decline around the age of thirty, whereas longitudinal studies show an increase or no change in intellectual performance until the age of fifty or sixty (Baltes, Reese, and Nesselroade, 1977). This difference has been attributed to what is called an *age-cohort effect*. In other words, longitudinal studies follow just one group or cohort of individuals over time, so all individuals within this cohort are experiencing similar environmental events. However, cross-sectional studies investigate a number of different groups of individuals or different cohorts. Because of changes in environmental events, these cohorts have not been exposed to similar experiences. For example, members of a fifty-year-old cohort would not have been

FIGURE 2.4

Change in intellectual performance as a function of the longitudinal versus the cross-sectional method.

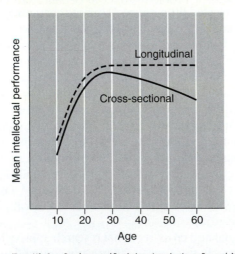

(From *Life-Span Developmental Psychology: Introduction to Research Methods* by P. B. Baltes, W. H. Reese, and J. R. Nesselroade. Copyright © 1977 by Brooks/Cole Publishing Company, Pacific Grove, CA 93950, a division of International Thomson Publishing Inc. By permission of the publisher.)

exposed to video games or computers when they were ten years old, but a group of eleven-year-olds would have. Such differences are confounded with actual age differences in cross-sectional studies.

The longitudinal approach is not subject to the age-cohort effect and is the preferred approach when testing age related effects, although it is more expensive and time consuming to conduct. The major problem with the longitudinal approach is that, due to its longitudinal nature, people die, move, or may decide to withdraw from the study prior to its conclusion. To counteract these difficulties, researchers who use the longitudinal approach must have the resources to travel in order to collect data, develop skill at persuasion to convince people to continue the study, and compare dropouts with those who remain in the study to provide insurance that the dropouts have not biased the final results.

Because of the constraints of time, attrition of participants, and cost in conducting the longitudinal study, the cohort-sequential design has been suggested as an alternative approach. This approach represents a compromise between the longitudinal and cross-sectional approaches and has been used with increasing frequency. The **cohort-sequential design** is a design in which groups of overlapping ages are tested longitudinally for several years. For example, Hetherington et al. (1992) were interested in identifying how mother–child negativity (e.g., degrees of conflict, punitiveness, and negative affect) changed over the years of early adolescence. To investigate this change they used a cohort-sequential design in which they identified five groups of children ages nine to thirteen years and assessed them contemporaneously three times over the next two years. If a longitudinal design had been used, the study would have taken five years to complete; the cohort-sequential design was completed in two years. Consequently, this design effects an economy in effort and provides more immediate rewards because differences in age groups are available in the first year of the study.

Although the cohort-sequential design is more efficient in terms of data collection, it does pose some interesting problems in terms of data analysis. These problems and issues are beyond the scope of this textbook. Anderson (1993) has provided an enlightening overview of these data analysis issues.

I have presented longitudinal, cross-sectional, and cohort-sequential studies as nonexperimental research approaches because most studies using either of these methods are in fact nonexperimental in nature. It is possible, however, to conduct an experimental longitudinal or cross-sectional study. There is currently a great deal of emphasis on prevention research. In a number of recent studies, a prevention technique has been used and then the individuals to whom the technique was administered are followed to determine, for example, whether they became drug abusers. Such research requires an experimental longitudinal approach.

Naturalistic Observation

Naturalistic observation is a technique that enables the investigator to collect data on naturally occurring behavior. Geller, Russ, and Altomari (1986), for example, were interested in determining the relationship among gender, group size, and the amount of beer consumed in a barroom setting. To obtain data to assess this

---

Cohort-sequential design

A developmental field study that measures the same characteristics at several selected time intervals in groups of individuals at different age levels

Naturalistic observation

A descriptive research technique for unobtrusively collecting data on naturally occurring behavior

relationship, 56 female and 187 male patrons drinking beer at either the Virginia Tech student center or any of five bars in Blacksburg, Virginia, were observed unobtrusively from a nearby table by one or two research assistants. The results of this study revealed that the patrons, who were predominantly college students with an estimated age of eighteen to twenty-five years, drank more beer in groups than when drinking alone. Males drank more than females. While this result may not be surprising and probably conforms to most people's expectations, Figure 2.5 reveals that the gender difference in beer consumption was a function of container type. There was little difference in number of ounces of beer consumed by male and female students when beer was consumed from a glass or bottle. When it was consumed from a pitcher, males consumed an average of 38.6 ounces versus 27.8 ounces for females, and this greater beer consumption occurred over a shorter interval of time.

The Geller et al. (1986) study is an example of a naturalistic observation designed to investigate a specific research question. However, in many instances such specific research questions do not exist; this is frequently the case when studies are done in

FIGURE 2.5

Ounces of beer consumed and minutes spent in a bar per patron as functions of gender and beer container.

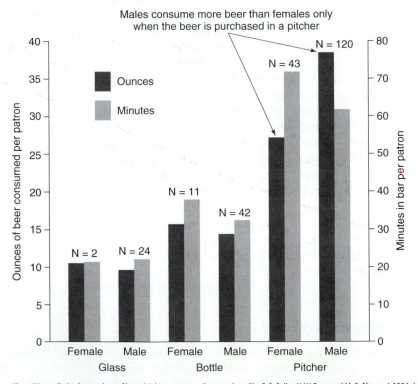

(From "Naturalistic observations of beer drinking among college students" by E. S. Geller, N. W. Russ, and M. G. Altomari, 1986, *Journal of Applied Behavior Analysis, 19,* pp. 391–396. Copyright 1986 by *Journal of Applied Behavior Analysis.* Reprinted by permission of the author.)

the wild and information is sought regarding the behavior of animals such as mountain gorillas or baboons. Sometimes this is the case with studies of humans. For example, Nikolaas Tinbergen did not have any specific research questions when he conducted his naturalistic observational study of autistic children. At the time he conducted this study (Tinbergen & Tinbergen, 1972), little was known about the behavior of autistic children, so he simply started observing and recording the behavior of these children. These observations revealed that the autistic children did not communicate with one another. Instead, they engaged in a variety of self-stimulating behaviors such as shaking their hands, hitting their head against the wall, or uttering unintelligible sounds.

Just recording behavior allows one to gain a global impression of the characteristics and range of behavior of the individuals or organisms studied. However, additional information is often obtained by identifying categories, such as sleeping, fighting, eating, arguing, and so on, and then recording the pattern of behavior representative of each of these categories. For example, Tinbergen identified the category of "an unfamiliar social situation" and observed that the abnormal behavior of the autistic children often occurred when they were in this type of situation. By looking at behavior in specific categories, one can get some idea of the significance of the behaviors. In this way naturalistic observation not only provides a description of the characteristics and range of behavior, but also the significance of the behavior.

These two studies demonstrate the primary characteristic of naturalistic observation—unobtrusiveness of the observer. Rather than taking an active part in the experiment, the observer must remain completely aloof in order to record natural behavior. If participants in the Geller et al. (1986) study had known they were being observed, their behavior probably would not have been the same. A second, related characteristic is the lack of artificiality of the situation. The participants are left in their natural environment so as to eliminate any artificial influence that might be caused by bringing them out of their natural habitat.

For certain types of studies, these characteristics are crucial. If a research project were directed at answering the question of what baboons do during the day, naturalistic observation would be the technique to use. Such research would also generate hypotheses that could be tested with field or laboratory experimentation. If we observe that baboons fight when conditions *a*, *b*, *c*, and *d* exist and we want to know why they fight, we could conduct an experiment to determine this. Condition *a* would be presented without *b*, *c*, or *d*, and we would observe whether fighting occurred. Then condition *b* would be presented without *a*, *c*, or *d*, and so forth, until all combinations of conditions had been presented. We have now moved from observation to experimentation.

Obviously, naturalistic observation is necessary in studying issues that are not amenable to experimentation. (It is not experimentally feasible, for example, to study suicide.)

Although there are many positive components of naturalistic observation, it also has a number of constraints. Naturalistic observation is excellent for obtaining an accurate description, but the causes of behavior are almost impossible to isolate using this method. Any given behavior could be produced by a number of agents operating independently or in combination, and observation does not provide any means of sorting these agents out. Thus, in no way could the Geller et al. (1986) study have isolated why males consume more beer only when the beer is served in a pitcher. In addition, the observational approach is very time consuming. Observers in the Geller et al. study spent three months recording the beer consumption of the 243 patrons. These are just a few of the difficulties encountered in conducting a study of this type.

Meta Analysis

Meta analysis

A quantitative technique that is used to integrate and describe a large number of studies

Meta analysis is a term that was introduced by Glass (1976) to describe a quantitative approach that could be used to integrate and describe the results of a large number of studies. In the field of psychology, we rarely find a single study that provides a complete answer to a research question. Not only is human behavior too complex to be explained within the framework of a single study, but the ability to control the research environment, the research participant sample, and the procedures used may vary from study to study. This means that a number of studies must be conducted in order to obtain a sufficiently definitive answer. Within the field of psychology, there has been a proliferation of studies investigating such research questions as the effectiveness of psychotherapy, leadership characteristics, and causes of obesity. These studies typically use different sets of definitions, participant samples, variables, and procedures; their conclusions may even be different. At some point, however, these studies need to be integrated and described. Prior to Glass's (1976) article, the traditional approach to accomplishing this task involved collecting the studies conducted on a given topic, categorizing them in some manner (for example, those that were methodologically sound versus those that contained obvious control problems), and then reaching a conclusion based on the proportion of studies that suggested a given outcome. Such an approach, however, maximizes the opportunity for the introduction of subjective judgments, preferences, and biases, which become obvious when two reviews of the same literature arrive at different conclusions. Meta analysis gets around this problem because it involves the analysis of analyses or the use of a variety of quantitative techniques to analyze the results of the studies in question.

There are actually two broad classes of meta-analytic techniques, and each provides an answer to a different research question. One technique involves determining if an overall significant result will emerge if the findings from many studies are combined in a statistical fashion. For example, assume that four different studies were conducted investigating the effectiveness of psychotherapy in treating depression. In two studies, a significant effect was not found; the probability (p) values attained in these studies were 0.10 and 0.08, respectively (a p value of 0.05 or less is necessary to conclude that a result is statistically significant). The other two studies indicated that psychotherapy was effective in treating depression, because p values of 0.04 and 0.001, respectively, were attained. It would be valuable to combine the studies to determine whether an overall significant effect emerged. Meta analysis can be used to combine the p values of these four studies to yield one overall p value that would be representative of the combined effect of all four studies.

The other meta-analytic technique deals with the size of the treatment effect produced. With this technique you are attempting to identify the magnitude or strength of the results. For example, if you conduct a study investigating the impact of some therapeutic intervention on depression, you want to know whether the treatment program was effective in reducing depression. You also want to know how much effect the treatment program had on depression—how large the effect was. Different studies investigating the same intervention technique would arrive at different estimates of the size of the effect. Consequently, it would be advantageous to be able to combine these effect sizes in order to come up with one overall effect size. This second meta-analytic technique enables the researcher to combine the results of several studies and arrive at a combined estimate of the size of the effect.

To illustrate the use of meta analysis, let us look at the research conducted on lunar effects. For centuries, a significant proportion of the population has believed that the moon influences behavior. The typical assumption is that a variety of behaviors—suicides, admissions to mental institutions, homicides—are more likely to occur during a full moon. Between 1961 and 1984 at least forty studies were conducted that investigated the lunar hypothesis—a surprisingly large number of studies given that most researchers are skeptical about the value of such investigations. However, the lunar hypothesis has a great deal of popular appeal and, if supported, would become a legitimate and valuable area for research. To determine whether the lunar hypothesis had any support, Rotton and Kelly (1985) collected all the studies between 1978 and 1984 that investigated the lunar hypothesis and then conducted a meta analysis of the results.

Rotton and Kelly first used the technique of combining the *p* values of these studies. The results of this meta analysis revealed that none of the combined *p* values were significant for studies that focused on activities taking place under a full moon or a new moon. Rotton and Kelly then focused on a meta analysis of the effect size computed for each of the studies identified. This analysis showed that the combined size of the effect of the moon is extremely small—so small, in fact, as to be considered negligible. Consequently, the results of this meta analysis indicated that the lunar hypothesis has no substance when the results of many studies are considered together. Exhibit 2.1 illustrates the use of meta analysis to identify the size of a treatment effect.

The Survey

Survey
A field study in which an interview technique is used to gather data on a given state of affairs in a representative sample of the population

The **survey** is a widely used nonexperimental research technique. It is often defined as a method of collecting standardized information by interviewing a representative sample of some population. In other words, the survey represents a probe into a given state of affairs that exists at a given time. Therefore direct contact must be made with the individuals whose characteristics, behaviors, or attitudes are relevant to the investigation.

Probably the most widely known surveys are those conducted by the Gallup organization. Gallup polls are frequently conducted to survey the voting public's opinions on such issues as the popularity of the president or a given policy or to determine the percentage of individuals who may be expected to vote for a given candidate at election time. Surveys are initially conducted to answer the questions "how many" and "how much." But collection of frequency data is only a preliminary phase of the research in many studies. Researchers often want to answer the questions "who" and

EXHIBIT 2.1

How Much of a Drug's Effect Is Due to a Placebo Response?

One of the most common treatments for depression is antidepressant medication, or drug therapy. Individuals who are depressed frequently take some type of antidepressant drug such as Prozac, and, frequently, their depression ameliorates within several weeks. The common assumption is that the amelioration of the depression is due to the active effect of the medication. However, we also know that there is such a thing as a placebo response, or the fact that amelioration of a disorder, such as depression, will occur if a person has a reason to expect that he or she will get better. Giving antidepressant medication to a depressed person creates such an expectation. This means that part of the response to taking antidepressant medication is probably a placebo response and part is due to the pharmacological properties of the drug.

Kirsch and Sapirstein (1998) were interested in finding out how much of a person's response to antidepressant medication is due to a placebo effect and how much is due to the pharmacological properties of the medication they are taking. To answer this research question, these investigators conducted a meta analysis. They identified nineteen studies that provided separate data for participants that received some form of antidepressant medication or an inactive placebo. They then calculated the average drug effect size (1.55) and the average placebo effect size (1.16) across the nineteen studies. This data revealed that the actual medication effect size was only 0.39 (1.55–1.16). This indicates that 75 percent of the amelioration in the depression experienced by the individuals in these studies was due to a placebo response. Only 25 percent was due to a true drug effect.

The meta analysis conducted by Kirsch and Sapirstein (1998) reveals a very significant finding and one that goes against what is commonly believed. We tend to believe that the medications we take are responsible for the beneficial effects we experience. However, this study reveals that, at least for antidepressant medications, most of the beneficial effect comes not from the drug itself but from a placebo response. This means that our expectations of getting better and the effect those expectations have on our physical well-being are more important and contribute more to ameliorating depression than do the pharmacological properties of antidepressant medications.

"why." Who votes for the Republican candidate, and who votes for the Democrat? Why do people buy a certain make of car or brand of product? Such information helps us to understand why a particular phenomenon occurred and increases our ability to predict what will happen.

For example, Table 2.2 on p. 53 presents the results to one question of a Gallup poll taken in 1998 concerning the drug Viagra. This question asked, "There is a new prescription drug on the market called Viagra. Without telling me the answer, specifically, do you know what this drug is used for or not?" The responses to this question revealed that only 64 percent of the individuals polled knew the use of the drug. However, knowledge of the drug's use varied according to the background characteristics of the respondents. White males, older individuals, individuals living in a suburban area, and in the East or West were more likely to be aware of the drug's use, as were more educated, married individuals. Responses to this question provide answers to the questions *who* and *how many* individuals are aware of Viagra's use.

TABLE 2.2

Response Obtained from a Gallup Poll to the Question "There is a new prescription drug on the market called Viagra. Without telling me the answer, specifically, do you know what this drug is used for or not?"

	Know its purpose? (%)		
	Yes	No	No opinion
National	64	33	3
Sex			
Male	69	29	2
Female	60	37	3
Age			
18–29 years	53	46	1
30–49 years	64	33	3
50–64 years	71	25	4
65 & older	70	27	3
Region			
East	74	23	3
Midwest	59	36	5
South	57	41	2
West	70	29	1
Community			
Urban	62	35	3
Suburban	70	28	2
Rural	54	42	4
Race			
White	67	30	3
Nonwhite	50	48	2
Education			
College postgraduate	89	11	0
Bachelor's degree only	76	22	2
Some college	66	31	3
High school or less	52	34	4
Ideology			
Liberal	63	35	2
Moderate	63	33	4
Conservative	66	32	2
Clinton approval			
Approve	64	33	3
Disapprove	64	33	3
Income			
$75,000 & over	64	14	2
$50,000 & over	77	21	2
$30,000–49,999	66	31	3
$20,000–29,000	62	35	3
Under $20,000	49	47	4
Marital status			
Married	67	29	4
Not married	60	38	2

The survey is a technique that is applicable to a wide range of problems. It is also a technique that is deceptively easy to use. The unsophisticated researcher may think that all that is needed is to construct a number of questions addressing the issue on which information is desired and then get a number of people to respond to these questions. Superficially, this is essentially all there is to the survey. However, completing these seemingly simple steps requires a lot of thought and work. Without this thought and work, the questions asked will elicit unreliable answers. For example, in 1936 the periodical *Literary Digest* set out to predict the winner of the presidential election. A sample of participants was selected from telephone directories and car registrations. This sample was surveyed to determine whom the participants would vote for in the 1936 election. Based on the results of this survey, the *Literary Digest* predicted that Alfred Landon would defeat Franklin Roosevelt by a wide margin. However, if you know your U.S. presidents, you know that Franklin Roosevelt won the election.

Why was such an error made? If you think about the climate that existed in 1936, you will realize that the United States was in the middle of the Great Depression. During this time many individuals did not have phones or cars simply because they couldn't afford them. Consequently, selecting a sample of individuals from telephone directories and car registrations provided a biased sample of individuals, which underrepresented the less affluent segment of the population and in doing so underestimated Roosevelt's popularity. To collect accurate data using the survey technique such errors must be eliminated. To give you an appreciation of the effort involved in conducting a good survey, several of the major types of decisions that must be made are discussed briefly here.

Methods of Data Collection   There are a variety of methods for collecting survey data. The most popular methods are face-to-face, telephone, mail, and increasingly, electronic. Each has its own set of advantages and disadvantages in terms of issues, such as cost and response rate. The **face-to-face method**, as the name suggests, is a person-to-person interview, which typically involves going to the interviewee's home and obtaining responses to the survey by conducting a personal interview. This technique has the advantages of allowing the interviewer to clear up any ambiguities in the question asked or to probe for further clarification if the interviewee provides an inadequate answer, and it generally gives a higher completion rate and more complete information. However, this technique is the most expensive. It is also possible that the interviewer may bias the responses. For example, an interviewer may (either consciously or unconsciously) spend more time with and probe more effectively an attractive interviewee of the opposite sex and thus bias the results.

With the **telephone method**, as the name suggests, the survey is conducted by means of a telephone interview. This method is about half as expensive as the face-to-face interview (Groves & Kahn, 1979), and some data (Rogers, 1976) demonstrate that the information collected is comparable to that obtained in a face-to-face interview. This seems to be particularly true with the use of random-digit dialing. In some areas 20–40 percent of customers elect not to list their phone numbers in telephone directories (Rich, 1977). Such unlisted numbers are accessible with the **random-digit dialing method**. In this method, telephone numbers are dialed through use

Face-to-face method
A survey method involving a personal interview, often conducted in the interviewee's home

Telephone method
A survey method involving a telephone interview

Random-digit dialing method
A survey method that involves dialing telephone numbers composed through a random process

of a random process, usually by a computer, which means that unlisted numbers are just as accessible as listed numbers. If a survey researcher has access to a computer-assisted telephone interview (CATI) system, the interviewer's questions are prompted on the computer screen and the interviewee's responses are put directly into the computer for analysis.

Mail method

A survey conducted by sending a questionnaire through the mail

The **mail method**, as the name suggests, involves sending questionnaires to interviewees through the mail and asking them to return the completed questionnaires, typically in envelopes provided by the organization conducting the survey. The primary advantage of this technique is its low cost. You can send a questionnaire anywhere in the world for the price of postage. However, the disadvantage is that most questionnaires are never returned. The return rate is typically 20–30 percent for the initial mailing (Nederhof, 1985), although the rate can be increased by use of techniques such as follow-up letters reminding the respondent of the survey and enclosing another copy of the questionnaire.

Electronic survey

Contacting people over the Internet and having them complete a survey on their computer

An **electronic survey** involves contacting people over the Internet and having them complete a survey on their computer. This type of survey has shown tremendous growth since the 1990s. Kaye and Johnson (1999) identified over 2,000 Web-based surveys several years ago, and the use of electronic surveys continues to grow (Shannon, Johnson, Searcy, and Lott, 2002).

There are currently two types of electronic surveys: e-mail surveys and Web-based surveys. An e-mail survey consists of sending an e-mail message with an appeal to complete a survey that is either a part of the message or in an attached file. The person who receives the e-mail message completes the survey and returns it to the sender. A Web-based survey is an electronic survey that is posted on the World Wide Web. Once the survey is constructed and posted, respondents are identified and sent an e-mail message inviting them to participate in the survey. If they agree, they are given a link with an Internet address to the survey. All they have to do is click on the link, which brings them to the Web site containing the survey, which they then proceed to complete.

One variation of the Web-based survey that has recently been introduced is the pop-up survey (Llieva, Baron, & Healey, 2002). This type of survey would appear in the browser's window while browsing various Web sites. The pop-up would invite the browser to participate in the survey and to click on a link that brings them to the Web site containing the survey. This type of survey has been viewed as a very positive contribution to Web site research (Llieva et al., 2002).

There are a number of significant advantages to conducting an electronic survey over other types of surveys. One of the major advantages is cost because electronic surveys do not require postage, printing costs, or involvement of interviewers. Anderson and Kanuka (2003) have estimated that electronic surveys cost about one-tenth of the cost of a comparable mail survey. Electronic surveys also have the advantages of having instant access to a wide audience, irrespective of their geographical location, being fast, capable of having responses downloaded into a spreadsheet or a statistical analysis program, and being flexible in terms of layout because of the kinds of response formats that can be incorporated particularly with Web-based surveys. While electronic surveys have a number of advantages over other survey methods, they do have disadvantages. The primary disadvantage is the inability to ensure privacy and anonymity, particularly with e-mail surveys, because the respondent's e-mail address is generally included in his or her response.

If you are considering conducting an electronic survey, you obviously must decide whether you will use the e-mail or the Web-based approach. This is an important choice because there are advantages and disadvantages to each approach. A Web-based survey is more appropriate if your goal is to sample a wide audience because all visitors to certain Web sites have an equal chance of linking to the Web site containing the survey. However, the researcher has little control over who enters and completes the Web-based survey. Therefore, if you want more control over who completes the survey, you should use the e-mail approach. This is a very important issue in many surveys. For example, if you wanted to survey college students regarding the quality of the education they received, you would not want to use a Web-based survey because you could not limit your respondents to college students. This would require an e-mail survey. Web-based surveys have the advantage over e-mail surveys in that the display of the survey is generally better because there is more flexibility in terms of layout and various kinds of response formats can be incorporated. However, to incorporate the different kinds of response formats requires considerable technological skill. If you need a rapid response to your survey, an e-mail survey would be the approach of choice, although use of pop-ups would increase the speed of response to Web-based surveys. Also, e-mail surveys generate better response rates than Web-based surveys and are more likely to avoid multiple entries to the same survey by the same person (Llieva et al., 2002).

Questionnaire Construction   In addition to deciding on the mode of data collection, it is necessary to construct a number of questions that will provide an answer to the research question. In constructing these questions, it is imperative that the researcher have an explicitly identified research question. An explicit research question states what the researcher wishes to know. For example, Veroff, Douvan, and Kulka (1981) conducted a survey "to determine in some detail how American people cope with problems of adjustment which arise in their lives." Given such a specific research question, a number of items directed at assessing coping mechanisms of the American public can be written.

Although specification of the research question is an essential beginning point for writing survey questions, there are a number of other factors that must be considered. Several of these factors are discussed next. More detailed discussions of these factors are found in Babbie (1990) and Sudman and Bradburn (1982).

Open-ended questions
Questions that enable respondents to answer in any way they please

Type of Question.   There are two types of questions that can be used in a survey: open-ended or closed-ended questions. An **open-ended question** enables respondents to answer in any way they please, whereas a **closed-ended question** requires respondents to choose from a limited number of predetermined responses. For example, if you wanted to find out what people do when they feel depressed, you could ask an open-ended question such as "What do you do when you feel depressed?" Alternatively, you could ask a closed-ended question such as

Closed-ended questions
Questions that require respondents to choose from a limited number of predetermined responses

What do you do when you feel depressed?

a. Eat
b. Sleep
c. Exercise
d. Talk to a close friend
e. Cry

The open-ended question requires the respondent to come up with the answer. Such a question is valuable when the researcher needs to know what people are thinking or when the dimensions of a variable are not well defined. However, the responses to an open-ended question must be coded and categorized, which takes time. Also, sometimes the responses given don't make sense and can't be categorized.

The closed-ended question requires the respondent to select one of the alternative answers given. Generally, closed-ended questions are appropriate when the dimensions of a variable are known. In such an instance the alternative responses can be specified and the respondent can select among these alternatives.

Question Wording. Once the type of question has been specified, the actual questions must be written. There are a number of pitfalls that must be avoided in writing the questions. **Double-barreled questions,** or questions that ask two things, must be avoided. A question such as "Do you agree that the president should focus his primary attention on the economy and foreign affairs?" includes two different issues: the economy and foreign affairs. Each issue may elicit a different attitude, and combining them into one question makes it unclear which attitude or opinion is being assessed. Leading and ambiguous questions must also be avoided. For example, a congressman used the following item in one of his mail surveys:

> A site in Ellis county, in your congressional district, is one of seven national finalists for the superconducting super collider (SCC) project. During this time of budget restraint, do you support programs vital to the future growth of our country such as the SCC?

This item is ambiguous—it is not clear whether it is trying to assess an attitude toward the SCC or toward the programs vital to the growth of the country. To identify the ambiguous or unclear items it is necessary to pilot test the questionnaire by administering it to a small sample of individuals who are instructed to identify any difficulties they have in responding to each item.

Ordering of the Questions. The ordering, or sequencing, of the questions must also be considered. When the questionnaire includes both positive and negative items, it is generally better to ask the positive questions first. Similarly, the more important and interesting questions should come first to capture the attention of the respondent. Roberson and Sundstrom (1990) found that placing the important questions first and demographic questions (age, gender, etc.) last in an employee attitude survey resulted in the highest return rates.

Questionnaire Length. There are many significant questions that can be asked in any survey, but every data-gathering instrument has an optimal length for the population

---

Double-barreled questions
Questions that cover two different issues at once

to which it is being administered. After a certain point, the respondents' interest and cooperation diminish. The survey researcher must therefore ensure that the questionnaire is not too long, even though some important questions may have to be sacrificed. It is impossible to specify the optimum length of any survey questionnaire because length is partially dependent on the topic and the method of data collection. As a general rule, telephone interviews should be no longer than fifteen minutes. However, a face-to-face interview may consume more time without making the interviewee feel uncomfortable.

Social desirability bias
Responding to look good rather than as one truly feels and believes

Response set
The tendency to respond in a specific way

Response Bias   There are several types of biases a person can have when responding to surveys. One of the most common is a **social desirability bias.** This bias occurs when people respond to a survey in a way that make them look the best rather than responding as they really feel or believe. Survey research must constantly be aware of this type of bias affecting individuals' responses and interpret the results with this bias in mind. Another type of bias is a specific **response set** or a tendency to respond in a specific manner to all questions. For example, a person may hesitate in giving extreme responses and tend to cluster his or her responses around a central choice. Other individuals may be "yea-sayers," tending to agree with every statement. Surveys need to be constructed so that biases such as these are eliminated or at least minimized.

Population
All the events, things, or individuals to be represented

Sample
Any number of individuals less than the population

Haphazard sampling
A nonprobability sampling technique whereby the sample of participants selected is based on convenience

Obtaining Participants   After the survey questionnaire has been constructed, it must be administered to a group of individuals to obtain a set of responses that will provide an answer to the research question. There are many ways in which a researcher can select the participants who will be given the survey questionnaire. Most research projects involve selecting a sample of participants from a population of interest. A **population** refers to all the events, things, or individuals to be represented, and a **sample** refers to any number of individuals less than the population. However, the manner in which this sample of participants is selected depends on the goals of the research project. If the research question focuses on identifying the relationship between variables, then a haphazard sampling technique will probably be used. However, if it is important that the results obtained from the sample mirror the results that would have been obtained if the total population had been included, then a random sampling technique must be used.

   Haphazard sampling is a nonprobability sampling technique whereby the sample of participants selected is based on convenience and includes individuals who are readily available. For example, a significant amount of psychological research is conducted using introductory psychology students as participants because these students are conveniently available to researchers. The obvious advantage of using the haphazard sampling technique is that participants can be obtained without spending a great deal of time or money. However, researchers usually want the results of their studies to generalize to "people in general" or at least to "a college student population." Making such a generalization from this sample of college students is hazardous because the sample is composed of students volunteering for the study who have elected to take introductory psychology during the semester in which the study was conducted.

Responses to electronic surveys also represent a type of haphazard sample because, in spite of the large number of individuals who are connected to the Internet, many people still are not connected to the Internet or choose not to use the Internet (Solomon, 2001). This means that any sample of responses to electronic surveys will be biased. Bias can be reduced by sampling from populations in which Internet access is extremely high, such as college students and university faculty within the United States, Canada, and western Europe. However, even these populations may produce a biased sample because of differing levels of experience and comfort with Internet-based tools such as Web browsers. This is one of the primary reasons that electronic surveying, although attractive, should be used with caution (Solomon, 2001).

Random sampling
Sampling in which every member of the population has an equal chance of being selected for the study

When the research question requires an accurate depiction of the general population, a **random sampling** technique must be used. When this technique is used, every member of the population has an equal chance of being selected for the study. (This technique is discussed in more detail in Chapter 9.) The advantage of this technique is that it provides a sample of participants whose responses represent those of the general population. For example, during presidential campaigns polls are frequently conducted to test the pulse of the voting public. These polls are taken to determine the popularity of the candidates as well as the influence of various issues, such as prior drug use, on the public's opinions of candidates.

When a true random sample of participants is obtained from the population, the results can be amazingly accurate. For example, in 1976 a *New York Times*–CBS poll correctly predicted that 51.1 percent of the voters would vote for Jimmy Carter and 48.9 percent would vote for Gerald Ford (Converse and Traugott, 1986). The prediction was made using a sample of less than 2,000 individuals selected from almost eighty million voters. This perfectly accurate prediction was unusual, but it illustrates the accuracy with which the population responses can be predicted from a sample of just a few individuals, if these individuals are selected randomly. In virtually all polls such as this there is sampling error, or error that arises from the fact that the sample of participants selected does not provide a perfectly accurate representation of the population. However, this error is typically quite small and much smaller than it would be if any other sampling technique were used.

STUDY QUESTION 2.2

- **What is nonexperimental quantitative research?**
- **What types of nonexperimental research methods have been discussed? Explain the purpose and design of each of these nonexperimental research methods and the limitations of each of these research methods.**

Qualitative Research

Qualitative research is an interpretative, multimethod approach that investigates people in their natural environment (Denzin & Lincoln, 1994). This definition has three primary components that are essential to understanding the nature of

Qualitative research
An interpretative, multimethod approach that investigates people in their natural environment

qualitative research. The first component is that qualitative research is interpretative. Remember that qualitative data consist of words, pictures, clothing, documents, or other non-numerical information. Once this information is collected, some meaning has to be extracted from it. For example, Schouten and McAlexander (1995) investigated the subculture of consumerism associated with Harley-Davidson motorcycles. Part of the data they collected was information on the general appearance and clothing worn by Harley-Davidson bikers. Many of the bikers had massive bellies or large biceps and exhibited loud, aggressive behavior. Their bikes were adorned with massive quantities of chrome and leather, and the bikers themselves wore leather clothing, heavy boots, and gauntlets as well as wallet chains, conches, chrome studs, and other similar hardware. What does this mean? This is where the interpretative component comes in. Schouten and McAlexander had to give some meaning to this behavior, general appearance, and clothing worn by the Harley-Davidson bikers because they were dominant characteristics of these individuals. It was as though you had to act and dress this way to be accepted as part of the in-group of Harley-Davidson bikers. Schouten and McAlexander interpreted this behavior and dress as an expression of machismo. The concept of *real men* seemed to pervade virtually every aspect of the biker experience from the clothing they wore to their general behavior and appearance. Even the Harley-Davidson bikes were reputedly the biggest, heaviest, loudest bikes, which meant that they were the manliest, even though they were not the fastest. All of this was interpreted as conveying a sense "of power, fearsomeness, and invulnerability to the rider" (p. 54).

The second component is that qualitative research is multimethod. This means that a variety of methods are used to collect data. These include such diverse data collection methods as an individual's account of a personal experience, introspective analysis, an individual's life story, interviews with an individual, observation of an individual or individuals, written documents, photographs, and historical information. In many qualitative studies, several of these data collection methods may be used to try to get the best description of an event and the meaning it has for the individual or individuals being studied. This use of several methods is referred to as triangulation because it is believed that the use of several methods provides a better understanding of the phenomenon being investigated. For example, Schouten and McAlexander (1995) collected their data from formal and informal interviews, observations, and photographs of the Harley-Davidson bikers.

The third component of qualitative research is that it is conducted in the field or in the person's natural surroundings, such as a school classroom, the playground, a board meeting, or a therapy setting. To meet this component of conducting the research in the natural surroundings of the research participants, Schouten and McAlexander attended rallies of the Harley Owners Group (HOG), as well as biker swap meets and certain club meetings. The final step involved purchasing Harley-Davidson bikes, the appropriate clothing (jeans, black boots, and black leather jackets) and wearing the clothing and using the bikes as their primary means of transportation. This heightened personal involvement increased the frequency of contact with other "bikers" and allowed the researchers to gain an empathic sense of the biker's identity, psyche, and everyday social interactions.

From this description of qualitative research, you should be able to see that it is an approach that uses many data collection methods requiring the interpretation of non-numerical data. This research approach is, however, plagued with a number of difficulties. Qualitative researchers have assumed that they can objectively and with clarity and precision report on their own observations of others, on the experiences of others, and, in some form, on their own experiences. These researchers have also believed that they could blend their observations of others and their own experiences with the observations provided by research participants through interviews, life stories, and personal experience to arrive at an accurate account of the meaning attached to research participants' various life experiences. Essentially, the researcher's observations and the verbal and written accounts provided by the research participants were assumed to represent a window into the life and the meaning of various life experiences that individuals can have (Denzin & Lincoln, 1994).

Recently, this position has come under attack from several different camps within the field of qualitative research. This attack has pointed out that any account provided by an individual is filtered through the lens of a person's language, gender, social class, race, and ethnicity. Every observation is partially determined by a person's social and cultural setting. In addition, qualitative researchers are recognizing that a person is seldom able to provide a full explanation of his or her actions or intentions. All he or she can provide is an account, and this account may or may not be accurate. This is why qualitative researchers employ many methods of collecting data to seek a better way to gain an understanding of the meaning and experience of the phenomenon they are investigating (Denzin & Lincoln, 1994).

These difficulties that qualitative researchers experience is one of the reasons why experimental research places so much emphasis on control of extraneous variables. However, just because qualitative research has difficulty providing a full explanation of a person's actions and intentions does not mean that qualitative research is not an appropriate research method or that it does not provide useful information. Rather, it indicates that qualitative research has its limitations just as every other research method does. If gaining an account of research participants' meanings and experiences of an event is desired, then qualitative research is the method to use.

Although qualitative research is used in many disciplines such as psychology, sociology, education, and anthropology, it has no specific theory or paradigm that it can claim as its own. Instead there are many paradigms that claim the use of qualitative research strategies with names such as constructivism, feminism, and post-structuralism (Denzin & Lincoln, 1994). Rather than spending time discussing the various paradigms used by qualitative researchers, I discuss next three qualitative research approaches or research strategies. You should realize that there are other qualitative research approaches such as grounded theory, the feminist approach, and historiography.

STUDY QUESTION 2.3

- **Define qualitative research and explain each of the components included in this definition.**
- **Discuss the difficulties and biases that can exist when doing qualitative research.**

Phenomenology

Phenomenology
The description of an individual, or group of individuals' conscious experience of a phenomenon

Phenomenology refers to the description of an individual's, or group of individuals', conscious experience of a phenomenon such as the death of a loved one, a counseling session, winning a championship football game, or experiencing a specific emotion such as guilt, love, anger, or jealousy. Phenomenological qualitative research attempts to describe, convey, and understand individuals' experience of a phenomenon such as guilt, death of a loved one, or terrorists acts such as that which occurred on the London underground transit. This means that phenomenologists focus not only on an individual's description of an experience, but also the meaning or interpretation of that experience. The description and interpretation of an experience are, however, intertwined and difficult to separate. Therefore, phenomenologists focus on how individuals put the phenomenon they experience together in a way that makes sense to them.

How do phenomenologists develop a description of an individual's or group of individuals' experience of a phenomenon? The primary method used by phenomenologists is in-depth interviews. For example, Rieman (1986) investigated the phenomenon of caring and noncaring interactions with nurses. To investigate this phenomenon, Rieman interviewed nonhospitalized individuals over the age of eighteen who had a prior interaction with a nurse. This interview requested that the research participants describe a personal interaction they had with a caring and noncaring nurse and to also describe how they felt during this interaction. From these interviews Rieman extracted the phrases and statements that directly pertained to caregiving. For example, some caring statements were "listened well," "empathetic," and "talked to me about things other than illness." Noncaring statements included "I felt as though my hands were being slapped," "didn't want to talk," and "she looked at the equipment instead of me."

Once these significant phrases and statements were extracted, meaning had to be formulated from them. Rieman arrived at the meaning of these statements by reading, rereading, and reflecting on the statements as they were presented by the research participants in the interview in an attempt to arrive at the research participant's meaning of the statement. For example, the meaning given to some of these statements are "Nurse's voluntary and unsolicited return to the client was highly indicative of a caring attitude" and "Nurse's caring made him feel comfortable, relaxed, secure, and in good hands, as though he was being taken care of by a family member." Meaning given to some noncaring statements include "The nurse's attitude of lack of interest in her as a person is interpreted by the client as the nurse viewing nursing as 'only a job,'" or "The nurse who does not pay any attention to the client's needs but views nursing as a job is perceived by the client as noncaring" (in Creswell, 1998, pp. 286–287). These formulated "meaning" statements are then organized into clusters or themes. Rieman formulated the clusters of "nurse's existential presence," "client's uniqueness," and "consequences" for the caring cluster. Finally, a description of the phenomenon was produced by integrating the statements, their meaning, and the clusters they formed. Rieman (1986) formed the following description of a caring nurse.

In a caring interaction, the nurse's existential presence i[s] more than just a physical presence. There is the aspect [of giving of] self to the client. This giving of oneself may be in resp[onse to a request,] but it is more often a voluntary effort and is unsolicite[d ...] willingness to give of oneself is primarily perceived by t[he ...] behavior of sitting down and really listening and resp[onding to the con]cerns of the individual as a person of value. The relaxa[tion and comfort] that the client experiences both physically and mentally are an immediate and direct result of the client's stated and unstated needs being heard and responded to by the nurse (in Creswell, 1998, p. 289).

Ethnography

Ethnography

The description and interpretation of the culture of a group of individuals

Ethnography refers to the description and interpretation of the culture of a group of people. The basic thesis of ethnography is that if a group of people are together long enough, a culture—patterns of behavior, customs, and ways of life of a group of people—will evolve. Ethnography, therefore, attempts to understand the "way of life" of a group of people.

Culture is often thought of as being associated with very large groups of individuals such as the Japanese or Chinese culture. However, the concept of culture can be used on a much smaller scale. We can study macro or micro cultures. Berg (1998) has even pointed out that a distinction is sometime made between micro- and macroethnography. At the macro level we might study the cultural characteristics of Japanese adolescents or the Ohio Amish. On the micro level, we might study the cultural characteristics of a street gang, a motorcycle group, a therapeutic setting, or the culture of the Trench Coat Mafia of which Eric Harris and Dylan Klebold were members. The primary difference in the two is the scope of the investigation. Obviously, studying the culture of Japanese adolescents is of greater scope than studying a therapeutic setting. However, regardless of the scope of the investigation, the primary concern is with describing the culture of the targeted setting.

Ethnographic Methods   Now that you have some knowledge of ethnography, let's take a look at how an ethnographer proceeds in describing a cultural setting. One technique that ethnographers use is in-depth interviews with members of the group being investigated. For example, Smith, Sells, and Clevenger (1994) conducted an ethnographic study of the use of reflecting teams or reflecting process in a family therapy setting. To acquire information about the culture of this therapeutic setting, Smith et al. conducted in-depth interviews with eleven couples and their therapists. These individuals were interviewed at least twice over a four-month period, and the interviews lasted up to two hours.

Participant observation

A research approach in which the researcher becomes an active participant in the group he or she is investigating

Although in-depth interviews are used in some ethnographic studies, participant observation is the more frequently used approach. **Participant observation** is a research approach in which the researcher becomes an active participant in the group he or she is investigating. Ellen (1984) has described the ethnographic process as subjective soaking or becoming immersed in the culture being studied. This immersion is accomplished primarily through participant observation. For example, Schouten and McAlexander (1995) in their ethnographic study of the subculture of consumption of Harley-Davidson bikers, not only went to rallies of the Harley Owners Group but also eventually bought Harley-Davidson bikes and the appropriate clothing, such as black boots, and used the bikes for their everyday transportation. Marquart (1983), in his study of the social control system that existed in the Texas Department of Corrections (TDC), went through the training program to become a prison guard and was employed as a prison guard for eighteen months in the maximum-security unit. During this period of time, he observed the behavior of the prison guards and inmates as he patrolled the cell blocks, showers, and dining halls, searched for weapons, and broke up fights.

Entry and Group Acceptance   One of the first tasks that must be accomplished when using the participant observation approach is to gain entry to the group or culture you wish to study. In some instances this is very easy. For example, if you wanted to conduct an ethnographic study of fraternity or sorority rush week, you might do so by actually participating in rush week, either as a bona fide participant or under the guise of wanting to belong to a sorority or fraternity. During rush week you would not only be a participant in the process, but you would also be observing and taking notes on the behavior and activity of other students involved in this process.

In other instances entry to the group or culture is not as easily accomplished. Gaining access to a local teenage street gang would, in most instances, be a rather difficult process. Similarly, access to elite groups, such as the super rich, is often very difficult because these individuals set up barriers to maintain their privacy and actively avoid scrutiny. Marquart, for example, had to get the approval of the Texas Department of Corrections (TDC) and the superintendent of the unit at which he was employed in order to conduct his study.

Before gaining entry into a group, you must decide whether this entry will be covert or overt. In some instances, the entry must be covert because this is the only way in which the research can be conducted. For example, Humphreys's (1970) study of casual homosexual encounters in a public restroom could not have been conducted if he had formally announced his identity as a researcher. In other instances entry can be overt, such as Marquart's study of the control system in the TDC or Schouten and McAlexander's study of Harley-Davidson bikers. However, even when entry is overt, you may have to get past gatekeepers, individuals who operate to protect, either formally or informally, the members of a group. Marquart, for example, had to secure the permission and approval of the warden of the prison unit in which he was employed.

Reactive effect
A change in the research participant's behavior created by the presence of the researcher or awareness of being in a study

Even when gatekeepers provide their approval, there frequently must be acceptance by the members of the group before valid information can be obtained. One of the difficulties with participant observation research is that a researcher's presence can create a **reactive effect**. By a reactive effect I mean that the presence of the research alters the behavior of the group members. For example, Marquart had to earn the trust of each inmate before the inmate would reveal his control techniques. Suspicion and paranoia run rampant in a prison environment. It would be virtually impossible for an unknown researcher to walk into a prison and expect the inmates or the guards to divulge their informal system of control. When Schouten and McAlexander (1995) first gained entry to a HOG chapter, they "were treated politely by some, standoffishly by others, and overly gregariously by others, but no one treated us as if we really belonged there" (p. 46). It was only after they stopped and rendered assistance to one of the members who had mechanical problems with his bike that an initial bond was formed and they began to be indoctrinated into the ways of HOG and eventually treated as one of the members.

Data Collection, Analysis, Report Writing   Once the researcher has gained entry and is accepted by the group members, data collection can begin because the observations made will be less influenced by a reactive effect. However, the researcher must be constantly aware of introducing biases into the data collected. When using the participant observation approach, the researcher plays two roles: researcher and participant. Even as the researcher is trying to make objective observations, he or she must also interact with those being observed. This dual role maximizes the chances for the observer to lose objectivity and allow personal biases to enter into the description. For example, if you were hired as a security guard in a prison, you would, over time, begin to take on the attitudes and behavior of the security guards with whom you worked. Researchers must, therefore, attempt to maintain a neutral posture with the goal of trying to understand what is going on around them, although this view is not universally accepted (Berg, 1998).

The ethnographer collects information on the patterns of behavior and social relations among the members of a group primarily through observing the behavior of the group members and listening to what they say. This means that ethnographers must keep a careful record of their observations and their conversations. In addition to maintaining a record of the behavior and conversation of group members, the ethnographer may interview some of the group members regarding specific topics. He or she may also take photographs of surroundings and note the clothing worn by the group members. Schouten and McAlexander not only recorded the behavior of Harley-Davidson bikers but also took pictures of their dress and their appearance (see Figure 2.6). Basically, the ethnographer makes use of any available data collection tool that will provide information about the culture of the group being studied.

Once these observations, appearance, and photographs have been collected, they must be analyzed. This means that some sense has to be made of the volumes of information that have been collected. Sense is extracted by trying to identify themes and patterns of behavior in the conversations and activities of the people depicted in the notes or other sources of information that has been gathered. Once these themes or behavior patterns has been identified, the ethnographer writes a narrative account that provides a description and interpretation of the culture being studied.

This narrative report may include the characteristics of the group, how members of the group interact with one another, what the group has in common, what some of the group's norms and rituals are, and what the group's identity is. Schouten and McAlexander's (1995) narrative report of their ethnographic study of Harley-Davidson bikers first discussed the structure of the various Harley-Davidson biker groups and then proceeded to present a narrative of the core values of each of the biker groups, such as the feeling of personal freedom and machismo surrounding the

FIGURE 2.6

Example of dress and appearance of Harley-Davidson bikers.

(Photograph courtesy of Harley-Davidson Photograph & Imaging. Copyright H-D.)

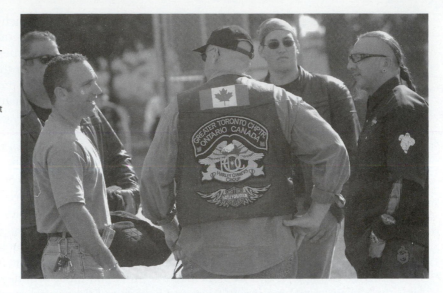

Harley-Davidson culture. The narrative report then continued with a discussion of how one becomes transformed into a biker and how, once a person has become a Harley-Davidson biker, he or she becomes committed to the consumption of products identified with being a biker.

Case Study

A **case study** is an intensive description and analysis of a single individual, organization, or event based on information obtained from a variety of sources, such as interviews, documents, test results, and archival records. There are several types of case studies: intrinsic, instrumental, and collective case studies (Stake, 1995). An **intrinsic case study** is an in-depth description of a particular individual, organization, or event conducted for the purpose of obtaining a better understanding of that particular case. Exhibit 2.2 provides a summary description of an intrinsic case study of an individual who engaged in autocastration. From reading this case, you should be able to see that it gives a description of a unique event that is both interesting and important, and it provides some understanding of possible reasons for the autocastration.

An **instrumental case study** is a case study conducted to provide insight into some issue or to refine or alter some theoretical explanation. In other words, the case study is undertaken to obtain a better understanding of some event. The specific case is not as important as gaining an understanding of the event that took place. For example, right after the Columbine tragedy, the media engaged in an intensive study of the lives of Eric Harris and Dylan Klebold to try to understand why they became killers. They looked at the type of behavior engaged in by these two and revealed that they had become obsessed with the violent video game Doom, an interactive game in which the players try to rack up the most kills. They were also members of a group

Case study

An intensive description and analysis of a single individual, organization, or event

Intrinsic case study

An in-depth description of a particular individual, organization, or event

Instrumental case study

An intensive analysis of an event to obtain a better understanding of that event

EXHIBIT 2.2

A Case Study of Autocastration

Meyer and Osborne (1982) described a case study of a twenty-nine-year-old male who castrated himself with a kitchen knife while immersed in the ocean because he thought the cool water would act as an anesthetic. He then returned home and handed his testicles to his mother, an act that he thought would return to her the life she had given him at birth. Subsequent in-patient psychiatric treatment revealed that this man had been emotionally disturbed during most of his childhood. When he was 17, he withdrew from social activities and was diagnosed as suffering from psychotic depression. Visual hallucinations were frequent, and he had the persistent delusion that he was draining his brain of nuclear material when he masturbated. During this time he frequented prostitutes and engaged in homosexual activities. These sexual exploits increased his feelings of guilt, anxiety, and depression. He considered suicide but chose castration instead because it would destroy the object of his guilt. The autocastration was interpreted by the subject's therapist as a substitute for suicide. The act was performed under sustained and mounting sexual tension. The male hormone testosterone was suggested as the possible cause of this tension because the man's sex drive and anxiety decreased sharply after he castrated himself.

known as the Trench Coat Mafia, a name given to the group by jocks who made fun of them and frequently taunted them. Harris and Klebold had been arrested in January of the previous year for breaking into a commercial van and stealing electronics. They were both enamored of Nazi culture and would berate their classmates in German. Their classroom writing assignments took on a more violent tone. These data were not examined because of an interest in describing the event of the killings at Columbine High School. Rather, they were examined to understand why the killings took place.

| Collective case study
| Intensive study of
| several individual
| cases or events

Collective case studies involve the extensive study of several individual cases. For example, a researcher might conduct a case study of three mildly retarded individuals who are placed in a general education class, several astronauts' reactions to being in space, or several cases of a rare clinical syndrome. When several case studies are conducted, the primary purpose is to gain a better understanding of the phenomenon being investigated. For example, Hippocrates (1931), Posidonius (cited in Roccatagliata, 1986, p. 143), and others have provided case study descriptions of individuals who suffer from seasonal affective disorder. These collective case studies have provided information about a general phenomenon that afflicts many people and verification of the fact that when a person is afflicted with this condition he or she will experience depression in the winter months. Collective case studies, therefore, provide some information on the ability to generalize to other cases. However, this ability to generalize is limited because the few cases investigated may represent a biased sample. Generalizing from one or several cases is possible only when there is no variability in the manifestation of the phenomenon being studied.

Case studies are important in providing a description of rare events, such as autocastration, as well as providing insight and understanding of a specific phenomenon, such as the Columbine High School shootings. However, case studies are limited because the cause of a specific event cannot be identified with any degree of certainty.

For example, it might seem logical to attribute the Columbine killings to the fact that Harris and Klebold belonged to the Trench Coat Mafia, and members of this group were frequently picked on, harassed, and excluded (Dority, 1999). Similarly, the case study of autocastration concluded that the decline in sexual tension was due to the decline in testosterone resulting from the castration. Although these interpretations may be correct, it is also possible that they are wrong. Membership in the Trench Coat Mafia may have given the members of this group a sense of identify, partially insulating them from the negative effect of being harassed. The decline in sexual tension following autocastration may have been due to a temporary decline in guilt, resulting from a belief that the object of the guilt, his testicles, had been destroyed. The most effective way to identify the cause of an event is through use of the experimental research approach.

STUDY QUESTION 2.4

- **List and then explain the purpose of the various qualitative research approaches discussed.**
- **Explain how to proceed in conducting a study using each of these qualitative research approaches.**

Summary

Since the 1990s research approaches have been dichotomized as either quantitative or qualitative. Quantitative research is research that focuses on the collection and analysis of numerical data, whereas qualitative research focuses on the collection and analysis of non-numerical information.

Quantitative research can be either experimental or nonexperimental. Experimental quantitative research attempts to ferret out cause-and-effect relationships, whereas nonexperimental research attempts to provide an accurate description or picture of a particular situation or phenomenon. Nonexperimental research approaches include the following.

1. Correlational studies provide a description of the degree of relationship that exists between two variables.

2. Ex post facto studies describe the relationship between a given behavior and a variable on which groups of research participants naturally differ, such as skin color.

3. Longitudinal and cross-sectional studies investigate changes that take place across time.

4. Naturalistic observation involves collecting data on naturally occurring behavior.

5. Meta analysis is a research approach involving the quantitative analysis of the results of many studies in order to integrate and describe the overall picture presented by these studies.

6. The survey describes a given state of affairs through use of the interview technique.

Qualitative research is an interpretative, multimethod approach that investigates people in their natural environment. Three research approaches used in conducting qualitative research are the following.

1. Phenomenology is the study of the conscious experience of a phenomenon such as death. This research approach attempts to describe, convey, and understand a person's experience of a phenomenon.

2. Ethnography describes and interprets the culture of a group of people, and through this description and interpretation attempts to understand the "way of life" of the group of people being studied.

3. A case study involves the description and analysis of a single individual, organization, or event. It is conducted either to provide a description of a particular individual, organization, or event or to provide a better understanding of some event.

Key Terms and Concepts

Experimental research	Electronic survey
Descriptive research	Open-ended questions
Quantitative research study	Closed-ended questions
Numerical data	Double-barreled questions
Qualitative research study	Social desirability bias
Non-numerical data	Response set
Nonexperimental quantitative research	Population
Correlational study	Sample
Ex post facto study	Haphazard sampling
Individual difference variable	Random sampling
Longitudinal study	Qualitative research
Cross-sectional study	Phenomenology
Cohort-sequential design	Ethnography
Naturalistic observation	Participant observation
Meta analysis	Reactive effect
Survey	Case study
Face-to-face method	Intrinsic case study
Telephone method	Instrumental case study
Random-digit dialing method	Collective case study
Mail method	

Related Internet Sites

www.mnstate.edu/wasson/ed603/ed603lesson11.htm
This Internet site provides a brief discussion of correlational research as well as the nature of correlation.

http://ecourse.amberton.edu/grad/RGS6035E1/READ4.htm
This Internet site discusses ex post facto research and experimental research and provides a good contrast between the two.

www.pitt.edu/~super1/lecture/lec3221/
This Internet site discusses in some depth the conduct of a meta analysis.

www.acenet.edu/bookstore/pdf/2002_access&persistence.pdf
This site contains the results of a longitudinal study focusing on college students.

http://psychology.wadsworth.com/workshops/workshops.html
This site consists of a series of workshops, two of which focus on surveys. To get to the survey research workshops first click on "Research Methods Workshops." This will bring up a Web page with many workshops. Click on "Surveys" and "Designing a survey."

www.phenomenologycenter.org/phenom.htm
This Internet site talks about phenomenology.

www2.chass.ncsu.edu/garson/pa765/ethno.htm
This Internet site discusses ethnographic research.

Practice Test

Answers to these questions can be found in Appendix A.

1. Dr. Jones wants to conduct a study to find out if smoking increases as alcohol consumption increases. Dr. Jones would be conducting what kind of study?
   a. Correlational
   b. Longitudinal
   c. Meta analysis
   d. Intensive case study
   e. Ex post facto

2. Dr. Smith took another approach to investigating the connection between cigarette smoking and alcohol consumption. He identified people who did not smoke and people who smoked at least a pack of cigarettes a day and then recorded the amount of alcohol they consumed to see if smokers drank more than nonsmokers. Dr. Smith conducted what kind of study?
   a. Correlational
   b. Longitudinal
   c. Meta analysis
   d. Intensive case study
   e. Ex post facto

3. Dr. Thomas had read reports of several studies that did find a connection between cigarette smoking and alcohol consumption and was convinced that a connection did exist. However, he wanted to find out how large the treatment effect might be. To answer this research question he would conduct what kind of study?
   a. Correlational
   b. Longitudinal
   c. Meta analysis
   d. Intensive case study
   e. Ex post facto

4. Dr. Marlboro was interested in another facet of smoking. He wanted to know what it was like to quit smoking. He had heard that some people have a very rough time, so he identified a person who had quit after having smoked for 20 years and investigated his experience with quitting. Dr. Marlboro conducted what kind of study?

a. Intensive case study
b. Phenomenological study
c. Ethnographic study
d. Survey
e. Naturalistic observation

5. Dr. Bourbon wanted to develop a better understanding of alcoholics, so he identified four individuals who met all criteria for being alcoholics. He then interviewed these individuals, tested them extensively, looked into their past behavior, and interviewed people with whom they had contact to develop this understanding. Dr. Bourbon was conducting what kind of study?

a. Phenomenological study
b. Ethnographic study
c. Survey
d. Collective case study
e. Naturalistic observation

Challenge Exercises

1. There are many beliefs about events in the world that different people hold, such as the following:

> When bones ache rain is coming.
> Blonds aren't very smart.
> People who live in the country move more slowly than people in the city.
> People who live in the South are not very smart.

Think about each of these beliefs and the various quantitative research designs. Identify the type of quantitative research design or designs (more than one design could be used to test some of these beliefs) that could be used to test each of these beliefs. Then explain why the design or designs you selected could test the belief. Also explain why the designs you did not select could not be used to test the beliefs.

2. Read the section in your textbook on surveys and pay particular attention to the material on writing questions. Then go to the Internet site www.cc.gatech.edu/classes/cs6751_97_winter/Topics/quest-design/ and read the material on survey design, again paying particular attention to the material on writing questions. After you have reviewed this material, identify a topic on which you might want to conduct a survey, such as:

Drinking on college campus
Sexual activity among college students
Drug use among a college population

After identifying your survey topic, write eight questions addressing the topic you have chosen. In writing each question make sure that each question addresses one of the eight issues discussed in this book (two issues) and the Internet site (six issues). First write each question so that it contains one of the problems addressed, and then rewrite it so that the problem is corrected.

3. Go to the library and find the following article:

    Rhoads, R. A. (1995). Whales tales, dog piles, and beer goggles: An ethnographic case study of fraternity life. *Anthropology and Education Quarterly, 26,* 306–323.

    This study is titled both an ethnographic study and a case study. Which is it, and why is it one and not the other? Or is it a combination of both an ethnographic study and a case study?

4. Give your students a brief introduction to phenomenology by having them engage in two behaviors. Have them throw some trash on the ground in a public place and in front of others. Also have them fix up public problems they come across in the course of their everyday activities such as picking up litter, fixing a street sign, cleaning a communal lounge such as one in their dorm, repairing public playground equipment, cleaning a public restroom, etc. After completing each of these activities, have them answer two questions:
    a. How did they feel when littering and how did they feel when fixing up a public problem?
    b. How did others around them react and how did they feel about the others' reaction?

3 The Experimental Research Approach

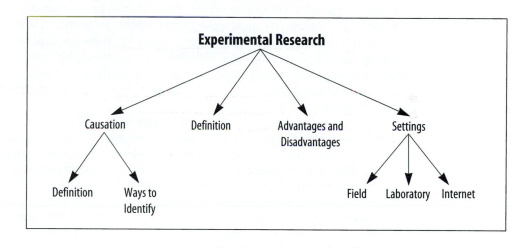

In June 1999, the American Psychological Association published a special issue of *The Monitor* on psychology and cancer. The thrust of this special issue was the contribution made by psychology in cancer research and cancer caregiving. At first glance, it may seem strange to focus on the role of psychology in cancer because cancer is typically thought of as a physical disorder with little or no psychological component. However, we are increasingly finding that the mind and the body are not separate entities but are interconnected. One has only to be associated with a cancer patient to realize the psychological impact of this illness.

Consider, for example, the case of Mrs. A, a forty-nine-year-old businesswoman. Mrs. A's mother was diagnosed with cancer when she was twelve. For the next five years, Mrs. A's mother underwent a series of treatments consisting of a radical mastectomy, radiation that burned and scarred her skin, and chemotherapy so toxic that it left her crouched on her hands and knees, vomiting onto newspapers by her bed. Mrs. A's mother was totally devastated by her illness and forced her daughter to be her only caregiver while at the same time forcing her husband out of the bedroom. By the time her mother died, Mrs. A had become her virtual slave. Today, Mrs. A is not only filled with rage at the disease that robbed her of her childhood, but she is also a patient at a high-risk clinic designed to educate women about breast cancer prevention and help them manage their emotions (Clay, 1999). This is just one example of the emotional turmoil that may accompany cancer.

So what kind of contribution can psychology make to cancer research and treatment? Remember that cancer can cause emotional turmoil not only in the cancer victim but also in the caregivers of the victim and other family members. Is it possible that a psychological intervention, or psychotherapy, can assist in preventing cancer or even prolong life in those that have cancer? We know that prolonged stress affects just about every system in the body. This leads to the question of whether individuals living in very stressful conditions are more susceptible to cancer. If research demonstrates that they are, can a stress management program reduce the risk of developing cancer? Many other legitimate questions could also be asked. These are questions that need to be asked and that are currently being researched.

How do we seek the answers to these questions? The primary way in which researchers have begun to provide answers to these questions is by conducting a psychological experiment or using the experimental research approach, the approach discussed in this chapter.

Chapter Preview

In the present chapter I discuss the experimental research approach. This is the research approach that is typically used to investigate causality. Although other approaches are used, the experimental approach is the primary one because of its characteristics. Because causality is the type of relationship investigated when using the experimental research approach, one might assume that we have a good understanding of the meaning of causality and how to identify causal relationships. This is an inaccurate assumption. To drive this point home, I first discuss the meaning of *causation* and, hopefully, convince you that it is difficult to identify causality. Then I discuss the characteristics of the experimental research approach, its advantages and disadvantages, and the settings in which psychological experiments are conducted.

Introduction

Experimental research approach
The research approach in which one attempts to discover the effects of presumed causes

The **experimental research approach** is a quantitative approach designed to discover the effects of presumed causes. The key feature of this approach is that one thing is deliberately varied to see what happens to something else, or to discover the effects of presumed causes. This is something that people do all the time. For example, individuals try different diets or exercise to see if they will lose weight. Others may get an education to see if that will lead to a better job. Still other individuals may change their diet to see if it will lower their blood cholesterol level. As you can see, both scientists and nonscientists use experimentation to try to identify causal relationships. However, scientific experimentation differs from nonscientific experimentation in that the scientist makes a deliberate attempt to make observations that are free of bias. Both approaches attempt to identify causal relationships. I therefore begin by exploring the concept of causation and then discuss scientific experimentation and the nature of causation that experiments test.

Causation

Causation
A term whose meaning is debated by philosophers, but that in everyday language seems to imply that manipulation of one event produces another event

Causation is one of those terms that people frequently use but often don't really understand. People ask questions like "What causes cancer?" "What causes a person to murder someone else?" "What causes a man to beat his wife?" What do they really mean? Common sense suggests that causality refers to a condition in which one event—the cause—generates another event—the effect. However, causality is much more complex.

When individuals discuss the effects of events, they tend to use the words *cause* and *effect* rather informally. People are likely to assume that manipulation is implicit in the concept of causation. If we manipulate or do something, we expect something else to happen. If something does happen, the thing or event we manipulate is called the *cause* and what happens is called the *effect*. For example, if we spank a child for coloring on a wall and then observe that he no longer colors on the wall, we assume that the spanking caused the child to stop the coloring. This temporal relationship between events such as spanking and ceasing a behavior such as coloring on a wall gives people an intuitive sense that they understand the meaning of cause and effect. However, the definition of these terms has eluded philosophers for centuries.

Cause

Cause
A contextually dependent event that makes something else exist

The intuitive definition most of us have is that a **cause** is something that makes something else exist. However, this intuitive definition of cause is far too simplistic because all causal relationships are contextually dependent. For example, depression can occur in many different ways. Eating a diet that does not contain the precursor of the central neurotransmitter serotonin, having a baby, being fired from a job, getting a divorce, and numerous other events can cause an onset of depression. However, none of these events by itself is sufficient to cause depression. Many women have babies without experiencing postpartum depression. For some individuals losing a job causes depression, whereas others view it as an opportunity to develop another stimulating career. The point is that many factors are usually required for an effect to occur, and we rarely know all of them and how they relate to each other. This means that any causal relationship occurs within the context of many factors and, if any of these other factors change, the causal relationship previously identified may or may not be replicated. This is why causal relationships are not deterministic but probabilistic (Shadish, Cook, & Campbell, 2002). In spite of the difficulty with identifying the cause of some event, it is still useful to think of cause as something that produces something else. However, we must never lose sight of the fact that any causal relationship occurs contextually and that the generalization of any effect is always an issue.

Effect

Effect
The difference between what would have happened and what did happen when a treatment is administered

An **effect** is the difference between what would have happened and what did happen. In an experiment, the effect is the difference between what did happen when a treatment was administered and what would have happened to *this same group of individuals* if the treatment had not been administered. Note the emphasis on the *same group* of individuals. However, it is impossible for the same group of people to both have and not have a treatment, so identifying a true effect is not possible. What we attempt to do within the context of an experiment is to obtain an imperfect measure of this difference by doing such things as having two different groups of individuals and administering the treatment to one group and not to the other group. The point is that it is never possible to obtain a true measure of an effect because this requires participants to both be exposed to something and not be exposed to something and that is not possible.

Causal Relationship

What kind of evidence is needed to know if a cause and effect are related? John Stuart Mill (1874), a British philosopher, set forth canons that could be used to experimentally identify causality. These canons form the basis of many of the approaches currently used.

Method of agreement

The identification of the common element in several instances of an event

Common element used in several instance of event

1. The first canon is the **method of agreement**, by which one identifies causality by observing the element common to several instances of an event. This canon can be illustrated by the frequently cited case of the man who wanted to find out scientifically why he got drunk. He drank rye and water on the first night and became drunk. On the second night, he drank scotch and water and became drunk again. On the third night, he got drunk on bourbon and water. He therefore decided that the water was the cause of his getting drunk because it was the common element each time. This method, as you can see, is inadequate for unequivocally identifying causation because many significant variables—such as the alcohol in the rye, scotch, and bourbon—may be overlooked.

Method of difference

The identification of the different effects produced by variation in only one event

Different aspect in one element

2. The second canon is the **method of difference,** by which one attempts to identify causality by observing the different effects produced in two situations that are alike in all respects except one. The method of difference is the approach taken in many psychological experiments. In an experiment designed to test the effect of a drug on reaction time, the drug is given to one group of participants while a placebo is given to another group of matched participants. If the reaction time of the drug-taking group differs significantly from that of the control group, the difference is usually attributed to the drug (the causal agent). This method provides the basis for a great deal of work in psychology aimed at identifying causality.

Joint methods of agreement and difference

The combination of the methods of agreement and difference to identify causation

3. The third canon set forth by Mill is the **joint methods of agreement and difference**. This method is exactly what its name implies. The method of agreement is first used to observe common elements, which are then formulated as hypotheses to be tested by the method of difference. In the case of the man who wanted to find out why he got drunk, the common element, water, should have been formulated as a hypothesis to be tested by the method of difference. Using the method of difference, researchers would give one group of participants water and a matched group another liquid (such as straight bourbon). Naturally, the group drinking only water would not get drunk, indicating that the wrong variable had been identified even though it was a common element.

Method of concomitant variation

The identification of parallel changes in two variables

4. The fourth canon is the **method of concomitant variation.** This method states that a variable is either a cause or an effect, or else is connected through some factor of causation if variation in the variable results in a parallel variation in another variable. Plutchik (1974) interprets this canon to be an extension of the method of difference in that, rather than just using two equated groups in an experiment, the researchers use three or more, with each group receiving a different amount of the variable under study. In the previously cited drug example, rather than just a placebo group and a drug group, one placebo and several drug groups could be used, with each drug group receiving a different amount of the drug. Reaction times could then be observed to determine if variation in the quantity of the drug results in a parallel variation in reaction time. If this parallel variation is found, then the drug is interpreted as being the cause of the variation in reaction time.

Some writers interpret this canon as including correlation studies. One is on extremely shaky ground in attempting to infer causative relationships from correlational studies because many correlational studies simply describe the degree of relationship. However, recent work is making strides in enabling causation to be inferred from correlational studies.

From looking at the works of such people as Mill, one gets the idea that we have a fairly adequate grasp of what causation is and how to obtain evidence of it. This belief is reinforced when we see that many studies of causation are based on Mill's canons. Such philosophizing and experimentation have not completely clarified the meaning of the word *cause,* however.

Exhibit 3.1 which presents Morison's (1960, pp. 193–194) review of the history of attempts to find the cause of malaria, illustrates the ambiguity of this word. Essentially, the method of agreement was used first to hypothesize that the bad air in the lowlands caused malaria because a common element among people living on top of the hills was better air. Subsequent investigation using the method of difference revealed that only individuals with the malaria parasite in their blood suffered from the disease. The problem with this second explanation is that it did not explain how the parasite came to exist in the bloodstream, until it was found that the mosquito transmitted it. As you can see, the various canons set forth by Mill enable us to identify the relationships that exist among a set of variables. However, they do not help us to name the single factor that causes an effect, just as they did not enable scientists to identify the single factor that causes malaria. This is because the identification of causation can occur only when *no* alternative interpretations for an effect exist other than the one specified. When we have reached this stage, we have essentially identified both the necessary and the sufficient conditions for the occurrence of an event. A **necessary condition** refers to a condition that must be present in order for the effect to occur. (To become an alcoholic, you must consume alcohol.) A **sufficient condition** refers to a condition that will always produce the effect. (Destroying the auditory nerve always results in a loss of hearing.)

A condition must be both necessary and sufficient to qualify as a cause because in such a situation the effect would never occur unless the condition were present and, whenever the condition was present, the effect would occur. If a condition were only *sufficient,* then the effect could occur in other ways. (There are several ways one can lose one's hearing in addition to destruction of the auditory nerve.) In like manner, a *necessary* condition does not mean that the effect will necessarily occur. (All people who consume alcohol do not become alcoholics, but one must consume alcohol to become an alcoholic.)

To state that we have found the cause for an event means that both the necessary and the sufficient conditions have been found. It means that a complete explanation of the occurrence of the event has been isolated and that, unlike the theory of malaria, the explanation *will never change.*

It is presumptuous to assume that we will ever find the conditions necessary and sufficient for the occurrence of an event, however, because the behavior of organisms is extremely complex. Seldom do we encounter situations or behaviors that cannot be explained in several different ways. Popper (1968) has perhaps been most explicit in his insistence on the necessity of ruling out alternative explanations. According to

Necessary condition
A condition that must exist for an effect to occur

Sufficient condition
A condition that will always produce the effect under study

EXHIBIT 3.1

Morison's Discussion of the History of Attempts to Find the Cause of Malaria

Whatever the reason, medical men have found it congenial to assume that they could find something called *The Cause* of a particular disease. If one looks at the history of any particular disease, one finds that the notion of its cause has varied with the state of the art. In general, the procedure has been to select as *The Cause* that element in the situation which one could do the most about. In many cases it turned out that, if one could take away this element or reduce its influence, the disease simply disappeared or was reduced in severity. This was certainly desirable, and it seemed sensible enough to say that one had got at the cause of the condition. Thus in ancient and medieval times malaria, as its name implied, was thought to be due to the bad air of the lowlands. As a result, towns were built on the tops of hills, as one notices in much of Italy today. The disease did not disappear, but its incidence and severity were reduced to a level consistent with productive community life.

At this stage it seemed reasonable enough to regard bad air as the cause of malaria, but soon the introduction of quinine to Europe from South America suggested another approach. Apparently quinine acted on some situation within the patient to relieve and often to cure him completely. Toward the end of the last century the malaria parasite was discovered in the blood of patients suffering from the disease. The effectiveness of quinine was explained by its ability to eliminate this parasite from the blood. The parasite now became *The Cause*, and those who could afford the cost of quinine and were reasonably regular in their habits were enabled to escape the most serious ravages of the disease. It did not disappear as a public health problem, however, and further study was given to the chain of causality. These studies were shortly rewarded by the discovery that the parasite was transmitted by certain species of mosquitoes. For practical purposes *The Cause* of epidemic malaria became the Mosquito, and attention was directed to control of its activities.

Entertainingly enough, however, malaria has disappeared from large parts of the world without anyone doing much about it at all. The fens of Boston and other northern cities still produce mosquitoes capable of transmitting the parasite, and people carrying the organism still come to these areas from time to time, but it has been many decades since the last case of the disease occurred locally. Observations such as this point to the probability that epidemic malaria is the result of a nicely balanced set of social and economic, as well as biological factors, each one of which has to be present at the appropriate level. We are still completely unable to describe these sufficient conditions with any degree of accuracy, but we know what to do in an epidemic area because we have focused attention on three or four of the most necessary ones.

inductive logic, science must be capable of deciding between the truth and falsity of hypotheses and theories. In other words, if we conduct a scientific experiment testing the hypothesis that depression can be treated with psychotherapy, we should be able to decide if this hypothesis is true or false. Popper rejects the notion of such inductive logic. He maintains that we cannot use the results of one or even several scientific experiments to infer that a given hypothesis or theory is true, or proven. Even if five experiments show the success of treating depressives with psychotherapy, this is not conclusive proof that psychotherapy can successfully treat depressives. The attained relationship could be due to flaws in the experiments or to unknown variables operating simultaneously with the psychotherapy. To Popper, a confirmation of an experiment states only that the hypothesis tested has survived the test. On the other hand, if the experiment fails to confirm a prediction or a theory, the prediction or theory being tested is falsified. Therefore, Popper focuses attention on a **position of falsification** rather than a position of confirmation. For him, a theory or prediction can only achieve the status of "not yet disconfirmed"; it can never be proved. In other words, if an experiment supports the prediction that psychotherapy is beneficial in treating depressives, Popper would not state that the prediction has been confirmed; he would merely state that this prediction has maintained the status of not yet disconfirmed. This status is very precious in science, however, because it means that the theory or prediction has passed the test of rigorous experimentation and thus only states one of the possible true explanations.

Deese (1972) provides yet another view of causation. He sees causation as a large network of cause-and-effect relations. Any given cause-and-effect relation that is isolated in a study is only one such relation embedded in a matrix of others. Consider the case of Morison's discussion of malaria, in which he illustrates the covariation between a number of events and malaria, each of which was once considered a specific cause-and-effect relationship. The bad air of the lowlands was found to covary with the incidence of malaria. Later it was found that the presence of a parasite covaried with the appearance of malaria, and even later it was found that a certain species of mosquito caused malaria because it carried the malaria parasite. Note that a number of specific cause-and-effect relationships, in terms of covariation of events, were involved in the history of trying to identify the cause of malaria. It is apparent that none of these specific relationships could be labeled as the cause of malaria, because many of the so-called causative events (such as the mosquitoes) still exist and yet the presumed effect of malaria no longer occurs. For a given effect to occur, as Morison pointed out, a nicely balanced system of interrelated conditions must exist. For malaria to occur, the mosquitoes and parasites must exist in a system of other specific social and economic conditions. Any one condition by itself is not sufficient to produce the effect. Proponents of this view of causation advocate study of the relationship among the levels or amounts of the variables operating within a system rather than study of the covariation between one variable, which can be labeled the cause, and another, which can be labeled the effect. Such a viewpoint sees any given study as representing only a small part of the overall system, and the relationship found in a given study exists only if certain relationships exist among the remainder of the elements of the system.

It is clear that causation is subject of quite a bit of debate. However, this debate (see Brand, 1976; White, 1990) exists primarily among philosophers of science and not among researchers. Philosophers of science are concerned with what causation is and the possibility that it is only a construction of the mind. Psychology is "concerned with how people understand and perceive causation, make causal inferences and attributions, and so forth" (White, 1990, p. 10). While these two concerns are related, psychological research takes a specific approach to seeking out causal processes. There is no inherent requirement stating that the approach used in research to seek out causal inferences has to adhere to the actual nature of causation, whatever that may

Position of falsification
The belief that the best that can be said about a theory or prediction is that it is "not yet falsified"

be. This is because the methods used by philosophers of science and those used by researchers are different.

The method used by philosophers of science is rationalism involving such things as imaginability, intelligibility, and freedom from ambiguity in an attempt to identify the nature of causation. The method used in psychological research is empirical, or makes use of objective observation to obtain evidence of some causal relationship. Philosophers of science and psychological researchers are, therefore, asking different kinds of questions although they both are focusing on causation. Philosophers of science are asking questions about the nature of causation whereas researchers are asking questions about the relationship between variables. The fact that they are both focusing on causation should not disguise their basic differences. One could not design a psychological study that would test a philosophical notion any more than one could establish the truth or falsity of a hypothesis by logic alone.

STUDY QUESTION 3.1

- **Why can we never identify the cause of an effect?**
- **Identify and discuss the different ways of viewing causation.**
- **What view or views of causation seem to be represented by the psychological experiment?**
- **Why is the debate about the nature of causation of little concern to researchers?**

The Psychological Experiment

John Stuart Mill, in his classic 1874 analysis, identified three criteria that must be met to identify a cause and effect relationship.

- The cause must precede the effect.
- The cause must be related to the effect.
- No plausible alternative explanations must exist for the effect other than the cause.

These three characteristics mirror what happens in the psychological experiment. Zimney (1961, p. 18) defines a **psychological experiment** as "objective observation of phenomena which are made to occur in a strictly controlled situation in which one *or more* factors are varied and the others are kept constant." This definition seems to be a good one because of the components that it includes, each of which are examined separately next. Analysis of this definition, with one minor alteration, should provide a definition of an experiment, an appreciation of the many facets of experimentation, and a general understanding of how experimentation meets the three criteria set forth by Mill to identify how a cause and effect enables causative relationships.

Psychological experiment
Objective observation of phenomena that are made to occur in a strictly controlled situation in which one or more factors are varied and the others are kept constant

1. Objective Observation   Impartiality and freedom from bias on the part of the investigator, or objectivity, was previously discussed as a characteristic that the scientist must exhibit. In order to be able to identify causation from the results of the experiment, the experimenter must avoid doing anything that might influence the outcome. Rosenthal (1966) has demonstrated that the experimenter is probably capable of greater biasing effects than one would expect. In spite of this, and recognizing that complete objectivity is probably unattainable, the investigator must strive for freedom from bias.

Science requires that we make empirical observations in order to arrive at answers to the questions that are posed. Observations are necessary because they provide the database used to attain the answers. To provide correct answers, experimenters must make a concerted effort to avoid mistakes, even though they are only human and therefore are subject to errors in recording and observation. For example, work in impression formation has revealed the biased nature of our impressions of others. Gage and Cronback (1955, p. 420) have stated that social impressions are "dominated far more by what the Judge brings to it than by what he takes in during it." Once scientists realize that they are capable of making mistakes, they can guard against them. Zimney (1961) presents three rules that investigators should follow to minimize recording and observation errors. The first rule is to accept the possibility that mistakes can occur—that we are not perfect, that our perceptions and therefore our responses are influenced by our motives, desires, and other biasing factors. Once we accept this fact, we can then attempt to identify where the mistakes are likely to occur—the second rule. To identify potential mistakes, we must carefully analyze and test each segment of the entire experiment in order to anticipate the potential sources and causes of the errors. Once the situation has been analyzed, then the third rule can be implemented—to take the necessary steps to avoid the errors. Often this involves constructing a more elaborate scenario or just designing equipment and procedures more appropriately. In any event, every effort should be expended to construct the experiment so that accurate observations are recorded.

2. Of Phenomena That Are Made to Occur   Webster's dictionary defines *phenomenon* as "an observable fact or event." In psychological experimentation, **phenomenon** refers to any publicly observable behavior, such as actions, appearances, verbal statements, responses to questionnaires, and physiological recordings. Focusing on such observable behaviors is a must if psychology is to meet the previously discussed characteristics of science. Only by focusing on these phenomena can we satisfy the demands of operationalism and replication of experiments.

Phenomenon
A publicly observable behavior

Defining a phenomenon as publicly observable behavior would seem to exclude the internal or private processes and states of the individual. In the introductory psychology course, such processes as memory, perception, personality, emotion, and intelligence are discussed. Is it possible to retain these processes if we study only *publicly* observable behavior? Certainly these processes must be retained because they also play a part in determining an individual's responses. Such processes are studied diligently by many psychologists. In studying these processes, researchers investigate publicly observable behavior and infer from their observations the existence of internal processes. It is the behavioral manifestation of the inferred processes that is observed. For example, intelligence is inferred from responses to an intelligence test, aggression from verbal or physical attacks on another person.

In the discussion of control as a goal of science, we saw that the psychologist does not have a direct controlling influence on behavior. The psychologist arranges the consequences and the antecedent conditions that result in the behavior of interest. In an experiment, the experimenter precisely manipulates one or more variables and objectively observes the phenomena *that are made to occur* by this manipulation. This part of the definition of experimentation refers to the fact that the experimenter is manipulating the conditions that cause a certain effect. In this way, experimenters identify the cause-and-effect relationships from experimentation by noting the effect or lack of effect produced by their manipulations.

3. In a Strictly Controlled Situation   This part of the definition refers to the need to eliminate the influence of variables other than those manipulated by the experimenter. As you have seen, control is one of the most pressing problems facing the experimenter and one to which considerable attention is devoted. Without control, causation could not be identified. Because of the magnitude of this issue, it is given extended coverage in later chapters.

4. In Which One or More Factors Are Varied and the Others Are Kept Constant   The ideas expressed in this phase of the definition are epitomized by the *rule of one variable,* which states that all conditions in an experiment must be kept constant except one, which is to be varied along a defined range, and the result of this variation is to be measured on the response variable. The two major ideas expressed in the rule of one variable are constancy and variation. *Constancy* refers to controlling or eliminating the influence of all variables except the one (or ones) of interest. This requirement is necessary to determine the cause of the variation on the response variable. If the constancy requirement is violated, the cause for the variation cannot be determined and the experiment is ruined. A learning experiment can easily illustrate the constancy component of the rule. Assume that you are interested in the effect of the length of a list of words on speed of learning. How does increasing the length influence the speed with which one learns that list of words? The length of the list of words could be systematically varied and related to the number of trials needed to learn the list. In such an experiment, some factors that could influence learning speed must be controlled, including the difficulty of the words, the participants' ability level, the participants' familiarity with the words, and the participants' motivation level. Only if these factors are held constant (and therefore do not exert an influence) can you say that the difference in speed of learning is a function of the change in the length of the list of words. The idea of *variation* means that one or more variables must be deliberately and precisely varied by some given amount to determine their effect on behavior. In the learning experiment, the length of the list of words must be changed by an exact, predetermined amount. The questions that frequently arise are *how* and *how much* is the variable to be varied? The answers to these questions will be discussed later in the book.

Advantages of the Experimental Approach

<u>Causal Inference</u>   The psychological experiment has been presented as a method for identifying causal relationships. Indeed, its primary advantage is the strength with

which a causal relationship can be inferred. However, in looking at this advantage, it is important to distinguish between causal description and causal explanation (Shadish et al., 2002). **Causal description** refers to describing the consequences attributable to deliberately varying a treatment. For example, many studies have demonstrated that drugs such as Prozac help ameliorate depression. Such a study is causal description because it describes the causal connection between administering the drug and the consequence of amelioration of depression. However, this study does not provide an explanation of why the drug worked. This is the purview of causal explanation.

Causal explanation refers to clarifying the mechanisms by which a causal relationship holds. In other words, causal explanation involves taking a causal relationship and identifying the features that produce the causal relationship. For example, identifying a causal descriptive relationship between Prozac and amelioration of depression is not sufficient. After identifying this causal descriptive relationship we want to know why the relationship holds. We want to know how Prozac works to affect depression. Currently we know that it has an influence on the central neurotransmitter serotonin and that serotonin is involved in depression. But how is serotonin involved and why does it take some time for Prozac to work when its effect on increasing serotonin is rather immediate? There are too many questions whose answers still remain unknown for us to have a full explanation of how the treatment (Prozac) mediates its influence on the outcome, the amelioration of depression.

The practical importance of causal explanation is emphasized when a person with depression obtains no relief from taking Prozac. Such instances not only emphasize the importance of causal explanation, but also help explain why the bulk of science is directed toward explaining why and how something happens. It also illustrates why it is easier to identify causal description and more difficult to achieve causal explanation.

Control   The inferential strength that the experimental approach has in identifying a causal relationship is, to a large degree, obtained from the degree of control that can be exercised. Control, as stated in Chapter 1, is the most important characteristic of scientific research, and the experimental approach enables the researcher to effect the greatest degree of control. In an experiment, one is seeking an answer to a specific question. In order to obtain an unambiguous answer, it is necessary to institute control over irrelevant variables by either eliminating their influence or holding their influence constant. Such control can be achieved by bringing the experiment into the laboratory, thereby eliminating noise and other potentially distracting stimuli. Control is also achieved by using such techniques as random assignment and matching, which are discussed in Chapter 9.

Ability to Manipulate Variables   An advantage of the experimental approach is the ability to manipulate precisely one or more variables of the experimenter's choosing. If a researcher is interested in studying the effects of crowding on a particular behavior, crowding can be manipulated in a very precise and systematic manner by varying the number of people in a constant amount of space. If the researcher is also interested in the effects of the gender of the participant and degree of crowding on some subsequent behavior, male and female participants can be included in both the

Causal description
Describing the consequences of deliberately varying a treatment

Causal explanation
Clarifying the mechanisms by which a causal relationship holds

crowded and noncrowded conditions. In this way, the experimenter can precisely manipulate two variables: gender of participant and degree of crowding. The experimental approach enables one to control precisely the manipulation of variables by specifying the exact conditions of the experiment. The results can then be interpreted unambiguously, because the research participants should be responding primarily to the variables introduced by the experimenter.

Disadvantages of the Experimental Approach

Does Not Test Effects of Nonmanipulated Variables   Although the experimental research approach is the best method we have for identifying causal relationships, it is limited to testing the effect of things that can be manipulated, such as the amount of attention parents give children, the severity of punishment administered, or the type of therapy used to treat people with depression. The world in which we live includes many events that are not capable of being controlled by an experimenter and, therefore, not capable of being deliberately manipulated. For example, we cannot deliberately manipulate people's ages, their raw genetic material, the weather, the appearance of sunspots, or terrorists' activities. We live in a world with many nonmanipulable events that produce effects. These nonmanipulable causal events are not capable of being investigated within the context of an experiment.

This does not mean that we cannot or should not investigate the effects of nonmanipulable events. We not only can but do investigate these nonmanipulate variables with ex post facto designs. Remember that ex post facto designs are used to investigate variables that are investigated after the fact. The destruction of the twin trade towers in New York City on September 11, 2001, had a significant psychological impact on many individuals' lives. Investigating one of the effects of this tragic event could be done by comparing the psychological impact of people who were near the twin towers when they collapsed with individuals who were more than one hundred miles away. Such a study would have to take place "after the fact" or after the event had taken place because it would not be possible for an experimenter to manipulate such an event. This means that an ex post facto design would have to be used and not an experimental design.

Artificiality   The most frequently cited and probably the most severe criticism leveled against the experimental approach is that laboratory findings are obtained in an artificial and sterile atmosphere that precludes any generalization to a real-life situation. The following statement by Bannister (1966, p. 24) epitomizes this point of view:

> In order to behave like scientists we must construct situations in which subjects are totally controlled, manipulated and measured. We must cut our subjects down to size. We must construct situations in which they can behave as little like human beings as possible and we do this in order to allow ourselves to make statements about the nature of their humanity.

Is such a severe criticism of experimentation justified? It seems to me that the case is overstated. Underwood (1959), taking a totally different point of view, does not see artificiality as a problem at all. The following are Underwood's words.

One may view the laboratory as a fast, efficient, convenient way of identifying variables or factors which are likely to be important in real-life situations. Thus, if four or five factors are discovered to influence human learning markedly, and to influence it under a wide range of conditions, it would be reasonable to suspect that these factors would also be important in the classroom. But, one would *not* automatically conclude such; rather, one would make field tests in the classroom situation to deny or confirm the inference concerning the general importance of these variables.[1]

The artificiality issue is a problem only when an individual makes a generalization from an experimental finding without first determining whether the generalization can be made. Ideally, competent psychologists rarely blunder in this fashion because they realize that laboratory experiments are contrived situations. Realistically, psychologists seem to frequently make risky generalizations from their work, although there are times when such generalizations are warranted. In most instances we cannot generalize from animals to humans. Instead, we must identify the effects on organisms such as rats and then verify the existence of such effects using humans as the research participants. Sulik, Johnston, and Webb (1981) present one of the more dramatic instances in which a direct generalization can be made from animals to humans. Figure 3.1 illustrates the similarity in the pattern of facial malformations that occur in the mouse and in humans as the result of maternal consumption of alcohol, a syndrome called *fetal alcohol syndrome*. This figure reveals that the pattern of facial malformations is strikingly similar, indicating a phenomenon that is common to humans and infrahumans.

Additional difficulties of the experimental approach include problems in designing the experiment and the fact that the experiment may be extremely time consuming. It is not unusual for an experimenter to have to go to extreme lengths to set the stage for, motivate, and occasionally deceive the research participant. Then, when the experiment is actually conducted, the experimenter and perhaps one or two assistants are often required to spend quite some time with each participant.

Inadequate Method of Scientific Inquiry   A final criticism that has been aimed at the experimental approach is that it is inadequate as a method of scientific inquiry into the study of human behavior. Gadlin and Ingle (1975) believe that a number of anomalies inherent in the experimental approach make it an inappropriate paradigm for studying human behavior. They state that the experimental approach promotes the view that humans are manipulable mechanistic objects because twentieth-century psychology mirrors the mechanistic method and assumptions of nineteenth-century physics. Gadlin and Ingle recommend the search for an alternative methodology that is not fraught with such inadequacies. It appears as though this criticism has been satisfied through the use of qualitative methodologies, although Kruglanski has pointed out that the mechanistic manipulable assumption exists only to the extent that the experimenter arranges a set of conditions that may direct the

---

[1]From "Verbal Learning in the Educative Process" by Benton J. Underwood, Spring 1959, *Harvard Educational Review, 29*, pp. 107–117. Copyright © by President and Fellows of Harvard College.

FIGURE 3.1

Malformation of facial features in the mouse and human caused by maternal alcohol consumption: (*a*) mouse embryo with fetal alcohol syndrome; (*b*) normal mouse embryo; (*c*) child with fetal alcohol syndrome.

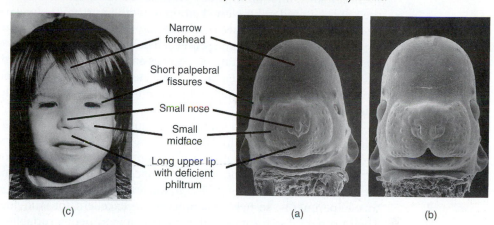

Narrow forehead

Short palpebral fissures

Small nose

Small midface

Long upper lip with deficient philtrum

(c) (a) (b)

(Reprinted from "Fetal Alcohol Syndrome: Embryogenesis in a Mouse Model" by K. K. Sulik, M. C. Johnston, and M. A. Webb, 1981, *Science, 214*, no. 4523, pp. 936–938 (figure on p. 937), November 20, 1981. © Copyright 1981 by the American Association for the Advancement of Science. Reprinted by permission.)

individual's behavior in a given manner. This in no way "suggests that the subject is an empty machine devoid of feelings, thoughts, or a will of his own" (Kruglanski, 1976, p. 656).

STUDY QUESTION 3.2

- **What is a psychological experiment? Explain the meaning of the components of this definition.**
- **What are the advantages and disadvantages of the psychological experiment?**

Experimental Research Settings

The experimental approach is used in laboratory settings, field settings, and, increasingly, on the Internet. Field, Internet, and laboratory experimentation use the experimental approach, but they have slightly different attributes that deserve mention.

Field Experimentation

Field experiment

An experimental research study that is conducted in a real-life setting

A **field experiment** is an experimental research study that is conducted in a real-life setting. The experimenter actively manipulates variables and carefully controls the influence of as many extraneous variables as the situation will permit. Regan and Llamas (2002), for example, wanted to find out if a female shopper's appearance influenced the amount of time it took for an employee of a store to approach and acknowledge her. The basic procedure they used was to have a female confederate dress either in formal work clothes and grooming (skirt, blouse, nylons, and dress shoes, with makeup and her hair down) or informal sports clothes and grooming (tights, T-shirt, and tennis shoes, with no makeup, and her hair in a ponytail) and then enter a randomly selected group of women's stores between the hours of 3:00 and 4:00 P.M. on two consecutive Thursdays. Upon entering the store, the confederate activated a stopwatch and proceeded down the first open aisle, giving the appearance of shopping for clothing. As soon as an employee approached and spoke to her she stopped the timer. As Figure 3.2 indicates, females dressed in formal work clothes were approached more quickly by store employees than were females dressed in informal sports clothing.

This is an example of a field study because it was conducted in the natural setting of a mall while engaging in daily activities. It also represents an experimental study because variable manipulation was present (type of dress) and control was present (the stores entered were randomly selected from those in the mall). Field experiments like this one are not subject to the artificiality problem that exists with laboratory experiments, so field experiments are excellent for studying many problems. Their primary disadvantage is that control of extraneous variables cannot be accomplished as well as it can be in laboratory experiments. In the Regan and Llamas study, even though the clothing stores were randomly selected from those available in the mall, the study was limited to only the types of store that rent from a mall. In addition, the store employees were not a random selection of possible employees. Consequently, a selection bias may have existed. Even though it is more difficult to exercise control in field experiments, such experiments are necessary.

FIGURE 3.2

Amount of time for a store employee to approach and acknowledge the confederate.

(Adapted from "Customer Service as a Function of Shopper's Attire" by P. C. Regan and V. Llamas, 2002, *Psychological Reports, 90,* pp. 203–204.)

Tunnell (1977) states that field experimentation should be conducted in a manner that makes all variables operational in real-world terms. The Regan and Llamas (2002) study included the three dimensions of naturalness identified by Tunnell: natural behavior, natural setting, and natural treatment. The natural behavior investigated was a store employee approaching a shopper. The setting was natural because the study took place in a mall; the natural treatment was type of dress. In reality, the treatment was imposed by a confederate, but it mirrored a behavior that could have occurred naturally. These are the types of behaviors Tunnell says we must strive for when we conduct field experimentation, as opposed to asking participants to provide self-reports or to recall their own behavior in some prior situation. Asking for such retrospective data only serves to introduce possible bias into the study.

Laboratory Experimentation

The laboratory experiment is the same type of study as the field experiment, but where the field experiment is strong the laboratory experiment is weak, and where the laboratory experiment is strong the field experiment is weak. The laboratory experiment epitomizes the ability to control or eliminate the influence of extraneous variables. This is accomplished by bringing the problem into an environment apart from the participants' normal routines. In this environment, outside influences (such as the presence of others and of noise) can be eliminated. However, the price of this increase in control is the artificiality of the situation created. This issue was covered in detail in the discussion of the disadvantages of the experimental approach. Even though precise results can be obtained from the laboratory, the applicability of these results to the real world must always be verified.

Laboratory experiment
An experimental research study that is conducted in the controlled environment of a laboratory

The **laboratory experiment** is a study that is conducted in the laboratory and in which the investigator precisely manipulates one or more variables and controls the influence of all or nearly all of the extraneous variables. For example, Kassin and Kiechel (1996) realized that there were police reports of individuals who confessed to crimes that they had not committed. They realized that there was no empirical proof of this phenomenon and were interested in determining if they could experimentally demonstrate that vulnerable individuals, under the right circumstances, would confess to an act that they did not commit and internalize this confession to the point that they would confabulate details in memory consistent with the confession. To investigate this phenomenon, Kassin and Kiechel had to construct a situation in which they manipulated the vulnerability of the research participants as well as the presence of a person falsely incriminating them. In addition, they had to control other variables such as the presence of witnesses, other individuals refuting or confirming the false accusation.

To precisely manipulate vulnerability and the presence of a witness and to control for the impact of extraneous variables, Kassin and Kiechel created a situation within the context of a laboratory setting in which the research participants had to perform a task at either moderate or rapid speed. A rapid-speed completion of the task created a vulnerable condition because the more rapidly the participants had to respond, the greater the likelihood of making a mistake. The results of this study revealed that individuals were more likely to confess to making a mistake they had not made in the vulnerable condition and when a confederate, or witness, said that the research participant had made the error. More important, these vulnerable individuals were more likely to internalize the false confession and tell others that they had committed the error.

Internet Experiments

Internet experiment
An experimental study that is conducted over the Internet

An **Internet experiment** is an experimental study that is conducted over the internet. An Internet experiment has the same characteristics as either a field or laboratory experiment in that the investigator precisely manipulates one or more variables and controls for as many extraneous confounding variables as possible. The Internet is unique because it is an object of research as well as a research tool or setting.

The precursor to conducting experiments over the Internet was probably the incorporation of computer automation in experimental research in psychology. As early as the 1970s, researchers were making use of computers in psychological experiments to perform tasks such as delivering a standardized and controlled presentation of stimuli and making accurate recordings of responses. This trend is not only continuing but, currently, most human experimental research in psychology is aided by computer automation.

The move to conduct human psychological experimentation on the Internet was made possible by the development, in 1990, of a new protocol, http, or HyperText Transfer Protocol. This protocol allowed an Internet browser, such as Netscape Navigator or Internet Explorer, to get a document it located on a server. This document or Web page is coded in a language known as HyperText Markup Language, or HTML, and this language permits the display of text, graphics, or other information on a Web page. With the ability to display such a combination of words, pictures, and sounds on Web pages, the Web grew at an astonishing rate. In 1997, Krantz, Ballard, & Scher conducted an Internet experiment investigating the determinants of female attractiveness and published it in a scientific journal (Musch & Reips, 2000). This is probably the first scientifically published study that was conducted over the Internet.

Since that time the number of studies conducted via the Internet has grown considerably and this growth rate is expected to continue given the many advantages it has over the common types of laboratory research conducted in the behavioral sciences (Birnbaum, 2001) especially relative to the fewer disadvantages (Reips, 2000). Some of the advantages identified by Reips (2000, p. 89) include the "(1) ease of access to demographically and culturally diverse participant population, including participants from unique and previously inaccessible target populations; (2) bringing the experiment to the participant instead of the opposite; (3) high statistical power by enabling access to large samples; (4) the direct assessment of motivational confounding *by noting the differential dropout rate between treatment conditions because participants in Web experiments are not induced to stay due to, for example, course credit* (italics mine); (5) cost savings of lab space, person-hours, equipment, and administration." The disadvantages identified by Reips (2000, p. 89) include issues "such as (1) multiple submissions, (2) lack of experimental control, (3) self-selection, and (4) dropout." Of these disadvantages, the most significant is lack of experimental control. However, as I will discuss in a later chapter, randomization is the most important technique to be included in the design of an experimental study. Reips (2000) points out that this technique can be incorporated into the design of an experiment with the use of "so-called CGIs, small computer programs that cooperate with the Web Server" (p. 107).

STUDY QUESTION 3.3 | **What are the different research settings in which experimental research is conducted and what are the advantages and disadvantages of each setting?**

Summary

The experimental approach is a quantitative research method in which one attempts to identify cause-and-effect relationships by conducting an experiment. However, the cause of an effect is difficult to identify because all causal relationships are contextually dependent. In spite of this, it is useful to think of a cause as something that produces something else. An effect is the difference between what would have happened without some treatment and what did happen when the treatment was administered. Although an exact measure of this difference is not possible to obtain, we approximate it within the context of the experiment.

To be able to state that a causal relationship exists, even though this relationship is contextually dependent, we need evidence. John Stuart Mill set forth four canons—the methods of agreement, difference, concomitant variation, and the joint methods of agreement and difference—that he said could be used in identifying causation. However, in order for one to be able to state that *the* cause of a given effect has been found, this condition must qualify as being both necessary and sufficient. Because behavior is multidetermined, it is highly unlikely that one can overrule all possible alternative explanations for behaviors. This is why Popper rejects the confirmationists' position and takes the position of falsification, maintaining that the best status a theory can attain is one of "not yet disconfirmed." Deese believes that causal relations are embedded in a matrix of other causal relations. A given relationship between a cause and an effect will continue to exist only if all the other variables within the matrix or system remain constant.

The psychological experiment achieves the goal of the experimental approach by allowing the researcher to observe, under controlled conditions, the effects of systematically varying one or more variables. The experimental approach has the primary advantage of being able to infer causal relationships. However, it is easier to identify causal description, which describes the consequences of deliberately varying a treatment, than it is to achieve a causal explanation, which clarifies the mechanisms by which a causal relationship holds. A second advantage of the experiment is that it controls for the influence of extraneous variables. Other advantages are that it permits the precise manipulation of one or more variables, produces lasting results, suggests new studies, and suggests solutions to practical problems. The experimental approach has the disadvantages of not being able to test for the effects of nonmanipulated variables, creating an artificial environment, and frequently being time consuming and difficult to design.

The experimental approach is used in both field and laboratory settings and on the Internet. In a field setting, the researcher makes use of a real-life situation and thereby avoids criticism for having created an artificial environment. Typically, however, there is not as much control over extraneous variables. In a laboratory setting, the experimenter brings the participants into the laboratory, where there is maximum control over extraneous variables; however, this usually means creating an artificial environment.

When conducting an experiment over the Internet the participants are recruited via the Internet, the stimulus conditions are presented via the Internet, and responses are recorded over the Internet. Conducting an experiment over the Internet has advantages such as being cost effective and being able to reach a diverse and difficult-to-reach population. However, there are some inherent disadvantages such as a lack of experimental control.

Key Terms and Concepts

Experimental research approach
Causation
Cause
Effect
Method of agreement
Method of difference
Joint methods of agreement and
    difference
Method of concomitant variation
Necessary condition

Sufficient condition
Position of falsification
Psychological experiment
Phenomenon
Causal description
Causal explanation
Field experiment
Laboratory experiment
Internet experiment

Related Internet Sites

www.pitt.edu/~super1/lecture/lec7741/
This site gives a discussion on the processes that is used to identify the cause of an effect through experimentation.

www.infidels.org/library/modern/quentin_smith/causation.html
This site gives a discussion of a variety of views of causation and discusses causation in a religious context.

Practice Test

Answers to these questions can be found in Appendix A.

1. To think of a cause as an event that produces some other event
   a. Is too simplistic a representation of cause.
   b. Refers to the contextual relationship between a cause and effect.
   c. Reveals that a cause is a probabilistic event.
   d. Refers to the difference between what would have happened and what did happen to something.

2. Assume that one hundred studies have indicated that alcoholics, to remain sober, must totally avoid alcohol. However, one study refutes this finding. If as a result of this one study you take the position that alcoholics do not necessarily have to avoid alcohol, you have based this position on which approach to causation?

   a. Method of difference
   b. Joint method of agreement and difference
   c. That alcohol is a necessary but not sufficient condition to become an alcoholic
   d. Position of falsification
   e. That alcoholism exists within a system of other factors

3. Dr. Zilstein knew that many children with Attention Deficit Hyperactivity Disorder take the drug Ritalin. He conducted another study in which he was trying to find out how the drug Ritalin worked in the brain to produce its beneficial effect. What was he trying to achieve with this study?

   a. Causal description
   b. Causal explanation
   c. Control of the effect of the drug
   d. Better description of the effect of the drug on children's behavior
   e. Causal prediction

4. The September 11, 2001, terrorist attack on the World Trade Center caused emotional turmoil for many individuals. Assume that you were interested in conducting an experimental study to assess the effects of this terrorist attack and I stated that you could not do so. I would have based my statement on what factor?

   a. The fact that the study would require you to identify individuals who lost loved ones in that attack
   b. The fact that the study would have to be conducted outside the context of a university-based laboratory
   c. The fact that you would not have control over the manipulation of the causal variable of interest
   d. The fact that individuals would probably not want to participate
   e. The fact that it is not possible to study such events

Challenge Exercises

The challenge exercises included in this chapter represent topics for discussion. Included are a couple Web sites (see the Related Internet Sites) that address the topic of causation. You may want to log in to these Web sites to get more information on this topic.

1. When we conduct our experiments we attempt to identify a cause-and-effect relationship. Is it more accurate to say that any relationship we find is deterministic or probabilistic? In other words, would it be more accurate to state that the presumed cause determined the effect or that the presumed cause increased the probability of the effect occurring? Make sure that you explain and defend your answer.

2. Prior to discussing the psychological experiment I stated that one of the criteria for identifying cause-and-effect relationships is that the cause must precede the effect. Is it possible for the effect to precede the cause and what would be necessary for this to happen?

3. Consider the two variables of inflation and unemployment. Should a causal relationship exist between these two variables, and which one should be the cause and which the effect?

4. Consider each of the following situations and identify the presumed cause and the presumed effect. Then discuss the likelihood that the presumed cause actually did produce the observed effect. Explain why someone might think these two variables were causally related and then consider the fact that other variables could also have produced the effect.

   a. The Republicans passed a law giving a tax break that benefits wealthy Americans. Shortly after the tax break went into effect, the stock market went down and the economy went into a recession. The Democrats claimed that the tax break caused the economic decline and attempted to repeal the tax break.

   b. Bill purchased a new piece of software for his computer and installed it immediately. The next time he started his computer, it froze up on him, so Bill concluded that it was the software that caused the computer to freeze.

4 Problem Identification and Hypothesis Formation

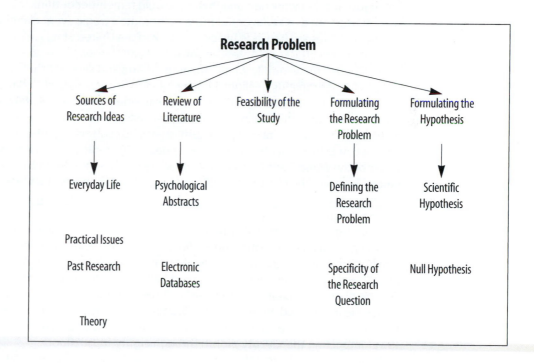

September 11, 2001, started as a typical Tuesday morning with every promise of being just another work day, one that few would remember or think much about. But what started out as an uneventful morning became a tragic event claiming thousands of innocent lives as 19 suicide hijackers attacked the United States in one of the biggest enemy attacks on American soil since Pearl Harbor.

It all began uneventfully when Mohammed Atta and several other suicide hijackers boarded American Airlines flight 11, scheduled to depart Boston's Logan Airport at 8 A.M. Flight 11 was a Boeing 767 capable of carrying more than 24,000 gallons of aviation fuel, enough to fill a swimming pool twenty-two feet in diameter to a depth of eight feet. Shortly after takeoff, men armed with box cutters and plastic knives hijacked flight 11. At 8:46 EDT, flight 11, traveling at nearly 500 mph, crashed into the north tower of the World Trade Center. The impact ripped a huge hole in the tower from the ninety-fourth to the ninety-eighth floor and spilled thousands of gallons of fuel from the aircraft wreckage, which ignited, cascading through vents and elevator shafts, and setting the building on fire.

Morning news programs immediately switched to live coverage of the tower, showing the gaping black hole in its upper floors, the thick smoke billowing out across lower Manhattan. At first, there was no thought that this was an attack on America. Rather, people wondered how such a thing could happen. Did the pilot have a heart attack? Did the plane's mechanical system fail? Eighteen minutes later, the answer became crystal clear as United Airlines flight 175, another Boeing 767, bound from Boston's Logan Airport to Los Angeles, banked in a graceful curve and slammed into the south tower impacting the seventy-eighth through eighty-fourth floors.

Instant replays showed the plane's last moments over and over, and the realization grew that this was not an accident but an attack on America. The horror grew as some of the victims trapped above the fires apparently decided that death by jumping was preferable to being burned by the fires. One by one, hand in hand, they jumped, falling for ten seconds or more before striking the ground.

At 9:59 A.M., the structural steel holding the north tower erect had become soft and pliable from the heat of the fire and was no longer able to support the building's weight. The steel buckled under the load and the floors containing the fire began to fall, each one smashing into the floor beneath it until the weight was more than the steel inner structure could bear. The collapsed floors drove the entire 110 stories of the north tower to the ground, trapping and killing all those who had not escaped as well as rescue workers. At 10:28 A.M., the south World Trade Center tower shuddered and fell, creating a gaping wound in the air where once there had been tall buildings. At the same time that these events were taking place in New York, a Boeing 757 slammed into the west wing of the Pentagon and a United Airlines flight bound from Newark, New Jersey, to San Francisco crashed in a field in rural Pennsylvania.

These repeated and coordinated crashes clearly demonstrated that America was under attack and that this was a planned attack by a group of terrorists. Throughout the day, people repeatedly asked, "Why?" "What?" and "How?" Why would anyone want to do this? What had motivated them to engage in such a destructive act? How had they orchestrated such an event? As the investigation of these terrorists acts continued, it became clear that they were orchestrated by a group of fanatical Muslims headed by Osama bin Laden and his al Qaeda fighters. However, if you were a social psychologist, you might want to search for reasons *why* such tragic events could take place. What would prompt a person to become a suicide terrorist? What would motivate a person to kill thousands of innocent people? What would a person hope to gain from acts such as these? What has America done to anger people halfway around the world so much that they want to destroy Americans? These are just some of the research questions that could be asked and that could become the topic of a research study.

Chapter Preview

The vignette about the events that happened on September 11, 2001, may give you the impression that research questions are easy to formulate. For the veteran researcher, this is typically true. Experienced researchers characteristically have more unanswered questions than they have time to investigate them. Beginning researchers, however, frequently have difficulty identifying a research problem suitable for investigation. In this chapter, I give you the information you need to develop a research question by discussing the origin of researchable problems, how to find information relating to research questions, and how to convert a problem you have identified into one that can be investigated experimentally.

Introduction

Up to this point in the text, I have discussed the general characteristics of scientific research. Using this approach, however, requires that we first have a problem in need of a solution. In the field of psychology, identification of a research idea should be relatively simple because psychology is the scientific study of behavior—including human behavior. Our behavior represents the focus of attention of a great deal of psychological investigation. To convert our observations of behavior into legitimate research questions, we must be inquisitive and ask ourselves why certain types of behavior occur. For example, assume that you hear a person express an extremely resentful, hostile, and prejudiced attitude toward Russians. The next day you see this person interacting with a Russian and note that she is both being very polite and courteous. You have seen a contradiction between the attitude expressed by this individual and her behavior. Two well-founded research questions are "Why is there a lack of correspondence between attitude and behavior?" and "Under what circumstance do attitudes *not* predict behavior?"

Let us now look at the major sources that can be used to generate research questions.

Sources of Research Ideas

Where do ideas or problems originate? Where should we look for a researchable problem? In all fields, there are a number of common sources of problems, such as existing theories and past research. In psychology, we are even more fortunate; we have our own personal experience and everyday events to draw from. The things we see, read about, or hear about can serve as ideas to be turned into research topics. But identifying these ideas as research topics requires an alert and curious scientist. Rather than just passively observing behavior or reading material relating to psychology, we must actively question the reasons for the occurrence of an event or behavior. If you ask, "Why?" you will find many researchable topics. Typically, problems originate from one of four sources: everyday life, practical issues, past research, and theory.

Everyday Life

As we proceed through our daily routine, we come into contact with many questions in need of solution. Parents want to know how to handle their children; students want to know how to learn material faster. When we interact with others or see others react, we note many individual differences. If we observe children on a playground, these differences are readily apparent. One child may be very aggressive and another much more reserved, waiting for others to encourage interaction. The responses of a particular person also vary according to the situation. A child who is very aggressive in one situation may be passive in another. Why do these differences exist? What produces these varying responses? Why are some people leaders and others followers? Why do we like some people and not others? Many such researchable questions can be identified from everyone's interactions and personal experiences.

In the late 1960s, Darley and Latané (1968) began a series of investigations that epitomize the use of life's experiences and the events taking place around us as a source of research problems. They were concerned about the fact that bystanders often do not lend assistance in emergencies. A case in point is the often-cited incident involving Kitty Genovese, who was stabbed to death in New York City. There were thirty-eight witnesses to the attack, which lasted more than half an hour, and no one even called the police. Many other similar and more recent cases can be recounted. For example, a woman was raped by four men on a barroom pool table while onlookers cheered her attackers on. In St. Louis, a thirteen-year-old girl was raped by two youths as several adults stood around and watched. It took a thirteen-year-old boy to finally summon the police. Darley and Latané asked why. They began to study the conditions that facilitate or inhibit bystander intervention in emergencies.

In fall 1995, the trial of O. J. Simpson finally concluded with a verdict of "not guilty." O. J. had been accused of murdering his estranged wife, Nicole Brown Simpson, and a friend of hers, Ron Goldman. The trial, which lasted a year, captured the attention of the American public and was billed as the "trial of the century." After hearing a year's worth of testimony, the prosecution and defense attorneys rested their case and turned the final verdict over to the jury. The attorneys left the court room thinking that the jury deliberations would last several days at least. Much to the surprise of everyone, the jury reached a verdict of "not guilty" within a matter of hours.

The majority of the black community was elated and agreed with the verdict. This was not the case among the white community. They felt that O. J. Simpson had gotten away with murder. From a scientist's point of view, this case could lead to a number of researchable ideas, such as "What was it about the case that led the jury to reach such a rapid verdict?" and "Why was there such a polarized reaction from white and black communities?"

Practical Issues

Many experimental problems arise from practical issues that require solutions. Private industry faces such problems as low employee morale, absenteeism, turnover, selection, and placement. Work has been and continues to be conducted in these areas. Clinical psychology is in need of a great deal of research to identify more efficient modes of dealing with mental disturbances. Units of the federal and state governments support experimentation designed to solve practical problems, such as finding a cure for cancer. Large expenditures are also being directed toward improving the educational process.

Law enforcement agencies are concerned not only with obtaining accurate eyewitness testimony, but also with extracting leads or clues from eyewitnesses. To that end, these agencies now use hypnosis, under the assumption that hypnosis can extract accurate evidence that otherwise would not be available. The validity of such an assumption was not tested until Sanders and Simmons (1983) asked eyewitnesses, some of whom were hypnotized and some of whom were not hypnotized, to identify a thief from a lineup. As Figure 4.1 reveals, hypnotized subjects, contrary to expectations, identified the thief *fewer* times than did the subjects who were not hypnotized. Such evidence suggests that hypnosis is not an effective technique for extracting accurate evidence.

Law enforcement agencies are also concerned with identifying and reducing the incidence of driving under the influence of alcohol. Although there has been increased legislation and stricter penalties for driving under the influence of alcohol, alcohol-impaired driving continues to plague American society. This is probably because intoxicated individuals are unlikely to change their driving plans even though they have been informed that their blood alcohol content is over the legal limit. Their resistance to changing their driving plans may be due to the fact that the alcohol has impaired their judgment. If this is true it would be better to intervene

FIGURE 4.1

Accuracy of eyewitness identification as a function of being hypnotized.

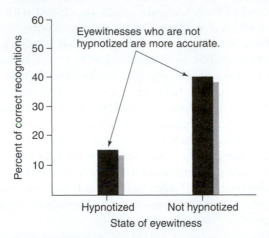

(Based on data from "Use of Hypnosis to Enhance Eyewitness Accuracy: Does It Work?" by G. S. Sanders and W. L. Simmons, 1983, *Journal of Applied Psychology, 68,* pp. 70–77.)

prior to the time in which judgment was seriously impaired. The best place to intervene is where the alcoholic beverages are sold.

Morine E. Chafety, founding director of the National Institute on Alcohol Abuse and Alcoholism developed a program entitled Training for Intervention Procedures by Servers of Alcohol, or TIPS. TIPS is a server intervention program that trains servers at bars to recognize the behavioral and physiological cues associated with alcohol consumption. They are then taught a variety of techniques to control the consumption of alcohol.

Russ and Geller (1987) were interested in determining whether a program such as TIPS really worked. Does it reduce the incidence of patrons leaving a bar with a blood alcohol content at or exceeding the legal limit of intoxication? To test the effectiveness of the TIPS program, Russ and Geller (1987) assessed the blood alcohol content of patrons who were served by individuals who had and had not participated in TIPS training. The results of this study demonstrated that none of the patrons served by trained servers left the bar legally intoxicated, whereas about 45 percent of those served by untrained servers were legally intoxicated. This study suggested that a program such as TIPS may be effective in reducing the incidence of patrons leaving a bar legally intoxicated.

Past Research

Previously conducted experiments are an excellent source of research ideas. This may sound like a contradiction because research is designed to answer questions, but one of the interesting features of research is that it tends to generate more questions than it answers. Although each well-designed study does provide additional knowledge, phenomena are multidetermined. In any experiment, only a limited number of variables can be studied. Investigation of these variables may lead to hypotheses about the effects of other variables. The multidimensional nature of phenomena is also frequently the cause of a lack of agreement among experimental results. An unidentified variable may be the source of conflict among various studies on a given problem, and experiments must be conducted to uncover this variable and thereby eliminate the apparent contradiction.

To illustrate this, consider the study conducted by Mellgren, Seybert, and Dyck (1978). They investigated the influence of presenting different orders of schedules of continuous reinforcement, nonreinforcement, and partial reinforcement on resistance to extinction. Previous research had revealed conflicting results when the resistance to extinction of participants who had received continuous reward and then partial reward was compared with that of participants given only partial reward schedules. Some studies indicated that resistance to extinction decreased, others indicated that it increased, and still others showed that the existence of an increase or decrease in resistance to extinction depended on the stage of extinction. Mellgren et al. attempted to resolve this inconsistency. The results of their study revealed that the greatest resistance to extinction occurred when a large number of nonreinforced trials preceded a partial reinforcement schedule. Although this study showed which schedule produced the greatest resistance to extinction, it left other questions unanswered. For example, it did not provide an explanation of why resistance to extinction increases if a large number of nonreinforced trials precedes partial reinforcement. This led to another study, which attempted to answer this new question. As you can see, each study leads to a subsequent study, so people can spend their whole lives investigating one particular area. Research is an ongoing process.

Theory

Theory
A group of logically organized and deductively related laws

A **theory**, defined by M. H. Marx (1963, p. 9) as "a group of logically organized (deductively related) laws," is supposed to serve a number of distinct functions. Marx states that theory is both a tool and a goal. The *goal* function is evidenced by the proposition that laws are ordered and integrated by theories; theories summarize and integrate existing knowledge. The *tool* function, evidenced by the proposition that theories guide research, is the function of interest to us. A good theory goes beyond the goal function to suggest new relationships and make new predictions. Thus, it serves as a source of researchable ideas.

Leon Festinger's (1957) theory of cognitive dissonance is an example of a theory that stimulated an extraordinary amount of research in the decade that followed its publication. From this theory, Festinger and Carlsmith (1959) hypothesized and validated the less-than-obvious prediction that, after completing a boring task, participants who were given $1 to tell a "stooge" that the boring task was interesting and fun actually stated that they had enjoyed the task more than did the participants who were given $20 to do the same thing.

The four sources of research ideas—everyday life, practical issues, past research, and theory—barely scratch the surface of circumstances that can inspire a creative idea. The important issue is not the identification of sources of ideas but the generation of these ideas as illustrated in Exhibit 4.1. This is the initial stage in the context of science. To develop these researchable ideas requires the development of a way of thinking. You have to develop a questioning and inquisitive approach to life. For example, Edwin H. Land invented the Polaroid Land Camera after his three-year-old daughter asked him why a camera could not produce pictures instantly. He could have dismissed this question and merely told her that this was not possible. However,

EXHIBIT 4.1

Finding the Cause and Treatment of Peptic Ulcer Disease

In the early part of the twentieth century, peptic ulcer disease was believed to be caused by stress and dietary factors. Treatment for the disease involved hospitalization, bed rest, and prescription of special bland foods. Later in the twentieth century, gastric acid was blamed for the disease. Antacids and medications that block acid production became the standard therapy. However, the incidence of peptic ulcer disease remained high and victims of this disease continued to battle it in spite of this treatment.

The real cause and an effective treatment did not appear on the medical scene until 1982 when Australian physicians Robin Warren and Barry Marshall (2002) first identified a link between *Helicobacter pylori* (*H. pylori*) and ulcers. These investigators concluded that the bacterium, not stress or diet, causes ulcers. However, the medical community was slow to accept this novel finding, and it was not until over ten years later that the National Institutes of Health Consensus Development Conference concluded that there was a strong association between *H. pylori* infections and ulcer disease. At this time, the conference also recommended that ulcer patients with *H. pylori* infection be treated with antibiotics. In 1996, the Food and Drug Administration approved the first antibiotic for treatment of ulcer disease (Centers for Disease Control, 2001).

Although we now know the cause and the effective treatment of peptic ulcer disease, this knowledge came only with Dr. Barry Marshall's boundless conviction that he was right when others doggedly pronounced him wrong. Marshall's initial investigation into this disease began when he was a medical resident at Royal Perth Hospital. He searched the literature and discovered that the presence of the spiral bacterium in the stomach had been reported as far back as the late 1800s and became convinced that this bacteria was the key to the cause and treatment of gastritis and ulcers. As a result of this conviction, he collaborated with Robin Warren, a staff pathologist at Royal Perth Hospital. Both of these individuals knew that the spiral bacterium was present in over half their patients but it had not been recognized as a common occupant of human gastric mucosa. This further stimulated their investigations into the relationship between this bacterium and peptic ulcer disease. At one point Marshall even infected himself with the ulcer-causing bacterium to create an experimental model to substantiate his hypothesis and challenge the accepted belief that mental or emotional disturbance or diet was responsible for peptic ulcer disease.

Persevering against the almost universal skepticism of his peers, Marshall's investigations proved the significance of *H. pylori* in peptic ulcer disease. And finally, in 1996, the Food and Drug Administration officially approved the first drug therapy for the treatment of this disorder, a combination of bismuth and the antibiotic tinidazole. Marshall continues to investigate the significance of this bacterium and has focused on its relationship to stomach cancer, which is also gaining acceptance.

Land asked himself why it couldn't be done. While out for a stroll he thought about this issue and came up with the ideas for a camera that could produce developed photographs.

Gender Bias in Research Ideas

Although there are many sources of ideas in psychology, it is important that we not overlook significant topics. To do so would lead us to develop a knowledge base that is incomplete. All scientists probably agree that we need to conduct research on all important topics. However, scientists are human, and the questions they ask are shaped not only by the particular topics they think are most significant but also by their gender roles. Because most scientists are males, the research topics they have selected to investigate have been those that males have considered to be most important. This has meant that some significant issues have been neglected or underresearched. Many of these issues are those that revolve about women. For example, feminists argue that menstrual cramps have not been taken seriously by the medical profession (Keller, 1984). Similarly, there is a lot of research focusing on the influence of mothers' working outside the home on their children's psychological welfare. Much less attention has focused on whether fathers' commitment to their work endangers their children's welfare or if the mothers' employment might even benefit their children (Hare-Mustin & Marecek, 1990). It appears that personal biases have influenced the selection of research questions and have led scientists to overlook important aspects of human behavior. Some (e.g., Unger & Crawford, 1992) have suggested that this is because of the preponderance of male scientists. If this is the case, then it is incumbent on both male and female scientists to constantly assess the most important issues for research. This continual assessment must incorporate listening to the community as well as other scientists. Any **gender bias** that exists is probably a natural outgrowth of belonging to a particular gender and not a deliberate attempt to avoid particular issues that may be important. To correct such bias and ensure that all topics of importance receive attention it is imperative that the scientific community include scientists of both genders.

Gender bias

The influence that a researcher's gender has on the identification and selection of his or her research topic

Ideas Not Capable of Scientific Investigation

Researchable ideas, as you have just seen, originate from a variety of sources. However, it is important to realize that not all ideas are subject to scientific investigation. One of the criteria that a scientific study must meet is that the research idea must be capable of being confirmed or refuted. There are some ideas that are very important, are debated vigorously, and consume inordinate amounts of time and energy but are not subject to scientific investigation. These ideas typically revolve about issues of morality and religion. Consider, for example, the issue of abortion. This is an issue that has been debated for decades and has polarized the population. A large segment of the population advocates a pro-choice position; another large segment advocates a pro-life position. Science can investigate the genesis of these positions and mechanisms for changing them, but it cannot resolve the issue of which position is the best or correct one.

STUDY QUESTION 4.1
- **Where can you get ideas for a research study?**
- **Explain how gender can influence the research ideas a person may develop**
- **Explain why some ideas you may have cannot be subjected to a scientific investigation.**

Review of the Literature

After a topic of research has been obtained from one of the sources just mentioned, the next step in the research process is to become familiar with the information available on the topic. For example, assume that you want to conduct research on the impact of environmental stress on AIDS. Before beginning to design such a research project, you should first become familiar with current information on both of these topics. Prior work has been conducted on practically all psychological problems, and the topics of AIDS and environmental stress are no exceptions.

At this point you might be asking yourself, "Why should I review the literature on my selected topic? Why not just proceed to the laboratory and find an answer to the problem?" There are several good reasons why you should do your homework in the form of a literature review before conducting any experiments. The general purpose of the library search is to gain an understanding of the current state of knowledge about the selected topic. Specifically, a review of the literature

1. Will tell you whether the problem you have identified has already been researched. If it has, you should either revise the problem in light of the experimental results or look for another problem, unless there is a good reason to replicate the study.

2. May give you ideas as to how to proceed in designing the study so that you can obtain an answer to your research question.

3. Can point out methodological problems specific to the research question you are studying.

4. Can identify whether special groups or special pieces of equipment are needed and perhaps give clues as to where to find the equipment or how to identify the particular groups of participants needed.

5. Will provide needed information for preparing the research report because this research report requires that you not only set your study in the context of prior studies but that you discuss the results in relation to other studies.

These are just a few of the more salient reasons for conducting a literature review.

Assuming you are convinced of the necessity of a literature review, you now need to know how to conduct such a review. Frequently, students don't know what kind of literature search is expected, where to start, how to get the best results from a search, what resources are available, or when to stop the search. To help in this process Marques (1998) has provided a number of guidelines such as those discussed next.

Getting Started

Before doing an effective search, you should know how to use the library. If you are unfamiliar with effective use of the library, you should ask your librarian to give you a guided tour and explain where and how to find documents related to psychology. You also need to define your topic area before beginning the search. This definition needs to be relatively narrow and specific to conduct an appropriate search. For example, you may be interested in depression. However, the topic of depression is very broad and would be unmanageable because it includes everything about depression from causes to treatment. If you narrow this topic to something like relapse of depression, you have a more manageable topic.

In conducting the search, be prepared to spend considerable time and effort. Effective searches frequently take many hours. When you search for journal articles, you will see abstracts of these articles. Do not rely only on the information in these abstracts. Abstracts should be used only to give you information about the content of the actual article so you can tell if you need to select that article for further reading. When you get an actual journal article, take detailed notes of its content as you read it. This includes a complete reference, details about the methodology, important findings, strengths and weaknesses, and any other thoughts or comments that may arise as you are reading the article.

Defining Objectives

Before starting the literature search it is helpful to define your objectives. For example, is the literature search being conducted to familiarize you with the topic area you want to investigate, or are you doing the literature search to help develop the methodology you need to use in conducting your research study? Identifying your objectives will show you that there are different reasons for doing a literature search and give you a focus when reading the literature.

Doing the Search

After you have developed some knowledge of how to find documents in your library and have defined the objectives of your search, you should be ready to do your literature search. There are many resources at your disposal that will give you more information than you ever thought existed or that you can digest. These resources consist of books, journal articles, computer databases, and the World Wide Web.

Books   Books have been written about most, if not all, areas in psychology. This is actually a good place to start your literature search because it will provide you with an introduction to your research topic and a summary of the literature published up to the time of the writing of the book. One book that is often very useful is the *Annual Review of Psychology*. Published yearly since 1950, it presents an expert's in-depth discussion of the principal work done during the preceding year on a variety of topics. One of the topics may relate to your own, so it is worthwhile to check this source. Other relevant books and chapters can be identified from a search of *Psychological*

Abstracts or PsycINFO (discussed later). After you have identified the book or books relating to your topic of interest from a search of PsycINFO, you should connect to your library's online catalogue to see if your library holds the book or books you are interested in. You should be able to connect to your library's online catalogue through the Internet. If your library does not have the books you are interested in, you should be able to request them through interlibrary loan.

Most books do not, however, provide a comprehensive review of all research conducted on a topic. The author has to be selective and present only a small portion of the literature. To be sure that the author has not presented a biased orientation, you should select and read several books on your chosen research topic.

Psychological Journals   Most of the pertinent information about a research topic is usually found in the psychological journals. Frequently, a review that has started with books leads to the journals. Because books are generally the outgrowth of work cited in journals, this progression from books back to journals is a natural one.

How should one proceed in reviewing the work cited in the journals? There are so many psychological journals that it would be impossible to go through each and every one looking for relevant information. This is where *Psychological Abstracts* comes in.

Psychological Abstracts is the primary reference source to the international literature in psychology. This hardbound reference source contains summaries of English-language journal articles, technical reports, book chapters, and books of works in psychology from 1927 to the present. These references are organized by subject area, which permits easy browsing. *Psychological Abstracts* is an appropriate resource to use if your goal is to identify several journal articles related to a specific topic area, such as anxiety or depression. However, if you want to conduct a more comprehensive search, the most efficient technique is to use an electronic or computerized database, because the accumulation of research in psychology continues at a staggering rate. More than 100,000 articles have been published in the past one hundred years in social psychology alone, and about 3,000 documents are added to this database each year (Richard, 1999). If you extrapolate that to the entire field of psychology, you can see that conducting a literature search without the help of something like a computerized or electronic database can quickly become overwhelming.

Computerized or Electronic Databases   **PsycINFO** is an electronic bibliographic database providing abstracts and citations to the scholarly literature in the behavioral sciences and in mental health. It is a department of the American Psychological Association and has the mission of locating and summarizing psychologically relevant documents from a variety of disciplines and disseminating these summaries in a form that is easy to access and retrieve. This mission was initially accomplished by publishing *Psychological Abstracts*. Although *Psychological Abstracts* remains a staple of library reference collections, PsycINFO is the electronic database and contains the same references as those found in *Psychological Abstracts,* plus some additional references.

The PsycINFO database contains more than 2 million references to the psychological literature accumulated from 1887 to the present day. It covers publications from over fifty countries and literature written in more than twenty-four languages. The

---

Psychological Abstracts
A journal that contains abstracts of books, journal articles, technical reports, monographs, and other scientific documents

PsycINFO
An electronic bibliographic database of abstracts and citations to the scholarly literature in psychology

database is updated weekly and more than 100,000 new records were added in 2004. Because of its depth and breadth of coverage, PsycINFO is the database of choice for a search of psychologically relevant material. For additional up-to-date information on PsycINFO, you can check out the Web site at www.apa.org/psycinfo/. This Web site will also give you information about other electronic products listed in Table 4.1.

On the outside chance that your library does not lease either of these databases, ask the librarian for the nearest library that does have this information available. If another library is not close by, your next option is to access the database directly through the PsycINFO Web site. You can log on to the Web site at www.psychinfo/products/pidirect.html, and if you follow the directions you can conduct a search for $11.95 a day. This is perhaps the easiest and cheapest way to conduct a search if your library does not subscribe to the database.

In searching PsycINFO, the basic procedure is to identify a list of search terms, enter them, and let the computer conduct the search for articles focusing on the issues relating to those terms. For example, if you were interested in literature focusing on the effect of food on a person's mood, you might select terms such as food and mood, carbohydrates and mood, and carbohydrate cravings. There are times when you might not know which terms to select for your search or you might think that there are more terms that should be used than you can think of. This is where the *Thesaurus of Psychological Index Terms* is helpful. This is an index of psychological terms as well as terms that describe interrelationships and related categories. For example, if you were interested in child welfare, the *Thesaurus of Psychological Index Terms* would provide a list of additional terms (adoption advocacy, child abuse, child day care, child neglect, child self-care, foster care, social casework, and social services) relevant to the topic of child welfare. These additional terms could also be searched to provide references to additional journal articles and books on the topic of child welfare. The thesaurus is available in a hardbound copy in most libraries. However, it can also be accessed from the PsycINFO main menu, so if you have access to PsycINFO you can first access the thesaurus to identify a list of appropriate search terms and then have PsycINFO conduct your search using these terms.

TABLE 4.1

Additional Electronic Products from PsycINFO

Product	Description
PsycARTICLES	Database containing full-text articles from fifty-five journals published by APA and allied organizations
PsycFIRST	Database containing the PsycINFO database for the most current three years
PsycBOOKS	Full text database of scholarly titles published by APA
PsycSCAN	Bibliographic citations and abstracts for specific topic areas including Applied Psychology, Behavior Analysis & Therapy, Developmental Psychology, Learning Disabilities and Mental Retardation, and Psychopharmacology

Once you have identified the terms you want to use in your search, you are ready to conduct your search. PsycINFO gives you the option of searching for articles that contain your key search terms in the title, in the author, in the subject, or anywhere. You could also do an author search if you know the author of a journal article of interest to you. In addition to searching by using relevant search terms, PsycINFO allows you to limit your search in a number of ways, such as searching only journal articles and not books or searching only animal literature and not human literature. These are specific things you can do to insure that you identify relevant literature. You will develop proficiency in using these options as you gain experience doing PsycINFO literature searches.

Assume you are interested in road rage and want to identify the literature on this topic area. You connect to PsycINFO and search the literature for the years 2000 to 2006, and your search identifies forty-one articles. Your next step is to read the abstracts of these articles and identify the ones that are of interest to you. Exhibit 4.2 presents the information provided by PsychINFO for one of these forty-one articles. If this abstract indicates that the article contains information of importance to you, then

EXHIBIT 4.2

Record: 1

Title: Is road rage increasing? Results of a repeated survey.

Author(s): Smart, Reginald G., Social, Prevention and Health Policy Research Department, Centre for Addiction and Mental Health, Toronto, ON, Canada, reg_smart@camh.net
Mann, Robert E., Social, Prevention and Health Policy Research Department, Centre for Addiction and Mental Health, Toronto, ON, Canada
Zhao, Jinhui, Social, Prevention and Health Policy Research Department, Centre for Addiction and Mental Health, Toronto, ON, Canada
Stoduto, Gina, Social, Prevention and Health Policy Research Department, Centre for Addiction and Mental Health, Toronto, ON, Canada

Address: Smart, Reginald G., Social, Prevention and Health Policy Research Department, Centre for Addiction and Mental Health, 33 Russell St., Toronto, ON, Canada, M5S 2S1, reg_smart@camh.net

Source: Journal of Safety Research, Vol 36(2), 2005. pp. 195–201.

Publisher: Netherlands: Elsevier Science
Publisher URL: http://elsevier.com

ISSN: 0022-4375 (Print)

Digital Object Identifier: 10.1016/j.jsr.2005.03.005

Language: English

Keywords: road rage; victimization; perpetration; demographics

EXHIBIT 4.2 (continued)

Abstract: Problem: We report on trends in road rage victimization and perpetration based on population survey data. Method: Based on repeated cross-sectional telephone surveys of Ontario adults between July 2001 and December 2003, logistic regression analyses examined differences between years in road rage victimization and perpetration in the previous year controlling for demographic characteristics. Results: The prevalence of any road rage victimization in the previous year decreased significantly from 47.5% in 2001 to 40.6% in 2003, while prevalence of any road rage perpetration remained stable (31.0% to 33.6%). Logistic regression analyses revealed that the odds of experiencing any road rage victimization was 33% higher in 2001 and 30% higher in 2002, than in 2003. Discussion: Survey data provide a valuable perspective on road rage trends, but efforts to track road rage incidents is also needed. Summary: In Ontario, the proportion of adults experiencing any road rage victimization decreased from 2001 to 2003 while the proportion reporting any road rage perpetration remained stable. Impact on industry: None. (PsycINFO Database Record (c) 2005 APA, all rights reserved)(journal abstract)

Subjects: *Aggressive Driving Behavior; *Demographic Characteristics; *Harassment; *Highway Safety; *Victimization

Classification: Transportation (4090)

Population: Human (10)
Male (30)
Female (40)

Location: Canada

Age Group: Adulthood (18 yrs & older) (300)
Young Adulthood (18–29 yrs) (320)
Thirties (30–39 yrs) (340)
Middle Age (40–64 yrs) (360)
Aged (65 yrs & older) (380)
Very Old (85 yrs & older) (390)

Tests & Measures: Computer Assisted Telephone Interview

Form/Content Type: Empirical Study (0800)
Quantitative Study (0890)
Journal Article (2400)

Publication Type: Peer Reviewed Journal (270); Print Format(s) Available: Print; Electronic

Release Date: 20050718

Accession Number: *2005-06225-010*

Number of Citations in Source: 20

Database: PsycINFO

TABLE 4.2

Guide for Reading Journal Articles

When you read scholarly articles you may have a difficult time comprehending much of the material. If you follow these simple steps, you will get the most out of the article.

1. Read and remember the title because it tells you what is being investigated in the article.

2. Read the abstract very carefully because it summarizes what is being investigated as well as what was found in the study.

3. As you read the introduction to the article, pay particular attention to the first paragraph because this typically gives a general statement of the topic area and problem being studied.

4. Toward the end of the introduction, typically in the last paragraph, the author(s) usually state the purpose of the study and, perhaps, the hypotheses being tested in the study. Keep these two in mind as you read the rest of the article and see how the author(s) go about testing the hypotheses or meeting the purpose of the study and what the results have to say about them.

5. As you read the Method section, make note of the type of research participants used and then pay particular attention to the Procedure section because this section tells you how the author(s) designed the study to test their hypotheses and meet the purpose of the study. Pay attention to what was done to the participants and what the participants were asked to do and then ask yourself if this tested the hypotheses of the study.

6. The Results section may be the hardest for you to read and comprehend because the author(s) may have used statistical procedures unfamiliar to you. Rather than spending time trying to understand the statistical analysis, look at what the authors say about the results of the statistical analysis. Look at any tables and figures presented and try to relate the information in them to the hypotheses and purpose of the study.

7. If you have difficulty with the Results section, read the first paragraph of the Discussion section. This typically summarizes the results of the study in a form that is easier to understand. In addition to helping understand the results, the Discussion section is where the author(s) explain why the study turned out as it did: Did it support the hypotheses? As you read this section, think about the purpose and hypotheses and look for the explanation of why the study did or did not support the hypotheses and fulfill the purpose of the study.

you retrieve the article. The information given identifies the author(s), title, and journal in which the article appeared, allowing you to seek and obtain a copy of the entire article. As you read the article, take notes to get as much as you can out of it. Scholarly articles are written for professionals, so there may be some parts that are difficult for you to understand. Table 4.2 gives some guidelines for reading journal articles.

You may want to search other databases (see Table 4.3) in addition to PsycINFO that incorporate psychological literature. This is particularly valuable if your research topic bridges other areas, such as medicine.

Internet Resources   The Internet is an additional resource that can be used to acquire psychological information. The Internet is best described as a "network of networks" consisting of millions of computers and tens of millions of users all over the world, all of which are joined into a single network to promote communication. It is probably an understatement to say that the Internet is revolutionizing communications much the way the telephone did many years ago. Now we can connect to the Internet and communicate with someone in another country just as easily as we can with our neighbor next door. The Internet has a number of tools that are of value to both the student and psychologists. In addition to the resources discussed here, there

TABLE 4.3

Databases Incorporating Psychological Publications

Database	Subject Coverage	Internet Address
PsycINFO	Psychology, mental health, biomedicine	Connect through your university library
MEDLINE	Medicine, biomedicine, health care	www.ncbi.nlm.nih.gov
Sociological Abstracts	Sociology and related disciplines	Connect through your university library

are conferences, debates, journals, and lists of references, as well as complete studies, on the Internet.

Electronic Mail. E-mail, or electronic mail, is probably one of the most frequent uses of the Internet. E-mail is an electronic means of sending messages as well as files and documents to another person over the Internet. It provides an unprecedented means of communication that avoids the problems of playing phone tag when trying to reach another person. Most, if not all, colleges and universities have connections to the Internet and provide a means for students to either become connected using their own computers or provide access to computers that are connected to the Internet. Regardless of the means of access to the Internet, once you have access, you must have a user ID, which is your Internet address. This address identifies your location on the Internet and allows e-mail to get to you. Similarly, to send an e-mail message to another person you must have their user ID or their address. Once you have a person's address, you can communicate with them regardless of where they are in the world.

Listserv. Discussion groups are also used for communication among researchers, students, and others interested in a particular topic, such as depression. Within psychology, there are many topics that are of interest to a particular group of individuals. These special interest groups use a variation of e-mail called a Listserv to communicate among all members of the group. A Listserv is a program that automatically distributes messages to all members of the list so it can be viewed as a discussion group organized around a particular topic. To become a participant in a Listserv you must first join or subscribe to the list. Once you have joined the list, the Listserv sends you all the messages posted by other subscribers. You can either just read these messages, reply to them, or send your own message. For example, if you are having difficulty finding information on a topic of interest, you might post a message on a Listserv asking for information relating to that topic. In a short period of time, you should get many replies from other participants giving you valuable, or not so valuable, information.

World Wide Web. Probably the most popular part of the Internet is the World Wide Web. The Web consists of hundreds of thousands of computers, each containing information, some of which may be useful and much of which is not. There is a wealth of information on the Web, and students and faculty alike enjoy surfing the

Web. However, the giant waves of information typically contain only a few drops of relevant information. This is why the Web can be a frustrating and time-consuming place to search for information. Therefore, you need a clear idea of what you are looking for to be able to mine the Web effectively.

One thing you need to know prior to beginning your search of the Web is that it will not search subscription or proprietary databases such as PsycINFO, MEDLINE, or ERIC. Although some databases, such as MEDLINE, are free and can be accessed by anyone, other databases, such as PsycINFO, are not and have to be accessed through your library because your library has paid the fee to permit your access. However, there is a vast amount of information available on the Web in addition to these databases.

To access material on the Web you need to make use of a browser such as Internet Explorer, Netscape, Safari, Opera, or Firefox. Browsers such as these allow a user to access Web pages stored on servers around the world and display them on the screen of their computer. If you know the address (the Uniformed Resource Locator or URL) of the Web page you are seeking, all you have to do is type in the address and the browser you are using will locate and display the Web page on your computer screen. In case you didn't know, the URL is the global address of documents and other resources on the World Wide Web.

In many instances you would not know the address or URL of Web pages containing information you desire. For example, if you were seeking information about support groups for people suffering from depression you probably would not know the address of such groups. To find Web pages with information about depression support groups you need to use a search engine. A **search engine** is a program that is designed to help find information stored on servers that are part of the World Wide Web. A listing of some of the search engines that can be used to search for information on the Web are listed in Table 4.4.

Search engine
A software program that seeks out Web pages stored on servers throughout the World Wide Web

TABLE 4.4
Internet Search Tools

Major Search Engines	Internet Address
Google	www.google.com
Yahoo!	www.yahoo.com
Ask Jeeves	www.askjeeves.com

Metacrawlers or Meta Search Engines	Internet Address
Dogpile	www.dogpile.com
Vivisimo	http://vivisimo.com/
Kartoo	www.kartoo.com
Mamma	http://mamma.com
SurfWax	http://surfwax.com

This list definitely does not exhaust the available search engines but it does represent the top choices identified by the staff of the Web site, www.searchengine watch.com. This Web site gives a comprehensive list of search tools, as well as a brief description of each, search tips, and ratings of major search engines. If you want to learn more about any of these search engines or about search procedures, you should log on to that site.

Search engines work by seeking out and then storing the information contained in Web pages stored on servers throughout the world. Most search engines seek out these Web pages using crawler-based search engines but a search engine can operate from a human-powered directory or a directory that depends on humans making submissions for its listings. Most of the time the result you get from a search will be the result of both types of listings (Sullivan, 2004). However, most of the information received from search engines is obtained from crawler-base search engines.

The listings or information obtained from a crawler-based search engine has three components. The first component is a spider that visits a Web page, reads it, stores the information, and then follows links to other pages within the site which are also read and stored. The second component of a search engine is for the information that is read by the spider to be brought back and placed in a database or index. The index is like a giant book containing a copy of every Web page the spider finds. Each Web page that is brought back is analyzed to determine how it should be indexed. For example, words from the title, heading, or special fields of the Web page are extracted and stored in an index database. Then, when a user, such as yourself, makes a query by typing in key words such as "child abuse," the third component of the search engine takes over. At this stage the search engine sifts the millions of pages recorded in the index to find matches to the key words you have provided and then gives a listing of the best-matching Web pages relating to these key words, usually with a short summary that includes the document's title and some of the text. Your task is to review the indexed Web pages and click on the link to the Web page that contains the information you desire. This will bring up the Web page for you to read and review.

For example, a search for information on *carbohydrates and depression* using the Google search engine produces 866,000 Web pages. From this, you should be able to see that a search engine such as Google will probably give links to more Web pages than you want and you must search through these Web pages to identify relevant information.

In spite of the vast amount of information provided by these search engines, none of the search engines has a database that even approaches all of the information on the Web. This is why for the most comprehensive search you must use several search engines; each search engine will have visited different Web pages and have a slightly different database.

In an attempt to provide a more comprehensive search of the information on the Web, meta search engines have been developed. These are search engines that submit your search to several search engine databases at the same time. The results are then blended together into one page.

The World Wide Web is a potentially valuable resource, giving you a wealth of information. Its tremendous advantage is that it is accessible twenty-four hours a day and can be accessed from the comfort of your own home, apartment, office, or dorm room. However, there are some significant disadvantages to conducting a Web search.

It can be very time consuming because much of the information is disorganized. Because the database of search engines consists of information gleaned from Web pages, a lot of the information you get will be irrelevant. Also, there is no controlling authority ensuring the accuracy or credibility of the information, so you must judge each Web site to determine if the information contained is reliable and accurate. Table 4.5 provides some guidelines for evaluating the accuracy of information obtained from the Web.

The World Wide Web is potentially a valuable resource. The challenge is to learn how to mine the Web to effectively use its vast information. There are books that

TABLE 4.5
Evaluating Web Pages

The main problem with the information received from the World Wide Web is its validity because anyone can establish a Web site and produce a Web page. The following criteria can help you differentiate good information from bad.

1. **Authority:** Authority exists if the Web page lists the author and his or her credentials and the address has a preferred domain such as .edu, .org, or .gov. Therefore, to assess the authority you should:
   a. Find the source of the document. A URL ending with .edu is from an institution of higher education, .gov is from some branch of the federal government, .org is from some nonprofit organization such as the American Psychological Association, .com is from a commercial vendor, and .net is from anyone who can afford to pay for space on a server.
   b. Identify the qualifications of the publisher of the Web document. You can get some of this information from the Web site itself by reading the "about us," "mission," or "Who we are" sections.

2. **Accuracy:** Accuracy is best when the Web page lists the author and institution that publishes the page and provides a way of contacting him or her. This means that you should do the following:
   a. Look at the credentials of the person who wrote the Web page and check for a link or an e-mail address that will permit you to contact this person.
   b. Identify the purpose of the information. Is it a public service announcement, advertising, sales, news, or a published research study? The purpose may suggest that a certain bias exists in the information.
   c. Determine if there is an acknowledgment of the limitations of the information, particularly if the information is the report of some study.

3. **Objectivity:** Objectivity is best when the Web page has little or no advertising and provides accurate and objective information. Therefore, you should do the following:
   a. Identify if there is any evidence of some sort of bias in the information presented.
      i. Is the information traceable to factual information presented in some bibliographic or internet reference? Such information may be less biased.
      ii. Do the authors express their own opinions? Authors opinions suggest bias.

4. **Currency:** Currency exists when the Web page and any links it provides are updated regularly. This means that you should determine
   a. When the Web page was produced
   b. When the Web page was updated and how up-to-date the links (if any) are

5. **Coverage:** Coverage is good when you can view the information on the Web page without paying fees or having additional software requirements.

describe the Internet and provide some instruction in searching for information. However, the best way to learn more about the Internet is to use it. As you spend more and more time navigating the Internet, you will become proficient at locating information and maximizing the tremendous resources available at your fingertips.

Obtaining Resources

Once you have obtained the list of books, journal articles, and other resources relevant to your topic of interest, you must obtain a copy of them. Obviously, the first choice is to search your library. Libraries purchase many books and subscribe to many journals and other documents, and it is possible that the books and journal articles you need are in your library. However, few libraries will contain all the resources you have selected, and in such cases you must use alternative means of securing documents.

Your first choice for securing documents not in your library should be through the interlibrary loan department. This is a department maintained by the library dedicated to obtaining documents from other locations, such as other libraries. In most instances they are reasonably efficient and can obtain documents within several weeks. The downside to using the interlibrary loan method is that you may be assessed a small fee for copies of journal articles. Rather than using interlibrary loan, you can contact the author of a journal article and request a reprint of that article. When authors publish journal articles, they typically receive a number of reprints that they distribute to individuals requesting copies.

There is also an increasing trend for libraries to provide a full-text electronic copy of journal articles and books. If your library provides full-text copies of journal articles you are interested in there will be a link, frequently at the end of the abstract, that says something like "linked full-text" or "check for full-text." If there is a "linked full-text" statement and you click on this link, you will retrieve the complete article which you can then print.

Additional Information Sources

The regional and national psychological association meetings are an excellent source of *current* information. I emphasize *current* because of the publication lag that exists in journals and books. A research study that appears in a book may be several years old, whereas studies presented at professional meetings are typically much more recent. An additional advantage of securing information at professional meetings is that frequently you can interact with the investigator. Exchanging ideas with the researcher is likely to generate added enthusiasm and many more research ideas.

Many times, the beginning researcher returns from meetings with renewed confidence in his or her developing research skills. Novices often feel that researchers at other institutions are more skilled or more adept, but when they attend professional meetings they find out that others use the same techniques and skills. It is recommended that psychology majors try to attend one of these national or regional meetings. Table 4.6 lists the various regional psychological associations, as well as a variety of other, more specialized psychological associations.

TABLE 4.6
Psychological Associations

National	Regional	Selected Others
American Psychological Association	New England Psychological Association Southwestern Psychological Association	Psychonomic Society Association for the Advancement of Behavior Therapy
American Psychological Society	Eastern Psychological Association Southeastern Psychological Association Western Psychological Association Midwestern Psychological Association Rocky Mountain Psychological Association	National Academy of Neuropsychologists International Neuropsychological Society

Information can also be gained from direct communication with colleagues. It is not unusual for researchers to call, write, or e-mail one another to inquire about current studies or methodological techniques.

STUDY QUESTION 4.2

- **Explain the purpose of a literature review.**
- **Discuss how you would go about conducting a literature review.**
- **Discuss all the resources available for conducting the literature review.**

Feasibility of the Study

After you have completed the literature search, you are ready to decide whether it is feasible for you to conduct the study. Each study varies in its requirements with respect to time, type of research participants, expense, expertise of the experimenter, and ethical sensitivity.

For example, you may want to study the effect of being sexually abused as a child on the stability of a person's later marital relationship. Although this is an excellent research question and one that has been investigated and needs further investigation, it is a difficult study to conduct and one that is not feasible for most students. This study requires the identification of sexually abused children, which would be difficult in the best of circumstances. In addition, it requires following the abused children for years until they marry, which would take an inordinate amount of time. Then an assessment of the couple's marital stability has to be obtained, which may require a level of expertise you do not have. In addition, this is an ethically sensitive topic because just revealing the fact that a person has been sexually abused could have a variety of consequences.

Contrast this with the study conducted by DePaulo, Dull, Greenberg, and Swaim (1989), in which they attempted to determine whether shy individuals seek help less frequently than people who are not shy. In conducting this study, the researchers administered a four-item shyness survey to introductory psychology students, and shy and not-shy individuals were selected on the basis of their survey scores. All participants were then given the impossible task of standing a stick on end when the end was slightly rounded. The number of times shy and not-shy individuals asked for help was recorded. This study was relatively simple to conduct, did not require any special skills on the part of the experimenters or the research participants, was relatively inexpensive, took only a moderate amount of time, and did not violate the participants' rights.

These two studies represent opposite ends of the continuum with respect to the issues of time, money, access to participant sample, expertise, and ethics. Although most studies fall somewhere between the two extremes, these examples serve to emphasize the issues that must be considered in selecting a research topic. If the research topic you have selected will take an inordinate amount of time, require funds that you don't have or can't acquire, call for a degree of expertise you don't have, or raise sensitive ethical questions, you should consider altering the project or selecting another topic. If you have considered these issues and find that they are not problematic, then you should proceed with the formulation of your research problem.

Formulating the Research Problem

You should now be prepared to make a clear and exact statement of the specific problem to be investigated. The literature review has revealed not only what is currently known about the problem but also the ways in which the problem has been attacked in the past. Such information is a tremendous aid in formulating the problem and in indicating how and by what methods the data should be collected. Unfortunately, novices sometimes jump from the selection of a research topic to the data collection stage, leaving the problem unspecified until after data collection. They thus run the risk of not obtaining information on the problem of interest. An exact definition of the problem is very important because it guides the research process.

Defining a Research Problem

Research problem
An interrogative sentence that states the relationship between two variables

What is a **research problem**? Kerlinger (1973, p. 17) defines a problem as "an interrogative sentence or statement that asks: 'What relation exists between two or more variables?'" For example, Milgram (1964a) asked, "Can a group induce a person to deliver punishment of increasing severity to a protesting individual?" This statement conforms to the definition of a problem, because it contains two variables—group pressure and severity of punishment delivered—and asks a question regarding the relationship between these variables.

Are all problems that conform to the definition good research problems? Assume that you posed the problem: "How do we know that God influences our behavior?" This question meets the definition of a problem, but it obviously cannot be tested. Kerlinger (1973) presents three criteria that good problems must meet. First, the variables in the problem should express a relationship. This criterion, as you can see, was contained in the definition of a problem. The second criterion is that the problem should be stated in question form. The statement of the problem should begin with "What is the effect of . . . ," "Under what conditions do . . . ," "Does the effect of . . . ," or some similar form. Sometimes only the purpose of a study is stated, which does not necessarily communicate the problem to be investigated. The purpose of the Milgram (1964a) study was to investigate the effect of group pressure on a person's behavior. Asking a question has the benefit of presenting the problem directly, thereby minimizing interpretation and distortion. The third criterion, and the one that most frequently distinguishes a researchable from a nonresearchable problem, states, "The problem statement should be such as to imply possibilities of empirical testing" (p. 18). Many interesting and important questions fail to meet this criterion and therefore are not amenable to scientific inquiry. Quite a few philosophical and theological questions fall into this category. Milgram's problem, on the other hand, meets all the criteria. A relation was expressed between the variables, the problem was stated in question form, and it was possible to test the problem empirically. Severity of punishment was measured by the amount of electricity supposedly delivered to the protesting individual, and group pressure was applied by having two confederates suggest increasingly higher shock levels.

Specificity of the Question

Specificity of the research question
The preciseness with which the research question is stated

In formulating a problem, **specificity of the research question** is an important consideration. Think of the difficulties facing the experimenter who asks the question "What effect does the environment have on learning ability?" This question meets all the criteria of a problem, and yet it is stated so vaguely that the investigator could not pinpoint what was to be investigated. The concepts of *environment* and *learning ability* are vague (what environmental characteristics? learning of what?). The experimenter must specify what is meant by *environment* and by *learning ability* to be able to conduct the experiment. Now contrast this question with the following: "What effect does the amount of exposure to words have on the speed with which they are learned?" This question specifies exactly what the problem is.

The two examples of questions presented here demonstrate the advantages of formulating a specific problem. A specific statement helps to ensure that the experimenters understand the problem. If the problem is stated vaguely, the experimenters probably do not know exactly what they want to study and therefore may design a study that will not solve the problem. A specific problem statement also helps the experimenters make necessary decisions about such factors as participants, apparatus, instruments, and measures. A vague problem statement helps very little with such decisions. To drive this point home, go back and reread the two questions given in the preceding paragraph and ask yourself, "What research participants should I use? What measures should I use? What apparatus or instruments should I use?"

How specific should one be in formulating a question? The primary purposes of formulating the problem in question form are to ensure that the researcher has a good grasp of the variables to be investigated and to aid the experimenter in designing and carrying out the experiment. If the formulation of the question is pointed enough to serve these purposes, then additional specificity is not needed. To the extent that these purposes are not met, additional specificity and narrowing of the research problem are required. Therefore, the degree of specificity required is dependent on the purpose of the problem statement.

STUDY QUESTION 4.3

- **What is meant by *research problem*, and what are the characteristics of a good research problem?**
- **Explain why a research problem should be stated in very specific and precise terms.**

Formulating Hypotheses

Hypothesis

The best prediction or a tentative solution to a problem

After the literature review has been completed and the problem has been stated in question form, you should begin formulating your **hypothesis.** For example, if you are investigating the influence of the number of bystanders on the speed of intervention in emergencies, you might hypothesize that as the number of bystanders increases, the speed of intervention will decrease. From this example you can see that hypotheses represent predictions of the relation that exists among the variables or tentative solutions to the problem. The formulation of the hypothesis logically follows the statement of the problem, because one cannot state a hypothesis without having a problem. This does not mean that the problem is always stated explicitly. In fact, if you survey articles published in journals, you will find that most of the authors do not present a statement of their specific problem. It seems that experienced researchers in a given field have such familiarity with the field that they consider the problems to be self-evident. Their predicted solutions to these problems are not apparent, however, and so these must be stated.

The hypothesis to be tested is often a function of the literature review, although hypotheses are also frequently formulated from theory. As stated earlier, theories guide research, and one of the ways in which they do so is by making predictions of possible relationships among variables. Hypotheses also (but less frequently) come from reasoning based on casual observation of events. In some situations it seems fruitless even to attempt to formulate hypotheses. When one is engaged in exploratory work in a relatively new area, where the important variables and their relationships are not known, hypotheses serve little purpose.

More than one hypothesis can almost always be formulated as the probable solution to the problem. Here again the literature review can be an aid because a review of prior research can suggest the most probable relationships that may exist among the variables.

Regardless of the source of the hypothesis, it *must* meet one criterion: A hypothesis must be stated so that it is capable of being either refuted or confirmed. In an experiment, it is the hypothesis that is being tested, not the problem. One does not test a question such as the one Milgram posed; rather, one tests one or more of the hypotheses that could be derived from this question, such as "group pressure increases the severity of punishment that participants will administer." A hypothesis that fails to meet the criterion of testability, or is nontestable, removes the problem from the realm of science. Any conclusions reached regarding a nontestable hypothesis do not represent scientific knowledge.

A distinction must be made between the scientific hypothesis and the null hypothesis. The **scientific hypothesis** represents the predicted relationship among the variables being investigated. The **null hypothesis** represents a statement of no relationships among the variables being investigated. For example, Hashtroudi, Parker, DeLisi, and Wyatt (1983) wanted to explore the nature of the memory deficits that occur due to the influence of alcohol. One of the research questions these investigators asked was whether the memory deficit induced by alcohol is decreased when intoxicated individuals are forced to generate a meaningful context for a word that is to be recalled. Although not specifically stated, these investigators' scientific hypothesis was that the generation of a meaningful context reduces the memory deficit produced by the alcohol. The null hypothesis predicted that no difference in recall is found between intoxicated participants who generated the meaningful context and those who did not.

Although an experimental study would seem to be directed toward testing the scientific hypothesis, this is not the case. In any study, it is the null hypothesis that is always tested, because the scientific hypothesis does not specify the exact amount or type of influence that is expected. To obtain support for the scientific hypothesis, you must collect evidence that enables you to reject the null hypothesis. Consequently, support for the scientific hypothesis is always obtained indirectly by rejecting the null hypothesis. The exact reason for testing the null hypothesis as opposed to the scientific hypothesis is based on statistical hypothesis-testing theory, which is beyond the scope of this text; but basically, the point is that it is necessary to test the null hypothesis in order to obtain evidence that will allow you to reject it so that, indirectly, you can get evidence supportive of the scientific hypothesis.

Why should hypotheses be set up in the first place? Why not just forget about hypotheses and proceed to attempt to answer the question? Hypotheses serve a valuable function. Remember that hypotheses are derived from knowledge obtained from the literature review of other experiments, theories, and so forth. Such prior knowledge serves as the basis for the hypothesis. If the experiment confirms the hypothesis, then, in addition to providing an answer to the question asked, it gives additional support to the literature that suggested the hypothesis. But what if the hypothesis is not confirmed by the experiment? Does this invalidate the prior literature? If the hypothesis is not confirmed, then either the hypothesis is false or some error exists in the conception of the hypothesis. If there is an error in conceptualization, it could be in any of a number of categories. Some of the information obtained from prior experiments may be false, or some relevant information may have been overlooked in the literature review. It is also possible that the experimenter misinterpreted some of the literature. These are a few of the more salient errors that could have taken place. In any event, failure to support a hypothesis may indicate that something is wrong, and it is up to the experimenter to discover what it is. Once the experimenter uncovers what he or she thinks is wrong, a new hypothesis is proposed that can be tested experimentally. The experimenter now has another study to conduct. Such is the

Scientific hypothesis
The predicted relationship among the variables being investigated

Null hypothesis
A statement of no relationship among the variables being investigated

continuous process of science. Even if the hypothesis is false, knowledge has been advanced, because for now an incorrect hypothesis can be ruled out. Another hypothesis must be formulated and tested in order to reach a solution to the problem.

- **What is a hypothesis and what specific criterion must a hypothesis meet?**
- **Distinguish between the scientific and null hypothesis.**
- **Explain how you would obtain support for the scientific hypothesis.**

Summary

In order to conduct research, it is first necessary to identify a problem in need of a solution. Psychological problems arise from several traditional sources: theories, practical issues, and past research. In addition, in psychology we have our personal experience to draw on for researchable problems because psychological research is concerned with behavior. Once a researchable problem has been identified, the literature relevant to this problem should be reviewed. A literature review will reveal the current state of knowledge about the selected topic. It will indicate ways of investigating the problem and will point out related methodological problems. The literature review should probably begin with books written on the topic and progress from there to the actual research as reported in journals. In surveying the past research conducted on a topic, the scientist can make use of an electronic database, one of which is operated by the American Psychological Association. In addition to using these sources, the researcher can search the World Wide Web and obtain information by attending professional conventions or by calling, writing, or e-mailing other individuals conducting research on the given topic.

When the literature review has been completed, the experimenter must determine whether it is feasible for him or her to conduct the study. This means that an assessment must be made of the time, research participant population, expertise, and expense requirements, as well as the ethical sensitivity of the study. If this assessment indicates that it is feasible to conduct the study, the experimenter must make a clear and exact statement of the problem to be investigated. This means that the experimenter must formulate an interrogative sentence asking about the relationship between two or more variables. This interrogative sentence must express a relation and be capable of being tested empirically. The question must also be specific enough to assist the experimenter in making decisions about such factors as participants, apparatus, and general design of the study.

After the question has been stated, the experimenter needs to set down hypotheses. These must be formalized because they represent the predicted relation that exists among the variables under study. Often, hypotheses are a function of past research. If they are confirmed, the results not only answer the question asked but also provide additional support to the literature that suggested the hypotheses. There is one criterion that any hypothesis must meet: It must be stated so that it is capable of being either refuted or confirmed. Always remember that it is actually the null hypothesis, and not the scientific hypothesis, that is being tested in a study.

Key Terms and Concepts

Theory
Gender bias
Psychological Abstracts
PsycINFO
Search engine

Research problem
Specificity of the research question
Hypothesis
Scientific hypothesis
Null hypothesis

Related Internet Sites

www.apa.org/science/lib.html
This site provides instruction on how to find relevant information on psychological topics in outlets ranging from newspaper articles to scientific journals. It also includes links to information about PsycINFO, PsycARTICLES, PsycBOOKS, etc.

http://library.albany.edu/internet/
This is a great site containing links to information relevant to just about anything you want to know about searching the World Wide Web, as well as links to information regarding evaluating information on the Web.

http://gateway.lib.ohio-state.edu/tutor/les1/checklist.html
This site provides a checklist of things to do in evaluating a Web site.

Practice Test   *Answers to the these questions can be found in Appendix A.*

1. Assume that you have just been to a demonstration by the psychic Uri Geller and watched him apply his psychic powers to do such things as bend spoons. Let's further assume that you are a skeptic and doubt that this was done by psychic powers. You want to conduct a study to determine if Uri Geller really has the ability to bend a spoon through use of his psychic powers. This research idea has originated from

   a. Everyday life
   b. A practical issue
   c. Past research
   d. Theory

2. Dr. Skeptic was interested in the following questions:

   - Is it ethical to experiment with animals?
   - Is there an afterlife?
   - What is science?

   The common element in all three of these questions is that they

   a. Arise from everyday life experience
   b. Arise from practical issues
   c. Arise from past research
   d. Arise from theory
   e. Are not capable of scientific investigation

3. If you are doing a literature search you can log on to the World Wide Web and conduct your search using one of the available search engines. Using this procedure to do your literature search has the disadvantage of
   a. Not providing any relevant information
   b. Being too slow
   c. Not providing enough information
   d. Providing too much information with questionable credibility
   e. Only being accessible through the university library

4. Consider the research question: "Does excessive drinking occur in animals other than rats?" This is considered a good research question because it
   a. Asks a question
   b. Focuses on a relationship between two variables
   c. Can be empirically tested
   d. Is stated specifically enough to specify the variables being tested and to aid in the design of the study
   e. All of the above

5. If you have stated your hypothesis in such a way that you predict no relationship between the variables being investigated, you have stated a
   a. Scientific hypothesis
   b. Null hypothesis
   c. Alternate hypothesis
   d. Formal hypothesis
   e. Experimental hypothesis

Challenge Exercises

1. Construct a research problem that could be experimentally investigated and then provide the following information about this research problem.

   a. My research problem is _____

   _____

   b. The relation expressed in my research problem is _____

   c. Does the research problem ask a question? If it does not, restate it in question form. _____

   _____

   d. The research problem can be empirically tested because _____

   _____

   e. The hypothesis I want to test is _____

   _____

2. Now that you have a research problem, you should conduct a literature review. Conduct this literature review using the databases specified here. You should get very different results, and this should illustrate to you the advantages and limitations of each.

   a. Conduct a mini-literature review of the information relating to your research topic using the PsycINFO database. Use the following approach when doing this literature review.
      1) List the search terms you want to use when searching PsycINFO
      2) Identify five articles related to your research problem. For each of these articles, provide the following information.
         a) Author(s)
         b) Title
         c) Journal
         d) Study hypothesis or purpose
         e) Results, or what the study found

   b. Conduct a mini-literature review using the World Wide Web. Use the following approach when conducting this search.
      1) Specify a search engine.
      2) Identify two Web pages that you think you can use for your literature review and answer the following questions regarding each Web page.
         a) What is the source of the information?
         b) What is the purpose of the Web page?
         c) Is the information accurate, and how can you tell that it is accurate?
         d) Does the Web page report the results of a study or a summary of several studies? Does it provide some acknowledgement of the limitations of the information?
         e) What type of information is being provided (scholarly, popular, trade, etc.)?

5 Ethics

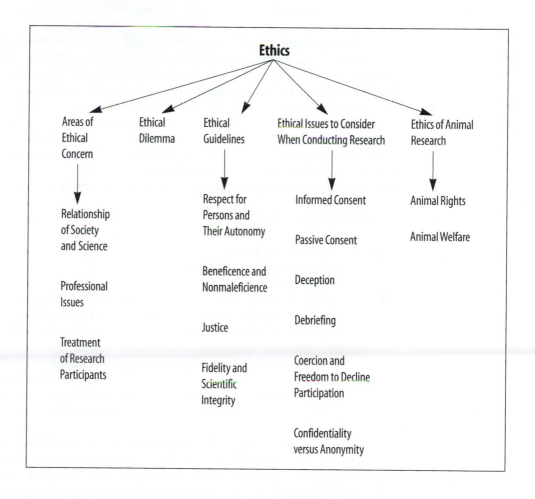

Ethics

Areas of Ethical Concern

Relationship of Society and Science

Professional Issues

Treatment of Research Participants

Ethical Dilemma

Ethical Guidelines

Respect for Persons and Their Autonomy

Beneficence and Nonmaleficience

Justice

Fidelity and Scientific Integrity

Ethical Issues to Consider When Conducting Research

Informed Consent

Passive Consent

Deception

Debriefing

Coercion and Freedom to Decline Participation

Confidentiality versus Anonymity

Ethics of Animal Research

Animal Rights

Animal Welfare

Riddick Bowe was the youngest son of thirteen children raised by his mother, Dorothy Bowe, in an impoverished and violent neighborhood. However, Bowe had an extraordinary gift as a fighter. As a youngster he won three Golden Gloves and later won a silver medal at the Olympics in Seoul, South Korea, in October 1988. He easily charmed almost everyone and was very protective of his mother, suggesting to some that he possessed a lot of character. His high school sweetheart described him as distinctive partially because he did not seem to be like the other guys in their neighborhood—the drug dealers and fast talkers with girls all over the place. On April 27, 1988, when she was twenty-one, she married Bowe. Everyone, however, was not taken in by Bowe's charm. Several of his trainers saw through his charm and correctly concluded that he was a difficult individual with a discipline and control problem. However, because of his enormous talent they continued to function as his trainers. Their efforts were not unrewarded. Four years after turning pro, Bowe was a champion, winning a twelve-round decision over Evander Holyfield in November 1992. His agent produced a lucrative HBO contract and a multimillion dollar endorsement deal with Fila, an athletic apparel company, and the media embraced him partly because reporters and broadcasters were weary of the unabashedly violent Mike Tyson.

Riddick Bowe's personal life, however, had a dark side. He was physically abusive to his wife. On one occasion he knocked her out in front of their three-year-old son and never thought anything of it. He could be a strict disciplinarian. One incident involved his ripping the cord from the television in his hotel suite, and, after using duct tape to bind his son's hands and feet, whipping him with the cord.

In 1997 Judy and Riddick Bowe separated. However, after a five-month separation Riddick Bowe decided he wanted to reunite his family and set about doing that in his own way. Armed with a buck knife, pepper spray, a flashlight, and duct tape, he and his brother drove to his wife's new home and abducted her and their five children during the early morning hours of February 1998.

Domestic violence such as is illustrated in the case of Riddick Bowe is not an isolated incident but one that is repeated multiple times every day in the United States and in virtually every other country in the world. It is also a research area that has attracted the attention of researchers, many of whom are psychologists. These individuals are trying to provide answers to questions such as why do people engage in domestic violence, what are the causes of such violence, and how can the incidence of such violence be reduced. Engaging in research such as this generates a variety of ethical concerns. One of the most serious ethical issues is the potential harmful effect the research may have on the participants. This could take the form of, for example, enraging either the husband or wife and causing an escalation of the already violent relationship by virtue of the fact that the abusive behavior is being reported to the researcher. In the course of conducting the research, an investigator may uncover a seriously abusive relationship in which the safety of the research participant is in jeopardy. In such an instance the investigator has the responsibility to protect the research participant, which may mean that the abusive behavior becomes public. Although this would be the appropriate behavior for the investigator, the researcher would have invaded the privacy of the couple.

Chapter Preview

Prior to conducting either a human or an animal research study, the investigator must determine if the study can be conducted in an ethically acceptable manner. This is a rather complicated process involving a review board that reviews all the material you will use in the study as well as the procedures involved in collecting your data. The primary goal of this review board is to ensure that your study does not harm the human participants and to ensure that the benefits of the study outweigh the liabilities that might be incurred. Although ethical considerations in animal research focus more on animal welfare, there is a focus on ensuring that animals do not suffer and that the benefits of the research outweigh the liabilities. Regardless of whether a research study uses animals or humans, there are many issues that go into conducting ethical research. In this chapter, I focus on the issues involved in the ethical conduct of both human and animal research. I discuss the meaning of research ethics and the areas that are pertinent to psychological research. I then present the American Psychological Association's code of ethics, which is to be used by psychologists for guidance in conducting research with human participants, and discuss some of the important points in this code of ethics. I conclude by discussing the ethics of conducting research with animals because animal research is also scrutinized and periodically criticized as being unethical. For example, it has been pointed out that animals are deprived of food, placed in stressful environments, shocked, and surgically altered— all in the name of science. Is it appropriate to subject animals to such treatment? This is a question that always confronts the scientist. Thus, psychological research has the potential for endangering the physical and psychological well-being of both animals and humans. If all scientific research consisted of innocuous studies, there would be little need to consider the welfare of research participants or the ethical issues surrounding the study. Unfortunately, as the foregoing examples illustrate, many psychological studies have been conducted that arouse ethical concerns.

Introduction

Once you have constructed your research problem and formulated the hypothesis, you are ready to begin to develop the research design. The design will specify how you will collect data that will enable you to test your hypothesis and arrive at some answer to the research question. However, at the same time that you are designing the research study, you must pay attention to ethical issues involved in research.

In their pursuit of knowledge relating to the behavior of organisms, psychologists conduct surveys, manipulate the type of experience that individuals receive, or vary the stimuli presented to individuals and then observe the research participants' reactions to these stimuli. Such manipulations and observations are necessary in order to identify the influence of various experiences or stimuli. At the same time, scientists recognize that individuals have the right to privacy and to protest surveillance of their behavior carried out without their consent. People also have the right to know if their behavior is being manipulated and, if so, why. The scientific community is confronted with the problem of trying to satisfy the public demand for solutions to problems such as cancer, arthritis, alcoholism, child abuse, and penal reform without infringing on people's rights. For a psychologist trained in research techniques, a decision *not* to do research is also a matter of ethical concern.

In order to advance knowledge and to find answers to questions, it is often necessary to impinge on well-recognized rights of individuals. Consideration of ethical issues is, therefore, integral to the development of a research proposal and to the conduct of research (Sieber & Stanley, 1988). It is very difficult to investigate such topics as child abuse, for example, without violating the right to privacy, because it is necessary to obtain information about the child abuser and/or the child being abused. Such factors create an ethical dilemma: whether to conduct the research and violate certain rights of individuals for the purpose of gaining knowledge or to sacrifice a gain in knowledge for the purpose of preserving human rights. Ethical principles are vital to the research enterprise because they assist the scientist in preventing abuses that may otherwise occur and delineate the responsibilities of the investigator.

Research Ethics: What Are They?

Research ethics
A set of guidelines to assist the experimenter in conducting ethical research

When most people think of ethics, they think of moralistic sermons and endless philosophical debates. However, **research ethics** should not be a set of moralistic dictates imposed on the research community by a group of self-righteous busybodies. Rather, they should be a set of principles that will assist the community of experimenters in deciding how to conduct ethical research.

Within the social and behavioral sciences, ethical concerns can be divided into three areas (Diener & Crandall, 1978): (1) the relationship between society and science, (2) professional issues, and (3) the treatment of research participants.

Relationship between Society and Science

The ethical issue concerning the relationship between society and science revolves about the extent to which societal concerns and cultural values should direct the course of scientific investigation. Traditionally, science has been conceived of as trying to uncover the laws of nature. It is assumed that the scientist examines the phenomenon being investigated in an objective and unbiased manner. However, the literature dealing with experimenter effects reveals that the scientist can never be totally objective. Similarly, the society surrounding the scientist dictates to a great extent which issues will be investigated. The federal government spends millions of dollars each year on research, and it sets priorities for how the money is to be spent. To increase the probability of obtaining research funds, investigators orient their research proposals toward these same priorities, which means that the federal government at least partially dictates the type of research conducted. AIDS research provides an excellent illustration. Prior to 1980, AIDS (acquired immunodeficiency syndrome) was virtually unheard of. Few federal dollars were committed to investigating this disorder. But when AIDS turned up within the U.S. population and its lethal characteristic was identified, it rapidly became a national concern. Millions of dollars were immediately earmarked for research to investigate causes and possible cures. Many researchers reoriented their interests and investigations to the AIDS problem because of the availability of research funds. Unfortunately, at times a more insidious and destructive federal influence affects science. The influence I am talking about is when legislators attempt to make decisions regarding studies they think are not meritorious of receiving federal funding by introducing legislation that targets specific research proposals and revokes funding for these proposals. See the example in Exhibit 5.1.

EXHIBIT 5.1

Congressional Influence on Research Studies

For three years in a row legislation has been introduced that would revoke funding for several behavioral research projects. In 2006 Randy Neugebarer introduced legislation targeting two behavioral research studies because, as his office stated, the funds that the National Institutes of Health (NIH) proposes to spend on these projects would be better spent on research on specific mental illness (Winerman, 2005). One of the studies that Neugebarer is attempting to eliminate from funding is a study that focuses on identifying which factors lead to successful marriages and which ones lead to divorce. Dr. Sandra Murray believes, and apparently so did the review panel of NIH, that this research is important because marital dissolution and breakdown are risk factors for depression.

This is not the first time Neugebarer has attached such an amendment to an appropriations bill and, according to Wasserman, one of the researchers whose research was targeted, this seems to be a pattern of his. Karen Studwell, a senior legislative and federal affairs officer in APA's Science Policy Office, correctly pointed out that this is congressional meddling in a peer-review process and congress does not have the responsibility of providing oversight of NIH. For a member of congress to attempt to legislate the elimination of funding that has been approved undermines the peer-review process and questions the priorities of NIH. Fortunately, there do seem to be some voices of reason among fellow members of congress. House Appropriations Committee chair Bill Young suggested that members who question a particular research project discuss their objections with the director of NIH rather than introduce legislation to kill the research project. While this is a very reasonable approach, there is no guarantee that similar legislation will not appear in subsequent years.

In the past thirty years, corporate support for research has increased from less than $5 million a year to hundreds of millions of dollars (Haber, 1996). Although this is substantial support, it frequently comes with a set of biases and restrictions. For example, most of the research sponsored by drug companies has focused on the development of variants of existing drugs with the goal of improving sales rather than developing new drugs. When comparisons are made between a new drug and a traditional therapy, 43 percent of the studies funded by a drug company and only 13 percent of the studies funded by other sources supported the new drug (Davidson, 1986). Drug companies obviously want their new patented drugs to turn out to be superior because this leads to sales of the new drug and increases the profit that can be made by the company.

For similar reasons, corporations may restrict the communication of research findings. Corporations sometimes award funds on the condition that research results cannot be published without their approval because they want to control what is and what is not communicated about their products. Unfavorable findings may be suppressed, which is what happened when the British pharmaceutical company Boots found that the results of a study they funded revealed that their popular synthetic thyroid medication was no better than three cheaper generic drugs (Leavitt, 2001).

Because funding is the lifeblood of scientists, they attempt to identify the priorities of various funding sources and then slant their proposals toward these priorities. In this way, corporate support drives a significant portion of the research that is conducted.

Societal and cultural values also enter into science to the extent that the phenomenon a scientist chooses to investigate is often determined by that scientist's own culturally based interests (for example, a female psychologist might study sex discrimination in the work force, or a black psychologist might study racial attitudes). The scientific enterprise is not value-free; rather, society's values as well as the scientist's own can creep into the research process in subtle and unnoticed ways.

Professional Issues

Research misconduct
Fabricating, falsifying, or plagiarizing the proposing, performing, reviewing, or reporting of research results

The category of professional issues includes the expanding problem of research misconduct. In December of 2000, the U.S. Office of Science and Technology Policy (OSTP) defined **research misconduct** as "fabrication, falsification, or plagiarism (FFP) in proposing, performing, or reviewing research, or in reporting research results" (OSTP, 2005). The attention fabrication, falsification, and plagiarism has received is understandable given that a scientist is trained to ask questions, to be skeptical, and to use the research process in the search for truth. This search for truth is completely antithetical to engaging in any type of deception. The most serious crime in the scientific profession is to cheat or present fraudulent results. Although fraudulent activity is condemned on all fronts, in the past decade there seems to have been an increase in the number of reports of scientists who forge or falsify data, manipulate results to support a theory, or selectively report data, as illustrated in Exhibit 5.2. In the past twenty years, the federal government has confirmed only two hundred cases of fraud, which works out to 1 case per 100,000 active researchers per year. However, this statistic may underrepresent the actual number because a 1987 study

EXHIBIT 5.2

Two Cases of Reportedly Fraudulent Research

Although most known cases of fraudulent research have occurred in the field of medicine, several very significant instances have recently been identified in the field of psychology. Two of the most infamous cases are described in this exhibit.

Cyril Burt, the first British psychologist to be knighted, received considerable acclaim in both Great Britain and the United States for his research on intelligence and its genetic basis. A biographical sketch published upon his death depicted a man with unflagging enthusiasm for research, analysis, and criticism. Shortly after his death, however, questions about the authenticity of his research began to appear. Ambiguities and oddities were identified in his research papers. A close examination of his data revealed that correlation coefficients did not change across samples or across sample sizes, suggesting that he may have fabricated data. Attempts to locate one of Burt's important collaborators were unsuccessful. Dorfman (1978) conducted an in-depth analysis of Burt's data and showed beyond a reasonable doubt that Burt fabricated his data on the relationship between intelligence and social class.

More recently, the National Institute of Mental Health (NIMH) conducted an investigation of alleged research fraud by one of its grantees, Steven E. Breuning. Breuning received his doctorate from the Illinois Institute of Technology in 1977 and several years later obtained a position at the Coldwater Regional Center in Michigan. At Coldwater, Breuning was invited to collaborate on an NIMH-funded study of the use of neuroleptics on institutionalized mentally disabled people. In January 1981 he was appointed director of the John Merck program at Pittsburgh's Western Psychiatric Institute and Clinic, where he continued to report on the results of the Coldwater research and even obtained his own NIMH grant to study the effects of stimulant medication on mentally disabled subjects. During this time Breuning gained considerable prominence and was considered one of the field's leading researchers. In 1983, however, questions were raised about the validity of Breuning's work. The individual who had initially taken Breuning on as an investigator started questioning a paper in which Breuning reported results having impossibly high reliability. This prompted a further review of Breuning's published work, and contacts were made with personnel at Coldwater, where the research had supposedly been conducted. Coldwater's director of psychology had never heard of the study and was not aware that Breuning had conducted any research while at Coldwater. NIMH was informed of the allegations in December 1983. Following a three-year investigation, an NIMH team concluded that Breuning "knowingly, willfully, and repeatedly engaged in misleading and deceptive practices in reporting his research." He reportedly had not carried out the research that was described, and only a few of the experimental subjects had ever been studied. It was concluded that Breuning had engaged in serious scientific misconduct (Holden, 1987).

at George Mason University found that one-third of the scientists interviewed suspected that a colleague had committed plagiarism. However, 54 percent of these did not report their suspicions to university officials (Brainard, 2000).

The cost of such fraudulent activity is enormous, both to the profession and to the scientist. Not only is the whole scientific enterprise discredited, but the professional career of the individual is destroyed. Breuning (see Exhibit 5.2) pleaded guilty to scientific misconduct in a plea bargain and was sentenced to sixty days in a halfway house, 250 hours of community service, and five years of probation. There is no justification for faking or altering scientific data.

Although fraudulent activity is obviously the most serious form of scientific misconduct, there is a broader range of less serious, although still unacceptable, practices that are receiving attention. These include such practices as overlooking others' use of flawed data; failing to present data contradicting one's own work; changing the design, methodology, or results of a study in response to pressure from a funding source; or circumventing minor aspects of human-participant requirements. While these practices do not approach the seriousness of fabrication, falsification, or plagiarism, they are of concern to the profession, especially as Martinson, Anderson, and de Vries (2005) have revealed that more than a third of U.S. scientists surveyed admitted to engaging in one or more of these practices in the past three years. This does not necessarily mean that the structure of the research process has eroded. However, these problems deserve attention as they do represent a form of research misconduct.

The increased frequency of and interest in scientific misconduct has naturally stimulated discussion about its cause and the type of action that needs to be taken to reduce the frequency of misconduct (Hilgartner, 1990; Knight, 1984). One of the best deterrents is probably the development of an institutional culture in which key faculty members model ethical behavior, stress the importance of research integrity, and translate these beliefs into action (Gunsalus, 1993). Jane Steinberg, Director of Extramural Activities and Research Integrity Officer at the National Institute of Mental Health, states that there are some specific strategies that can be used to prevent fabrications of data. She advocates instituting prevention strategies (Steinberg, 2002), such as those listed in Table 5.1, that make it difficult to engage in scientific misconduct.

Additionally, the National Institutes of Health (NIH) require that all investigators who receive funding from NIH, as well as other key personnel such as co-investigators and study coordinators, complete an education module on the protection of human participants. Most universities, including my own, extend this requirement to all investigators, including other key personnel such as graduate and

TABLE 5.1
Strategies for Preventing Scientific Misconduct

- Have the faculty member or project investigator make it clear that he or she personally checks and verifies data that are collected. This must be followed by an actual check of the collected data.

- If appropriate and reasonable, ask participants if you may recontact them and then contact some who should have been seen by each data collector.

- If animals were used in the research study, check to make sure that the animals were purchased and used in the study and that lab notes were maintained.

- Do not tolerate any deviations from the approved design, and discuss any improvements in the context of another study.

- Watch for individuals who complete data collection in record time. Some people may be better at, for example, recruitment, but it is best to check on everyone.

- Teach the standard of conduct in research in classes and review cases of misconduct, discussing the ramifications it has for researchers, the field, and public trust.

- Provide guidelines detailing how to handle suspected misconduct.

undergraduate students, who are conducting research with human participants whose research does not receive NIH funding.

Treatment of Research Participants

The treatment of research participants is the most fundamental issue confronted by scientists. The conduct of research with humans can potentially create a great deal of physical and psychological harm. For example, in September 1995, *U.S. News & World Report* (Pasternak & Cary, 1995) published an article on once-secret records of government-sponsored or -funded radiation experiments carried out between 1944 and 1974. During this time, more than 4,000 radiation experiments were conducted on tens of thousands of Americans for the dual purpose of learning more about the effects of radiation on humans and the potential medical benefits of radiation on cancer.

From a scientific perspective this research appears legitimate because cancer was and is a dreaded disease in need of a cure. Radiation was viewed as a potential weapon in the fight against cancer. There was a curiosity and legitimate question regarding the effect of radiation on the human body. Radiation experiments could, therefore, serve the dual purpose of investigating their benefit in the fight against cancer and revealing the effect of radiation on the body. This dual-use rationale was used to justify many of the experiments conducted. However, in most of these experiments the welfare of the research participant was disregarded in favor of science. Finding a cure for cancer was used as the rationale to justify experiments designed to test the effect of radiation on the human body.

One of the most controversial experiments funded by the defense establishment was TBI or Total-body Irradiation. This procedure involved irradiating a large portion of the body using cobalt-60 gamma rays. The Defense Department was interested because these experiments would provide data on the effects of radiation on soldiers. One way of obtaining such data was to observe the effect of radiation on people who could potentially benefit from such exposure. These were individuals with terminal cancer.

The cancer patients receiving the treatments were told that the radiation might cure their cancer. Documents, however, suggested that many of these treatments were conducted only to gather data on the effect of radiation on humans. Other radiation studies were conducted on patients with cancer resistant to radiation. In these experiments Dr. Saenger, the principal investigator, even stated that he was experimenting and not treating the patients' disease. There was a 25 percent mortality rate.

When the experiments conducted by Saenger were publicized in the Cincinnati press, some of the children of his research participants recognized their parents' cases. These children recalled that their parents experienced extensive physical and psychological pain and distress. The patients reported aching throughout their body, getting violently ill, bleeding from various orifices, and pleading to have the treatment stopped. In spite of these pleas, Dr. Saenger encouraged the patients to continue, using the argument that radiation exposure was beneficial.

Many of these radiation experiments were clearly unethical and inflicted extensive harm and psychological pain on the research participants. Other examples of experiments that created physical and psychological harm are illustrated in Exhibit 5.3.

EXHIBIT 5.3

Psychological Experiments That Have the Potential for Creating Physical or Psychological Harm

A number of experiments that have been conducted in the field of psychology have the potential for creating either physical or psychological harm. Three such experiments are described here.

Humphreys (1970) was interested in learning about the motives of individuals who commit fellatio in public restrooms. To accomplish this purpose, Humphreys offered to serve as "watchqueen"—the individual who keeps watch and gives a warning when a police car or a stranger approaches. In this capacity, Humphreys observed hundreds of impersonal sexual acts. He even gained the confidence of some of the men whom he observed and persuaded them to tell him about the rest of their lives and their motives. In other cases, he recorded the automobile license numbers of the men and then obtained their addresses from the Department of Public Safety. At a later time he appeared at their homes, claiming to be a health service interviewer and then interviewed them about their marital status, jobs, and so on. Clearly Humphreys deceived the men he observed and questioned, creating the potential for anger, embarrassment, and even more extreme reactions from the subjects.

Berkun, Bialek, Kern, and Yagi (1962) reported on a variety of studies conducted by the military to investigate the impact of stress. In one experiment, army recruits were placed in a DC-3 that apparently became disabled and was preparing to crash-land. Before the impending crash, the recruits were asked to complete a questionnaire that assessed their opinions regarding the disposition of their earthly possessions in case of death, their knowledge of emergency landing procedures, and so forth. After all the questionnaires had been completed, the responses were jettisoned in a metal container so as not to be destroyed, and then the plane landed safely. Only then did the recruits realize that the whole incident was an experiment.

Middlemist, Knowles, and Matter (1976) investigated the impact of an invasion of personal space on physical responses. In collecting data on this topic, the authors used hidden periscopes to study the effect of closeness of others on the speed and rate of urination by men in a public lavatory. To manipulate the closeness variable, a confederate appearing to urinate was stationed either one or two urinals away from the subject.

Experiments designed to investigate important psychological issues may subject participants to humiliation, physical pain, and embarrassment. In planning an experiment, a scientist is obligated to consider the ethics of conducting the necessary research. Unfortunately, some studies cannot be designed in such a way that the possibility of physical and psychological harm is eliminated. Hence, the researcher often faces the dilemma of having to determine whether the research study should be conducted at all. Because it is so important, we will consider this issue in some detail.

STUDY QUESTION 5.1

- **What is meant by the term *research ethics?***
- **Discuss the areas of ethical concern to the social and behavioral sciences.**
- **What are the ethical issues in each of these areas and which area is of most concern?**

Ethical Dilemmas

Ethical dilemma
The investigator's conflict in weighing the potential cost to the participant against the potential gain to be accrued from the research project

The scientific enterprise in which the research psychologist engages creates a special set of dilemmas. On the one hand, the research psychologist is trained in the scientific method and feels an obligation to conduct research; on the other hand, doing so may necessitate subjecting research participants to stress, failure, pain, aggression, or deception. Thus, there arises the **ethical dilemma** of having to determine if the potential gain in knowledge from the research study outweighs the cost to the research participant (see Exhibit 5.4). In weighing the pros and cons of such a question, the researcher must give primary consideration to the welfare of the participant.

EXHIBIT 5.4

Documenting That Stuttering Can Be a Learned Disorder: Did the Benefit of This Study Outweigh the Harm to the Participants?

In 1939, an experimental study was conducted demonstrating that stuttering could be created by constantly badgering a person about the imperfections in his or her speech (Monster experiment, June 2001). This experiment led to a theory that helped thousands of children overcome their speech impediment. However, the experiment affected the participants negatively, creating significant lifelong pain and suffering.

The experiment was designed by Dr. Wendell Johnson, who theorized that stuttering was not an inborn condition but something children learned from parents who seized on minor speech imperfections. As children became aware of their speech, he believed, they could not help but stutter. To validate his theory he experimented with twenty-two orphans at an Iowa orphanage. Half of the orphans were given positive speech therapy and the other half were induced to stutter by his graduate assistant Mary Tudor. Tudor induced stuttering by badgering the orphans about their speech even if it was nearly flawless. Through this process, eight of the eleven orphans who were constantly badgered became chronic stutterers. One of the orphans who had developed stuttering wrote Tudor a letter in 2001 and called her a "monster" and "Nazi." She stated that Tudor had destroyed her life and left her nothing. Fortunately, she had married a man who helped her piece together her self-confidence. However, after

he died in 1999, she resumed stuttering and placed a Do Not Disturb sign on her door, rarely venturing outdoors.

Clearly, this experiment caused significant grief and pain for the orphans who developed stuttering. It is also something that has bothered Tudor while and after she conducted the experiment. At the time she conducted the experiment, she didn't like what she was doing. After the conclusion of the experiment, Tudor returned to the orphanage three times to try to reverse the orphans' stuttering with little success. Since that time, she has remained extremely ambivalent of her participation in the study because the results have helped countless individuals but at the same time the study caused considerable pain for the participants. She remembers how the orphans greeted her, running to her car and helping her carry in materials for the experiment. She got them to trust her and then she did this horrible thing to them. However, countless individuals have overcome their stuttering problems as a result of the knowledge acquired from this experiment.

There are tremendous benefits and costs that have accrued from this study. This is the reason for Tudor's current ambivalent feelings. She conducted an experiment that created a knowledge base that was very beneficial. It is also very clear that the cost was considerable to the participants.

Unfortunately, there is no formula or rule that can help investigators. The decision must be based on a subjective judgment, which should not be made entirely by the researcher or his or her colleagues, because such individuals might become so involved in the study that they might tend to exaggerate its scientific merit and potential contribution. Investigators must seek the recommendations of others, such as scientists in related fields, students, or lay individuals.

At the present time the recommendations regarding the cost–benefit relationship in a study comes from the Institutional Review Board (IRB). This is a board that exists at all institutions that receive federal funds for research and reviews research proposals involving human participants.

In reviewing the research proposals, members of the IRB are required to make judgments regarding the ethical appropriateness of the proposed research by ensuring that protocols are explained to the research participants and that the risks of harm are reasonable in relation to the hoped-for benefits. To make this judgment, the IRB members must have sufficient information about the specifics of the research protocol. This means that the investigator must submit a research protocol that the IRB can review. This research protocol must provide the information listed in Table 5.2. A sample research protocol submitted to an IRB appears in Exhibit 5.5.

From the information contained in the research protocol, IRB members must make a judgment as to the ethical acceptability of the research. In making this judgment the primary concern of the IRB is the welfare of the research participants. Specifically, the IRB will review proposals to ensure that research participants provide informed consent (see sample in Exhibit 5.5) for participation in the study and that the procedures used in the study do not harm the participants. This committee has particularly difficult decisions to make when a procedure involves the potential for harm. Some procedures, such as administering an experimental drug, have the potential for harming participants. In such instances the IRB must seriously consider the potential benefits that may accrue from the study relative to the risks to the participant. Figure 5.1 (p. 139) presents a decision plane that provides a conceptual view of how the cost–benefit analysis should work. Studies falling in the areas labeled A and D can be easily decided on. Area A studies have high costs and low benefits and

TABLE 5.2

Information That Must Be Presented in a Research Protocol Presented to the IRB

- Purpose of the research
- Relevant background and rationale for the research
- Participant population
- Experimental design and methodology
- Incentives offered, if any
- Risks and benefits to the participants and precautions to be taken
- Privacy and confidentiality

EXHIBIT 5.5

Sample Research Protocol

Title of Protocol: The Relationship of Attributional Beliefs, Self-Esteem, and Ego Involvement to Performance on a Cognitive Task.

Primary Investigator: Jane Doe
Department   Psychology
Address   Psychology Bldg.
Phone Number   123-4567

Purpose of the Research: The present investigation is designed to determine the potential individual differences in the ego-involvement effect. It is possible that some people are more at risk for the debilitating effects of ego-involving instructions than others. It is predicted that individuals with low self-esteem and negative attributional beliefs will be influenced negatively by ego-involving instructions.

Relevant Background for the Research: Recent research suggests that the way in which a cognitive task is presented influences performance on the task. Nicholls (1985) suggested that ego involvement often resulted in diminished task performance. He described ego involvement as a task orientation in which the goal is to either demonstrate one's ability relative to others or avoid demonstrating a lack of ability. This ego orientation is in contrast to task involvement in which the goal is simply to learn or improve a skill. In support of the Nicholls position, Graham and Golan (1991) found that ego-involving instructions resulted in poorer recall in a memory task than task-involving instructions. Apparently, the focus on performance detracted from the necessary information processing.

Participant Population: Two hundred students will be recruited from the Department of Psychology research participant pool. The pool consists of students enrolled in Psychology 120 who choose to participate in the research option to fulfill a course requirement.

The Experimental Design and Methodology:
The research will be conducted in a large group setting (approximately 30 students) in a classroom on campus. Students choosing to participate in the research will first read and sign the consent from. Students will then complete an attributional questionnaire and a self-esteem questionnaire. These materials will then be collected and a cognitive task will be distributed. Students will be given one minute to read the instructions and three minutes to solve twenty anagrams. (The experimenter will announce when to start and end each activity). The packets containing the instructions and the anagrams will be randomly ordered so that half of the participants in each session will receive the ego instructions and half will receive the task instructions. The ego instructions explain that the anagram task is a test of ability and that the researchers want to see how each person rates in comparison to his or her peers. The task instructions explain that the anagram task is an opportunity to learn how to solve anagrams and that practice helps people improve. The attributional questionnaire is designed to assess the students' beliefs about the importance of different causal factors (e.g., effort, ability, luck, and powerful others) in academic performance. The self-esteem questionnaire is designed to measure global self-worth.

The data will be analyzed through multiple regression with attributions, self-esteem, gender, and instructional format as predictors of the criterion variables (number of anagrams solved, number of codes completed).

Potential Benefit to Participant, Humankind, or General Knowledge: The present literature on ego and task involvement indicates that ego instructions can negatively affect performance. It is important to determine the individual differences in this phenomenon. It is possible that females, individuals with low self-esteem, and individuals with negative attributional beliefs may be especially at risk for the debilitating effects of ego-

(*continued*)

EXHIBIT 5.5 (continued)

involving instructions. If this is the case, one could reduce these individual differences in performance (and support optimal learning) by presenting tasks primarily in a task-involvement format.

Risks, Hazards, and Precautions to Be Taken:
The risks are minimal. It is possible that students will be discouraged by not having time to complete all of the tasks. However, at the end of the session, we will make it clear to the group of students that the tasks were designed so that no one could complete them in the time allotted.

Assurance of Confidentiality, Including Description of Means of Such Assurance:
Participants will remain anonymous. Each packet (questionnaires and cognitive tasks) will have a number. Participants will be identified only by this number. Students will not be asked to put their name on any form (other than the consent form). All data will be stored securely. Only the principal investigator and her assistants will have access to the data.

Consent to Participate in Research

Primary Investigator: Jane Doe
Department: Psychology
Telephone Number: 123-4567

The purpose of this research is to determine the role of beliefs about success and failure and about self-esteem in cognitive tasks. If you agree to participate in this research, you will be asked to complete two questionnaires. The attributional questionnaire includes sixty questions concerning the possible causes of academic success and failure. The self-esteem questionnaire includes ten questions designed to measure an individual's global sense of self-worth or self-acceptance.

After completing both questionnaires, you will be asked to read a set of instructions and then try to solve as many anagrams as possible in a limited amount of time. Anagrams are jumbled letters that can be reordered to form a word (e.g., rlyibar = library).

Your participation in this research is entirely voluntary. You may change your mind and withdraw at any time without affecting your grade in the class.

The information gathered from this study will be strictly confidential and your privacy will be carefully protected. Code numbers will be used to record all test results and responses to questionnaires. Your name will not be used. Should the results of this research be published or presented in any form, your name or other identifying information will not be revealed.

This research has been approved by the chair of the Department of Psychology and the Institutional Review Board of the University of USA. Any questions you might have should be directed to Dr. Jane Doe, who can be reached at 123-4567. Should you have unresolved questions relating to your rights as a research participant, you may contact the Institutional Review Board at 246-8910.

I have read or have had read to me and understand the above research study and have had an opportunity to ask questions that have been answered to my satisfaction. I agree voluntarily to participate in the study as described.

_____
Participant's Name

_____
Date

_____
Signature of Consenting Party

_____
Date

_____
Signature of Investigator

FIGURE 5.1

A decision-plane model representing the costs and benefits of research studies.

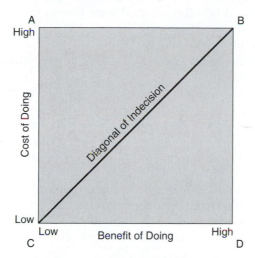

(From "Hedgehogs, Foxes and the Evolving Social Contract in Science: Ethical Challenges and Methodological Opportunities" by R. L. Rosnow, 1997, *Psychological Methods, 2,* pp. 345–356. Copyright by the American Psychological Association. Reprinted by permission of the author.)

would *not* be approved. Area D studies would have high benefit and low cost and would be approved. The difficulty in deciding to approve or disapprove a study increases as a study moves into the areas labeled B and C. Studies in area C create difficulty because, although they create little potential cost to the participant, they are also likely to yield little benefit. Studies in area B create difficulty because, although the benefit accruing from the study is high, costs to the participants is also high. An example of such a study appears in Exhibit 5.4.

Sometimes the board's decision is that the risks to the research participants are too great to permit the study; in other instances the decision is that the potential benefits are so great that the risks to the research participants are deemed to be acceptable. Unfortunately, the ultimate decision seems to be partially dependent on the composition of the IRB; Kimmel (1991) has revealed that males and research-oriented individuals who worked in basic areas were more likely to approve research proposals than were women and individuals who worked in service-oriented contexts and were employed in applied areas.

Even if the IRB approves the research protocol prepared, the investigator must always remember that no amount of advice or counsel can alter the fact that the final ethical responsibility lies with the researcher conducting the study.

STUDY QUESTION 5.2 | **What is the ethical dilemma researchers are faced with in psychology and how is this dilemma resolved?**

Ethical Guidelines

Nazi scientists during World War II conducted some grossly inhumane experiments that were universally condemned as being unethical. For example, they immersed people in ice water to determine how long it would take them to freeze to death, performed mutilating surgery, and deliberately infected many individuals with lethal pathogens. In 1946, twenty-three of the physicians went on trial at Nuremberg for the crimes they committed against these prisoners of war. During this trial the fundamental ethical standards for the conduct of research were set forth in what has become known as the Nuremberg Code. This code set forth ten conditions that must be met to justify research involving human participants. Of the ten conditions, the two most important were voluntary informed consent and a valid research design that had the potential of yielding valuable results.

One would logically think that the Nuremberg trial and the ethical standards resulting from this trial would have led to the conduct of ethical research with human participants. However, this was not the case, although the abuses (e.g., falsifying data) were not as profound as those committed by the Nazi physicians. In the 1960s there was not only an increase in funding for medical research and a corresponding increase in human participants, but also an increase in the attention given to human rights and the publicizing of research abuses.

In the medical field, Pappworth (1967) cited numerous examples of research that violated the ethical rights of human participants. One issue of *Daedalus* in 1969 was devoted to the ethics of human experimentation, particularly as it related to medical research. The Tuskegee experiment (Jones, 1981), described in Exhibit 5.6, probably epitomizes the type of unethical experimentation that was conducted within the medical field. There was an equal concern about the violation of the rights of human participants in psychological research. Kelman (1967, 1968, 1972) has been by far the most outspoken on this issue, although others, such as Seeman (1969) and Beckman and Bishop (1970), have also contributed. Entire books have been devoted to this issue (for example, Kimmel, 1996). This widespread concern led to the development of several sets of guidelines, such as the Belmont Report (Office for Protection from Research Risks [OPRR], 1979) and the American Psychological Association's *Ethical Principles in the Conduct of Research with Human Participants* (APA, 1982), for researchers to use when conducting their research. The APA guidelines were directed toward psychological research and the issues of concern at that time, such as deception and confidentiality. Although these issues are still important, the ethical issues faced by current researchers are much broader and have expanded into field settings and biomedical contexts. Investigations involve a broad range of populations, such as children, elderly adults, teenage mothers, individuals with chronic illnesses, and sexually abused individuals, that raise special concerns. Many research questions focus on sensitive issues such as incest, sexual abuse, and domestic violence that create a tension between participants' right to privacy and the need for knowledge. Studies using the Internet raise new ethical issues not addressed in previous guidelines or standards.

These new and emerging issues have dated the prior guidelines and ethical codes. In an effort to respond to these emerging issues, the American Psychological Association convened a task force with the charge of addressing them. This task force cre-

EXHIBIT 5.6

The Tuskegee Syphilis Experiment

In July 1972 the Associated Press released a story that revealed that the U.S. Public Health Service (PHS) had for forty years been conducting a study of the effects of untreated syphilis on black men in Macon County, Alabama. The study consisted of conducting a variety of medical tests (including an examination) on 399 black men who were in the late stages of the disease and on 200 controls. Although a formal description of the experiment could never be found (apparently one never existed), a set of procedures evolved in which physicians employed by the PHS administered a variety of blood tests and routine autopsies to learn more about the serious complications that resulted from the final stages of the disease.

This study had nothing to do with the treatment of syphilis; no drugs or alternative therapies were tested. It was a study aimed strictly at compiling data on the effects of the disease. The various components of the study, and not the attempt to learn more about syphilis, made it an extremely unethical experiment. The participants in the study were mostly poor and illiterate, and the PHS offered incentives to participate, including free

physical examinations, free rides to and from the clinic, hot meals, free treatment for other ailments, and a $50 burial stipend. The participants were not told the purpose of the study or what they were or were not being treated for. Even more damning is the fact that the participants were monitored by a PHS nurse, who informed local physicians that those individuals were taking part in the study and that they were not to be treated for syphilis. Participants who were offered treatment by other physicians were advised that they would be dropped from the study if they took the treatment.

As you can see, the participants were not aware of the purpose of the study or the danger it posed to them, and no attempt was ever made to explain the situation to them. In fact, participants were enticed with a variety of inducements and were followed to ensure that they did not receive treatment from other physicians. This study seems to have included just about every possible violation of our present standard of ethics for research with humans.

(From Jones, 1981.)

ated a book, *Ethics in Research with Human Participants,* edited by Bruce D. Sales and Susan Folkman (2000), to serve as an educational document that researchers and students can use in solving ethical dilemmas that arise in the conduct of research studies. This book, although not endorsed as the official position of the APA, specifies five basic moral principles (respect for persons and their autonomy, beneficence and nonmaleficence, justice, trust, and fidelity and scientific integrity) that should be adhered to when conducting research with human participants.

Respect for Persons and Their Autonomy

An autonomous person is a person who is capable of making decisions and following through on those decisions. Within the context of research, this means that a prospective research participant has the right to choose to participate in a research study. Denial of this choice shows a lack of respect for that person. This principle is adhered to in research studies by obtaining the prospective participant's informed consent. This means that the prospective participant is given all the information about a research study that may influence his or her willingness to participate. Once they have this information, they can make an informed choice whether to participate. Although adherence to this principle seems simple and straightforward, difficulties arise when the target population of a research study has limited or diminished capacity to understand the consent agreement, as may exist with young children, the mentally handicapped, or individuals with a mental disorder. In these instances, the interests of the participant must be appropriately represented and an assurance must be provided that they will not be placed at risk. This assurance is typically obtained by having a proxy, such as a parent or guardian, provide the informed consent.

Although informed consent is the standard that must be followed in most studies, there are situations in which informed consent is not required, for example, in the limited situation where participation in the study is deemed to involved no risk. However, the judgment of no risk can be difficult. These issues surrounding informed consent are discussed in more detail later in the chapter.

Beneficence and Nonmaleficence

Beneficence means doing good and *nonmaleficence* means doing no harm. This principle states that we should design and conduct our research studies in a way that minimizes the probability of harm to the participant and maximizes the probability that the participants receive some benefit. This is obviously a laudable goal and one that we should strive for. However, the costs and benefits of research studies vary considerably and seldom can we, in advance, anticipate all the costs and benefits that may accrue from a particular study. However, this is the task that is given to the IRB. Remember that a researcher planning to conduct a study using human participants must prepare and submit a proposal to the IRB detailing the elements of the research. From reading this proposal, the IRB members attempt to determine the costs and benefits of the research and then either approve or disapprove the research based on this determination.

There are actually three categories of review that a proposal can receive from the IRB. These categories relate directly to the potential risk of the study to the participant. Studies can receive exempt status, expedited review, or review by the full IRB board (OPRR, 2001). Exempt studies are studies that appear to involve no risk to the participants and do not require review by the IRB. However, studies involving fetal participants and prisoners are never exempt. Also, children involved in surveys, interview procedures, or the observation of their public behavior are never exempt unless the study involves observing these participants in the absence of any type of intervention. In making the decision to place a study in the exempt category, the IRB staff makes use of the exempt categories set forth in the OPRR (2001) reports and listed in Table 5.3.

The second category of review, expedited review, is a process whereby a study is rapidly reviewed by fewer members than constitute the full IRB board. Studies receiving expedited review are typically those involving no more than minimal risk such as the following:

1. Research involving data, documents, records, or specimens that have been collected or will be collected solely for nonresearch purposes.

TABLE 5.3
Exempt Categories

1. Research conducted in established or commonly accepted educational settings, involving normal educational practices, such as (a) research on regular and special education instructional strategies or (b) research on the effectiveness of or the comparison among instructional techniques, curricula, or classroom management methods.

2. Research involving the use of educational tests (cognitive, diagnostic, aptitude, achievement), survey procedures, interview procedures, or observation of public behavior, unless:
   a. information obtained is recorded in such a manner that the participants can be identified, directly or through identifiers linked to the participants; and
   b. any disclosure of the participants' responses outside the research could reasonably place the participant at risk of criminal or civil liability or be damaging to the participants' financial standing, employability, or reputation.

3. Research involving the use of educational tests (cognitive, diagnostic, aptitude, achievement), survey procedures, interview procedures, or observation of public behavior that is not exempt under item 2 above if
   a. the participants are elected or appointed public officials or candidates for public office, or
   b. federal statute(s) require(s) without exception that the confidentiality of the personally identifiable information will be maintained throughout the research and thereafter.

4. Research involving the collection or study of existing data, documents, records, pathological specimens, or diagnostic specimens if these sources are publicly available or if the information is recorded by the investigator in such a manner that participants cannot be identified, directly or through identifiers linked to the participants.

5. Research and demonstration projects that are conducted by or subject to the approval of Department or Agency heads and that are designed to study, evaluate or otherwise examine:
   a. Public benefit or service programs
   b. Procedures for obtaining benefits or services under those programs
   c. Possible changes in or alternatives to those programs or procedures
   d. Possible changes in methods or levels of payment for benefits or services under those programs

2. Research involving the collection of data from voice, video, digital, or image recordings made for research purposes.

3. Research on individual or group characteristics or behavior or research employing survey, interview, oral history, focus groups, program evaluation, human factors evaluation, or quality assurance methodologies when they present no more than minimal risk to participants.

Many of the studies conducted by students and psychology faculty probably fall into the minimal risk category and should receive expedited review.

The third category of review is full board review. This is a review by all members of the IRB. Any proposal that involves more than minimal risk raises red flags and must receive full board review.

Justice

The moral principle of justice is perhaps one of the more difficult ones to accomplish and is unlikely to be fully achieved (Sales & Folkman, 2000) in our imperfect world.

In the research arena, justice asks the question: Who should receive the benefits of the research and who should bear its burdens? Go back and reread Exhibit 5.4. In this study, the research participants not only did not benefit from participation in the study but were harmed. It seems clear that there was not a sense of fairness in the distribution of the benefits of this study. This brings up a difficult question for researchers. How should the benefits that may accrue from a study be distributed? Should all research participants receive equal benefits, and should the research participants benefit as much as nonparticipants? It seems fair that they should. However, the benefits from participation in the various components of a study are not known prior to the completion of the study, just as the benefits that might accrue from the research study are not known prior to its completion.

Consider, for example, a study investigating the effectiveness of a new drug for treating depression. A typical design might involve a comparison of the new drug with an old drug that represents a standard pharmacological treatment for depression. Because both groups received treatment, would this represent a fair and just distribution of benefit? If both drugs were equally effective, the benefits would seem to be equally distributed. However, what if the new drug was much more effective? What if the new drug had serious negative side effects? Now what is your assessment of the benefits and burdens? Should a placebo control group be included to determine if either drug was more effective than no treatment? Kirsch and Sapirstein (1998) have shown that up to 75 percent of an antidepressant drug's effect is due to a placebo effect. As you should be able to see, equally distributing the benefit and burden of a study can be a difficult and, perhaps, impossible task. In our imperfect world, the best we can do is remain conscious of this principle and try to adhere to its basic tenet.

Trust

The moral principle of trust states that researchers should establish and maintain a relationship of trust with the research participants. This should not only be an obvious relationship but one that should be easy to accomplish. In fact, the necessity of requiring the research participants' informed consent would seem to dictate that participants be told what they are getting into. However, in our society there has developed a mistrust of science and public institutions (Sales & Folkman, 2000). This mistrust has probably been precipitated by the disclosures in the media of studies such as the Tuskegee study in Exhibit 5.6 and the stuttering study summarized in Exhibit 5.4. In 2002, there was a repeated disclosure of fraudulent activity by executives of corporations such as Enron and World Com that probably further contributed to this mistrust.

Within the context of the psychological experiment, the principle of trust can be compromised in several ways. Some studies incorporate deception to maximize the probability that valid unbiased data are collected. Whenever deception is incorporated the principle of trust is violated. The principle of trust can also be violated when the confidentiality of the information collected from research participants is not maintained. Safeguards need to be incorporated into each study to deal with these issues to reduce compromising the principle of trust. These two issues are discussed later in this chapter.

Fidelity and Scientific Integrity

The principle of fidelity and scientific integrity refers to the goal of discovering valid knowledge. Behavioral scientists conduct studies to uncover the mysteries of behavior—to acquire knowledge that will advance our understanding of behavior. To accomplish this goal, the scientist must not only conduct quality research but must truthfully report the research he or she conducts. Both of these components are integral to the discovery and promulgation of truth. Poorly designed and executed studies lead to questionable information, whereas well-designed studies lead to valid information that contributes to the psychological knowledge base. Truthfully reporting the results of research also contributes to a valid knowledge base. This moral principle speaks directly to the issue of presenting fraudulent results that I discussed earlier in this chapter. As stated earlier, faking or altering scientific results has no place in science.

Although the principle of fidelity and scientific integrity is accepted by the scientific community and promoted by the vast majority, some violate this principle for personal gain. During my term as an IRB member, the board encountered a violation of this principle. The chair of the physiology department, also an IRB member, investigated one of his faculty member's research. This faculty member published extensively every year. The department chair became suspicious because the faculty member was not supported by grant funds and he was curious about how the faculty member could conduct so many studies without significant financial support. As he further investigated this faculty member, he found that the equipment needed to conduct this research was still packed in its shipping boxes. He also counted the number of animals the faculty member stated he used in his research and then contacted the animal-holding facility to see if the faculty member had purchased an equivalent number of animals. He had not. All of these investigations led to the conclusion that the faculty member could not have conducted the studies he had published, so the data reported in the studies had to have been fraudulently produced. This meant that information had been presented to the scientific community that was probably not valid information. This faculty member was found guilty of violating the principle of fidelity and scientific integrity and released from his position at the university.

APA Ethical Standards for Research

Any psychologist conducting research must ensure that the dignity and welfare of the research participants are maintained and that the investigation is carried out in accordance with federal and state regulations and with the standards set forth by the American Psychological Association. Although the APA code of ethics has always included a section pertaining to the conduct of research, a major advance in providing guidance in this arena was the publication of a set of ten guiding principles to direct the behavior of research psychologists. These ten principles were published as a document, *Ethical Principles in the Conduct of Research with Human Participants,* in 1973 and revised in 1982. When these documents were published, primary concern focused on areas such as the use of deception, the potential coercive nature of departmental participant pools, and confidentiality. Although these issues remain important, many additional issues have developed as psychologists have moved into other areas such as biomedical research. Rather than continuing to update *Ethical Principles in the Conduct of Research with Human Participants,* the American Psychological Association has chosen to expand the section of the code of ethics dealing with research to include the issues previously identified as important and the emerging issues of importance.

The code of ethics was first published in 1953 (APA, 1953) and was the outcome of about fifteen years of discussion within APA. Since that time, the code has been revised several times. The most recent revision was approved in October of 2002. Exhibit 5.7 presents the section of the code of ethics pertaining to research and publication.

EXHIBIT 5.7

Ethical Standards Pertaining to Research and Publication

Section 8 of the code of ethics gives the standards psychologists are to adhere to when conducting human and animal research and publishing the results of this research. These standards are as follows.

8.01 Institutional Approval

When institutional approval is required, psychologists provide accurate information about their research proposals and obtain approval prior to conducting the research. They conduct the research in accordance with the approved research protocol.

8.02 Informed Consent to Research

(a) When obtaining informed consent as required in Standard 3.10, Informed Consent, psychologists inform participants about

(1) the purpose of the research, expected duration, and procedures

(2) their right to decline to participate and to withdraw from the research once participation has begun

(3) the foreseeable consequences of declining or withdrawing

(4) reasonably foreseeable factors that may be expected to influence their willingness to participate such as potential risks, discomfort, or adverse effects

(5) any prospective research benefits

(6) limits of confidentiality

(7) incentives for participation

(8) whom to contact for questions about the research and research participants' rights. They provide opportunity for the prospective participants to ask questions and receive answers.

(b) Psychologists conducting intervention research involving the use of experimental treatments, clarify to participants at the outset of the research

(1) the experimental nature of the treatment

(2) the services that will or will not be available to the control group(s) if appropriate

(3) the means by which assignment to treatment and control groups will be made

(4) available treatment alternatives if an individual does not wish to participate in the research or wishes to withdraw once a study has begun

(5) compensation for or monetary costs of participating including, if appropriate, whether reimbursement from the participant or a third-party payer will be sought.

8.03 Informed Consent for Recording Voices and Images in Research

Psychologists obtain informed consent from research participants prior to recording their voices or images for data collection unless

(1) the research consists solely of naturalistic observations in public places, and it is not anticipated that the recording will be used in a manner that could cause personal identification or harm

(2) the research design includes deception, and consent for the use of the recording is obtained during debriefing.

EXHIBIT 5.7 (continued)

8.04 Client/Patient, Student, and Subordinate Research Participants

(a) When psychologists conduct research with clients/patients, students, or subordinates as participants, psychologists take steps to protect the prospective participants from adverse consequences of declining or withdrawing from participation.

(b) When research participation is a course requirement or opportunity for extra credit, the prospective participant is given the choice of equitable alternative activities.

8.05 Dispensing with Informed Consent for Research

Psychologists may dispense with informed consent only

(1) where research would not reasonably be assumed to create distress or harm and involves

(a) the study of normal educational practices, curricula, or classroom management methods conducted in educational settings

(b) only anonymous questionnaires, naturalistic observations, or archival research for which disclosure of responses would not place participants at risk of criminal or civil liability or damage their financial standing, employability, or reputation; and confidentiality is protected

(c) the study of factors related to job or organization effectiveness conducted in organizational settings for which there is no risk to participants' employability and confidentiality is protected

(2) where otherwise permitted by law or federal or institutional regulations.

8.06 Offering Inducements for Research Participation

(a) Psychologists make reasonable efforts to avoid offering excessive or inappropriate financial or other inducements for research participation when such inducements are likely to coerce participation.

(b) When offering professional services as an inducement for research participation, psychologists clarify the nature of the services, as well as the risks, obligations, and limitations.

8.07 Deception in Research

(a) Psychologists do not conduct a study involving deception unless they have determined that the use of deceptive techniques is justified by the study's significant prospective scientific, educational, or applied value and that effective nondeceptive alternative procedures are not feasible.

(b) Psychologists do not deceive prospective participants about research that is reasonably expected to cause physical pain or severe emotional distress.

(c) Psychologists explain any deception that is an integral feature of the design and conduct of an experiment to participants as early as is feasible, preferably at the conclusion of their participation, but no later than at the conclusion of the data collection, and permit participants to withdraw their data.

8.08 Debriefing

(a) Psychologists provide a prompt opportunity for participants to obtain appropriate information about the nature, results, and conclusions of the research, and they take reasonable steps to correct any misconceptions that participants may have of which the psychologists are aware.

(b) If scientific or humane values justify delaying or withholding this information, psychologists take reasonable measures to reduce the risk of harm.

(c) When psychologists become aware that research procedures have harmed a participant, they take reasonable steps to minimize the harm.

8.09 Humane Care and Use of Animals in Research

(a) Psychologists acquire, care for, use, and dispose of animals in compliance with current federal, state, and local laws and regulations, and with professional standards.

(b) Psychologists trained in research methods and experienced in the care of laboratory animals supervise all procedures involving animals and are responsible for ensuring appropriate consideration of their comfort, health, and humane treatment.

(c) Psychologists ensure that all individuals under their supervision who are using animals

EXHIBIT 5.7 (continued)

have received instruction in research methods and in the care, maintenance, and handling of the species being used, to the extent appropriate to their role.

(d) Psychologists make reasonable efforts to minimize the discomfort, infection, illness, and pain of animal subjects.

(e) Psychologists use a procedure subjecting animals to pain, stress, or privation only when an alternative procedure is unavailable and the goal is justified by its prospective scientific, educational, or applied value.

(f) Psychologists perform surgical procedures under appropriate anesthesia and follow techniques to avoid infection and minimize pain during and after surgery.

(g) When it is appropriate that an animal's life be terminated, psychologists proceed rapidly, with an effort to minimize pain and in accordance with accepted procedures.

8.10 Reporting Research Results

(a) Psychologists do not fabricate data.

(b) If psychologists discover significant errors in their published data, they take reasonable steps to correct such errors in a correction, retraction, erratum, or other appropriate publication means.

8.11 Plagiarism

Psychologists do not present portions of another's work or data as their own, even if the other work or data source is cited occasionally.

8.12 Publication Credit

(a) Psychologists take responsibility and credit, including authorship credit, only for work they have actually performed or to which they have substantially contributed.

(b) Principal authorship and other publication credits accurately reflect the relative scientific or professional contributions of the individuals involved, regardless of their relative status. Mere possession of an institutional position, such as department chair, does not justify authorship credit. Minor contributions to the research or to the writing for publications are acknowledged

appropriately, such as in footnotes or in an introductory statement.

(c) Except under exceptional circumstances, a student is listed as principal author on any multiple-authored article that is substantially based on the student's doctoral dissertation. Faculty advisors discuss publication credit with students as early as is feasible and throughout the research and publication process as appropriate.

8.13 Duplicate Publication of Data

Psychologists do not publish, as original data, data that have been previously published. This does not preclude republishing data when they are accompanied by proper acknowledgment.

8.14 Sharing Research Data for Verification

(a) After research results are published, psychologists do not withhold the data on which their conclusions are based from other competent professionals who seek to verify the substantive claims through reanalysis and who intend to use such data only for that purpose, provided that the confidentiality of the participants can be protected and unless legal rights concerning proprietary data preclude their release. This does not preclude psychologists from requiring that such individuals or groups be responsible for costs associated with the provision of such information.

(b) Psychologists who request data from other psychologists to verify the substantive claims through reanalysis may use shared data only for the declared purpose. Requesting psychologists obtain prior written agreement for all other uses of the data.

8.15 Reviewers

Psychologists who review material submitted for presentation, publication, grant, or research proposal review respect the confidentiality of and the proprietary rights in such information of those who submitted it.

- **What are the five basic moral principles that psychologists should follow when conducting research? Explain what is meant by each of these principles.**
- **What are the categories of review that a research proposal can receive and what are the criteria used to determine in which category a research proposal falls?**

Ethical Issues to Consider When Conducting Research

Section 8 of the code of ethics was adopted by the American Psychological Association in October 2002 as its official position on research and publication and, therefore, represents the standards to be used by psychologists conducting animal and human research. Included in these standards are a number of important issues focusing on research with human participants that are worthy of further discussion. These include the issues of institutional approval, informed consent, deception, and debriefing. In addition to these issues are the issues of freedom to decline to participate in or to withdraw from the study at any time and of confidentiality and anonymity. There is also the issue of the ethics of Internet research that has not been addressed by the APA code of ethics.

Institutional Approval

Most, if not all, institutions that have active research programs have a requirement that all human research is reviewed by an IRB. The requirement that all human research be reviewed by an IRB dates back to 1966. At the time there was a concern for the way in which medical research was designed and conducted. As a result of this concern, the surgeon general initiated an institutional review requirement at the Department of Health, Education, and Welfare (DHEW). This policy was extended to all investigations funded by the Public Health Service that involved human participants, including those in the social and behavioral sciences. By 1973 the DHEW regulations governing human research required a review by an IRB for all research receiving Public Health Service funds. This meant that virtually all institutions of higher education had to establish an IRB and file an assurance policy with the Office for Protection from Research Risks of the Department of Health and Human Services. This assurance policy articulates the responsibilities and purview of the IRB within that institution. Although the Public Health Service mandated only that federally funded projects be reviewed by an IRB, most institutions extended the scope of the IRB to include all research involving human participants, even those falling into the exempt category. Once this assurance policy is approved, it becomes a legal document to which the institution and researchers must comply. If your institution receives funds from one of the federal granting agencies, such an assurance policy probably exists, which means that any research involving human participants must be submitted to and approved by your institution's IRB prior to conducting the research.

Ethical Standard 8.01 of the code of ethics specifies that, when such institutional approval is required, psychologists must provide accurate information about their research proposal (see Table 5.2), receive approval from the IRB, and then conduct the research in accordance with the approved protocol.

Informed Consent

Informed consent
Informing the research participant of all aspects of the study that may influence his or her willingness to volunteer to participate

Informed consent refers to fully informing the research participants about all aspects of the study. Standards 8.02 to 8.04 of the code of ethics (Exhibit 5.7) states that fully informing the research participants means that you inform them of all aspects of the research, from the purpose and procedures to any risks and benefits, including such things as incentives for participation. With this information, the research participant can make an informed decision and choose to either decline to participate in the study or give his or her informed consent.

Gaining a participant's informed consent is considered to be vital because of the sacredness of the principle that individuals have a fundamental right to determine what is done to their minds and bodies. Once a person is provided with all available information, it is assumed that he or she can make a free decision as to whether to participate, and in this manner participants can avoid experimental procedures they consider objectionable. In this way, the basic principle of "respect for persons and their autonomy," discussed early in this chapter, is achieved.

Dispensing with Informed Consent   Although the ideal procedure is to fully inform research participants of all features of the study that may affect their willingness to participate, the current code of ethics recognizes that there may be times when it is appropriate to dispense with informed consent. There is a good reason to dispense with informed consent in some studies because the integrity of the data can be compromised. Consider the study by Resnick and Schwartz (1973). These investigators attempted to determine the impact of following the informed consent principle to its logical extreme in a simple but widely used verbal conditioning task developed by Taffel (1955). The control, or noninformed, group was given typical instructions, which gave them a rationale for the study and informed them of the task that they were to complete. The experimental, or informed, group received *complete* instructions regarding the true reason for conducting the experiment and the *exact* nature of the Taffel procedure. Figure 5.2 depicts the results of the data obtained from the fourteen participants in each treatment condition. The uninformed participants performed in the expected manner, demonstrating verbal conditioning. The informed group, however, revealed a reversal in the conditioning rate. Such data show that maintaining maximum ethical conditions alters the knowledge that we accumulate. This altered information might represent inaccurate information, which would create a *lack* of external validity.

In addition to finding a drastic difference in response on the part of the informed participants, Resnick and Schwartz also found that informing participants of the entire experiment apparently destroys any incentive to participate in the study. Uninformed participants were enthusiastic and appeared at the scheduled time, but informed participants were generally uncooperative and "often haughty, insisting that they had only one time slot to spare which we could either take or leave" (p. 137). It actually took Resnick and Schwartz five weeks to collect the data on the fourteen

FIGURE 5.2

Verbal conditioning data obtained by Resnick and Schwartz.

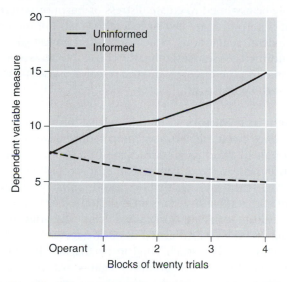

(Adapted from "Ethical Standards as an Independent Variable in Psychological Research" by J. H. Resnick and T. Schwartz, 1973, *American Psychologist, 28,* p. 136. Copyright 1973 by the American Psychological Association. Reprinted by permission of the author.)

informed participants for such reasons! These researchers suggested that completely informing participants makes some participants very suspicious and may cause them to stay away. For most participants, however, a full disclosure of the research causes them to lose interest, which "suggests that people enjoy an element of risk and nondisclosure and become bored rapidly with the prospect of participating in something of which they already have full knowledge" (Resnick & Schwartz, 1973, p. 137). This view is supported by a survey of student opinion conducted by Epstein, Suedfeld, and Silverstein (1973). They found that more than 70 percent of the college students they surveyed did not expect to be told the purpose of the experiment and that deception, although not desirable, was not an inappropriate feature of the research setting.

Informed consent is not necessary in some studies (e.g., those that use census data) and impossible in others (e.g., some field experiments). For example, Rind and Bordia (1996) had a male and female server in a restaurant-diner either draw or not draw a happy face on the back of customer checks prior to delivering them to determine if the happy face influenced the size of the tips received. They found that the happy face increased tips only for the female server. The purpose of the study was explained to the servers and the owner of the restaurant who gave their consent to proceed. The research participants (customers), however, were not informed because doing so would have destroyed the credibility of the manipulation and rendered the experiment meaningless.

Federal guidelines as well as the American Psychological Association's code of ethics, Standard 8.05, recognize the necessity of sometimes forgoing the requirement of informed consent. However, the code of ethics specifies that informed consent may be dispensed with only under specific and limited conditions in which the research will not reasonably be assumed to create distress or harm or where dispensing with informed consent is permitted by law or federal or institutional regulations. This is consistent with federal regulations which state that investigators can waive the requirement of informed consent if signing the consent form would be the only thing linking the participant to the research and the research presents no more than minimal risk of harm to the participant.

Informed Consent and Minors   The principle of informed consent refers to the fact that a person, once given the pertinent information, is competent and legally free to make a decision as to whether to participate in a given research study. Minors, however, are presumed to be incompetent and cannot give consent. In such instances, Standard 3.10(b)(4) states that permission must be obtained from a legally authorized person, if this substitute consent is permitted or required by law. In most instances, the substitute consent is obtained from the minor's parents or legal guardians after they have been informed of all the features of the study that may affect their willingness to allow their child to participate. In addition to obtaining informed consent from the minor's parents or legal guardians, Standard 3.10(b)(1 & 2) of the code of ethics specifies that the minor be given an appropriate explanation of the study and that the minor give his or her assent. **Assent** means that the minor agrees to participate in the research after receiving an appropriate explanation. By appropriate, I mean that the explanation is one that is in language that the minor can understand.

> **Assent**
> Agreement from a minor to participate in research after receiving an age-appropriate explanation of the study

Federal regulations (OPRR, 2001) state that provisions should be made for soliciting the assent of a minor when, in the judgment of the IRB, the minor is capable of providing assent. However, the age at which a person is capable of providing assent can differ among children. To provide assent, the child must be able to understand what is being asked, to realize that permission is being sought, and to make choices free from outside constraints. This depends on the cognitive capabilities of the child. Unfortunately, the cognitive capabilities of children develop at different rates, making it difficult to state an age at which a child is capable of providing assent. Individuals over the age of nine generally have sufficient cognitive ability to make a decision concerning participation in research, and individuals over the age of fourteen seem to make the same decisions as adults (Leikin, 1993). This should not be taken to mean that assent should definitely be obtained from individuals over age fourteen, possibly from individuals over age nine, and not from individuals age nine or less. Rather, most individuals (e.g., Leikin, 1993) and the ethical guidelines provided by the Society for Research in Child Development (2003) state that assent should be obtained from all children. Assent occurs when "the child shows some form of agreement to participate without necessarily comprehending the full significance of the research necessary to give informed consent" (Society for Research in Child Development, 2003). Not only is it ethically acceptable to obtain the assent of minors, but it may also enhance the validity of the study. Insisting that minors participate when they have clearly stated that they do not want to can alter their behavioral responses and represent a confounding influence on the data collected.

Passive versus Active Consent   The discussion of consent has, up to this point, focused on active consent. **Active consent** involves consenting to participate in a research study by verbally agreeing and signing a consent form. When minors are used as research participants, consent is typically obtained from the minor's parent or legal guardian. If consent is desired from school-age children, a common way in which consent is obtained is to provide the parent or legal guardian with a consent form by some means, such as mailing the consent form or sending it home with the minor. Ideally, the parent reads the consent form and either gives or refuses consent and returns the consent form to the researcher. However, studies (e.g., Ellickson, 1989) have revealed that only 50–60 percent of parents return consent forms even when follow-up efforts are made. One interpretation of the failure to return consent forms is that the parents have denied consent. However, there are a number of other reasons why parents may not return consent forms. They may not have received the consent form, they may forget to sign and return the consent form, or they may not take enough time to read and consider the request. The existence of any or all of these possibilities reduces the sample size and possibly bias the results.

> **Active consent**
> Verbally agreeing and signing a form consenting to participate in research

To increase participation in research studies, Ellickson (1989) recommended the use of passive consent. **Passive consent** is a process whereby parents or legal guardians give consent by not returning the consent form. They return the consent form only if they do *not* want their child to participate in the research. Passive consent has been promoted by some investigators as a legitimate means of securing parental consent. Ethical concerns have been raised when passive consent procedures are used because these studies may include children whose parents actually oppose their participation in the research but did not return the consent form or perhaps did not receive it. However, studies (e.g., Ellickson & Hawes, 1989; Severson & Ary, 1983) have revealed that active and passive consent procedures yield comparable rates of participation when the active consent procedures used extensive follow-up techniques. This suggests that nonresponse to passive consent represents latent consent. When this is combined with the fact that the use of the active consent process, in the absence of extensive follow-up, results in a lower level of participation of low socioeconomic status and minority participants, the use of passive consent seems legitimate. This conclusion seems to be particularly true because the lower participation stems primarily from a failure to respond rather than an explicit desire to not participate. Requiring active consent would, therefore, run counter to federal guidelines to increase minority participation in research. In addition, passive consent, because it increases low socioeconomic status and minority participation, leads to less biased results than does the use of active consent. Exhibit 5.8 provides an example of a passive consent form.

> **Passive consent**
> Consent is received from a parent or guardian by not returning the consent form

Although there seems to be a place for passive consent and some cogent arguments for its use in certain situations, I recommend that you use active consent whenever possible. This is the best form of consent. Passive consent should be considered only when the integrity of the study would be seriously compromised by requiring active consent. The APA code of ethics does not directly address passive consent so it is imperative that you inform the IRB whenever you want to use passive consent and receive their approval prior to making use of this technique.

EXHIBIT 5.8

Example of a Passive Consent Form

Dear Parent or Legal Guardian:

I am a faculty member in the Psychology Department at Excel University. I am interested in finding the best method of teaching mathematical concepts. To identify the best method, I am planning a study that will compare two different methods of teaching mathematical concepts. Both teaching methods are acceptable and standard methods of teaching these concepts, but we do not know which is the more effective method. My research will identify the more effective method.

To identify the more effective method, during the next six weeks I will be presenting material in two different ways to separate classes. To test the effectiveness of each method I will measure students' performance by giving them a standard math test.

Your child's responses will remain confidential and will be seen only by me and my research assistant.

No reports about this study will contain your child's name. I will not release any information about your child without your permission.

Participation in this study is completely voluntary. All students in the class will take the test. If you do **not** wish your child to be in this study, please fill out the form at the bottom of this letter and return it to me. Also, please tell your child to hand in a blank test sheet when the class is given the mathematics test so that he or she will not be included in this study.

I will also ask the children to participate and tell them to hand in a blank test sheet if they do not want to be included in the study. Your child may choose to stop participating at any time.

If you have any questions about the study, please contact professor John Doe, Excel University, Department of Psychology, Good Place, AL 12345, Phone 251–246–8102. You may also contact me at (provide address and phone number).

Thank you,

Tom Thumb

Return this portion only if you do not want your child to participate in the study described above.

I do not wish for my child _____ to be in the research study on the teaching of math concepts being conducted in his/her classroom.

_____   _____
Parent's Signature   Date

STUDY QUESTION 5.4

- **What is meant by *informed consent* and why is this considered a vital component of a research protocol?**
- **When is it appropriate for you to dispense with informed consent?**
- **What is meant by *assent* and when should it be obtained?**
- **What is the difference between active consent and passive consent?**
- **When should you try to obtain passive consent and what ethical issues are associated with it?**

Deception

Deception refers to deceit. The use of deception in psychological research is counter to the requirement of fully informing the research participants of the nature of the research in which they are asked to participate. It also runs counter to the basic moral principle of trust that psychologists should adhere to when conducting research with humans. However, psychologists must also conduct their research with fidelity and scientific integrity. This means that they must conduct well-designed and executed studies to advance our understanding of behavior. To conduct such studies requires, in some instances, the use of deception. This requirement is acknowledged by the code of ethics. However, the code of ethics does not permit the unfettered use of deception. Rather, the use of deception is limited to studies in which alternative procedures arc not available and the study has the potential of producing important knowledge. If deception is used, the participants are informed of its use as early as is feasible. In addition, deception cannot be used in studies that can be expected to cause harm or severe emotional distress.

Active deception
Deliberately misleading research participants by giving them false information

Passive deception
Withholding information from the research participants by not giving them all the details of the experiment

In social and behavioral research, deception can be either active or passive deception (Rosnow & Rosenthal, 1998). **Active deception** refers to deception by commission, when the experimenter deliberately misleads the research participants such as when they are given false information about the purpose of the experiment or when they are deliberately led to believe that a confederate is a research participant. **Passive deception** refers to deception by omission, when certain information is withheld from the research participants, such as not giving the research participants all the details of an experiment. Both active and passive deception are incorporated in the design of many psychological experiments. In fact, a number of investigators have attempted to determine the extent to which deception is used in psychological studies. Table 5.4, which summarizes the results of these surveys, reveals that the use of deception increased from the late 1940s to the late 1960s. This increase occurred primarily within the fields of personality and social psychology. The percentage of deception studies in the leading social psychology journals *Journal of Abnormal and Social Psychology* prior to the mid-1960s and *Journal of Personality and Social Psychology* after its inception in the mid-1960s increased from 14.3 percent in 1948 to 66 percent in 1969. From 1969 to 1987, the percent of deception studies declined to a low of 24 percent. If attention is focused only on the percentage of deception studies in these two journals, the trend seems to suggest that there was an initial increase followed by a more recent decline in the use of deception.

If this suggested trend is true, it may imply that the objections to deception and the more rigid ethical standards (Nicks, Korn, & Mainieri, 1997) have been acknowledged by researchers, and they have turned to alternative methods for investigating important psychological phenomena. Unfortunately, this does not seem to be the case. Sieber, Iannuzzo, and Rodriguez (1995) have revealed that any change in the percentage of studies using deception has been an outgrowth of the type of study conducted. Such topic areas as attribution, environmental psychology, and sex roles were popular in 1978 and 1986. These are topic areas in which deception is seldom used and corresponds to the years in which the percentage of deception studies declined.

TABLE 5.4
Use of Deception in Psychological Research

Author(s)	Journals	Year	Percentage of Deception Studies
Seeman (1969)	Journal of Abnormal and Social Psychology	1948	14.3
Seeman (1969)	Journal of Personality	1948	23.8
Seeman (1969)	Journal of Consulting Psychology	1948	2.9
Seeman (1969)	Journal of Experimental Psychology	1948	14.6
Menges (1973)	Journal of Abnormal and Social Psychology	1961	16.3
Seeman (1969)	Journal of Abnormal and Social Psychology	1963	36.8
Seeman (1969)	Journal of Personality	1963	43.9
Seeman (1969)	Journal of Consulting Psychology	1963	9.3
Seeman (1969)	Journal of Experimental Psychology	1963	10.8
Carlson (1971)	Journal of Personality and Journal of Personality and Social Psychology	1968	57.0
Sieber, Iannuzzo, and Rodriguez (1995)	Journal of Personality and Social Psychology	1969	65.9
Menges (1973)	Journal of Personality and Social Psychology	1971	47.2
Menges (1973)	Journal of Abnormal and Social Psychology	1971	21.5
Menges (1973)	Journal of Educational Psychology	1971	8.3
Menges (1973)	Journal of Consulting Psychology	1971	6.3
Menges (1973)	Journal of Experimental Psychology	1971	3.1
Levenson, Gray, and Ingram (1976)	Journal of Personality	1973	42.0
Levenson, Gray, and Ingram (1976)	Journal of Personality and Social Psychology	1973	62.0
Sieber, Iannuzzo, and Rodriguez (1995)	Journal of Personality and Social Psychology	1978	46.8
Adair, Dushenko, and Lindsay (1985)	Journal of Personality and Social Psychology	1979	58.5
Nicks, Korn, and Mainieri (1997)	Journal of Personality and Social Psychology	1983	41.2
Nicks, Korn, and Mainieri (1997)	Journal of Personality	1983	17.4
Nicks, Korn, and Mainieri (1997)	Journal of Experimental Social Psychology	1983	67.6
Sieber, Iannuzzo, and Rodriguez (1995)	Journal of Personality and Social Psychology	1986	31.7
Nicks, Korn, and Mainieri (1997)	Journal of Personality and Social Psychology	1987	24.1
Nicks, Korn, and Mainieri (1997)	Journal of Personality	1987	10.7
Nicks, Korn, and Mainieri (1997)	Journal of Experimental Social Psychology	1987	42.9
Nicks, Korn, and Mainieri (1997)	Journal of Personality and Social Psychology	1989	29.9
Nicks, Korn, and Mainieri (1997)	Journal of Personality	1989	11.1
Nicks, Korn, and Mainieri (1997)	Journal of Experimental Social Psychology	1989	65.5
Sieber, Iannuzzo, and Rodriguez (1995)	Journal of Personality and Social Psychology	1992	46.7
Nicks, Korn, and Mainieri (1997)	Journal of Personality and Social Psychology	1994	31.3
Nicks, Korn, and Mainieri (1997)	Journal of Personality	1994	16.6
Nicks, Korn, and Mainieri (1997)	Journal of Experimental Social Psychology	1994	50.0

In 1992 there were fewer studies focusing on these topic areas, and the result was that the percentage of deception studies increased.

Although the use of the deception occurs most frequently in personality and social psychology, it is important to remember that it also occurs in other areas. For example, in the early 1990s the CBS TV news program *60 Minutes* staged an elaborate deception in its investigation of the use of polygraph tests by private employers (Saxe, 1991). The staff from *60 Minutes* randomly selected four polygraph examiners from the telephone directory and hired them to examine four people who supposedly worked for the CBS-owned magazine *Popular Photography.* The polygraphers were instructed to examine the four employee suspects in an attempt to determine if one of them had stolen $500 worth of camera equipment. All four polygraphers were told that all suspects had access to the stolen camera, and each polygrapher was told that a different person was probably the guilty party. Unbeknownst to the polygraphers, there had been no theft of property and the four suspects were confederates who were to be paid $50 if they could convince the polygraphers of their innocence. In addition, the office in which the polygraph examinations were to be conducted was modified to enable surreptitious filming. Much to the delight of the *60 Minutes* team, all four polygraphers fingered as the guilty party the individual whom they had been told was the suspect, although none of the confederates had stolen anything or confessed to a theft.

Given that deception is here to stay and that alternatives to deception, such as role playing (Kelman, 1967), are inadequate substitutes (Miller, 1972), we need to take a look at the effect of deception on research participants because it has been stated that deception will affect their behavior in unintended ways (Ortmann & Hertwig, 1997). More than four decades ago Kelman (1967) predicted that the persistent use of deception would cause research participants to become distrustful of psychologists and undermine psychologists' relations with them. Fortunately, this prediction has not come true. Sharpe, Adair, and Roese (1992) revealed that current research participants are as accepting of arguments justifying the use of deception as they were twenty years ago. Soliday and Stanton (1995) found that mild deception had no effect on attitudes toward researchers, science, or psychology. Fisher and Fyrberg (1994) even found that most of the student research participants in their study believed that the deception studies they evaluated were scientifically valid and valuable. Most also believed that the use of deception was an important methodology to retain even when other methodologies, such as role playing or questionnaires, were available.

It also seems to be generally accepted that deception has a significant potential for wronging and harming participants. Sieber's (1982) stance perhaps epitomizes this view. According to her, a study that deceived participants and did not obtain their informed consent involves an invasion of privacy, denial of self-determination, concealment, and lying. Expositions such as those presented by Sieber give the impression that deception is not only ethically objectionable but potentially harmful as well. However, these writings seem to be based on the authors' opinions, which may or may not conform to reality. The only way to determine whether such expositions represent moral philosophizing or actual ethical objections is to investigate the perceptions of participants who have been subjected to deception.

Christensen (1988) summarized the results of studies investigating the reactions of participants to deception experiments. The literature consistently revealed that research participants do not perceive that they were harmed and do not seem to mind having been misled. For example, in a follow-up investigation of people who had participated in a series of studies that included deception and potential physical and mental stress, Pihl, Zacchia, and Zeichner (1981) found that only 19 percent of those contacted reported being bothered by any aspect of the experiment and only 4 percent said they were bothered by the deception. The components that upset the participants were mostly rather trivial (one participant felt that using a cloth holder for a drinking glass was unsanitary). The greatest distress surrounded the type of alcohol consumed, the dose, and the speed with which it had to be consumed. One participant reported being bothered for several days because "laboratory and not commercial alcohol was consumed" (Pihl et al., 1981, p. 930). Interestingly, this participant was in a placebo group that had not even consumed alcohol. It is also interesting to note that the distress surrounding the deception and averse stimuli variables lasted less time than did the distress surrounding other seemingly trivial variables such as boredom. As is illustrated in Figure 5.3, the duration of distress over the deception or shock was only one hour or less, whereas the dissatisfaction with the alcohol lasted an average of twenty hours.

Smith and Richardson (1983) found that the participants who had taken part in deception experiments reported enjoying the experiment more, felt that they had received more educational benefit from the experiment, and perceived their participation in the research as being more satisfactory than did other participants. Not only

FIGURE 5.3

Average length of distress for four categories of complaints.

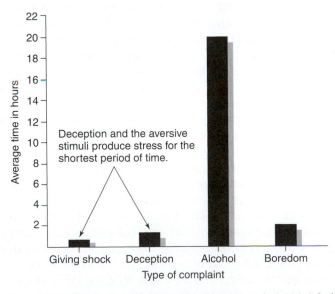

(Based on data from "Follow-up Analysis of the Use of Deception and Aversive Contingencies in Psychological Experiments" by R. O. Pihl, C. Zacchia, and A. Zeichner, 1981, *Psychological Reports, 48*, pp. 927–930.)

did Smith and Richardson not find support for the notion that deception is harmful—they provided data suggesting that deception may be advantageous. Kimmel (1998) concludes that deception does not negatively influence participants' perception of psychology or science in general.

Although research participants consistently report that they do not mind having been misled and were not harmed by deception experiments, a case could be made for the view that the detrimental effects of deception depend on the type of study being conducted. Christensen (1988) pointed out that deception is viewed as less acceptable ethically if the study investigates private behaviors such as sexual experiences or if the experimental procedure has significant potential to harm the research participant. Deception research raises special ethical concerns when it involves private behaviors or behaviors that are perceived as negative and may result in harm to the research participant (Sieber et al., 1995). This is consistent with the code of ethics, which states that deception should not be used in research expected to cause pain or severe emotional distress.

Debriefing

Debriefing

A postexperimental discussion or interview about the details of the study, including an explanation for the use of any deception

Debriefing refers to a postexperimental interview or discussion with the participant about the purpose and details of the study, including an explanation for the use of any deception. APA code of ethics Standard 8.08 specifies that psychologists must debrief participants as soon as possible following completion of a study and that if this information must be delayed measures must be taken to reduce any risk of harm. In addition, if the research procedures may have harmed the participant, steps must be taken to minimize the harm. Debriefing participants is not only required by the code of ethics but can be beneficial to the researcher in many ways. I elaborate on the beneficial use of debriefing in Chapter 13. Here I focus on deception and the use of debriefing because considerable attention has been focused on this issue.

The evidence shows that deception is not necessarily the harmful component many individuals assume it to be. This does not mean that the potentially harmful effects of deception can be forgotten, however. One of the primary modes used to eliminate any harmful effects of deception is debriefing. All the studies that investigated the impact of deception incorporated a debriefing procedure, and, if such a procedure does in fact eliminate any harmful effects of deception, this may explain the positive findings of these experiments.

Milgram (1964b) reported that, after extensive debriefing, only 1.3 percent of his participants reported any negative feelings about their experiences in the experiment. Such evidence indicates that the debriefing was effective in eliminating the extreme anguish that these participants apparently experienced. Ring, Wallston, and Corey (1970) in their quasi-replication of Milgram's 1963 experiment, found that only 4 percent of the participants who had been debriefed indicated they regretted having participated in the experiment and only 4 percent believed that the experiment should not be permitted to continue. On the other hand, about 50 percent of the participants who had not been debriefed responded in this manner. Berscheid, Baron, Dermer, and Libman (1973) found similar ameliorative effects of debriefing on consent-related responses. Holmes (1973) and Holmes and Bennett (1974) took an even more convincing approach and demonstrated that debriefing reduced the arousal generated in a stress-producing experiment (expected electric shock) to the prearousal level, as assessed by both physiological and self-report measures.

Smith and Richardson (1983) asserted that their deceived participants received better debriefings than did their nondeceived participants and that this more effective debriefing may have been the factor that caused the deceived participants to have more positive responses than did the nondeceived participants.

This suggests that debriefing is quite effective in eliminating the stress produced by the experimental treatment condition. However, Holmes (1976a, 1976b) has appropriately pointed out that there are two goals of debriefing and both must be met for debriefing to be maximally effective: dehoaxing and desensitizing. **Dehoaxing** refers to debriefing the participants about any deception that the experimenter may have used. In the dehoaxing process, the problem is one of convincing the participant that the fraudulent information given was, in fact, fraudulent. **Desensitizing** refers to debriefing the participants about their behavior. If the experiment has made participants aware that they have some undesirable features (for example, that they could and would inflict harm on others), then the debriefing procedure should attempt to help the participants deal with this new information. This is typically done by suggesting that the undesirable behavior was caused by some situational variable rather than by some dispositional characteristic of the research participant. Another tactic used by experimenters is to point out that the research participants' behavior was not abnormal or extreme. The big question is whether or not such tactics are effective in desensitizing or dehoaxing the participants. In Holmes's (1976a, 1976b) review of the literature relating to these two techniques, he concluded that they were effective. Fisher and Fyrberg (1994) support this conclusion. Over 90 percent of their student research participants were of the opinion that the dehoaxing would be believed.

This means only that effective debriefing is *possible*. These results hold only if the debriefing is carried out properly. A sloppy or improperly prepared debriefing session may very well have a different effect. In addition, the beneficial impact of debriefing can be experienced only if the experimental procedure includes a debriefing session. Adair, Dushenko, and Lindsay (1985), in their survey of the literature, found that only 66 percent of all the deception studies reported in the *Journal of Personality and Social Psychology* in 1979 included debriefing. This suggests that researchers should be more diligent about debriefing their research participants.

One more point needs to be made about debriefing. Perhaps debriefing should not be universally applied in all experiments. Aronson and Carlsmith (1968) and Campbell (1969) have discussed the potentially painful effects that debriefing can have if the participant learns of his or her own gullibility, cruelty, or bias. Fisher and Fyrberg (1994) have revealed that at least half of their research participants thought that a person would be embarrassed once the deception was revealed. These feelings would not be revealed to the investigator for fear of further embarrassment.

For this reason Campbell (1969) suggested that debriefing be eliminated when the experimental treatment condition falls within the participant's range of ordinary experiences. This recommendation has also been supported by survey data collected by Rugg (1975). Debriefing may also be inadvisable when the participants are children or individuals with mental retardation.

Dehoaxing
Debriefing the participants about any deception that was used in the experiment

Desensitizing
Eliminating any undesirable influence that the experiment may have had on the participant

STUDY QUESTION 5.5 | **What is deception, and what are the ethical issues involved with the use of deception in psychological research? In answering this question, consider the effect of deception on the research participant and the use of debriefing.**

Coercion and Freedom to Decline Participation

Standard 3.08 of the code of ethics explicitly states that psychologists should not exploit the individuals over whom they have some authority. This includes students and clients/patients. The concern with coercion has probably been expressed most frequently over the widespread use of research participant pools and the nature of the relationship between professors and students. Professors may present situations where students may feel coercive pressure to participate, such as providing extra-credit for participation. Leak (1981) found that students who were induced to participate by means of an offer of extra-credit points were divided on their perception of the coercive nature of the means used for attaining participation. However, they did not resent or object to being offered the extra credit for participation and, overall, viewed the research experience as being worthwhile.

Britton (1979) reached the same conclusion. He found that students evaluated their experience as research participants very favorably and that only 4 percent acknowledged experiencing any discomfort from the experience. Such evidence implies not that concern about the coercive influence surrounding the participant pool should be diminished, but rather that the current procedures to minimize coercion must be operating effectively. This may be because researchers are following the code of ethics and providing a choice of equitable alternative activities to research participation.

In addition to the issue of coercion, individuals must always feel free to decline to participate in or free to withdraw from the research at any time. This principle seems quite reasonable and relatively innocuous. Gardner (1978), however, has asserted that such a perception, although ethically required, can influence the outcome of some studies. The subtle influence of telling research participants that they were free to discontinue participation was discovered quite accidentally. Gardner had been experimenting on the detrimental impact of environmental noise. Prior to the incorporation of a statement informing potential participants that they could decline to participate without penalty, he always found that environmental noise produced a negative aftereffect. After he incorporated this statement, however, he could not produce the effect. In order to verify that a statement regarding freedom to withdraw was the factor causing the elimination of the negative aftereffect of environmental noise, Gardner replicated the experiment, telling participants in one group that they could decline to participate at any time without penalty and not making this statement to participants in another group. As Figure 5.4 illustrates, the environmental noise caused a decline in performance under the old procedures but not under the new procedures. This study indicates the very subtle effects that ethical principles can have and suggests that such effects should be considered when prior results are not replicated and the only difference in procedure is the incorporation of the ethical principles.

FIGURE 5.4

Accuracy of performance of participants during silence or environmental noise conditions after being instructed or not instructed that they can decline to participate.

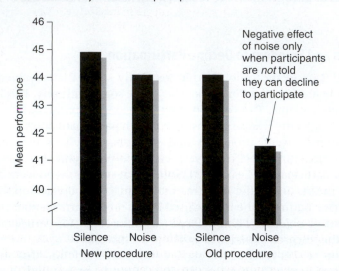

(Based on data from "Effects of Federal Human Subjects Regulations on Data Obtained in Environmental Stressor Research" by G. T. Gardner, 1978, *Journal of Personality and Social Psychology, 36,* pp. 628–634.)

Confidentiality, Anonymity, and the Concept of Privacy

Privacy
Having control of others access to information about you

Privacy refers to controlling other people's access to information about a person. There are two aspects to privacy that must be considered (Folkman, 2000). The first involves a person's freedom to identify the time and circumstances under which information is shared with or withheld from others. For example, a person might not want information about their sexual behavior shared with others, or they may agree to share this information only if it is aggregated with others' information so they cannot be identified. The second is the person's right to decline receiving information that he or she does not want. For example, a person may not want to know if they performed worse on a task than the average person.

While respecting the privacy of research participants is at the heart of the conduct of ethical research, constitutional and federal laws have not been passed that would protect the privacy of information collected within the context of social and behavioral research. So how do we protect the privacy of research information? Researchers attempt to ensure the privacy of research participants by either collecting anonymous information or ensuring that information collected is kept confidential. Anonymity is an excellent way of protecting privacy because **anonymity** refers to keeping the identity of the research participants unknown. In the context of a research study, anonymity is achieved if the researcher cannot connect the data collected with any specific participant. For example, if you were conducting a survey of the sexual behavior of college students, you might ask every person taking a psychology course during the fall semester to complete the survey. If the research participants did not put any identifying information on the survey, anonymity would be

Anonymity
Keeping the identity of the research participant unknown

obtained. However, Picou (1996) has revealed that removing all identifiers from data files may not be sufficient to maintain research participants' anonymity because a careful examination of participant responses may allow a third party to deduce a participant's identity. This was a hard lesson he learned during a year in federal court.

Confidentiality is the other means that researchers use to protect the privacy of research participants. **Confidentiality**, in the context of a research study, refers to an agreement with research investigators about what may be done with the information obtained about a research participant. Typically, this means that the information obtained, although known to the research group, will not be revealed to anyone other than the researcher and his or her staff. The APA code of ethics is very explicit in stating that information obtained about a research participant must be kept confidential because to do otherwise represents a violation of the right to privacy.

Confidentiality
Not revealing information obtained from a research participant to anyone outside the research group

This promise to keep information confidential is provided in the context of the informed consent. However, investigators must be careful about what they promise for several reasons. The APA code of ethics permits disclosure of confidential information without consent to protect others from harm; and some states, such as California, mandate that therapists protect potential victims from harm. Also, all states have mandatory reporting of child abuse or neglect and many mandate reporting of elder abuse or neglect. This means that researchers should be familiar with state and federal laws to determine what can and cannot be kept confidential, and this information should be included in the informed consent.

Because information collected by researchers is not protected by law, confidentiality can be difficult to maintain. Research records can be subpoenaed by a court to be turned over to the party that wants them. However, courts have typically been willing to protect the identity of participants who have been promised confidentiality (Holder, 1993). Also, research data are rarely subpoenaed because they typically do not provide information central to the issue being litigated. If you think your data may be subject to litigation and subpoenaed, you could obtain a "certificate of confidentiality" from the U.S. Department of Health and Human Services. Obtaining such a certificate provides immunity from the requirement to reveal names or identifying information in a legal proceeding.

As the above indicates, ensuring the privacy of research participants is littered with obstacles, some of which are not under the control of the researcher. This means that researchers should carefully consider the nature of the study they are conducting and the probability of the data collected being the subject of some type of litigation and incorporate as many controls as seems prudent to ensure the privacy of the research participants. It is also incumbent upon the researcher to inform the research participants of the limits of their ability to maintain the privacy of the information collected.

Ethical Issues in Electronic Research

Over the past decade researchers have increasingly turned to the Internet as a medium for conducting research investigating important psychological issues. For example, Smucker, Earleywine, & Gordis (2005) made use of the Internet in their study examining the relationship between alcohol consumption and cannabis use.

The increasing use of the Internet in the conduct of psychological studies is logical given the advantages it offers. Internet studies can access not only a large number of individuals in a short period of time, but also individuals with diverse backgrounds. This is contrasted with numerous psychological studies that are limited to their universities' "subject or participant pool" consisting primarily of college sophomores. Psychology experiments conducted on the Internet are also much more cost effective and capable of reaching individuals anywhere in the world.

The ease with which many studies can be conducted with the Internet medium also raises ethical issues. These issues focus on topics such as informed consent, privacy, and debriefing. While these issues are recognized and have been discussed by organizations such as the American Association for the Advancement of Science (see www.aaas.org/spp/sfrl/projects/intres/report.pdf) and the Association of Internet Research (see www.aoir.org/reports/ethics.pdf), the development of a firm set of guidelines has not been established. Although these guidelines have not been established, I do want to elaborate on some of the ethical issues surrounding Internet research.

Before getting into the thorny and difficult issues, I do want to point out that the absence of an experimenter in Internet research removes the probability of coercion (Nosek, Banaji, & Greenwald 2002) as a source of concern which is an advantage. Because Internet studies are not conducted in a face-to-face environment and the researcher has no obvious power over the potential participant, there is little possibility for the participant to feel coerced into participating. In fact, it is extremely easy for the potential participant to hit the "delete" button on his or her computer if they do not want to participate.

Informed Consent and Internet Research   Obtaining the informed consent of participants is one of the vital components of conducting ethical research because this is the component that recognizes the autonomy of research participants. Obtaining informed consent and answering questions participants may have regarding consent is a relatively simple process in the context of most experiments. However, when conducting research over the Internet there are a variety of issues that must be confronted, such as when is informed consent required, how should informed consent be obtained, and how can you make sure that the participant actually provided informed consent.

The issue of when informed consent should be obtained is complicated because it involves a determination of what is public and what is private behavior. Informed consent may not be needed with data collected from the public domain. For example, data collected from television or radio programs, or from books or conferences are definitely within the public domain. However, is the data that could be obtained from newsgroups, listservs, and chat rooms within the public or private domain? Some see these components of cyberspace as being in the public domain because they are there for anyone to read. Others disagree because, although the communications are public, the cyberspace participants may perceive and expect a degree of privacy in their communications. This is one of those issues that has not been resolved.

If it is determined that a study requires informed consent, there is the issue of how it should be obtained. Informed consent has three components: providing the information to participants, ensuring that they comprehend it, and then obtaining their voluntary consent to participate. Obviously a consent form can be placed online with a request that the participant read the consent form and then check a box next to a statement such as "I agree to the above consent form." However, there are the accompanying issues of ensuring that the participant comprehends the information contained in the consent form and answering any questions he or she may have. If a study is online, it is accessible twenty-four hours a day but researchers are not. To try to deal with this issue, Nosek et al. (2002) suggested that consent forms be accompanied by FAQs (frequently asked questions) that anticipate potential questions and concerns.

Privacy and Internet Research   Maintaining the privacy of the research data collected from participants is essential to the conduct of an ethical study, as participants can be harmed when their privacy is invaded or when there is a violation of confidential information. This is an important issue when conducting research over the Internet because there are limits to the ability to maintain the privacy and confidentiality of information collected. Privacy and confidentiality can be compromised during data transmission and storage in a multitude of ways—from hackers to someone sending an e-mail to the wrong address. However, Nosek et al. (2002) point out that it may be possible to guarantee a greater degree of privacy of research data collected over the Internet than in standard studies. Data transmitted over the Internet can be encrypted and if no identifying information is collected, the only connection that could possibly lead to a participant is the Internet Protocol (IP) address. However, IP addresses identify machines and not individuals, so the only way an IP address could be connected to a participant is if the participant is the sole user of the machine or computer. If identifying data is obtained, assurance of privacy and confidentiality is not as great if the information is stored in a file that is on an Internet-connected server. However, most of the data collected in psychological studies would be of little interest to hackers, so I suspect that it would run little risk of being compromised. In spite of this, individuals conducting Internet research must consider this, and take as many precautions as necessary to prevent such a possibility.

Debriefing and Internet Research   To conduct an ethical study it is necessary to debrief participants following completion of the study. To be most effective, debriefing should be interactive, with the researcher providing a description of the study including its purpose and the way in which the study was conducted. The researcher is also available to answer any questions the participant may have, and, more importantly, to ensure that the participant is adequately dehoaxed if deception is used and desensitized if made to feel uncomfortable. However, the Internet can create difficulties in effectively debriefing participants for a variety of reasons. The study could be terminated early because of a computer or server crash, a broken Internet connection, or a power outage. Also, the participant may become irritated with the study or decide to voluntarily terminate due to boredom or frustration. All of these are real possibilities that could preclude the possibility of conducting debriefing. Nosek et al. (2002) has anticipated such difficulties and has identified several options researchers can use to maximize the probability of debriefing in the event that a study is terminated early.

1. Require the participant to provide an e-mail address so that a debriefing statement can be sent to them.
2. Provide a "leave the study" radio button on every page that will direct them to a debriefing page.
3. Incorporate a debriefing page into the program driving the experiment that directs the participant to this page if the study is terminated prior to completion.

As you can see, researchers conducting research on the Internet encounter a number of ethical issues that do not have a perfect solution. If you are going to conduct a study using the Internet you must consider the issues of privacy, informed consent, and debriefing just discussed and identify the best way to accomplish each. In doing this you must keep the general principles of the Code of Ethics in mind. Also keep in mind that data collected over the Internet is potentially available to anyone if it is not encrypted.

Ethical Issues in Preparing the Research Report

Throughout this chapter I have concentrated on various ethical issues that must be considered in designing and conducting an ethical study. After you have completed the study, the last phase of the research process is to communicate the results of the study to others. Communication most frequently takes place through professional journals in a field. This means that you must write a research report stating how the research was conducted and what was found. In writing the research report the two moral principles of justice and fidelity and scientific integrity are involved. Justice involves the decision of authorship, or who receives credit for the research. Fidelity and scientific integrity in the preparation of the research report refers to the accurate and honest reporting of all aspects of the study.

Authorship Authorship is important because it is used to identify the individual or individuals who are responsible for the study. This is important because it represents a record of a person's scholarly work and, for the professional, relates directly to decisions involving salary, hiring, promotion, and tenure. For the student, it can have direct implications for getting into a graduate program or for securing a job upon completion of doctoral studies. Authorship, therefore, has serious implications for all those involved. However, everyone that makes a contribution to the research study should not receive authorship. The person or persons who receive authorship should be confined to individuals who have made a substantial contribution to the conceptualization, design, execution, analysis, or interpretation of the study being reported. The order of authorship of these individuals is typically such that the person who made the most substantial contribution is listed as the first author. Anyone who has made a contribution of a technical nature, such as collecting, coding, entering data into a computer file, or running a standard statistical analysis under the supervision of someone else does not warrant authorship. These individuals' contributions are generally acknowledged in a footnote.

Writing the Research Report   The primary ethical guideline that must be followed in writing the research report is honesty and integrity. You should never fabricate or falsify any information presented and you should report the methodology used in collecting and analyzing the data as accurately as possible and in a manner that allows others to replicate the study and draw reasonable conclusions about its validity. In writing this research report it is necessary to make use of the work of others both in the introduction section where you set down the rationale for the study and in the discussion section where you discuss your study's findings and relate them to the findings of others.

When making use of the contributions of others, it is essential that you give credit to them. To make use of the contributions of others without giving them credit constitutes plagiarism. **Plagiarism** occurs when you copy someone else's work but do not give them credit. When you do not give them credit, you are giving the reader the impression that the work you have copied is yours. This constitutes a type of scholarly thievery and is totally unethical.

To appropriately give credit to a person whose work you are using, you could make use of quotation marks or you could indent the material and then give a citation for the material you have quoted. If you were using some of the material presented in the Nosek et al. (2002) article discussing many issues involved in Internet research, you could put the material you were using in quotation marks and then give the authors credit as follows: Nosek, Banaji, and Greenwald (2002) have stated that "The potential of the information highway to advance understanding of psychological science is immense . . ." (p. 161). If you wanted to use a longer quote you would indent the quoted material as follows: Nosek et al. (2002) have stated that

> The potential of the information highway to advance understanding of psychological science is immense, and it is likely that the Internet will decisively shape the nature of psychological research. Yet as any researcher who has attempted to use the Internet to obtain data will have discovered, a host of methodological issues require consideration because of differences between standard laboratory research and Internet-based research concerning research methodology. (pp. 161–162)

While I have only addressed plagiarism with regard to the written work, it is equally important that you give appropriate credit if you use tables or figures taken from someone else's work, including something you find on the Internet. The basic principle you must use is that if you use something someone else has done you must give them credit for that work.

Plagiarism
Using work produced by someone else and calling it your own

STUDY QUESTION 5.6

- **Defend or refute the position that participants in most psychological research studies are coerced to participate.**
- **Explain privacy and how confidentiality and anonymity relate to privacy.**
- **What are the ethical issues involved in conducting research on the Internet?**
- **What is the difference between privacy, confidentiality, and anonymity?**

Ethics of Animal Research

Considerable attention has been devoted to the ethics of human research. In about 7–8 percent of the studies they conduct, however, psychologists use animals as their research participants in order to gain control over many potentially contaminating factors (Gallup and Suarez, 1985) or to investigate the influence of a variable that might be judged too dangerous to test on humans. Of the animals used by psychologists, 90 percent have been rodents and birds. Only about 5 percent are monkeys and other primates. Dogs and cats are rarely used.

Animal Rights

During the late 1970s and early 1980s, such animal rights groups as People for the Ethical Treatment of Animals (PETA), the Animal Rights Coalition, and the Animal Liberation Front (ALF) were formed to protest the use of animals in research. This movement began through the efforts of Henry Spira as a calculated, deceptive, and deductive campaign to win the sympathy and financial support of the American public (Johnson, 1990). In the mid-1970s Spira took a continuing education course on animal liberation from the philosopher Peter Singer. Singer's (1975) arguments that animals are capable of suffering and enjoyment and are worthy of moral considerations struck Spira as rational, defensible, and as a basis for a program of protest and action.

Spira was a veteran of labor and civil rights battles and realized that the promotion of a movement required a specific target with an achievable goal and a well-publicized victory. To identify this target, Spira and other similarly minded individuals began to review scientific abstracts and grant proposals. From this review they learned that the American Museum of Natural History's Department of Animal Behavior was conducting experiments on the neurological basis of sexual behavior. These experiments involved removing parts of the brain, severing nerves in the penis and destroying the sense of smell.

For Spira, this was the ideal target. Not only should taxpayers be shocked to find that their tax dollars are being used to support the mutilation of cats to observe sexual behavior, but the protest was against a popular museum. This should attract broad public interest and media attention.

In spring 1976, Spira launched his campaign and organized demonstrations at the museum. Activists waved placards saying, "Curiosity kills cats," and "Castrate the Scientists." Press headlines ranged from passive criticism to hostile descriptions that cats were tortured in vicious experiments. The final result was that the research was stopped and the cat laboratory was dismantled (Jasper & Nelkin, 1992).

Since the museum victory, organizations devoted to animal rights have proliferated. The four most prominent, PETA, ALF, In Defense of Animals (IDA), and Animal Legal Defense Fund (ALDF), represent the new generation of organizations. As these organizations have become more popular, there has been a corresponding rise in membership. For example, PETA membership rose from less than one hundred in 1980 to more than three hundred thousand in 1990. In 1989 PETA's budget was $6.5 million (Jasper & Nelkin, 1992).

The basic philosophy of these organizations, derived from Regan (1983), is that humans and other mammals are similar and that they have a value of their own independent of their utility for humans. Because they have worth, animals have a right to live their life with respect and harmony. Rights are absolute, and those who accept the rights view will not be satisfied with anything less than the total abolition of the harmful use of animals in all domains including education, toxicity testing, and research.

This is the philosophy advocated by the leaders of the animal rights groups. They believe that the rights accorded humans should be extended to nonhuman animals (Dewsbury, 1990) and that we should not require anything of animals that we would not require of humans, as illustrated in Figure 5.5. This position is articulated most effectively by one of the codirectors of People for the Ethical Treatment of Animals, who stated that "There is no rational basis for separating out the human animal. A rat is a pig is a dog is a boy. They're all mammals" (McCabe, 1986).

The topic on which animal rights groups have been most vocal is the use of animals in research. Using research as a target was promoted because scientists have been an easy target (Johnson, 1990). Fundamentalists in the animal rights movement want to abolish all research regardless of its merits or potential benefit. They argue that the use of animals in research is immoral, is of no value in treating human disorders, and is unacceptably cruel (Greenough, 1991). To support their arguments, animal rights brochures and magazines are filled with shocking images of maimed and tortured animals. They have produced videotapes documenting the experiments of a team of researchers studying the effects of severe head injury. These edited tapes portray bantering among researchers and joking about injured animals. Posters at demonstrations portray experiments as cruel and painful (Jasper & Nelkin, 1992).

They also have engaged in a variety of activities from letter writing and distortion of the truth to harassment, burglary, and violence in an attempt to eliminate the use

FIGURE 5.5
Antivivisectionists' cartoon of mice performing the type of experiments on Watson that he performed on the mice.

(From the Journal of Zoophily, 1907, vol. 16 (issue 6), page 65.)

DREAM OF THE MEDICAL VIVISECTIONIST CRANK WHO WANTONLY AND CRUELLY OPERATED ON RATS, TO SEE THE EFFECT, FROM A "SCIENTIFIC" VIEW-POINT, OF THE LOSS OF THE DIFFERENT SENSES.

of animals in research. The director of the Washington, D.C., office of the National Anti-Vivisection Society has stated that seventy million animals are used each year in research (Pardes, West, & Pincus, 1991). The actual figure is between seventeen and twenty-two million, 90 percent of which are rats. Promoting violence and causing deliberate harm to others are also tactics that have been used. The Animal Liberation Front is listed by the FBI as one of the country's ten most dangerous organizations (Pardes et al., 1991). An animal activist was convicted of attempted murder, possession of explosives, and bomb manufacturing after planting a remote-controlled pipe bomb near the parking space of the chairman of the U.S. Surgical Corporation. Trans Species Unlimited, a Pennsylvania-based animal rights group, picketed the laboratory of a noted drug researcher, made constant phone calls, and wrote letters condemning her experiments, causing her to forfeit a $530,000 three-year grant.

Herzog (1995) has suggested that interest in animal rights may have peaked because the number of newspaper and magazine articles devoted to animal welfare and animal rights has declined more than 50 percent since 1990. However, this conclusion is based totally on the attention this issue has received in the media. Other evidence suggests that interest in animal rights has not declined and that some groups are shifting their emphasis to include lobbying and litigation, to the dismay of the scientific community. Animal rights advocates have even formed a political-action committee, Humane U.S.A., to provide financial support for their activities (Southwick, 2000). One group has sued the National Institutes of Health for failing to disclose information about a research project it funded at Ohio State University (Southwick, 2002). The animal rights groups are extremely tenacious and are growing politically sophisticated, and they are not about to give up their cause. For example, Associated Press writer Dionne Walker reported in September 2005 that PETA had developed a campaign using a series of images comparing animal abuse with those of slavery. Some of these images juxtaposed pictures of black individuals in chains with shackled elephants. Another involved a black civil rights protester being beaten at a lunch counter beside a photo of a bludgeoned seal. Although this campaign was temporarily halted after the exhibit was accused of being racist, it was resumed later because PETA concluded that the complaints about the exhibit boiled down to "not wanting to be compared to animals." This, according to a PETA spokeswoman, was the exact type of bias she said they were trying to challenge. As a result of their activities, the Agriculture Department, the chief watchdog for the Animal Welfare Act, has shown increasing interest in enforcing federal standards for the care of laboratory animals. However, animal rights groups are not winning all the battles. For several years, animal rights groups had lobbied congress to cover birds and rodents under the Animal Welfare Act. In 2002 they experienced a stinging defeat when Congress exempted rodents and birds from the Animal Welfare Act.

Alternatives to the Use of Animals

The allegations of animal rights groups have not gone unnoticed and alternative procedures have been proposed, including the use of plants, tissue cultures, computer simulations, naturalistic observation, and embryos. Gallup and Suarez (1985) reviewed these alternatives and concluded that they are complements to the use of animals but not substitutes. In fact, researchers who use animals are legally and ethically required to consider the possibility of using alternatives to nonhuman animals. However, alternatives are typically inadequate or not available. Psychologists study psychological constructs such as depression, alcoholism, abuse, violence, and cognitive deficiencies. These are phenomena that do not exist among plants or tissue cultures. Similarly, plants do not have a physiological system that can be used to study human characteristics and computer simulations would have to be programmed with knowledge acquired from living organisms. Regardless of which alternative is suggested, at present there seems to be no adequate substitute for the use of animals as research participants. This does not mean that researchers have a license to subject animals to any procedure that can be justified in the name of research. Rather, it places an additional burden on the researcher to provide humane care and treatment of the animals and to minimize the pain and suffering they may experience.

Safeguards in the Use of Animals

There are many safeguards that have been instituted to ensure that laboratory animals receive humane and ethical treatment. The Animal Welfare Act, enforced by the Department of Agriculture, governs the care and use of many research animals and conducts unannounced inspections of both public and private animal research facilities. In addition, institutions conducting animal research, and covered by the Act, are required to have an Institutional Animal Care and Use Committee (IACUC) that reviews each research protocol. This committee reviews the researcher's rationale for the proposed experiment, the conditions of animal care during the experiment, the rationale for the number of animals that will be used, as well as the researcher's assessment of the pain and suffering that might be involved in the experiment and the approach that the researcher uses for alleviating any pain and suffering.

Professional societies whose members conduct animal research also have a set of ethical standards and guidelines to which their members must adhere. The American Psychological Association code of ethics (see Exhibit 5.7, section 8.09) includes principles for the humane and ethical treatment of research animals. All APA members are committed to upholding these principles.

STUDY QUESTION 5.7

- **What are the basic position and goal of animal rights activists and how have they attempted to fulfill their goal?**
- **What safeguards currently exist to ensure that laboratory animals receive humane and ethical treatment?**
- **What alternatives are there to the use of animals and how useful are they?**

Animal Research Guidelines

In reading the guidelines in Exhibit 5.7 you should be aware of the fact that they focus primarily on animal welfare and not animal rights. **Animal welfare** is concerned with improving laboratory conditions and reducing the number of animals

Animal welfare
Improving the laboratory conditions in which animals live and reducing the number of animals used in research

Animal rights
The belief that animals have rights similar to humans and should not be used in research

needed in research (Baldwin, 1993). **Animal rights** focuses on the rights of animals. This position states that animals have the same rights as humans and should not be used in research. Because there is no substitute for the use of animals as research participants, the focus of attention is on animal welfare, which concerns the humane treatment of animals.

The acquisition, care, housing, use, and disposition of animals should be in compliance with the appropriate federal, state, local, and institutional laws and regulations and with international conventions to which the United States is a party. APA authors must state in writing that they have complied with the ethical standards when submitting a research article for publication. Violations by an APA member should be reported to the APA Ethics Committee, and any questions regarding the guidelines should be addressed to the APA Committee on Animal Research and Ethics (CARE) at science@apa.org.

I. Justification of the Research   Research using animals should be undertaken only when there is a clear scientific purpose and a reasonable expectation that the research will increase our knowledge of the processes underlying behavior, increase our understanding of the species under study, or result in benefits to the health or welfare of humans or other animals. Any study conducted should have sufficient potential importance to justify the use of animals, and any procedure that produces pain in humans should be assumed to also produce pain in animals.

The species chosen for use in a study should be the one best suited to answer the research question. However, before a research project is initiated, alternatives or procedures that will minimize the number of animals used should be considered. Regardless of the type of species or number of animals used, the research may not be conducted until the protocol has been reviewed by the IACUC. After the study has been initiated, the psychologist must continuously monitor the research and the animals' welfare.

II. Personnel   All personnel involved in animal research should be familiar with the guidelines. Any procedure used by the research personnel must conform with federal regulations regarding personnel, supervision, record-keeping, and veterinary care. Both psychologists and their research assistants must be informed about the behavioral characteristics of their research animals so that unusual behaviors that could forewarn of health problems can be identified. Psychologists should ensure that anyone working for them when conducting animal research receives instruction in the care, maintenance, and handling of the species being studied. The responsibilities and activities of anyone dealing with animals should be consistent with his or her competencies, training, and experience regardless of whether the setting is the laboratory or the field.

III. Care and Housing of Animals   The psychological well-being of animals is a topic that is currently being debated. This is a complex issue because the procedures that may promote the psychological well-being of one species may not be appropriate for another. For this reason, the APA does not stipulate any specific guidelines but rather states that psychologists familiar with a given species should take measures, such as enriching the environment, to enhance the psychological well-being of the species. For example, the famous Yerkes Laboratory and New York University's LEM-SIP (Laboratory for Experimental Medicine and Surgery in Primates) have constructed wire-mesh tunnels between the animals' cages to promote social contact.

In addition to providing for the animals' psychological well-being, the facilities housing the animals should conform to current U.S. Department of Agriculture ([USDA], 1990, 1991) regulations and guidelines and are to be inspected twice a year (USDA, 1989). Any research procedures used on animals are to be reviewed by the Institutional Animal Care and Use Committee (IACUC) to ensure that they are appropriate and humane. This committee essentially supervises the psychologist who has the responsibility for providing the research animals with humane care and healthful conditions during their stay at the research facility.

IV. Acquisition of Animals   Animals used in laboratory experimentation should be lawfully purchased from a qualified supplier or bred in the psychologist's facility. When animals are purchased from a qualified supplier, they should be transported in a manner that provides adequate food, water, ventilation, and space and that imposes no unnecessary stress on the animals. If animals must be taken from the wild, they must be trapped in a humane manner. Endangered species should be used only with full attention to required permits and ethical concerns.

V. Experimental Procedures   The design and conduct of the study should involve humane consideration for the animals' well-being. In addition to the procedures governed by guideline I, "Justification of the Research," the researcher should adhere to the following points.

1. Studies, such as observational and other noninvasive procedures, that involve no aversive stimulation and create no overt signs of distress are acceptable.

2. Alternative procedures that minimize discomfort to the animal should be used when available. When the aim of the research requires use of aversive conditions, the minimal level of aversive stimulation should be used. Psychologists engaged in such studies are encouraged to test the painful stimuli on themselves.

3. It is generally acceptable to anesthetize an animal prior to a painful procedure if the animal is then euthanized before it can regain consciousness.

4. Subjecting an animal to more than momentary or slight pain that is not relieved by medication or some other procedure should be undertaken only when the goals of the research cannot be met by any other method.

5. Any experimental procedure requiring exposure to prolonged aversive conditions, such as tissue damage, exposure to extreme environments, or experimentally induced prey killing, requires greater justification and surveillance. Animals that are experiencing unalleviated distress and are not essential to the research should be euthanized immediately.

6. Procedures using restraint must conform to federal guidelines and regulations.

7. It is unacceptable to use a paralytic drug or muscle relaxants during surgery without a general anesthetic.

8. Surgical procedures should be closely supervised by a person competent in the procedure, and aseptic techniques that minimize risk of infection must be used on warm-blooded animals. Animals should remain under anesthesia until a procedure is ended unless there is good justification for doing otherwise. Animals should be given postoperative monitoring and care to minimize discomfort and prevent infection or other consequences of the procedure. No surgical procedure can be performed unless it is required by the research or it is for the well-being of the animal. Alternative uses of an animal should be considered when they are no longer needed in a study. Multiple surgeries on the same animal must receive special approval from the IACUC.

9. Alternatives to euthanasia should be considered when an animal is no longer required for a research study. Any alternative taken should be compatible with the goals of the research and the welfare of the animal. This action should not expose the animal to multiple surgeries.

10. Laboratory-reared animals should not be released because, in most cases, they cannot survive or their survival may disrupt the natural ecology. Returning wild-caught animals to the field also carries risks both to the animal and to the ecosystem.

11. Euthanasia, when it must occur, should be accomplished in the most humane manner and in a way that ensures immediate death and is in accordance with the American Veterinary Medical Association panel on euthanasia. Disposal of the animals should be consistent with all relevant legislation and with health, environmental, and aesthetic concerns and should be approved by the IACUC.

VI. Field Research   Field research, because of its potential for damaging sensitive ecosystems and communities, must receive IACUC approval, although observational research may be exempt. Psychologists conducting field research should disturb their populations as little as possible and make every effort to minimize potential harmful effects on the population under investigation. Research conducted in inhabited areas must be done so that the privacy and property of any human inhabitants are respected. The study of endangered species requires particular justification and must receive IACUC approval.

VII. Educational Use of Animals   Discussion of the ethics and value of animal research in all courses is encouraged. Although animals may be used for educational purposes after review of the planned use by the appropriate institutional committee, some procedures that may be appropriate for research purposes may not be justified for educational purposes. Classroom demonstrations using live animals can be valuable instructional aids—as can videotapes, films, and other alternatives. The anticipated instructional gain should direct the type of demonstration.

STUDY QUESTION 5.8

- **What is the distinction between animal welfare and animal rights?**
- **What basic guidelines have been adopted by APA for the care and use of research animals?**

Summary

The ethical concerns surrounding the conduct of psychological research can be divided into the three areas of the relationship between society and science, professional issues, and the treatment of research participants. The area involving the relationship between society and science focuses on the extent to which societal concerns and cultural values direct scientific investigations. Because research is an expensive enterprise, both federal and corporate funding directs a large portion of the research that is conducted.

Professional issues include a variety of areas such as overlooking others' use of flawed data. However, the most serious professional issue is research misconduct—scientists must not forge or falsify data. The treatment of research participants is the most important and fundamental ethical issue confronted by scientists. Research participants have certain rights, such as the right to privacy, that must be violated if researchers are to attempt to arrive at answers to many significant questions. This naturally poses a dilemma for the researcher as to whether to conduct the research and violate the rights of the research participant or abandon the research project. To address the ethical concerns of researchers, the American Psychological Association has developed a code of ethics that includes a set of standards that psychologists must adhere to when conducting research studies. Inherent in the code of ethics are the five basic moral principles of respect for persons and their autonomy, beneficence and nonmaleficence, justice, trust, and fidelity and scientific integrity that should be adhered to when conducting research with human participants. The specific issues addressed by Section 8 of the code of ethics include getting institutional approval, informed consent, deception, and debriefing.

Approval must be obtained from the IRB prior to conducting any study involving human participants. If the research falls into the exempt category the research protocol must still be submitted to the IRB because this is the board that must approve its exempt status.

The code of ethics requires that research participants be fully informed about all aspects of the study so that they can make an informed decision to choose or to decline to participate. However, the code of ethics recognizes that there are instances in which it is appropriate to dispense with informed consent. This may occur only under specific and limited conditions in which it is permitted by law or federal or institutional regulations. If the research participant is a minor, informed consent must be obtained from the minor's parent or legal guardian. If consent is given, assent must be obtained from the minor. Although most consent involves active consent, some individuals recommend the use of passive consent in certain situations, such as when the research participants are school-age children and the research is conducted in the school. This is an issue that the APA code of ethics has yet to address.

Some studies require the use of deception to insure the integrity and fidelity of their research study. Although deception runs counter to the necessity of informed consent, the code of ethics recognizes that, in some studies, deception is necessary.

A number of individuals have suggested alternatives to deception, such as role playing, but research studies have shown that such alternatives are poor substitutes. Therefore deception remains a part of numerous psychological studies, and its potential effects must be considered. It is generally assumed that deception creates stress and that this stress or invasion of privacy is ethically objectionable and perhaps harmful to the research participants. Yet research indicates that participants do not view deception as detrimental and that those who have been involved in deceptive studies view their research experience as more valuable than do those who have not. This phenomenon may be due to the increased attention given in deception studies to debriefing, which seems to be effective in eliminating the negative effects of deception as well as any stress that may have occurred.

Although there does not seem to be a negative effect resulting from deception or from the use of research participant pools, it has been demonstrated that informing participants that they are free to withdraw at any time without penalty can influence the outcome of some experiments.

Investigators also are quite concerned about coercing students to become research participants. Experiments investigating the perceptions of research participants drawn from a research participant pool reveal that they generally view their research experience quite positively.

A significant ethical concern involves ensuring the privacy of the information obtained from research participants because privacy is at the heart of conducting ethical research. Anonymity is an excellent way of ensuring privacy because the identity of the research participant is unknown. If anonymity is not possible, the information obtained must be kept confidential. However, the information collected by researchers is not protected by law, so confidentiality may be difficult to maintain if researchers are subpoenaed by a court of law. If this is a possibility, a researcher could obtain a "certificate of confidentiality" that would provide immunity from the requirement to reveal names or identifying information.

In recent years there has been an increasing use of the Internet as a medium for conducting psychological research. Use of this medium has many advantages such as reduced cost, access to many individuals, and the reduction of feeling of being coerced into participation. However, there are many ethical issues that accompany use of this medium such as obtaining informed consent from the participants, ensuring the privacy of the data collected, and debriefing the participants following completion of the study.

When preparing a research report of a completed study, ethically, only those individuals who made a substantial contribution should receive authorship. Also, honesty and integrity should be followed when writing the research report. This means that you should not plagiarize because this is a form of scholarly thievery.

There is concern for the ethical treatment of animals in research. Spearheading this concern are a variety of animal rights groups who claim that psychologists have treated their research animals in an inhumane manner. Although a survey of the literature demonstrates that the claims of animal rights groups are unfounded, their efforts have resulted in the development of institutional animal care and use committees and a set of guidelines adopted by the American Psychological Association for use by psychologists working with animals. These guidelines address various issues, ranging from where the animals are housed to how the animals are disposed of. Psychologists using animals for research or educational purposes should be familiar with these guidelines and adhere to them.

Key Terms and Concepts

Research ethics
Research misconduct
Ethical dilemma
Informed consent
Assent
Active consent
Passive consent
Active deception
Passive deception

Debriefing
Dehoaxing
Desensitizing
Privacy
Anonymity
Confidentiality
Plagiarism
Animal welfare
Animal rights

Related Internet Sites

www.nap.edu/readingroom/books/obas/
This site reproduces a book online that includes a discussion of most of the topics relating to the ethical conduct of research.

www.apa.org/ethics/
This is the American Psychological Association's site for information on ethics. It contains links to the code of ethics and information on ethics in the use of animals.

www.psychologicalscience.org/teaching/tips/tips_0902.html
This site is maintained by the American Psychological Society and provides information relevant to teaching ethics. There are many brief cases at this site that can be used for the discussion of ethics in the conduct of research and in the delivery of psychological services.

www.psychology.org
To get to the site that is applicable to this chapter, you must, when the home site opens, click on the "Resources" link and then the "Ethical Issues" link. This will bring you to a site with links to online books and other discussions of ethical issues involved in the conduct of psychological research.

Practice Test

The answers to these questions can be found in Appendix A.

1. The National Institutes of Mental Health funded Dr. Doom's study of the effect of treating obsessive-compulsive disorder with a new drug produced by one of the biotechnology companies. Dr. Doom reported that his research found that the new drug was more effective than any prior treatment of this disorder. However, a detailed investigation of Dr. Doom's research revealed that he fudged and manipulated some of the data to show these results. This ethical issue falls under which of the following areas:

   a. The relationship between society and science
   b. Professional issues
   c. Treatment of research participants
   d. Trust
   e. Autonomy

2. Obtaining informed consent meets the moral principle of
   a. Respect for persons and their autonomy
   b. Beneficence and nonmaleficence
   c. Justice
   d. Trust
   e. Fidelity and scientific integrity

3. Assume that you are a member of the IRB and are presented with a research protocol stating that the researcher wants to test a new treatment for autistic children. Although the new treatment holds out a promise of benefiting the children in the study and yielding new knowledge, it also includes some troublesome components that may create severe emotional stress for the children. Having to consider of the benefits of the research as well as the distress that it may cause
   a. Involves the moral principle of trust
   b. Involves the moral principle of fidelity and scientific integrity
   c. Creates an ethical dilemma
   d. Will result in disapproval because the children could be harmed
   e. Will result in approval because the children may benefit from the research

4. When you are proposing a research study that uses minors as the research participants, you must
   a. Gain their trust
   b. Get the informed consent of their parent or guardian
   c. Get the child's assent to participant in the research study
   d. Incorporate additional safeguards to insure that the child is not harmed
   e. Both b and c

5. Animal rights groups focus on _____, whereas researchers and professional organizations concerned with animals in research focus on

   _____.
   a. Animal welfare; the integrity of the research being proposed
   b. Animal rights; the integrity of the research being proposed
   c. Primates and household pets; rodents and birds
   d. The use of violence; the use of legislation
   e. Animal rights; animal welfare

Challenge Exercises

1. This challenge exercise is intended to give you some practice and experience in recognizing and dealing with scientific fraud. For this exercise, we will focus on the case of Steven E. Breuning. Read the article

   Holden, C. (1987). NIMH finds a case of "serious misconduct." *Science, 235,* 1566–1567.

Read some of the other articles that are provided in the reference section as well, and then answer the following questions.

a. What evidence led to the exposure of Breuning's scientific misconduct?
b. What ethical principles were violated by Bruening's behavior?
c. What were the consequences to Bruening of his behavior?
d. What are the possible consequences of his misconduct to his colleagues, to the organization in which he worked, to other scientists, and to the general public?

2. This challenge exercise is intended to give you some practice reviewing a research protocol and then acting like an IRB member, scrutinizing the protocol and making a decision as to whether the research should receive approval. Assume that you received a protocol having the following characteristics.

Dr. Smith is interested in studying the resilience of some individuals to the effects of exposure to maladaptive environments. The basic research question she poses is: Why are some individuals able to fend off the negative consequences of adverse environmental conditions whereas others are not? Dr. Smith proposes to study sixth, seventh, and eighth graders who have been exposed to violent and stressful home and community environments.

The research participants will be assessed at six-month intervals for the next three years by means of surveys and individual interviews. These outcome measures will assess the extent and frequency of exposure to violence and stress both in the home and in the community. Additional outcome measures will assess psychological stability (anxiety, depression, suicidal thoughts, and social support), academic achievement, and psychological and behavioral coping responses.

Dr. Smith has received the approval of the local school system as well as the principal of the school in which the study is to be conducted. She proposes to obtain passive consent from the students' parents and to provide the school system with a summary of the outcome of the study.

As an IRB member, evaluate this study from the perspective of

a. The investigators—what are the important items to consider?
b. The nature of the study—what are the important aspects of the study design that must be considered?
c. The research participants—what are the important considerations regarding who they are and how they are recruited?
d. Confidentiality—what information should be kept confidential and what can be revealed?
e. Debriefing—what should these children be told about the study?

3. This challenge exercise pertains to an aspect of research that is new and has been given little consideration even by the current APA code of ethics. However, it is becoming a common event and one that should be considered—it is research conducted over the Internet. Think about a study that is being conducted via the Internet regardless of whether this is a survey or an experimental study.

a. What are the ethical issues that must be considered and that may create difficulty in conducting such a study? In answering this question, consider the five moral principles discussed in this chapter as well as the code of ethics presented in Exhibit 5.7.

b. Is the current code of ethics sufficient to cover research conducted in cyberspace?

4. This challenge exercise involves more of a debate than a specific exercise. There has been considerable emotion devoted to the issue of the use of animals in research. The basic questions are: Should they be used and is the harm and suffering inflicted on them justified by the benefit achieved? Animal rights people say no to both, but researchers say yes. For this exercise, form two groups, one to argue the animal rights' and one to argue the researchers' point of view. Take about ten minutes to form your positions and then debate the issue for another ten minutes. After the debate, consider this general issue: What limits should we place on our scientific curiosity in our use of animals in research?

6 Variables Used in Experimentation

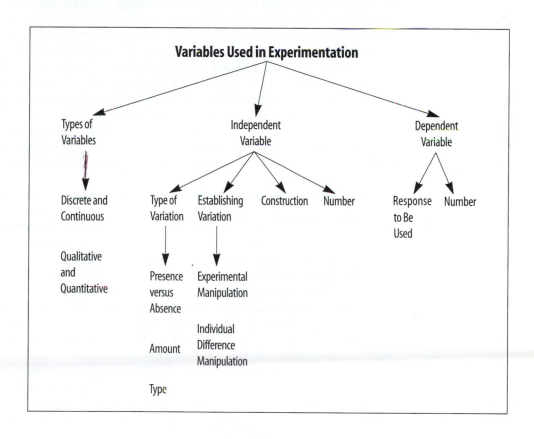

Every year many people have a limb amputated as a result of disease or an accident. Many of these individuals, when they awake from surgery and recover from the anaesthetic, have the feeling that the surgery has not been performed. This feeling is so vivid that they are frequently shocked when they try to look at the limb that seems to be there only to see that it has indeed been amputated. This realization does nothing to subdue the sensation of the presence of the limb, a phenomenon known as *phantom limb*. The phantom limb experience is often accompanied by a presence or absence of pain. The nonpainful variety is typically accompanied by a tingling or pins and needles experience. However, more than 70 percent of amputees experience phantom limb pain, described as pain traveling up and down the limb, a cramped or unnatural posture of the limb causing pain, or an intense burning pain. Unfortunately, this pain typically lasts for decades.

In the last century, numerous psychological and neurological explanations have been proposed to account for phantom limbs and particularly the pain associated with them. Katz (1992) has summarized these explanations as well as his own. Katz has suggested that the central nervous system is extremely plastic and can change in response to various sensory inputs. Specifically, Katz believes that phantom limb experience is a biopsychosocial phenomenon consisting of the neural integration of a variety of sensory processes including cognitive and emotional processes.

If you were interested in assessing Katz's biopsychosocial explanation of phantom limb pain, you would design a psychological experiment to test one or more components of this explanation. Designing the experiment would require you to make a variety of decisions. You would have to choose the variables that would be investigated in the experiment. Specifically, you would have to identify the cognitive or emotional variables to investigate. You would also have to identify the variables that may introduce a confounding influence and the techniques that must be employed in order to eliminate such a confounding influence. Only after making such decisions can you describe the final design of the experiment.

Chapter Preview

To conduct a psychological experiment you must first identify the variable or variables that are to produce the effect you are interested in and the variable or variables that are to measure this effect. In this chapter, you will learn that the variable that produces the effect is called the *independent variable* and the variable that is measuring this effect is called the *dependent variable*. You will also learn how the independent variable can be varied to enable the experimenter to identify its effect. However, the effect created by an independent variable must be measured in some way, and this is the role of the dependent variable. In this chapter, you will find out what responses can be used as dependent variables and that the criteria that needs to be used in the selection of the dependent variable(s) are that they must not only be sensitive to the effect of the independent variable but that they must also be reliable and valid.

Introduction

Variable
Any characteristic or phenomenon that can vary across organisms, situations, or environments

Independent variable
One of the antecedent conditions manipulated by the experimenter

Dependent variable
The response of the organism; the variable that measures the influence of the independent variable

One of the first decisions that must be made after the research problem and the hypothesis have been specified is which variable or variables are to serve as the independent variable and which variable or variables are to serve as the dependent variable. By **variable** I mean any characteristic of an organism, environment, or experimental situation that can vary from one organism to another, from one environment to another, or from one experimental situation to another. Therefore, independent and dependent variables can be any of the numerous characteristics or phenomena that can take on different values, such as IQ, speed of response, number of trials required to learn something, or amount of a particular drug consumed. The researcher's task is to select one or more of these variables as the independent variable and another of these variables as the dependent variable. The **independent variable** is the variable that the experimenter changes within a defined range; it is the variable in whose effect the experimenter is interested. The **dependent variable,** on the other hand, is the variable that measures the influence of the independent variable. For example, if you are studying the effectiveness of several teaching techniques, the task of the dependent variable is to assess effectiveness. Consequently, the dependent variable is linked to the independent variable.

In any given study, there are many possible independent and dependent variables that could be used. How do we identify the ones that are to be included? The independent and dependent variables for a study are specified by the research problem. For example, one of the research questions Flaherty and Checke (1982) asked was whether the concentration of a solution of sugar and water was important in determining the extent to which rats would decrease their consumption of a solution of saccharin and water. Such a research question specifies which variable must be independent and which must be dependent. Because Flaherty and Checke varied the sugar–water concentration consumed, it was the independent variable. The influence of the sugar–water concentration was assessed by observing the degree to which it reduced the consumption of the saccharin–water solution. The magnitude of this decrease represented the response of the organisms (albino rats, in this instance) and measured the influence of the sugar–water concentration. Therefore, the suppression measure was the dependent variable.

Although the research problem may specify both the independent and the dependent variables, it is not always a simple task to design an experiment that uses these independent and dependent variables. For example, assume that a research problem involves the investigation of aggression in rats. If aggression is specified to be the independent variable, you must identify ways to vary aggression. If it is specified to be the dependent variable, you have to identify ways of measuring aggression. As you can see, many decisions and a great deal of thought may be involved in the development of these variables. This chapter discusses the types of variables and the factors that must be considered when constructing the independent and the dependent variables for an experiment.

Types of Variables

Within the field of psychology, many different areas are investigated. Studies have been conducted on such topics as attraction, learning, types of abnormal behavior, and child development. Within each topic area there are a number of variables that can be studied. For example, the topic of child development focuses on such variables as stranger anxiety, attractiveness, ethnic background, and language development. Ethnic background and language development are not, however, the same type of variable. To understand the nature of variables and how variables are used in psychological research, it is important to understand the distinctions made among types of variables. We will consider two approaches often used in psychological research to distinguish between variables.

Discrete variable
A variable that comes in whole units or categories

Continuous variable
A variable that forms a continuum and that can be represented by fractional and whole units

One way to distinguish between variables is to categorize them as either discrete or continuous. **Discrete variables** are variables that come in whole units or categories. A family has a specific number of children. A person is either sick or well, male or female. A stimulus can be either present or absent. **Continuous variables,** on the other hand, are variables that form a continuum and can be represented by both whole and fractional units. Attitudes toward President Bush, for example, vary from extremely positive to extremely negative. The latency period prior to making a response can be measured in minutes, seconds, or milliseconds. Consequently, a continuous variable can be measured with varying degrees of precision. The precision with which it is measured is limited only by the precision of the measuring instrument. For example, if latency to responding were measured by a clock that recorded only hours, minutes, and seconds, then the most precise measurement we could obtain would be in seconds. Another, more precise instrument might measure latency in milliseconds.

Qualitative variable
A variable that varies in kind

Quantitative variable
A variable that varies in amount

Variables can also be distinguished by categorizing them as either quantitative or qualitative. **Qualitative variables** are variables that vary in kind. Psychiatric patients, for example, are given one of several diagnoses, such as bulimia or anorexia. Individuals can be labeled attractive or nonattractive. **Quantitative variables** are variables that vary in amount. Loudness is measured in decibels; latency to responding is measured in seconds, minutes, or some other time measurement.

These are just two of the dimensions on which variables can be categorized. Others could be identified. Any one variable may fit into several different categories on different dimensions. For example, using the variable of hair color, one might classify people as blond, brunette, or redhead. Such a classification is representative of a discrete variable, because a person can be placed into only one of these categories. However, the variable of hair color also represents a qualitative variable, because the three hair colors vary in kind.

- **Define *variable*.**
- **Distinguish between an independent and a dependent variable.**
- **What are the different ways to distinguish between variables?**

The Independent Variable

The independent variable has been defined as the variable manipulated by the experimenter. It is of interest to the investigator because it is the variable hypothesized to be one of the causes of the presumed effect. To obtain evidence of this predicted causal relationship, the investigator manipulates this variable independently of the others. In the Flaherty and Checke (1982) experiment, sucrose concentration was the independent variable manipulated by the experimenter. Marks-Kaufman and Lipeles (1982) investigated the influence of chronic self-administration of morphine on the food rats ate. In this study, rats either were allowed or were not allowed to administer the morphine to themselves, so the ability to self-administer morphine was the independent variable. In an experiment that examines the influence of rate of presentation of words on speed of learning, the independent variable is speed of presentation. Variation in the rate of presentation from one to three seconds provides an independent manipulation that, along with the control of other factors, such as ability, enables one to identify the effect of rate of presentation on learning speed.

These examples demonstrate the ease with which one can pick out the independent variable from a study. They also illustrate the requirements necessary for a variable to qualify as an independent variable. In all of the foregoing examples, the independent variable involved variation—variation in rate of presentation of words, sucrose concentration, or self-administration of morphine. This variation was not random but was under the direct control of the experimenter. In all cases, the experimenter created the conditions that provided the type of variation desired. Here we have the two requirements necessary for a variable to qualify as an independent variable: variation and control of the variation. We shall look at each requirement separately and also discuss other issues related to the independent variable.

Variation

To qualify as an independent variable, a variable must be manipulable. The variable must be presented in at least two forms. There are several ways in which the desired variation in the independent variable can be achieved. We will take a look at each of these.

Presence versus Absence The presence-versus-absence technique for achieving variation is exactly what the name implies: One group of research participants receives the treatment condition and the other group does not. The two groups are then compared to see if the group that received the treatment condition differs from the group that did not. A drug study such as the one illustrated in Figure 6.1 illustrates this type of variation. One group of research participants is given a drug, and a second group is given a placebo. The two groups of participants are then compared on some measure, such as reaction time, to determine if the drug group had significantly

FIGURE 6.1
Illustration of presence-versus-absence variation in the independent variable.

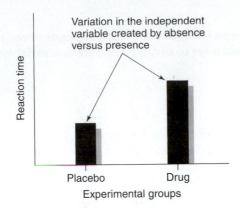

different reaction times than did the placebo group. If it did, then the difference is attributed to the drug.

A study investigating the phantom limb phenomenon could also represent a good example of the presence-versus-absence technique for manipulating the independent variable. The group of research participants with an amputated limb would represent the *presence* condition, and the group of research participants that did not receive this surgery would represent the absence condition.

Amount of a Variable   A second basic technique for achieving variation in the independent variable is to administer different amounts of the variable to each of several groups. For example, Ryan and Isaacson (1983) varied the amount of the drug ACTH administered to rats to determine the minimum dose of ACTH required to induce excessive grooming. Rats were injected with either 0, 20, 50, 80, or 1,000 nanograms of ACTH in the area of the brain known as the nucleus accumbens. One to two minutes following injection of ACTH, the rats' grooming behavior was recorded. As can be seen from Figure 6.2, the results reveal that even a dose of ACTH as low as 20 nanograms induced excessive grooming.

This study shows not only variation in the amount of a variable but also presence–absence variation because the first condition consisted of injecting zero nanograms of ACTH, or an absence of ACTH. (Actually, one microliter of a saline solution was injected in order to create a placebo condition.) This combination of techniques is frequently necessary so that the experimenter can tell not only whether the independent variable has an effect but also what influence varying amounts of the independent variable may have. Using a combination of the amount and the presence-versus-absence techniques, Ryan and Isaacson could tell not only that ACTH induced grooming but also that grooming behavior was affected by different amounts of ACTH. However, you should not assume that all studies varying the amount of the independent variable also use a presence–absence technique—in some studies this is not possible. For example, if you were investigating the influence of exposure durations on recognition of different types of words, all participants would have to be exposed to the words for some period of time. It would not make sense to ask people to identify a word to which they had never been exposed. Consequently,

FIGURE 6.2

Illustration of variation of the independent variable by amount of a variable.

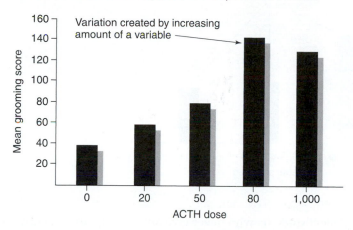

(Based on data from "Intraaccumbens Injections of ACTH Induce Excessive Grooming in Rats" by J. P. Ryan and R. L. Isaacson, 1983, *Physiological Psychology, 11,* pp. 54–58.)

you could only vary the amount of time of exposure to the various words and could not include an absence condition.

One question that comes up with regard to establishing variation concerns the number of levels of variation to induce. An exact answer cannot be given, other than that there must be at least two levels of variation and that these two must differ from one another. The research problem, past research, and the experience of the investigator should provide some indication as to the number of levels of variation that should be incorporated in a given experiment.

Also, the type of inference that is to be drawn from the results of the study will suggest the number of levels of variation that need to be included. If, for example, the objective of a particular drug study is to determine if a drug produces a given effect, you would probably use only two levels of variation. One group of research participants would receive a large dose of the drug, and another group would receive the placebo. But if you were concerned with identifying the specific drug dosage that produced a given effect, you would probably have many levels of variation, ranging in small increments from none to a massive dose.

Type of a Variable   A third means of generating variation in the independent variable is to vary the type of variable under investigation. Assume that you were interested in determining whether or not a person's reactions to others were affected by the label these others were given. Such a study could be conducted by having a school psychologist and a teacher discuss the teacher's pupils at the beginning of a school year. In this discussion, the school psychologist could let the teacher know the type of student he or she would be facing. As illustrated in Figure 6.3, some of the students would be labeled as troublemakers, some would be portrayed as average, run-of-the-mill students who may occasionally create a disturbance, and a third group would be

FIGURE 6.3
Illustration of variation in the independent variable created by type of a variable.

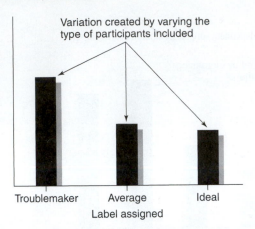

labeled ideal students who never give any trouble. In actuality, a matched group of students would have been randomly assigned to the three groups. Some time after the school term had begun, the teacher would be required to assess the students in terms of problem behavior. The teacher might be asked to rate the students in terms of the degree to which they were considered to be problem children or perhaps to rank the students in order from those who never gave any trouble to those who were constantly a problem. If the assessments initially provided by the school psychologist were confirmed by the teacher's ratings or rank ordering, then support would be given to the hypothesis that giving a child a certain type of label tends to generate the type of behavior labeled. In this hypothetical example, variation was generated in the type of behavioral label given to each child.

Establishing Variation in the Independent Variable

You have just seen that there are three basic techniques for creating variation in the independent variable. These techniques seem straightforward and relatively simple. Remember, however, that the variation created must be under the control of the experimenter. It is much easier to establish this controlled variation for some variables than for others. In drug studies, it is relatively easy to establish controlled variation because different doses of a drug can be measured quite accurately. If a presence-versus-absence form of variation were used, a placebo could be administered to one group and a specific amount of the drug to the other group. In this way, exact control would be maintained over the independent variable—the amount of the drug administered.

It is not always so easy to establish controlled variation, however. Assume that you want to investigate the influence of anxiety or fear on the desire of individuals to be together. You have decided to use the presence-versus-absence technique for varying the level of anxiety or fear. How do you create a controlled variation of this independent variable? Do you tell the participants that you are going to hurt them in the hope that this anticipation will create anxiety or fear? Or do you try to create anxiety or fear in some other manner? Clearly, it seldom suffices to state that you are going to achieve variation by a certain technique. You must identify exactly how you plan to establish the variation—by presence or absence, amount, or type.

Next, we look at two concrete ways in which variation can be achieved and the difficulties each technique produces.

| **Experimental manipulation** The controlled adjustment of the independent variable

Experimental Manipulation   The term **experimental manipulation** of an independent variable refers to a situation in which the experimenter administers one specific controlled amount of a variable to one group of individuals and a different specific controlled amount of the same variable to a second group of individuals. For example, one of the research questions Shuell (1981) wanted to investigate was: What is the influence of type of practice on long-term retention? Shuell identified two types of practice: distributed and massed. Shuell operationally defined massed practice as six learning trials administered on the same day and distributed practice as six learning trials distributed over three days. He had one group of research participants learn a list of words using massed practice and another group learn a list of words using distributed practice. The experimenter not only defined the independent variable of massed or distributed practice operationally but also had total control over the administration of the practice schedule. Thus the researcher, in a controlled manner, experimentally manipulated the independent variable.

The two basic ways of experimentally manipulating the independent variable are instructional manipulation and event manipulation.

| **Instructional manipulation** Varying the independent variable by giving different sets of instructions to the participants

Manipulation of Instructions.   One of the techniques available for creating variation in the independent variable is **instructional manipulation.** One group of participants receives one set of instructions, and another group receives another set of instructions. Barlow, Sakheim, and Beck (1983), for example, investigated the hypothesis that increases in anxiety level increases sexual arousal. In order to create a variation in anxiety, experimenters, as illustrated in Figure 6.4(*a*), told one group of participants that there was a 60 percent chance they would receive an electric shock when a light came on. Participants in a second group were told that there was a 60 percent chance they would receive an electric shock if their level of arousal was less than the average of all of the research participants. The last group was the control group, who were told that the light had no meaning. In reality, no participant received an electric shock. The instructional set was administered only to generate the anticipation of possibly receiving shock. Because shock is unpleasant and anxiety-provoking to most individuals, it is probably safe to assume that this instructional manipulation generated anxiety in those who were told they had a 60 percent chance of getting shocked. Those participants who were not given such instructions would not become anxious in anticipation of shock. Thus, instructional manipulation can enable the researcher to establish experimental manipulation.

Manipulation of variables through instruction is not without its dangers, two of which can be readily identified. First, there is the risk that some participants will be inattentive when the instructions are given. These participants will miss part or all of the instructions and therefore will not be operating according to the appropriate manipulation, thereby introducing error into the results. The second danger is the possibility that participant-to-participant variation exists in the interpretation of the

FIGURE 6.4
Experimental manipulation (*a, b*) and individual difference manipulation (*c*).

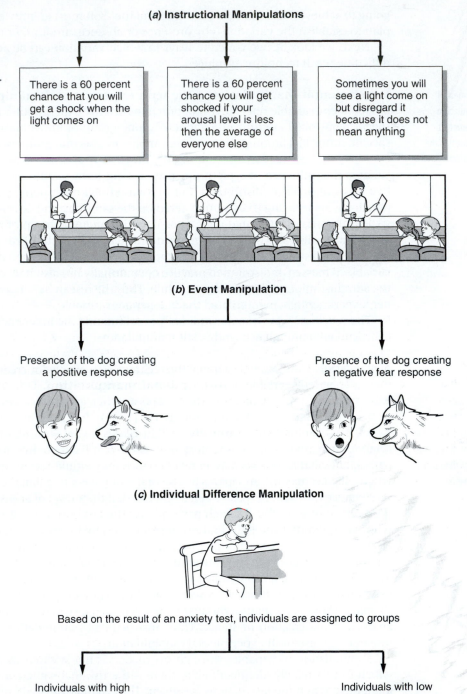

(a) Instructional Manipulations

There is a 60 percent chance that you will get a shock when the light comes on

There is a 60 percent chance you will get shocked if your arousal level is less then the average of everyone else

Sometimes you will see a light come on but disregard it because it does not mean anything

(b) Event Manipulation

Presence of the dog creating a positive response

Presence of the dog creating a negative fear response

(c) Individual Difference Manipulation

Based on the result of an anxiety test, individuals are assigned to groups

Individuals with high test anxiety scores

Individuals with low test anxiety scores

instructions. Some participants may interpret the instructions to mean one thing, and others interpret them in a different way. In this case, an unintentional variation is introduced that represents error, or, actually, an uncontrolled variable. The danger of misinterpretation can be minimized if instructions are kept simple, given emphatically, and related to the activity at hand. Probably no more than one variable should be manipulated through instructions. Manipulation of more than one variable will often result in instructions that are too complex and too long, rendering the manipulations ineffective by virtue of increasing inattentiveness, misinterpretation, and forgetfulness.

Event manipulation
Varying the independent variable by altering the events that participants experience

Manipulation of Events.   A second means of establishing variation in the independent variable is **event manipulation.** Event manipulation involves exposing different individuals to different events. For example, as illustrated in Figure 6.4(*b*), you might vary the level of fear or anxiety of individuals by exposing one group of individuals to a mild-mannered dog and another group of individuals to a ferocious growling dog. In order to investigate the behavioral effects of surgically cutting the corpus callosum, it is necessary either to identify humans who have undergone this surgery for medical reasons or to actually perform this surgery on animals and then subject them to a variety of behavioral tests. Drug research varies such events as drug dosages, and learning experiments vary such events as meaningfulness of the material presented to participants. Most human experiments and almost all animal experiments use event manipulation to achieve variation. Communication skills have been developed in chimpanzees (Fouts, 1973), enabling researchers to use instruction with these primates. When a choice exists between using instructions and events to create the variation, the best choice in most cases is to use events, because events are more realistic and thus have more impact on the participant.

Individual difference manipulation
Varying the independent variable by selecting participants that differ in the amount or type of a measured internal state

Individual Difference Manipulation   **Individual difference manipulation** refers to the situation in which the independent variable is varied by selecting participants that differ in terms of some internal state (for example, self-esteem or anxiety level). The assumption underlying such a manipulation is that each individual possesses a certain amount of a variety of variables, commonly labeled *personality variables.* One efficient means of achieving a manipulation is to select participants having different levels of a given variable (such as anxiety) and then look for effects of the difference. As illustrated in Figure 6.4(*c*), the typical procedure is to administer an instrument measuring the internal state of interest. From the test results, two smaller groups of participants are selected: one group that has scored high on the variable of interest and one group that has scored low. These two groups are required to perform a task, and then the two groups are compared to determine if a difference exists in the task performance. If a difference does exist, it is typically attributed to the differences in the internal states. Ritchie and Phares (1969) were interested in the relationship among internal–external control, communicator status, and attitude change. To examine this relationship, researchers first had to classify research participants as internals or externals, so they administered the Locus of Control Scale to 152 female participants, from whom 42 internals and 42 externals were chosen. The degree of attitude change of these two groups of participants was compared for different levels of communicator status. Results indicated that a high-prestige communicator produces more change in externals than in internals. This result was attributed to the externals' higher expectancy of reinforcement.

What is wrong with such an experiment? It seems to be appropriately designed and statistically analyzable. The difficulty lies in the fact that the states—internal and external control—were not experimentally manipulated. Research participants were not randomly assigned to conditions but were nonrandomly assigned, or selected, on the basis of their test scores. Thus, it is possible that another variable, correlated with the internal and external states, produced the differences in performance. If, in a learning experiment, motivation was highly correlated with tested anxiety, then it would be impossible to determine whether the difference in performance between a high-anxiety and a low-anxiety group was due to the anxiety factor or to motivation. In the Ritchie and Phares study, if some other variable was highly correlated with the participants' locus of control, then, similarly, one could not determine if the observed effect was caused by the perceived locus of control (internal or external) or by the other correlated variable. An experiment that tries to manipulate variables in this way is therefore an ex post facto type of study, even though it may be conducted in a laboratory, with control over other variables. In fairness to Ritchie and Phares, it must be stated that they did manipulate the communicator status variable, so the study they conducted actually did include both an ex post facto component and an experimental component. I should also add that individual difference manipulations are not inherently undesirable. A great deal of high-quality research has been generated through the use of such manipulations. However, you should remain aware of their limitations when using them.

STUDY QUESTION 6.2

- **What are the different ways of varying the independent variable?**
- **Discuss the different ways of establishing variation in the independent variable.**

Constructing the Independent Variable

In addition to deciding how variation in the independent variable is to be achieved, the researcher must also decide how the independent variable is to be constructed or operationally defined. In an experiment, we are trying to determine if the independent variable actually produces the hypothesized effect. In order to test the hypothesis and achieve the necessary variation, we must translate the independent variable into concrete operational terms; in other words, we must specify the exact empirical operations that define the independent variable. If the independent variable represents different learning techniques, then we must operationally define each one of the learning techniques. The ease with which the independent variable is translated into operational terms varies greatly among research problems. For example, if the independent variable consists of a drug, then there is no difficulty in operationally defining the independent variable because a specific empirical referent exists in the form of the drug. All that is needed is to obtain the drug and then to administer different dosages to different groups of research participants. Similarly, if the independent variable consists of either the length of time participants are exposed to various words or the area of a rat's brain that is destroyed, it is simple to translate the independent variables into concrete operations. The only decision that must be made is the length of time the participants should be exposed to the words or the area of the brain that must be destroyed.

Difficulty in translating the independent variable into concrete operational terms arises when the independent variable consists of some abstract construct, such as attitude, frustration, anxiety, learning, or emotional disturbance. The problem stems from the fact that there is no one single definition or empirical referent for such constructs. For example, learning in albino rats could be operationally defined as speed of acquisition, number of trials to extinction, or latency of response. Aggression in some instances may be defined as including "intent to harm," whereas in other instances "intent to harm" may be irrelevant. The scientist's task is to identify the specific empirical referents that correspond to the meaning denoted by the way the construct is used as the independent variable in the research question. For example, if we were investigating the aggressiveness with which women pursue their jobs, the component "intent to harm" would probably not be included in the operational definition of aggressiveness. However, if we were investigating the influence of children's aggressive responses on their popularity, then the empirical referent "intent to harm" probably would be included.

For some types of research, operationally defining a conceptual variable that does not have specific empirical referents is not a major problem because standard agreed-on techniques exist. A study of the effect of schedules of reinforcement on strength of a response requires the construction of the different reinforcement patterns. The schedules of reinforcement identified by Skinner are standard and accepted in the field (the interested student is referred to Ferster and Skinner, 1957). These could immediately be incorporated into the study.

In other areas of research, such as social psychology, difficulty is frequently encountered in constructing conditions that represent a realization of the independent variable specified in the problem. The reason is that relatively few standard techniques exist for manipulating the conceptual variable in such areas. Few of the manipulations of such variables as conformity, commitment, and aggression are identical. Aronson and Carlsmith (1968, p. 40) state that this lack of development of specific techniques is a function of the fact that the variables with which the social psychologist works must be adapted to the particular population with which he or she is working. A standard technique would not work with all populations. Therefore, the researchers must use ingenuity in accomplishing the task, capitalizing on previous work by borrowing ideas and innovations and incorporating them. The problem is that many researchers simply use prior ideas and innovations without creating a better translation of the abstract concept. They "cling to settings and techniques that have been used before" (Ellsworth, 1977). Every translation has had its own quirks and characteristic sources of error, and, as Stevens (1939) has pointed out, each operational definition or translation of an abstract concept represents merely a partial representation of that concept. Therefore, one should not automatically assume that prior translations are the best or even the most appropriate. In fact, in any translation the investigator has to compromise, sacrificing some methodological advantages for others.

Given the problem of translating abstract concepts into operational terms, you should first determine how the topic or phenomenon has been studied in the past. Once that has been determined, you should then decide whether or not any of these translations are appropriate for your study. In making this decision, consider the overall research that has been conducted on the topic. It may be that most prior studies have focused on only a narrow but typical translation of an abstract concept. If this is the case, then it would be appropriate to identify another translation that would help approximate a more complete representation of the concept. For example, fear has typically been studied in the laboratory. However, the range of fear that can be generated in this setting is limited by the ethical restrictions on imposing stimuli that may create extreme fear. Given this situation, it may be more appropriate to search for a setting in which extreme fear is created naturally.

In other areas of research, the problem is not so much *how* the conceptual variable will be translated into specific experimental operations but *which* of the many available techniques will be used. Plutchik (1974) lists eight different techniques (including approach–avoidance conflict and physiological measures) that Miller (1957) identified for either producing or studying fear in animals. If you were to study the conceptual variable of fear in animals, which one should you use? What specific operations will be used to represent this conceptual variable of fear? To answer this question, you have to determine which techniques most adequately represent the variable. This issue is discussed later in the chapter.

Why do several different techniques exist for constructing a single variable such as learning, emotion, or fear? Variables such as fear refer to a general state or condition of the body. Therefore, there is probably no single index that is the way to produce such a concept. Some ways are probably better than others, but no one index can provide complete understanding. To obtain a better understanding of the concept, you should investigate several indexes, even though they may initially seem to give contradictory results. As our knowledge of the idea increases, the initial results that appear to be contradictory will probably be integrated.

Number of Independent Variables

How many independent variables should be used in an experiment? In looking through the literature in any area of psychology, you will find some studies that used only one independent variable and others that used two or more. What criterion dictated the number used in each study? Unfortunately, no rule can be stated to answer this question. We do know that behavior is multidetermined and inclusion of more than one independent variable is often desirable because of the added information it will give. For example, Mellgren, Nation, and Wrather (1975) investigated the relationship between the magnitude of negative reinforcement and schedule of reinforcement for producing resistance to extinction. As predicted, they found that the effect of magnitude of reinforcement was dependent on the schedule of reinforcement used. The participants (albino rats) that were performing under a partial reinforcement schedule revealed greater resistance to extinction when receiving a large negative reinforcer; rats performing under a continuous schedule of reinforcement displayed greater resistance to extinction when receiving a small negative reinforcer.

In other words, the effect of reinforcement magnitude was dependent on the schedule of reinforcement. If the second variable of reinforcement schedule had not been included, the study would probably have revealed, as demonstrated by other studies, that no difference existed between magnitudes of negative reinforcement in terms of the ability to affect resistance to extinction. Inclusion of this variable showed that the magnitude of negative reinforcement did affect resistance to extinction, but its effect depended on the schedule of reinforcement. Experiments like the one conducted by Mellgren et al. reveal the advantage and even the necessity of varying more than one independent variable.

Although theoretically and statistically there is no limit to the number of variables that can be varied, realistically there is. From the research participant's point of view, as the number of variables increases, there are more things to be done, such as participating in more events or taking more tests. The participant is apt to become bored, irritated, or resentful and thereby introduce a confounding variable into the experiment. From the experimenter's point of view, as the number of variables increases, the difficulty in making sense out of the data increases along with the difficulty in setting up the experiment. Aronson and Carlsmith (1968, p. 51) give the following rule of thumb. They say that the experiment "should only be as complex as is necessary for the important relationships to emerge in a clear manner."[1] In other words, do not use the "why not" approach, in which a variable is included in the experiment because there is no real reason not to include it. Only include those variables that seem to be necessary to reveal the important relationships.

STUDY QUESTION 6.3

- **What issues must be considered in operationally defining the independent variable?**
- **Why would you want to include more than one independent variable in a study, and what determines the limit of the number of independent variables that can be included?**

The Dependent Variable

The dependent variable has been defined as the behavioral variable designed to measure the effect of the variation of the independent variable. This definition, like the definition of the independent variable, seems straightforward and simple enough. Also, like the independent variable, the dependent variable is relatively easy to identify in a given study. Aronson and Mills (1959) wanted to investigate the influence of severity of initiation on liking for a group. Liking for a group was the dependent variable. Ritchie and Phares (1969) investigated attitude change as a function of communicator status and locus of control. Attitude change was their dependent variable. However, many decisions must be made to secure the most appropriate measure of the effect of the variation in the independent variable.

[1]Reprinted by special permission from "Experimentation in Social Psychology" by E. Aronson and J. M. Carlsmith, in *The Handbook of Social Psychology*, 2nd edition, volume 2, edited by G. Lindzey and E. Aronson, 1968, p. 51. Reading, Mass.: Addison-Wesley.

A psychological experiment is conducted to answer a question (What is the effect of . . . ?) and to test the corresponding hypothesis (A certain change in *x* will result in a certain change in *y*). In order to answer the question and test the hypothesis, the researcher varies the independent variable to determine whether it produces the desired or hypothesized effect. The experimenter's concern is to make sure that he or she actually obtains an indication of the effect produced by the variation in the independent variable. To accomplish this task, the experimenter must select a dependent variable that will be sensitive to, or able to pick up, the influence exerted by the independent variable. Often, researchers believe that an effect was produced because they think they saw behavioral change exhibited, yet their study indicated that the independent variable produced no effect. Such a case may indicate distorted perception, or it may mean that the dependent variable was not sensitive to the effects produced by the independent variable.

The initial observations of the impact of split-brain surgery on humans are a good example of failing to observe the appropriate dependent variables. It was assumed at first that split-brain surgery left the person unchanged because there seemed to be little alteration in personality or behavior. This conclusion was reached because the dependent variables assessed consisted primarily of observations of individuals performing their daily activities. This assessment revealed that the individuals could continue their normal daily activities with little, if any, apparent change. But when Roger Sperry and others changed the test environment and assessed these participants' responses on a variety of specific dependent variables, they demonstrated that split-brain surgery has a rather significant impact. For example, Zaidel and Sperry (1974) focused on the dependent variable of short-term memory and demonstrated that split-brain participants have a deficiency in this area.

It is the task of the dependent variable to determine whether the independent variable did or did not produce an effect. If an effect was produced, the dependent variable must indicate whether the effect was a facilitating one or an inhibiting one and must reveal the magnitude of this effect. If the dependent variable can accomplish these tasks, the experimenter has identified and used a good, sensitive dependent variable. The first decision for the experimenter, then, is what specific measure to use to assess the effect of the independent variable. In making this decision it is important to consider the gender of the research participants. This is an important issue because the gender of the participants can influence their response to the dependent variable measure. Consider, for example, a study that investigated the influence of siblings on empathy. In this study empathy was the dependent variable and the presence of siblings was the independent variable. Assume further that the operational definition you selected for the dependent variable was a self-report in response to the question "When your best friend is feeling sad, do you feel sad?" A gender bias might arise from the use of such an assessment of the dependent variable because males may be more hesitant than females to report empathic feelings (Matlin, 1993). In such an instance, the dependent variable of empathy does not represent an appropriate assessment of the independent variable (the presence of siblings) for males. Such a biased assessment of the dependent variable would result in data that would lead one to conclude incorrectly that females are more empathic than males, when the truth may be that there are no differences. To demonstrate such a difference, a gender-neutral measure would have to be used—perhaps assessment of people's facial expressions when they looked at a sad movie (Matlin, 1993).

Once the dependent variable has been selected, the experimenter still confronts several problems. The experimenter must somehow ensure that the research participant is taking the measurement seriously and is doing his or her best. The experimenter must also make sure that the research participant is responding in a truthful manner rather than "cooperating" with the experimenter by responding in a manner that he or she feels will be most helpful to the experimenter. The last two problems are most crucial in human experiments.

Response to Be Used as the Dependent Variable

What response should be selected as the dependent variable? We just saw that the foremost criterion for the dependent variable is sensitivity to the effect of the independent variable. To my knowledge, there is no specific rule that will tell you how to select a dependent variable. Psychologists use as dependent variables a wide variety of responses, ranging from questionnaire responses to verbal reports, overt behavior, and physiological responses. The task is to select the response that is the most sensitive to the effect produced by the independent variable. In most experiments, there are several different measures that could be used, and the experimenter must choose among them. For example, attitudes can be measured by a response to a questionnaire, by a physiological response, or by observation of a participant's response.

The difficulty in identifying the most appropriate dependent variable seems to stem from the fact that psychologists study processes, attitudes, or outcomes of the human and infrahuman organism. When an independent variable is introduced, our task is to determine the effect of the independent variable on phenomena such as learning, attitudes, or intelligence. Are these processes, attributes, or outcomes facilitated, inhibited, or affected in some other way? The problem is that the processes, attributes, or outcomes are not directly observable. Because direct observation is not possible, some result of the construct under study that can be observed must be selected for observation to allow inference back to the construct.

Consider learning as an example. It is impossible to study the learning process directly. But if a student sits down and studies certain material for an hour and then can answer questions he or she previously could not, we say that learning has taken place. In this case, learning is inferred from an increase in performance. In such a way, we can acquire information about a phenomenon. The decision that the scientist faces is selecting the aspect or type of response that will provide the best representation of change in the construct as a result of the variation in the independent variable. Previous experimentation can help one make such a decision. Prior research has been conducted on most phenomena, and many dependent variables have been used in these studies. The results of these studies should provide clues to the responses that would be most sensitive.

Aronson and Carlsmith (1968, p. 54) address the problem of selecting the dependent variable with research conducted on humans. They discuss some of the advantages and disadvantages of various techniques that can be used to measure the dependent variable in social psychological research. One very significant point they make is that the more commitment demanded of the participant by the dependent variable, the greater the degree of confidence we can have in the results of our experiment. Why is this so? First, making a commitment to a course of action reduces the probability of faking on the part of the participant because it helps to ensure that participants take the dependent variable measure seriously. If we wanted to find out which person in a group is most liked by a particular individual, we could have that individual rate each of the group members on a liking rating scale. Or we could have him or her choose a member of the group as a roommate for the next year, with the contingency that the person picked will in fact be the roommate. In this case, if the request were credible, the participant would be motivated to respond truthfully, because he or she would have to live with the decision. The second advantage of requiring the participant to make a commitment is that it often increases one's confidence that the dependent variable of interest is really being measured. Recording the frequency with which fights are initiated is a better index of aggression than having a participant verbally state that he or she is angry or evaluate the degree of anger on a rating scale.

Behavior that involves a commitment is probably the best type of dependent variable to use. But because of cost, time, or some other constraint, sometimes it is not feasible to use such a dependent variable. In that case, a questionnaire or a verbal report must be used instead. Although questionnaires and verbal reports yield a great deal of useful data, there is an increased likelihood of error with these measures, because the participants either may not take the measure seriously or may "cooperate" with the experimenter by producing the results they think the experimenter desires.

Reducing Participant Error

Once a decision has been made as to what the dependent variable will be, the experimenter using human research participants must make sure that the participant is taking the measure seriously and not trying to fake the responses. The difficulty of this task increases as the degree of commitment decreases. For example, in filling out a questionnaire, some participants will undoubtedly race through it, reading questions in a haphazard manner and checking off answers without putting much thought into them. One way of decreasing such errors is to disguise the measure of the dependent variable. In addition to increasing the likelihood that the participant takes the measure seriously, the disguise also helps guard against the possibility that the participant will cooperate with the experimenter.

Aronson and Carlsmith (1968, p. 58) present a number of techniques useful for disguising the dependent variable. One technique is to assess the dependent variable outside the context of the experiment. Carlsmith, Collins, and Helmreich (1966) solicited the aid of a consumer research analyst to assess the dependent variable after the participant had supposedly completed the experiment and left the room. Another technique is to assess behavior of significance to the participant, such as the selection of a roommate. A third technique is to construct the experiment in such a way that the participant does not realize that the dependent variable is being observed. Lefkowitz, Blake, and Mouton (1955) observed the frequency with which people jaywalked or disobeyed signs upon introduction of various levels of an independent variable. A fourth method that is often used in attitude-change experiments is to embed key items in a larger questionnaire in hopes that the key items will not be recognized and falsely reported on. A similar technique is to disguise the reason for interest in a particular dependent variable. Aronson (1961) was interested in finding out whether the attractiveness of several colors varied as the effort expended in getting them varied. For this study, he needed a measure of attractiveness. When he asked the participants to rate the attractiveness of colors, he told them that he was investigating a relationship between color preference and a person's performance. Using unsuspicious participants such as young children is also a very good way to reduce or eliminate cooperation. Young children are very straightforward and do not have devious motives. A sixth technique is to use what Aronson and Carlsmith call the family of "whoops" procedures. The typical procedure is to collect pretest data and then claim that something happened to them so that posttest data can be collected. Christensen (1968) used this method in collecting test–retest reliability data on ratings of a series of concepts. A seventh procedure is to have a confederate collect the data. Karhan (1973) had the learner, a member of the experiment who had supposedly received electric shock for errors made, make a request of the research participant. The dependent variable was the participant's response to the confederate's request. Another technique is to use a physiological measure that is presumable not under the participant's conscious control. However, a number of individuals have presented data indicating that these measures may be consciously influenced by the research participant.

Number of Dependent Variables

Should more than one dependent variable be used in a psychological experiment? This is a very reasonable question, particularly when more than one dependent variable could be used to measure the effect of variation of a given independent variable. In a learning experiment using rats, the dependent variable could be the frequency, amplitude, or latency of response. Likewise, in an attitude experiment, the dependent variable could be measured by a questionnaire, by observing behavior, or by a physiological measure. When more than one dependent variable can be used, the scientist usually selects only one and proceeds with the experiment. If the scientist elects to use more than one dependent variable, certain problems arise. Assuming the scientist knows how to measure each of the dependent variables, he or she must be concerned with the relationship among them. If the various dependent variable measures are very highly correlated (for example, 0.95 or above), there is reasonable assurance that they are identical measures, and all but one can be dropped. If they are not so highly correlated, the experimenter must ask why not. The lack of correspondence could be due to unreliability of the measures or to the fact that they are not measuring the same aspect of the construct under study. Two different measures of learning may evaluate different aspects of the learning process. These difficulties must be resolved, but all too often the scientist does not have the necessary data. As a field advances, more and more of the aspects of a phenomenon are unraveled and problems such as these are resolved. Such cases support the notion that multiple dependent variables should be used in some experiments because they contribute to the understanding of a phenomenon, which is the goal of science.

The fact that the constructs we are attempting to measure, such as learning or anxiety, can be measured by several different techniques indicates that they are multidimensional. In order to get a good grasp of the effect that our independent variable has on our multidimensional dependent variable, we must use several different measures. Multidimensional statistical procedures have been developed to handle the simultaneous use of several dependent variables in the same study. When several independent variables and several dependent variables are manipulated in one experiment, a more elaborate statistical technique called *multivariate analysis of variance* must be used to analyze the results. This approach allows us to take the correlation between the dependent variables into account (Kerlinger and Pedhazur, 1973). Analyzing each dependent variable separately would violate one of the underlying assumptions of the statistical test if a correlation did exist between the different dependent variable measures. Using several dependent variables in a study and appropriately analyzing them can, therefore, increase our knowledge of the complex relationship that exists between antecedent conditions and behavior.

STUDY QUESTION 6.4
- **What is the primary purpose of the dependent variable?**
- **What criterion should be used in selecting the dependent variable?**
- **What can be done to ensure that participants are responding seriously to the dependent variable?**
- **Why would you want to use more than one dependent variable in a study?**

Summary

In seeking an answer to a research question, one must develop a design that will provide the necessary information. Two primary ingredients in a research design are the independent and dependent variables. Before the research design can be finalized, it is necessary to make a number of decisions about these two variables.

For the independent variable, the investigator must first specify not only the number of independent variables to be used but also the exact concrete operations that will represent the conceptual variable or variables. For some independent variables, this is easy because specific empirical referents exist; others, however, are not so easily translated. In either case, the conceptual independent variable must be operationally defined. In addition to translating the independent variable, the investigator must also specify how variation is to be established in the independent variable. Generally, variation is created by a presence-versus-absence technique or by varying the amount or type of the independent variable. The investigator must determine, within the framework of one of these techniques, the exact mode for creating the variation. Will the variation be created by manipulating instructions or events or by measuring the internal states of the organism?

In addition to making decisions about the independent variable, we must make decisions about the dependent variable. The investigator must select a dependent variable that is sensitive to the effect of the independent variable. This is a difficult process because, in most instances, there are many dependent variable measures that could be selected and no one measure is a perfectly accurate measure because the outcomes we are interested in are processes or constructs. In selecting the dependent variable, we must be concerned with ensuring that the participants are taking the measure seriously and we must decide on the number of dependent variable measures to use because some constructs are more accurately measured using several dependent variables.

Key Terms and Concepts

Variable	Quantitative variable
Independent variable	Experimental manipulation
Dependent variable	Instructional manipulation
Discrete variable	Event manipulation
Continuous variable	Individual difference manipulation
Qualitative variable	

Related Internet Sites

www.wadsworth.com/psychology_d/templates/student_resources/workshops/workshops.html
This site contains a variety of workshops focusing on research methods. The one that contains material relevant to this chapter is The Experimental Method (Independent and Dependent Variables).

www.parmly.luc.edu/hearing/ExpMethod.htm
This site provides a definition of the independent and dependent variables and gives an exercise to illustrate each of these variables.

Practice Test

The answers to these questions can be found in Appendix A.

1. If you manipulate the independent variable by giving one group of research participants an impossible task and another group of research participants a task that is relatively easy to complete, you have manipulated the independent variable by

   a. The presence-versus-absence technique
   b. The amount of the independent variable administered
   c. An individual difference manipulation
   d. An event manipulation
   e. An instructional manipulation

2. What criterion should be used when selecting the dependent variable?

   a. You should select a behavior and not a mentalistic concept.
   b. You should select a response measure that is sensitive to the effect of the independent variable.

    c. You should select a response that cannot be faked by the research participants.

    d. You should select a response that has face validity.

    e. You should select an uncomplicated response.

3. Dr. Nutrition wanted to find out if carbohydrate cravers exhibit a greater degree of obsessive-compulsive behavior than do non-carbohydrate cravers. So he identified a group of carbohydrate cravers and non-cravers and then administered the SCL-90 to all of these individuals and scored the obsessive-compulsive scale of the SCL-90. When comparing the cravers to the non-cravers, he found that the cravers scored significantly higher than the non-cravers on this scale. In this study the obsessive-compulsive scale of the SCL-90 was the _____ and craving for carbohydrates was the _____.

    a. Independent variable; dependent variable

    b. Discrete variable; continuous variable

    c. Quantitative variable; continuous variable

    d. Dependent variable; independent variable

    e. Experimental variable; descriptive variable

4. Which of the following variables would create the greatest amount of difficulty when translating into concrete operational terms?

    a. Drug amount

    b. Amount of violence demonstrated

    c. Time taken to perform a task

    d. Weight loss

    e. Temperature decline in a biofeedback task

5. How many independent variables should be used in a study?

    a. However many are needed to reveal the important relationships

    b. No more than two because of the difficulty in interpretation

    c. As many as can be used to identify the complex human relationships

    d. At least four to have a valid study

Challenge Exercise

1. For each of the following research examples, identify

    a. The independent variable

    b. The levels of the independent variable

    c. The method used to manipulate the independent variable

    d. The dependent variable

    A. Asch (1952) conducted an experiment in which he wanted to determine if a person's impression of another individual is influenced more by information they receive immediately after being introduced or by information they receive later in the conversation. Asch presented a series of positive and negative adjectives to two groups of individuals. One group received the positive adjectives first and the other group received the negative adjectives first. After reading both lists of adjectives, each group gave their impression of the hypothetical person.

B. A study was conducted to determine if men think the women in a bar get more attractive as closing time approaches. This was a field study in which the researcher asked patrons of the bar to evaluate the attractiveness of various women in the bar at four different times in the evening, with the last evaluation being ten minutes prior to closing.

C. Benbow and Stanley (1980) wanted to find out if gender could be used in trying to differentiate mathematical ability, so they compared the test scores on the mathematics portion of the SAT of 9,927 seventh- and eighth-grade boys and girls. In this study, they used only the scores of boys and girls who had the same number of mathematics courses. When they compared the SAT mathematics test scores of the boys and girls, they found that the boys scored significantly higher than the girls. In addition, they found that more than 50 percent of the boys scored above 600, whereas none of the girls scored that high.

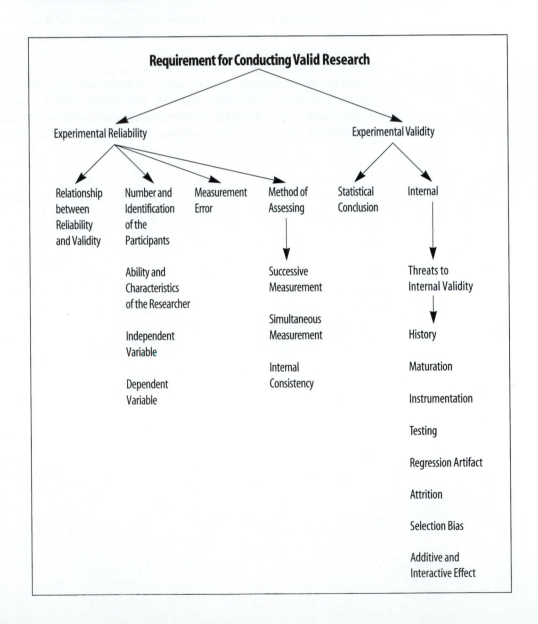

7   Reliability and Validity in Experimental Research

Requirement for Conducting Valid Research

Experimental Reliability

Experimental Validity

Relationship between Reliability and Validity

Number and Identification of the Participants

Measurement Error

Method of Assessing

Statistical Conclusion

Internal

Ability and Characteristics of the Researcher

Independent Variable

Dependent Variable

Successive Measurement

Simultaneous Measurement

Internal Consistency

Threats to Internal Validity

History

Maturation

Instrumentation

Testing

Regression Artifact

Attrition

Selection Bias

Additive and Interactive Effect

Jacqueline Gavagan was one of those fortunate individuals who seemed to have the perfect life. She had a satisfying profession as a speech pathologist, a loving husband, and two healthy young children with a third due in seven weeks. On September 11, 2001, her world came tumbling down. Jacqueline's husband was a bond broker working in the World Trade Center on that fatal morning when terrorists crashed hijacked planes into the north and south towers. By midmorning, Jacqueline's husband and many of their closest friends were entombed in a million tons of burning rubble.

The trauma of a loss such as this causes one to grieve and experience feelings of anger, fear, guilt, hopelessness, and chronic fear. For some individuals, these emotions continue for years. Others, such as Jacqueline Gavagan, are much more resilient. Did Gavagan grieve? Of course she did and still does. However, some individuals have the ability to bounce back from even the most severe setbacks. In the year after Jacqueline's husband was killed, she managed to restore meaning and even some joy to her life. She began this effort by starting a fund in her husband's name that might save a child's life. Earlier that year, surgeons at NYU Medical Center had successfully repaired a defect in her toddler's heart and she wanted to sponsor similar operations for families that couldn't afford it. Through her efforts, the money flowed in and by April 2002 sufficient funds had been donated to allow her to sponsor a similar operation for the son of a woman from Kosovo (Cowley, 2002).

Psychologists have for years expended most of their time and research effort on understanding illness and developing treatments for disorders, including individuals who have experienced traumatic events such as that experienced by Gavagan. In doing so they have neglected a focus on the other side of the spectrum. It was not until the 1990s that a movement was initiated to direct attention to studying positive emotions such as optimism and contentment and why some individuals are so resilient in the face of adversity. This new emphasis has attracted the attention of many psychologists who are uncovering interesting findings, such as that there seems to be a large genetic component in one's mood and temperament and that the circumstances in life have little to do with the satisfaction we experience. Health, wealth, good looks, and status seem to have little effect on what researchers call *subjective well-being*. For example, although people living in extreme poverty are, on average, less happy than those whose basic needs are met, once they cross over that threshold to security the greater wealth they possess does not contribute to making their life more satisfying.

So what does contribute to happiness? According to Martin Seligman (2002), happiness is not about managing our moods but about outgrowing our concern with how we feel. We need to have some gratification and fulfillment that comes from developing one's strengths and putting them to positive use, as Jacqueline Gavagan did in developing the fund to assist families with children in need of heart surgery.

Where did we gain this interesting knowledge about positive psychology? Obviously we gained it from the efforts of research psychologists who have conducted valid research studies. The key here is that the studies were valid. It is only when valid research studies are conducted that we can reach firm conclusions and believe the results.

Chapter Preview

The opening vignette to this chapter describes an interesting line of research on positive psychology that has attracted the attention of many research psychologists. These individuals have focused their attention on why some individuals maintain their optimism and positive outlook even in the face of adversity, whereas others experience depression, guilt, and feelings of hopelessness. These studies have yielded some interesting findings and may contribute to identifying ways in which people can increase the probability of their feeling happy. However, the research that is conducted must be valid for it to yield useful findings. A valid research study is one that produces results that are both reliable and valid. These are two very important concepts that permeate all components of a research study. In this chapter I will discuss the concepts of reliability and validity as they relate to the psychology experiment.

Introduction

Reliability
The consistency, stability, or repeatability of a behavior

Experimental reliability
The consistency, stability, or repeatability of the results of an experimental study

Validity
The correctness or truthfulness of an inference

Reliability refers to consistency, stability, or repeatability. **Experimental reliability** refers to the consistency, stability, or repeatability of the results of an experimental study. An experimental study is reliable if it always gave the same results regardless of when it was conducted. For example, one of my graduate students and I (Christensen and Brooks, in press) investigated the relationship between mood state and consumption of food and found that when females are experiencing something distressing, such as finding out that their boyfriend cheated on them, they increase their consumption of carbohydrate-rich foods. The results of this study are reliability if I would get the same results if I repeated or replicated the study. Reliability of research studies relates to the ability to replicate the results of a study. If the study results can be replicated then evidence exists that the results are reliable because when they are reliable they are repeatable.

It is important to recognize that experimental reliability says absolutely nothing about the conclusions or inferences that can be made from the results of a study. This is where the concept of validity comes in. All reliability states is that the results obtained are repeatable.

Validity refers to the correctness or truth of an inference. **Experimental validity** refers to the correctness or truthfulness of an inference that is made from the results of an experiment. For example, the field of comparative or evolutionary psychology has asked a number of very broad and significant questions such as "What does it mean to be human?" and "What characteristics appear to be uniquely human?" (Povinelli & Bering, 2002, p. 115). Researchers have then conducted many

Experimental validity
The correctness or truthfulness of an inference that is made from the results of an experiment

experiments to try to answer these questions. From the results of many of these experiments, Suddendorf and Whiten concluded that "the gap between human and animal mind has been narrowed" (2001, p. 644). De Waal has stated that the chimpanzee is "inching closer to humanity" (1999, p. 635). Statements such as these are inferences that are made from empirical data collected in the research studies. Validity asks the question: Are these inferences accurate and correct? Validity, therefore, is a property of inferences. This is the important point you need to keep in mind. Experimental validity is not something inherent in a research design, in a test, or a method. It is concerned only with the accuracy of the inferences we make from some type of evidence. The evidence researchers use is their research studies.

Relationship between Reliability and Validity

The two prerequisites needed for conducting valid experimental research are reliability and validity. The relationship between the two prerequisites is a one-way street in that experimental reliability must exist for experimental validity to exist. However, a study can have experimental reliability without having experimental validity. To illustrate this one-way relationship between reliability and validity, consider the speedometer on your car. When the car comes from the factory, the speedometer is calibrated so that the speed recorded on the speedometer is accurate or valid. This means that you can make the correct inference that you are going 50 mph when the speedometer says you are traveling that fast. To make such a correct inference the speedometer must be reliable and valid. This means that it must consistently (reliability) record 50 mph when you are going 50 mph (validity).

Now assume that you put larger tires on the car than were called for by the car manufacturer. Putting larger tires on the car would cause the speedometer to read lower than the car was actually traveling. The speedometer would record that you were traveling at, say, 60 mph when you were actually going 62 mph. This means that you would make an invalid or inaccurate inference if you said you were going 60 mph because that is what the speedometer read. However, the reading of 60 mph would be very reliable in that every time the car was traveling at 62 mph the speedometer would read 60 mph. It just would not be an accurate or valid indication of your actual speed. As you should be able to see, just because a measure is reliable doesn't mean that it is valid. Reliability does not indicate validity.

Validity or making a correct inference, however, does require reliability. Every time the car is traveling at 60 mph the speedometer must record 60 mph for you to make a valid or correct inference that the car is traveling at 60 mph. If the speedometer reading is unreliable it will sometimes record speeds greater than 60 mph and sometimes less than 60 mph when the car is actually going 60 mph. In such instances you would make an incorrect inference every time the speedometer recorded a speed other than 60 mph.

When conducting psychological research we investigate many different constructs such as attitudes, stress, depression, and learning. To conduct a study investigating such psychological constructs requires that we measure these constructs. These measures must be both reliable and valid to be able to make a valid inference from the study results just as the speedometer in your car must be reliable and valid to make a correct inference about the speed you are traveling.

- **What is meant by reliability and validity?**
- **What is the difference between experimental reliability and experimental validity?**
- **What is the relationship between reliability and validity?**

Experimental Reliability

How can you construct a study in which you maximize the probability that the results are reliable or repeatable? To conduct a study that produces reliable results, all the various components of the study must be reliable. The components I am talking about are the number of participants taking part in the study and the identification of these participants, the ability and characteristics of the researcher, and the independent and dependent variables.

Reliability and the Number and Identification of the Participants

The reliability of the results of any study is partially dependent on the number of participants that are included. Generally speaking, the more participants included in a study the more confidence we have in the results. By confidence I mean that the results are reliable or that we would get the same results if we repeated the study. For example, assume that you wanted to identify the percentage of people on your campus who were bulimic, so you randomly selected two individuals from the campus phone book and called them. If both of them told you they were bulimic, I don't think that you would conclude that everyone on campus was bulimic. However, if you randomly selected and called 1,000 people and found out that 10 percent of them stated that they were bulimic, you could be more confident in concluding that about 10 percent of the students on your campus were bulimic. Using a larger number of participants gives more confidence because the results would be less likely to be influenced by random or chance factors. This means that the results would be more reliable.

In addition to having a sufficient number of participants to ensure the reliability of the results, it is also necessary to be able to reliably identify the type of participant investigated in the study. Any human psychological study that is conducted makes use of a certain type of participant. Many studies, because of the particular research problem being investigated, require the identification of participants with certain characteristics such as depression, an eating disorder, Alzheimer's, schizophrenia, or impoverishment. To identify the participants for a given study, the investigator selects one or more indices as indicators of the type of person that should be included in the study. For example, if a depression study was conducted, you might use a score of 25 or above on the Beck Depression Inventory as an indicator of a depressed person and select for your study anyone that scores above 25 on this psychological inventory. Reliability of the participant sample would exist if the indicators used in the selection of the sample select people with the same characteristics whenever they are used. For example, if everyone making a score of 25 or above on the Beck Depression Inventory was depressed, then you could use this index to select a sample of depressed individuals. In other words, you could reliably select a sample of individuals with the same characteristics regardless of when the study was conducted. If this has been accomplished, you have a reliable means for selecting a participant sample. Remember, however, that reliability says nothing about the type of characteristics a person has. Selecting people with a score of 25 or above on the Beck Depression Inventory may result in selecting depressed individuals; however, it may also result in selecting individuals with high anxiety levels—some who may be depressed and some who may not. Reliability addresses only the consistency with which people with certain characteristics can be identified. It says nothing about the nature of these characteristics.

Reliability and the Ability and Characteristics of the Researcher

The reliability or consistency of the data collected in any study is partially dependent on the ability as well as the characteristics of the researcher. Let's take a look at the characteristics of the researcher first. Assume that you are a male and are participating in a study investigating the effect of sleep deprivation on heart rate. Also assume that the researcher is an attractive blond who has to touch you to connect you to the equipment that will measure your heart rate. What effect do you think this might have on your heart rate? I suspect that it would increase. Now consider another situation where the researcher is a male doing the same thing. What effect do you think the male will have on your heart rate? Very little I would predict. From this example, you should be able to see that the characteristics of the experimenter can influence the data that is collected and this differential influence must be eliminated to collect reliable data. One way of maximizing the probability of collecting reliable data is to make sure that the same researcher collects the data from all participants. Then whatever influence the researcher has will be the same for every participant. Also, to ensure experimental reliability, researchers with the same characteristics should be employed in any replication study.

The ability of the researcher can also influence experimental reliability. If a researcher does not use the same procedure when collecting data from all participants, reliable data will not be obtained. To provide a more concrete illustration, assume that you were conducting an EEG experiment. To conduct this type of study, you must place electrodes on the scalp of the participant and ensure that you are getting good recordings prior to collecting the data. It takes some skill and training to be able to connect the electrodes properly to get "good" data. If you do not have the proper training in connecting the electrodes and in collecting the data once the electrodes are connected, you will get data that is contaminated in a variety of ways. As the degree of contamination increases the data that is collected will vary. Therefore, as the degree of contamination increases, the data becomes less consistent or more unreliable. This is why considerable emphasis is given to ensuring that the person collecting the data is well trained to insure that good data is collected and collected in the same manner from all participants.

Reliability and the Independent Variable

The independent variable is the variable that is manipulated by the experimenter. It is also the variable that is supposed to create some psychological state or phenomenon through a set of concrete operations. For example, if your study required that you create different mood states in individuals you might use the set of concrete operations specified by Velten (1968). The concrete operations involved in the Velten (1968) mood induction procedure involve having the research participant read a set of statements (e.g., you have nothing to live for) and to feel and place themselves in that situation. This procedure has been used to create a depressed or elated mood state depending on the set of statements read. If this set of concrete operations produces a similar mood state every time it is applied then we have a reliable independent variable. Note that reliability says nothing about the nature of the mood state induced. It only addresses the consistency of whatever mood state is created. For example, if participants reading the depressive statements experience about the same level of depression every time the mood induction procedure is applied, the procedure produces a reliable independent variable effect. If the procedure produces severe depression sometimes, mild depression at other times, and no depression at yet other times, then an unreliable independent variable effect is produced. Reliability of the independent variable, therefore, pertains to the consistency with which a psychological construct, such as mood, is created in the participants. If the operations used to create the different levels of the independent variable are not reliable then we need a different and better set of operations.

Reliability and the Dependent Variable

The dependent variable is the variable that measures the effect of the independent variable. If the effect measured by the dependent variable is about the same every time it is measured, the dependent variable is reliable. For example, assume you wanted to assess the effect of different mood states on the score a person makes on the ACT. The dependent variable, or ACT in this example, would be reliable if it produced repeatable results. If you participated in this study on three different occasions and got a score of exactly 24 on the ACT on each of the three testing occasions, you would have perfectly reliability results because the outcome was the same every time you took the ACT. However, we never get such perfect repeatability. A more realistic outcome would be scores of 24, 25, and 22, on the three testing occasions. Although these scores are not identical, they are very similar and this similarity still represents consistency or reliability. It is only when the scores are very dissimilar, for example, as if they were 9, 38, and 22, that they are considered unreliable. Any measure of behavior is never perfectly reliable. There is always some inconsistency in the results. This inconsistency is due to measurement error.

Measurement Error

Measurement error
The inaccuracy that exists when measuring a psychological characteristic or behavior

Measurement error refers to the inaccuracy that is introduced into the measurement of a behavior. There are a multitude of factors that could cause measurement error such as fatigue, a car accident, or being emotionally upset. Factors such as these cause us to respond differently on different occasions. For example, if you participated in an experiment on bystander intervention when you were fatigued, you might take longer to intervene than if you had participated when you were well rested.

Reliability is directly related to the amount of measurement error. As measurement error is reduced reliability increases, and as measurement error increases reliability decreases. Every measurement is a combination of a true score plus an error score. For example, if it took you six seconds to intervene in an emergency, part of that score would be your true score of the length of time to intervention and another part would be the error due to variables such as fatigue or having other things on your mind. How much is error is not known. However, if you get similar scores on repeated assessments, such as the following:

5 seconds, 7 seconds, 6 seconds, 8 seconds, 7.5 seconds

you can assume that most of the score represents your true score because the scores are very similar. However, if the following scores were obtained

5 seconds, 12 seconds, 3 seconds, 18 seconds, 10 seconds

you can see that the variability is much greater, indicating more measurement error and less reliability. The ideal situation is for the error score to be very small so that most of what we measure is a person's true score.

Although the issue of reliability is very important in ensuring that we have good measures of behavior, calculating the reliability of our behavioral measures is seldom done in experimental research. This is because most experiments are conducted as single-occasion events. This means that the behavior of interest in the experiment is measured only once. According to Epstein (1981), if reliability could be measured, low reliability (usually less than 0.30) would exist for a variety of measures including self-ratings, other ratings, behavioral responses, personality test results, and physiological responses. However, as shown in Figure 7.1, Epstein (1979) found that the stability of each of these responses increased as they were averaged over several days. In other words, the reliability of the responses increased as the responses were aggregated over time. The lowest reliability existed when reliability was assessed by

FIGURE 7.1

Reliability coefficients as a function of the number of days.

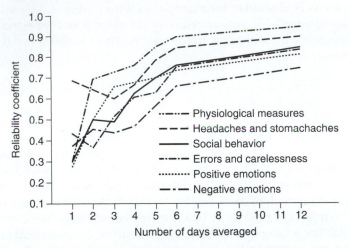

(From "The Stability of Behavior: I. On Predicting Most of the People Much of the Time" by S. Epstein, 1979, *Journal of Personality and Social Psychology, 37,* pp. 1097–1126. Copyright 1979 by the American Psychological Association. Reprinted by permission of the author.)

correlating the responses obtained on one day with those obtained a second day. When reliability was assessed by correlating the average response obtained over one twelve-day period with the average response obtained over another twelve-day period, excellent reliability was found to exist.

Such evidence strongly suggests that most behaviors measured in the traditional single-occasion experiment are unreliable. This in turn means that the results obtained from our single-session studies do not produce stable findings and are therefore suspect. Where does this leave us? The results of Epstein's study indicate that, for our findings to be reliable, we must repeat each experiment a number of times and then use the average response as our dependent variable. Many studies cannot be repeated on the same group of research participants, however, because the repetition would alter the participants' responses. So in many instances we are locked into the single-occasion experiment. Although Epstein's study strongly suggests that a single study, by itself, should not be given much credence, replication of the results of single-occasion studies provides a good measure of the reliability of our measures because replication of an effect cannot be attained if the dependent variable measure is unreliable. Thus, the results from any one study should not be considered seriously except as those results contribute to a population of studies; it is the results from such a population of studies that give us reliable information.

STUDY QUESTION 7.2

- **What do you need to do to maximize the probability that a study has experimental reliability?**
- **Why is experimental reliability dependent on having a sufficient number of people in the study and being able to identify the participants' need for the study?**
- **How can the ability and characteristics of the researcher affect experimental reliability?**
- **Why is it necessary to have a reliable independent and dependent variable to have experimental reliability?**
- **What is measurement error and how does it influence reliability?**

Methods of Assessing Reliability

While most experiments are single-occasion events and do not make allowance for the assessment of reliability, we could and do assess the reliability of many of the components of any experimental study.

I have defined reliability as referring to consistency or stability and experimental reliability as consistency or the ability to replicate the results of an experiment. Assessing experimental reliability is a rather straightforward process of determining if the results of an experiment can be duplicated or replicated. However, I also discussed the many different components of an experiment that also must be reliable for the experimental results to be reliable. Psychological researchers make use of psychological tests, electronic equipment, surveys, questionnaires, and observations to identify the participant sample, to administer the independent variable and to provide a measure of the dependent variable. For example, there are psychological tests that have been constructed to measure constructs such as personality, intelligence, attitudes, eating disorders, pathology, and cognitive styles, all of which could be used for either identifying a participant sample or as a measure of the dependent variable. All of the psychological tests as well as the electronic equipment that is used within the context of the psychological experiment must be reliable to have an experiment that produces reliable results. There are several specific ways that have been used to assess reliability. I will provide a brief description of each of these.

Successive Measurement

Successive measurement
Assessing reliability by comparing the data obtained from the same group of individuals on two successive measurements

Successive measurement assesses reliability by comparing the data obtained from the same group of individuals on two successive measurements using the same procedure. There are actually two ways in which you could obtain an index of reliability using successive measurements. The first is **test–retest reliability** which involves comparing the scores obtained from the same group of individuals who are measured on two different occasions. They take the test or measurement once and then again after a time interval has elapsed (e.g., one month). If the scores on the two testing occasions are very similar, then the test or measurement is reliable. If they are very different, then the test or measurement is unreliable. Reliability is typically computed by calculating a statistical technique called a *correlation* that gives a quantitative index of the consistency of the two sets of scores.

A second way of obtaining an index of reliability using successive measurement is equivalent forms. **Equivalent forms** assess reliability by comparing the consistency of the data obtained from people who have been measured on two equivalent forms of the same measurement. The individuals take both forms, measuring the same thing on the same occasion and then the data from the two measurements are compared. Because both forms of the measurement were constructed to be equivalent, they should yield similar results. If they do, then evidence exists that the measurements are reliable. The difficulty with this method is developing two forms that are truly equivalent measures.

Simultaneous Measurement

Simultaneous measurement assesses reliability by comparing the data obtained from at least two simultaneous measures of the same behavior. For example, Woods et al. (2004) had six neuropsychologists independently provide ratings of neuropsychological impairment of 30 individuals with advanced HIV-infection to assess the reliability of the clinical rating of the extent of their impairment. When two or more people are assessed on the same behavior, we want consistency among the raters. This study found excellent consistency or reliability among the six individual ratings of the presence and severity of neuropsychological impairment. This means that the same results would have been obtained regardless of which individual provided the ratings.

There are two general ways of assessing reliability using the simultaneous measurement method, interrater reliability and interobserver agreement. **Interrater reliability** involves assessing the consistency of ratings made by different observers. If different observers give the same or similar ratings, then interrater reliability exists. This is the type of reliability used in the Woods et al. (2004) study and should be used any time behavior is assessed by means of some type of rating. **Interobserver agreement** involves assessing the percentage of times raters agree. For example, you might have two individuals observe children and record the incidence of violent behavior. Each observer would record a child's behavior as being either violent or not violent. The measure of reliability would be the percentage of time, e.g., 92 percent or 95 percent, that the two observers agreed. Calculating reliability using the interobserver agreement method is, therefore, simple to calculate and understand.

Internal Consistency

Internal consistency refers to the consistency with which test items provide a measure of the intended construct. For example, psychological research is conducted on constructs such as learning, shyness, love or any of various personality dimensions such as dominance or extraversion. To obtain a measure of these constructs, we typically devise a test or scale composed of a variety of items. No single item is assumed to be able to provide a sufficient measure of the construct, so many items are constructed—each of which are assumed to contribute to the measure of the construct. For example, when you are tested on the material in this book, your instructor devises a test composed of many items that are assumed to contribute to the measure of the extent to which you have learned the material. If it is true that all items making up the test contribute to the measure of a specific construct, then there should be some consistency between these items or the items should be internally consistent. One measure of the internal consistency of a test or scale is the split-half method. The **split-half** method assesses internal consistency reliability by dividing the test items into two equal halves. Each half is then scored and the results from the two halves are compared. If equivalent results are obtained from each half, then the test is assumed to be reliable. Although this method is useful, the assessment of reliability is affected by the reduction in length. Reliability is affected by the length of the test—as the test gets longer it becomes more reliable. Consequently, the split-half method artificially reduces the estimate of the reliability of the test because its length is reduced. This deficiency can be overcome with a statistical correction.

| **Spit-half**
| The consistency with
| which each half of a
| test measures a
| construct

One drawback to the use of the split-half method is that the reliability coefficient obtained depends on how the items comprising the test are split. The typical manner is to do an odd-even split or have the odd numbered items represent one-half of the test and the even numbered items represent the other half of the test. However, the test items could be split in many other ways—such as randomly splitting them. The scores obtained from the two halves of the test would partially depend on the items comprising each half of the test, so the reliability estimate would also depend on the way the items were split. One way to get around this problem is to compute Cronbach's alpha. **Cronbach's alpha** computes a reliability coefficient that is equivalent to the average of all possible split-half reliability estimates. This is a coefficient that can be calculated directly from a formula which is easily done with the use of a computer. Cronbach's alpha is a more accurate estimate of internal consistency so it is more frequently used.

| **Cronbach's alpha**
| A measure of internal
| consistency that is the
| average of all possible
| split-half reliability
| estimates

STUDY QUESTION 7.3

- **Identify and define the three ways of assessing reliability.**
- **What is the difference between test–retest reliability and equivalent forms reliability?**
- **What is the difference between interrater and interobserver reliability?**
- **How is reliability computed using the split-half method and how is Cronbach's alpha related to the split-half method?**

Experimental Validity

Earlier in this chapter I defined experimental validity as referring to the correctness or truthfulness of an inference that is made from the results of an experiment.

Because the validity of the inferences we make is a function of empirical data we collect in a research study, we must make sure that the study's empirical findings are as accurate and truthful as possible. The best way to ensure that a research study yields empirical findings from which accurate inferences can be made is to try to

TABLE 7.1
Types of Validity in Experimental Research

Validity Types	Description
Statistical conclusion validity	Validity of the inference made about whether the independent and dependent variables covary
Internal validity	Validity of the inference that the independent and dependent variables are causally related
Construct validity	Validity of the inference about the higher-order constructs from the operations used to represent them
External validity	Validity of the inference about whether the causal relationship holds over people, settings, treatment variables, measurement variables, and time

ensure that the study has the four types of validity listed in Table 7.1 (Shadish et al., 2002) because they are so important to collecting data from which valid inferences can be made. However, do not think that you must or can achieve all four types of validity in any one study. Any single study will do a good job achieving only some of these types of validity. This is because we cannot incorporate all the methods and procedures that would enable us to simultaneously achieve all four types of validity and, frequently, incorporating a method to achieve one type of validity reduces our chances of achieving another type of validity. This seems to be particularly true for internal and external validity.

In this chapter I will discuss statistical conclusion and internal validity. Construct and external validity will be covered in Chapter 8.

Statistical Conclusion Validity

Statistical conclusion validity
The validity of inferences made about the covariation of the independent and dependent variables

Statistical conclusion validity refers to the validity with which we can infer that the independent and dependent variables covary. By *covary* I mean that with every variation in the independent variable there is a corresponding variation in the dependent variable. We make this inference about covariation from the results of the statistical analysis computed on the data collected in our experiment. Statistical conclusion validity, therefore, is concerned with the extent to which accurate inferences or conclusions are made from the statistical analysis of the data collected in a study. For example, Shi and Werker (2001) wanted to find out if six-month-old infants could discriminate between lexical and grammatical words by recording the amount of time spent looking at the two different types of words. When they completed the study, they statistically analyzed the data they had collected (looking time in seconds) and found that their infants looked significantly longer at lexical words after first seeing grammatical words. The statistical analysis, therefore, indicated that time spent looking at the words covaried with the type of word. Based on this statistical analysis, Shi and Werker inferred that there was a relationship between these two variables. If this inference about the covariation between these two variables is correct, then the study has statistical conclusion validity.

There are times when we are wrong about the inferences we make from our statistical analysis. For example, if a study does not have a sufficient number of research participants the statistical test used may not have sufficient power to detect the covariation that really exists between the dependent and independent variables, leading to the wrong conclusion. This is just one of the many factors that can threaten statistical conclusion validity. However, understanding these threats requires a statistical background and will not be reviewed here. If you are interested in them, see Shadish et al. (2002).

STUDY QUESTION 7.4

- **If I have stated that my experimental results are valid, what does that mean?**
- **What is statistical conclusion validity?**

Internal Validity

Internal validity
The extent to which we can accurately infer that the independent and dependent variables are causally related

Internal validity refers to the extent to which we can accurately infer that the independent variable caused the effect observed on the dependent variable. When conducting an experiment, we want to identify the effect produced by the independent variable. If the observed effect, as measured by the dependent variable, is caused only by the variation in the independent variable, then internal validity has been achieved. We make this inference when we have evidence that the presumed cause precedes the effect, when the presumed cause and effect are related, and when no other explanations for the relationship are plausible. The first requirement, cause preceding effect, is easily handled in psychological experiments because experiments force the manipulation of the independent variable to precede the dependent variable. The second requirement, demonstrating that the cause and effect covary, is handled by using statistics to determine whether the independent and dependent variables covary. This leaves the third requirement of ensuring that no other plausible explanations exist for the relationship—so internal validity boils down to ensuring that the observed effect, as measured by the dependent variable, is caused *only* by the variation in the independent variable. This requirement is difficult to achieve because the dependent variable could be influenced by variables other than the independent variable. For example, if we were investigating the influence of tutoring (independent variable) on grades (dependent variable), we would like to conclude that any improvement in the grades of the students who received the tutoring over that of those who did not was in fact a result of the tutoring. However, if the tutored students were brighter than those who were not tutored, the improvement in grades could be due to the fact that the tutored students were brighter. In such an instance, intelligence would represent another explanation for the relationship observed between the independent and dependent variables. This other explanation is an **extraneous variable** that confounds the results of the experiment. If this type of extraneous variable creeps into an experiment, we can no longer draw any conclusions regarding the causal relationship that exists between the independent and dependent variables.

Extraneous variable
Any variable other than the independent variable that influences the dependent variable

Confounding
When an extraneous variable systematically varies with variations in the independent variable

Confounding, therefore, occurs when the experiment contains a variable that systematically varies with the independent variable. This is an important point because extraneous variables may or may not introduce a confound within an experiment. The only extraneous variables that introduce a confound are variables that *systematically* vary with the independent variable. If the tutored students are brighter than the students who are not tutored, intelligence level varies systematically with the independent variable of tutoring. Any difference in the dependent variable of grades could, therefore, be due to the tutoring, the difference in intelligence levels of the tutored and nontutored students, or some combination of these two variables. The important point is that it is impossible to tell what caused the grade difference because the influence of the extraneous variable of intelligence was confounded with the influence of tutoring.

If the extraneous variable of intelligence did not systematically vary with the independent variable of tutoring, it would not represent a confounding extraneous variable. If the students that received and did not receive tutoring were of the same intelligence level, any difference in grades could not be attributed to intelligence. Intelligence level, in this case, would represent an extraneous variable but it would not represent a confounding extraneous variable. It is necessary to control only for the influence of confounding extraneous variables in order to attain internal validity.

Threats to Internal Validity

Extraneous variables that confound the results of an experiment must be controlled to achieve internal validity and correctly infer that the independent variable manipulation caused the effect observed in the dependent variable. Controlling for the effect of confounding extraneous variables does not mean totally eliminating the influence of a variable because eliminating the influence of most of the variables we investigate—such as intelligence, past experience, or history of reinforcement—is not possible. What we can do is eliminate any *differential* influence that these variables may have across the various levels of the independent variable. This means that we must keep the influence of these variables **constant** across the various levels of the independent variable. For example, Wade and Blier (1974) investigated the differential effect that two methods of learning have on the retention of lists of words (they actually used consonant-vowel-consonant trigrams). In this study, they had to control for the associations that participants had with these words because it has been shown that association value influences rate of learning. Therefore, they chose words that had previously been shown to have an average association value of 48.4 percent for research participants. In this manner, they held the association value of the words constant across the two groups of participants and eliminated any differential influence that this variable might have had.

Constancy
Stability, or absence of change, in the influence exerted by an extraneous variable across all treatment conditions

How is constancy achieved? That is, how do we arrange factors in an experiment so confounding extraneous variables do not differentially influence the result of the experiment? The only way is through control. Control means exerting a constant influence. Thus, if we wanted to hold constant the trait of dominance, we would attempt to make sure that this trait had an equal influence on all groups of participants.

Control, or achieving constancy of potential extraneous variables, is often relatively easy to accomplish once the confounding extraneous variables have been identified. The difficulty frequently lies in identifying these variables. Shadish et al. (2002) have identified a number of extraneous variables that can affect a study. These extraneous variables are threats to the internal validity of a study and must be controlled to accurately infer that a causal relationship exists between the independent and dependent variables.

History
Any event occurring after the experimental treatment is introduced that could produce the observed outcome

History **History** refers to any event that occurs between the beginning of experimental treatment and the measurement of the dependent variable that could produce the observed outcome. For example, Shadish and Reis (1984) revealed that women who participated in the federal Women, Infants, and Children (WIC) program to improve their pregnancy outcome by improving their nutritional intake were also eligible for and probably participated in the food stamps program. Because the availability of food stamps could also lead to better nutrition, participation in this program could also improve pregnancy outcomes and represents a real history threat in studies attempting to demonstrate the efficacy of the WIC program, as illustrated in Figure 7.2(a).

FIGURE 7.2
Illustration of extraneous history events.

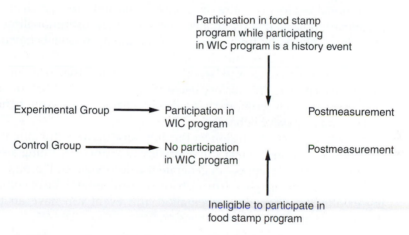

A. History event occurring after initiation of the experimental treatment

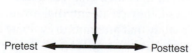

B. History event occurring between the pre- and the postmeasurement of the dependent variable

A history threat can also occur in a study that is designed to have both a pre- and postmeasurement of the dependent variable, as illustrated in Figure 7.2(*b*). For example, Schoenthaler (1983) investigated the impact of a dietary change on violent and aggressive behaviors of institutionalized juveniles. A record of such behaviors was maintained for each inmate for three months prior to, as well as three months after, dietary change. The results of this study revealed that the mean number of violent and aggressive behaviors exhibited during the three months prior to the dietary change was significantly greater than the mean number of such behaviors exhibited after the dietary change. Schoenthaler concluded that the dietary change was responsible for the significant reduction in violent and aggressive behavior. Although this may be true, it is also important to realize that six months had elapsed between the beginning of the pretesting and the completion of the posttesting, and many other events that took place during this time could have accounted for the alteration in behavior. Schoenthaler also realized this and considered a variety of alternative explanations, such as system-wide changes that coincided with the introduction of the dietary alteration. Although these rival hypotheses did not seem to be supported by facts and apparently could not explain the observed change in violent and aggressive behavior, there was one alternative explanation that was not controlled and that could explain the observed results. The juveniles who participated in the study were institutionalized for the entire six-month period and participated in both the pre- and postdietary phases. It is reasonable to assume that institutionalization itself should, over time, reduce the frequency of violent and aggressive behavior and that a six-month period should be sufficient to induce such a reduction. Consequently, such a history event serves as a rival hypothesis for the effect that Schoenthaler attributed to the dietary change. This history event must be controlled before one can conclude with any degree of certainty that a dietary change can have a beneficial impact on violent and aggressive behavior.

Generally speaking, the longer the time lapse between treatment implementation and the posttest, the greater the possibility of history becoming a rival explanation. But even short time lapses can generate the history effect. If group data are collected and an irrelevant, unique event such as an obstreperous joke or comment occurs during or after treatment implementation, this event can have an influence on the posttest, making it a rival hypothesis.

Maturation

Changes in biological and psychological conditions that occur with the passage of time

Maturation   **Maturation** refers to changes in the internal conditions of the individual that occur as a function of the passage of time. The changes involve both biological and psychological processes, such as age, learning, fatigue, boredom, and hunger, that are not related to specific external events but reside within the individual. To the extent that such changes affect the individual's response to the experimental treatment, they create internal invalidity.

Consider a study that attempts to evaluate the benefits achieved from a Head Start program. Assume the investigator gave the participants a preachievement measure at the beginning of the school year and a postachievement measure at the end of the school year. In comparing the pre- and postachievement measures, she found that significant increases in achievement existed and concluded that Head Start programs are very beneficial. Such a study is internally invalid because there was no control for the maturational influence. The increased achievement could have been due to the changes that occurred with the passage of time. A group of children who did not participate in Head Start may have progressed an equal amount. In order to determine the effect of a program such as Head Start, a control group that did not receive the treatment would also have to be included to control for the potential rival influence of maturation.

Instrumentation
Changes in the assessment of the dependent variable

Instrumentation   **Instrumentation** refers to changes that occur over time in the measurement of the dependent variable. This class of confounding extraneous variables does not refer to participant changes but to changes that occur during the process of measurement. Unfortunately, many of the techniques that we use to measure our dependent variable are subject to change during the course of the study. The measurement situation that is most subject to the instrumentation source of error is one that requires the use of human observers. Physical measurements show minor changes, but human observers are subject to such influences as fatigue, boredom, and learning processes. In administering intelligence tests, the tester typically gains facility and skill over time and collects more reliable and valid data as additional tests are given. Observers and interviewers are often used to assess the effects of various experimental treatments. As the observers and interviewers assess more and more individuals, they gain skill. The interviewers may, for example, gain additional skill with the interview schedule or with observing a particular type of behavior, producing shifts in the response measure that cannot be attributed to either the participant or the treatment conditions. This is why studies that use human observers to measure the behavioral characteristics of interest typically use more than one observer and have each of the observers go through a training program. In this way, some of the biases inherent in making observations can be minimized, and the various observers can serve as checks on one another to ensure that accurate data are being collected. Typically, the data collected by the various observers must coincide before they are considered valid.

Testing
Changes in a person's score on the second administration of a test as a result of previously having taken the test

Testing   **Testing** refers to changes in the score a participant makes on the second administration of a test as a result of previously having taken the test. In other words, the experience of having taken a test on one occasion can alter the results obtained on a second administration of the same test. Taking a test does a number of things that can alter a person's performance on a subsequent administration of the same test. Taking a test gives you practice with taking the test and familiarizes you with the content of the test. After taking a test, you may think about the errors you made that could be corrected if the test were taken over. When the test is administered a second time, you are already familiar with it and may remember some of your prior responses. This can lead to an enhanced performance entirely tied to the initial or pretest administration. Any alteration in performance as a result of a testing effect threatens the internal validity of a study because it serves as a rival hypothesis to the treatment effect or experimental manipulation. This means that whenever the same test is administered on multiple occasions, some control needs to be implemented for a testing rival hypothesis.

Regression Artifact   Many psychological experiments (such as attitude change experiments) require pre- and posttesting on the same dependent variable measure or some other equivalent form for the purpose of measuring change. In addition, these studies sometimes select only two groups of research participants having the extreme scores, such as high and low attitude scores. The two extreme scoring groups are then given an experimental treatment condition, and a posttest score is obtained. A variable that could cause the pre- and posttest scores of the extreme groups to change is a regression artifact. **Regression artifact** refers to the fact that extreme scores in a particular distribution will tend to move, or regress, toward the mean of the distribution as a function of repeated testing. The scores of the high groups may become lower, not because of any treatment condition introduced, but because of the regression artifact phenomenon. Also, low scores could show increases on retesting because of the regression artifact and not because of any effect of the experimental treatment. This regression phenomenon exists because the first and second measurements are not perfectly correlated. In other words, there is some degree of unreliability in the measuring device.

This regression artifact is illustrated in Table 7.2. A total of twelve participants were pretested, and the scores of these participants ranged from 46 to 123. A group of three extremely high scorers and four extremely low scorers was selected from the original twelve participants. These high- and low-scoring participants were then posttested. The scores of participants with high pretest scores declined on posttesting, whereas those of participants with low pretest scores increased on posttesting. In this example, an experimental treatment condition was not administered to the participants that could cause a change in their scores. Rather, the decline in the scores of the high-scoring group and the increase in the scores of the low-scoring group were caused entirely by the regression artifact resulting from unreliability of the measuring device.

Regression artifact
The tendency for extreme scores to become less extreme on a second assessment

TABLE 7.2
Illustration of the Regression Artifact Effect

Participant	Pretest Score	Selected Participant	Pretest Score	Selected Participant	Posttest Score
S_1	110	S_1	110	S_1	103
S_2	46	S_3	123	S_3	116
S_3	123	S_8	105	S_8	98
S_4	92				
S_5	59				
S_6	73				
S_7	99				
S_8	105				
S_9	67	S_2	46	S_2	57
S_{10}	84	S_5	59	S_5	63
S_{11}	61	S_9	67	S_9	70
S_{12}	96	S_{11}	61	S_{11}	65

Regression artifacts may exist in many research settings. For example, a study investigating the efficacy of a new type psychotherapy for treating depression may be most attractive to individuals when they are feeling very depressed. Because they come to the study when they are extremely depressed, they are likely to be less depressed on subsequent occasions as illustrated in Figure 7.3. Such a decline in depression is due to a regression artifact and threatens the internal validity of a study such as this one. Regression artifacts constitute a real source of possible internal invalidity and must be controlled if a valid inference is to be drawn regarding the cause of the observed effects.

Attrition
Some people do not show up for the study or do not complete it

Attrition **Attrition** refers to the fact that some individuals do not complete the experiment for a variety of reasons such as failure to show up at the scheduled time and place or not participating in all phases of the study. Most psychological experiments, both human and infrahuman, must contend with this potential source of bias at some time. Physiological experiments involving electrode implantation sometimes experience participant loss because of the complications that arise from the surgical procedures. Human experiments must contend with participants who do not show up for the experiment at the designated time and place or do not participate in all the conditions required by the study. The difficulty arises not just because participants are lost but because the loss of participants may produce differences in the groups that cannot be attributed to the experimental treatment. Consider the following example. Assume that you want to test the effect of a certain treatment condition on conformity. You know that past research has demonstrated that females conform to a greater degree than males do, so you control for this factor by assigning an equal

FIGURE 7.3
Illustration of a regression artifact.

number of males and females to two groups. When you actually run the experiment, however, half of the females assigned to the group that does not receive the treatment condition do not show up and half of the males assigned to the other group (the one receiving the treatment condition) do not show up. Statistical analysis reveals that the group receiving the treatment condition conforms significantly more than does the group not receiving any treatment. Can you conclude that this significantly greater degree of conformity is caused by the independent variable administered? Such an inference is incorrect because more females were in the group receiving the experimental treatment and past research indicates that females exhibit a greater degree of conformity. This variable, and not the independent variable, may have produced the observed significant difference.

Selection
The choice of participants for the various treatment groups is based on different criteria

Selection   **Selection** exists when a differential selection procedure is used for placing research participants in the various comparison groups. Ideally, a sample of participants is randomly chosen from a population, and then these participants are randomly assigned to the various treatment groups. When this procedure cannot be followed and the assignment to groups is based on some different procedure, possible rival hypotheses are introduced. Assume that you wanted to investigate the relative efficacy of a given type of therapy on various types of psychotic behaviors. For your research participants, you selected two groups of psychotic patients. After two months, the progress in therapy was evaluated and you found that the participants exhibiting one type of psychotic reaction improved significantly more than those with the other type. With these results, one is tempted to say that the therapy technique used is the agent that produced the difference in improvement between the two groups of psychotic patients. But there may be other differences between the two groups that would provide a better explanation of the observed difference. The psychotic patients who improved most may possess characteristics that predispose them toward more rapid improvement with almost any type of therapy. If this is the case, then it is these characteristics and not the type of therapy that caused the more rapid improvement. Such difficulties are encountered when participants are differentially selected based on a criterion such as type of psychosis because the independent variable manipulation represents an individual difference manipulation. Therefore, a study with a selection bias boils down to an ex post facto study, with all of its inherent difficulties.

Additive and interactive effects
The combined effect of several threats to internal validity

Additive and Interactive Effects   **Additive and interactive effects** refer to the fact that the threats to internal validity can combine to produce complex biases. Validity threats do not necessarily operate in isolation; they can operate simultaneously. For example, selection can combine with a maturation, history, or instrumentation effect. To illustrate a selection–maturation effect, suppose you want to teach the concepts of good and bad to five-year-old children with and without hearing difficulties. In doing so, you find that the normal children learn these concepts much faster than do the children with hearing difficulties. From this study you might conclude that the ability of children who have hearing difficulties to learn these concepts is somehow impaired. However, as Figure 7.4 shows, Kusche and Greenberg (1983) revealed that children with hearing difficulties gain an understanding of the concepts of good and bad more slowly than do children who can hear normally. If these maturational differences are not known, a study that attempted to teach the concepts of

FIGURE 7.4

The evolution of the concepts of good and bad as a function of age and hearing status.

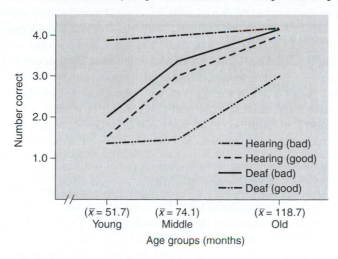

(From "Evaluative Understanding and Role Taking Ability: A Comparison of Deaf and Hearing Children" by C. A. Kusche and M. T. Greenberg, 1983, *Child Development, 54,* pp. 141–147. © The Society for Research in Child Development, Inc. Reprinted by permission.)

good and bad to deaf and to hearing children might conclude that the instructional program was more effective for the hearing children. However, the difference in response is strictly a result of a selection–maturation effect and not a result of the instructional program. Similar effects can occur if a selection–history or a selection–instrumentation effect exists. For example, if a history effect influenced one of two treatment groups, a difference might exist between the two groups not because of the treatment effect but because of the impact of history on only one of the groups.

STUDY QUESTION 7.5

- **What is meant by internal validity?**
- **What is a confounding extraneous variable and how do these variables affect internal validity?**
- **How are threats to internal validity and the principle of constancy related?**
- **Identify each of the threats to internal validity and explain how each threatens internal validity.**

Summary

To obtain useful information from a research study, the finding obtained must be reliable and valid. Reliable results are results that are consistent or repeatable so experimentally reliable results would be results that can be replicated. Validity refers to the accuracy or correctness of an inference so experimentally valid results are results that allow us to make a correct or accurate inference from the results of an experiment. Validity is partially a function of reliability because it is impossible for something to be valid if it is not reliable. Therefore, one prerequisite for experimental validity is experimental reliability. However, just because something is reliable does not mean that it is valid.

To maximize the probability of achieving experimental reliability a sufficient number of participants must be included in the study because the reliability of the results increases as the number of participants increases. Experimental reliability is also influenced by the consistency with which the participants can be identified and the ability and characteristics of the researcher. The consistency of the effect created by the independent variable and the consistency with which the dependent variable is measured influences experimental reliability. Ideally, the independent variable should create the same effect in participants every time it is implemented and the dependent variable should consistently measure a given state regardless of when it is measured. Unreliability or inconsistency in the measurement of a behavior or construct is due to measurement error. Measurement error is introduced by anything, such as fatigue, distress, or a situational event, such as a death in the family, that creates variability in response.

Reliability is measured in several general ways including successive measurements, simultaneous measurements, and internal consistency. Successive measurement involves assessing reliability by comparing the data obtained from two successive measurements. Test–retest reliability and equivalent forms are two ways of obtaining a successive measurement index of reliability. Simultaneous measurement assesses reliability by comparing the data obtained from two simultaneous measurements of the same behavior. Interrater reliability and interobserver agreement are two ways of obtaining a simultaneous measurement of reliability. Internal consistency measures reliability by assessing the consistency with which test items measure a construct. Internal consistency is measured by the split-half method or Cronbach's alpha which is a measure of the average of all possible split-half reliability estimates.

One of the most important tasks confronting the experimenter is to ensure that the experiment is valid because this is the best way to ensure that the study will yield results from which accurate inferences can be made. There are four types of validity that are relevant to psychological experimentation: statistical conclusion validity, internal validity, construct validity, and external validity.

Statistical conclusion validity is concerned with inferences regarding whether the independent and dependent variables covary. We make an inference about the covariation of these two variables from the statistical analysis we compute on the data collected. If the statistical analysis reveals that the independent and dependent variables covary, and they really do covary, then we have made a correct inference and we have statistical conclusion validity.

Internal validity refers to our ability to make a causal statement that the independent variable produces the effect observed in the dependent variable. To make this causal inference and attain internal validity, the experimenter must control for the influence of extraneous variables that could serve as rival hypotheses explaining the effect of the independent variable. Controlling for the influence of extraneous variables refers to holding the influence of the extraneous variables constant across the various levels of the independent variable. Some of the more salient variables that could influence the experiment and serve as rival hypotheses are as follows:

History. Any event that occurs between the beginning of the experimental treatment and the measurement of the dependent variable that could have produced the observed outcome

Maturation. Any of the many conditions internal to the individual that change as a function of the passage of time

Instrumentation. Any changes that occur as a function of measuring the dependent variable

Testing. Changes that may occur in a participant's scores on the second administration of a test as a result of previously having taken the test

Regression artifact. Extreme scores becoming less extreme on a retest of the original measure or on other related measures

Attrition. Individuals not completing the experiment for reasons such as failure to show up at the scheduled time and place or not participating in all phases of the study

Selection. Any change due to the differential selection procedure used in placing participants in various groups

Additive and interactive effects. Any change due to the combined effect of several of the threats to internal validity

Key Terms and Concepts

Reliability
Experimental reliability
Validity
Experimental validity
Measurement error
Successive measurement
Test–retest reliability
Equivalent forms
Simultaneous measurement
Interrater reliability
Interobserver agreement
Internal consistency
Split-half
Cronbach's alpha

Statistical conclusion validity
Internal validity
Extraneous variable
Confounding
Constancy
History
Maturation
Instrumentation
Testing
Regression artifact
Attrition
Selection
Additive and interactive effects

Related Internet Sites

www.wadsworth.com/psychology_d/templates/student_resources/workshops/index.html

This site contains a variety of workshops focusing on research methods. To get to the one on reliability and validity, click on the "Research Methods Workshop" link. Then click on the "reliability and validity" workshop link.

http://psych.athabascau.ca/html/centre/general.shtml

This site has an internal validity link on the left-hand side of the page that will bring you to a tutorial on internal validity. The tutorial exposes the student to each of the threats to internal validity discussed by Campbell and Stanley (1963).

Practice Test

1. Assume you conducted a study and found that a delay in helping others in trouble increases when several other people are available to help versus when there is only one person available to help. You decided to see if you could replicate this study and therefore conducted a second study using the exact procedure. In this second study you got the same result. This indicates that the study
   a. Is valid
   b. Has experimental validity
   c. Has experimental reliability
   d. Has construct reliability
   e. Has internal reliability

2. If you have divided a test into two equal halves, scored each half of the test, and then assessed the consistency of the scores from the two halves of the test, you have assessed
   a. Reliability using equivalent forms
   b. Reliability using the split-half method
   c. Reliability using construct validity
   d. Validity using the split-half method
   e. Validity using equivalent forms

3. If you gave a person a test of intelligence on five different occasions and got the scores of 105, 109, 104, 108, and 110, the difference in the scores received on the different testing occasions would be due to
   a. A lack of validity of the test
   b. A lack of construct assessment
   c. Measurement error
   d. An invalid test
   e. Failure to control for measurement error

4. When we talk about the validity of psychological research studies we are referring to
   a. Statistical conclusion validity
   b. Internal validity
   c. Construct validity
   d. External validity
   e. All of the above

5. If a research study revealed that the independent and dependent variables covary and they really do covary, the study has
   a. Been demonstrated to be worthwhile
   b. Revealed a causal relationship
   c. Internal validity
   d. Statistical conclusion validity
   e. Experimental validity

6. If a research study permits you to accurately infer that the independent variable is the cause of the changes observed in the dependent variable, then you have a study

   a. That is worthwhile
   b. That has internal validity
   c. That has statistical conclusion validity
   d. That has construct validity
   e. That has external validity

Challenge Exercise

1. For each of the following research examples, identify the threat to internal validity that could also explain the improvement in math performance. Because a pretest–posttest design is used and the same test is used at both pre- and posttest assessment in many of the examples, there is naturally a potential testing threat. However, there is also another potential threat in each example and it is this other threat that I want you to identify.

   a. Dr. Brown was investigating the effect of a compensatory education program in mathematics for first-grade students. This study gave a standardized math achievement test to all first-grade students and, based on the results of this test, identified the first-grade students that scored in the lowest quartile on this test. He then placed these students in the compensatory education program and administered the program for the next six months. At the end of the six-week period he again administered the standardized math achievement test to these students and found that they had significantly increased their math score and concluded that the compensatory program was effective in remediating poor math performance.

   b. Dr. Brown was investigating the effect of a compensatory education program in mathematics for first-grade students. This study gave a standardized math achievement test to all first-grade students and administered the program to all students for the next six months. During this six-month period a number of families moved and withdrew their children from this school. Most of the students that were withdrawn from school were poor math students which allowed the teacher of the compensatory education program to progress faster and provide more benefit to the remaining students. At the end of the six-week period Dr. Brown again administered the standardized math achievement test to these students and found that they had significantly increased their math score and concluded that the compensatory program was effective in remediating poor math performance.

   c. Dr. Brown was investigating the effect of a compensatory education program in mathematics for first-grade students. This study gave a standardized math achievement test to all first-grade students and then placed these students in the compensatory education program and administered the program for the next six weeks. At the end of the six-week period he again administered the standardized math achievement test to these students. However, the company from which he purchased the standardized math achievement test had developed an updated and revised form which was supposed to be better, so he used the new form for the posttest and found that the students had significantly increased their math score at posttesting time. Therefore, Dr. Brown concluded that the compensatory program was effective in remediating poor math performance.

d. Dr. Brown was investigating the effect of a compensatory education program in mathematics for first-grade students. This study gave a standardized math achievement test to all first-grade students and administered the program to these students for the entire year. At the end of the year he again administered the standardized math achievement test to these students and found that they had significantly increased their math score and concluded that the compensatory program was effective in remediating poor math performance.

e. Dr. Brown was investigating the effect of a compensatory education program in mathematics for first-grade students. This study gave a standardized math achievement test to all first-grade students and then placed these students in the compensatory education program and administered the program for the next six weeks. During this six-week period Sesame Street ran a special program on mathematics concepts which many of the students watched. Dr. Brown encouraged the students to watch this program and even used examples from this program when he was teaching to emphasize the concepts he used in his compensatory math program. At the end of the six-month period he again administered the standardized math achievement test to these students and found that they had significantly increased their math score and concluded that the compensatory program was effective in remediating poor math performance.

8 Construct and External Validity in Experimental Research

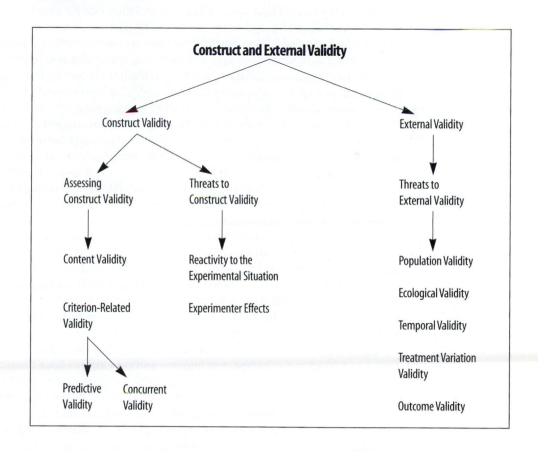

Construct and External Validity

Construct Validity

External Validity

Assessing Construct Validity

Threats to Construct Validity

Threats to External Validity

Content Validity

Reactivity to the Experimental Situation

Population Validity

Criterion-Related Validity

Experimenter Effects

Ecological Validity

Predictive Validity

Concurrent Validity

Temporal Validity

Treatment Variation Validity

Outcome Validity

Construct and External
Validity in Experimental
Research
8

Imagine that you are stretching your jaws open with a wide gape, taking a deep breath that is followed by a short exhalation, and then closing your jaws. What are you doing? If you haven't figured it out, you would be yawning. Yawning is one of the most common behavioral acts, and one that we have in common with mammals and most other animals with backbones such as fish, turtles, crocodiles, and birds (Provine, 2005). This is something that we all start very early in life. It is present by the end of the first trimester of prenatal development and can readily be seen in newborn children.

Why do we yawn? Robert Provine has been investigating this subject for some time. Based on his own research and that of others, Provine has suggested that yawning and having a sexual climax may share a neurobehavioral heritage because a yawnlike facial expression exists during sexual climax. This connection is supported by the fact that "yawning is triggered by androgens and oxytocin and is associated with other sex-related agents and acts" (Provine, 2005, p. 534). This suggestion is supported by research revealing that the chemical agents that produce yawning in rats also produce penile erection. Some individuals taking antidepressants such as Prozac to ameliorate their depression also experience the side effect of having an orgasm when yawning. Additionally, yawning makes one feel good. People give yawning a rating of 8.5 on a scale of 1 to 10 with 10 being good and 1 being bad. Based on the similarities between sexual orgasm and yawning, Provine believes that it is perfectly reasonable to consider both a sexual orgasm and yawning a "climax." As further evidence of both being a climax, Provine points to fact that being unable to complete a sexual climax or a yawn is frustrating and disturbing to those who experience it.

As you can see from this brief description of yawning and the research that has been conducted, some unexpected findings and conclusions have been made. The conclusions are inferences made from data collected from studies conducted with a variety of species including both rats and humans. The significant issue from the results of this research is whether the investigators have made the correct inferences. Are the inferences made from the data collected relevant to the construct of yawning; and can the data collected from not only the humans who participated in the research study but also the data collected from rats be generalized to other humans?

Chapter Preview

The opening vignette to this chapter discussed the results of research conducted on yawning. While this is something that we all do, it is a topic that has attracted little research. Most students do not immediately think of yawning when they are asked to think about a topic for research. The studies on yawning have revealed some interesting parallels to other behaviors, such as the potential connection with sexual orgasm. To draw these parallels, the data obtained from the studies investigating yawning and sexual orgasm must actually be investigating these constructs. This is an issue involved with construct validity. Additionally, if the results of these investigations are expected to exist for people or organisms other than those participating in the research studies, these studies must have external validity. Construct and external validity are very important and contribute to the experimental validity of any study. These are the two types of validity that will be discussed in this chapter.

Introduction

In the last chapter I defined experimental validity as existing when a correct or accurate inference is made from the experimental data. In that chapter I stated that there were four types of validity that are applied to research studies but focused on only two of them—statistical conclusion validity and internal validity. The other two types of validity that are applied to research studies are construct validity and external validity. For construct validity to exist in a study, the operations used to represent a construct must be an accurate representation for the study to provide any information about the intended construct. For example, Melinder, Barch, Heydebrand, and Csernansky (2005) investigated phonologic fluency in schizophrenics. Their operationalization of phonologic fluency was to have each of the participants in their study name as many words beginning with a certain letter of the alphabet as they could within a prescribed time limit. If the person who can name more words beginning with a certain letter is more phonologically fluent than one who cannot, then construct validity exists. Similarly, for external validity to exist, the generalizations one makes from a study must be correct and accurate. In this chapter I will discuss both of these important types of validity.

Construct Validity

Construct validity
The validity of inferences we make about higher-order constructs from the operation we use to represent them

In Chapter 7 I defined **construct validity** as the extent to which we can infer higher-order constructs from the operations we use to represent them. Creating operations from which we can accurately infer higher-order constructs is very important because constructs can be incorporated in every phase of the experiment from participant selection to the experimental setting. For example, when we talk about individuals diagnosed with schizophrenia, obsessive-compulsive disorder, or an eating disorder we are dealing with the constructs of schizophrenia, obsessive-compulsive disorder, and eating disorder. Constructs are also used sometimes to refer to the experimental setting such as an impoverished setting, enriched setting, or a poverty neighborhood. Conducting an experiment may, therefore, involve the use of constructs when considering the research participant, the independent and dependent variables, and the setting of the experiment. For example, if you are investigating the effect of being depressed on marital discord among disadvantaged people living in an impoverished neighborhood you have a construct representing the research participant (disadvantaged people), the independent variable (depression), the dependent variable (marital discord), and the setting of the experiment (a poverty neighborhood). For each of these constructs, you must identify a set of operations that represent the construct. The difficulty arises in identifying a set of operations that will allow you to accurately infer each of these constructs.

For example, disadvantaged people might be operationally defined as individuals who have had incomes below the poverty level for the past six months and who participate in government welfare programs. The independent variable depression might be operationalized as persons scoring above 20 on the Beck Depression Inventory (Beck, Ward, Mendelson, Mock, & Erbaugh, 1961). The dependent variable of marital discord could be operationalized by a count of the number of arguments the couple had per day, and the setting of a poverty neighborhood could be based on the type and condition of the homes and other buildings in the neighborhood in which the participants lived.

The important issue with respect to construct validity is whether these operations are a correct representation of the intended construct. Does the person who has had an income below the poverty level for the past six months and who participates in government welfare programs really representative of a disadvantaged person? Is a person who scores above 20 on the Beck Depression Inventory really depressed? These are the questions that must be asked to determine if construct validity exists.

How does an investigator determine if construct validity exists or if the inferences made from our operational representations are accurate? The accuracy of an inference is an empirical question. This means that we have to collect evidence indicating that the inference we make is correct. Schachter and Singer (1962) used the concrete operations of having research participants watch a confederate waltz around the room shooting rubber bands, playing with a hula hoop, and practicing hook shots in a wastebasket with wadded paper to create the state of euphoria. They inferred that the participants would develop the state of euphoria from watching the confederate engage in these behaviors as illustrated in Figure 8.1. However, the concrete operations of shooting rubber bands, playing with a hula hoop, and practicing hook shots says nothing about the validity of the construct that is inferred. Construct validity is based on evidence revealing that the target construct can validly be inferred from the concrete operations.

Assessing Construct Validity

Given that construct validity is so important, how do we obtain evidence that it has been achieved? Shadish et al. (2002) have identified several ways in which construct validity is fostered. The first step is to have a clear definition of the constructs of interest. Accomplishing this step involves identifying the prototypical features of the constructs of interest. This, however, is very difficult because of the constructs we deal with, such as violence, attitudes, helping, depression, and productivity. What, for example, are the prototypical features of a construct such as violence? Does it only involve physical characteristics such as hitting or can it also involve verbal characteristics such as swearing at someone? If it does involve hitting, then there are unique

FIGURE 8.1
Illustration of the requirements for construct validity.

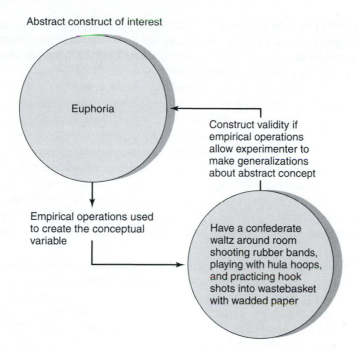

Abstract construct of interest

Euphoria

Construct validity if empirical operations allow experimenter to make generalizations about abstract concept

Empirical operations used to create the conceptual variable

Have a confederate waltz around room shooting rubber bands, playing with hula hoops, and practicing hook shots into wastebasket with wadded paper

components of hitting that must be decided on. Is any type of hitting representative of violence or must one take intention into consideration to eliminate accidental hitting from the prototypical features of violence? Because of the difficulty in identifying the prototypical features of most of our psychological constructs, there will never be a one-to-one relationship between the operations used in a study and the corresponding construct. All we can do is carefully select instances that match the constructs. This is greatly facilitated by having a detailed description of the constructs, and this description should identify as many of the prototypical elements of the constructs as possible.

The second step in assessing construct validity is to assess the match between the constructs and the operations used to represent them. This step involves collecting evidence indicating that the operations used to represent the constructs are accurate representations of these constructs. This evidence comes from all sources and is a continuing process because no one piece of evidence will definitively assess the accuracy of the match between the constructs and the operations used to represent them. Content validity and criterion-related validity are two common sources of evidence, but there are many others.

Content validity
Judgment of the degree to which the items or tasks adequately sample the target domain

Content Validity   **Content validity** refers to a judgment of the degree to which the items, tasks, or questions adequately sample the target domain. Content validity is a procedure that is much more applicable to the dependent variable than to the independent variable because the dependent variable involves the measurement of behavior. Often the behavior of interest is an attitude or a psychological state, such as depression, loneliness, love, shyness, or cognitive style. One of the primary ways in which these psychological states are measured is by a psychological test. The test that is developed must sample the content of the thing that is being measured. For example, if a test of depression has content validity, then the items on the test sample the domain of things that are representative of depression. Depression includes characteristics such as fatigue, anxiety, lack of appetite, and lack of motivation. The items on any test of depression must include these characteristics to have content validity.

Whether a test or any other measure of a psychological construct has content validity is generally a matter of judgment by experts in the area. These experts generally review the content domain of the construct being measured. For the construct of depression they review the characteristics and type of behavior that can be exhibited by depressed individuals. Then they look at the items in the test and make a judgment as to whether the items adequately sample and represent the characteristics and type of behavior exhibited by depressed individuals. If, in the judgment of the experts, the test adequately samples the content domain, the test has content validity.

Criterion-related validity
A judgment of the extent to which the procedures or behavioral measures can be used to infer or predict some criterion

Criterion-Related Validity   **Criterion-related validity** refers to a judgment of the extent to which the procedures or behavioral measures can be used to infer or predict some criterion, such as a specific behavior or performance. If they can, then criterion-related validity exists. There are actually two different types of criterion-related validity: predictive validity and concurrent validity. The only difference between these two types is time. Predictive validity involves using our procedures or behavioral measures to predict some future criterion performance; concurrent validity involves using our procedures or behavioral measures to predict some concurrent criterion performance.

The Velton mood induction procedure (1968) was developed to enable investigators to create various mood states in research participants. If this procedure is used to create a state of depression in a group of individuals, then we predict that these individuals will have negative thoughts, will score high on tests of depression, will feel fatigued, and will be pessimistic. If this mood induction procedure is used to create elation in another group of research participants, we predict that these individuals will feel vigorous, will score low on tests of depression, and will be optimistic. If these predictions are verified and the people in the depressive group are tired, pessimistic, and depressed, and the people in the elated group do feel vigorous, optimistic, and have no depression, then the mood induction procedure has criterion-related validity. In other words, the mood induced by using the Velton mood induction procedure correctly predicts a variety of different behavioral responses. Now note the difference between concurrent and predictive validity. If the criterion measures of pessimism or optimism, fatigue, and level of depression are assessed concurrently with the induction of the mood state we have established concurrent validity. If they are measured at some later time we have established predictive validity.

Other Sources of Evidence of Construct Validity   While content and criterion-related validity are sources of evidence for construct validity, the assessment of construct validity includes any method and any source of information that provides data indicating the match between a set of operations and the constructs that these operations are to represent. To drive this point home, let us consider examples of both the independent variable and dependent variable.

Evidence supporting the construct validity of the independent variable depends on the type of independent variable you are manipulating. If the independent variable is different types of treatment for depression, you have to collect evidence indicating that the different types of treatment have been administered as they should be according to theory or some specific manual of treatment. One type of treatment may be cognitive-behavior therapy and the other type may be interpersonal therapy. To ensure that these therapy constructs have been accurately applied, there should be some check or some type of data collected that measures the extent to which the various therapies have been applied appropriately.

Evidence supporting the construct validity of the dependent variable also depends on the type of dependent variable being measured. If the dependent variable construct is being measured by a psychological test, evidence indicating construct validity can be obtained from correlations with other tests designed to measure the same construct. A high correlation between the test you selected as your dependent variable and another test measuring the same construct indicates that both tests are measuring the same thing. Therefore, if the other test is measuring the dependent variable construct, then the test you selected is also measuring the construct. If the dependent variable is a response measure such as encephalographic recordings from the brain, you want to ensure that the recordings you have measured are only brain recordings and not some other artifact such as reaction to an eye-blink response.

From these examples, you can see that construct validity evidence comes from a multitude of sources. The source used is dependent on the nature of the construct you are trying to represent. This is why I can only provide examples of types of evidence that can be collected. Construct validity embraces all forms of validity evidence and construct validation should be viewed as an evolving and never-ending process (Messick, 1995).

STUDY QUESTION 8.1

- **What is construct validity and why is it so important?**
- **Why is it difficult to develop a clear definition of most psychological constructs?**
- **Identify and describe the sources of evidence that can be used to indicate that construct validity exists.**

Threats to Construct Validity

Construct validity is concerned with the extent to which set of operationalizations represent and, therefore, can be used to infer the higher-order constructs they describe. For example, is a person who has had an income below the poverty level for 6 months a good representation of the construct of a disadvantaged person? In other words, is there a match between the construct and the operations used in your study? Sometimes our operationalizations are good representations and sometimes there are other factors that affect these operationalizations that reduce the accuracy with which the operations represent the intended construct. Shadish et al. (2002) have identified a number of reasons why we may be incorrect in the inferences we make about constructs from our study operations. These reasons, presented in Table 8.1, are considered to be threats to construct validity. Two of these threats, reactivity to the

TABLE 8.1
Threats to Construct Validity

- *Inadequate explanation of the construct*—if a construct is not adequately explained and analyzed, it can lead to a set of operations that do not represent the construct adequately.
- *Construct confounding*—the operations used in a study represent more than one construct.
- *Mono-operation bias*—a study uses only one operationalization of a construct. This typically results in an underrepresentation of the construct and lowers construct validity.
- *Mono-method bias*—a study uses only one method (e.g., physiological recording) to operationalize a construct. When this occurs, the method used may influence the results.
- *Confounding constructs with level of constructs*—a study investigates only a few levels of a construct (e.g., three doses of a drug), but makes inferences about the overall construct (e.g., the overall effect of the drug).
- *Treatment-sensitive factorial structure*—an instrumentation change that occurs because of the experimental treatment.
- *Reactive self-report changes*—changes that a research participant may make on self-report measures as a result of a motivational shift after being included in the experimental study.
- *Reactivity to the experimental situation*—research participants' perceptions and motives can affect the responses they make to the dependent variable and these responses can be interpreted as part of the treatment construct being tested.
- *Experimenter effects*—the experimenter's attributes and expectancies can influence the responses made by the research participants and these responses can be interpreted as part of the treatment construct being tested.
- *Novelty and disruption effects*—research participants usually respond better to a new and novel situation and poorly to one that disrupts their routine. These effects are part of the overall treatment effect.
- *Compensatory equalization*—individuals try to provide the same benefits or services to the control group that are received by the experimental group.
- *Compensatory rivalry*—individuals resent being assigned to the control group and respond more negatively than would be expected, because of the resentment they feel.
- *Treatment diffusion*—individuals in one treatment group receive some or all of another group's treatment.

Reactivity to the experimental situation
Research participants' motives and perceptions that can influence the responses they make to the dependent variable

experimental situation and experimenter effects, are discussed next in more detail because a considerable amount of research has been devoted to them documenting the biasing effect that they can have on the outcome of experimental studies.

Reactivity to the Experimental Situation   **Reactivity to the experimental situation** refers to the fact that the motives and perceptions that research participants bring with them to the experiment can influence their perception of the experiment and the responses they make to the dependent variable. When agreeing to take part in an experiment, a person is making an implicit contract to play the role of the participant. Theoretically, this means that the participant will listen to the instructions and perform the tasks requested to the best of his or her ability and as truthfully as possible. In reality, such an ideal situation does not always exist because participants are not passive responders to the experimental instructions and manipulations. As Kihlstrom (1995) has stated, participants "are sentient curious creatures, constantly thinking about what is happening to them, evaluating the proceedings, figuring out what they are supposed to do, and planning their responses" (p. 10). These cognitive activities may interact with the experimental procedures, confounding the results of the experimental manipulation and threatening the construct validity of the experimental treatment.

Participant Effect. In an experiment, the researcher would like to have ideal participants—participants who bring no preconceived notions to the laboratory and who, once in the laboratory, accept instructions and are motivated to respond in as truthful a manner as possible. Although such a situation would be wonderful, it exists only in the experimenter's mind. When participants enter the experiment, they are generally naive regarding its purpose or the task required of them. Once they appear for the experiment, however, they receive information from the way the experimenter greets them, from the instructions given regarding the experiment, from the task required of them, from the laboratory setting (including the available equipment), and from any rumors they have heard about the experiment. This information, called the **demand characteristics** of the experiment (Orne, 1962), defines the experiment from the participants' point of view. It provides the participants with the information from which they create their perceptions of the purpose of the experiment and the task required. Once the participants identify this task, they are motivated to perform it. It is in the performance of the experimental task that the participants' perceptions can influence the outcome of the experiment.

In the past, it was thought that participants assumed a specific role (Orne, 1962; Rosenberg, 1969; Fillenbaum, 1966; Masling, 1966) and attempted to portray this role when performing the experimental task. Increasingly, this view is being rejected (for example, Carlston & Cohen, 1980; Carlopia, Adair, Lindsay, & Spinner, 1983). It has been replaced by the notion that participants respond to the experimental task as they perceive it. If the experiment involves a learning task, the participant will attempt to learn the material presented. However, participants do not take an uninvolved, neutral approach because often their performance implies something about them. For example, a learning task indirectly says something about the participants' intelligence. If they learn the material rapidly, this suggests that they are intelligent. Most individuals have a desire to appear intelligent, so they will try to learn as rapidly as possible. Similarly, if the task suggests something about emotional stability, participants will respond in such a way as to appear most emotionally stable (Rosenberg, 1969). Consequently, although participants seem to approach an experiment with the motivation to perform the task requested, superimposed on this desire is the wish to make a **positive self-presentation** (Christensen, 1981). This means that participants use their perceptions of the experiment to determine how to respond to the experimental task in such a way that they appear most positive.

Consider the experiment conducted by Christensen (1977). In this experiment, an attempt was made to verbally condition the research participants—to increase the

Demand characteristics
Any of the cues available in an experiment, such as the instructions, the experimenter, rumors, or the experimental setting

Positive self-presentation
Participants' motivation to respond in such a way as to present themselves in the most positive manner

participants' use of certain pronouns such as *we* and *they* by saying "good" whenever the participants used one of them. Some participants interpreted the experimenter's reaction of saying "good" as an attempt to manipulate their behavior. These participants resisted any behavioral manifestation of conditioning. This resistance was caused by their viewing being manipulable as negative—if they did not demonstrate any conditioning, then they would show that they could not be manipulated and, in this way, present themselves most positively. Similarly, Bradley (1978) has revealed that individuals take credit for desirable acts but deny blame for undesirable ones in order to enhance themselves.

Conditions Producing a Positive Self-Presentation Motive.   In order to control the interactive effects that exist between the research participants' behavior and their role in an experiment, it would be advantageous to know the conditions that alter participants' behavior in their attempt to attain favorable self-presentations. Only when such conditions are identified can one construct conditions that control for this construct validity threat.

Tedeschi, Schlenker, and Bonoma (1971) provide some insight into the general conditions that may determine whether or not the self-presentation motive will exist within an experiment. They state that this motive arises only when the behavior in which the participant engages is indicative of the participant's true intentions, beliefs, or feelings. If participants believe that others view their behavior as being determined by some external source not under their control, then the positive self-presentation motive is not aroused. However, our experiments are seldom constructed so that the research participants believe that others think their behavior is externally determined. Thus it seems that the positive self-presentation motive will exist in most research studies.

Implication for Research.   The implication of the positive self-presentation motive is that experimenters must try to ensure that constant participant perceptions exist throughout all phases of the experiment. When such constancy is not maintained, artifactual confounding can be expected to occur from the interaction of the motive of positive self-presentation with the experimental treatment condition. There appear to be two types of interaction that can exist (Christensen, 1981): an intertreatment and an intratreatment interaction. An **intertreatment interaction** exists when research participants' perceptions of the different experimental treatment conditions suggest to them different ways of presenting themselves in a positive manner. For example, Sigall, Aronson, and Van Hoose (1970) found that in one treatment condition participants increased their performance when told that they were responding to a dull, boring task under decreased illumination levels. However, in another treatment condition, participants decreased their performance when told that rapid performance of the task indicated obsessive-compulsive performance. In the first experimental task, participants apparently perceived that they could appear most positive by overcoming the obstacles of low illumination and a dull, boring task by performing rapidly. In the other treatment condition, participants believed that they would appear most positive by performing slowly in order not to seem obsessive-compulsive.

Intertreatment interaction Perception by participants in different treatment groups that they can fulfill the positive self-presentation motive by responding in different ways

Intratreatment interaction
Perception by participants in the same treatment condition that they can fulfill the positive self-presentation motive by responding in different ways

An **intratreatment interaction** exists when different participants in the same treatment condition perceive different ways of presenting themselves in the most positive light. For example, Turner and Solomon (1962) found that some participants participating in an avoidance conditioning paradigm failed to learn to move a lever to avoid shock. Investigation of the perceptions of these participants disclosed that they perceived the purpose of the study to be one of determining who could tolerate the shock. Consequently, these participants apparently believed that they would appear most positive if they could demonstrate their capacity to endure the shock. When the instructions were changed to eliminate this perception, all participants demonstrated avoidance conditioning. If these instructions had not been altered, the internal validity of the study would have been compromised because the obtained results would have been due to the combined factors of participants' perceptions and avoidance conditioning and not just the avoidance conditioning paradigm.

Experimenter Effects   We have just seen that the participants who are used in psychological research are usually not apathetic or willing to passively accept and follow the experimenter's instructions. Rather, they have motives that can have an effect on the experimental results and threaten the validity of the inferences we make about the independent variable construct. In a like manner, the experimenter is not just a passive, noninteractive observer but an active agent who can influence the outcome of the experiment. These are called the **experimenter effects**.

Experimenter effects
The experimenter's attributes and expectancies influence the responses made by the research participants

Let's take a look at the motives that the experimenter brings with him or her. First, the experimenter has a specific motive for conducting the experiment. The experimenter is a scientist attempting to uncover the laws of nature through experimentation. In performing this task, he or she develops certain perceptions of the experiment and the research participant. Lyons (1964, p. 105) states that the experimenter wants research participants to be perfect servants—intelligent individuals who will cooperate and maintain their position without becoming hostile or negative. It is easy to see why such a desire exists. The scientist seeks to understand, control, and predict behavior. To attain this goal, the scientist must eliminate the research participant effect, and so he or she dreams of the ideal research participant, who does not have any bias. Also, the experimenter has expectations regarding the outcome of the experiment. He or she has made certain hypotheses and would like to see these confirmed. Although this aspect of science is legitimate and sanctioned, it can, as we shall see, lead to certain difficulties. In addition, journals have a bias toward publishing primarily positive results, which essentially means that studies supporting hypotheses have a greater chance of being accepted for publication. Knowing this, the experimenter has an even greater desire to see the hypotheses confirmed. Can this desire or expectancy bias the results of the experiment so as to increase the probability of attaining the desired outcome? Consider the fascinating story of Clever Hans. Clever Hans was a remarkable horse that could apparently solve many types of arithmetic problems. Von Osten, the master of Clever Hans, gave Hans a problem, and then Hans gave the correct answer by tapping with his hoof (see Figure 8.2). Pfungst (1965) observed and studied this incredible behavior. Careful scrutiny revealed that von Osten would, as Hans approached the correct answer, look up at Hans. This response of looking up represented a cue for Hans to stop tapping his foot. The cue was unin-

FIGURE 8.2
Picture of Clever Hans
and his owner,
Wilhelm von Oster.

(From Archives of the
History of American
Psychology—The University
of Akron.)

tentional and not noticed by observers, who attributed mathematical skills to the horse.

Observations such as those made by Pfungst of Clever Hans seem to indicate that one's desires and expectancies can somehow be communicated to the participant and that the participant will respond to them. The research has suggested that research participants are motivated to present themselves in the most positive manner. If this is true, then the subtle cues presented by the experimenter in the experimental session may very well be picked up by the participants and influence their performance in the direction desired by the experimenter. Consequently, the experimenter may represent a demand characteristic.

The experimenter, zealous to confirm his or her hypothesis, may also unintentionally influence the recording of data to support the prediction. Kennedy and Uphoff (1939) investigated the frequency of misrecording of responses as a function of research participants' orientation. Participants, classified on the basis of their belief or disbelief in extrasensory perception (ESP), were requested to record the guesses made by the receiver. The receiver was supposedly trying to receive messages sent by a transmitter. Kennedy and Uphoff found that 63 percent of the errors that were in the direction of increasing the telepathic scores were made by believers in ESP, whereas 67 percent of the errors that were in the direction of lowering the telepathic scores were made by disbelievers. Such data indicate that biased recording, unintentional as it may be, exists in some experiments.

In addition, the experimenter is an active participant in social interaction with the research participant. The role behavior of the research participant can vary slightly as a function of the experimenter's attributes. McGuigan (1963), for example, found that the results of a learning experiment varied as a function of the experimenter.

Some of the nine researchers used to test the effectiveness of the same four methods of learning found significant differences, whereas the others did not. Such research shows that certain attributes, behavior, or characteristics of the experimenter may influence the research participants' responses in a particular manner.

The ways in which the experimenter can potentially bias the results of an experiment can be divided into two types: bias arising from the attributes of the experimenter and bias resulting from the expectancy of the experimenter.

Experimenter attributes
The physical and psychological characteristics of an experimenter that may create differential responses in participants

Experimenter Attributes.   The term **experimenter attributes** refers to the physical and psychological characteristics of an experimenter that may interact with the independent variable to cause differential performance in research participants. Rosenthal (1966) has proposed that at least three categories of attributes exist. The first is *biosocial attributes,* which include factors such as the experimenter's age, sex, race, and religion. The second category is *psychosocial attributes.* These attributes include the experimenter's psychometrically determined characteristics of anxiety level, need for social approval, hostility, authoritarianism, intelligence, and dominance and social behavior of relative status and warmth. The third category is *situational factors,* which include whether or not the experimenter and the participant have had prior contact, whether the experimenter is a naive or experienced researcher, and whether the participant is friendly or hostile.

Although experimenter attributes can influence the outcome of an experiment, this does not mean that they will. Sufficient information does not exist to identify when and under what conditions experimenter attributes will influence the outcome of an experiment. However, because we know that they can have an effect, controls for experimenter attribute effects need to be incorporated into our studies.

Experimenter expectancies
The influence of the experimenter's expectations regarding the outcome of an experiment

Experimenter Expectancies.   The term **experimenter expectancies** refers to the biasing effects that can be attributed to the expectancies the experimenter has regarding the outcome of the experiment. As noted earlier, experimenters are motivated by several forces to see their hypotheses validated. Therefore, they have expectancies regarding the outcome of the experiment. These expectancies can lead the experimenter to behave unintentionally in ways that will bias the results of the experiment in the desired direction. These unintentional influences can operate on the experimenter to alter his or her behavior and on the research participants to alter their behavior.

> *Effect on the Experimenter.* It has been well documented that the expectancies we have can color our perceptions of our physical and social worlds. Research in social perception has repeatedly demonstrated the biased nature of our perceptions of others. In light of this research, it would be naive to assume that the expectancies of the experimenter did not have a potential influence on his or her behavior. In fact, there are several documented ways in which these expectancies have actually influenced the outcome of experiments. The expectancies of the experimenter can lead him or her to record responses inaccurately in the direction that supports the expectancies, as was noted in the ESP experiment conducted by Kennedy and Uphoff (1939), discussed earlier.

Rosenthal (1978) summarized the results of twenty-one studies relating to the expectancy issue. These studies showed that, on the average, 60 percent of the recording biases favored experimenter expectancies. In one study, 91 percent of the recording biases supported the experimenter's expectancies. Impressive as these percentages are, it is important to understand that these recording errors, both biased and unbiased, represent only a small portion of the overall number of observations made. Generally speaking, only about 1 percent of all observations are misrecorded, and of these about two-thirds support the experimenter's expectancies (Rosenthal, 1978). Such a rate of misrecordings, even if the majority of them support the expectancies of the experimenters, is so small that it seldom affects the conclusions reached in a given study. But just because recording errors occur infrequently does not mean that experimenters can stop worrying about them, because when we relax we run the risk of increasing such errors. Reviews such as the one conducted by Rosenthal reveal that when we attempt to avoid recording errors we are relatively successful—at least successful enough to avoid reaching an unfounded conclusion that can be directly traced to recording errors.

Effect on the Research Participants. It is relatively easy to believe that the experimenter's expectancies may cause them to behave in ways that support their expectancies. It is harder to see how these same expectancies can influence the research participant to behave in a way that would support them, yet there is a body of research that demonstrates just this phenomenon. Remember that research participants seem to be motivated toward positive self-presentation. How do they know what response will maximize the possibility of achieving such a positive self-presentation? Somehow they make use of the demand characteristics surrounding the experiment, one of which seems to be the experimenter. The researcher has certain expectancies that lead him or her unintentionally to behave in ways that convey these expectancies. Research participants pick up these subtle cues and respond accordingly. Von Osten, for example, conveyed to Clever Hans when he should stop tapping his foot. Rosenthal and his associates have demonstrated in many studies that experimenters definitely can influence the results of the study in the direction of their hypotheses; that is, the experimenter can influence the research participants' responses in such a way that they will support the experimenter's hypothesis. For example, Rosenthal and Fode (1963) found that researchers who expected to get high success ratings on photographs previously judged to be neutral actually got significantly higher ratings than did researchers who were led to expect that they would get low success ratings.

Do these biasing effects exist in different types of experiments in psychology? One might initially think that the biasing effects of the expectancies of the experimenter on the research participants' responses would be limited to human types of experimentation—more specifically, to human experiments in such areas as social and personality psychology. However, when Rosenthal and Rubin (1978) summarized the studies conducted on expectancy, they found, as shown in Table 8.2, that the expectancy effect had been demonstrated in eight different

TABLE 8.2
Number of Experimenter Expectancy Studies Conducted in Eight Different Research Areas

Research Area	Number of Studies Conducted	Proportion Demonstrating Expectancy
Reaction time	9	0.22
Inkblot tests	9	0.44
Animal learning	15	0.73
Laboratory interviews	29	0.38
Psychophysical judgments	23	0.43
Learning and ability	34	0.29
Person perception	119	0.27
Everyday situations	112	0.40

Source: Based on Table 1 in "Interpersonal Expectancy Effects: The First 345 Studies" by R. Rosenthal and D. B. Rubin, 1978, *The Behavioral and Brain Sciences, 3*, pp. 377–415.

research areas. Perhaps the most revealing bit of information contained in Table 8.2 is that the expectancy effect is not confined to human experiments—not only has it been demonstrated in animal experiments, but a greater proportion of animal studies display the expectancy effect.

Mediation of Expectancy. The evidence presented by Rosenthal and others is consistent in indicating that the problem of the biasing effects of the experimenter is serious and needs to be dealt with. To deal most effectively with such biases, we must know what is causing them. In other words, just how is the experimenter transmitting expectancies? In addressing this question, Rosenthal (1976) considers the possibility of recording errors, particularly those biased in the direction of the expectancy. He found that although recording errors can account for some of the expectancy effect in some studies, they cannot account for all of it. To further support the fact that the experimenter expectancy bias cannot be reduced to a recording bias, Rosenthal (1976) reviewed thirty-six studies that employed special techniques for the control of recording errors and deliberate cheating. He found that these studies were *more* rather than less likely to demonstrate the experimenter expectancy effect. Exactly why such studies should be more susceptible to an experimenter expectancy effect is not known. It may be that the investigators not only provided safeguards against cheating and recording errors but also reduced the influence of other errors, thereby creating a more powerful and precise test of the expectancy effect.

If recording errors and intentional biases are insufficient to account for expectancy effects, then how can they be explained? Lack of an explanation of expectancy effects is the primary shortcoming of this research area (Adair, 1978). In all probability, these effects do not work in a unitary fashion because they have been demonstrated to exist in both animal and human research. In animal studies, differences in animal handling seem to be important (Rosenthal and Fode, 1963). In human studies, important factors seem to be nonverbal cues (Rosenthal, 1980), such as facial or postural signals (Barber, 1976); intonation, such as emphasizing different key sections of the instructions (Adair, 1973); or a nod, smile, or glance (Rosenthal, 1969). However, as Rosenberg (1980) stated and as I emphasize earlier, we must also consider the research participant when discussing the mediating influence of expectancy effects, because it is the research participants' responses that ultimately demonstrate these effects. The participants are motivated to present themselves in the most positive manner. In doing so, they use the demand characteristics of the experimental situation—including the behavior of the experimenter—to define the most appropriate way of responding to induce a positive self-presentation. Consequently, participants apparently make use of many nonverbal cues transmitted by the experimenter to define the responses that will maximize the probability that they will present themselves in the most positive manner.

The important point is that expectancy effects represent a communication process involving both the experimenter and the research participant. This interactive process is epitomized in Cooper and Hazelrigg's (1988) review of the personality factors moderating expectancy effects. Their meta-analytic review of this literature revealed that the personalities of the experimenter and research participant contribute to the existence of an expectancy effect although the size of this effect is small. Experimenters with a high need to influence others and research participants who were most influenceable and adept at decoding the experimenters' nonverbal cues were most likely to generate expectancy effects. Hazelrigg, Cooper, and Strathman (1991) supported this conclusion by revealing that experimenters with a high need for social influence and research participants with a high need for social approval produced the greatest expectancy effects.

Although we have some information on when expectancy effects are likely to be produced and who is most likely to produce them, no complete conceptual integration or theoretical statement has been proposed to explain the communication of experimenter expectancies. Therefore, we do not know when expectancy effects might occur or what may mediate them; the evidence merely tells us that these effects are real possible sources of bias. However, it is precisely because we do not know when expectancy effects are likely to occur that we must always protect ourselves against them as a potential source of bias (Ellsworth, 1978).

Magnitude of the Expectancy Effects. The influence of experimenter expectancies has been demonstrated repeatedly in a wide variety of contexts. Table 8.2 illustrates that, of the studies conducted, about one-third showed a significant expectancy effect. This rate is about seven times greater than would be expected if the effect did not exist (Rosenthal, 1976). However, if the effect of experimenter expectancies were extremely small (but real), it might not pose a significant threat to construct validity, which would mean that researchers need not concern themselves with this potential bias. Rosenthal (1978) reviewed five studies that directly addressed this issue. These studies compared the effect produced by the experimental treatment condition with the effect produced by expectancy. In three of these five studies, the expectancy effect

FIGURE 8.3

Discrimination learning of lesioned and nonlesioned rats as a function of experimenter expectancy.

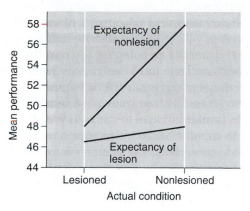

(Based on data from "Interpersonal Expectancy Effects: The First 345 Studies" by R. Rosenthal and D. B. Rubin, 1978, *The Behavioral and Brain Sciences, 3*, pp. 377–415.)

was greater than the treatment condition. For example, Burnham (in Rosenthal and Rubin, 1978) compared lesioned rats with nonlesioned (sham surgery) rats on a discrimination learning task. Half of the lesioned and half of the nonlesioned rats were assigned to experimenters who were told that they had received lesioned rats. The remainder were assigned to researchers who were told that they had received nonlesioned rats. Figure 8.3 shows that all the rats tested by experimenters who were told that the rats were nonlesioned performed better than did the rats tested by experimenters who were told that the rats were lesioned. This evidence indicates that expectancy effects can be quite large and that precautions should be taken against them.

STUDY QUESTION 8.2

- **List the threats to construct validity.**
- **What is meant by *reactivity to the experimental situation* and how does this bias a psychological experiment?**
- **What is meant by the *experimenter effect* and how does this bias the results of a psychological experiment?**

External Validity

External validity refers to the extent to which the results of the experiment can be generalized across variations in people, settings, treatments, outcomes, and times. External validity is an inferential process because it involves making broad statements based only on limited information. For example, stating that a study conducted on twenty college students in a psychology laboratory is externally valid implies that the results obtained from this experiment are also true for all college students responding in a variety of settings to variations in the treatment and outcome measures, and at different times. Such inference is a necessary component of the scientific process because all members of a defined population can seldom be studied in all settings, with all the possible variations in the treatment and outcome measures, and at all times. In order to generalize the results of a study, we must identify a target population of people, settings, treatment variations, outcome measures, and times and then randomly select individuals from these populations so that the sample will be representative of the defined population. For a variety of reasons (cost, time, accessibility), most studies do not randomly sample the specified population. Failure to randomly sample the population means that a study may contain characteristics that threaten its external validity. Such threats fall into five broad categories: lack of population validity, ecological validity, treatment variation validity, outcome validity, and time validity (Bracht and Glass, 1968; Shadish et al., 2002; Wilson, 1981). Making an inference that the results of a study can be generalized across variations in people, settings, treatments, outcomes, and times really boils down to a test of interactions. If one attitude change procedure works best with females and another works best with males, then the results are specific to each gender. The threats to external validity, therefore, are interactions of the effect of the independent variable with the variations in people, settings, treatments, outcomes, and times.

Population Validity

Population validity refers to the ability to generalize from the sample on which the study was conducted to the larger population of individuals in which one is interested. The **target population** is the larger population (such as all college students) to whom the experimental results are generalized, and the **experimentally accessible population** is the one that is available to the researcher (say, the college students at the university at which the investigator is employed). Two inferential steps are involved in generalizing from the results of the study to the larger population, as illustrated in Figure 8.4. First, we have to generalize from the sample to the experimentally accessible population. This step can be easily accomplished if the investigator *randomly* selects the sample from the experimentally accessible population. If the sample is randomly selected, it should be representative, which means that the characteristics of the experimentally accessible population can be inferred from the sample. If you conduct an experiment on a sample of fifty participants randomly selected from a given university, you can say that the obtained results are characteristic of students at that university.

The second step in the generalization process requires moving from the experimentally accessible population to the target population. This ultimate generalization seldom can be made with any degree of confidence because only rarely is the experimentally accessible population representative of the target population. For example, assume you are conducting a study using college students as the target population. You want to be able to say that the results of the study will hold for all college students. To be able to make such a statement, you would have to select randomly from the target population, which is rarely possible. Therefore, you probably will have to settle for randomly selecting from the nonrepresentative, experimentally accessible population.

FIGURE 8.4
Two-step inferential process involved in generalizing from the sample to the target population.

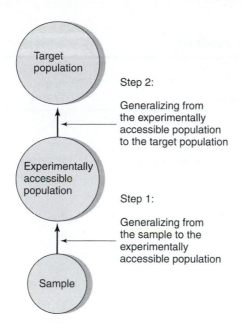

It is difficult to select randomly even from the experimentally accessible population. This is why experimenters select participants based on availability or precedent. The two categories of organisms that have most often been used in psychological studies are the albino rat and the college student taking an introductory psychology course. A number of individuals have attacked the use of these two categories of organisms. Beach (1950, 1960), Boice (1973), Eysenck (1967), Kavanau (1964, 1967), Richter (1959), and Smith (1969) have all questioned the degree to which the research results produced from laboratory rats can be generalized to other animals. Also, as Sidowski and Lockard (1966) point out, the rats that are used in a given study are definitely not a random sample of the experimentally accessible population.

Even more attention has been directed toward research conducted on human participants, much of which has been aimed at identifying laws governing human behavior. Implicit in this objective is the notion that the results from the sample of research participants on which the research was conducted will generalize to all humans—the target population. There is increasing suspicion among behavioral researchers that the participants in research studies are not representative of humans in general. Table 8.3 summarizes the results of surveys that have computed the percentage of studies using college students. You can see from this table that, at least for the journals surveyed, the percentage of psychological studies using college students is considerable.

The potential lack of generalizability when college students are used as the predominant source of research participants in psychological experiments is illustrated by Oakes (1972). He showed that he could not replicate, using a non–college student population, a reinforcement effect that had reliably been demonstrated on college students. Steele and Southwick (1985) found that college students behaved less emotionally and impulsively in laboratory studies than did the general population.

TABLE 8.3

Percentage of Studies Using College Students as Research Participants

Author	Source	Year(s)	Percentage Using College Students
Christie (1965)	*Journal of Abnormal and Social Psychology*	1949	20
Christie (1965)	*Journal of Abnormal and Social Psychology*	1959	49
Smart (1966)	*Journal of Abnormal and Social Psychology*	1962–1964	73
Smart (1966)	*Journal of Experimental Psychology*	1963–1964	86
Schultz (1969)	*Journal of Personality and Social Psychology*	1966–1967	70
Schultz (1969)	*Journal of Experimental Psychology*	1966–1967	84
Carlson (1971)	*Journal of Personality and Social Psychology* and *Journal of Personality*	1968	66
Higbee and Wells (1972)	*Journal of Personality and Social Psychology*	1969	76
Levenson, Gray, and Ingram (1976)	*Journal of Personality and Social Psychology*	1973	72
Levenson, Gray, and Ingram (1976)	*Journal of Personality*	1973	74
Sears (1986)	*Journal of Personality and Social Psychology, Personality and Social Psychology Bulletin,* and *Journal of Experimental Social Psychology*	1980	82

The lack of generalizability of experimental results is not restricted to research conducted using college students. For example, we now find that men and women have very different reactions to drugs (Neergaard, 1999). Morphine controls pain much better in women than in men. However, women reject heart transplants more often than men do, which may be due to the fact that anti-rejection drugs such as cyclosporine clear out of women's body faster. Aspirin seems to thin men's blood much better than women's. These gender differences have resulted in the Food and Drug Administration's requiring drug manufacturers to analyze how different sexes respond to experimental therapies. These examples illustrate that the generalizability of the results of a study is not a function of the population sampled. It is a function of the interaction of the characteristics of the research participants and the particular behavioral phenomenon being investigated. Population validity, therefore, boils down to a selection by treatment interaction. If a selection by treatment interaction (Campbell and Stanley, 1963) exists, the experiment is externally invalid or cannot be generalized to the target population. This means that the particular sample of research participants selected for use in a study may respond differently to the experimental treatment condition than would another sample of participants with different characteristics.

Ecological Validity

Ecological validity
The extent to which the results of a study can be generalized across settings or environmental conditions

Ecological validity refers to the generalizability of the results of the study across settings or from one set of environmental conditions to another. For example, the environmental setting of an experiment may require a specific arrangement of the equipment, a particular location, or a certain type of experimenter. If the results of a laboratory experiment that requires such a setting can be generalized to other settings (such as a therapy setting or a labor relations setting), then the experiment possesses ecological validity. Consequently, ecological validity exists to the extent that the treatment effect is independent of the experimental setting. If a treatment effect depends on the experimental setting, then ecological validity does not exist. Kazdin (1992), for example, described a treatment program for drug abusers that did not have ecological validity because the treatment program was effective for individuals living in rural areas but not for individuals living in urban areas. Ecological validity, therefore, boils down to a selection by treatment interaction. If a selection by treatment interaction exists, ecological validity does *not* exist. However, if a selection by treatment interaction does not exist, then the study has ecological validity.

Temporal Validity

Temporal validity
The extent to which the results of an experiment can be generalized across time

Temporal validity refers to the extent to which the results of an experiment can be generalized across time. Most psychological studies are conducted during one time period. Carlson (1971), for example, found that 78 percent of the studies published in the *Journal of Personality and Social Psychology* and the *Journal of Personality* were based on only a single session. Five years later, Levenson, Gray, and Ingram (1976) found that 89 percent of the articles published in the same two journals were based on a single session. If these two periodicals are representative of most of the work being conducted in psychology, we are not taking the time variable into consideration. Experimenters seem to be assuming that the results of an experiment remain invariant across time.

It has been demonstrated, however, that the results of an experiment can vary depending on the amount of time that elapses between the presentation of the independent variable and the assessment of the dependent variable. Walster (1964) asked army draftees to rate the attractiveness of ten different jobs to which they could be assigned during their two-year enlistment period. After rating the ten jobs, each person was asked to choose between two jobs that had been rated similarly and were moderately attractive. After selecting one of the two, the recruits were asked to rate the attractiveness of the two jobs once again. For one group of recruits, this second rating took place immediately after the job choice was made. For the other three groups, the choice was delayed four, fifteen, or ninety minutes. Figure 8.5 illustrates the change in attractiveness of the chosen job over time. Immediately after making the choice, the draftees found the chosen job more attractive. Within four minutes, however, the recruits apparently experienced some degree of regret or had second thoughts about the jobs they had chosen because they rated the job as less attractive. This regret then dissipated rather rapidly. Ratings of the chosen job reached their

FIGURE 8.5

Illustration of how the attractiveness of a chosen job changes across time.

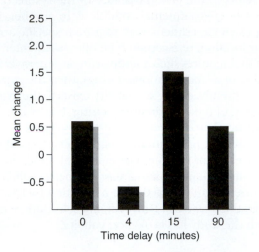

(Based on data from "The Temporal Sequence of Post-Decision Processes" by E. Walster. In L. Festinger, *Conflict, Decision, and Dissonance*. Stanford: Stanford University Press, 1964.)

highest level after fifteen minutes, only to return to their original postchoice level within ninety minutes.

Experiments such as this one vividly demonstrate that experimental results can vary across time. The time variable does not merely refer to the passage of time but also to variations as a function of different points in time. For example, Willson (1981) has pointed out that a **seasonal variation**, or a variation that appears regularly over time, can threaten external validity. Seasonal variations refer to events such as the winter months versus summer months or various holiday periods. Studies conducted during one of these seasonal variations may not generalize to other seasonal variations. For example, the automobile accident rate is probably greater in the winter than in the summer months in states such as Minnesota. A **cyclical variation**, or the regular variation that occurs in people or other organisms, can also threaten external validity. Just consider the circadian (approximately twenty-four hour) rhythm on which our pulse rate, temperature, and endocrine and kidney functions operates (Conroy and Mills, 1970) and the effect that variations in this rhythm can have on the results of some experiments. The many cyclical variations that can exist within the organisms on which we conduct our experiments can potentially alter the influence of the experimental treatment or interact with the experimental treatment. If such an interaction takes place, the results of the experiment are generalizable only to the specific point in the cycle during which the experiment was conducted.

These examples clearly illustrate that failure to consider the time variable can threaten the external validity of experiments.

Seasonal variation

A variation that occurs at regular time intervals

Cyclical variation

A regular variation that occurs within people and other organisms

Treatment Variation Validity

Treatment variation validity refers to the generalizability of results across variations of the treatment. Treatment variation validity is an issue because the administration of a treatment can vary from one administration to the next. For example, many studies have been conducted demonstrating that behavior therapy is effective in treating depression. However, these studies have typically been conducted in a way that has provided maximum assurance that the therapists are competent and have delivered the therapy in the prescribed manner. Therapists who administer behavior therapy to the general public, however, vary considerably in their competency and the extent to which they deliver the therapy in the prescribed manner. This means that there is considerable variation in the way behavior therapy is administered. If behavior therapy produces a beneficial effect for the treatment of depression across these different variations in the way it is delivered, treatment variation validity exists. If behavior therapy is beneficial only when administered exactly as prescribed and is not beneficial when administered in a slightly different way, then treatment variation validity does not exist.

Outcome Validity

Outcome validity refers to the generalizability of results across different but related dependent variables. Many studies investigate the effect of an independent variable on more than one dependent variable. Outcome validity refers to the extent to which the same effect is measured by all related outcome measures. For example, a job-training program is expected to increase the likelihood of a person's getting a job after graduation. This is probably the primary outcome measure of interest. However, an equally important issue is keeping the job. This means that the person must arrive on time, not miss work, and follow orders, as well as demonstrate an acceptable level of performance. The effectiveness of the job-training program may increase the probability of getting a job but have no effect on job retention because it has little impact on these other essential adaptive job skills. If this is the case, the job-training program does not have outcome validity. However, if the job-training program increases the probability of getting a job and also increases the other essential adaptive job skills necessary to keeping a job, the training program has outcome validity.

STUDY QUESTION 8.3

- **What is meant by *external validity* and why is it important to experimental research?**
- **What characteristics of an experiment could threaten external validity?**
- **Explain each of the ways in which the external validity of an experiment can be threatened.**

Cautions in Evaluating the External Validity of Experiments

Mook (1983) has appropriately pointed out that experiments are conducted for a variety of purposes and that some of these purposes do not attempt to relate to real-life behavior. The issue of external validity is moot for such experiments. For example, we may conduct an experiment in order to determine if something *can* happen and not necessarily if it really does happen. Person–perception studies have revealed that people wearing glasses are judged as more intelligent when seen for only fifteen seconds. If these same people are viewed for five minutes, however, the glasses make no difference. The temporary effect of the glasses seems to have no meaning in real life. If the experiment had not been conducted, however, this temporary effect would not have been identified. Although it says little about real-life behavior, it does say something about humans as judges, so the experimental results are important.

A second significant point made by Mook (1983) is that the component of an experiment that is to be generalized is often the theoretical process that is being tested or the understanding that accrues from the experiment. For example, consider the difference between a study investigating the influence of a new teaching technique and a study investigating the influence of the presence of weapons. Researchers investigating a new technique for teaching basic arithmetic to seven-year-old children would like to have their results generalize to all seven-year-olds. Contrast their situation with that of Berkowitz and LePage (1967), who found that if a weapon was present on the table a research participant delivered more shocks as an indication of not liking a partner's ideas. In no way would they want to generalize the specific procedure of this experiment to other people, settings, or times. A person in a setting other than the laboratory might indeed give more shocks to a partner if a weapon were placed on the table. Such a situation, however, would seldom exist in real life, and it was not Berkowitz and LePage's intention to generalize the specific experimental procedure. Rather, it is an understanding of the impact of the presence of weapons that is to be extracted from the study, not the specific procedure.

One must also exercise caution in placing too much emphasis on the setting in which the experiment is conducted. Laboratory research has been criticized because of the artificiality of the setting, and this artificiality can impose a severe restraint on the external validity of the experiment. Because of the intuitive logic inherent in this criticism, a number of investigators have advocated that psychologists move out of the laboratory and into a real-world setting, such as a mental health clinic. The assumption seems to be that if we change the experimental setting, we will enhance external validity. For example, some people believe that if industrial psychologists conduct their research in an organizational setting, both the setting and the research participants will be more representative of the real-world population. Dipboye and Flanagan (1979) have demonstrated that such an assumption is not valid. They showed that the field research conducted in industrial organizational psychology has been performed on male, professional, technical, and managerial personnel in productive economic organizations through the use of self-report inventories. Thus, in at least this one area of psychology, the assumption of the greater external validity of field research has not been supported, because the field research has used a limited sample of individuals in limited field settings over one time period.

Relationship between Internal and External Validity

Given our knowledge of the classes of variables that threaten external validity, it would seem logical to design experiments using a diverse sample of research participants, treatment variations, outcome measures, and settings across several different time periods in order to increase external validity. The problem with this strategy is that there tends to be an inverse relationship between internal and external validity. When external validity is increased, internal validity tends to be sacrificed; when internal validity is increased, external validity tends to suffer (Kazdin, 1980).

To gain insight into this relationship between internal and external validity, consider the following characteristics of a well-designed study. From the previous chapters, you know that a well-designed study attempts to control for the effects of all extraneous variables. The researcher selects as research participants a specific subsample of the population, such as females or sixth-grade children, in order to control for variation in different subsamples of individuals or to create a more homogeneous sample so as to maximize the possibility of detecting a treatment effect. The experimenter conducts the experiment within the confines of a controlled laboratory setting in order to present a specific amount of the treatment condition and to eliminate the influence of extraneous variables, such as the presence of noise or weather conditions. While in the laboratory setting, the research participants receive a set of standardized instructions delivered by one experimenter or perhaps by some automated device and complete outcome measures at one specific point in time. But these same features that maximize the possibility of attaining internal validity—using a restricted sample of research participants and testing them in the artificial setting of a laboratory at one specific time—limit the external validity (Kazdin, 1980) by excluding different people, treatment variations, settings, and times. However, if an experimenter tried to maximize external validity by conducting the experiment on diverse groups of individuals and treatment variations in many settings and at different points in time, the experiment's internal validity would decrease. As the number of settings, treatment variations, or types of research participants is increased, the control of the extraneous variables that may influence the independent variable decreases, decreasing the likelihood that the study will identify the influence produced by the independent variable. This does not, however, mean that external validity should be disregarded. Rather, it suggests that which type of validity is most important is a function of the purpose of the research study. If your primary purpose is to determine if the relationship between two variables is causal, then internal validity takes priority. However, if prior research has established that a causal relationship exists between the two variables, then the purpose of the study may be to assess the external validity of the causal relationship.

STUDY QUESTION 8.4 | **Explain why there is an inverse relationship between internal and external validity.**

Summary   Construct and external validity are two types of validity that are relevant to psychological experimentation in addition to statistical conclusion and internal validity that were discussed in Chapter 7. Construct validity refers to the extent to which we can infer higher-order constructs from the operations we used to represent them in psychological research. Effectively assessing whether the operations used are accurate representations of the intended construct is fostered by having a clear definition of the construct of interest. This is very difficult to accomplish because it is difficult to identify the prototypical features of many of the constructs investigated. The best that can typically be accomplished is to identify as many of the prototypical elements of the constructs as possible. The next step in assessing construct validity is to obtain evidence that there is a match between the constructs and the operations used to represent them. This involves collecting evidence indicating that this match exists. This evidence comes from all sources such as obtaining evidence of content validity and criterion-related validity as well as any other source of evidence indicating that a match exists.

In spite of a person's best effort at accurately representing a specific construct with a given set of operations, there are a number of reasons why we may not be correct in the inferences we make about the higher-order constructs from the operations used in the experiment. These reasons are considered threats to construct validity. Two of the threats that have received attention are the research participant's reactivity to the experimental situation and experimenter effects. Reactivity to the experimental situation refers to the fact that participants come into experiments with their own motives and perceptions and these motives and perceptions partially determine their response to the dependent variable. The responses observed on the dependent variable are, therefore, due to the independent variable *and* the research participants' motives and perceptions. So any inference that the observed response is due only to the independent variable treatment construct is incorrect. The primary reactive factor affecting participants' responses is their positive self-presentation motive (their desire to present themselves in the most positive light).

Experimenter effects refer to the influence that the experimenter can have on the responses of the research participant, therefore becoming part of the treatment construct being tested. The two primary ways in which the experimenter influences the research participants' response is by their attributes and by the expectancies they have that are communicated to the research participant. The attributes that may influence the research participants' response are biosocial, psychosocial, and situational factors. Experimenter expectancies refer to the expectancies that the experimenter has regarding the outcome of the experiment. These expectancies can lead the experimenter to record responses inaccurately in the direction that supports the hypothesis. However, this is a relatively minor source of bias. The primary way experimenter expectancies bias the outcome of a study is that these expectancies are subtly communicated to the research participant and the research participant acts on them in a way that can support the experimenter's hypothesis.

External validity refers to the extent to which the results of an experiment can be generalized across variations in people, settings, treatments, outcomes, and times. To be able to make such an inference a random sample must be obtained from the target population of people, settings, treatment variations, outcome measures, and times. For many reasons, such as cost, such a random sample cannot be obtained. This means that a study may contain characteristics that threaten its internal validity. These threats fall into the following categories:

Population validity. The ability to generalize from the sample on which the study was conducted to the larger target population. Population validity is threatened because most studies do not randomly select research participants from the target population.

Ecological validity. The generalizability of the results of the study across settings. Ecological validity is threatened when the experiment is not conducted in a random selection of settings.

Temporal validity. The extent to which the results of the experiments can be generalized across time. Temporal validity is threatened if the experiment is completed at one point in time.

Treatment variation validity. The ability to generalize across variations of the treatment. Treatment variation validity is threatened if the study is conducted using only one variation of the treatment.

Outcome validity. The ability to generalize across different but related dependent variables. Outcome validity is threatened if the treatment effect is demonstrated with some but not all related outcome measures.

One of the important criteria for a study is external validity. However, studies are conducted for a variety of purposes and for some studies external validity is a moot issue. The purpose of a particular study must be examined prior to assessing its external validity.

Key Terms and Concepts

Construct validity
Content validity
Criterion-related validity
Reactivity to the experimental situation
Demand characteristics
Positive self-presentation
Intertreatment interaction
Intratreatment interaction
Experimenter effects
Experimenter attributes
Experimenter expectancies

External validity
Population validity
Target population
Experimentally accessible population
Ecological validity
Temporal validity
Seasonal variation
Cyclical variation
Treatment variation validity
Outcome validity

Related Internet Sites

www.socialresearchmethods.net/kb/constval.htm
This site discusses construct validity and gives a variety of links that help in understanding construct validity and the threats to construct validity.

www.socialresearchmethods.net/kb/external.htm
This site provides a brief discussion of external validity as well as a brief discussion of threats to external validity.

Practice Test

1. Dr. Brown conducted a study to determine if rats can count. His study revealed that rats pressed a bar many more times when they were shocked three times to avoid a fourth shock than they did when shocked only once to avoid a second shock. He concluded from this experiment that rats can indeed count. If he is correct in this conclusion the study has

   a. Content validity
   b. Experimental validity
   c. Experimental reliability
   d. Developed an inappropriate hypothesis because only humans can count
   e. Demonstrated criterion-related validity

2. Dr. Future wanted to demonstrate that a score of greater than 25 on the Conners scale was representative of children with hyperactivity so he identified ten children under the age of 5 with a score greater than 25. Dr. Future then predicted that these children, when they entered the first grade would have the classic symptoms of hyperactivity consisting of such things as not being able to sit still at their desks. If this prediction turns out to be true,

   a. Concurrent validity exists
   b. Test–retest reliability exists
   c. Experimental validity exists
   d. Test validity exists
   e. Predictive validity exists

3. John Brown has signed up for a social psychology study. His friend just completed the study and told him that he experienced smoke coming into the room while they were completing some questionnaires. His friend told him that he thought the study was investigating a reaction to the smoke and not the response to the questionnaires. When John arrived at the experimental site and heard the experimenter's instructions, he evaluated the things he was told to see if the experiment was actually about the reaction to smoke. John's behavior

   a. Represents a positive self-presentation attempt
   b. Represents an example of use of demand characteristics
   c. Represents experimental curiosity
   d. Represents an example of confounding extraneous variables influencing the experiment
   e. Represents an inappropriate behavior on the part of John's friend

4. Dr. Prediction conducted an experiment investigating future predictions of violent behavior and found that children that hurt animals are more likely to become spouse abusers. From the results of this study he wrote a book which had as its thesis the fact that parents should use children's behavior toward pets as an indication of their future behavior toward others, and if they see them consistently abuse pets they should get their children some help. In presenting this advice to parents, Dr. Prediction assumes that his study

a. Has external validity
b. Has construct validity
c. Has experimental reliability
d. Has internal validity
e. Has eliminated all confounding variables

5. If you are conducting a study investigating premenstrual symptoms and find that women change their eating pattern over their monthly cycle you would have identified a

a. Gender related effect
b. Cyclical variation
c. Treatment variation
d. Outcome variation
e. Hormonal effect

6. Dr. Know conducted an experiment on youth violence and found that his treatment was effective when he conducted it at the Strickland Youth Center; so he also tried it at the Boys Club, testing which threat to external validity?

a. Population validity threat
b. Ecological validity threat
c. Temporal validity threat
d. Outcome validity threat
e. Treatment variation validity threat

Challenge Exercise

1. For each of the following research examples, identify

a. The independent variable
b. The dependent variable
c. The constructs being investigated
d. The operations used to represent these constructs
e. How you would collect evidence indicating the construct validity of the operations

A. Logue and Anderson (2001) were interested in determining whether experienced administrators were more likely than individuals training to be administrators to consider the long-term consequences of their actions. The experienced group of administrators consisted of forty-four provosts (chief academic officers) of colleges and universities and the trainees consisted of fourteen individuals enrolled in the American Council on Education Fellows Program (a program that trains individuals to be college and university administrators). One of the measures of long-term consequences was that all participants made a series of fifty-nine hypothetical choices between two monetary alternatives. These alternatives always took the form of "The administrator to whom you report will give your unit $X right now or The administrator to whom you report will give you $20,000 in Y time." The $X amounts varied from $20 to $20,000 in increments of $666 and the Y time periods were 1 week, 10 weeks, 5 months, 10 months, 1.5 years, 3 years, 6 years, and 12 years. The participants had to select one of the two alternatives. Interestingly, when given the choice between choosing a smaller but immediate amount of money versus a larger amount to be received at some time in the future, the experienced administrators were more likely to choose the immediate funding, whereas the trainees were more likely to select the larger future funding.

B. Blascovich, Spencer, Quinn, and Steele (2001) wanted to test the hypothesis that stereotype threat causes an increase in blood pressure among African Americans but not among European Americans. To test this hypothesis, African American and European American participants were randomly assigned to a high-stereotype or low-stereotype threat condition. In the high-stereotype condition the experimenter was a European-American man presumably from Stanford University who informed the participants about the debate regarding standardized tests—whether they were biased toward particular subcultural groups—and that a new test of intelligence had been developed and asked the participants to take the new test to obtain a nationally representative sample. In the low-stereotype condition, the experimenter was an African American man presumably from Stanford University. He noted the debate about the use of standardized tests and said he wanted them to take a new culturally unbiased test. He further noted that prior studies had indicated that the test was unbiased. All participants then completed the Remote Associates Test, which consists of presenting three words and asking the participants to generate a fourth word related to the three they see. Arterial blood pressure of the participants was taken prior to hearing the instructions and continuously while they took the Remote Associates Test.

Control Techniques

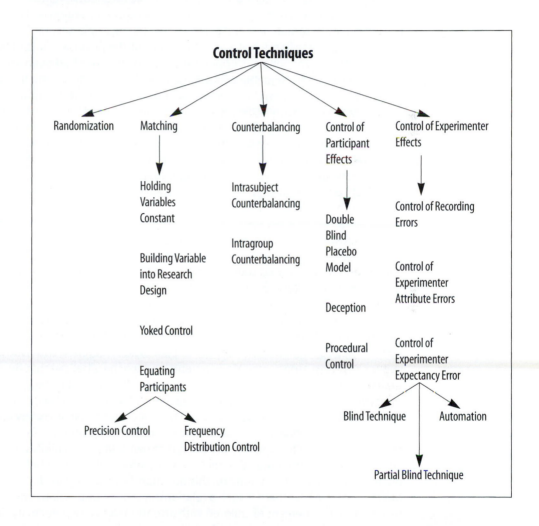

Control Techniques

Randomization

Matching
- Holding Variables Constant
- Building Variable into Research Design
- Yoked Control
- Equating Participants
  - Precision Control
  - Frequency Distribution Control

Counterbalancing
- Intrasubject Counterbalancing
- Intragroup Counterbalancing

Control of Participant Effects
- Double Blind Placebo Model
- Deception
- Procedural Control

Control of Experimenter Effects
- Control of Recording Errors
- Control of Experimenter Attribute Errors
- Control of Experimenter Expectancy Error
  - Blind Technique
  - Automation
  - Partial Blind Technique

One of the areas that has attracted considerable attention over the past several decades is the effect of diet on behavior. The increased attention and interest have come from both researchers and practitioners. For example, several years ago a colleague stopped me in the hall and inquired about the possible effect of breakfast on a student's classroom behavior. Apparently, this psychologist had been approached regarding the unmanageable behavior of a specific child. According to teacher reports, the child's behavior, when he arrived at school, was considered normal. The child was responsive to instructions, did his schoolwork, and in general was like all the rest of the children in the classroom. But at about 10:00 A.M. his whole demeanor changed. Instead of being a pleasant, responsive child, he became extremely disruptive. He would get out of his seat and roam around the classroom, talk back to the teacher, and make strange sounds. Inquiry into the child's eating habits revealed that he typically ate a breakfast consisting of very high-carbohydrate foods such as pancakes and syrup. Could this high-carbohydrate diet have the effect of triggering disruptive behavior several hours after its consumption? Possibly, but many other variables, including other dietary substances, could have caused the disruptive behavior.

Let's look at another actual case. Several years ago the parents of a four-year-old child found that he would suddenly become extremely disobedient and even rather violent. He would start running around in circles, and, when his parents tried to restrain him, would run away from them as fast as he could, run straight into a wall, bounce off it, pick himself up, and do the same thing again and again until his parents finally caught him and physically restrained him. Eventually it was established that this behavior was elicited when the child consumed Kool-Aid sweetened with Nutrasweet (the sugar substitute aspartame). Many parents and teachers believe that the diet their children eat and whether or not they have eaten a decent breakfast have an impact on their later behavior. In fact, a survey of teachers (McLoughlin & Nall, 1988) has revealed that 90 percent of the teachers surveyed believed that sugar adversely affected children's classroom behavior and academic performance despite the fact that there is little, if any, evidence to support the notion that restriction of a child's sugar intake is of any benefit. Does this mean that diet does not affect subsequent behavior? Little high-quality research has been done on this question, but the studies that have been conducted indicate that there is such a relationship. For example, Boris and Mandel (1994) revealed that 73 percent of children with attention deficit hyperactivity disorder demonstrated an improvement when placed on a diet restricting a variety of foods such as dairy products, wheat, eggs, and peanuts.

Any investigation into an area like this, however, is littered with variables that must be controlled. For example, a maturational variable such as the age of the participant may influence the outcome of a diet–behavior study because younger individuals who are still maturing may be more susceptible to the impact of dietary manipulations. In addition, other variables—previous dietary habits, the food combinations ingested, the personality of the participants, or their metabolic rate—may have an impact on the effect of a specific diet or even on whether skipping meals has any impact. The influence of such variables must be controlled for us to reach a conclusion regarding the impact of a specific dietary variable.

Chapter Preview

When we conduct a psychological experiment, one of the primary goals is to determine whether the independent variable causes the changes observed in the dependent variable. To make this causal inference, we must control for the influence of extraneous variables that could confound the results and serve as rival hypotheses. If we have controlled for the influence of the extraneous variables, then internal validity is achieved. However, there are many different extraneous variables that could creep into an experiment and threaten internal validity, such as those presented in Chapter 8. The influence of these extraneous variables has to be held constant across the different levels of the independent variable. The most frequently used way of accomplishing this is to include control techniques into the design of our experiment. Many techniques have been developed over the years that enable the researcher to control the influence of confounding extraneous variables. In this chapter, I discuss a number of the more commonly used control techniques.

Introduction

In order to infer that the manipulation of the independent variable caused the effect observed in the dependent variable, the experiment must have internal validity. This means that some procedure must be incorporated into the study that will eliminate any differential influence that confounding extraneous variables may have on the dependent variable. There are three general methods of achieving the desired level of control. First, control can be attained through appropriate design of the experiment. In fact, one of the purposes of experimental design is to eliminate the differential influence of extraneous variables. (The control function of appropriate designs becomes evident in Chapter 10.) A second means of attaining control involves making statistical adjustments by using techniques such as analysis of covariance. These techniques, however, are beyond the scope of the present text and therefore will not be discussed. A third means of acquiring the desired control is to incorporate one or more of the available control techniques into the design of the experiment. This method is intimately related to control through the appropriate design of the experiment because any control technique must be incorporated into the design of the experiment. However, control techniques are discussed separately in this chapter to allow a more effective illustration of the variables that they control and the way they control these unwanted sources of variation.

All the following techniques cannot and should not be incorporated into one study. Indeed, it would be impossible to do so. By the same token, it is often possible and advisable to use more than one of the techniques. The researcher must decide which of the possible extraneous variables could influence the experiment and, given this knowledge, select from the available techniques those that will allow the desired control. Failure to do so will create internal invalidity.

Randomization

Randomization
A control technique that equates groups of participants by ensuring every member an equal chance of being assigned to any group

Randomization, the most important and basic of all the control methods, is a statistical control technique designed to assure that extraneous variables, known or unknown, will not systematically bias the study results. It is the only technique for controlling unknown sources of variation. As Cochran and Cox (1957) have stated, "Randomization is somewhat analogous to insurance, in that it is a precaution against disturbances that may or may not occur and that may or may not be serious if they do occur. It is generally advisable to take the trouble to randomize even when it is not expected that there will be any serious bias from failure to randomize. The experimenter is thus protected against unusual events that upset his expectations" (p. 8).

How does randomization eliminate systematic bias in the experiment? Randomization refers to the use of some clearly stated procedures such as tossing coins, drawing cards from a well-shuffled deck, or using a table of random numbers. To provide for maximum control of any systematic bias in the process of selecting the sample of research participants on which the study is conducted, one should select participants randomly from a population. *Population,* if you recall, refers to all of something, such as all college students in the United States or all females. Randomly selecting research participants from a population provides maximum assurance that a systematic bias does not exist in the selection process and that you have selected for the study a sample that is representative of the total population. By **representative** I mean that the sample participants have the same characteristic as the people in the population. If the average IQ in the population is 120, then the average IQ of the participants in the sample should also be 120. Only in this way can the results of the study say something about the total population.

Representative
When the sample participants have the same characteristics as the people in the population

For example, assume that you want to conduct a study focusing on interpersonal attraction among college professors. In this instance the population of interest is all college professors, and you want the results of the study to say something about all college professors and not just those who participate in your study. One way to ensure that the study results say something about all college professors is to include all of them in the study. However, including the total population is seldom, if ever, possible, so you must select a sample from the population on which to conduct the study. A sample, if you recall, is any number less than the population. Whenever you select a sample for a study, you run the risk of getting an unusual group of individuals who do not represent the population of interest. For example, if you conduct the study only on female college professors, you will have excluded the responses of male college professors. This will provide a biased representation of interpersonal attraction among college professors and the results will say little about the overall population—something you want to avoid.

How do you select a sample of research participants that is representative of the population? The only way in which this can be done is to select a random sample. A random sample is a sample of participants that is selected in such a way that each person has an equal chance of being selected and the selection of one does not affect the selection of another.

Once participants have been randomly selected for a study, they should be randomly assigned to the same number of groups as there are experimental treatment conditions, as illustrated in Figure 9.1. The experimental treatment conditions should then be assigned to the experimental treatment groups. Although this is the ideal arrangement, one can seldom select research participants randomly from a population. For example, just think of the difficulty of randomly selecting a sample of college professors from all professors within the United States. This would simply be not just difficult to do but next to impossible—unless you were independently wealthy or had a research grant to either go to all the various universities to test these participants or have them come to your university. Consequently, the random selection of participants from a population is an ideal that is seldom achieved. Fortunately, the random selection of participants from a population is not the crucial element needed to achieve control over the influence of extraneous variables. Random assignment of the research participants to treatment conditions is essential. There is a basic differ-

FIGURE 9.1
Illustration of the ideal procedure for obtaining participants for an experiment.

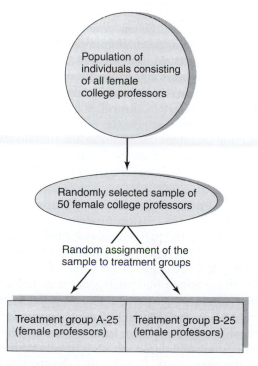

Population of individuals consisting of all female college professors

Randomly selected sample of 50 female college professors

Random assignment of the sample to treatment groups

Treatment group A-25 (female professors)

Treatment group B-25 (female professors)

Random selection
Selection of people at random from a defined population

Random assignment
Randomly assigning a sample of individuals to a specific number of comparison groups

ence between random selection and random assignment. **Random selection** involves selecting people at random from a defined population. **Random assignment** involves randomly assigning a specific group of participants to a set number of conditions. The group of participants that are randomly assigned does not have to be, and typically is not, randomly selected from a target population. Random selection of participants provides assurance that your sample is *representative* of the population from which it was drawn. It therefore has implications for generalization of the results of the experiment back to the population. Random assignment provides assurance that the extraneous variables are controlled and contributes to the internal validity of the study.

The key word in this whole process of selecting and assigning participants is *random*. The term *random* "may be used in a theoretical sense to refer to an assumption about the equiprobability of events. Thus, a random sample is one such that every member of the population has an equal probability of being included in it" (Ferguson, 1966, p. 133). In a random selection of a sample of one hundred participants from a population of, say, college freshmen, every freshman has an equal chance of being included in the sample of one hundred. In like manner, random assignment of participants to the experimental groups assures that each sample participant has an equal opportunity of being assigned to each group.

In order to provide equiprobability of events when randomly assigning participants to treatment conditions, it is necessary to use a randomization procedure, such as the one presented in Exhibit 9.1 on page 267. When such a procedure is used, maximum assurance is provided that any systematic bias will be eliminated from the experimental results. This is because the random assignment of participants to treatment conditions is assumed to result in random distribution of all extraneous variables. Consequently, the distribution and influence of the extraneous variables should be about the same in all groups of participants.

Consider the following example using the random assignment of participants. Professor X was conducting a study on learning. Intelligence naturally is correlated with learning ability, so this factor must be controlled for, or held constant. Let us consider two possibilities—one that provides for the needed control through the use of random assignment and one that does not. Assume first that no random assignment of participants existed (no control) but that the first ten participants who showed up for the experiment were assigned to treatment Group A and the second ten participants were assigned to treatment Group B. Assume further that the results of the experiment revealed that treatment Group B learned significantly faster than treatment Group A. Is this difference caused by the different experimental treatment conditions that were administered to the two groups or by the fact that the participants in Group B *may* have been more intelligent than those in Group A? Suppose that the investigator also considers the intelligence factor to be a possible confounding variable and therefore gives all participants an intelligence test. The left-hand side of Table 9.1 depicts the hypothetical distribution of IQ scores of these twenty participants. From this table, you can see that the mean IQ score of the people in Group B is 10.6 points higher than that of those in Group A. Intelligence is, therefore, a potentially confounding variable and serves as a rival hypothesis for explaining the observed performance difference in the two groups. To state that the treatment conditions pro-

EXHIBIT 9.1

Procedure for Randomly Assigning Participants to Experimental Treatment Conditions

The most common procedure for randomly assigning participants to experimental treatment conditions is to use a list of random numbers such as the following list of two hundred numbers. A larger list of random numbers appears in Appendix D.

This list consists of a series of twenty rows and ten columns. The number in each position is random because each of the numbers from 0 to 9 had an equal chance of occupying that position and the selection of one number for a given position had no influence in the selection of another number for another position. Therefore, because each individual number is random, any combination of the numbers must be random.

Now let's look at the procedure you should follow when using this list of random numbers or the random number table in Appendix D. Let's assume that you want to conduct an experiment that investigates the effect that thoughts about a prior lover have on a person's physiological responses. To investigate this relationship, you identify twenty people who have had lovers in the past and want to randomly assign them to two groups of ten participants each so that you can test one group of ten when they are thinking about their past lover and the other group of ten when they are thinking about a friend who was not a lover. To randomly assign the twenty participants to the two groups you complete the following steps.

Step 1. Number the participants from 0 to 19.

Step 2. Block the list of random numbers into columns of two, because the maximum number of participants you have is a two-digit number. This blocking has been done in the list of random numbers in this exhibit. The same procedure should be used if you are using the random numbers in Appendix D.

Step 3. Randomly select the first group of ten participants by reading down the first two columns until you come to a number less than 20. The first number encountered that is less than 20 is 00.

Therefore, the first participant randomly selected from this group of 20 is the participant assigned the number 00. Proceed down the columns until you encounter the other numbers less than 20, which are 18 and 03. Participants numbered 18 and 03 represent the second and third randomly selected participants. When you reach the bottom of the first two columns, start at the top of the next two columns. With this procedure, the participant numbers 05, 06, 09, 10, 01, 14, and 07 are selected, which represent the remaining eight of the first ten randomly selected participants. Note that if you encounter a number that has already been selected (as we did with the numbers 03, 06, and 14), you must disregard it.

Step 4. If you have to randomly assign the research participants to more than two groups, continue step 3 for the third and subsequent groups. However, the last group will be the remaining participants. In our example, we randomly selected ten of the twenty participants for one group, so the remaining ten participants represent the second group as follows:

Group 0		Group 1	
00	01	02	04
03	05	08	11
06	07	12	13
09	10	15	16
14	18	17	19

Step 5. After the participants have been randomly assigned to the same number of groups as there are treatment conditions, the groups should ideally be randomly assigned to the treatment conditions. In this case, this is accomplished by using only one column of the table of random numbers because there are only two groups of participants. The two groups are numbered 0 and 1. If you proceed down the first column you can see that the first number encountered that is less than 2 is 0, so group 0 (the first group of participants) is assigned

(*continued*)

EXHIBIT 9.1 (continued)

to the first treatment group. This means that group 1, the second group of randomly assigned participants, is assigned to the second treatment group as follows:

Treatment Condition

A_1	A_2
Group 0	Group 1

Random Number List

	1	2	3	4	5	6	7	8	9	10
1	8	1	4	5	5	6	9	8	7	3
2	2	7	9	6	5	4	6	4	8	3
3	0	0	0	5	5	8	9	7	6	9
4	7	8	3	4	7	0	7	7	5	2
5	8	5	8	6	3	5	4	2	2	2
6	7	3	5	3	6	8	0	7	3	3
7	1	8	6	0	1	0	7	4	4	7
8	7	9	5	3	0	1	5	5	5	1
9	5	6	6	7	8	5	8	1	1	9
10	3	0	3	3	9	1	9	9	1	9
11	9	7	4	7	8	4	7	1	0	9
12	5	6	4	5	1	4	5	4	1	1
13	5	7	4	0	4	2	5	9	6	7
14	8	6	0	5	6	9	4	4	3	2
15	6	7	6	7	3	3	7	1	8	9
16	2	6	0	6	7	3	3	0	6	9
17	6	7	5	5	1	4	7	4	1	2
18	6	3	0	9	9	9	5	3	8	0
19	0	3	7	3	0	3	0	6	8	6
20	7	1	6	8	2	0	5	3	2	1

duced the observed effect, researchers must control for potentially confounding variables such as the IQ difference.

One means of eliminating such a bias is to randomly assign the twenty participants to the two treatment groups as they show up for the experiment. The right-hand side of Table 9.1 depicts the random distribution of the twenty participants and their corresponding hypothetical IQ scores. Now note that the mean IQ scores for the two groups are very similar. There is only a 0.2 point IQ difference as opposed to the prior 10.6 point difference. For the mean IQ scores to be so similar, both groups of participants have to have a similar distribution of IQ scores, the effect of which is to control for the potential biasing effect of IQ. The IQ scores in Table 9.1 have been rank ordered to show this similar distribution.

Random assignment produces control by virtue of the fact that the variables to be controlled are distributed in approximately the same manner in all groups (ideally the

TABLE 9.1

Hypothetical Distribution of Twenty Research Participants' IQ Scores

Group Assignment Based on Arrival Sequence				Random Assignment of Participants to Groups			
Group A		Group B		Group A		Group B	
Participants	IQ Scores	Participants	IQ Scores	Participants	IQ Scores	Participants	IQ Scores
1	97	11	100	1	97	3	100
2	97	12	108	2	97	4	103
3	100	13	110	11	100	6	108
4	103	14	113	5	105	12	108
5	105	15	117	13	110	7	109
6	108	16	119	9	113	8	111
7	109	17	120	15	117	14	113
8	111	18	122	10	118	16	119
9	113	19	128	19	128	17	120
10	118	20	130	20	130	18	122
Mean IQ score	106.1		116.7		111.5		111.3

Mean difference between the two groups: 10.6   Mean difference between the two groups: 0.2

distribution would be exactly the same). When the distribution is approximately equal, the influence of the extraneous variables is held constant because they cannot exert any differential influence on the dependent variable. Does this mean that randomization will *always* result in equal distribution of the variables to be controlled? The control function of randomization stems from the fact that random selection and assignment of participants also results in the random selection and assignment of most extraneous variables. Because every participant, and therefore the extraneous variables present, have an equal chance of being selected and then assigned to a particular group, the extraneous variables to be controlled are distributed randomly. But because chance determines the distribution of the extraneous variables, it is also possible that, by chance, these variables are not equally distributed among the various groups of participants. In other words, bias can still exist when one uses the randomization procedure. The smaller the number of research participants, the greater the risk that this will happen. However, randomization still decreases the probability of creating a biased distribution, even if one has access only to a small group of participants. Because the probability of the groups' being equal is so much greater with randomization, it is an extremely powerful method for controlling extraneous variables. And because it is really the *only* method for controlling unknown variables, it is necessary to randomize whenever and wherever possible, even when another control technique is being used.

There are, however, several extraneous variables that are not controlled for by randomization, including the research participant effect and the experimenter effects. The potential influences of the participants' motive of positive self-presentation and the experimenter's expectancies and attributes are not randomly distributed. Instead, these potential biasing effects are a function of how participants perceive the experiment or the expectations researchers have regarding the outcome of the experiment. Consequently, these extraneous variables must be controlled by the use of techniques other than randomization.

STUDY QUESTION 9.1

- **Why is randomization the most important control technique?**
- **How does it control for the confounding effect of extraneous variables?**

Matching

Matching

Using any of a variety of techniques for equating participants on one or more variables

Although randomization does provide the best guard against interpreting differences in the dependent variable as being the result of variables other than the independent variable, it is not the best technique for increasing the sensitivity of the experiment. In any study, it is desirable to demonstrate the influence of the independent variable, regardless of how small its effect may be. Suppose we want to isolate the potential effect of televised aggression on children's behavior. Assume that the effect is one of increasing aggressive behavior in children (this has been found in a number of studies) but the amount of increase is small. In order to isolate and detect this small effect, we need to construct an experiment that will be as sensitive as possible. The sensitivity of an experiment can be increased by **matching** the participants in the various experimental treatment groups. An explanation of how matching accomplishes this requires a discussion of the way in which statistical techniques operate, which is beyond the scope of this book. For our purposes, you need only remember that one of the benefits of matching is that the sensitivity of the experiment is increased. A second benefit of matching is that the variables on which participants are matched are controlled in the sense that constancy of influence is attained. If participants in all treatment conditions are matched on intelligence, then the intelligence level of the research participants is held constant and therefore controlled for all groups.

Here we have two definite benefits that can accrue from matching. It is important to remember, however, that matching is no substitute for randomization. Randomization should still be incorporated whenever possible, because one cannot attain an exact match on most variables, and it is impossible to identify and match on all variables that could affect the results of the experiment. The sections that follow present a number of ways in which matching can be accomplished.

Matching by Holding Variables Constant

One technique that can be used to increase the sensitivity of the experiment and control an extraneous variable is to hold the extraneous variable constant for all experimental groups. This means that all participants in each experimental group will have the same degree or type of extraneous variable. If we are studying conformity, then gender of participants needs to be controlled because conformity has been shown to vary with the gender of the participant. As illustrated in Figure 9.2, the gender variable can be controlled simply by using only male participants in the experiment. This has the effect of matching all participants in terms of the gender variable so that the sensitivity of the experiment is increased. Hauri and Ohmstead (1983) used only insomniacs in their investigation of estimates of the length of time required to fall asleep. This matching procedure creates a more homogeneous participant sample because only participants with a certain amount or type of the extraneous variable are included in the participant pool.

Although widely used, the technique of holding variables constant is not without its disadvantages. Two can readily be identified. The first disadvantage is that the technique restricts the size of the participant population. Consequently, in some cases, it may be difficult to find enough participants to participate in the study. Consider a study that was conducted to investigate the influence of assistance given to single parents (assistance with child care or with household chores) on their attitudes and perceived interactions with their child or children. The study was limited to single parents, and researchers had to find volunteers. After two weeks of advertising, eighteen single parents had volunteered to participate in the study. If the study had not been limited to single parents, the participant pool from which researchers could have drawn would have been much larger, with the probable effect that more individuals would have volunteered their help.

FIGURE 9.2 Illustration of matching by holding variables constant.

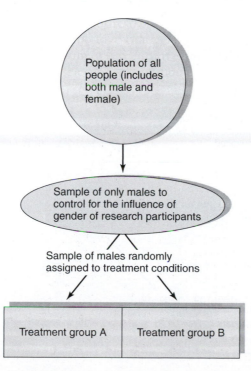

The second disadvantage is more serious. The results of the study can be generalized only to the type of participant who participated in the study. The results obtained from the single-parent study can be generalized only to other single parents. If someone wanted to know whether two-parent families would derive the same benefit from receiving this type of assistance, he or she would have to conduct a similar study using two-parent families. Conclusions from such a study might indeed be the same as those obtained from the single-parent study, but this is an empirical question. The only way we can find out if the results of one study can be generalized to individuals of another population is to conduct an identical study using representatives of the second population as research participants.

Matching by Building the Extraneous Variable into the Research Design

A second means of increasing the sensitivity of an experiment is to build the extraneous variable into the research design. Assume that we were conducting a learning experiment and wanted to control for the effects of intelligence. Also assume that we had considered the previous technique of holding the variable constant by selecting only individuals with IQs of 110 to 120, but thought it unwise and inexpedient to do so. In this case, we could select several IQ levels (for example, 90 to 99, 100 to 109, and 110 to 120), as illustrated in Figure 9.3, and treat them as we would an indepen-

FIGURE 9.3
Illustration of matching by building the extraneous variable into the research design.

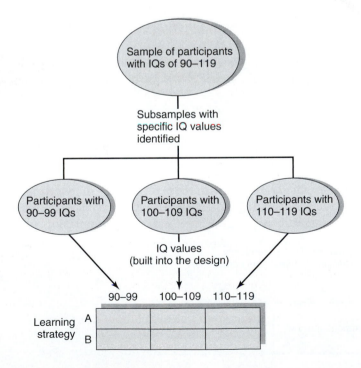

dent variable. This would allow us to identify and extract the influence of the intelligence variable. Intelligence, therefore, would not represent a source of random fluctuation, and the sensitivity of the experiment would be increased.

To provide further insight into this control technique, consider a study conducted by Kendler, Kendler, and Learnard (1962) that investigated the influence of the participants' age on their use of internal mediating responses. Prior research conducted on this topic indicated that rats do not use mediational processes, whereas college students do, and that three- and four-year-old children do not use the mediational process, whereas nearly half of the children between ages five and seven do. Such data suggested that a developmental process was involved in the use of internal mediating responses, which must be controlled for in order to avoid attaining contradictory results from various studies. Realizing this, Kendler et al. controlled for age by building it into the design of their study. Children at five chronological age levels—three, four, six, eight, and ten years of age—were required to engage in a task that would elicit mediational responses. Thus the researchers controlled for the age factor by matching the five different age groups and then used these age groupings as an independent variable. In this way, the age variable was controlled and its influence on mediational responses was displayed.

Building the extraneous variable into the research design seems like an excellent technique for achieving control and increasing sensitivity. But the technique is recommended only if one is interested in the differences produced by the various levels of the extraneous variable or in the interaction between the levels of the extraneous variable and other independent variables. In the hypothetical learning experiment, one might be interested in the differences produced by the three levels of intelligence and how these levels interact with the learning strategies. The primary reason Kendler et al. conducted their study was to investigate the differences produced by research participants of different ages. If they had not been interested in such conditions, then another control technique would probably have been more efficient. When such conditions are of interest, the technique is excellent because it isolates the variation caused by the extraneous variable. This control technique takes a factor that can operate as an extraneous variable, biasing the experiment, and makes it focal in the experiment as an independent variable.

Matching by Yoked Control

Yoked control
A matching technique that matches participants on the basis of the temporal sequence of administering an event

The **yoked control** matching technique controls for the possible influence of the temporal relationship between an event and a response. Consider the study conducted by Brady (1958) in which he investigated the relationship between emotional stress and development of ulcers. Brady trained monkeys to press a lever at least once during every 20-second interval to avoid receiving electric shock. The monkeys learned this task quite rapidly, and only occasionally did they miss a 20-second interval and receive a shock. In order to determine whether the monkeys developed ulcers from the psychological stress rather than the physical stress resulting from the cumulative effect of the shocks, Brady had to include a control monkey that received an equal number of shocks. This was easily accomplished, but there was still one additional variable that needed to be controlled—the temporal sequence of administering the shocks. It may be that one temporal sequence produces ulcers whereas another does not. If the experimental and the control monkeys received a different temporal sequence of shocks, this difference and not the stress variable could be the cause of the ulcers. Consequently, both monkeys had to receive the same temporal sequence to control this variable. Brady placed the experimental and the control monkeys in yoked chain, whereby both monkeys received a shock when the experimental monkey failed to press the lever during the 20-second interval. However, the control animal could not influence the situation and essentially had to sit back and accept the fact that sometimes the shock was going to occur. The only apparent difference between these animals was the ability to influence the occurrence of the shock. If only the experimental monkey got ulcers, as was the case in this experiment, the ulcers could be attributed to the psychological stress.

Matching by Equating Participants

A third technique for controlling extraneous variables and also increasing the sensitivity of the experiment is to equate research participants on the variable or variables to be controlled. If intelligence needs to be controlled, then the investigator must make sure that the participants in each of the treatment groups are of the same intelligence level.

Matching by equating participants is very similar to matching by building the extraneous variable into the study design: Both techniques attempt to eliminate the influence of the extraneous variable by creating equivalent groups of participants. The difference lies in the procedure for creating the equivalent groups. The previously discussed method creates equivalent groups by establishing categories of the extraneous variable into which participants are placed, thereby creating another independent variable. The present method does not build the extraneous variable into the design of the study but matches participants on the variable to be controlled, where the number of participants is always some multiple of the number of levels of the independent variable. There are two techniques that are commonly used to accomplish this matching, which Selltiz, Jahoda, Deutsch, and Cook (1959) labeled the precision control technique and the frequency control technique.

Precision control
A matching technique in which each participant is matched with another participant on selected variables

Precision Control   The technique of **precision control** requires the investigator to match participants in the various treatment groups on a case-by-case basis for each of the selected extraneous variables. Scholtz (1973) investigated the defense styles used by individuals who attempted suicide versus those used by individuals who did not attempt suicide. All participants were neuropsychiatric patients. The suicide participants were identified as those individuals who, among other things, had attempted suicide during the past year. The other participants had evidenced "no history of a suicide attempt nor marked suicidal ideation" (p. 71). For a non–suicide attempter to be included in the study, the participant had to be of the same age, gender, race, marital status, diagnosis, and education as a suicide attempter. Matching on these variables on a case-by-case basis resulted in thirty-five pairs of participants.

The Scholtz study illustrates the various advantages and disadvantages of the precision control matching technique. Before discussing them, I should point out that the Scholtz study was an ex post facto study because the participants assigned themselves to the various groups; they could not be randomly assigned after being paired. In a truly experimental study, research participants would be matched and then randomly assigned to the different groups, as illustrated in Figure 9.4. As stated before, matching is never a substitute for random assignment.

The principal advantage of the precision control technique is that it increases the sensitivity of the study by ensuring that the participants in the various groups are equal on at least the paired variables. If sensitivity is to be increased, the variables on which participants are matched must be correlated with the dependent variable. How much of a correlation should exist? Kerlinger (1973) states that matching is a waste of time unless the variables on which participants are matched correlate greater than 0.5 or 0.6 with the dependent variable (this criterion holds only for linearly related variables). This corresponds to the data Billewicz (1965) obtained from his simulation experiments.

The precision control technique has three major disadvantages. First, it is difficult to know which are the most important variables to match. In most instances, there are many potentially relevant variables. In his study, Scholtz selected age, gender, race, marital status, diagnosis, and education, but many other variables could have been selected. The variables selected should be those that show the lowest intercorrelation but the highest correlation with the dependent variable.

A second problem encountered in precision control matching is that the difficulty in finding matched participants increases disproportionately as the number of

FIGURE 9.4
Illustration of matching by the precision control technique.

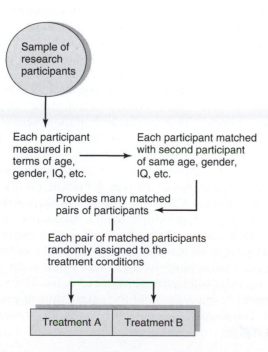

variables increases. Scholtz matched on six variables, which must have been very difficult. His task would have been much easier if matching had been attempted on only two variables, such as gender and age. In order to match individuals on many variables, one must have a large pool of individuals available in order to obtain a few who are matched on the relevant variables. Fortunately, the relevant variables are generally intercorrelated, so the number that can be used successfully to increase precision is limited. Matching also limits the generality of the results of the study. Assume that you are matching on age and education and that the participants in your final sample of matched participants are between the ages of twenty and thirty and have only high school educations. Because this is the type of participant included in the study, you can generalize the results only to other individuals having the same characteristics.

A third disadvantage is that some variables are very difficult to match. If having received psychotherapy was considered a relevant variable, an individual who had received psychotherapy would have to be matched with another person who had also received psychotherapy. A related difficulty is the inability to obtain adequate measures of the variables to be matched. If we wanted to equate individuals on the basis of the effect of psychotherapy, we would have to measure such an effect. Matching can only be as accurate as the available measurement.

Frequency Distribution Control   The precision control technique of matching is excellent for increasing sensitivity, but many participants must be eliminated because they cannot be matched. **Frequency distribution control** attempts to overcome this disadvantage while retaining some of the advantages of matching. This technique, as the name implies, matches groups of participants in terms of the overall distribution of the selected variable or variables rather than on a case-by-case basis. If IQ were to be matched in this fashion, the two or more groups of participants would have to have the same average IQ, as well as the same standard deviation and skewness of IQ scores, as illustrated in Figure 9.5. This means that, generally speaking, the investigator would select the first group of participants and determine the mean, standard deviation, and so forth of their IQ scores. Then another group having the same statistical measures would be selected. If more than one variable was considered to be a relevant variable on which to match participants, the groups of participants would have to have the same statistical measures on both of these variables. The number of participants lost using this technique would not be as great as the number lost using the precision control method because each additional participant would merely have to contribute to producing the appropriate statistical indexes rather than be identical to another participant on the relevant variables. Consequently, this technique allows more flexibility in terms of being able to use a particular participant.

The major disadvantage of matching by the frequency distribution control method is that the combinations of variables may be mismatched in the various groups. If age and IQ were to be matched, one group might include old participants with high IQs and young participants with low IQs, whereas the other group might be composed of the opposite combination. In this case, the mean and distribution of the two variables would be equivalent but the participants in each group would be completely different. This disadvantage obviously exists only if matching is conducted on more than one variable.

Frequency distribution control
A matching technique that matches groups of participants by equating the overall distribution of the chosen variable

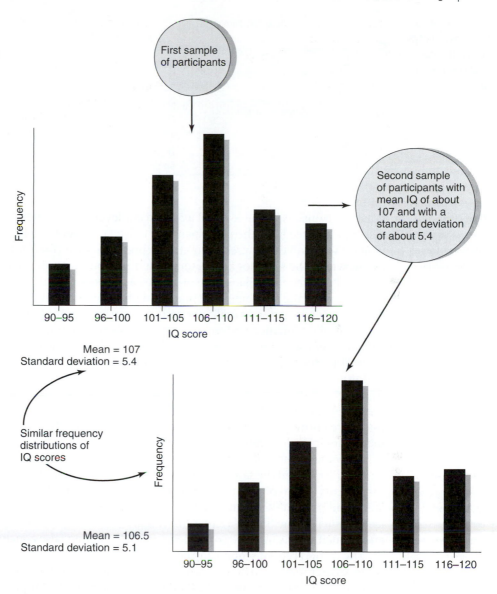

FIGURE 9.5
Illustration of the frequency distribution control technique.

Counterbalancing

Counterbalancing
A technique used to control sequencing effects

Counterbalancing is the technique used to control for sequencing effects. Sequencing effects can occur when the investigator elects to construct an experiment in which all participants serve in each of several experimental conditions. (See Figure 9.6.) Under these conditions, there are two types of effects that can occur. The first is an **order effect,** which arises from the order in which the treatment conditions are administered to the participants. Suppose that you are conducting a verbal learning experiment in which the independent variable is rate of presentation of nonsense

FIGURE 9.6
Illustration of the type of design that may include sequencing effects.

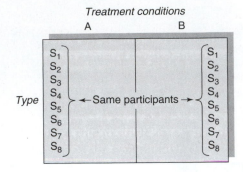

Order effect
A sequencing effect arising from the order in which the treatment conditions are administered to participants

syllables. Nonsense syllables with a 50 percent level of meaningfulness are randomly assigned to three lists. The participant has to learn sequentially list S (the slow list, in which the syllables are presented at 6-second intervals), then list M (the moderate list, in which the syllables are presented at 4-second intervals), and finally list F (the fast list, in which the syllables are presented at 2-second intervals). In such an experiment, there is the possibility that practice with the equipment, learning the nonsense syllables, or just general familiarity with the surroundings of the experimental environment may enhance performance. Let us assume that one or more of these variables does enhance performance and that the increment due to the order effect is four units of performance for participants progressing from list S to M and two units of performance for participants progressing from list M to list F. The left half of Table 9.2 depicts these order effects. As you can see, order effects could affect the conclusions reached because performance increments occurred in the learning of these two lists that were entirely the result of order effects. You should also be aware that when the increment in performance is caused by order effects, the particular sequence of the list is irrelevant. If the order of the lists were reversed, the increments in performance would still occur in the same ordinal position, as is shown in the right half of Table 9.2. Increments due to order effects are strictly the result of participants' increased familiarity and practice with the whole experimental environment. Other experimental factors, such as the time of testing (morning, noon, or night), may produce the order effect. Such effects must be controlled to avoid reaching false conclusions.

Carry-over effect
A sequencing effect that occurs when performance in one treatment condition affects performance in another treatment condition

The second type of sequencing effect that can occur is a carry-over effect. A **carry-over effect** occurs when performance in one treatment condition is partially dependent on the conditions that precede it. D'Amato (1970) provides an excellent

TABLE 9.2
Hypothetical Order Effects

	List Learned			Reversed Order of List		
	S	M	F	F	M	S
Increment in performance	0	4	2	0	4	2

example of carry-over effects in his simulated experiment designed to investigate the influence of monetary reward (5, 10, or 15 cents) on performance. In this type of study, it is possible that when research participants serve in all three conditions, performance in a particular treatment condition may be partially a function of the conditions that precede it (a dime may be more rewarding when it is preceded by 5 cents than when it is preceded by 15 cents). "Let us simplify the analysis by assuming that the carry-over effects from one condition to another will be directly proportional to the difference in the monetary rewards of the two conditions. We will assume that going from A (5 cents) to B (10 cents) or from B to C (15 cents) results in a positive carry-over (increment in performance) of two units, whereas traveling in the reverse direction results in the same amount of carry-over effect but negative in sign, i.e., leads to a decrement in performance of two units. Transitions from A to C and from C to A both result in four units of carry-over effects, positive and negative, respectively" (p. 53). Table 9.3 illustrates that the carry-over effects for any one treatment condition are a function of the preceding treatment conditions. Such effects need to be controlled to identify unambiguously the effects due to the independent variable.

The order effects and the carry-over effects are potential sources of bias in any studies in which the participant partakes of several treatment conditions. In such cases, the sequencing effects need to be controlled, and researchers often resort to counterbalancing.

Intrasubject Counterbalancing: The ABBA Technique

Intrasubject counterbalancing controls for sequencing effects by having each participant take the treatment conditions first in one order and then in the reverse order. Suppose that you were conducting a Pepsi challenge experiment to find out if people preferred Pepsi over Coke. In this experiment, the treatment conditions would

TABLE 9.3
Calculation of Assumed Carry-Over Effects in Six Sequences

Sequence	A (5 cents)	B (10 cents)	C (15 cents)
	Value of the Independent Variable		
ABC	0	2	2
ACB	0	−2	4
BAC	−2	0	4
BCA	−4	0	2
CAB	−4	2	0
CBA	−2	−2	0
Total	−12	0	12

Source: From *Experimental Psychology Methodology: Psychophysics and Learning* by M. R. D'Amato. Copyright 1970, McGraw-Hill. Used with permission of McGraw-Hill Book Co.

Intrasubject counterbalancing Administering the treatment conditions to each individual participant in more than one order

consist of the two colas. Research participants would make an assessment of liking after tasting first the Pepsi (cola A) and then the Coke (cola B), in AB order. Participants would then taste the Coke (cola B) a second time, followed by the Pepsi (cola A), and make a liking assessment after each, making the sequence ABBA. In other words, each participant would taste each cola drink twice and make an assessment of liking after each tasting. The results of the liking assessment obtained from the two Pepsi tastings would be combined for each participant, as would the results of the two Coke tastings, once again making the study a two-treatment-condition experiment. The Pepsi-liking assessment would then be compared to the Coke-liking assessment to determine whether one cola was liked more than the other. Any observed difference could not be attributable to carry-over or order effects because they would have been equalized, or held constant, across groups.

To illustrate how intrasubject counterbalancing controls for carry-over and order effects, let us assume that each research participant increments his or her liking assessment by one unit for each treatment condition in which he or she participates solely because of sequencing effects. If the ABBA technique is employed, these sequencing effects will be constant across treatment conditions and will therefore be controlled. This constant influence is illustrated in the top half of Table 9.4. For both the A and the B treatment condition, liking was increased by a constant amount of three units. Therefore, sequencing was controlled. Note, however, that the sequencing effect was linear in the sense that a constant increment was added to liking in each successive position in the sequence.

Would the ABBA technique control for carry-over and order effects if they were not linear? The answer is no. The ABBA method is based on the assumption that the sequencing effects are linear, or constant for each successive position in the sequence. (This assumption is also made for the incomplete counterbalancing method discussed later.) If a constant effect is not attained, the sequencing effect will differentially affect the results, as shown in the bottom half of Table 9.4. In this case, the sequencing

TABLE 9.4
Sequencing Effects for the ABBA Technique

	Treatment Condition			
	A	B	B	A
Linear sequencing effect	0	1	2	3
Sequence effect				
A sequence effect 0 + 3 = 3				
B sequence effect 1 + 2 = 3				
Nonlinear sequencing effect	0	4	6	8
Sequence effect				
A sequence effect 0 + 8 = 8				
B sequence effect 4 + 6 = 10				

TABLE 9.5

Control for Order Effects Using Intrasubject Counterbalancing

	Sequence I				Sequence II			
	A	B	B	A	B	A	A	B
Order effect	0	2	3	4	0	2	3	4

Total A order effect $0 + 4 + 2 + 3 = 9$

Total B order effect $2 + 3 + 0 + 4 = 9$

effects were not controlled because liking increased by ten units for condition B but only eight units for condition A. This is because the sequence effect was twice as powerful for progression from the first A condition to the first B condition as it was for progression through the remainder of the conditions. Can such differential sequence effects be controlled? The answer depends on whether you are considering carry-over effects or order effects.

Differential order effects can be held constant by having each treatment condition appear in every possible position in the sequence. This means that in addition to an ABBA sequence a BAAB sequence must be included to control nonlinear order effects. Half of the research participants can then be assigned to each sequence. Let us assume that each participant increments two units of liking after tasting the first cola and one unit of liking after tasting each subsequent cola just because of order effects. If both the ABBA and the BAAB sequences are employed, the results in Table 9.5 will occur. The total order effects for both treatment conditions are equal, which means that the effect is held constant. This actually represents a combining of intrasubject with intragroup counterbalancing.

It is not as easy to control for differential carry-over effects. These effects frequently defy control because the carry-over may vary as a function of the preceding treatment conditions. Such a condition was illustrated earlier in the example of a simulated experiment designed to test the influence of monetary reward on performance. Table 9.3 shows the assumed carry-over effects. Note that the carry-over effect for any one treatment condition varies as a function of the particular treatment conditions that precede it. Also note that the total carry-over effects for the treatment conditions are not identical. Here, then, is a case in which carry-over effects are not controlled. When carry-over effects are linear, they can be controlled by the ABBA sequence, but in nonlinear cases such as this, they cannot. The investigator who suspects such a situation should consider using some other technique, such as precision control; otherwise, the carry-over effects serve as a rival hypothesis.

Intragroup Counterbalancing

A primary disadvantage of using the intrasubject counterbalancing technique is that each treatment condition must be presented to each research participant more than once. As the number of treatment conditions increases, the length of the sequence of conditions each participant must take also increases. For example, with the three treatment conditions A, B, and C, each participant must take a sequence of six treatment conditions—ABCCBA. Intragroup counterbalancing allows the experimenter to avoid this time-consuming process. **Intragroup counterbalancing** differs from intrasubject counterbalancing in that groups of participants rather than individuals are counterbalanced. Because the intragroup technique attempts to control sequencing effects over groups, it represents a more efficient technique, particularly when more than two treatment conditions exist.

Incomplete Counterbalancing The intragroup counterbalancing technique used most frequently is **incomplete counterbalancing,** which derives its name from the fact that all possible sequences of treatment conditions are not enumerated. The first criterion that incomplete counterbalancing must meet is that, for the sequences enumerated, each treatment condition must appear an equal number of times in each ordinal position. Also, each treatment condition must precede and be followed by every other condition an equal number of times.

Assume that you are conducting an experiment to determine whether caffeine affects reaction time. You want to administer 100, 200, 300, and 400 mg of caffeine (conditions A, B, C, and D, respectively) to participants to see whether reaction time increases as the amount of caffeine consumed increases. You know that, if each participant takes all four doses of caffeine, sequencing effects could alter the results of your experiment, so you want to counterbalance the order in which the dosages are administered to the participants. Whenever the number of treatment conditions is even, as is the case with the four caffeine dosages, then the number of counterbalanced sequences equals the number of treatment conditions. The sequences are established in the following way. The first sequence takes the form 1, 2, n, 3, $(n-1)$, 4, $(n-2)$, 5, and so forth, until we have accounted for the total number of treatment conditions. In the case of the caffeine study with four treatment conditions, the first sequence would be ABDC, or 1, 2, 4, 3. If an experiment consisted of six treatment conditions, the first sequence would be ABFCED, or 1, 2, 6, 3, 5, 4. The remaining sequences of the incomplete counterbalancing technique are then established by incrementing each value in the preceding sequence by 1. For example, for the caffeine study, in which the first sequence is ABDC, the second sequence is BCAD. Naturally, to increment the last treatment condition, D, by 1, you do not proceed to E but go back to A. This procedure results in the following set of sequences for the caffeine study.

Participant	Sequence			
1	A	B	D	C
2	B	C	A	D
3	C	D	B	A
4	D	A	C	B

If the number of treatment conditions is odd, as with five treatment conditions, the criterion that each value must precede and follow every other value an equal

Intragroup counterbalancing Administering the treatment conditions to various members of each group of participants in more than one order

Incomplete counterbalancing Enumerating fewer than all possible sequences, and requiring different groups of participants to take each of the enumerated sequences

number of times is not fulfilled if the above procedure is followed. For example, the foregoing procedure would give the following set of sequences:

		Sequence		
A	B	E	C	D
B	C	A	D	E
C	D	B	E	A
D	E	C	A	B
E	A	D	B	C

In this case, each treatment condition appears in every possible position; but, for example, D is immediately preceded by A twice but never by B. To remedy this situation, we must enumerate five additional sequences that are exactly the reverse of the first five sequences. In the five-treatment-condition example, the additional five sequences appear as follows:

		Sequence		
D	C	E	B	A
E	D	A	C	B
A	E	B	D	C
B	A	C	E	D
C	B	D	A	E

When these ten sequences are combined, the criteria of incomplete counterbalancing are met. Consequently, the incomplete counterbalancing technique provides for control of order effects.

How well does the incomplete counterbalancing technique control for sequencing effects? The influence of order effects is controlled because every treatment condition occurs at each possible position in the sequence. In other words, every condition (A, B, C, and D) precedes and follows every other condition an equal number of times. However, carry-over effects are controlled only if they are linear for all sequences. If they are not, then incomplete counterbalancing is inadequate.

STUDY QUESTION 9.2
- **List and define each of the matching control techniques discussed.**
- **Explain how the technique controls for each type of extraneous variable.**

Control of Participant Effects

We have seen that participants' behavior in an experiment can be influenced by the perceptions and motives they bring with them. It seems as though research participants are motivated to present themselves in the best possible light. If the demand characteristics suggest that a particular type of response will allow participants to fulfill this motive, the participants' responses will be a function of this motive in addition to the experimental treatment conditions. Such a situation will produce internal validity if the demand characteristics that operate in the experiment suggest to the participants that the self-presentation motive can be fulfilled in different ways. For internal validity to be created, there must be constancy in the participants' perceptions of the way in which the positive self-presentation motive can be fulfilled. Only then can we state with certainty that the independent variable has caused the variation in the participants' responses to the dependent variable.

The experimenter can use a number of control techniques to try to ensure identical perceptions in all participants. The following techniques cannot be used in all types of experiments; they are presented so that the experimenter can choose the most appropriate one for the particular study being conducted.

Double Blind Placebo Model

Double blind placebo model
A model in which neither the experimenter nor the research participant is aware of the treatment condition administered to the participant

One of the best techniques for controlling demand characteristics is the **double blind placebo model.** This model requires that the experimenter "devise manipulations that appear essentially identical to research participants in all conditions"[1] and that the experimenter not know which group received the placebo condition or the experimental manipulation.

If you were conducting an experiment designed to test the effect of aspartame on disruptive behavior in young children, you would have to administer this sweetener to one group of children and a placebo to another group. Because both groups would think that they had received the aspartame, expectancies would be held constant. The experimenter also must not know whether a given participant received the aspartame, expectancies would be held constant. The experimenter also must not know whether a given participant received the aspartame or the placebo in order to avoid communicating the expectancy of generating disruptive behavior. Therefore, the experimenter as well as the participant must be blind to the treatment condition that a given participant received. For some time, drug research has recognized the influence of patients' expectations on their experiences subsequent to taking a drug. Thus drug research consistently uses this model to eliminate participant bias.

Using this technique, Beecher (1966) found no difference in pain alleviation between a placebo group that was administered a weak saline solution and a drug group that was administered a large dose of morphine. Such results ran counter to a large body of previous research. However, Beecher communicated with another experienced drug researcher, who revealed that demand characteristics probably existed in the prior studies. This researcher said that he "found that as long as he knew what the subject [research participant] had received, he could reproduce fine dose-effect curves; but when he was kept in ignorance, he was no more able than we were to distinguish between a large dose of morphine and an inert substance such as saline" (p. 841). In the former cases, the participant knew the correct response and acted accordingly.

---

[1]Reprinted by special permission from "Experimentation in Social Psychology" by E. Aronson and J. M. Carlsmith, in *The Handbook of Social Psychology,* 2nd edition, volume 2, edited by G. Lindzey and E. Aronson, 1968, p. 62. Reading, Mass.: Addison-Wesley.

Use of the double blind placebo model is a way to eliminate the development of differential participant perceptions because all participants are told that they are given (and appear to be given) the same experimental treatment. And because the researcher does not know which participants have received the experimental treatments, he or she cannot communicate this information to the participants. Therefore, the demand characteristics surrounding the administration of the treatment conditions are controlled by the double blind placebo model.

Unfortunately, many types of experiments cannot use such a technique because all conditions cannot be made to appear identical in all respects. In such cases, other techniques must be employed.

Deception

Deception
Giving the participant a bogus rationale for the experiment

One of the more common methods used to solve the problem of participant perceptions is the use of deception in the experiment. **Deception** involves providing all research participants with a hypothesis that is unrelated to or orthogonal to the real hypothesis. Almost all experiments contain some form of deception, ranging from minor deceit (an omission or a slight alteration of the truth) to elaborate schemes. Christensen, Krietsch, White, and Stagner (1985), in their investigation of the impact of diet on mood disturbance, told research participants that the double blind challenges in which they had participated had isolated certain food substances as the causal factors in their mood disturbance. But the particular foods mentioned to the participants were ones that actually had not been investigated in the challenges to which they had participated. Participants were given this bogus information to induce the perception that the offending foods had been isolated and that the remaining foods could be eaten without inducing any detrimental effect on mood states. At the other end of the continuum, there are experiments in which participants are given unrelated or bogus hypotheses to ensure that they do not discover the real hypothesis.

Aronson and Mills (1959) repeatedly used deception in their study; at just about every stage of the experiment, some type of cover for the real purpose was given. For example, rather than telling the research participants that the experiment was investigating the effect of severity of initiation, the researchers said that the study was investigating the "dynamics of the group discussion process." Is it better to use such deception or simply to refrain from giving any rationale for the tasks to be completed in the experiment? It seems as though providing participants with a false, but plausible, hypothesis is the preferred procedure because the participants' curiosity may be satisfied so that they do not try to devise their own hypotheses. If different participants perceive the study to be investigating different hypotheses, their responses may create a source of bias.

The rationale underlying the deception approach is "to provide a cognitive analogy to the placebo."[2] In a placebo experiment, all research participants think they have received the same independent variable. In the deception experiment, all

[2]Reprinted by special permission from "Experimentation in Social Psychology" by E. Aronson and J. M. Carlsmith, in *The Handbook of Social Psychology,* 2nd edition, volume 2, edited by G. Lindzey and E. Aronson, 1968, p. 63. Reading, Mass.: Addison-Wesley.

Retrospective verbal report
An oral report in which the participant retrospectively recalls aspects of the experiment

Postexperimental inquiry
An interview of the participant after the experiment is over

Concurrent verbal report
A participant's oral report of the experiment that is obtained as the experiment is being performed

Sacrifice groups
Groups of participants that are stopped and interviewed at different stages of the experiment

Concurrent probing
Obtaining a participant's perceptions of the experiment after completion of each trial

Think-aloud technique
A method that requires participants to verbalize their thoughts as they are performing the experiment

participants receive the same false information about what is being done, which should produce relatively constant participant perceptions of the purpose of the experiment. Therefore, deception seems to be an excellent technique for controlling the potential biasing influence that can arise from research participants' differential perceptions regarding the hypothesis of the experiment. The one problem with deception is that it frequently prompts objections on ethical grounds (see Chapter 5).

Procedural Control, or Control of Participant Interpretation

The techniques just discussed are excellent for controlling some of the demand characteristics of the experiment. "However, these control techniques seem to be limited to ensuring that subjects [research participants] have a unified perception of the treatment condition they are in, whether or not they receive a given treatment, and the purpose of the experiment" (Christensen, 1981, p. 567). There is little recognition of the fact that the participants' perceptions are also affected by the many demand characteristics surrounding the whole procedure. For example, it has been demonstrated that participants respond differently to a verbal conditioning task depending on how they interpret the verbal reinforcer (Christensen, 1977). To provide adequate control of participant perceptions and the positive self-presentation motive, we need to know the types of situations and instructions that will alter participants' perceptions of how to create the most positive image. The literature on this issue, however, is in its infancy. At the present time, therefore, it is necessary to consider each experiment separately and try to determine if the participants' perceptions of the experiment might lead them to respond differentially to the levels of variation in the independent variable.

A variety of techniques that can be used to gain insight into participants' perceptions of the experiment are summarized in Christensen (1981) and Adair and Spinner (1981). These methods can be grouped into two categories: retrospective verbal reports and concurrent verbal reports. A **retrospective verbal report** consists of a technique such as the **postexperimental inquiry,** which is exactly what it says it is: questioning the participant regarding the essential aspects of the experiment after completion of the study. What did the participant think the experiment was about? What did he or she think the experimenter expected to find? What type of response did the participant attempt to give, and why? How does the participant think others will respond in this situation? Such information will help to expose the factors underlying the participant's perception of his or her response.

Concurrent verbal reports include such techniques as Solomon's sacrifice group (Orne, 1973), concurrent probing, and the think-aloud technique (Ericsson and Simon, 1980). In Solomon's **sacrifice groups,** each group of participants is sacrificed by being stopped at a different point in the experiment and probed regarding the participants' perceptions of the experiment. **Concurrent probing** requires participants to report, at the end of each trial, the perceptions they have regarding the experiment. The **think-aloud technique** requires participants to verbalize any thoughts or perceptions they have regarding the experiment as they are performing the experimental task. Ericsson and Simon (1980) consider this the most effective technique because it does not require the participant to recall information and hence eliminates distortions in reporting due to failure to remember or due to the biasing influence that may result from the experimenter's probing.

Although Ericsson and Simon (1993) promote the think-aloud technique as a valid source of verbal-report data, it does have its limitations. The most serious limitation is the potential reactive effect of these verbalizations. A number of studies (see Wilson, 1994) suggest that verbalizations can be reactive by focusing a person's attention on information that is accessible and easily verbalized, resulting in a change in the psychological state under investigation. For example, if you ask individuals to think about the reasons they hold a certain attitude, they will focus on things such as the attributes (e.g., laziness or violence) of the attitude object. This focus has the effect of changing the underlying attitude. This is why Ericsson and Simon (1993) recommended that research participants report only their actual thoughts. They should not try to analyze, explain, or interpret them.

In light of the recent work on the think-aloud technique, Wilson (1994) makes the following recommendation. The think-aloud technique should be used to study only the content of consciousness or what comes into conscious awareness. It is also excellent for generating hypotheses because a person's conscious thoughts can be a rich source of inspiration. Verbal protocols cannot, however, tap cognitive processes that never reach conscious awareness. If you are planning to use the think-aloud technique, you should read Ericsson and Simon's (1993) book and Payne's (1994) article. These two sources provide guidelines in the use of this technique.

None of the techniques is foolproof or without disadvantages. However, the use of these methods will provide some evidence regarding research participants' perceptions of the experiment and will enable you to design an experiment in such a way as to minimize the differential influence of the participants' motive of positive self-presentation.

STUDY QUESTION 9.3

- **List and describe the control techniques that can be used to create, in the research participants, identical perceptions of the experiment.**
- **Assume you want to identify the research participants' perception of the purpose of the experiment. Explain the various ways in which you could accomplish this purpose.**

Control of Experimenter Effects

Experimenter effects
The biasing influence that can be exerted by the experimenter

Experimenter effects have been defined in Chapter 8 as the unintentional biasing effects that the experimenter can have on the results of the experiment. The experimenter is not a passive, noninfluential agent in an experiment, but an active potential source of bias. This potential bias seems to exist in most types of experiments, although it may not be quite as powerful as Rosenthal (1976) maintains.

Page and Yates (1973) have shown that 90 percent of the respondents they surveyed felt that the implications of experimenter bias for psychology were serious. In addition, 81 percent of the respondents felt that the presence of experimenter-related controls should be a major criterion for publishability of studies. Such data suggest that psychologists in general consider the experimenter bias effect to be of importance in psychological research and see the need to incorporate techniques to control for such potential effects. According to Wyer, Dion, and Ellsworth (1978), such problems as experimenter bias are widely understood in social psychology, and it is assumed "that most persons who submit papers to JESP avoid these problems as a matter of course" (p. 143). However, Silverman (1974) concluded from his survey that "despite all of the rhetoric and data on experimenter effects, it appears that psychologists show little more concern for their experimenters as sources of variance than they might for the light fixtures in their laboratories" (p. 276). His findings indicate that it is important to present and emphasize the use of controls for experimenter bias.

Control of Recording Errors

Errors resulting from the misrecording of data can be minimized if the person recording the data remains aware of the necessity of making careful observations to ensure the accuracy of data transcription. An even better approach is to use multiple observers or data recorders. If, for example, three individuals independently recorded the data, discrepancies could be noted and resolved to generate more accurate data. Naturally, all data recorders could err in the same direction, which would mask the error, but the probability of this occurring is remote. This procedure could be improved even further if the data recorders were kept blind regarding the experimental conditions in which the participant was responding (Rosenthal, 1978).

The best means for controlling recording errors, although not possible in all studies, is to eliminate the human data recorder and have responses recorded by some mechanical or electronic device. In some research laboratories, the participants' responses are automatically fed into a computer.

Control of Experimenter Attribute Errors

At first glance, there seems to be a simple and logical solution to the problem created by experimenter attributes. Throughout much of this book, I have referred to control in terms of constancy. Because most extraneous variables cannot be eliminated, they are held constant so that a differential influence is not exerted on the participants' responses in the various treatment groups. In like manner, the influence of experimenter attributes could be held constant across all treatment conditions. Some experimenters, because of their attributes, may obtain more of an effect than other experimenters. But this increased effect should be constant across all treatment groups. Therefore, the influence of experimenter attributes should not significantly affect the *mean differences* among treatment groups. Assume that a cold and a warm experimenter independently conduct the same learning study and that the warm experimenter obtains an average of 3 more units of learning from participants in each of the two treatment groups than does the cold experimenter, as shown in the top half of Table 9.6. Note that the mean difference between Groups A and B is identical for both experimenters, indicating that they would have reached the same conclusions even though each obtained different absolute amounts of learning. In such a situation, the effects of the experimenter attributes do not have any influence on the final conclusion reached.

TABLE 9.6

Hypothetical Data Illustrating the Mean Difference in Learning Obtained from a Warm and a Cold Experimenter

Experimenters	Experimental Group		Mean Difference
	A	B	
Experimenter attributes controlled			
Warm	10	20	10
Cold	7	17	10
Experimenter attributes not controlled			
Warm	8	21	13
Cold	17	17	0

Control through the technique of constancy does imply that the variable being held constant—experimenter attributes, in this case—produces an equal effect on all treatment groups. If this assumption is not accurate or if the experimenter's attributes interact with the various treatment effects, control has not been achieved. If, in the foregoing example, a warm experimenter obtained an average of 8 units of performance from participants in Group A and 21 units of performance from participants in Group B, whereas the cold experimenter obtained identical performance from participants in both treatment groups (as shown in the bottom half of Table 9.6), we have not controlled for the influence of experimenter attributes. In this case, the two experimenters have produced conflicting results. Unfortunately, we do not know which attributes interact with numerous independent variables that exist in psychology. Because we do not know how much difference is exerted by various experimenters, a number of individuals (for example, McGuigan, 1963; Rosenthal, 1966) have suggested that several experimenters be employed in a given study. (The ideal but impractical recommendation is that a random sample of experimenters be selected to conduct the experiment.)

If more than one experimenter were employed, evidence could be acquired as to whether there was an interaction between the treatment conditions and an experimenter's attributes. If identical results were produced by all experimenters, we would have increased assurance that the independent variable and the experimenter attributes did not interact. If the experimenters produced different results, however, we would know that an interaction existed and could perhaps identify the probable cause of the interaction.

Based on his review of the literature, Johnson (1976) has found that the experimenter attributes effect can be minimized if one controls for "those experimenter attributes which correspond with the psychological task" (p. 75). In other words, if the experimenter attribute is correlated with the dependent variable, then it should be controlled. On hostility-related tasks, it is necessary to hold the experimenters' hostility level constant. In a weight reduction experiment, the weight of the therapist may be correlated with the success of the program. Therefore, to identify the relative effectiveness of different weight reduction techniques, it would be necessary, at the very least, to make sure the therapists were of approximately the same weight. Such an attribute consideration may not, however, have an artifactual influence in a verbal learning study. At the present time, it is necessary for the investigator to use his or her judgment as well as any available research to ascertain whether the given attributes of the experimenters may have a confounding influence on the study.

Control of Experimenter Expectancy Error

Rosenthal and his associates have presented a strong argument for the existence of experimenter expectancy effects in most types of psychological research. Despite the fact that certain individuals, notably Barber and Silver (1968), have presented counterarguments against Rosenthal, it seems important to devise techniques for eliminating bias of this type. There are a number of techniques that can be used for eliminating or at least minimizing expectancy effects. Generally, they involve automating the experiment or keeping the experimenter ignorant of the condition the participant is in so that appropriate cues cannot be transmitted. Rosenthal (1966) discusses such techniques, several of which will now be presented.

Blind technique
A method whereby knowledge of each research participant's treatment condition is kept from the experimenter

The Blind Technique   The **blind technique** actually corresponds to the experimenter's half of the double blind placebo model. In the blind technique, the experimenter knows the hypothesis but is blind as to which treatment condition the research participant is in. Consequently, the experimenter cannot unintentionally treat groups differently.

Rosenthal (1966) has suggested that we need a professional experimenter—a trained data collector analogous to the laboratory technician. This person's interest and emotional investment would be in collecting the most accurate data possible and not in attaining support of the hypothesis. The scientist would not attempt to keep the hypothesis from this individual because it would be very difficult to do so (Rosenthal, Persinger, Vikan-Kline, & Mulry, 1963) and, in any case, the experimenter would probably just develop his or her own. However, because this person's primary interest would be in collecting accurate data, he or she would have less incentive to bias the results and therefore would probably not be as much of a biasing agent. As Rosenthal pointed out, this idea has already been implemented with survey research and may have merit for experimental psychology. However, Page and Yates (1973) have indicated that most psychologists are not favorably disposed toward this alternative.

At present, the blind technique is probably the best procedure for controlling experimenter expectancies. But there are many studies in which it is impossible to remain ignorant of the condition the participant is in, and in those cases the next best technique should be employed—the partial blind technique.

Partial blind technique
A method whereby knowledge of each research participant's treatment condition is kept from the experimenter through as many stages of the experiment as possible

The Partial Blind Technique   In cases where the blind technique cannot be employed, it is sometimes possible to use the **partial blind technique,** whereby the experimenter is kept ignorant of the condition the research participant is in for a portion of the study. The experimenter could remain blind while initial contact was made with the participant and during all conditions prior to the actual presentation of the independent variable. When the treatment condition was to be administered to the participant, the experimenter could use some technique (such as pulling a number out of a pocket) that would designate which condition the participant was in. Therefore, all instructions and conditions prior to the manipulations would be standardized and expectancy minimized. Aronson and Cope (1968) used this procedure in investigating the attraction between two people who share a common enemy. The experimenter explained the purpose of the study and instructed each participant in the performance of a task. After the task had been completed, the participant was randomly assigned to one of two experimental conditions. This was accomplished by having the experimenter unfold a slip of paper—given to him or her just prior to using the participant—that stated the participant's experimental condition. Only at this point did the experimenter learn the participant's experimental condition.

Although this procedure is only a partial solution, it is better than the experimenter's having knowledge of the participant's condition throughout the experiment. If the experimenter could leave the room immediately following administration of the independent variable and allow another person (who was ignorant of the experimental manipulations administered to the participant) to measure the dependent variable, the solution would come closer to approaching completeness. Again, in many experiments this is not possible because the independent and dependent variables cannot be temporally separated.

Automation A third possibility for eliminating expectancy bias in animal and human research is total **automation** of the experiment. Indeed, numerous animal researchers currently use automated data collection procedures. Many human studies could also be completely automated by having instructions written, tape recorded, filmed, televised, or presented by means of a computer, and by recording responses via timers, counters, pen recorders, computers, or similar devices. These procedures are easily justified to the participant on the basis of control and standardization, and they minimize the participant–experimenter interaction.

Psychological experiments are becoming increasingly automated. With each passing year, we find more electronic devices manufactured for use in our experiments. At present, however, few of them totally remove the researcher from the experimental environment. Complete automation, through such approaches as the use of computers and the Internet, is restricted by such practical considerations as cost of equipment and programming. In most animal research, the experimenter must transport the animals to and from the home cages as well as feed and care for them; seldom is this operation totally automated. With human research, Aronson and Carlsmith (1968) make the point that the experimenter sometimes eliminates bias rather than acting as a biasing agent. Rosenthal (1966) states that when the experimenter's participation is considered vital, his or her behavior should be as constant as possible and experimenter–participant contact and interaction should be minimal.

Automation
The technique of totally automating the experimental procedures so that no experimenter–participant interaction is required

---

STUDY QUESTION 9.4

What techniques can be used to control for experimenter recording errors, experimenter attribute errors, and experimenter expectancy errors? Explain how each one produces the necessary control.

Likelihood of Achieving Control

So far we have looked at several categories of extraneous variables that need to be controlled and a number of techniques for controlling them. Do these methods allow us to achieve the desired control? Are they effective? The answer to these questions seems to be both yes and no. The control techniques are effective, but not 100 percent effective. Actually, we do not know exactly how effective they are. If we are controlling by equating participants on some characteristic, then the effectiveness of the control is dependent on such factors as the ability to measure (for example, the ability of an intelligence test to measure intelligence). Likewise, the effectiveness of control through randomization depends on the extent to which the random procedure equated the groups. Because participants were randomly assigned to groups, it is also possible that the factors affecting the experiments were unequally distributed among the groups, which would result in internal invalidity.

The point is that we can never be certain that complete control has been effected in the experiment. All we can do is increase the probability that we have attained the desired control of the confounding extraneous variables that would be sources of rival hypotheses.

Summary

In conducting an experiment that attempts to identify a causal relationship, the experimenter must accomplish one important task: controlling for the influence of extraneous variables. This is usually accomplished by using an available control technique. The technique of randomization is extremely valuable because it provides control for unknown as well as known sources of variation by distributing them equally across all experimental conditions so that the extraneous variables exert a constant influence.

Matching is a control technique that is less powerful than randomization in its ability to equate groups of research participants on all extraneous variables. The prime advantage of the matching technique is that it increases the sensitivity of the experiment while providing control of those extraneous variables that are matched. There are four basic matching techniques. One technique, matching by holding variables constant, produces control by including in the study only participants with a given amount or type of an extraneous variable. Certain extraneous variables are therefore excluded from the study, which means they cannot influence the results. A second matching technique involves building the extraneous variable into the design of the experiment. In this case, the extraneous variable actually represents another independent variable, so its effect on the results is noted and isolated from the effects of other independent variables. The yoked control matching technique is very restrictive in that it controls only for the temporal relationship between an event and a response. It accomplishes this by having a yoked control participant receive the stimulus conditions at exactly the same time as does the experimental research participant. The last matching technique involves equating participants in each of the experimental groups either on a case-by-case basis (precision control) or by matching the distribution of extraneous variables in each experimental group. Regardless of which approach is used, the matching technique represents an attempt to generate groups of research participants that are equated on the extraneous variables considered to be of greatest importance.

The counterbalancing technique represents an attempt to control for both order and carry-over sequencing effects. Order effects exist where a change in performance arises from the order in which the treatment conditions are administered, whereas carry-over effects refer to the influence that one treatment condition has on performance under another treatment condition. Two counterbalancing techniques that can provide some control over sequencing effects are intrasubject counterbalancing, which involves counterbalancing participants, and intragroup counterbalancing, which involves counterbalancing groups of participants. These techniques are effective in controlling for all sequencing effects except nonlinear carry-over effects.

Research participants and experimenters have also been shown to be potential sources of bias in psychological experiments. The biasing influence of participants is the result of their differential perceptions regarding the most effective mode for presenting themselves in the most positive manner. Use of the double blind placebo model, deception, disguising the experiment, and obtaining an independent measurement of the dependent variable are all effective ways of creating constant perceptions of the experimental hypothesis, the purpose of the experiment, and knowledge of being in the experiment. However, differential participant perceptions can be caused by other procedural aspects of the experiment. To determine whether these other procedures create differential perceptions, we must use a technique such as the retrospective or concurrent verbal report. Experimenter effects can be minimized by using some technique that either conceals from the experimenter the treatment condition that the participant is in or else eliminates experimenter–participant interaction. Such techniques include automation, the blind technique, and the partial blind technique.

Even after all of these control techniques have been considered for a given study and the appropriate ones have been used, we still cannot be completely sure that all extraneous variables have been controlled. The only sure thing that can be said is that more control is gained with the use of these techniques than would be without their use.

Key Terms and Concepts

Randomization
Representative
Random selection
Random assignment
Matching
Yoked control
Precision control
Frequency distribution control
Counterbalancing
Order effect
Carry-over effect
Intrasubject counterbalancing
Intragroup counterbalancing

Incomplete counterbalancing
Double blind placebo model
Deception
Retrospective verbal report
Postexperimental inquiry
Concurrent verbal report
Sacrifice groups
Concurrent probing
Think-aloud technique
Experimenter effects
Blind technique
Partial blind technique
Automation

Related
Internet Sites

www.randomizer.org
This site permits the user, or student, to randomly sample participants from a defined population or to randomly assign participants to an experimental treatment condition.

www.psychology.uiowa.edu/Faculty/wasserman/Glossary/yoke.html
This site has a short tutorial on the yoked control design.

http://skepdic.com/experimentereffect.html
This site gives a good example of experimenter expectancy effects and how they can influence the outcome of a study.

Practice Test   *The answers to these questions can be found in Appendix A.*

1. If you could only use one control technique, which one should you use?

a. Random assignment of participants to groups
b. Matching by holding variables constant
c. Matching by yoked control
d. Double blind placebo model
e. Counterbalancing

2. Assume that you wanted to investigate the effect of caffeine on a person's ability to identify the number of times the letter *q* appeared in a page filled with a random list of letters. To control for the effect of a person's reaction time, you divided people into those that had high and low reaction times and then included this difference in reaction time as another independent variable in the design of your study. By controlling for the possible influence of reaction time in this way you used

a. Random assignment of participants to reaction time groups
b. Yoked control by yoking the reaction time to identification of the letter *q*
c. Counterbalancing by having participants in each reaction-time group
d. Matching by including the extraneous variable into the design of the study
e. Use of the blind technique because the people did not know if their reaction times were fast or slow

3. If you identify extraneous variables that are correlated with the dependent variable and control for them by matching participants on an individual basis and then randomly assign the matched participants to groups, you have used which control technique?

a. Random assignment
b. Yoked control
c. Precision control
d. Frequency distribution control
e. Procedural control

4. Assume you wanted to find out if alcohol increased a person's aggressiveness. To test this hypothesis you wanted to test people's aggressiveness while under the influence of alcohol and while not under the influence of alcohol. However, you know that you are asking people to perform under two conditions and that performing once may change their performance on the second occasion. To control for this effect you elect to

   a. Randomly select the research participants from the larger group of people who volunteer for the study
   b. Match the people who participate in terms of their sensitivity to alcohol
   c. Administer the alcohol in a double blind fashion
   d. Assess the participants' perceptions of whether they can tell they are drinking alcohol
   e. Counterbalance the administration of the alcohol and no alcohol conditions

5. If you wanted to control for the expectancies that the experimenter might have regarding the outcome of the experiment you might

   a. Use deception
   b. Counterbalance the treatment conditions so that any change due to expectancies is distributed equally across groups of participants
   c. Automate the experimental procedure so that the experimenter does not interact with the research participant
   d. Randomly assign participants to treatment conditions so that the expectancies are distributed equally across groups
   e. Match participants so that the expectancies are the same for all participants

Challenge Exercises

1. You want to conduct an experiment to test the effect of a new drug for treating children with Attention Deficit Disorder. You have decided to test four different amounts of the new drug—5 mg, 10 mg, 15 mg, and 20 mg. The parents of forty children with Attention Deficit Disorder have volunteered their child to participate in the study. Randomly assign the forty children to the four drug conditions using the table of random numbers in Appendix D, describing each step taken in this procedure and what you did in each step.

   a. Step 1
   b. Step 2
   c. Step 3
   d. Step 4

Participants Randomly Assigned to Groups

Group 1	Group 2	Group 3	Group 4

   e. Step 5

2. You want to test the effect of a new drug for treating children with Attention Deficit Disorder, but this time you want all the children to take a placebo—5 mg, 10 mg, 15 mg, and 20 mg on different days. You know that using this procedure may result in either carry-over or order effects, so you want to counterbalance the order of presentation of the five dosages. Construct the different counterbalanced order of treatment conditions using the incomplete counterbalancing technique.

3. Dr. Know developed a new type of therapy for treating individuals' depression. He wanted to find out if the therapy technique he had developed was effective and resulted in an amelioration of depression. Assume that he enlisted your aid in setting up a study that would test the effectiveness of this therapy. Identify the extraneous variables that could confound the results of this experiment, explain how the confounding would take place, and identify how you would control for these extraneous variables.

10 Experimental Research Design

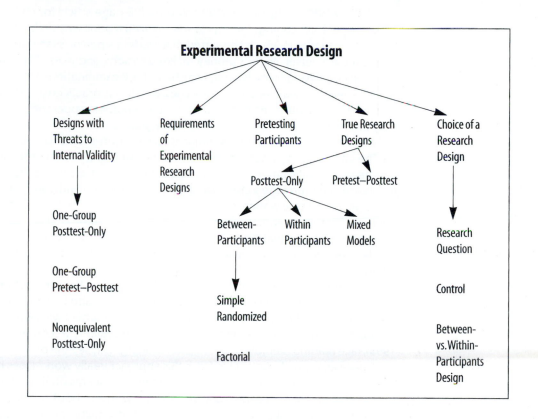

In February 1999, Cathy Hainer (1999) wrote a full-page article for *USA Today* on the ancient art of face reading. This article summarized a book written by Rose Rosetree, a leading face reader, in which she stated that reading a person's face can tell you things such as "how a person spends money, makes decisions, and works." Face reading, which is also called physiognomy, is similar to phrenology, examination of the bumps on the skull of a person's head for personality cues, which was practiced in psychology around the turn of the century. The difference is that face reading apparently does not require touching. Many face readers work from photographs.

According to Rose Rosetree, prominent facial features signal personality characteristics. The position of a person's ears, whether they sit high, low, or in the middle of a person's head, is significant because it reveals the speed with which a person makes decisions. Eyelids provide a clue to a person's emotionality and aggressiveness. Straight lower eyelids indicate wariness, suspicion, and shyness. Curved lower lids indicate an emotionally open person. The fullness of lips is an indication of the degree of comfort in talking about personal issues. People with full lips are more comfortable talking openly about private issues, whereas people with thin lips don't like to share personal details.

In reading such assertions, different people will have different reactions. Some will consider it total garbage; others will place considerable faith in it and make decisions based on the conclusions drawn from face readers. Yet others will, perhaps, be skeptical but open enough to consider that it may have some validity. According to Cathy Hainer (1999), face reading is enjoying a renaissance along with several other ancient Chinese arts. However, the real question is: Does this approach really work? Does it accurately reveal the personality characteristics of individuals? It seems obvious that Rose Rosetree is convinced of its accuracy because she has written a book advocating this approach, and she makes use of it in identifying personality characteristics of individuals. However, just because some individuals are convinced of and believe in a certain approach does not make it valid. There are many people who believe in the accuracy of palm reading, handwriting analysis, tarot cards, and astrology. Most scientists, however, place little faith in the accuracy of these techniques because there is little objective data to support the conclusions drawn. Psychology gave up phrenology decades ago because it did not provide a window into a person's personality.

How do we determine if face reading accurately portrays a person's personality characteristics? To do this we must test experimentally the conclusions drawn from face reading to determine its accuracy. This means that we must formulate a research design that can be used to answer this research question. On the basis of the material presented in the previous chapters, you know that answering such a research question requires that you first identify the independent and dependent variables. For the face reading question, you might test the hypothesis that people with ears located high, low, or in the middle of the head differ in the speed with which they make decisions. In testing this research question, your independent variable is the location of the ears on the head and the dependent variable is the speed of decision making. You also have to identify the variables that must be controlled in order to ensure internal validity and the techniques that must be used to control for the influence of these extraneous variables. For example, you want to control for the intelligence of the individuals comprising the three levels of the independent variable, which might be accomplished by matching individuals' intellectual levels. Only after these decisions are made would you construct a design that would incorporate the independent and dependent variables and the control techniques. This design would provide a strategy for collecting data that will give an answer to the research question regarding the validity of conclusions drawn from face reading about the location of ears on a person's head.

Chapter Preview

After a research topic has been selected and decisions have been made about the independent and dependent variables, it is necessary to develop a strategy for testing the effect of the independent variable. This means that some plan has to be developed for collecting information from which the relationship between the independent and dependent variables can be inferred. This plan is the design of the experiment. In this chapter, I cover the basic characteristics of experimental designs. I start with a discussion of several weak designs that do not provide the best control for various threats to internal validity. These designs are presented to demonstrate how threats to internal validity operate within some studies and to show that these threats can be eliminated by incorporating control elements into the experimental designs. I then continue with coverage of the basic characteristics of strong designs that control for the threats to internal validity and provide information about the causal relationship between the independent and dependent variable. After presenting these basic characteristics, I discuss some of the more complex research designs that incorporate more than one independent variable. These designs enable researchers to test for the interactive effect of several independent variables, and this interactive effect is explained in detail to enable you to understand what an interaction means. The chapter ends with a few comments on some of the factors you need to consider in choosing a research design.

Introduction

Research design refers to the outline, plan, or strategy specifying the procedure to be used in seeking an answer to the research question. It specifies such things as how to collect and analyze the data. One purpose of the design is to control unwanted variation, which is accomplished by incorporating one or more of the control techniques discussed in Chapter 9 or by incorporating a control group. The significance of the

Research design
The outline, plan, or
strategy used to
investigate the
research problem

control group is discussed in detail later in the chapter, and the manner in which it assists in achieving control is discussed in conjunction with the various research designs.

To illustrate the purposes of research design, let us evaluate the study conducted by Ossip-Klein et al. (1983) in which they attempted to determine if switching to low tar/nicotine/carbon monoxide cigarettes actually decreases a smoker's level of carbon monoxide. Forty adult smokers were recruited through advertising in newspapers, television, radio, and posters. The research participants were randomly assigned to two groups: control and experimental. Members of the control group were told to continue smoking their usual brand of cigarettes, whereas those in the experimental group were instructed to smoke a low tar/nicotine/carbon monoxide brand. Study results revealed that the level of carbon monoxide in the body was not altered by switching to a low tar/nicotine/carbon monoxide cigarette.

The procedure specified in the design selected by Ossip-Klein et al., depicted in Figure 10.1, is quite simple. First, the forty participants were to be randomly assigned to the two groups, and then each group was to be assigned a different brand of cigarettes to smoke. All participants were to be tested for carbon monoxide levels before and after smoking their designated brand. The design also suggests which statistical test to use in analyzing the data. Because there were to be two groups and these two groups were assessed twice, a factorial design based on a mixed model was called for. (This design is discussed later in this chapter.) Note the intimate connection between research design and statistics.

The design of the experiment also suggests the conclusions that can be drawn. With the design illustrated in Figure 10.1, a statistical test could be computed to determine if differences existed between the two groups of research participants, if the pre- and postmeasurements of the carbon monoxide level varied, and if the differences between the pre- and postmeasurements depended on the group being considered (an interaction effect that is discussed in more detail later).

The design also shows how the controls for extraneous variables are incorporated. In the Ossip-Klein et al. experiment, the randomization control technique was incorporated by randomly assigning participants to the two groups. Before being assigned, participants were matched on several variables, such as number of cigarettes smoked per day.

Because the design suggests which observations will be made and how these observations will be analyzed, it determines whether valid, objective, and accurate answers to research questions will be obtained. Whether designs are good or bad depends on whether they enable one to attain the answers sought. It is usually much easier to

FIGURE 10.1
Design of the
Ossip-Klein et al.
(1983) study.

	Preresponse measure	Treatment condition	Postresponse measure
Experimental group	Carbon monoxide measure	Smokes low tar/nicotine cigarettes	Carbon monoxide measure
Control group	Carbon monoxide measure	Smokes usual brand of cigarettes	Carbon monoxide measure

design an experiment inappropriately, because careful thought and planning are not required. To the extent that the design is faulty, however, the results of the experiment will be faulty. How does one go about conceiving a good research design that will provide answers to the questions asked? It is no simple task, and there is no set way of instructing others in how to do it. Designing a piece of research requires thought—thought about the components to include and pitfalls to avoid. We will look first at some faulty research designs and then at some appropriate research designs.

STUDY QUESTION 10.1 | **What is a research design, and what is its purpose?**

Research Designs with Threats to Internal Validity

In seeking solutions to questions, the scientist conducts experiments, devising a certain strategy to be followed. Ideally, these experiments control for all threats to internal validity and support a conclusion that the independent and dependent variables are causally related. However, sometimes this is not possible and the threats to internal validity cannot be eliminated. As Shadish et al. (2002) have pointed out, sometimes researchers have to use designs that do not control for various threats to internal validity such as when the focus of attention is on external validity or when ethical considerations preclude including design elements that would control for various threats to internal validity. In cases such as these, it becomes more difficult, but not impossible, to infer a causal relationship between the independent and dependent variables. The first few designs that I present do not control for all threats to internal validity.

One-Group Posttest-Only Design

One-group posttest-only design
Research design in which the influence of a treatment condition on only one group of individuals is investigated

In the **one-group posttest-only design,** a single group of research participants is measured on a dependent variable after having undergone an experimental treatment (see Figure 10.2). Consider a hypothetical situation in which an institution starts a training program X (the treatment condition). The institution wants to evaluate the effectiveness of the program, so on completion of the program it assesses behaviors, the Y measure (for example, the opinions, attitudes, and perhaps performance of the individuals who went through the program). If the Y measures are positive and if the individuals' performances are good, then the validity of the program is thought to have been established.

FIGURE 10.2
One-group posttest-only design.

Treatment	Response measure
X	Y

(Adapted from *Experimental and Quasi-Experimental Designs for Research* by D. T. Campbell and J. C. Stanley, 1963. Chicago: Rand McNally and Company. Copyright 1963, American Educational Research Association, Washington, D.C.)

For yielding scientific data, the design in Figure 10.2 is rarely useful because without a pretest it is difficult to know if the treatment effect produced a change and without a no-treatment control group it is difficult to know what would have happened in the absence of the treatment. Also, just about all the threats to internal validity apply, so it is difficult to know if any effect is due to the treatment or to some confounding extraneous variable. However, as Shadish et al. (2002) point out, this design does have merit in the rare cases where specific background information exists on the dependent variable. For example, in 1966 the Canadian province of Ontario initiated a program to prevent phenylketonuria (PKU), a disorder that causes retardation. This program consisted of screening and treating infants born with this disorder. After the screening and treating program was initiated, only three out of forty-seven infants born with PKU showed any evidence of retardation, and two of these had been missed by the screening program (Webb et al., 1973). Prior to initiating this program, there was a much higher rate of retardation due to PKU.

This study used the type of design depicted in Figure 10.2. Based on the evidence obtained from the study the authors concluded that the program successfully prevented PKU-based retardation. This conclusion was reached only because background information existed about the rate of PKU prior to the initiation of the screening program and other extraneous variables, such as history and maturation, are unlikely to have caused the reduction in the incidence of PKU retardation. This combination of events, background information available on the dependent variable and an absence of threats to internal validity, rarely exists in psychological research, so this design would rarely, if ever, be used by psychologists.

One-Group Pretest–Posttest Design

One-group pretest–posttest design
Research design in which a treatment condition is interjected between a pre- and posttest of the dependent variable

Most researchers recognize the deficiencies in the one-group posttest-only design and attempt to improve on it by including a pretest. For an evaluation of a curriculum or training program, some measure of improvement is necessary. Some individuals, however, assume they need only include a pretest that can be compared with a test taken after administration of some treatment condition. Figure 10.3 depicts such a plan, which corresponds to the **one-group pretest–posttest design.**

A group of research participants is measured on the dependent variable, Y, prior to administration of the treatment condition. The independent variable, X, is then administered, and Y is again measured. The difference between the pre- and posttest scores is taken as an indication of the effectiveness of the treatment condition.

FIGURE 10.3
One-group pretest–posttest design.

(Adapted from *Experimental and Quasi-Experimental Designs for Research* by D. T. Campbell and J. C. Stanley, 1963. Chicago: Rand McNally and Company. Copyright 1963, American Educational Research Association, Washington, D.C.)

The Liddle and Long (1958) study represents an example of the use of this design. Liddle and Long selected eighteen slow learners, who were administered an intelligence test and assigned a reading grade placement score (pre-Y) prior to being placed in the experimental classroom. After students had spent approximately two years in the experimental classroom, the Metropolitan Achievement Tests were administered (post-Y) and these scores were compared with the previously assigned placement scores. This comparison indicated "an improvement of about 1.75 years in less than 2 school years" (p. 145). Such a study has intuitive appeal and at first seems to represent a good way to accomplish the research purpose—a change in performance can be seen and documented. In actuality, this design represents only a small improvement over the one-group posttest-only study because of the many uncontrolled rival hypotheses that could also explain the obtained results.

In the Liddle and Long (1958) study, almost two years elapsed between the pre- and posttests. Consequently, the uncontrolled rival hypotheses of history and maturation could account for some, if not all, of the observed change in performance. In order to determine conclusively that the observed change was caused by the treatment effect (the experimental classroom) and not by any of these rival hypotheses, researchers should have included an equated group of slow learners who were not placed in the experimental room. This equated group's performance could have been compared with the performance of the children who received the experimental treatment. If a significant difference had been found between the scores of these two groups, it could have been attributed to the influence of the experimental classroom because both groups would have experienced any history and maturation effects that had occurred and, therefore, these variables would have been controlled. The design of the study was inadequate, not so much because the sources of rival hypotheses *can* affect the results, but because we do not know if they did.

Although the one-group pretest–posttest does not allow us to control or to test for the potential influence of these effects, it is not totally worthless. In situations in which it is impossible to obtain an equated comparison group, the design can be used to provide some information. However, the confidence one has in concluding that the treatment produced the observed effect is totally dependent on the success of identifying the possible threats to internal validity and then collecting data demonstrating that these threats do not occur. For example, Jason, McCoy, Blanco, and Zolik (1981) found that a campaign to reduce dog litter by distributing educational material and pooper-scoopers with plastic bags resulted in a dramatic decrease in dog litter. However, the extent to which the reduction in dog litter can be tied to the campaign requires identifying plausible alternative hypotheses such as bad weather causing fewer dogs to be on the streets or an increase in local crime keeping residents indoors, and then collecting data demonstrating that these plausible hypotheses did not confound the results.

Nonequivalent posttest-only design
Research design in which the performance of an experimental group is compared with that of a nonequivalent control group

Nonequivalent Posttest-Only Design

The primary disadvantage of the previous two designs is the impossibility of drawing any unambiguous conclusions as to the influence of the treatment condition. The **nonequivalent posttest-only design** makes an inadequate attempt to remedy

FIGURE 10.4
Nonequivalent posttest-only design.

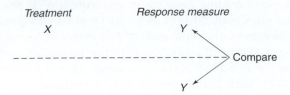

(Adapted from *Experimental and Quasi-Experimental Designs for Research* by D. T. Campbell and J. C. Stanley, 1963. Chicago: Rand McNally and Company. Copyright 1963, American Educational Research Association, Washington, D.C.)

this deficiency by including a comparison group. In this design, one group of research participants receives the treatment condition (X) and is then compared on the dependent variable (Y) with a group that did not receive this treatment condition. Figure 10.4 depicts the design.

Brown, Wehe, Zunker, and Haslam (1971) conducted a study that illustrates the use of this scheme. They wanted to evaluate the influence of a student-to-student counseling program on potential college freshman dropouts. One group of potential dropouts received the student-to-student counseling, and another matched group—the comparison group—did not. Following the series of counseling sessions, all students were administered several tests designed to evaluate the effects of the program. First-semester grade point averages were also obtained. Results revealed that, on all dependent variable measures, the group receiving the counseling performed in a superior manner.

The design of this study appears to be adequate. A comparison group was included to evaluate the influence of the treatment condition, and participants in both groups were matched. Why, then, is this design included as an example of one that has threats to internal validity? The reason is that the two groups are *assumed* to be equated on variables other than the independent variable. Granted, Brown et al. (1971) did match the groups on a number of variables such as age, gender, and ACT composite scores. Matching, however, is no assurance of having attained equated groups. As Campbell and Stanley (1963, p. 12) have stated, "Matching on background characteristics other than O [the dependent variable] is usually ineffective and misleading. . . ." The only way one can have any assurance that the groups are equated is to assign participants randomly to the two groups. As indicated by the dashed lines in Figure 10.4, random assignment is not included in the nonequivalent posttest-only design. In studies in which it is not possible to assign participants randomly, the next best technique is to match on relevant variables. However, matching is no substitute for random assignment because it does not control for other variables such as motivation. This design, therefore, does not exclude possible selection effects from the treatment effect.

STUDY QUESTION 10.2

Describe each of the research designs with threats to internal validity and explain why these threats exist.

Requirements of Experimental Research Designs

The designs just presented are weak designs because, in general, they do not provide a way of isolating the effect of the treatment condition; rival hypotheses are not excluded. What, then, is a strong research design? Three criteria need to be met in a research design. The first criterion is that the design answer the research question and adequately tests the hypothesis. Periodically, one encounters a situation in which an investigator designs a study and collects and analyzes the data, only to realize when he or she attempts to interpret the data that there is no answer to the research question. Such instances can been avoided if, after the study is designed, the researcher asks, "What conclusion or conclusions can I draw from this experiment?" Remember that the design of the study suggests the statistical tests that can be performed on the data, which in turn determine the conclusions that can be drawn. If the design allows us to conduct statistical tests that will provide an answer to the research question, the first criterion has been met.

The second criterion for a strong research design is that extraneous variables be controlled. In order to achieve internal validity, we must eliminate potential rival hypotheses. This can be accomplished by two means: control techniques or a control group. Of the control techniques discussed in Chapter 9, the most important is randomization because this is the only means by which unknown variables can be controlled.

The second means of effecting control is the inclusion of a control group. A **control group** is a group of research participants that does not receive the independent variable, receives zero amount of it, or receives a value that is in some sense a *standard* value, such as a typical treatment condition. An **experimental group** is a group of research participants that receives some amount of the independent variable. In the study conducted by Aronson and Mills (1959) on severity of initiation, the group that did not have to take the embarrassment test was the control group, whereas the other two groups, which had to read either embarrassing or not very embarrassing material, were the two experimental groups. In a drug study, the participants receiving a placebo are the control group and the participants receiving the drug are the experimental group.

A control group serves two functions. First, it serves as a source of comparison. The one-group posttest-only and the one-group pretest–posttest designs are considered weak primarily because there was no way to tell whether the treatment condition, *X*, caused the observed behavior, *Y*. To arrive at such a conclusion, we must have a comparison group or a control group that did not receive the treatment effect. Only by including a control group—assuming all other variables are controlled—can we get any concrete indication of whether the treatment condition produced results different from those that would have been attained in the absence of the treatment. Consider a hypothetical case of a father whose daughter always cries for candy when they go into a store. The parent does not like the behavior so, in order to get rid of it, he decides to spank the child whenever she cries for candy in the store and also to refuse to let her have any candy. After two weeks, the child has stopped the crying behavior, and the parent concludes that the spanking was effective. Is he correct? Note that the child also did not receive any candy during the two weeks, so a rival

Control group
The group of participants that serves as a standard of comparison for determining whether the treatment condition produced any effect

Experimental group
The group of participants that receives the treatment condition

hypothesis is that crying was extinguished. To determine whether it was the spanking or extinction that stopped the behavior, we would also have to include a control child who did not receive the spanking. If both stopped crying in two weeks, then we would know that the spanking was not the variable causing the elimination of the crying behavior.

This hypothetical example also demonstrates the second function of a control group—that is, to serve as a control for rival hypotheses. All variables operating on the control and experimental groups must be identical, except for the one being manipulated by the experimenter. In this way, the influence of extraneous variables is held constant. The extinction variable was held constant across the child who did receive the spanking and the child who did not and therefore did not confound the results. In the one-group pretest–posttest design, extraneous variables such as history and maturation can serve as rival hypotheses unless a control group is included. If a control group is included, these variables will affect the performance of both the control participants and the experimental participants, effectively holding their influence constant. It is in this way that a control group also serves a control function.

Before we leave the topic of the control group, one additional point needs to be made. A necessary requirement of the control group is that the research participants in the group be similar to those in the experimental group. If this condition does not exist, the control group cannot act as a baseline for evaluating the influence of the independent variable. The responses of the control group must stand for the responses that members of the experimental group would have given if they had not received the treatment condition. The participants in the two groups must be as similar as possible so that theoretically they would yield identical scores in the absence of the introduction of the independent variable.

The third criterion of a true research design is generalizability, or external validity. Recall from Chapter 8 that generalization asks the question: Can the results of this experiment be applied to individuals other than those who participated in the study, in other settings, at different times, using different but related outcome measures, and with variations in administration of the treatment? If the answer is yes, complete generalization exists. Remember, however, that it is difficult if not impossible to achieve this ultimate generalization within the confines of a single study. In all cases, we would like to be able to generalize beyond the confines of the actual study. Whether we can generalize and how far we can generalize our results, however, is never completely known.

The foregoing three criteria represent the ideal. Naturally, the first criterion must be met by all studies, but the degrees to which the second and third are met will vary from one study to another. Basic research focuses primarily on the criterion of internal validity because its foremost concern is the examination of the relations among variables. Applied research, on the other hand, places equal emphasis on external and internal validity because the central interest of such research is to apply the results to people and to situations.

STUDY QUESTION 10.3
- **What are the criteria that need to be met to have a good research design?**
- **What function is served by the control group?**

Pretesting Participants

One means of obtaining information about the pretreatment condition of the organism is to pretest the research participants, as was done in the one-group pretest–posttest design. The experimenter can then directly observe change in the participants' behavior as a result of the treatment effect. But one may legitimately question the need to pretest. Is it not sufficient and appropriate to assign participants randomly to experimental and control groups and forget about pretesting? One can then assume comparability of the participants in the two groups, and those in the control group provide the comparison data. Hence a pretest is unnecessary. However, there are several reasons (Lana, 1969; Selltiz et al., 1959) for including a pretest in the experimental design. These are as follows:

1. *Increased sensitivity.* One can increase the sensitivity of the experiment by matching participants on relevant variables. Such matching requires pretesting (see Chapter 9).

2. *Ceiling effect.* Another reason for pretesting is to determine if there is room for the treatment condition to have an effect. Suppose you were investigating the efficiency of a particular persuasive communication for improving attitudes toward environmental protection. If, by chance, all participants in the experiment already had extremely positive attitudes toward environmental protection, there would be no room for the treatment condition to have an effect. Pretesting enables the investigator to identify the existence of a possible ceiling effect and take it into consideration when evaluating the effects of the independent variable.

3. *Initial position.* Many psychological studies are conducted in which it is necessary to know a person's initial position on the dependent variable because it may interact with the experimental condition. A treatment condition that tries to induce hostility toward a minority group may find that the effectiveness of this treatment condition is a function of the subjects' initial level of hostility. The treatment may be very successful with individuals having little hostility but unsuccessful with extremely hostile individuals. With such conditions, it is very helpful to pretest subjects.

4. *Initial comparability.* Another reason for pretesting is to assure that participants are initially comparable on relevant variables. Ideally, participants are randomly assigned to conditions. Although random assignment provides the greatest assurance possible of comparability of research participants, it is not infallible. Should randomization fail to provide comparability, comparison of the subgroups' pretest mean scores would tell us so.

   In field research, we cannot always assign participants randomly; rather, they must be taken as intact groups. Educational experiments, for example, are sometimes restricted to using one intact class for one group of participants and another class for another group of participants. In such instances, it is advisable to make sure that participants do not differ initially on the independent variable. This kind of compromise occasionally has to be made. We must also recognize that the results of the experiment could be caused by group differences on characteristics other than the pretested variables. The pretest does, however, give some indication that the observed differences result from the treatment condition.

5. *Evidence of change.* Perhaps the most common reason for pretesting is to gain an empirical demonstration of whether the treatment condition succeeded in producing a change in the research participants. The most direct way of gaining such evidence is to measure the difference obtained before and after a treatment is introduced.

As you can see, there are several legitimate reasons for including a pretest in the study design. Unfortunately, there are also some difficulties that accompany pretesting (Oliver and Berger, 1980). First, pretesting may increase the amount of time or money required to complete the investigation. A more serious problem is that it may sensitize research participants to the experimental treatment condition. For example, pretesting participants' opinions may alert them to the fact that they are participating in an attitude experiment, and this knowledge could heighten their sensitivity to the independent variable. Pretested participants may therefore produce results that are not representative of those that would be obtained from a population that had not been pretested. However, this pretesting effect appears to depend on the type of study being conducted. If the posttest score involves recall of previously learned material, the effect on the posttest scores is probably facilitative. In attitude research any effect of a pretest will be to depress the posttest measure of the effect of the treatment condition (Lana, 1969).

STUDY QUESTION 10.4 | **Why would you want to pretest research participants on the dependent variable?**

Experimental Research Designs

Experimental design
A design in which the influence of extraneous variables is controlled for while the influence of the independent variable is tested

In this section we will consider some experimental research designs. To be an **experimental design,** a research design must enable the researcher to maintain control over the situation in terms of assignment of research participants to groups, in terms of who gets the treatment condition, and in terms of the amount of the treatment condition that participants receive. In other words, the researcher must have a controlled experiment in order to have confidence in the relations discovered between the independent and dependent variable. There are two basic types of experimental research designs: the posttest-only design and the pretest–posttest design.

Posttest-Only Design

Posttest-only design
An experimental design in which the experimental and the control groups' posttest scores are compared to assess the influence of the treatment condition

The **posttest-only design** contains the basic components of most research plans used in the field of psychology. Its name is derived from the fact that the dependent variable is measured only once and this measurement occurs after the experimental treatment condition has been administered to the experimental group, as depicted in Figure 10.5. From this figure, you can see that the responses obtained from an experimental condition are compared with the responses obtained from a control condition after the treatment has been administered. However, the format illustrated here represents only the basic structure of the posttest-only design. The exact structure of the

FIGURE 10.5
Posttest-only design.

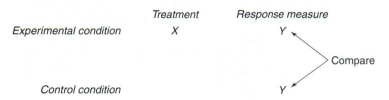

(Adapted from *Experimental and Quasi-Experimental Designs for Research* by D. T. Campbell and J. C. Stanley, 1963. Chicago: Rand McNally and Company. Copyright 1963, American Educational Research Association, Washington, D.C.)

final design depends on several factors, such as the number of independent variables included in the investigation, the number of levels of variation of each independent variable, and whether the same or different participants are to be used in each treatment condition. Posttest-only designs are usually dichotomized in terms of this last factor. If different participants are used in each experimental treatment condition, then the posttest-only design is typically labeled a *between-participants* design. If the same participants are used in each experimental condition, then the posttest-only design is labeled a *within-participants* design.

Between-participants posttest-only design
A type of posttest-only research design in which research participants are randomly assigned to the experimental and control groups

Between-Participants Posttest-Only Design In the **between-participants posttest-only design,** the research participants are randomly assigned to as many groups as there are experimental treatment conditions. For example, if a study was investigating only one independent variable and the presence-versus-absence form of variation was being used with this independent variable, participants would be randomly assigned to two treatment groups, as illustrated in Figure 10.6. This design is similar in appearance to the nonequivalent posttest-only design, but with one basic and important difference. Remember that the nonequivalent posttest-only design was criticized primarily from the standpoint that it does not provide any assurance of equality among the various groups. This between-participants posttest-only design provides the necessary equivalence by randomly assigning participants to the two groups. If enough participants are included to allow randomization to work, then, theoretically, all possible extraneous variables are controlled (excluding those such as experimenter expectancies).

The study conducted by Cialdini, Cacioppo, Bassett, and Miller (1978) illustrates the use of the between-participants posttest-only research design. The experiment

FIGURE 10.6
Two-group between-participants posttest-only design.

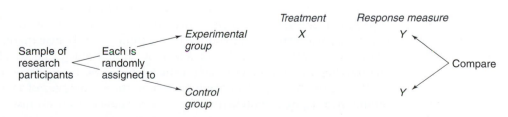

that these investigators conducted represented an attempt to determine whether the tactic used by new-car dealers to entice a customer to pay more for an automobile really worked. In order to investigate this tactic, the researchers had to simulate, in the laboratory, the same type of psychological ploy that the car dealers used. This simulation involved contacting students by phone, explaining a psychological experiment to them, and asking them if they would be willing to participate in it. If they agreed to participate, they were told that the experiment was being conducted at 7:00 A.M. on Wednesday and Friday mornings. The experimenter then asked if it was possible to schedule the participant for one of these mornings. In this way the experimenter simulated the tactic used by the new-car dealers: He or she obtained a commitment from the participant to participate in the experiment prior to increasing the cost of participation. Once the commitment was received, the cost was increased. The key issue was whether the participant would still agree to participate, as with the assumption of the new-car dealers that the customer, once committed to buying the car, will still agree to buy it even after the price is raised. Consequently, the dependent variable was the percentage of individuals agreeing to participate in the experiment. To determine if this tactic worked, however, it was necessary to include a control group that was not subjected to this tactic. This control group consisted of a group of research participants who were contacted by phone and asked to participate in a psychological experiment that began at 7:00 A.M. Note that these participants were told that the experiment began at 7:00 A.M. *before* being asked to participate, like a customer who is told the real price of a car and then allowed to make a decision to purchase. Consequently, this experiment involved two groups, a control and an experimental group, and the participants for each group were randomly selected from class rolls in order to control for the influence of extraneous variables. Therefore, the experiment was a between-participants posttest-only research design. The results of this experiment revealed that the tactic worked: 56 percent of the participants in the experimental group agreed to participate, whereas only 31 percent of the participants in the control group did so.

Two difficulties can be identified in the design just presented. First, randomization is used to produce equivalence between the two groups. Although this is the best control technique available for achieving equivalence, it does not provide complete assurance that the necessary equivalence has been attained. (This is particularly true when the group of participants being randomized is small.) In the Cialdini et al. (1978) experiment there were over thirty participants randomly selected for each group. This is a large enough group to provide reasonable assurance that randomization produced the necessary group equivalence. If there is any doubt, it is advisable to combine matching with the randomization technique. Second, it is not the most sensitive design for detecting an effect caused by the independent variable. As discussed earlier, matching is the most effective technique for increasing the sensitivity of the experiment, and so these difficulties with the posttest-only design can be eliminated by matching participants prior to randomly assigning them to the experimental treatment groups. However, the benefits of matching should always be weighed against the accompanying disadvantages, such as the limitation of the available participant pool.

When, in the opinion of the investigator, the advantages of matching outweigh the disadvantages, a matched between-participants posttest-only design should be

FIGURE 10.7
Matched between-participants posttest-only design.

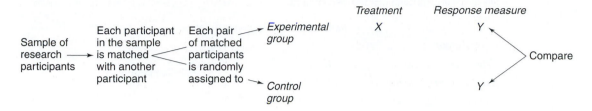

used. As illustrated in Figure 10.7, this design requires that each member of the sample of participants be matched with another participant on the variable or variables that are correlated with the dependent variable. The matched participants are then randomly assigned to the experimental groups. Note that matching takes place *in addition* to randomization; it does not replace randomization. Using the two techniques increases both the sensitivity of the experiment and the probability that the groups are equivalent on the extraneous variables that must be controlled.

The two-group between-participants posttest-only design just discussed illustrates the basic conceptual structure of the between-participants design. However, experiments are seldom confined to two levels of variation of one independent variable. Instead, most studies use several levels of variation of one or more independent variables, and their schemes are extensions of the between-participants posttest-only design. The two primary extensions are represented by the simple randomized participants design and the factorial design.

Simple randomized participants design
A between-participants design in which the influence of several levels of variation on the independent variable is investigated

Simple Randomized Participants Design. The **simple randomized participants design** is a between-participants posttest-only type of design that has been extended to include several levels of the independent variable. There are many situations in which it is desirable to give varying amounts or degrees of an independent variable to different groups of participants. In drug research, the investigator may want to administer different amounts of a drug to see if they produce differential reactions to the dependent variable. In such a case, participants will be randomly assigned to the various treatment groups. If there were three experimental groups and one control group, participants will be randomly assigned to the four groups, as shown in Figure 10.8. A statistical test will then be used to determine if a significant difference existed in the average responses of the four groups of participants to the dependent variable.

Sigall et al. (1970) used the simple randomized participants design in attempting to determine whether participants are motivated to look good or whether they are motivated to cooperate with the experimenter to produce the results that he or she wants. To investigate these motives, they had a control group and three experimental groups. In one experimental group, the participants were led to believe that they should increase performance; in another group, the participants were led to believe that they should decrease performance; and in a third group, evaluative apprehension was generated by telling the participants that increased performance was indicative of obsessive–compulsive behavior. The design of this experiment is depicted in Figure 10.8.

FIGURE 10.8

Simple randomized participants design with four levels of variation of the independent variable. *R* indicates that the four groups of participants were randomly assigned.

	Treatment	Response measure
Control group		Y
Experimental group I	X_1	Y
Experimental group II	X_2	Y
Experimental group III	X_3	Y

R → Compare

The analysis by Sigall et al. of their data revealed significant differences among the various groups. Additional statistical tests showed that the three experimental groups differed significantly from the control group and that the evaluative apprehension group differed significantly from the other two experimental groups. From this they concluded that a research participant's primary motive is to look good rather than to cooperate with the experimenter. They arrived at this conclusion because the obsessive–compulsive group performed more slowly than any other group, whereas the other two experimental groups performed better than either the control or the obsessive–compulsive experimental group.

The simple randomized subjects design considers only one independent variable. In psychological research, as in other types of research, we are frequently interested in the effect of several independent variables acting in concert. In research on instructional effectiveness, researchers are interested in methods of instruction (for example, tutorial, discussion, lecture) as well as in other factors such as instructor attitude or experience. The simple randomized participants design does not enable us to investigate several independent variables simultaneously, but a factorial design does.

STUDY QUESTION 10.5

- **Diagram a posttest-only research design and explain why it is called a *between-participants* design.**
- **Explain why a simple randomized design is a between-participants design and how it is similar to and different from the posttest-only research design.**

Factorial design

A between-participants design that enables us to investigate the independent and interactive influences of more than one independent variable

Cell

A specific treatment combination in a factorial design

Factorial Design. In a **factorial design,** two or more independent variables are simultaneously studied to determine their independent and interactive effects on the dependent variable. Let us look at a hypothetical example that considers the effect of two independent variables, A and B. Assume that variable A has three levels of variation (A_1, A_2, and A_3) and that variable B has two levels of variation (B_1 and B_2). Figure 10.9 depicts this design, in which there are six possible combinations of the two independent variables—A_1B_1, A_1B_2, A_2B_1, A_2B_2, A_3B_1, and A_3B_2. Each one of these treatment combinations is referred to as a **cell.** There are six cells within this design to which the participants are randomly assigned. The participants randomly assigned to A_1B_1 receive the A_1 level of the first independent variable and the B_1 level of the second independent variable. In like manner, the participants randomly assigned to the other cells receive the designated combination of the two independent variables.

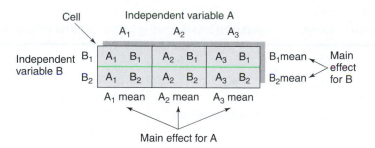

Main effect

The influence of one
independent variable
in a factorial design

In an experiment that uses the design shown in Figure 10.9, two types of effects need to be analyzed: main effects and interaction effects. A **main effect** refers to the influence of one independent variable. The term *main effect* did not arise in the simple randomized experiment or in the two-group between-participants posttest-only experiment because only one main effect or one independent variable existed. However, more than one independent variable exists in a factorial design, and the separate effects of each independent variable must be identified. To distinguish the influence of the different independent variables, we refer to each one as a separate main effect. In Figure 10.9, the two independent variables A and B each have a main effect. The main effect for A simply tells us if A produced a significant influence on behavior or if there was a significant difference among the three A mean scores. Similarly, the main effect for B tells us if B had a significant impact on behavior or if there was a significant difference between the two B mean scores.

Interaction effect

The influence of one
independent variable
on a second
independent variable

An **interaction effect** refers to the influence that one independent variable has on another. The concept of interaction is rather difficult for most students to grasp, so I will digress in order to clarify this idea. First, I will present a number of possible outcomes that could accrue from an experiment having the design shown in Figure 10.9. Some of the outcomes represent interactions and others do not, so that you can see the difference in the two situations. I will set up a progression from a situation in which one main effect is significant to a situation in which both main effects and the interaction are significant. The letter A will always represent one independent variable, and the letter B will always represent a second independent variable. Table 10.1 and Figure 10.10 depict these various cases. For the sake of clarity, the hypothetical scores in the cells will represent the mean score for the participants in each cell.

Parts (*a*), (*b*), and (*d*) of Figure 10.10 represent situations in which one or both of the main effects are significant. In each case, the mean scores for the level of variation of at least one of the main effects differ. This can readily be seen from both the numerical examples presented in Table 10.1 and the graphs in Figure 10.10. Note also from Figure 10.10 that the lines for levels B_1 and B_2 are parallel in each of these three cases.

Interaction

The effect of one
independent variable
depends on the
level of another
independent variable

In such a situation an interaction cannot exist, because an **interaction** means that the effect of one variable, such as B_1, depends on the level of the other variable being considered, such as A_1, A_2, or A_3. In each of these cases, the B effect is the same at all levels of A.

Part (*c*) depicts the classic example of an interaction. Neither main effect is significant, as indicated by the fact that the three-column means are identical and the two-row means are identical and reveal no variation. However, if the A treatment effect is

TABLE 10.1

Tabular Presentation of Hypothetical Data Illustrating Different Kinds of Main and Interaction Effects

	A_1	A_2	A_3	Mean
B_1	10	20	30	20
B_2	10	20	30	20
Mean	10	20	30	

(a) A is significant; B and the interaction are not significant

	A_1	A_2	A_3	Mean
B_1	20	20	20	20
B_2	30	30	30	30
Mean	25	25	25	

(b) B is significant; A and the interaction are not significant

	A_1	A_2	A_3	Mean
B_1	30	40	50	40
B_2	50	40	30	40
Mean	40	40	40	

(c) Interaction is significant; A and B are not significant

	A_1	A_2	A_3	Mean
B_1	10	20	30	20
B_2	40	50	60	50
Mean	25	35	45	

(d) A and B are significant; interaction is not significant

	A_1	A_2	A_3	Mean
B_1	20	30	40	30
B_2	30	30	30	30
Mean	25	30	35	

(e) A and the interaction are significant; B is not significant

	A_1	A_2	A_3	Mean
B_1	10	20	30	20
B_2	50	40	30	40
Mean	30	30	30	

(f) B and the interaction are significant; A is not significant

	A_1	A_2	A_3	Mean
B_1	30	50	70	50
B_2	20	30	40	30
Mean	25	40	55	

(g) A, B, and the interaction are significant

considered only for level B_1, we note that the scores systematically increase from level A_1 to level A_3. In like manner, if only level B_2 is considered, then there is a systematic decrease from level A_1 to A_3. In other words, A is effective but in opposite directions for levels B_1 and B_2, or the effect of A depends on which level of B we are considering. This is the definition of *interaction*. I find graphs to be more helpful than tables in depicting interaction, but you should use whichever mode better conveys the information.

Parts (e) and (f) show examples of situations in which a main effect and an interaction are significant; part (g) shows a case in which both main effects and the interaction are significant. These illustrations exhaust the possibilities that exist in a factorial design having two independent variables. The exact nature of the main effects or the interaction may change, but one of these types of conditions will exist. Before we leave this section, one additional point needs to be made regarding the interpretation of significant main and interaction effects. Whenever either a main or an interaction effect *alone* is significant, you naturally have to interpret this effect. When *both* main and interaction effects are significant, however, and the main effect is contained in the interaction effect, then only the interaction effect is interpreted because the significant interaction effect qualifies the meaning that would arise from the main effect alone.

FIGURE 10.10

Graphic presentation of hypothetical data illustrating different kinds of main and interaction effects.

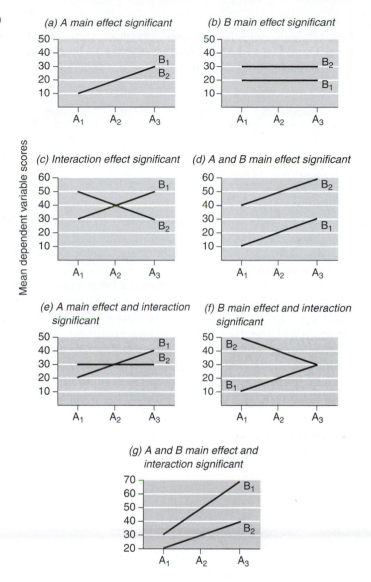

A design similar to that just discussed was used by Swann, Wenzlaff, Krull, and Pelham (1992) to investigate the type of feedback preferred by depressed individuals. It was hypothesized that depressed people preferentially seek to interact with others who provide unfavorable feedback, whereas the nondepressed seek out others who provide positive feedback. In investigating this hypothesis, Swann et al. used two independent variables: level of depression and type of feedback. Three levels of depression were established for the first independent variable: nondepressed, dysphoric, and depressed. Similarly, three levels of feedback were established for the second independent variable: positive, neutral, and negative. This gives a 3×3 factorial

FIGURE 10.11
Design of the Swann
et al. (1992) study.

Type of feedback	Level of depression		
	Nondepressed (A₁)	Dysphoric (A₂)	Depressed (A₃)
Positive (B₁)	A_1B_1	A_2B_1	A_3B_1
Neutral (B₂)	A_1B_2	A_2B_2	A_3B_2
Negative (B₃)	A_1B_3	A_2B_3	A_3B_3

design (three levels of one independent variable times three levels of the other) with nine cells, as shown in Figure 10.11.

Figure 10.12 displays a graph of the data collected from one portion of this study. This figure shows that an interaction exists between the type of evaluator and the level of depression. Depressed individuals have a greater desire to interact with unfavorable evaluators or others who provide negative feedback, whereas nondepressed and dysphoric individuals have a greater desire to interact with favorable evaluators who provide positive feedback.

So far, the discussion of factorial designs has been limited to those with two independent variables. There are times when it would be advantageous to include three or more independent variables in a study. Factorial designs enable us to include as many independent variables as we consider important. Mathematically or statistically, there is almost no limit to the number of independent variables that can be included in a study. Practically speaking, however, there are several difficulties associated with increasing the number of variables. First, there is an associated increase in the number of research participants required. In an experiment with two indepen-

FIGURE 10.12
Self-verification and depression.

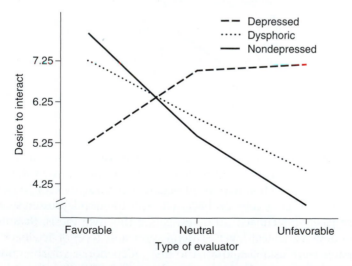

(From "Allure of Negative Feedback: Self-verification Strivings among Depressed Persons" by W. B. Swann, Jr., R. M. Wenzlaff, D. S. Krull, and B. W. Pelham, 1992. *Journal of Abnormal Psychology, 101*, pp. 293–306. Reprinted by permission.)

dent variables, each of which has two levels of variation, a 2×2 arrangement is generated, yielding four cells. If ten participants are required for each cell, the experiment requires a total of forty participants. In a three-variable design, with two levels of variation per independent variable, a $2 \times 2 \times 2$ arrangement exists, yielding eight cells, and eighty participants are required in order to have ten participants per cell. Four variables mean that sixteen cells and 160 participants are required. As you can see, the required number of participants increases rapidly with an increase in the number of independent variables. This difficulty, however, does not seem to be insurmountable; many studies are conducted with large numbers of research participants.

A second problem with factorial designs incorporating more than two variables is the increased difficulty of simultaneously manipulating the combinations of independent variables. In an attitude study, it is harder to simultaneously manipulate the credibility of the communicator, type of message, gender of the communicator, prior attitudes of the audience, and intelligence of the audience (a five-variable problem) than it is just to manipulate the credibility of the communicator and prior attitudes of the audience.

A third complication arises when higher-order interactions are significant. In a design with three independent variables, it is possible to have a significant interaction among the three variables A, B, and C. Consider a study that includes the variables of age, gender, and intelligence. A three-variable interaction means that the effect on the dependent variable is a joint function of the participants' age, gender, and intelligence level. The investigator must look at this triple interaction and interpret its meaning, deciphering what combinations produce which effect and why. Triple interactions can be quite difficult to interpret, and interactions of an even higher order tend to become unwieldy. Therefore, it is advisable to restrict the design to no more than three variables.

In spite of these problems, factorial designs are very popular because of their overriding advantages when appropriately used. The following four advantages of factorial designs are adapted from Kerlinger (1973, p. 257).

The first advantage is that more than one independent variable can be manipulated in an experiment, and therefore more than one hypothesis can be tested. In a one-variable experiment, only one hypothesis can be tested: Did the treatment condition produce the desired effect? In an experiment with three independent variables, however, seven hypotheses can be tested: one regarding each of the three main effects—A, B, and C—and one regarding each of the four interactions—$A \times B$, $A \times C$, $B \times C$, and $A \times B$ C.

A second positive feature is that the researcher can control a potentially confounding variable by building it into the design. This, as noted in Chapter 9, is a mechanism for eliminating the influence of an extraneous variable. Naturally, the decision whether to include the extraneous variable (such as gender) in the design will be partially a function of how many independent variables are already included. If three or four are already included, it may be wise to effect control in another manner (perhaps by including only females). If only one or two independent variables exist, then the decision in most cases should be to include the extraneous variable in the design. Including the extraneous variable not only controls it but also may provide valuable information about its effect on the dependent variable.

The third advantage of the factorial design is that it produces greater precision than does an experiment with only one variable, for reasons discussed earlier.

The final benefit of the factorial design is that it enables the researcher to study the interactive effects of the independent variables on the dependent variable. This advantage is probably the most important because it enables us to hypothesize and test interactive effects. Testing main effects does not require a factorial design, but testing the interactions does. It is this testing of interactions that lets us investigate the complexity of behavior and see that behavior is caused by the interaction of many independent variables. Lana (1959), for example, specifically set out to test an interactive hypothesis put forth by Solomon (1949) and Campbell (1957). They stated that pretests have a potentially sensitizing effect on attitudes. Using the four-group design to test this interactive hypothesis, Lana found no significant interaction, so pretesting apparently did not have the hypothesized sensitizing effect on attitudes.

STUDY QUESTION 10.6

- **What is a factorial design and why would you want to use this design instead of a simple randomized design?**
- **What are main and interaction effects in a factorial design?**
- **Describe an interaction between learning and anxiety.**
- **What are the advantages and disadvantages of a factorial design?**

Within-participants posttest-only design
A type of posttest-only design in which the same research participants are repeatedly assessed on the dependent variable after participating in all experimental treatment conditions

Within-Participants Posttest-Only Design   In the **within-participants posttest-only design,** the same research participants participate in all experimental treatment conditions (see Figure 10.13). Actually, this is a repeated measures design because all participants are repeatedly measured under each treatment condition. Haslerud and Meyers (1958) used this scheme in their investigation of the transfer value of individually derived principles. All research participants were first trained on problems in which rules were given and on problems in which the participants had to derive their own rules. After this training, *all* participants solved problems using both the rules they had been given and the rules they had derived. In other words, participants served under both conditions.

FIGURE 10.13
Within-participants posttest-only design.

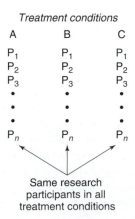

Treatment conditions

A	B	C
P_1	P_1	P_1
P_2	P_2	P_2
P_3	P_3	P_3
•	•	•
•	•	•
•	•	•
P_n	P_n	P_n

Same research participants in all treatment conditions

Among the benefits of using the within-participants posttest-only design is the fact that the investigator need not worry about creating equivalence in the research participants because the same participants are involved in each treatment condition. In other words, participants serve as their own control, and variables such as age, gender, and prior experience remain constant over the entire experiment. Because the participants serve as their own control, the participants in the various treatment conditions are perfectly matched, which increases the sensitivity of the experiment. Therefore, the within-participants design is maximally sensitive to the effects of the independent variable.

Also, the within-participants design does not require as many participants as does the between-participants design. In the former, with all participants participating in all treatment conditions, the number of participants needed for an entire experiment is equal to the number of participants needed for one experimental treatment condition. In the between-participants design, the number of research participants needed equals the number of participants required for one treatment condition times the number of treatment conditions. If ten participants are needed in each treatment condition and there are three treatment conditions, then ten participants are needed in a within-participants design, whereas thirty participants are needed in a between-participants design.

With all these advantages, one might think that the within-participants design would be used more than the between-participants design. Actually, the reverse is true because of the disadvantages that also accompany the within-participants design. The most serious handicap of this design is the confounding influence of a sequencing effect. Remember that a sequencing effect can occur when participants participate in more than one treatment condition. Because the primary characteristic of a within-participants design is that all participants participate in all experimental treatment conditions, a sequencing rival hypothesis is a real possibility. In order to overcome the sequencing effect, investigators frequently use one of the counterbalancing techniques discussed earlier. However, counterbalancing controls only linear sequencing effects; if the sequencing effects are nonlinear, then a confounding sequencing influence exists even if counterbalancing is used. Even if the sequencing effect can be overcome through counterbalancing, in a within-participants design there is no way to identify any impact of the extraneous variables of history, maturation, and statistical regression.

As you can see, there are some serious problems associated with the within-participants design, and they are generally more difficult to control than those in the between-participants design. As a result, the within-participants design is not the most commonly used.

Factorial design based on a mixed model
A factorial design that represents a combination of the within-participants and the between-participants designs

Combining Between- and Within-Participants Designs   Many times in psychological research there are several variables of interest, of which one or more would fit into a between-participants design and the others would fit into a within-participants design. Does this mean that two separate studies must be conducted, or can they be combined? As you probably suspected, they can be incorporated into one design called a **factorial design based on a mixed model.** The simplest form of such a design involves a situation in which two independent variables have to be

FIGURE 10.14
Factorial design based
on a mixed model,
with two independent
variables.

Within-participants
independent variable

		A_1	A_2	A_3
		P_1	P_1	P_1
		P_2	P_2	P_2
	B_1	P_3	P_3	P_3
		P_4	P_4	P_4
Between-participants independent variable		P_5	P_5	P_5
		P_6	P_6	P_6
		P_7	P_7	P_7
	B_2	P_8	P_8	P_8
		P_9	P_9	P_9
		P_{10}	P_{10}	P_{10}

varied in two different ways. One independent variable requires a different group of research participants for each level of variation. The other independent variable is constructed in such a way that all participants have to take each level of variation. Consequently, the first independent variable requires a between-participants design, and the second independent variable requires a within-participants design. When these two independent variables are included in the same scheme, it becomes a factorial design based on a mixed model, as illustrated in Figure 10.14.

In this design, participants are randomly assigned to the different levels of variation of the between-participants independent variable. All participants then take each level of variation of the within-participants independent variable. Therefore, we have the advantage of being able to test for the effects produced by each of the two independent variables, as well as for the interaction between the two independent variables. In addition, we have the advantage of needing fewer participants because all participants take all levels of variation of one of the independent variables. Therefore, the number of participants required is only some multiple of the number of levels of the between-participants independent variable.

The discussion of the factorial design based on a mixed model has been limited to the consideration of only two independent variables. In no way is this meant to imply that the design cannot be extended to include more than two independent variables. As with the factorial designs, we can include as many independent variables as are considered necessary. We can include any combination of the between-participants type of independent variable with the within-participants type of independent variable. If we are conducting a study with three independent variables, two of which require all participants to take each level of variation of both the independent variables, our design will include two independent variables of the within-participants variety and one of the between-participants variety.

STUDY QUESTION 10.7
- **Describe a within-participants research design.**
- **Describe a factorial design based on a mixed model.**
- **List the advantages and disadvantages of each design.**

Pretest–Posttest Design

Pretest–posttest design
A true experimental design in which the treatment effect is assessed by comparing the difference between the experimental and control groups' pre- and posttest scores

The pretest–posttest design differs from the one-group pretest–posttest design in two important respects: The former incorporates a control group and randomization. In a **pretest–posttest design,** participants are randomly assigned to groups and then pretested on the dependent variable, *Y*. The independent variable, *X*, is administered to the experimental group, and the experimental and control groups are posttested on the dependent variable, *Y*. The differences between the pre- and posttest scores for the experimental and control groups are then tested statistically to assess the effect of the independent variable. Figure 10.15 depicts this design.

The pretest–posttest design is also a good experimental design and does an excellent job of controlling for rival hypotheses such as history and maturation. Whereas the similar one-group pretest–posttest design was said to have been contaminated by extraneous variables, including history and maturation, the pretest–posttest design neatly controls for many of these rival hypotheses. The history and maturation variables are clearly controlled because any history events that may produce a difference in the experimental group also will produce a difference in the control group. Note, however, that an intragroup history effect can exist in this or any design that includes more than one group of research participants. If all the participants in the experimental group were treated in one session and all the participants in the control group were treated in another session, it is possible that events took place in one group that did not take place in the other. If a differential event did take place (for example, laughter, a joke, or a comment about the experimental procedure), there would be no way of eliminating its influence, and it may produce an effect that was picked up by the dependent variable. Such an event would have to be considered a possible cause for any significant difference noted between the groups.

The intragroup history effect can be controlled by individually testing participants who are randomly assigned to the treatment groups and by randomly determining when a control and an experimental treatment will be administered. If group administration of each level of variation of the independent variable is essential, then each separate group potentially has a different intrasession history. In this case, it will be necessary to test the various groups statistically to determine whether differences exist as a function of intrasession history. In other words, the groups have to be included as another independent variable.

FIGURE 10.15
Pretest–posttest design.

		Preresponse measure	*Treatment*	*Postresponse measure*	*Difference*	
Experimental group	*R*	*Y*	*X*	*Y*	Pre-*Y* – Post-*Y*	Compare
Control group		*Y*		*Y*	Pre-*Y* – Post-*Y*	

(Adapted from *Experimental and Quasi-Experimental Designs for Research* by D. T. Campbell and J. C. Stanley, 1963. Chicago: Rand McNally and Company. Copyright 1963, American Educational Research Association, Washington, D.C.)

Maturation and instrumentation are also controlled in this design because they should be equally manifested in both the experimental group and the control group. Equal manifestation of the testing effect in experiments that use observers or interviewers to collect the dependent variable data does, however, assume that the observers are randomly assigned to individual observation sessions. This ensures that the instrumentation effect is randomly distributed across groups. When this assumption cannot be met, a double blind model should be used, with each available observer used in both experimental and control sessions.

Regression and selection variables are controlled by virtue of the fact that participants are randomly assigned to both the experimental and the control groups. Randomization ensures initial equality of groups as well as equality in the extent to which each group regresses toward the mean. Because participants are randomly assigned, each group should have the same percentage of extreme scores and, therefore, should demonstrate the same degree of regression toward the mean. Selection bias is naturally ruled out because random assignment has assured the equality of the experimental and control groups at the time of randomization. As stated earlier, randomization does not provide 100 percent assurance, and one will occasionally be wrong. It is, however, our *best* protection against the selection rival hypothesis.

STUDY QUESTION 10.8 | **Describe the pretest–posttest research design and explain how it controls for extraneous variables such as history, maturation, instrumentation, and statistical regression.**

Choice of a Research Design

It is your task to choose which type of research design is most appropriate for a particular research study. There are some straightforward factors to consider in making the design selection. The choice requires a thorough knowledge of the research problem, of the extraneous variables to be controlled, and of the advantages and disadvantages inherent in the alternative designs available.

Research Question

First and foremost, you must select a design that will give you an answer to your problem. There are times when investigators try to force a problem into a specific research design. This is an example of the tail wagging the dog and seldom allows you to arrive at an appropriate answer. Thus the primary criterion in design selection is whether the design will enable you to arrive at an answer to the research question.

Control

The second factor to consider in selecting a research design is whether you can incorporate control techniques that will allow you to arrive unambiguously at a conclusion. If you have the choice of several designs that will enable you to answer your research question, then you should select the design that will provide maximum control over variables that can also explain the results. Control, therefore, is the second most important criterion.

Between- versus Within-Participants Design

The third factor to consider is the nature of the research design. Generally speaking, this means that you must select either a between-participants or a within-participants design. In making this decision, you must take into consideration the advantages and disadvantages of each and choose the design that provides the most sensitive and unconfounded test of the independent variable. This means that you must consider both the nature of the problem and the confounding extraneous variables to be controlled. For example, if you wanted to find out which of two methods, active recitation or passive learning, required fewer trials to learn a list of words, you would use a within-participants design. This is because the list of words would be so difficult that no one could recall them the first time they tried. It would, therefore, take each research participant several attempts, or trials, to correctly recall the list of words.

Remember that a sequencing effect exists in a within-participant design. However, in the learning study, carry-over and order effects are desirable and expected because you want practice and exposure on prior trials to affect performance on subsequent trials. This is the nature of learning. You would be testing whether these carry-over and order effects were greater when a person used the active recitation or passive learning methods.

If you were testing the effect of consuming 0, 100, 200, or 400 mg of caffeine on alertness, you would want to use a between-subjects design. If you used a within-subjects design and assessed arousal after each research participant consumed all four caffeine doses, the measure of arousal after each caffeine dose would be confounded with the effect of the preceding dose, a sequencing effect. To obtain an unconfounded measure of the effect of each dose of caffeine, a separate group of participants needs to take each caffeine dose. Thus, a between-participants design must be used.

Using a between-subjects design results in a less sensitive test of the independent variable of caffeine dose. However, this is necessary to obtain internal validity and control of the rival hypothesis of a sequencing effect. Consequently, sensitivity is sacrificed in favor of control of a rival hypothesis. This is the appropriate trade-off because internal validity is the first requirement of good science.

As you can see, selection of the appropriate research design is often a compromise. You must consider the advantages and disadvantages of the possible research designs and select the one that provides the best and most sensitive test of the independent variable.

When the options are a between- or a within-participants design, the decision is usually made in favor of the latter. This is because, as mentioned earlier, the within-participants design provides a more sensitive test of the independent variable.

Summary

The design of a research study is the basic outline of the experiment, specifying how the data will be collected and analyzed and how unwanted variation will be controlled. The design determines to a great extent whether the research question will be answered. Studies based on designs such as the one-group posttest-only design, the one-group pretest–posttest design, and the nonequivalent posttest-only design do not provide the desired answers because they do not control for the influence of the many extraneous variables that can affect the results of an experiment.

An experimental research design satisfies three criteria. First, the design must test the hypotheses advanced. Second, extraneous variables must be controlled so that the experimenter can attribute the observed effects to the independent variable. Third, it must be possible to generalize the results. These three criteria represent the ideal; seldom will a study satisfy them all.

In designing a study that attempts to meet the conditions just stated, many investigators use a pretest. There are a number of good reasons for administering a pretest. It can be used to match research participants and thereby increase the sensitivity of the experiment. It can also be used to determine if a ceiling effect exists or to test a participant's initial position on a variable to see if the variable interacts with the independent variable. Other reasons include testing for initial comparability of participants and establishing that participants actually changed as a result of the independent variable.

The posttest-only and the pretest–posttest designs are experimental research designs because they have the ability to eliminate the influence of extraneous variables that serve as sources of rival hypotheses for explaining the observed results. These designs can control for unwanted variation because they include a comparison control group and because participants are randomly assigned to the experimental and control groups. The posttest-only design represents the prototype of most research designs. Although the basic posttest-only design is not commonly used, its variants—the between-participants posttest-only design and the within-participants posttest-only design—are very popular. The between-participants type is used when participants must be randomly assigned to the various experimental treatment groups. The within-participants type is used when participants must participate in all treatment groups. When different participants must participate in some experimental treatment conditions and all participants must participate in other experimental treatment conditions, a combination of the between- and the within-participants designs is called for.

Key Terms and Concepts

Research design
One-group posttest-only design
One-group pretest–posttest design
Nonequivalent posttest-only design
Control group
Experimental group
Experimental design
Posttest-only design
Between-participants posttest-only design

Simple randomized participants design
Factorial design
Cell
Main effect
Interaction effect
Interaction
Within-participants posttest-only design
Factorial design based on a mixed model
Pretest–posttest design

Related Internet Sites

www.wadsworth.com/psychology_d/templates/student_resources/workshops/index.html

This site has several tutorials maintained by Wadsworth. When you get to this site click on research methods workshops and then on the icon for True Experiments and Between versus Within Designs.

www.socialresearchmethods.net/kb/expfact.htm

http://web.umr.edu/~psyworld/between_subjects.htm

These two sites provide instruction on factorial designs and interactions.

Practice Test

The answers to these questions can be found in Appendix A.

1. The one-group posttest-only design, the one-group pretest–posttest design, and the nonequivalent posttest-only design have in common
   a. Their frequent use by research psychologists
   b. The fact that they do not control for threats to internal validity
   c. The fact that they are more typically used by research in applied areas
   d. The fact that they are more typically used in animal (versus human) research
   e. The fact that they do not use a control group

2. A control group is needed
   a. To control for some rival hypotheses
   b. To serve as a comparison
   c. To control for attrition effects
   d. To control for experimenter expectancy effects
   e. Both a and b are correct.

3. The between- and within-participants designs are distinguished on the basis of
   a. The number of independent variables they can test
   b. Whether they can test for the effect of an interaction
   c. The number of main effects they can test
   d. Whether the various treatment combinations use different or the same participants
   e. The type of dependent variables that can be used

4. If I have studied the effect that three dosages—5 mg, 10 mg, and 15 mg—of the drug Prozac has on depressed people and people with an eating disorder and find that the lower dosages are most effective with people with eating disorders and the higher dosages are most effective with people with depression, I have identified
   a. An interaction between the drug dosage and the type of disorder
   b. A main effect of drug dosage
   c. A main effect of type of treatment
   d. A main effect of both drug dosage and type of treatment
   e. A design with three cells

5. If I have conducted an experiment that requires me to randomly assign twenty participants to two levels of one independent variable and then all of these twenty participants take all three levels of a second independent variable, I have used what type of design?

   a. Pretest–posttest design
   b. Simple randomized design
   c. Factorial design
   d. Within-participants posttest-only design
   e. Factorial design based on a mixed model

Challenge Exercises

1. For each of the follow experimental briefs:

   a. Identify the type of design used to test the hypothesis of the study
   b. Explain why this design is used
   c. Identify the threats to internal validity.

   A. College students are used to test the hypothesis that carbohydrate cravings increase as a person's level of depression increases. To test this hypothesis, the experimenter randomly assigns participants to three groups and then administers a mood-induction technique that will induce several different types of moods. One version of the mood-induction technique is administered to one group to induce a depressed mood, another version is used to induce an elated mood in a second group, and a third version is administered to the third group to ensure that their mood does not change. After the mood-induction procedure has been administered to each group, the participants provide an assessment of the extent to which they experience carbohydrate cravings.

   B. Hillary wants to find out if nicotine patches really help people quit smoking, so she identifies twenty people who have been smoking at least a pack of cigarettes a day for the past ten years and want to quit. She has them all wear a nicotine patch for a month and sign a form agreeing to stop smoking. At the end of the month, she monitors their cigarette smoking and finds that 25 percent of these individuals have stopped smoking completely and another 30 percent have reduced their smoking by at least 50 percent. Hillary concludes that the nicotine patches are effective in helping people quit or reduce their consumption of cigarettes.

   C. Dr. Cane was interested in determining if there was an association between a person's gender and the tendency to report a false memory. To test this hypothesis, male and female participants were interviewed about a real emotional event that happened to them (a serious accident) between the ages of four and ten and about a false event (getting lost). Two weeks later these same individuals were interviewed about both events and the interviewers attempted to elicit both memories using guided imagery, context reinstatement, and mild social pressure. The results of this experiment revealed that 100 percent of females and males recalled the real emotional event. However, 55 percent of females and 28 percent of males recalled the false event.

2. Basketball players naturally want to increase their accuracy in shooting foul shots so they hire a sports psychologist who hypothesizes that either anxiety reduction or mental imagery could help them. The sports psychologist randomly assigns sixty basketball players to six groups. These six groups of basketball players then shoot twenty free throws under one of three anxiety conditions—high, moderate, or low—and one of two imagery conditions—imaging that the shot is going through the hoop or imaging that the shot is missing the hoop. The mean number of shots that are made by each group of basketball players is as follows

		Anxiety conditions		
		High	**Moderate**	**Low**
Imagery condition	Making shot	15	14	6
	Missing shot	9	12	17

a. Does there seem to be an anxiety main effect? If there is, what does it mean?
b. Does there seem to be an imagery main effect? If there is, what does it mean?
c. Does there seem to be an interaction? If there is, graph the interaction and explain what it means.

3. Assume that you wanted to examine the motivational factors responsible for the retention of novice and experienced teachers. You wanted to examine three motivational factors of extrinsic motivation (e.g., salary received), intrinsic motivation (e.g., the satisfaction of seeing students progress), and altruistic motivation (e.g., helping students learn and get an education). This study produced the following data.

		Types of motivation		
		Extrinsic	**Instrinsic**	**Altruistic**
Teaching experience	Novice	33	4	29
	Experienced	13	83	44

a. Does there seem to be a motivation main effect? If there is, what does it mean?
b. Does there seem to be a teaching experience main effect? If there is, what does it mean?
c. Does there seem to be an interaction? If there is, graph the interaction and explain what it means.

11 Quasi-Experimental Designs

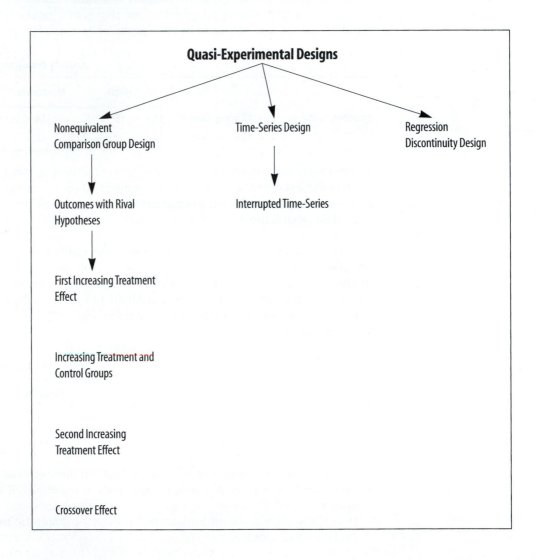

One of the most significant changes occurring in the life of many Americans during the last several decades of the twentieth century was the advent of the personal computer. In August 2000, 51 percent of all U.S. households had one or more computers and 41 percent of households had access to the Internet (Newburger, 2001). The Internet is a marvelous technological development providing easy access to information and communication in a way unparalleled by anything we have known in the past. People use the Internet to obtain information previously inaccessible, to increase technological skills, and to conduct commercial transactions all in the comfort of their homes. The Internet is also used for social purposes, to communicate and socialize with colleagues, friends, and family through electronic mail and to join social groups through distribution lists, newsgroups, and chat rooms. There is some evidence (Kraut, Mukhopadhyay, Szczypula, Kiesler, & Scherlis, 1998) that the Internet is used primarily for communication with others. This has led some researchers to ask questions about the behavioral and psychological effect of the Internet. These questions seem to be particularly important because of numerous reports of individuals becoming addicted to the Internet and this addiction leading to divorce, child neglect, job termination, debt, flunking out of school, and legal trouble.

Young (1996), for example, cites the case of a homemaker who initially spent a few hours per week scanning a variety of chat rooms. During the next three months, she continued to increase the time spent conversing or chatting online with other individuals, peaking at fifty to sixty hours per week. Frequently she spent more than the intended two hours online with some sessions lasting up to fourteen hours. This obsession with participating in chat rooms eventually resulted in her reducing her involvement with her family, eliminating social activities, and ceasing to perform routine chores such as cooking, cleaning, and grocery shopping. The end result was that she became estranged from her two daughters and separated from her husband within one year of the purchase of her home computer.

The repeated occurrence of stories such as the one just mentioned and research (Kraut, Patterson, et al., 1998) demonstrating the negative social impact of extensive use of the Internet has led some individuals, such as Harvard psychologist Maressa Hecht Orzack (Potera, 1998) to develop a treatment for this problem. Dr. Orzack's approach is to treat Internet addiction like binge eating, where the client is taught to set limits, balance activities, and schedule time. However, this treatment has not, as yet, been empirically validated or demonstrated to be effective through sound, empirically based experimental studies. It is appropriate, therefore, to ask the question: Is this treatment effective? On the basis of the material you have learned in previous chapters, you should realize that this research question could be answered using a good experimental design. A sample of individuals meeting specified criteria for excessive use of the Internet could be randomly assigned to a control group that did not receive Orzack's treatment or an experimental group that did receive the treatment. Following treatment, the two groups could be compared to determine if the experimental group gained more control over their Internet addiction than did the control group.

The problem with using such an approach is that many treatment programs will not allow a researcher to come in and determine randomly whether a person can or cannot receive treatment. Rather, the treatment program states that their mission is to treat individuals, such as those with an addiction to the Internet, and they will accept anyone who requests treatment. It would be unethical to do otherwise. This is one of the primary difficulties encountered in moving out of the laboratory and into the real world. Outside the laboratory setting, it is more difficult to use control techniques and therefore harder to control for the influence of extraneous variables. But in such cases investigators need not throw up their hands and abandon the research. Rather, they must turn to the use of quasi-experimental designs—designs that enable researchers to investigate problems that preclude the use of procedures required by a true experimental design.

Chapter Preview

When researchers move out of the controlled confines of the laboratory they frequently encounter difficulties in incorporating the design and control techniques that are needed to eliminate the influence of confounding extraneous variables. One of the most frequent difficulties encountered is the lack of ability to randomly assign participants to the various treatment conditions. This means that researchers are precluded from using their most important control technique. Rather than throwing up their hands and walking away from important research projects, researchers do the best they can. They design their studies so as to control for as many confounding extraneous variables as possible but recognize that there is some slippage in their designs. This is why the designs are called quasi-experimental designs. Because the researchers know that confounding extraneous variables can creep into their studies when using a quasi-experimental design, they make a concerted effort to identify these potential confounding extraneous variables and then do something to handle them, such as collect data indicating whether the potential confounding extraneous variables actually did represent a confound. In this chapter, I discuss the most frequently used quasi-experimental designs and the way in which confounding extraneous variables are handled. You will see that when the potential confounding extraneous variables are appropriately dealt with, these quasi-experimental designs can yield accurate causal inferences.

Introduction

A **quasi-experimental design** is an experimental design that does not meet all the requirements necessary for controlling the influence of extraneous variables. In most instances the requirement that is not met is that of random assignment of participants

Quasi-experimental design
A research design in which an experimental procedure is applied but all extraneous variables are not controlled

to groups. For example, several years ago the head of the probation department in a large metropolitan area approached a group of investigators, of which I was a part, and asked us to design a study to investigate the validity of the hypothesis that the food eaten by juvenile delinquents is causally related to their delinquent behavior. This administrator said that we could use the juveniles who had been committed to one of the detention facilities as our research participants. Because these youngsters were required to spend all their time at this detention facility and the food available to them was prepared there, this was an ideal setting in which to test the nutrition–behavior hypothesis. Once we started designing the experiment, however, we encountered some of the constraints that investigators may find when moving out of the laboratory and into the real world. We were told that we could not randomly assign the juveniles into experimental and control groups; they all had to be treated in the same manner. Consequently, we realized at the outset that it would be impossible to conduct a true experiment and that we had to settle for a design that would not provide maximum assurance that the experimental and control groups were equated. In other words, we had to settle for a quasi-experimental design.

You may ask whether it is possible to draw causal inferences from studies based on a quasi-experimental design, because such a design does not rule out the influence of all rival hypotheses. Making a causal inference from a quasi-experiment requires meeting the same basic requirements needed for any causal relationship: cause must covary with the effect, cause must precede effect, and rival hypotheses must be implausible. The first two requirements, cause covarying with effect and cause preceding effect, are easy to handle because quasi-experiments, like randomized experiments, manipulate conditions so that covariation between the cause and effect is tested with statistical analysis and the cause is forced to precede the effect. The third requirement, ruling out rival hypotheses, is more difficult because quasi-experiments do not use random assignment. This means that rival hypotheses or alternative explanations for the observed effect frequently exist when quasi-experiments are conducted.

Causal inferences can be made using quasi-experimental designs, but these inferences are made only when data are collected that render rival interpretations implausible. If a friend of yours unknowingly stepped in front of an oncoming car and was pronounced dead after being hit by the car, you would probably attribute her death to the moving vehicle. Your friend might have died as a result of numerous other causes (a heart attack, for example), but such alternative explanations are not accepted because they are not plausible. In like manner, the causal interpretations are made from quasi-experiments only when rival explanations have been shown to be implausible. Shadish et al. (2002) have identified three principles, presented in Table 11.1, to address rival explanation and show that they are implausible. The first principle, identification and study of plausible threats to internal validity, is the one we focus on in this chapter. The discussion of the other two principles is beyond the scope of this book; Shadish et al. (2002) have an extended discussion of these two principles.

STUDY QUESTION 11.1

- **How does a quasi-experimental research design differ from an experimental research design?**
- **How are rival hypotheses ruled out in quasi-experimental designs?**

TABLE 11.1

Principles Used to Rule out Rival Explanations in Quasi-Experiments

1. *Identification and study of plausible threats to internal validity:* This principle involves identifying plausible rival explanations and then probing and investigating them to determine how likely it is that they can explain the covariation between the treatment and the outcome.

2. *Control by design:* This principle involves adding design elements, such as additional pretest time points or additional control groups, to either eliminate a rival explanation or obtain evidence about the plausibility of the rival explanation.

3. *Coherent pattern matching:* This principle can be used when a complex prediction can be made about a causal hypothesis and there are few, if any, rival explanations that would make the same prediction. If the complex prediction is supported by the data, most rival explanations are eliminated. The more complex the prediction, the less likely it is that a rival explanation can explain the prediction and the more likely that the independent variable is producing the effect.

Nonequivalent Comparison Group Design

Nonequivalent comparison group design

A quasi-experimental design in which the results obtained from nonequivalent experimental and control groups are compared

The **nonequivalent comparison group design** is probably the most common of all quasi-experimental designs (Shadish et al., 2002). This design includes both an experimental and a control group, but participants are not randomly assigned. The fact that participants in the control and experimental groups are not equivalent on all variables may affect the dependent variable. These uncontrolled variables operate as rival hypotheses to explain the outcome of the experiment, making these designs quasi-experimental designs. But when a better design cannot be used, some form of a nonequivalent control group design is frequently recommended. The basic scheme, depicted in Figure 11.1, consists of giving an experimental group and a control group first a pretest and then a posttest (after the treatment condition is administered to the experimental group). The pre- to posttest difference scores of the two groups are then compared to determine if significant differences exist. The design appears identical to the pretest–posttest experimental design. However, there is one basic difference that makes one a *true* experimental design and the other a *quasi*-experimental design. In

FIGURE 11.1

Nonequivalent comparison group design.

	Preresponse measure	Treatment	Postresponse measure	Difference	
Experimental group	Y_1	X	Y_2	$Y_1 - Y_2$	
					Compare
Control group	Y_1		Y_2	$Y_1 - Y_2$	

(Adapted from *Experimental and Quasi-Experimental Designs for Research* by D. T. Campbell and J. C. Stanley, 1963. Chicago: Rand McNally and Company. Copyright 1963, American Educational Research Association, Washington, D.C.)

the pretest–posttest design, participants are randomly assigned to the experimental and control groups, whereas in the nonequivalent comparison group design they are not. The absence of random assignment is what makes a design quasi-experimental.

Consider the study conducted by Becker, Rabinowitz, and Seligman (1980), which was concerned with the impact of the billing procedure on energy consumption. Because of the large energy bills resulting from increased energy costs, a number of utility companies have given their customers the option of using an equal monthly payment plan. This scheme requires the utility company to bill the resident for one-twelfth of the yearly utility cost each month, as opposed to billing for the actual amount consumed. Although such a plan apparently produces a great deal of customer satisfaction, it runs the risk of increasing energy use because there is no direct connection between energy used and the size of the monthly bill. The study conducted by Becker et al. was designed to determine if the equal monthly payment plan actually led to an increased use of energy.

In conducting such a study, we would ideally assign participants randomly to either the equal monthly payment plan or the conventional payment plan (in which energy is paid for as it is consumed). For a variety of reasons, however, the utility companies contacted would not allow such random assignment, so the investigators had to formulate two groups without randomization. This meant that a quasi-experimental design had to be used, and Becker et al. selected the nonequivalent comparison group type. Figure 11.2 shows that the design of the Becker et al. (1980) study consisted of pretesting both groups on consumption of electricity prior to the implementation of the equal payment plan. Following this pretesting (which occurred during the summer months), the treatment plan was implemented for the experimental group and consumption of electricity was measured for both groups during the following summer.

In formulating the experimental and control groups, Becker et al. did not have the opportunity to assign participants randomly, although they were aware of the need to have equated groups. Consequently, they devised a system that seemed to match the participants on the variables that would influence electrical consumption. One of the companies whose customers were used in the study maintained records in such a way that it was possible to identify next-door neighbors. The investigators reasoned that next-door neighbors would be more likely to have similar-size homes and to be more similar on other variables that may affect electrical consumption than would a random sample of individuals not on the equal monthly payment plan. Therefore, the control group consisted of next-door neighbors of those individuals who were on the equal monthly payment plan.

FIGURE 11.2
The design of the Becker et al. (1980) study.

	Pretest response	Treatment conditions	Posttest response
Experimental group	Magnitude of electricity consumed	Equal monthly payment plan	Magnitude of electricity consumed
Control group	Magnitude of electricity consumed	Conventional payment plan	Magnitude of electricity consumed

FIGURE 11.3

Average daily electricity consumption for two payment plans.

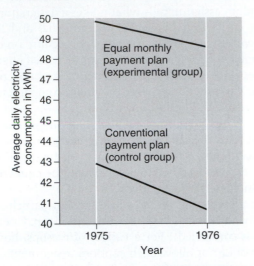

(Based on data from "Evaluating the Impact of Utility Company Billing Plans on Residential Energy Consumption" by L. J. Becker, V. C. Rabinowitz, and C. Seligman, 1980, *Evaluation and Program Planning, 3*, pp. 159–164.)

The results of this study for one company are depicted in Figure 11.3, which shows that a difference in electrical consumption existed between the two groups at pretesting time. However, the change in consumption between pretesting and posttesting was about the same for both groups. The question now becomes one of interpreting these results. The pretest component of the nonequivalent comparison group design is very important because it tells us how the groups compared initially. There is an assumption that the larger the initial difference, the greater the likelihood of a strong selection bias (Shadish et al., 2002). In the Becker et al. (1980) study there was a large difference between the control and experimental groups, strongly suggesting that a selection bias existed. In addition to demonstrating a selection bias, pretesting allows for a testing and examination of other biases such as those listed in Table 11.2. The list of potential threats to internal validity is large. Shadish et al. (2002) have pointed out that the possibility of an extraneous variable confounding the results of a study depend on the characteristics of the design and the pattern of results obtained from the study. Naturally, some studies have a greater possibility of threats existing, such as the nonequivalent comparison group design as opposed to a randomized design. However, the possibility of identifying threats in the outcome pattern of a study is not as apparent, so let us take a look at several outcomes and see how threats are more or less plausible, depending on the outcome.

STUDY QUESTION 11.2

- **Diagram the nonequivalent comparison group design, and explain why it is a quasi-experimental design.**
- **What potential threats to internal validity exist when using this design?**

TABLE 11.2
Possible Biases That Exist in the Nonequivalent Comparison Group Design

1. *Selection bias*—Because groups are nonequivalent there will always be a potential selection bias. However, the pretest allows the exploration of the possible size and direction of the bias on any variables measured at pretesting.

2. *Attrition bias*—The pretest allows examination of the nature of attrition to see if there is a difference between those that drop out or do not complete the experiment and those that do.

3. *Selection–maturation bias*—This may exist if one group of participants becomes more experienced, tired, or bored than participants in the other group.

4. *Selection–instrumentation bias*—This may exist if the nonequivalent groups of participants start at different points on the pretest, particularly if the measuring instrument does not have equal intervals.

5. *Selection–regression bias*—This may exist if the two groups are from different populations, such as the experimental treatment group being from a population of individuals with a reading disability and the comparison group being from a population of individuals without a reading disability.

6. *Selection–history bias*—This may exist if an event occurring between the pretest and posttest affects one group more than the other group.

First increasing treatment effect
An outcome in which the experimental and the control groups differ at pretesting and only the experimental group's scores change from pre- to posttesting

Outcomes with Rival Hypotheses

Outcome I: First Increasing Treatment Effect   In the **first increasing treatment effect,** illustrated in Figure 11.4, the control group scores reveal no change from pretest to posttest, but the experimental group starts at a higher level and shows a significant positive change. Such an outcome appears to suggest that the experimental treatment was effective. However, this outcome could also have occurred as a result of a selection–maturation effect or a selection–history effect.

FIGURE 11.4
First increasing treatment effect.

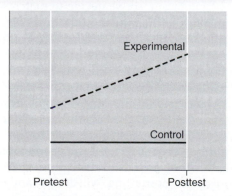

(From "The Design and Conduct of Quasi-Experiments and True Experiments in Field Settings" by T. D. Cook and D. T. Campbell, in *Handbook of Industrial and Organizational Psychology,* edited by M. D. Dunnette. Copyright © Rand McNally College Publishing Company, 1976.)

Selection–maturation effect
The result of selecting one of two groups in such a way that its participants develop faster than those in the other group

A **selection–maturation effect** refers to the fact that one of the two groups of participants was selected in such a way that its participants were growing or developing faster than the participants in the other group. One group may progress faster because its members are more intelligent or capable than those in the other group. In the Becker et al. (1980) study, an increasing treatment effect would have been indicated if the experimental group had consumed more electricity during pretesting and had continued to increase consumption between pre- and posttesting while control group consumption remained stable. Such an increase could have been caused by the type of payment plan used by the experimental group, but it could also have been caused by the fact that the salary level of this group was increasing, so that these participants were less concerned with electrical costs. If this were the case, then the posttest increase could be accounted for by the fact that the selection procedure happened to place in the experimental group individuals whose salary levels were increasing more rapidly.

In an attempt to eliminate the potential biasing of this type of selection–maturation effect, many investigators try to match research participants. This procedure is supposed to equate participants on the matched variables not only at the time of matching but also during the remainder of the study. If matching is conducted during the pretest, then experimental and control participants should not differ on the dependent variable measure. If they do not, then it is assumed that they are equated. This equality is supposed to persist over time, so any difference observed during a posttest is attributed to the experimental treatment effect. However, evidence (Campbell and Boruch, 1975; Campbell and Erlebacher, 1970) has revealed that such an assumption could be erroneous because of a regression artifact phenomenon that may occur within the two groups of participants. This regression phenomenon increases the difference between the two matched groups on posttesting, apart from any experimental treatment effect. Such a difference could be misinterpreted as being due to a treatment effect or a failure to find a treatment effect, depending on which of the matched groups operated as the experimental group and which operated as the control group.

Assume that we are conducting a study designed to investigate the influence of a Head Start program on children's subsequent school performance. We consider the attitudes of the mothers to be important, so we decide to match on this variable to eliminate its influence. Assume further that the attitude scores obtained from mothers of Head Start children and of non–Head Start children are distributed in the manner shown in Table 11.3. From this table, it is readily apparent that most of the Head Start mothers have lower attitude scores than do the non–Head Start mothers. Therefore, matching involves selecting for the experimental group those Head Start mothers with the highest attitude scores and for the control group those non–Head Start mothers with the lowest attitude scores. In other words, we include only participants with an extreme score—the participants most susceptible to the regression artifact phenomenon. This would not be a serious factor if the distributions of scores of the two groups were the same, but they are not. The regression artifact dictates that the Head Start mothers' scores, upon posttesting, will decline and regress toward the mean of their group and that the control participants' scores will regress or increase toward their group's mean (also illustrated in Table 11.3). Such a regression phe-

TABLE 11.3
Hypothetical Attitude Scores

Head Start Participants	Head Start Mothers' Pretest Attitudes	Mothers' Posttest Attitudes	Non–Head Start Participants	Non–Head Start Mothers' Pretest Attitudes	Non–Head Start Mothers' Posttest Attitudes
S_1	5		S_{16}	25	28
S_2	7		S_{17}	27	30
S_3	9		S_{18}	29	32
S_4	11		S_{19}	31	34
S_5	13		S_{20}	33	36
S_6	15		S_{21}	35	
S_7	17		S_{22}	37	
S_8	19		S_{23}	39	
S_9	21		S_{24}	41	
S_{10}	23		S_{25}	43	
S_{11}	25	22	S_{26}	45	
S_{12}	27	24	S_{27}	47	
S_{13}	29	26	S_{28}	49	
S_{14}	31	28	S_{29}	51	
S_{15}	33	30	S_{30}	53	

Matched Participants

nomenon could indicate that the experimental treatment is detrimental when it actually may not have any effect. If the treatment does have a positive effect, this regression effect might lead us to underestimate it.

Another way of attempting to equate participants by eliminating the selection–maturation bias artifact is to use a variety of statistical regression techniques, such as analysis of covariance and partial correlation. Campbell and Erlebacher (1970) and Campbell and Boruch (1975) have pointed out the fallacy of such an approach, but a discussion of this fallacy is beyond the scope of this book. Suffice it to say that these researchers and others (Cronbach and Furby, 1970; Lord, 1969) have found that such statistical adjustments cannot equate nonequivalent groups unless there is no error in the dependent measures given to the research participants.

Selection-history effect

The result of an extraneous event's influencing either the experimental or the control group, but not both groups

A second rival explanation of the increasing treatment effect is a **selection-history effect** (Cook and Campbell, 1976). A general history effect, discussed in Chapter 7, is controlled in the nonequivalent comparison group design by inclusion of a control group. However, the design is still susceptible to a selection-history effect, in which some event affects either the experimental or the control group, but not both. A selection-history effect could have operated in the Becker et al. (1980) study—if the participants in the control group had purchased additional insulation for their homes, the control group would have decreased consumption of electricity not because of the type of payment plan but because of the additional insulation. Such a variable would represent a rival hypothesis for any difference observed between the control and the experimental groups.

Increasing treatment and control groups
An outcome in which the experimental and the control groups differ at pretesting and both increase from pre- to post-testing, but the experimental group increases at a faster rate

Outcome II: Increasing Treatment and Control Groups   In **increasing treatment and control groups**, both the control group and the experimental group show an increment in the dependent variable from pre- to posttesting, as is depicted in Figure 11.5. The difference between the increased growth rates could be the result of an actual treatment effect, but it could also be due to a type of selection–maturation interaction. Figure 11.5 indicates that participants in both groups are increasing in performance. Note, however, that at the time of pretesting, the treatment group scored higher on the dependent variable. This could mean that the participants in the experimental treatment group were just naturally increasing faster on the dependent variable than were the control participants. The greater difference between groups of participants at posttesting might simply reflect the fact that the experimental participants continued to increase faster on the dependent variable than did the control participants. For example, assume that the dependent variable consisted of a measure of problem-solving ability and that the participants were six years old at the time of pretesting and eight years old at the time of posttesting. Also assume that the experimental participants were brighter and therefore increasing in problem-solving ability more rapidly than were the control participants. If this were the case, then we would expect the two groups of participants to differ somewhat at pretest time. However, participants would not stop increasing in problem-solving ability at age six, and thus an even greater difference would exist at posttest time, independent of any treatment effect. Where such a differential growth pattern occurs, we may interpret a greater posttest difference as being the result of a treatment effect when it is really an artifact of a selection–maturation interaction.

FIGURE 11.5
Increasing treatment and control groups.

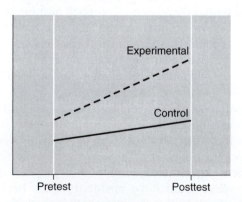

(From "The Design and Conduct of Quasi-Experiments and True Experiments in Field Settings" by T. D. Cook and D. T. Campbell, in *Handbook of Industrial and Organizational Psychology*, edited by M. D. Dunnette. Copyright © Rand McNally Publishing Company, 1976.)

Evidence of the existence of a selection–maturation interaction can be seen by looking at the variability of the participants' scores at pretest and posttest time. Random error dictates that the variability of the scores should be the same on both occasions. A growth factor dictates that the scores should increase in terms of variability, however. Thus an increase in the variability of the scores for the experimental and control groups from pretest to posttest suggests the possibility of the existence of a selection–maturation interaction.

Second increasing treatment effect
An outcome in which the control group performs better than the experimental group at pretesting, but only the experimental group improves from pre- to posttesting

Outcome III: Second Increasing Treatment Effect   The **second increasing treatment effect**, depicted in Figure 11.6, is an outcome in which the control group and experimental treatment group differ rather extensively at pretest time. However, the experimental group starts lower than the control group at pretest and improves over time, presumably because of the experimental treatment, so that the posttest difference is decreased. Such an outcome would be desired when the experimental group was a disadvantaged group and the experimental treatment was designed to overcome the disadvantage. For example, Head Start was initiated to overcome the environmental deprivation experienced by many children in the United States and bring the performance of these disadvantaged individuals up to that of nondisadvantaged children. If a study were conducted to compare the pretest and posttest performances of a group of control individuals (who had not experienced the environmental deprivation) with those of a group of environmentally disadvantaged children who had received the Head Start experimental treatment, we would hope to find the type of effect illustrated in Figure 11.6. However, before we can interpret the increase in performance of the experimental treatment group as being the result of the Head Start experience, several rival hypotheses must be ruled out. The first is a selection–history effect that affects only one of the two groups of participants. The second and more likely rival hypothesis is a regression artifact effect—a likely source

FIGURE 11.6
Second increasing treatment effect.

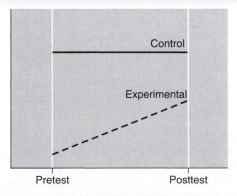

(From "The Design and Conduct of Quasi-Experiments and True Experiments in Field Settings" by T. D. Cook and D. T. Campbell, in *Handbook of Industrial and Organizational Psychology,* edited by M. D. Dunnette. Copyright © Rand McNally College Publishing Company, 1976.)

of confounding because the participants in the experimental treatment group are typically selected based on their unusually poor performance or low scores. Consequently, the regression artifact would predict that the scores of this group should increase during posttesting. The regression artifact could, therefore, produce the outcome depicted in Figure 11.6, an outcome that the unwary investigator would interpret as a treatment effect. Therefore, designs that involve administering an experimental treatment to a disadvantaged group should provide a check for the possibility of such a regression artifact.

One indicator of the existence of a regression artifact is the instability of the deprived group's scores in the absence of the experimental treatment. If the deprived group's scores stay consistently low over time, this suggests that the low scores represent the true standing of the individuals. In such cases, a pretest-to-posttest increment would probably represent a true experimental effect or at least an effect not confounded by the influence of a regression artifact.

Crossover effect
An outcome in which the control group performs better at pretesting but the experimental group performs better at posttesting

Outcome IV: Crossover Effect   Figure 11.7 depicts the **crossover effect,** an experimental outcome in which the treatment group scores significantly lower than the control group at pretest time but significantly higher at posttest time. This outcome represents the typical interaction effect and is much more readily interpreted than the others discussed because it renders many of the potential rival hypotheses implausible. Statistical regression can be ruled out because it is highly unlikely that the experimental treatment group's lower pretest scores would regress enough to become significantly higher than those of the control group on posttesting. Second, a selection–maturation effect is improbable because it is typically the higher scoring pretest participants who gain faster. The outcome depicted in Figure 11.7 shows that the participants scoring lower on the pretest increased their scores more rapidly than

FIGURE 11.7
Crossover effect.

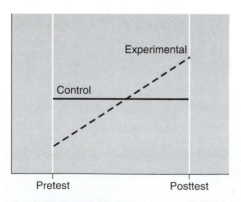

(From "The Design and Conduct of Quasi-Experiments and True Experiments in Field Settings" by T. D. Cook and D. T. Campbell, in *Handbook of Industrial and Organizational Psychology,* edited by M. D. Dunnette. Copyright © Rand McNally College Publishing Company, 1976.)

did the control group, which scored higher on the pretest. This is the opposite of what a selection–maturation outcome would suggest.

Causal Inference from the Nonequivalent Comparison Group Design

The nonequivalent comparison group design, as we have just discussed, is susceptible to producing biased results because of the potential existence of a number of threats to internal validity. The existence of these potential threats suggests that the results obtained from this quasi-experimental design are likely to be biased and produce results that are different from that which would be obtained from one of the randomized experimental designs. Heinsman and Shadish (1996) conducted a meta analysis comparing the effect-size estimates from randomized experimental designs and the nonrandomized nonequivalent comparison group design to determine the extent to which similar results could be obtained from studies using these two designs. This analysis suggested that if the randomized experimental design and the nonequivalent comparison group design were equally well designed and executed, they yielded about the same effect size. In other words, the nonequivalent comparison group design gave about the same results as the randomized experimental design.

The result of this meta analysis is a strong endorsement of the nonequivalent comparison group design. However, this strong endorsement exists only when the nonequivalent comparison group design is as well designed and executed as the randomized experimental design. As Heinsman and Shadish (1996) have pointed out, it is probably very difficult in many studies to design and execute the nonequivalent comparison group design as well as the randomized experimental designs. Therefore, in many studies, the nonequivalent comparison group design will give biased results.

There seem to be two design components that researchers must focus on when designing and conducting quasi-experiments to ensure that results are not biased. The first component focuses on the way participants are assigned to groups. To obtain unbiased results, experimenters must not let the participants self-select into groups or conditions. The more they self-select into the treatment conditions, the more biased the results will be. The second component focuses on pretest differences. Big differences at the pretest will lead to big differences at the posttest. This means that the researcher should try to reduce any pretest differences by matching the comparison groups on variables correlated with the dependent variable. When it is not possible to match, you should consider statistically adjusting the posttest scores for any pretest differences (e.g., using analysis of covariance, ANCOVA). If the experimenter focuses on these two design characteristics, the results obtained from the nonequivalent comparison group design will be a closer approximation to the randomized experimental research design.

STUDY QUESTION 11.3

- **Identify and discuss the rival hypotheses that could explain the various outcomes that could occur in a nonexperimental comparison group design.**
- **Why is the crossover effect not readily explained by rival hypotheses?**
- **What design components should be used to reduce bias in quasi-experiments?**

Time-Series Design

In research areas such as psychotherapy and education, it is very difficult to find an equivalent group of research participants to serve as a control group. Is the one-group pretest–posttest design (discussed in Chapter 10) the only available design in such cases? Is there no means of eliminating some of the rival hypotheses that arise from this design? Fortunately, there is a means for eliminating some of these hypotheses, but to do so one must think of mechanisms other than using a control group. "Control is achieved by a network of complementary control strategies, not solely by control-group designs" (Gottman, McFall, and Barnett, 1969, p. 299). These complementary strategies are detailed next.

Interrupted Time-Series Design

Interrupted time-series design
A quasi-experimental design in which a treatment effect is assessed by comparing the pattern of pre- and posttest scores of one group of research participants

The **interrupted time-series design** requires the investigator to take a series of measurements both before and after the introduction of some treatment condition, as depicted in Figure 11.8. The result of the treatment condition is indicated by a discontinuity in the recorded series of response measurements. Consider the study conducted by Lawler and Hackman (1969) in which they tried to identify the benefit derived from employee participation in the development and implementation of an employee incentive plan. Prior research had investigated a variety of payment plans and found that a given plan (say, a bonus plan) may be successful in one instance and not in another, indicating that the success of pay incentive plans is a function of factors other than just the plan itself. Lawler and Hackman hypothesized that a particular pay incentive plan would be more effective if the employees participated in its development, as opposed to having a plan dictated by management. To assess the validity of this theory, Lawler and Hackman had three work groups meet and develop a bonus incentive plan for reducing absenteeism. Absenteeism rates for these work groups were measured before and after the incentive plan was developed. The rates were then converted to a percentage of the number of scheduled hours that the employees actually worked. The average percentage of scheduled hours actually worked for all participants appears in Figure 11.9. From this figure, you can see that there was a rise in this average percentage and that this rise persisted over the sixteen weeks during which data were collected. All this is just a visual interpretation, however. Now it is necessary to ask two questions. First, did a significant change occur following the introduction of the treatment condition? Second, can the observed change be attributed to the treatment condition?

FIGURE 11.8
Interrupted time-series design.

Preresponse measure	Treatment	Postresponse measure
Y_1 Y_2 Y_3 Y_4 Y_5	X	Y_6 Y_7 Y_8 Y_9 Y_{10}

(Adapted from *Experimental and Quasi-Experimental Designs for Research* by D. T. Campbell and J. C. Stanley, 1963, American Educational Research Association, Washington, D.C.)

FIGURE 11.9

Mean attendance of the participative groups for the twelve weeks before the incentive plan and the sixteen weeks after the plan. (Attendance is expressed in terms of the percentage of hours scheduled to be worked that were actually worked.)

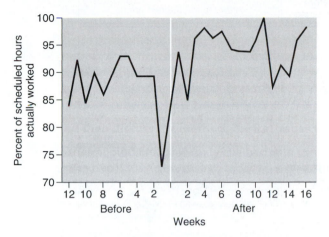

(From "Impact of Employee Participation in the Development of Pay Incentive Plans: A Field Experiment" by E. E. Lawler and J. R. Hackman, 1969, *Journal of Applied Psychology, 53,* pp. 467–471. Copyright 1969 by the American Psychological Association. Reprinted by permission of the author.)

The answer to the first question naturally involves tests of significance because, as Gottman et al. (1969, p. 301) have stated, "The data resulting from the best of experimental designs is of little value unless subsequent analyses permit the investigator to test the extent to which obtained differences exceed chance fluctuations." However, before presenting the specific tests of significance, I want to follow the orientation set forth by Campbell and Stanley (1963) and Caporaso and Ross (1973) and discuss the possible outcome patterns for time series that reflect a significant change resulting from an experimental alteration. Let us first take a look at the data that would have been obtained from Lawler and Hackman's (1969) study and a study conducted by Vernon, Bedford, and Wyatt (1924) if they had used only a one-group pretest–posttest design. The Vernon et al. study was concerned with investigating the influence of introducing a rest period on the productivity of various kinds of factory workers. These data are presented in Figure 11.10. Note that in *both* studies beautiful data

FIGURE 11.10

A one-group pretest–posttest representation of a portion of the Vernon et al. (1924) data and Lawler and Hackman (1969) data.

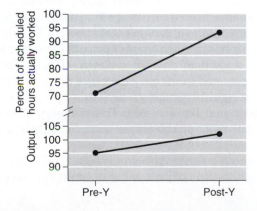

FIGURE 11.11

Effect of a ten-minute rest pause on worker productivity.

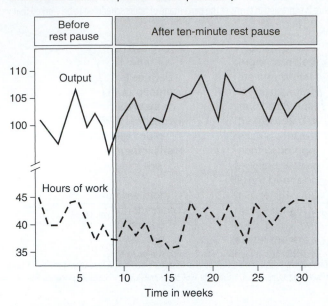

(Reprinted from *Two Studies of Rest Pauses in Industry* by H. M. Vernon, T. Bedford, and S. Wyatt, 1924. Medical Research Council, Industrial Fatigue Research Board No. 25. London: His Majesty's Stationery Office.)

seem to support the hypothesis that the experimental treatment condition produced a beneficial effect. Remember, however, that the one-group pretest–posttest design does not include a comparison group, so the increase in performance could have been due to many variables other than the experimental treatment condition.

One means of eliminating some of the sources of rival hypotheses is to take a number of pre- and postmeasurements or to conduct an interrupted time-series analysis. When this kind of study is undertaken, we find the data depicted in Figure 11.9 for Lawler and Hackman's (1969) study and the data depicted in Figure 11.11 for the Vernon et al. (1924) study. The data suggest that the treatment condition investigated by Lawler and Hackman was influential but that the treatment condition investigated by Vernon et al. was not. The pattern of responses obtained by Vernon et al. seems to represent a chance fluctuation rather than a real change in performance.

Visual inspection of a pattern of behavior can be very helpful in determining whether an experimental treatment had a real effect. Caporaso and Ross (1973) have presented a number of additional possible patterns of behavior, shown in Figure 11.12, that could be obtained from time-series data. Note that the first three patterns reveal no treatment effect but merely represent a continuation of a previously established pattern of behavior. Lines D, E, F, and G represent *true* changes (I am assuming that they are statistically significant) in behavior, although line D represents only a temporary shift.

Now let us return to our original question of whether a significant change in behavior followed the introduction of the treatment condition. Such a determination

FIGURE 11.12
Possible pattern of behavior of a time-series variable.

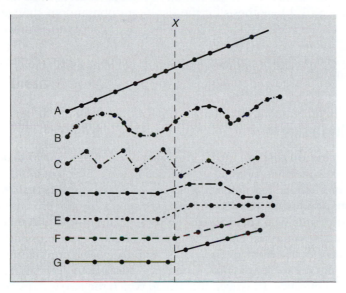

(From *Quasi-Experimental Approaches: Testing Theory and Evaluating Policy,* edited by J. A. Caporaso and L. L. Ross, Jr. © 1973 by Northwestern University Press. Reprinted by permission.)

involves tests of significance. The most widely used and, I believe, the most appropriate statistical test is the Bayesian moving average model (Box and Jenkins, 1970; Box and Tiao, 1965; Glass, Tiao, and Maguire, 1971; Glass, Willson, and Gottman, 1975). Basically, this method consists of determining whether the pattern of postresponse measures differs from the pattern of preresponse measures. To make such an assessment using the moving average model requires many data points. Glass et al. (1975) recommend that at least fifty data points be obtained. This relatively large number of data points can typically be obtained when conducting experiments using animals. However, it frequently cannot be obtained when conducting research with humans. When fewer data points are obtained, the probability of concluding that a treatment is effective when it really is not, a Type I error, is increased. This difficulty has resulted in a limited use of the moving average model in analyzing time-series data. Fortunately, Tryon (1982) and Crosbie (1993) have developed statistical procedures that are effective with as few as ten data points. A valid statistical analysis can, therefore, be conducted on almost any study using a time-series analysis.

Lawler and Hackman's analysis of their data revealed a significant difference between the patterns of pre- and postresponse measures. This led them to conclude that a nonrandom change occurred following the introduction of the incentive plan. This brings us to the second question: Can this significant change be attributed to the employees' participation in the incentive plan? The primary source of weakness in the interrupted time-series design is its failure to control for the effects of history. Considering Lawler and Hackman's study, assume that at about the same time the treatment condition was introduced, some extraneous event occurred that could also have led to an increase in the number of hours worked. Such an extraneous event serves as a rival hypothesis for the significant nonrandom change. The investigator must consider all the other events taking place at about the same time as the experimental event and determine whether they might be rival hypotheses. Actually, Lawler and Hackman included several other control groups in their study to rule out such effects.

Regression Discontinuity Design

Regression discontinuity design
A design used to determine whether individuals meeting some predetermined criteria profit from receiving some special treatment

The **regression discontinuity design** is a design that is used to determine whether individuals meeting some predetermined criteria profit from receiving some special treatment. This design, depicted in Figure 11.13, consists of measuring all participants on a preassignment measure and then selecting a cutoff score based on this measure. All participants who score above the cutoff score receive the special treatment and participants who score below the cutoff score do not receive the special treatment. After the special treatment is administered, the posttest measure is obtained and the two groups are compared on the outcome measure to determine if the special treatment was effective. However, the way in which the two groups are compared in the regression discontinuity design is different than that of any other design we have considered so far. A treatment effect is demonstrated by a discontinuity in the regression line that would have been formed if no treatment effect existed.

Figure 11.14 illustrates a continuity in the regression line. Notice that there is a continuous increase of scores from a low of about 41 to a high of about 58 and a cutoff score of 50 separating the control group from the treatment group. The straight line pushed through these scores is the regression line. Note that this regression line is continuous and that the individuals that received the special treatment made a score higher than 50 on the preassignment variable. The continuous regression line indicates that there was no effect of the treatment because the scores of the people above the cutoff of 50 who received the treatment continued the pattern of scores of people below the cutoff of 50 who did not receive the treatment.

Now look at Figure 11.15. This figure shows a regression line for the people above the cutoff score of 50 that is not a continuation of the regression line established for the people with a cutoff score below 50. In other words, there is a discontinuity of the

FIGURE 11.13

Structure of the regression discontinuity design. Y_p is the preassignment measure; C indicates the preassignment measure cutoff score used to assign participants to conditions, where participants with scores above the cutoff are assigned to the treatment condition and participants with scores below the cutoff are assigned to the control condition; X refers to a treatment condition; and Y refers to the posttest measure or the outcome or dependent variable.

Experimental group	Y_p	C	X	Y
Control group	Y_p	C		Y

FIGURE 11.14

Regression discontinuity experiment with no treatment effect.

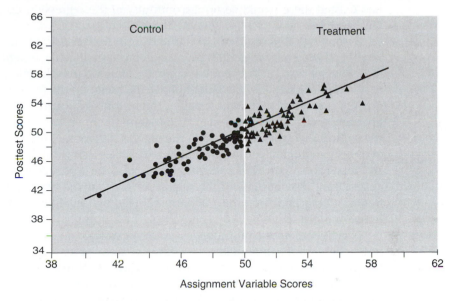

(From Shadish, W. R., Cook, T. D. and Campbell, D. T. *Experimental and Quasi-Experimental Designs for Generalized Causal Inference.* © 2002. Houghton Mifflin Co. Used with permission.)

FIGURE 11.15

Regression discontinuity experiment with an effective treatment.

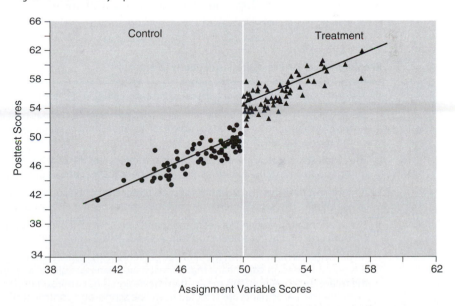

(From Shadish, W. R., Cook, T. D. and Campbell, D. T. *Experimental and Quasi-Experimental Designs for Generalized Causal Inference.* © 2002. Houghton Mifflin Co. Used with permission.)

regression line for the people with a cutoff score below and above 50. This discontinuity indicates that the treatment had an effect because if no treatment effect had existed there would be no discontinuity of the regression line, as illustrated in Figure 11.14.

Braden and Bryant (1990) used the regression discontinuity design to determine whether a program for gifted students enhanced their achievement more than regular school placement. The cutoff score to be admitted into the gifted program was set at two or more standard deviations above the mean on the Stanford-Binet or WISC-R intelligence tests. Students meeting this cutoff score were admitted to the gifted program and students referred to the program but not meeting the cutoff score were the control group and remained in the regular classroom. Three years after initiation of the gifted program, outcome data were collected using the California Achievement Test total battery percentile. Statistical analysis of the outcome data demonstrated that a significant discontinuity of the regression lines for the two groups of students did not exist, indicating that the gifted program did not enhance academic achievement of the bright students.

The regression discontinuity design is an excellent design that can be used when researchers want to investigate the efficacy of some program or treatment but cannot randomly assign participants to comparison groups. However, there are a number of criteria, listed in Table 11.4, that must be adhered to for the design to effectively assess the effectiveness of a treatment condition. When these criteria are met, the regression discontinuity design is a very good design to use for testing the effect of a treatment condition and is typically more powerful than other quasi-experimental designs.

Any threat to the validity of the regression discontinuity design would have to cause a sudden discontinuity in the regression line that coincides with the cutoff. As Shadish et al. (2002) have pointed out, this is implausible, although possible. The

TABLE 11.4
Requirements of the Regression Discontinuity Design

- Assignment to comparison groups must be based only on the cutoff score.
- The assignment variable must be at least an ordinal variable and it is best if it is a continuous variable. It cannot be a nominal variable such as sex, ethnicity, religious preference, or status as a drug user or nonuser.
- The cutoff score ideally should be located at the mean of the distribution of scores. The closer the cutoff score is to the extremes, the lower the statistical power of the design.
- Assignment to comparison groups must be under the control of the experimenter to avoid a selection bias. This requirement rules out most retrospective uses of the design.
- The relationship between the assignment and outcome variables (whether it is linear, curvilinear, etc.) must be known to avoid a biased assessment of the treatment effect.
- All participants must be from the same population. With respect to the regression discontinuity design, this means that it must have been possible for all participants to receive the treatment condition. This means that the design is not appropriate, for example, if the experimental participants are selected from one school and control participants are selected from another school.

primary threat that could produce such an effect is a contemporaneous history effect. However, this history effect would have to be one that affected only participants on one side of the cutoff, which makes it quite unlikely. Of the other threats to internal validity I discussed in Chapter 8, attrition is about the only other serious threat. However, this is a threat to any design, including experiments with random assignment.

STUDY QUESTION 11.4

- **Describe the interrupted time-series design, and explain how rival hypotheses are eliminated in this design.**
- **What is the primary rival hypothesis that cannot be controlled when using the interrupted time-series design?**
- **Describe the regression discontinuity design.**
- **What rival hypotheses are controlled in the regression discontinuity design?**

Summary

This chapter has deviated considerably from the orientation taken in the previous chapters by presenting a number of quasi-experimental designs, which represent approximations of true experimental designs in the sense that they use the experimental mode of analysis in investigating areas that do not allow for complete control of extraneous variables. Quasi-experimental designs are the best type of design available for use in some field studies in which one wants to make causal inferences. The quasi-experimental designs presented are the pretest–posttest design, the time-series design, and the regression discontinuity design.

The nonequivalent comparison group design is the one most frequently used. It is exactly like the pretest–posttest experimental design except that participants are not randomly assigned to the experimental and control groups, which means that we do not have the necessary assurance that the two groups of participants are equated. We could attempt to equate participants on the important variables using matching techniques. However, this still does not assure us that the participants are totally equated, and it may produce a regression effect. However, this design does give results that are of about the same effect size as a randomized experiment when the two are equally well designed and executed.

The time-series design attempts to eliminate rival hypotheses without the use of a control group. In the interrupted time-series design, a series of measurements is taken on the dependent variable both before and after the introduction of some experimental treatment condition. The effect of that condition is then determined by examining the magnitude of the discontinuity produced by the condition in the series of recorded responses. The primary source of error in this design is the possible history effect.

The regression discontinuity design is used when the goal is to determine if individuals meeting some predetermined criteria profit from receiving some special treatment. The effect of the treatment condition is determined by examining the regression line. A treatment effect is inferred if there is a discontinuity in the regression line that would have been formed if no treatment effect existed.

Key Terms and Concepts

Quasi-experimental design
Nonequivalent comparison group
   design
First increasing treatment effect
Selection–maturation effect
Selection-history effect

Increasing treatment and control groups
Second increasing treatment effect
Crossover effect
Interrupted time-series design
Regression discontinuity design

Related Internet Sites

www.socialresearchmethods.net/kb/quasiexp.htm
This site provides a brief discussion of quasi-experimental design and has links to other designs such as the nonequivalent groups design and the regression-discontinuity design as well as other issues relevant to this topic.

www.wadsworth.com/psychology_d/templates/student_resources/workshops/index.html
When this page appears, click on the "research methods workshops" link. Then click on "nonexperimental approaches" and this will bring you to a site that starts out with a brief description of some quasi-experimental designs.

Practice Test

The answers to these questions can be found in Appendix A.

1. The primary difference between a quasi-experimental design and a randomized experimental design is
   a. The number of independent variables that can be manipulated
   b. That quasi-experimental designs are used in field research and randomized designs are used in laboratory research
   c. The ability of the design to control for potential threats to internal validity
   d. The ability of the design to generalize the results of the study
   e. The size of the treatment effect that can be expected

2. The primary threat to internal validity in the nonequivalent comparison group design is
   a. History
   b. Selection
   c. Testing
   d. Instrumentation
   e. Regression

3. The outcome from a nonequivalent comparison group design that gives us the most confidence that the treatment produced the observed effect is
   a. An increasing treatment effect
   b. An effect in which both the experimental and control groups increase but the experimental group increases more

   c. An effect in which the experimental group increases but the control group does not change

   d. A crossover effect

   e. An effect in which the experimental group increases and the control group decreases

4. Most of the threats to internal validity are ruled out in the time-series design

   a. As a result of the discontinuity in the regression line

   b. As a result of the change in level corresponding with the introduction of the treatment

   c. When the pre- and posttesting outcomes differ significantly

   d. As a result of the multiple pretests and posttests

   e. As a result of the multiple pretests

5. A school principal wants to decrease the amount of truancy that exists in his school system. He requires all students who have missed coming to school an average of twice every week for the past year to participate in a special program designed to make school more enjoyable and rewarding. To test the effectiveness of this special program he would probably use which design?

   a. Randomized experimental design

   b. Regression discontinuity design

   c. Nonequivalent comparison group design

   d. Time-series design

   e. Multimodal design

Challenge Exercises

1. For each of the following design briefs, identify

   a. The type of quasi-experimental design used

   b. The potential threat to internal validity that may exist in concluding that the treatment produced the observed effect

     A. The National Institutes of Health wanted to improve the research careers of promising young scientists by giving them a significant grant to allow them to devote time to their research careers. They requested and received applications from one hundred scientists who were assistant professors and had been in their first job for less than five years. From this pool of one hundred applicants, they selected the twenty-five most promising individuals in terms of number of publications, school from which they had received their terminal degree, and letters of recommendation. After five years had elapsed, they compared the performance of the twenty-five applicants who had received the award with the applicants who had not. It was found that the applicants who received the award were more productive in terms of number of publications, more of them had been promoted to associate professor, and their salary was higher than those who did not receive the award. Based on this evidence it was concluded that the program should be continued because it was a great success.

B. MADD (Mothers against Drunk Drivers) has lobbied for tougher laws against drunk drivers for years. Assume that it was successful in convincing the legislators in your state to pass a tougher law against drunk drivers that required a mandatory jail sentence of at least six months, loss of driver's license for five years, and a fine of at least $10 thousand. You want to test the effect of this tougher law, so you record the number of people arrested and convicted for DUI (driving under the influence of alcohol) for five years prior to the passage of this law and for five years after passage of this law. You find that the number of arrests and convictions decreased after the law was passed, so you conclude that the tougher laws are effective.

C. School systems frequently provide special instruction and classes for individuals who are behind in particular subjects. You want to determine if a special reading program is effective for children with reading difficulties, so you test all second-grade children on reading ability. The children who score below 30 on your test of reading ability are required to participate in the special reading program. After these children have been in the special reading program for a time, you again test all the second-grade children on reading ability. You find that the children given the special program improved more than would be expected and conclude that it indicates that the program was effective.

2. A youth center wants to improve the family life for teenagers at risk for violence. One of the current programs that is being implemented is a type of therapy called Functional Family Therapy. To assess the effectiveness of this type of therapy in reducing violence among youth, two youth centers are selected. One provides Functional Family Therapy to the families of teenagers who have been at the youth center and are being released back into the care of their parents; the other youth center continues its standard practice of follow-up and brief counseling of parents. For each teenager who is being released to his or her family, data are collected on the number of violent encounters with other teenagers, the law, and other family members for one month before and after the treatment program was initiated. The following shows four different outcomes that could occur.

a. Graph each outcome.
b. State whether the treatment condition seems to have been effective.
c. Identify the rival hypotheses that may explain the observed effect.

First Outcome:	Experimental group:	Pretest = 27	Posttest = 13
	Control group:	Pretest = 10	Posttest = 10
Second Outcome:	Experimental group:	Pretest = 16	Posttest = 4
	Control group:	Pretest = 10	Posttest = 27
Third Outcome:	Experimental group:	Pretest = 14	Posttest = 27
	Control group:	Pretest = 5	Posttest = 10
Fourth Outcome:	Experimental group:	Pretest = 4	Posttest = 13
	Control group:	Pretest = 15	Posttest = 15

12 Single-Case Research Designs

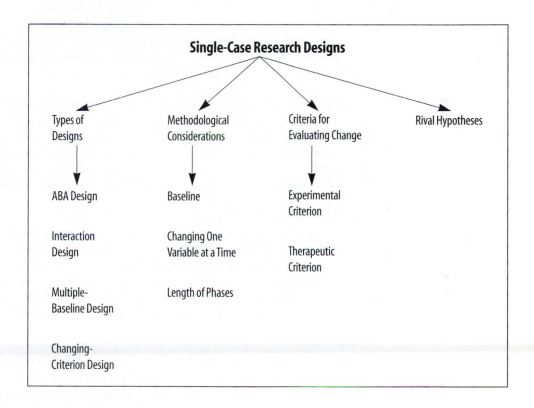

Single-Case Research Designs

Types of Designs	Methodological Considerations	Criteria for Evaluating Change	Rival Hypotheses
ABA Design	Baseline	Experimental Criterion	
Interaction Design	Changing One Variable at a Time	Therapeutic Criterion	
Multiple-Baseline Design	Length of Phases		
Changing-Criterion Design			

Dr. Kathleen Baynes of the University of California at Davis gave an intelligent businessman, H.W., a picture depicting a specific event and asked him to describe it. The following (cited in Gazzaniga, Ivry, & Mangun, 2002, p. 338) is the description provided by this individual. Read the description and see if you can identify who is in the picture and what the people in the picture are doing.

> First of all this is falling down, just about, and is gonna fall down and they're both getting something to eat … But the trouble is this is gonna let go and they're both gonna fall down … I can't see well enough but I believe that either she will have some food that's not good for you and she's to get some for her, too … and that you get it there because they shouldn't go up there and get it unless you tell them that they could have it. And so this is falling down and for sure there's one they're going to have for food and, and this didn't come out right, the, uh, the stuff that's uh, good for, it's not good for you but it, but you love, um mum mum (H.W. intentionally smacks lips) … and so they're … see that, I can't see whether it's in there or not … I think she's saying, I want two or three, I want one, I think, I think so, and so, so she's gonna get this one for sure it's gonna fall down there or whatever, she's gonna get that one and, and there, he's gonna get one himself or more, it all depends with this when they fall down … and when it falls down there's no problem, all they got to do is fix it and go right back up and get some more."

After reading this description I suspect that you are having a difficult time identifying the individuals and the activities they were engaged in. About the only thing you probably know is that something or someone was falling down and that food was involved. However, if you saw the picture you would see that it depicts a boy falling off a stool while reaching for cookies in a jar on a shelf and handing one to his sister. So what is missing from H.W.'s description? He accurately described a number of aspects of the scene, but he left out any reference to nouns, making the information useless. For example, he said "this" instead of "the stool" or "the chair"; he substituted "food" for "cookie" even though he knew it was a cookie, that it tasted good, and that it is considered bad for children; and he never mentioned the fact that the people in the picture were a male and female child.

This individual suffered from a stroke in his left hemisphere damaging an area called Wernicke's area, or a part of the cortex surrounding Wernicke's area, producing a disorder called *anomia,* the inability to name things or a difficulty in labeling objects. However, as his description indicates, comprehension is intact and speech is unaffected.

Cases such as this are relatively rare and provide glimpses into the operation of various areas of the brain, so scientists are very interested in using these individuals as research participants in investigations of brain structures that contribute to processes such as language. Because individuals with cortical damage in specific areas, such as Wernicke's area, are rare, investigations are typically limited to a single individual.

Chapter Preview

Up to this point in the book, the designs that have been discussed have involved groups of different individuals. However, as the vignette at the beginning of this chapter reveals, there are times when large groups of individuals are not available on which to test some treatment effect. To make the situation even more difficult, there are times when it is necessary to assess the effect of a treatment on a single individual. This means that we cannot use either random assignment or inclusion of a control group, the primary techniques that are typically used to control for the influence of rival hypotheses. How can we control for the influence of rival hypotheses when conducting an experiment on only one participant? The answer is to make use of single-case designs—designs constructed for use with only one participant and in a manner that controls for the influence of most rival hypotheses.

This chapter presents the most frequently used single-case designs and demonstrates how each of them enables the investigator to assess the impact of an independent variable while at the same time controlling for the influence of rival hypotheses. The chapter concludes with a discussion of specific methodological issues that must be considered when designing a single-case research study.

Introduction

Single-case research designs
Research design in which a single participant or a single group of individuals is used to investigate the influence of a treatment condition

Single-case research designs are designs that use only one participant or one group of individuals to investigate the influence of some experimental treatment condition. The unique feature of this design is the capacity to conduct experimental research with one participant or with one group of individuals such as a community, a group of employees, or a group of juveniles. Although single-case research designs can be used with a group of participants as well as with a single participant, they are most frequently used with single participants. In discussing these designs I therefore focus attention on their use in experimentation with single participants.

Encountering these designs for the first time, most people tend to equate them with case studies, but this is incorrect: Single-case designs experimentally investigate a treatment effect, whereas case studies provide an in-depth description of an individual. Dukes (1965) found that only 30 percent of all single-case studies are case studies; the great majority are of the experimental variety. A brief look at the history of experimental psychology reveals that psychological research actually began with the intensive study of a single organism. Wundt's (1902) use of the method of introspection required a highly trained single participant. Ebbinghaus (1913) conducted his landmark studies on memory using only one participant—himself. Pavlov's (1928) basic findings were the result of experimentation with a single organism, a dog (see Exhibit 12.1), but were replicated on other organisms. As you can see, single-case research was alive and well during the early history of psychology. In 1935, however, Sir Ronald Fisher published a book on experimental design that altered the course of psychological research. In it, Fisher laid the foundation for conducting and analyzing multiparticipant experiments. Psychologists quickly realized that the designs and statistical procedures elaborated by Fisher were very useful and began to adopt them. With the publication of Fisher's (1935) work, psychologists turned from single-case studies toward multiparticipant designs. The one notable exception to this tradition was B. F. Skinner (1953), his students, and his colleagues. They developed a general approach that has been labeled the *experimental analysis of behavior*. This method is devoted to experimentation with a single participant (or with only a few participants) on the premise that the detailed examination of a single organism under rigidly controlled conditions will yield valid conclusions about a given experimental treatment condition. The use of this approach led to the development of a variety

EXHIBIT 12.1

Pavlov with His Laboratory Apparatus

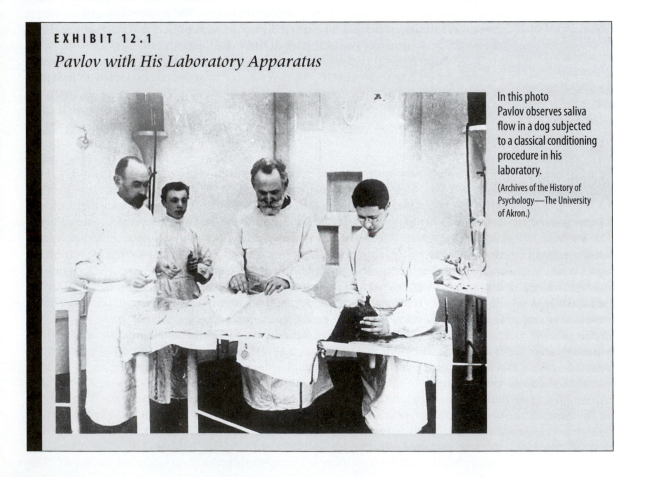

In this photo Pavlov observes saliva flow in a dog subjected to a classical conditioning procedure in his laboratory.

(Archives of the History of Psychology—The University of Akron.)

of single-case experimental designs that form the basis of the single-case research designs.

The single-case research designs developed by Skinner (1953) and his colleagues and explicated by Sidman (1960) probably would not have experienced the level of acceptability that they currently enjoy without the growth in the popularity of behavior therapy (Hersen and Barlow, 1976). In psychotherapy, the case study was initially the primary method of investigation (Bolger, 1965). During the 1940s and 1950s researchers grounded in experimental methodology attacked the case study method on methodological grounds (Hersen and Barlow, 1976). This led some investigators to focus on the percentage of clients who were successfully treated by a given psychotherapy. Eysenck (1952) demonstrated the inadequacy of this method, however, by showing that the percentage of successes achieved by psychotherapy was no greater than that achieved by a spontaneous remission of symptoms. This disturbing evidence led researchers to focus even more on the multiparticipant design, and they found many difficulties in applying this approach (Bergin and Strupp, 1972). More significantly, they found "that these studies did not prove that psychotherapy worked" (Hersen and Barlow, 1976, p. 12). Such evidence left researchers perplexed, and some (e.g., Hyman and Berger, 1966) wondered if psychotherapy could be evaluated. Other researchers lapsed into naturalistic studies of the therapeutic process; still others engaged in process research, which emphasizes what goes on during therapy and deemphasizes the outcome of therapy. These efforts did little to advance knowledge of psychotherapy. By the 1960s, there was tremendous dissatisfaction with clinical practice and research, prompting the search for other alternatives. Bergin (1966) thought that the multiparticipant designs failed to demonstrate the effectiveness of therapy because the results were averaged. In the studies he reviewed, he noted that some clients improved and some got worse; when the results for these two types of clients were averaged, however, the effects canceled one another out, indicating that therapy had no effect. Given such evidence, along with the fact that process research was not beneficial in increasing effectiveness of therapy, some researchers (Bergin and Strupp, 1970) began to advocate returning to the use of experimental case studies, which employ an experimental analogue. Research was making a change back to single-case research. During the 1960s, however, an appropriate methodology for experimentally investigating the single participant was not apparent. It took the growing popularity of behavior therapy to provide a vehicle for the use of the appropriate methodology. Because behavior therapy involved the application of many of the principles of learning that had been identified in the laboratory, it was but a small step for these applied researchers also to borrow the procedures used to identify these principles. This methodology, successfully used in applied settings, has become accepted for use in identifying the influence of antecedents on individual behavior.

STUDY QUESTION 12.1

• **Discuss the historical use of single-case research designs.**
• **Explain why single-case research designs have become popular with researchers in recent decades.**

Single-Case Designs

When planning an experimental study that uses only one participant, it is necessary to use some form of time-series design. Recall that the time-series design requires that repeated measurements be taken on the dependent variable both before and after the treatment condition is introduced. This is necessary to permit detection of any effect produced by the treatment condition because it is not possible to include a control group of participants. For example, assume we wanted to determine if caffeine was the cause of the emotional disturbance experienced by a truck driver. Here, there is only one participant, and we want to know whether caffeine caused his emotional disturbance. We could administer the caffeine and measure the participant's level of emotional stability, but then we would have no basis for determining whether the caffeine produced the effect because we would not know how stable the participant was when he was not consuming the caffeine. Without such a comparison, it is impossible to infer any effect of the treatment condition.

What can we use as a basis of comparison in a single-case design? Because there is only one participant in the study, the comparison responses have to be the participant's own pretreatment responses. In other words, the investigator has to record the participant's responses before and after administration of the independent variable. In the caffeine experiment, we would have to record the participant's level of emotional stability prior to and after consuming caffeine. If we take only one pre- and postresponse measure, we will have a one-group pretest–posttest design, which has many disadvantages. To overcome some of those problems (such as maturation), we must obtain multiple pre- and postresponse measures. For example, we could measure the truck driver's level of emotional stability each day over a period of two weeks prior to consuming caffeine and while consuming caffeine. Now we have a time-series design using one participant, which represents descriptive experimentation because it furnishes a continuous record of the organism's responses during the course of the experiment. Using this procedure, we would have a continuous record of the truck driver's level of emotional stability over the course of the entire experiment. This technique is also experimental because it permits us to interject a planned intervention—a treatment condition such as caffeine—into the program. Consequently, it allows us to evaluate the effect of an independent variable.

Although the basic time-series design can be used in single-case research, we must remember that it is only a quasi-experimental design. Taking repeated pre- and postintervention measures of the dependent variable does allow us to rule out many potential biasing effects, but it does not rule out the possibility of a history effect. Risley and Wolf (1972) have pointed out that the ability to detect a treatment effect with the time-series design hinges on the ability to predict the behavior of the participant if the treatment condition had not been administered. When using the time-series design, we collect both pre- and postintervention measures of the dependent variable. In determining whether the treatment or intervention had any effect on behavior, we compare the pre- and post-dependent variable measures to see if there is a change in the level or the slope of the responses. However, in this assessment, the underlying assumption is that the pattern of preresponse measures would have continued if the treatment intervention had not been applied. In other words, the pretreatment responses are used to forecast what the posttreatment responses would have been in the absence of the treatment. If this forecast is inaccurate, then we cannot adequately assess the effects of the treatment intervention because the pretreatment responses do not serve as a legitimate basis for comparison. The basic time-series design, then, is truly limited in unambiguously identifying the influence of an experimental treatment effect.

STUDY QUESTION 12.2	**Explain why single-case research designs have to represent a time-series type of design.**

ABA Design

In order to improve on the basic time-series design in an attempt to generate unambiguous evidence of the causal effect of a treatment condition, a third phase has been added. This third phase, a withdrawal of the experimental treatment conditions, makes the design an **ABA design**. The ABA design, depicted in Figure 12.1, represents the most basic of the single-case research plans. As the name suggests, it has three separate conditions. The A condition is the baseline condition, which is the target behavior as recorded in its freely occurring state. In other words, **baseline** refers to a given behavior as observed prior to presentation of any treatment designed to alter this behavior. The baseline behavior thus gives the researcher a frame of reference for assessing the influence of a treatment condition on this behavior. The B condition is the experimental condition, wherein some treatment is deliberately imposed to try to alter the behavior recorded during baseline. Generally, the treatment condition is continued for an interval equivalent to the original baseline period or until some substantial and stable change occurs in the behaviors being observed (Leitenberg, 1973).

After the treatment condition has been introduced and the desired behavior generated, the A condition is then reintroduced. There is a return to the baseline conditions—the treatment conditions are withdrawn and whatever conditions existed during baseline are reinstated. This second A condition is reinstituted in order to determine if behavior will revert back to its pretreatment level. It is generally assumed that the effects of the treatment are reversible, but this is not always the case. Reversal of the behavior back to its pretreatment level is considered to be a crucial element for demonstrating that the experimental treatment condition, and not some other extraneous variable, produced the behavioral change observed during the B phase of the experiment. If the plan had included only two phases (A and B), as in the typical time-series design, rival hypotheses could have existed. However, if the behavior reverts back to the original baseline level when the treatment conditions are withdrawn, rival hypotheses become less plausible.

ABA design

A single-case design in which the response to the treatment condition is compared to baseline responses recorded before and after treatment

Baseline

The target behavior of the participant in its naturally occurring state or prior to presentation of the treatment condition

FIGURE 12.1
ABA design.

A	B	A
Baseline measure	Treatment condition	Baseline measure

Consider the study conducted by Walker and Buckley (1968). These researchers investigated the effect of using positive reinforcement to condition attending behavior in a nine-year-old boy named Phillip. A bright, underachieving child, Phillip was referred to the investigators because he exhibited deviant behavior that interfered with classroom performance. Specifically, Phillip demonstrated extreme distractability, which often kept him from completing academic assignments. The investigators first took a baseline measure of the percentage of time that Phillip spent on his academic assignment. After the percentage of attending time had stabilized, the treatment condition was introduced, which consisted of enabling Phillip to earn points if no distraction occurred during a given time interval. These points could then be exchanged for a model of his choice. When Phillip had completed three successive ten-minute distraction-free sessions, the reinforcement of being able to earn points was withdrawn. Figure 12.2 depicts the results of this experiment. During the first baseline (A) condition, attending behavior was very low. When the treatment contingency (B) of being able to earn points was associated with attending behavior, percentage of attending behavior increased dramatically. When the contingency was withdrawn and baseline conditions were reinstated (A), attending behavior dropped to its pretreatment level.

In this case, the ABA design seems to provide a rather dramatic illustration of the influence of the experimental treatment conditions. However, there are several problems with this design (Hersen and Barlow, 1976). The first of these is that the design ends with the baseline condition. From the standpoint of a therapist or other individual who desires to have some behavior changed, this is unacceptable because the

FIGURE 12.2

Percentage of attending behavior in successive time samples during the individual conditioning program.

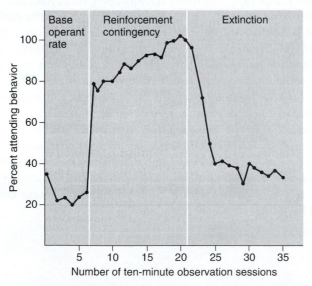

(From "The Use of Positive Reinforcement in Conditioning Attending Behavior" by H. M. Walker and N. K. Buckley, 1968, *Journal of Applied Behavior Analysis, 1*, p. 247. Copyright 1968 by the Society for the Experimental Analysis of Behavior, Inc.)

FIGURE 12.3
ABAB design.

A	B	A	B
Baseline measure	Treatment condition	Baseline measure	Treatment condition

benefits of the treatment condition are denied. Fortunately, this limitation is easily handled by adding a fourth phase to the ABA design in which the treatment condition is reintroduced. We now have an ABAB design, as illustrated in Figure 12.3. The participant thus leaves the experiment with the full benefit of the treatment condition.

Quattrochi-Tubin and Jason (1980) provide a good illustration of the ABAB design. Their study actually used the responses from a single *group* of participants rather than from a single participant. Remember that with single-case designs the case can be a single group or a single participant. Quattrochi-Tubin and Jason investigated a means for getting residents of a nursing home to increase attendance and social interaction in the lounge area instead of remaining in their rooms or passively watching television. (Such increased activity is considered important to the mental and physical well-being of the elderly.) The experiment was divided into four phases, with each phase consisting of four days. The first four days were the baseline phase, during which the experimenters merely recorded, on two different occasions, the number of residents present in the lounge, the number of those present watching television, and the number of those present engaged in social interaction. The second phase was the treatment phase, during which an announcement was made on the public-address system that coffee and cookies were available in the lounge. After four treatment days, the third phase (the baseline conditions) was instituted, which meant that the refreshments were no longer offered. In the fourth phase, refreshments (the treatment condition) were again served. Figure 12.4 depicts the number of elderly

FIGURE 12.4

Attendance, television watching, and social interaction during baseline and refreshment phases in the lounge.

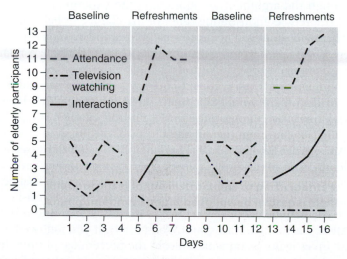

(From "Enhancing Social Interactions and Activity among the Elderly through Stimulus Control" by S. Quattrochi-Tubin and L. A. Jason, 1980, *Journal of Applied Behavior Analysis, 13,* pp. 159–163. Copyright 1980 by the Society for the Experimental Analysis of Behavior, Inc.)

residents present in the lounge as well as those engaged in social interaction or watching television during each of the four phases of the experiment. Apparently, attendance and social interaction increased and television watching decreased when refreshments were offered, suggesting that a simple act of incorporating coffee and cookies in a nursing home routine can alter the behavior of its residents.

A second problem with the ABA design is not so easily handled. As previously stated, one of the basic requirements of the ABA design is that the situation revert to the baseline conditions when the experimental treatment condition is withdrawn. This requirement is necessary in order to rule out rival hypotheses such as history because, if the behavior did not revert to baseline, we would have an AB, or time-series, design. Quattrochi-Tubin and Jason (1980) needed to demonstrate that the attendance, television watching, and social interactions returned to baseline levels once the refreshments were taken away in order to show that the behavior was modified by the experimental treatment.

The problem with the ABA design is that a reversal to baseline does not occur with all behavior. Hewett, Taylor, and Artuso (1969) found that the removal of a token program increased the target behaviors rather than returning them to baseline. Without the reversal, the experimenter cannot be sure that the change in behavior following introduction of the treatment condition was not caused by some other extratreatment factor. Failure to reverse may be due to a carry-over effect across phases, whereby the treatment condition was maintained so long that a relatively permanent change in behavior took place. In fact, Bijou, Peterson, Harris, Allen, and Johnston (1969) have recommended that short experimental periods be used to facilitate obtaining a reversal effect. This is in line with Leitenberg's (1973, p. 98) statement that "single-case experimental designs are most pertinent to the discovery of short-term effects of therapeutic procedure while they are being carried out." Once the influence of the experimental treatment has been demonstrated, attention can then be placed on its persistence.

Although the argument for shortening the experimental treatment to facilitate reversal (thereby demonstrating cause of the change in behavior) is valid, it applies only to behaviors that will in fact reverse. When the investigator is interested in nontransient effects, none of these arguments is valid because a relatively permanent change is instated.

Withdrawal
Removal of the treatment condition

Reversal design
A design in which the treatment condition is applied to an alternative but incompatible behavior so that a reversal in behavior is produced

A last issue concerns a distinction between a reversal and a withdrawal ABA design. In discussing the ABA design, I have described **withdrawal**, in which the treatment condition is removed during the third (second A) phase of the design. Leitenberg (1973) states that the ABA withdrawal design should be distinguished from an ABA **reversal design**. The distinction occurs in the third (second A) phase of the ABA design. In the withdrawal design, the treatment condition is withdrawn; in the reversal design, the treatment condition is applied to an alternative but incompatible behavior. For example, assume that you were interested in using reinforcement to increase the play behavior of a socially withdrawn four-and-a-half-year-old girl, as were Allen, Hart, Buell, Harris, and Wolf (1964). If you followed the procedure used by these investigators, you would record the percentage of time the girl spent interacting with both children and adults during the baseline phase. During treatment (the B phase), praise would be given whenever the girl interacted with other children, and isolated play and interaction with adults would be ignored. During the third phase of the experiment (the second A phase), the true reversal would take place. Instead of being withdrawn, the contingent praise would be shifted to interactions with adults so that any time the child interacted with adults she would be praised, and interactions with other children would be ignored. This phase was implemented to see if the social behavior would reverse to adults and away from children as the reinforcement contingencies shifted. Although the ABA reversal design can reveal rather dramatic results, it is more cumbersome and thus is used much less frequently than the more adaptable withdrawal design. Therefore, most of the single-case ABA designs that you encounter will be of the withdrawal variety.

STUDY QUESTION 12.3

- **Diagram the ABA single-case research design and explain how this design rules out confounding extraneous variables.**
- **Explain why the ABA design is often extended to an ABAB design and the circumstances under which the ABA or ABAB design is ineffective in identifying a treatment effect.**
- **Explain the difference between a reversal and a withdrawal of the treatment effect.**

Interaction Design

A survey of the literature on single-case designs shows that researchers have not been content to stick to the basic ABA design but instead have extended this basic design in a variety of ways. One intriguing and valuable extension is used to identify the interactive effect of two or more variables. In discussing multiparticipant designs, I described interaction as the situation that exists when the influence of one independent variable depends on the specific level of the second independent variable. This definition of interaction was presented because multiparticipant designs allow us to include several levels of variation for each independent variable being investigated. In a single-case design, we do not have that degree of flexibility. One of the cardinal rules in single-case research (Hersen and Barlow, 1976) is that only one variable can be changed from one phase of the research to another. For example, in the ABAB design, we can introduce a specific type or level of reinforcement when changing from the baseline phase to the treatment phase of the experiment. However, only one level of reinforcement can be implemented. Therefore, when I discuss an **interaction effect in single-case research**, I am referring to the combined influence of two or more specific levels of two or more different independent variables. For example, we could investigate the interaction effect of a concrete reinforcement (giving of tokens) and verbal reinforcement (the experimenter saying "good"). It would not be practical to investigate the interaction of different forms of material reinforcement (tokens, points, and candy) with different forms of praise. Therefore, interaction typically refers to the combined influence of two specific variables.

Interaction effect in single-case research The combined influence of two or more specific levels of two or more independent variables

In order to isolate the interactive effect of two variables from the effect that would be achieved by only one of these variables, it is necessary to analyze the influence of each variable separately and in combination. To complicate the issue further, we must

FIGURE 12.5

Single-participant interaction design.

	Baseline	Single treatment	Baseline	Single treatment	Combined treatment	Single treatment	Combined treatment
Sequence 1	A	B	A	B	BC	B	BC
Sequence 2	A	C	A	C	BC	C	BC

do this by changing only one variable at a time. Thus the sequence in which we test for the influence of each variable separately and in combination must be such that the influence of the combination of variables (interaction effect) can be compared with that of each variable separately. Figure 12.5 illustrates this design. In sequence 1, the effect of treatment B is independently investigated, and then the combined influence of treatments B and C is compared to the influence of treatment B alone. In like manner, sequence 2 enables the investigation of the influence of treatment C independently, and then the combined influence of treatments B and C is compared to treatment C. In this way, it is possible to determine whether the combined influence of B and C was greater than that of B or C. If it was, then an interactive effect exists. However, if the combined effect was greater than that of one of the treatment variables (C) but not the other (B), then an interactive effect does not exist because the effect can more parsimoniously be attributed to treatment B.

One of the more useful illustrations of a test of an interaction effect is found in the combined studies of Leitenberg, Agras, Thompson, and Wright (1968) and Leitenberg, Agras, Allen, Butz, and Edwards (1975). In the first study, Leitenberg et al. (1968) used feedback and praise to overcome a severe knife phobia in a fifty-nine-year-old woman. The dependent variable measure was the amount of time the subject could spend looking at an exposed knife. Following the completion of a trial, the participant was given feedback and/or praise regarding the amount of time spent observing the knife. Praise consisted of verbally reinforcing the participant when she looked at the knife for progressively longer periods of time. Feedback consisted of telling the participant how much time had been spent observing the knife. The specific design of this study is depicted in Figure 12.6. Although it does not correspond exactly to an interaction design, it is close enough to demonstrate the essential components.

The results of this study appear in Figure 12.7. Feedback resulted in an increase in mean viewing time. This increase does not appear to have been altered by the introduction of praise, suggesting that praise had no effect on the knife phobia. During the

FIGURE 12.6

Design of two studies used to test the interaction of feedback and praise.

		Experimental condition				
	B	BC	B	A	B	BC
Leitenberg et al. (1968)	Feedback	Feedback and praise	Feedback	Baseline	Feedback	Feedback and praise
Leitenberg et al. (1975)	Praise	Feedback and praise	Praise	Baseline	Praise	

FIGURE 12.7

Time in which a knife was kept exposed by a phobic patient as a function of feedback, feedback plus praise, and no feedback or praise conditions.

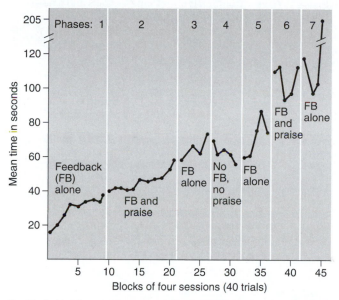

(From "Feedback in Behavior Modification: An Experimental Analysis in Two Phobic Cases" by H. Leitenberg, W. S. Agras, L. E. Thompson, and D. E. Wright, 1968 *Journal of Applied Behavior Analysis, 1*, p. 136. Copyright 1968 by the Society for the Experimental Analysis of Behavior, Inc.)

third phase of the experiment, when praise was withdrawn, the same increase persisted, lending even more support to the notion that praise was ineffective. Therefore, feedback seems to have been the controlling agent. The second half of the study, during which feedback was presented independently and in combination with praise, provides additional support for the notion that feedback is the controlling agent.

Although the apparent conclusion of the Leitenberg et al. (1968) study is that feedback is the sole agent responsible for the reduction in the knife phobia, this is only one of two possible conclusions. As Hersen and Barlow (1976) have pointed out, an alternative interpretation is that praise had an effect but that it was masked by the effect of feedback. Feedback may have been so powerful that it enabled the participant to progress at her optimal rate. If such were the case, then there would have been no room for the effect of praise to manifest itself, which would lead us to conclude erroneously that praise was ineffective when actually it did have some effect. This is one reason that both of the sequences depicted in Figure 12.5 must be incorporated in order to isolate an interaction effect.

In accordance with this requirement, Leitenberg et al. (1975) conducted another experiment on a second knife-phobic patient. In this study, praise was presented independently and then in combination with feedback, as illustrated in Figure 12.6. Otherwise, the procedure of the study was identical to that of the Leitenberg et al. (1968) study. Figure 12.8 depicts the results of the second study. As you can see, the participant made no progress when only praise was administered. When feedback was

FIGURE 12.8

Mean time looking at phobic stimulus as a function of praise and feedback plus praise conditions: Subject I.

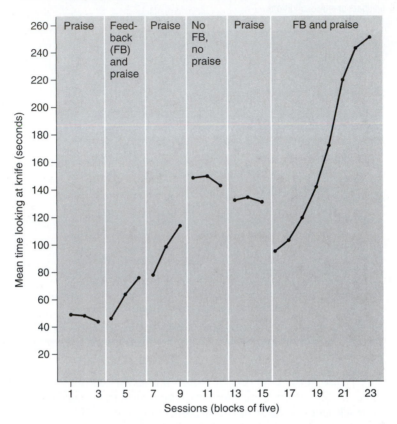

(From "Feedback and Therapist Praise during Treatment of Phobia" by H. Leitenberg, W. S. Agras, R. Allen, R. Butz, and J. Edwards, 1975, *Journal of Consulting and Clinical Psychology, 43,* p. 397. Copyright 1975 by the American Psychological Association. Reprinted by permission of the author.)

combined with praise, progress was made. Interestingly, this progress was maintained even when feedback was subsequently discontinued in the third phase of the study. In the fifth and sixth phases of the study, again no progress was made unless feedback was combined with praise.

Taken together, these two studies reveal that feedback alone was the primary agent in helping the patient overcome the knife phobia because praise alone had no appreciable effect and adding praise to feedback did not produce a marked increase in progress toward overcoming the phobia. These two studies also show the necessity of testing each variable (such as feedback and praise) separately and in combination in order to isolate any interactive effect. Herein lie what may be considered the disadvantages of testing for an interaction effect. First, at least two research participants are typically required because a different participant will have to be tested on each of the two sequences depicted in Figure 12.5. Second, the interaction effect can be demonstrated only under conditions in which each variable alone (for example, feedback) does *not* produce maximum increment in performance on the part of the participant. As pointed out, in the Leitenberg et al. (1968) study it was possible that praise was effective in overcoming knife phobia, but the feedback variable was so potent that it enabled the participant to respond at the maximum level, thus precluding any possibility of demonstrating an interactive effect. In such cases, the proper conclusion would be that the two variables being tested were equally effective, and the addition of the second variable was not beneficial. Note that a conclusion could not be drawn regarding the possible interactive effect of the two variables because this effect could not be tested. In this case, the interaction design is quite useful in demonstrating the continued effects of two or more variables.

STUDY QUESTION 12.4
- **Diagram the interaction single-case research design.**
- **Explain how an interaction in a single-case design is different from that of a multiparticipant design.**

Multiple-Baseline Design

One of the primary limiting components of the ABA design is its failure to rule out a history effect in situations in which the behavior does not revert back to baseline level when the treatment condition is withdrawn. If you suspect that such a situation may exist, the multiple-baseline design is a logical alternative because it does not entail withdrawing a treatment condition. Therefore, its effectiveness does not hinge upon a reversal of behavior to baseline level.

Multiple-baseline design
A single-case design in which the treatment condition is successively administered to several participants or to the same participant in several situations after baseline behaviors have been recorded for different periods of time

In the **multiple-baseline design**, depicted in Figure 12.9, baseline data are collected on two or more different behaviors for the same individual, on the same behavior for two or more different individuals, or on the same behavior across two or more different situations for the same individual. After the baseline data have been collected, the experimental treatment is successively administered to each target behavior. If the behavior exposed to the experimental treatment changes while all others remain at baseline, this provides some evidence for the efficacy of the treatment condition. It becomes increasingly implausible that rival hypotheses would contemporaneously influence each target behavior at the same time as the treatment was administered.

Saigh (1986) used the multiple-baseline design in a study investigating the use of an imagery-based flooding procedure in the treatment of a six-and-a-half-year-old boy suffering from posttraumatic stress disorder. Joseph experienced this disorder after being exposed to a bomb blast in a war zone where he lived. His reaction to the bomb blast included trauma-related nightmares, recollections of the trauma, depression, and avoidance behavior.

FIGURE 12.9
Multiple-baseline design.

		T_1	T_2	T_3	T_4
Behaviors, people, or situations	A	Baseline	Treatment		
	B	Baseline	Baseline	Treatment	
	C	Baseline	Baseline	Baseline	Treatment
	D	Baseline	Baseline	Baseline	Baseline

To treat Joseph, five scenes were developed that evoked anxiety (for example, a scene of injured people and debris and another where he approached specific shopping areas). When Joseph saw each scene he rated his level of anxiety to obtain a measure of discomfort to each scene. During therapy sessions Joseph was trained to relax and then he was exposed to each scene for an extended period of time (over twenty minutes). During each exposure the therapist asked Joseph to imagine the exact details of the scene. The five scenes were incorporated into treatment in a multiple-baseline design. The results of this treatment for four of the five scenes is depicted in Figure 12.10.

FIGURE 12.10

Joseph's ratings of discomfort referred to as Subject Units of Disturbance (SUDS) where 5 = *maximum discomfort* and 0 = *no discomfort*. Assessment was conducted to measure discomfort for each scene during the treatment sessions. Treatment (graphed as open circles) reflects the period in which imagery-based exposure (flooding) focused on the specific scene.

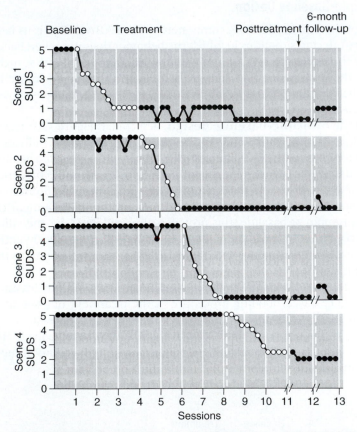

(From "In vitro flooding in the treatment of a 6-year-old-boy's posttraumatic stress disorder," by P. S. Saigh, 1986, *Behavior Research and Therapy, 24,* p. 687. Reprinted with kind permission from Elsevier Science Ltd, The Boulevard, Langford Lane, Kidlington OX516B, UK.)

Figure 12.10 reveals that four baseline ratings of discomfort were obtained for scene 1, 16 for scene 2, 24 for scene 3, and 32 for scene 4. Immediately after obtaining the baseline measure for each scene, the relaxation treatment was implemented. Figure 12.10 reveals that Joseph's rating of discomfort began to decline soon after relaxation treatment was implemented. Also note that the treatment produced a decline of ratings of discomfort only in response to the targeted scene. Consequently, a change in behavior did not occur until the treatment condition was administered providing convincing evidence that the relaxation was the cause of the reduction in anxiety and discomfort. In this study there was the additional component of a six-month follow-up that further confirmed the efficacy of the treatment by demonstrating that the decline in ratings of discomfort persisted over time.

Although the multiple-baseline design avoids the problem of reversibility, it has another basic difficulty. For this design to be effective in evaluating the efficacy of the treatment condition, the target behaviors must not be highly interrelated. This means that there must not be **interdependence of behaviors** being investigated such that a change in one behavior alters the other behaviors. Figure 12.10 indicates that this requirement was satisfied in the Saigh (1986) study because a reduction in ratings of discomfort occurred only when the experimental treatment was administered. However, such independence is not always found. Kazdin (1973), for example, noted that the classroom behaviors of inappropriate motor behavior, inappropriate verbalizations, and inappropriate tasks are interrelated and that a change in one response can result in a change in one of the other responses. In like manner, Broden, Bruce, Mitchell, Carter, and Hall (1970), using a multiple-baseline design across individuals, found that contingent reinforcement changed not only the inattentive behavior of the target participant but also that of an adjacent peer.

Interdependence of behaviors
The influence of one behavior on another

The problem of interdependence of behaviors is real and needs to be considered before the multiple-baseline design is selected because interdependence will destroy much of the power of this design, resting as it does on its ability to demonstrate change whenever the treatment condition is administered to a given behavior. If administering the experimental treatment to one behavior results in a corresponding change in all other behaviors, then when the experimental treatment is administered to the remaining behaviors, it will have less impact and produce less change because the behavior has previously been altered. In such a case, it is not clear what caused the change in behavior. Which behaviors are interrelated is an empirical question. Sometimes data exist on this interdependence, but where none exist the investigators must collect their own.

Kazdin and Kopel (1975) provide several recommendations for cases in which independence cannot be achieved. The first is to select behaviors that are as independent as possible. Because it may be difficult to predict in advance which behaviors are independent, one should consider using different individuals or situations; their behaviors will probably be more distinct than different behaviors of the same individual.

In attempting to select independent behaviors, investigators often correlate the baseline behaviors. If a low correlation is obtained, they tend to infer that the behaviors are independent. Although this could be an indication of independence, it may suggest a level of independence that does not exist. If the baseline behaviors are quite stable or do not change much, a low correlation could result from this limited fluctuation in behavior. Then we might conclude that the behaviors were independent when they really were not. Even if we have good, valid evidence that baseline behaviors are independent, this does not provide any assurance that they will remain independent after implementation of the treatment condition. For example, implementing a time-out procedure for disruptive behavior with one child in a classroom could affect other children's behavior. Therefore, the consideration of independence should take place during the treatment phase as well as during the baseline phase.

A second recommendation made by Kazdin and Kopel (1975) for decreasing ambiguity in the multiple-baseline design is to use several baselines (specifically, four or more) to decrease the possibility of dependence across all baselines. Even though some baseline behaviors will be dependent, those that are independent can demonstrate the treatment effect relationship.

A third recommendation is to implement a reversal on one of the baseline behaviors. If this leads to a generalized reversal effect (reversal on other behaviors), then one has added evidence for the effect of the treatment, as well as evidence for a generalized treatment effect.

STUDY QUESTION 12.5

- **Diagram the multiple-baseline single-case research design.**
- **Explain how confounding extraneous variables are ruled out.**
- **Discuss the concept** *interdependence of behaviors* **in the context of this design.**

Changing-Criterion Design

Changing-criterion design

A single-case design in which a participant's behavior is gradually shaped by changing the criterion for success during successive treatment periods

The **changing-criterion design,** depicted in Figure 12.11, requires an initial baseline measure on a single target behavior. Following this measure, a treatment condition is implemented and continued across a series of intervention phases. During the first intervention or treatment phase, an initial criterion of successful performance is established. If the participant successfully achieves this performance level across several trials, or if the participant achieves a stable criterion level, the criterion level is increased. The experiment moves to the next successive phase, in which a new and more difficult criterion level is established while the treatment condition is continued. When behavior reaches this new criterion level and is maintained across trials, the next phase, with its more difficult criterion level, is introduced. In this manner, each successive phase of the experiment requires a step-by-step increase in the criterion

FIGURE 12.11
Changing-criterion design. T_1 through T_4 refer to four different phases of the experiment.

T_1	T_2	T_3	T_4
Baseline	Treatment and initial criterion	Treatment and criterion increment	Treatment and criterion increment

measure. "Experimental control is demonstrated through successive replication of change in the target behavior, which changes with each stepwise change in criterion" (Kratochwill, 1978, p. 66).

Hall and Fox (1977) provide a good illustration of the changing-criterion design in a study of a child named Dennis who refused to complete arithmetic problems. To overcome this resistant behavior, the investigators first obtained a baseline measure of the average number of assigned arithmetic problems (4.25) that he would complete during a forty-five-minute session. Then Dennis was told that a specified number of problems had to be completed correctly during the subsequent session. If he completed them correctly, he could take recess and play with a basketball; if he did not, he had to miss recess and remain in the room until they were correctly completed. During the first treatment phase, the criterion number of problems to be solved was set at five, which was one more than the mean number completed during the baseline phase. After successfully achieving the criterion performance on three consecutive days, Dennis had to finish an additional problem. The recess and basketball contingencies were maintained. The results of this experiment, shown in Figure 12.12, reveal that Dennis's performance increased as the criterion level increased. When a change in behavior parallels the criterion change so closely, it rather convincingly demonstrates the relative effects of the treatment contingency.

Hartmann and Hall (1976) indicate that the successful use of the changing-criterion design requires attention to three factors: the length of the baseline and treatment phases, the magnitude of change in the criterion, and the number of treatment phases or changes in the criterion. With regard to the length of the treatment and baseline phases, Hartmann and Hall state that the treatment phases should be of different lengths; or, if they are of a constant length, then the baseline phases should

FIGURE 12.12
Number of math problems solved in a changing-criterion design.

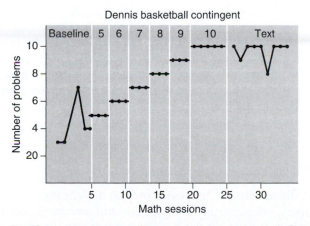

(From "Changing-Criterion Designs: An Alternative Applied Behavior Analysis Procedure" by R. V. Hall and R. G. Fox, in *New Developments in Behavioral Research: Theory, Method, and Application.* In honor of Sidney W. Bijou, edited by C. C. Etzel, G. M. LeBlanc, and D. M. Baer, 1977. Hillsdale, N.J.: Lawrence Erlbaum Associates. Copyright 1977 by Lawrence Erlbaum Associates. Reprinted by permission of the authors.)

be longer than the treatment phases. This is necessary to ensure that the step-by-step changes in the participant's behavior are caused by the experimental treatment and not by some history or maturational variable that occurs simultaneously with the criterion change. In addition, the baseline data should be stable or changing in a direction opposite to that of the treatment condition in order to establish unambiguously that only the treatment condition produced the observed change. With regard to the actual length of each treatment, the rule of thumb is that each treatment phase must be long enough to allow the behavior to change to its new criterion level and then to stabilize. In other words, the new criterion level must be consistently achieved across trials. If the behavior continues to fluctuate between the new and the old criterion level, stability has not been achieved.

The second consideration is the magnitude of the criterion change. Naturally, it must be large enough so that a detectable change can occur. If the behavior is difficult to change, the criterion change should be small enough so that it can be achieved but still large enough to be noticed. If the behavior varies wildly from trial to trial, then the criterion change must be rather large in order to allow the experimenter to detect any change.

Hartmann and Hall (1976) state that two criterion changes may be adequate. This issue is, however, directly dependent on the number of replications that are required to demonstrate convincingly that the behavioral change is the result of the treatment condition. For this reason, Kratochwill (1978) recommends at least four criterion changes. When the participant's behavior is quite variable, Hall and Fox (1977) suggest including a reversal in one of the treatment phases. This reversal could consist of reverting back to baseline or to a former criterion level. Such a reversal would provide additional evidence of the influence of the treatment condition.

The changing-criterion design seems to be a useful design in studies that require shaping of behavior over a period of time (Hall and Fox, 1977) or in cases in which step-by-step increases in accuracy, frequency, duration, or magnitude are the therapeutic goals (Hartmann and Hall, 1976), as may be the case in learning to write or read.

STUDY QUESTION 12.6

- **Diagram the changing-criterion design, and identify the type of situation in which this design would be appropriate to use.**
- **Discuss the factors of length of baseline and treatment phases, magnitude of change in the criterion, and the number of treatment phases as they relate to this research design.**

Methodological Considerations in Using Single-Case Designs

The preceding discussion of single-case research designs by no means represents an exhaustive survey, but presents the most basic and commonly used designs. Regardless of which design is used, there are several common issues that one must consider when attempting to conduct a single-case study.

Baseline

Baseline has been defined as the target behaviors in their freely occurring state. Repeatedly, investigators (such as Gelfand & Hartmann, 1968) have emphasized the importance of the baseline data in single-case research. A prime concern is obtaining a **stable baseline** because the baseline data serve as the standard against which change induced by the experimental treatment condition is assessed. A stable baseline is characterized by an absence of trend (or slope) in the data and only a slight degree of variability (Kazdin, 1992). An absence of trend (or slope) means that the baseline data should not demonstrate an increase or decrease over time. Although this is the ideal, sometimes it is impossible to eliminate a baseline trend.

Stable baseline
A set of responses characterized by the absence of any trend and by little variability

If the trend occurring during the baseline phase is opposite that which is expected during the intervention phase when the experimental treatment condition is administered, the experiment demonstrates that the treatment condition is powerful enough not only to produce an effect but also to reverse a previous trend. If the baseline change is in the same direction as is expected from the intervention, it is difficult to draw an unambiguous conclusion regarding the influence of the treatment condition. In such a case, it is best to wait for the baseline to stabilize before introducing the treatment condition. If this cannot be done, one can resort to an alternating-treatments design in which the two treatments are designed to change the trend in opposite directions.

A stable baseline is also characterized by having little variability in the baseline data. Excessive variability during baseline, or other phases of a single-case design, can interfere with one's ability to draw valid conclusions about a treatment. However, the definition of excessive variability is relative because variability is excessive only if it interferes with one's ability to draw conclusions about the treatment effect, and drawing valid conclusions depends on many factors, such as the initial level of behavior during baseline and the magnitude of change when the intervention is implemented. In general, variability will be more of a problem with human participants than with animals because a greater degree of control can generally be exercised over the animals. McCullough, Cornell, McDaniel, and Mueller (1974), for example, found that the number of irrelevant comments made by high school students during a fifty-minute class period ranged from 17 to 104 during an eight-day period. Although this may be somewhat atypical, it does illustrate the extent to which baseline data can fluctuate with humans. When extreme fluctuations or unsystematic variations exist in the baseline data, one should check all components of the study and try to identify and control the sources of the variability. Sometimes the fluctuation can be traced to sources that are important to the validity of the experiment, such as unreliability in scoring participant behavior. When the sources cannot be identified or controlled, one can artificially reduce the variability by averaging data points across consecutive days or sessions. This averaging substantially reduces variability and allows the effect of the treatment condition to be accurately assessed. However, it does distort the day-to-day pattern of performance.

There is one additional problem to be considered in obtaining baseline frequencies on humans: the potential reactive effect of the assessment on the behavior under study (Webb, Campbell, Schwartz, and Sechrest, 1966). The fact that baseline data are being taken may itself have an effect on the behavior. This was vividly demonstrated by McFall (1970) and Gottman and McFall (1972), who showed that monitoring one's own behavior can have a significant influence on that behavior. If one monitors frequency of smoking, one increases the number of cigarettes smoked, whereas if one monitors the frequency of not smoking, one smokes less.

Changing One Variable at a Time

A cardinal rule in single-case research is that only one variable can be changed from one phase of the experiment to the next (Hersen and Barlow, 1976). Only when this rule is adhered to can the variable that produced a change in behavior be isolated. Assume that you want to test the effect of reinforcement on increasing the number of social responses emitted by a chronic schizophrenic. In an attempt to employ an ABA design, you first measure baseline performance by recording the number of social responses. Following baseline, you give the schizophrenic a token (which can be redeemed for cigarettes) and say "good" after each social response. At this point you are violating the rule of one variable because two types of reinforcement are being administered. If the number of social responses increases, you will not know which type of reinforcement is responsible for changing the behavior. In fact, it may not be either reinforcer independently but the combined (interactive) influence that is the catalyst. To isolate the separate and combined influences of the two reinforcers, you would need an interaction design.

Length of Phases

An issue that must be given consideration when a single-case study is being designed is the length of each phase of the study. Although there are few guidelines to follow, most experimenters advocate continuing each phase until some semblance of stability has been achieved. Although this is the ideal, in many clinical studies it is not feasible. In addition, following this suggestion leads to unequal phases, which Hersen and Barlow (1976) consider to be undesirable. According to these investigators, unequal phases (particularly when the treatment phase is extended in time to demonstrate a treatment effect) increase the possibility of a confounding influence of history or maturation. For example, if the baseline phase consisted of recording responses for seven days and the treatment phase lasted fourteen days, we would have to entertain the possibility of a history or maturation variable affecting the data if a behavioral change did not take place until about the seventh day of the treatment phase. Because of such potential confounding influences, Hersen and Barlow suggest using an equal number of data points for each phase of the study.

There are two other issues that relate directly to the length of phases: carry-over effects and cyclic variations (Hersen and Barlow, 1976). Carry-over effects in single-case ABAB designs usually appear in the second baseline phase of the study as a failure to reverse to original baseline level. When such effects do occur or are suspected, many single-case researchers (for example, Bijou et al., 1969) advocate using short treatment condition phases (B phases). These effects become particularly problematic in a single-case drug study.

Hersen and Barlow (1976) consider cyclic variations a neglected issue in the applied single-case literature. It is of paramount concern when participants are influenced by cyclic factors, such as the menstrual cycle in females. Where the data may be influenced by such cyclical factors, it is advisable to extend the measurement period during each phase to incorporate the cyclic variation in both baseline and treatment phases of the study. If this is not possible, then the results must be replicated across participants that are at different stages of the cyclic variation. If identical results are achieved across participants regardless of the stage of the cyclic variation, then meaningful conclusions can still be derived from the data.

STUDY QUESTION 12.7 | **List and then discuss the methodological issues that must be considered when designing a single-case study.**

Criteria for Evaluating Change

The single-case designs discussed in this chapter attempt to rule out the influence of extraneous variables by strategies such as replicating the intervention effect over time, which is quite different from the control techniques employed by multiparticipant experimental designs. Similarly, single-case designs use different criteria for evaluating treatment effects than do multiparticipant designs. The two criteria that are usually used in single-case research are an experimental criterion and a therapeutic criterion (Kazdin, 1978).

Experimental Criterion

Experimental criterion
In single-case research, repeated demonstration that a behavioral change occurs when the treatment is introduced

The **experimental criterion** requires a comparison of pre- and postintervention behavior. In making this comparison, most experimenters using a single-case design do not employ statistical analyses, which is definitely a source of controversy, as illustrated in Exhibit 12.2. Instead of using statistical analysis, these researchers rely on replicating the treatment effect over time.

When it can be demonstrated that behavior repeatedly changes as the treatment conditions change, the experimental criterion has been fulfilled. In actual practice, the experimental criterion is considered to be met if the behavior of the participant during the intervention phase does not overlap with his or her behavior during the baseline phase or if the trend of the behavior during baseline and intervention phases differs.

Therapeutic Criterion

Therapeutic criterion
Demonstration that the treatment condition has eliminated a disorder or has improved everyday functioning

The **therapeutic criterion** refers to the clinical significance or value of the treatment effect for the participant. Does the treatment effect eliminate some disorder for the participant or does it enhance the participant's everyday functioning? This criterion is much more difficult to demonstrate than is the experimental criterion. For example, a self-destructive child may demonstrate a 50 percent reduction in

EXHIBIT 12.2

Analysis of Data Obtained from Single-Case Designs

In the past, when single-case research designs were conducted predominantly by Skinner, his colleagues, and his students, statistical analysis of single-case data was shunned. It was deemed to be unnecessary because the studies were conducted on infrahumans and sufficient experimental control of extraneous variables could be established to enable the experimental effect to be determined by visual inspection of the data.

As single-case designs have become more popular, some people have insisted on the need for statistical analysis of the data. This point of view is by no means universal, however.

The arguments against the use of statistical analysis are as follows.

1. Statistical analysis of the data provides evidence of a treatment effect only by demonstrating if the effect is statistically significant. It offers no evidence regarding the treatment's clinical effectiveness. For example, even though a treatment condition that was applied to reduce irrational thought patterns in schizophrenic individuals produces a statistically significant decline in such thought patterns, the patient may not have improved enough to operate effectively outside of an institutional setting.

2. Statistical tests hide the performance of the individual because they lump participants together and focus only on average scores. Consequently, a treatment condition that benefited only a few individuals might not achieve statistical significance and would therefore be considered ineffective when in fact it was beneficial for some individuals.

There are two basic arguments that support the use of statistical analysis.

1. Visual inspection of the data obtained from single-case designs will not provide an accurate interpretation when a stable baseline cannot be established. When data are not statistically analyzed, investigators must use the trend and the variability of the data to reach a conclusion as to whether the treatment condition produced an effect. If the baseline data and the treatment data have different trends or different levels of performance, then a decision is typically made that the treatment condition produced an effect, particularly if there is a stable baseline. However, if there is a great deal of variability in the data, it is difficult to interpret the data without statistical analysis. Statistical analysis can analyze extremely variable data more objectively than can individuals.

2. Visual inspection of the data leads to unreliable interpretation of the treatment effects. For example, Gottman and Glass (1978) found that the thirteen judges given data from a previously published study disagreed on whether the treatment effect was significant. Seven said a treatment effect existed, and six said it did not.

The proponents and opponents of statistical analysis each have valid points to make. However, doctrinaire positions that unequivocally advocate one strategy to the exclusion of the other seem to do more harm than good. When a stable baseline and limited variability can be achieved, statistical analysis probably adds little to the interpretation of the data. When they cannot, statistical analysis should be used in addition to visual analysis. Visual inspection and statistical analysis should be viewed as complementary tools in the development and verification of hypotheses using single-case designs.

Social validation
Determination that the treatment condition has significantly changed the participant's functioning

Social comparison method
A social validation method in which the participant is compared with nondeviant peers

Subjective evaluation method
A social validation method in which others' views of the participants are assessed to see whether those others perceive a change in behavior

self-destructive acts following treatment but still engage in fifty instances of such behavior every hour. Even though the experimental criterion has been satisfied, the child is still far from reaching a normal level of behavior.

In an attempt to resolve this problem, researchers have included a procedure known as social validation in some experiments. **Social validation** of a treatment effect consists of determining if the treatment effect has produced an important change in the way the client can function in everyday life. (For example, after treatment, can a claustrophobic client ride in an elevator?) This validation is accomplished by either a social comparison method or a subjective evaluation method.

The **social comparison method** involves comparing the behavior of the client before and after treatment with the behavior of his or her nondeviant peers. If the participant's behavior is no longer distinguishable from that of the nondeviant peers, then the therapeutic criterion has been satisfied. The **subjective evaluation method** involves assessing whether the treatment has led to qualitative differences in how others view the participant. Individuals who normally interact with the participant and are in a position to assess the participant's behavior may be asked to provide a global evaluation of the client's functioning on an assessment instrument, such as a rating scale or a behavioral checklist. If this evaluation indicates that the client is functioning more effectively, then the therapeutic criterion is considered to have been satisfied. Each of these methods has its limitations, but both provide additional information regarding the therapeutic effectiveness of the experimental treatment condition.

STUDY QUESTION 12.8 | **Discuss the criteria that have been used for evaluating treatment effects in single-case research designs.**

Rival Hypotheses

When discussing and reading literature on single-case designs, one gets the distinct impression that these designs can effectively identify causal relationships. However, it seems wise to heed Paul's (1969, 51) claim that only multiparticipant designs are capable of establishing causal relationships:

> This is the case because the important classes of variables for behavior modification research are so closely intertwined that the only way a given variable can be "systematically manipulated" alone somewhere in the design is through the factorial representation of the variables of interest in combination with appropriate controls.

Paul does admit that the reversal and multiple-baseline designs provide the strongest evidence of causal relationships that can be attained from single-case designs.

What types of rival hypotheses exist in the single-case designs presented? The issues of nonreversible changes and interdependence of behavior have already been discussed. A number of studies (for example, Packard, 1970) have shown that instructions alone can change behavior. If different instructions are given for the baseline and experimental treatment phases, it is difficult to determine whether the effect was due to the treatment, the instructions, or some combination of the two. The best we can do is to maintain constant instructions across the treatment phases while introducing, withdrawing, and then reintroducing the therapeutic treatment condition (Hersen, Gullick, Matherne, and Harbert, 1972). Experimenter expectancies are another source of error in single-case designs. In most studies, the researcher is acutely aware of the time periods devoted to baseline and to the experimental treatment, which may lead to differential reactions on his or her part. These differential reactions may lead the participant's behavior to change in the desired direction. A last possible biasing effect has to do with sequencing. Because the same participant must perform in all phases of the experiment, order effects and carry-over effects may exist. It is difficult to separate the effects of the particular sequence of conditions from the effect of the treatment condition. If a change in behavior occurs, it could be the result of the sequence effect, the treatment effect, or some combination of the two.

STUDY QUESTION 12.9 | **Identify the rival hypotheses that may operate in single-case research designs that are not specific to a particular design.**

Summary

In conducting an experimental research study that uses only one participant, you must reorient your thinking because extraneous variables cannot be controlled by using a randomization control technique nor can they be handled by the inclusion of a control group. To begin to rule out the possible confounding effect of extraneous variables, you must take some form of a time-series approach. This means that multiple pre- and postmeasures on the dependent variable must be made in order to exclude potential rival hypotheses such as maturation. The most commonly used single-case design is the ABA type, which requires the investigator to take baseline measures before and after the experimental treatment effect has been introduced. The experimental treatment effect is demonstrated by a change in behavior when the treatment condition is introduced and a reversal of the behavior to its pretreatment level when the experimental treatment condition is withdrawn. The success of this design depends on the reversal.

Many extensions of the basic ABA design have been made. One valuable extension attempts to assess the combined or interactive effect of two or more variables. The influence of each variable is assessed separately and in combination. In addition, the influence of the combination of variables, or the interaction of the two or more variables, must be compared with that of each variable separately. This means that at least two participants must be used in the study.

A third type of single-case design is the multiple-baseline design. This design avoids the necessity for reversibility required in the ABA design by calling for successive administration of the experimental treatment condition to different participants. The influence of the treatment condition is revealed if a change in behavior occurs simultaneously with the introduction of the treatment condition. Although the multiple-baseline design avoids the problem of reversibility, it requires that the behaviors under study be independent.

The changing-criterion design is useful in studies that require a shaping of behavior over a period of time. This plan requires that, following the baseline phase, a treatment condition be implemented and continued across a series of intervention phases. For each intervention phase the criterion that must be met in order to advance to the next intervention phase is progressively more difficult. In this way, behavior can gradually be shaped to a given criterion level.

In addition to a basic knowledge of the single-case designs, you should also have a knowledge of some of the methodological considerations required to appropriately implement the plans. These include the following:

1. *Baseline.* A stable baseline must be obtained, although some variation will always be found in the freely occurring target behaviors.

2. *Changing one variable at a time.* A cardinal rule in single-case research is that only one variable can be changed from one phase of the experiment to another.

3. *Length of phases.* Although there is some disagreement, the rule seems to be that the length of the phases should be kept equal.

4. *Criteria for evaluating change.* An experimental or a therapeutic criterion must be used to evaluate the results of a single-case design to determine whether the experimental treatment condition produced the desired effect.

5. *Rival hypotheses.* Alternative theories must be considered, including the effect of variables such as instructions, experimenter expectancies, and sequencing effects.

Key Terms and Concepts

Single-case research designs
ABA design
Baseline
Withdrawal
Reversal design
Interaction design
Interaction effect in single-case research
Multiple-baseline design

Interdependence of behaviors
Changing-criterion design
Stable baseline
Experimental criterion
Therapeutic criterion
Social validation
Social comparison method
Subjective evaluation method

Related Internet Sites

http://userwww.service.emory.edu/~evanman/smallnlect.html
This site provides information relevant to the history of single-case design and the advantages and disadvantages of these designs as well as examples of most of the designs covered in your textbook.

www.msu.edu/user/sw/ssd/issd01.htm
This site discusses the basic single-case designs and other methodological issues such as the characteristics of single-case evaluation including how to determine whether a treatment is effective.

Practice Test   *The answers to these questions can be found in Appendix A.*

1. Single-case research designs are a type of
   a. Time-series design
   b. Quasi-experimental design
   c. Multimodal design
   d. Mixed model design
   e. Case study

2. When the ABA cannot be used because the targeted behavior does not return to baseline after the treatment is implemented, a good alternative is to use the
   a. Changing-criterion design
   b. Interaction design
   c. Alternating treatments design
   d. Multiple-baseline design
   e. ABAB design

3. Which of the single-case designs would you use if you wanted to test the combined effect of two treatment conditions?
   a. ABA design
   b. Interaction design
   c. Multiple-baseline design
   d. Changing-criterion design
   e. Alternating treatments design

4. If you used the experimental criterion for evaluating the effectiveness of a treatment effect you would
   a. Ensure that the baseline behavior was stable before administering the treatment condition
   b. Determine whether the participant could function effectively in society after the treatment
   c. Determine whether the behaviors seen during baseline and treatment overlap
   d. Determine whether the trend of the behaviors during baseline and treatment differed
   e. Use both c and d

5. Rival hypotheses are ruled out in the single-case designs by
   a. The repeated measurements during baseline and following treatment
   b. The withdrawal of treatment in the ABA design
   c. The administration of the treatment condition at different times to different participants in the multiple-baseline design
   d. All of the above are correct.

Challenge Exercises

1. Assume that you conducted a study using an ABA design in which you tested the effectiveness of turning off the television every time a ten-year-old boy sucked his thumb. Construct a graph depicting

   a. The effectiveness of the denial of watching TV on the reduction of thumb sucking
   b. A reduction in thumb sucking when the TV was turned off but an inability to verify that the reduction in thumb sucking was due *only* to the turning off the TV

2. Assume you wanted to test the effectiveness of a specific treatment of stuttering. You identified three children that stuttered and used the multiple-baseline design to demonstrate that the treatment worked. Construct a graph depicting

   a. The effectiveness of the treatment
   b. An interdependence of behaviors that would reduce your ability to conclude that the treatment was effective

3. Assume that you wanted to evaluate the effectiveness of a program designed to help people get over their claustrophobia. This program consisted of having them give you $50.00. Each day they were able to stay in a small enclosed room for an additional ten minutes you returned $10.00 until they were able to remain in there for a total of fifty minutes. The first day that they stayed in the room ten minutes they received $10.00. Then they had to stay in the room twenty minutes to receive another $10.00, and so forth, until they were able to remain for fifty minutes and get the last $10.00.

   a. Construct a graph depicting the effectiveness of this strategy.
   b. Specify the type of design used.

4. Assume a mother came to you with the following problem. Every time her child was around other kids he bit them severely. She did not know how to eliminate this problem and wanted your help. You suggest that a combination of reinforcement and punishment would probably work. Construct a single-case design that will test the effectiveness of the combined effects of reinforcement and punishment in eliminating this child's biting of other children.

13 Data Collection

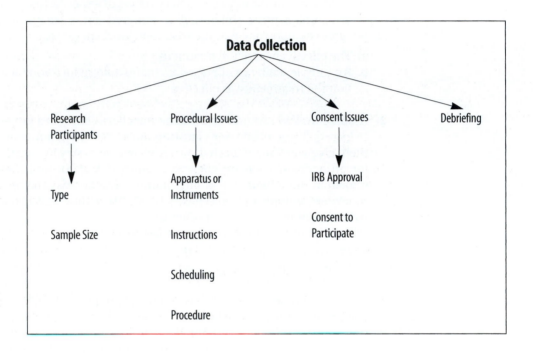

Data Collection

- Research Participants
  - Type
  - Sample Size
- Procedural Issues
  - Apparatus or Instruments
  - Instructions
  - Scheduling
  - Procedure
- Consent Issues
  - IRB Approval
  - Consent to Participate
- Debriefing

Plastic surgery has definitely come of age. What was once viewed as something sought after by individuals who may have psychiatric issues (Dittmann, 2005) is currently something that is in vogue. According to the American Society for Aesthetic Plastic Surgery, 11.9 million cosmetic procedures were conducted in 2003. Tori DeAngelis (2005) reports that "breast implants are becoming an increasingly popular high school graduation gift for teenage girls" (p. 41) and that some females are even having cosmetic surgery to improve the appearance of their genitals. This upsurge in cosmetic surgery has even spilled over into the entertainment industry with the appearance of reality TV shows. For example, Fox's reality show transformed a captain in the Army Reserve who complained of looking too masculine into a beauty queen following the completion of a number of surgical procedures including a brow lift, lower eye lift, midface lift, tummy tuck, breast lift, and liposuction, as well as several other procedures. Following these procedures she competed in a beauty pageant which she won (Dittmann, 2005).

While the number of cosmetic procedures that are being performed are increasing at an exponential rate, the outcome is not always positive. While it is true that people report feeling more satisfied with the body part on which they had surgery and research has consistently demonstrated that physically attractive people often receive preferential treatment, surgery could have adverse effects. For example, DeAngelis (2005) talks about a female who regretted the breast reduction she had as a teenager because now, as a young woman, she will never be able to nurse a baby and will never again have any sensation in her nipples. Cases such as this emphasize the need for research focusing on the psychosocial effects of plastic surgery. Studies need to be conducted to determine if plastic surgery makes patients feel better, how it affects those with whom the recipients interact, its effect on children and teenagers, and when changing a person's appearance qualifies as body dysmorphic disorder (Dittman, 2005).

In conducting such studies researchers naturally have to design their studies to answer their research question. This means that they have to identify relevant independent and dependent variables and control for the confounding effect of extraneous variables. After these basic design and control decisions have been made, there are still many more that must be made regarding the actual collection of the data that will be used to answer the research question. For example, if you were going to conduct a study on the effect of receiving plastic surgery you would have to decide on your source of research participants. Where will you get a sample of individuals who are going to receive plastic surgery? Once you have identified the source of the research participants, you must decide on whether you are going to use people who are planning any type of plastic surgery or only those individuals who are planning a specific type of plastic surgery such as breast enhancement. In addition, the age of the participants could range from teenagers to the elderly. Both males and females also elect to have plastic surgery. Will you include individuals of any age or will you limit your sample to a specific group such as teenagers? Will you limit your sample to female teenagers or will you also include male teenagers? These are just some of the decisions that you will have to make prior to beginning data collection.

Chapter Preview

The vignette at the beginning of this chapter points out that many decisions have to be made after the basic design of the experiment has been specified. The researcher has to determine what types of participants are to be used in the study, from where they are to be obtained, and how many should be used. The researcher must decide if human participants are to be used and, if they are, what instructions should be given. The design of any experiment provides only the framework of the study. Once established, this outline must be filled in and implemented. In this chapter, I discuss the issues that must be addressed to actually conduct the study. I address these issues in a general way because each study has its own unique characteristics; however, the discussion should provide the information you will need when conducting your own study.

Introduction

The first time you have to make all the decisions that are required to conduct a study you may feel somewhat intimidated and tentative. However, the only way to overcome this feeling and approach the task with confidence is to actually make the decisions and then follow through with the actual conduct of the experiment. Each section in this chapter gives you some guidelines that can help in making the decisions that are required to conduct the experiment according to the design selected.

Research Participants

Psychologists investigate the behavior of organisms, and there are a wealth of organisms that can potentially serve as research participants. What determines which organism will be used in a given study? In some cases, the question asked dictates the type of organism used. If, for example, a study is to investigate imprinting ability, then one must select a species, such as ducks, that demonstrates this ability. In most studies, however, the primary determining factor is precedent: Most investigators use research participants that have been used in previous studies. As Sidowski and Lockard (1966, pp. 7–8) state:

Most of the common laboratory animals are mammals; man, several species of monkey, numerous rodents, a few carnivores, and one cetacean, the porpoise. Other than mammals, teleost fishes and one species of bird, the pigeon, have mainly represented the other classes of chordates; amphibians and reptiles have been rare. The 21 phyla below the chordates have been underrepresented. . . .[1]

Other than humans, precedent has established the albino variant of the brown rat as the standard laboratory research animal. The concentrated use of the albino rat in infrahuman research has not gone without criticism. Beach (1950) and Lockard (1968) have eloquently criticized the fact that psychologists have focused too much attention on the use of this particular animal. As Lockard has argued, rather than using precedent as the primary guide for selecting a particular organism as a participant, one should look at the research problem and select the type of organism that is best for its study.

Obtaining Animals (Rats)

Once a decision has been made regarding the type of organism to be used, the next question is where to get the participants. Researchers who use rats typically select from one of three strains: the Long-Evans hooded, the Sprague-Dawley albino, and the Wistar albino. The researcher must decide on the strain, sex, age, and supplier of the albino rats because each of these variables can influence the results of the study.

Once the albino rats have been selected, ordered, and received, they must be maintained in the animal laboratory. The Animal Welfare Act, most recently amended in 1985, regulates the care, handling, treatment, and transportation of most animals used in research. The National Academy of Sciences Institute of Laboratory Animal Research (ILAR) developed a *Guide for the Care and Use of Laboratory Animals* (1996). The purpose of this guide was to assist scientific institutions in using and caring for laboratory animals in professionally appropriate ways. The recommendations in this publication are the ones suggested by National Institutes of Health policy. They are also the standards used by the American Association for the Accreditation of Laboratory Animal Care (AAALAC) for its accreditation of institutions. Therefore, the guidelines suggested in this manual are the ones that all researchers should adhere to when caring for and using laboratory animals.

Obtaining Human Participants

Researchers selecting humans as their research participants experience varying degrees of ease in finding participants. In most university settings, the psychology department has a participant pool consisting of introductory psychology students. These students are motivated to participate in a research study because they are frequently offered this activity as an alternative to some other requirement, such as

---

[1]From *Experimental Methods and Instrumentation in Psychology* by J. B. Sidowski and R. B. Lockard. Copyright © 1966 by McGraw-Hill, Inc. Used with permission of McGraw-Hill Book Co.

writing a term paper. Participant pools provide a readily available supply of participants for the researcher. Another source of human participants that is being used with increasing frequency is the Internet. While the participant pool that exists within psychology departments is a convenient sample, there is a continuous concern that the findings obtained from these participants are not generalizable to a non-college student population. Just consider the fact that college students are bright individuals, all of whom have graduated from high school but not from college. This represents a rather unique segment of the population. The Internet provides access to a more heterogeneous sample. It is capable of reaching individuals from other cultures and individuals who may be inaccessible due to time and cost constraints, such as disabled individuals. If you wanted to conduct a study investigating some aspect of unique populations such as identical twins you could recruit such individuals via the World Wide Web or Internet from online groups such as Mothers of Twins Clubs. Such online groups exist for many special populations. For example, a student of mine and I are designing a study investigating the motives for and psychosocial consequences of having gastric bypass surgery for weight loss. We are planning to make use of online support groups to access individuals who have had such surgery. Without the availability of the Internet and such online groups we would have to contact physicians who conduct such surgery and seek their cooperation and assistance in identifying such individuals. Additionally, our participant sample would be limited to individuals in the area who volunteered to participate in the study. With the Internet we have immediate access to a larger sample of individuals not confined to our geographic location.

While the Internet and the departmental participant pool can provide access to many individuals, there are other types of studies in which neither of these are appropriate. For some studies the necessary participant pool is one other than a college population and cannot be solicited via the Internet. For example, a child psychologist who wishes to study kindergarten children usually will try to solicit the cooperation of a local kindergarten. Similarly, to investigate incarcerated criminals, one must seek the cooperation of prison officials as well as the criminals.

When one has to draw research participants from sources other than a departmental participant pool, a new set of problems arises. Assume that a researcher is going to conduct a study using kindergarten children. The first task is to find a kindergarten that will allow her or him to collect the data needed for the study. In soliciting the cooperation of the individual in charge, the researcher must be as tactful and diplomatic as possible because many people are not receptive to psychological research. If the person in charge agrees to allow the researcher to collect the data, the next task is to obtain the parents' permission to allow their children to participate. This frequently involves having parents sign permission slips that explain the nature of the research and the tasks required of their children. Where an agency is involved, such as an institution for mentally disabled persons, one might be required to submit a research proposal for the agency's research committee to review.

Internet studies offer different challenges in terms of contacting and obtaining research participants. For example, if your strategy is to contact individuals and ask them to participate in your study, you must identify a mechanism for contacting these individuals. If the research participants belong to an organization or association, you could contact the organization or association and ask for a list of e-mail addresses of their members. You could also post a request to a selected number of e-mail lists, Usenet groups, or open discussion groups. Another mechanism is to purchase a list of e-mail users from Net-based white page services. The address of one such Internet address finder is www.iaf.net.

Alternatively, if your strategy is to post a research study on the Internet and have participants log on to the Web site and complete the study, you could post the study on one of several Web sites that specialize in advertising such opportunities. One of these sites is hosted by the Social Psychology Network, www.socialpsychology.org/expts.htm, and another is hosted by the American Psychological Society, http://psych.hanover.edu/research/exponnet.html. There are also commercial services, such as Survey Sampling, www.surveysampling.com, that will identify and select specific samples of individuals for your study.

After identifying the participant population, the researcher must select individual participants from that group. Ideally, this should be done randomly. In a study investigating kindergarten children, a sample should be randomly selected from the population of kindergarten children. However, this is often impractical—not only in terms of cost and time but also in terms of the availability of the participants. Not all kindergartens or parents will allow their children to participate in a psychological study. Therefore, human participants are generally selected on the basis of convenience and availability. The kindergarten children used in a study will probably be those who live closest to the university and who cooperate with the investigator.

Because of this restriction in participant selection, the researcher may have a built-in bias in the data. For example, the children whose parents allow them to participate may perform differently than would children whose parents restrict their participation. The participants who volunteer to participate in an Internet study may perform differently than those who do not. Rosenthal and Rosnow (1975) have summarized research exposing the differences in the responses of volunteer and nonvolunteer research participants. If random selection is not possible, the next best solution is to assign participants randomly to treatment conditions. In this way, the investigator is at least assured that no systematic bias exists among the various groups of available participants. Because of the inability to select participants randomly, the investigator *must* report the nature of participant selection and assignment, in addition to the characteristics of the participants, to enable other investigators to replicate the experiment and assess the compatibility of the results. For example, in a study on depression, the depressed individuals who were used as research participants had to meet a variety of inclusion and exclusion criteria after they had volunteered to participate in the study. The inclusion criteria included meeting the research diagnostic criteria for a current episode of a Major Depressive Disorder and having a score of at least 14 on the Hamilton Rating Scale for depression. Exclusion criteria included the presence of other psychiatric disorders such as panic disorders, alcoholism, or drug use. Consequently, the participants for this study were not selected randomly but were chosen on the basis of whether they volunteered and whether they met certain criteria.

Gender Bias

Before leaving this section on participant selection I want to alert you briefly to one additional source of bias. This is the tendency of most studies to make use of male participants. Most animal studies are conducted on male rats (Keller, 1984). The most reasonable explanation for this practice is that female rats have a four-day estrus cycle that complicates experiments, but Keller (1984) does not believe that this explanation is justification for the preponderant use of male rats. A similar situation seems to exist with regard to human research. Males seem to be overrepresented in psychological research (Unger & Crawford, 1992). In some entire areas of study, such as achievement motivation, findings are based totally on males (McClelland, 1953). This apparent bias with regard to choice of participants does not lead to inaccurate information. Rather, it leads to a psychology of predominately male behavior rather than human behavior. To the extent that females respond differently than males, data obtained only from males is an inaccurate representation of the behavior of females. This is a problem of generalization.

STUDY QUESTION 13.1

- **What factors frequently determine the selection of the research participant used in a study, and which is the most important factor that should be used?**
- **What problems may exist in using research participants who are not attending college?**

Sample Size

After you have decided which type of organisms will be used in the research study and have obtained access to a sample of such participants, you must determine how many participants are needed to test the hypothesis adequately. This decision must be based on issues such as the design of the study and the variability of the data. The relationship between the design of the study and sample size can be seen clearly by contrasting a single-case and a multiparticipant design. Obviously, a single-case design requires a sample size of one, so sample size is not an issue. In multiparticipant designs, however, the sample size is important because the number of participants used can theoretically vary from two to infinity. We usually want more than two participants, but it is impractical and unnecessary to use too many participants. Unfortunately, few guidelines exist for deciding how large the sample size must be. The primary guide used by most researchers is precedent, which may be just as inappropriate in sample size selection as in research participant selection (Beach, 1950; Lockard, 1968). The issue surrounding sample size in multiparticipant designs really boils down to the number of participants needed in order to detect an effect caused by the independent variable, if such an effect really exists. As the number of participants within a study increases, the ability of our statistical tests to detect a difference increases; that is, the power of the statistical test increases. Power, therefore, is an important concept in determining sample size.

Power

Power
The probability of rejecting a false-null hypothesis

Power is defined as the probability of rejecting a false-null hypothesis. Any time we reject a false-null hypothesis we are correctly saying that the treatment condition produced an effect. This is the type of decision we want to make. Because power increases as the number of participants increases, some investigators may state that the larger the sample size, the better the study. As the sample size increases, however, the cost in terms of both time and money also increases. From an economic standpoint we would like a relatively small sample. Researchers must balance the competing desires of detecting an effect and reducing cost. They must select a sample size that is within their cost constraints, but that still provides the ability to detect an effect produced by the independent variable. A power analysis seems to be the best method for resolving these competing desires and determining the appropriate sample size to use for a study.

Effect size
The correlation between the independent and dependent variables

The power of a statistical test is determined by the probability level, the sample size, and the effect size (**effect size** is the magnitude of the relation between the independent and dependent variable expressed by the correlation between these two variables) used in a study. These three variables are related so that, for a given level of power, when any two of them are known, the third is determined. Therefore, for a given power level, if you know the effect size of the study you are contemplating and the alpha level that you will use, you can identify the sample size needed. Table 13.1 summarizes this relationship when using an alpha level equal to 0.05. For example, if you wanted power to equal 0.8, the level recommended by Cohen (1988), you

TABLE 13.1
Total Sample Size Needed to Detect Effects at Alpha = 0.05, Two-Tailed

Power	Effect Size Correlation								
	0.10	0.20	0.30	0.40	0.50	0.60	0.70	0.80	0.90
0.25	167	42	20	12	8	6	5	4	3
0.50	385	96	42	24	15	10	7	6	4
0.60	490	122	53	29	18	12	9	6	5
0.67	570	142	63	34	21	14	10	7	5
0.70	616	153	67	37	23	15	10	7	5
0.75	692	172	75	41	25	17	11	8	6
0.80	783	194	85	46	28	18	12	9	6
0.85	895	221	97	52	32	21	14	10	6
0.90	1047	259	113	62	37	24	16	11	7
0.95	1294	319	139	75	46	30	19	13	8
0.99	1828	450	195	105	64	40	27	18	11

Source: From *Statistical Power Analysis for the Behavioral Sciences,* 2nd ed., by J. Cohen. Copyright © 1988, Lawrence Erlbaum Associates, Inc. Used by permission.

would need 194 research participants to reject the null hypothesis at the 0.05 alpha level if the anticipated effect size of your study was 0.20. However, if the anticipated effect size of your study was 0.60, you would need only eighteen research participants to reject the null hypothesis at the 0.05 alpha level.

In using information such as that in Table 13.1, it is necessary to know the alpha level, the anticipated effect size, and the desired power. Identification of the alpha level is easy because the conventional and recommended alpha level used is 0.05. In addition, if you follow the recommendation of Cohen (1988), you will use a power level of 0.8. That leaves identification of the anticipated effect size. The identification of the anticipated effect size can be based on a review of the literature. A literature review should uncover studies that have investigated independent and dependent variables similar to those you are investigating. The effect size found in these studies will give some idea of the magnitude of the effect size you can expect in your study. Therefore, the effect size found in other similar studies would represent the effect size you would anticipate in your study. The other way of identifying an anticipated effect size is to compute an effect size on data collected from a small number of research participants and then use this effect size to determine the sample size to be used and complete the study using this sample size.

STUDY QUESTION 13.2 | **Explain how you would determine the sample size to use in a multiparticipant design.**

Apparatus and/or Instruments

In addition to securing research participants, the investigator must identify the manner in which the independent variable will be presented and the way in which the dependent variable will be measured. In some studies the presentation and manipulation of the independent variable requires the active participation of the investigator, and the measurement of the dependent variable involves the administration of a variety of psychological assessment instruments. For example, Nezu (1986) investigated the effectiveness of two different types of therapy in treating depression. These treatment modalities required active intervention on the part of the experimenter, which meant that the investigator was actively participating in the manipulation of the independent variable. To assess the effectiveness of the various treatment modalities, Nezu administered several different depression inventories. Consequently, psychological assessment instruments were used as dependent variable measures. In other studies, a specific type of apparatus must be used to arrive at a precise presentation of the independent variable and to record the dependent variable. For example, assume that you were conducting a study in which the independent variable involved presenting words on a screen for different periods of time. You could try to control manually the length of time during which the words were presented, but because it is virtually impossible for a human to consistently present words for a very specific duration of time, a tachistoscope is typically used. Similarly, if the dependent variable is the recorded heart rate, we could use a stethoscope and count the number of times per minute a participant's heart beats. It is, however, much more accurate and far simpler to use an electronic means for measuring this kind of dependent variable. The use of such automatic recording devices also reduces the likelihood of making a recording error as a function of experimenter expectancies or some type of observer bias.

Microcomputers are also used frequently in experimentation both for the presentation of stimulus material and for the recording of dependent variable responses. The use of microcomputers in the laboratory has given the experimenter an extremely flexible tool. The microcomputer can be programmed to present as many different independent variables and record as many different types of responses as creativity will allow. In addition, the researcher is not tied to one specific computer. Rather, the role of the computer in stimulus presentation and recording of responses is preserved in the computer program, and this program is typically saved on a CD or hard drive, which enables the researcher to reconfigure any compatible computer at a moment's notice. Finally, the computer has enabled researchers to investigate areas previously inaccessible to behavioral scientists.

In addition to the use of microcomputers, advances in technology and interdisciplinary research have enabled psychologists to conduct research that would have been impossible several decades ago. For example, psychologists have been measuring brain waves for more than fifty years. However, it is only recently that we have used the measurement of brain waves, or the electroencephalograph (EEG) to study the way brain systems respond to various stimulus conditions such as written words. This research has progressed to the point where recordings are taken from a configuration of eighty or more electrodes placed on the scalp of a research participant's head (see Figure 13.1). This electrical activity of the brain is then transformed into a series of

FIGURE 13.1
Illustration of subject wearing the geodesic sensor net of 64 electrodes.

(From IMAGES OF THE MIND by Michael I. Posner and Marcus E. Raichle, © 1994 by Scientific American Library. Reprinted by permission of Henry Holt and and Company, LLC.)

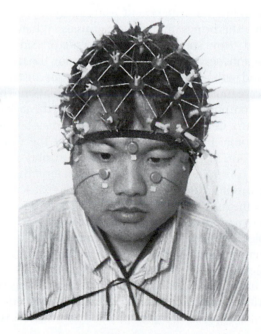

pictures, or maps of the brain, which depict the degree of activity of various areas of the brain. Areas of the brain that are very active are shown as bright spots and are interpreted as the areas that are stimulated by the independent variable that was presented, such as seeing a word presented on a computer screen. To further confirm that the area identified by the EEG produced *brain maps* that do represent the brain area stimulated by the independent variable, psychologists have teamed up with physicians. Through this collaboration, research participants have had positron emission tomography (PET) and/or magnetic resonance imaging (MRI) scans while participating in an experiment and responding to the presentation of an independent variable such as word presentation. The areas that are found to be active in PET scans are also the same areas found to be active with the EEG brain maps, at least in terms of response to stimuli such as word presentation. Psychologists, particularly cognitive neuropsychologists, in collaboration with physicians, are increasingly combining the technological tools of brain imaging from EEG recordings and PET and MRI scan to investigate the brain systems involved in a variety of behavioral activities and disorders.

Because the apparatus for a given study can serve a variety of purposes, the investigator must consider the particular study being conducted and determine the type of apparatus that is most appropriate. One journal, *Behavioral Research Methods, Instruments, and Computers,* is devoted specifically to apparatus and instrumentation. If you have difficulty identifying an instrument or a computer program that will perform a certain function, you might find it helpful to consult this journal and the previous research conducted in your area of investigation.

Instructions

The investigator who conducts an experiment using human participants must prepare a set of instructions. This brings up such questions as "What should be included in the instructions?" and "How should they be presented?" Sidowski and Lockard (1966) state that instructions serve the purposes of defining the task, directing attention, developing a set, and perhaps motivating the participant. Instructions are important, and considerable care must be exercised in their formulation. They must include a clear description of the purpose, or disguised purpose, and the task that the research participants are to perform. Certain types of instructions may be ineffectual in producing the desired outcome. Instructions requesting that the research participant "pay attention," "relax," or "ignore distractions" are probably ineffective because research participants are constrained by other factors that limit their ability to adhere to the commands. Instructions sometimes request that the participants perform several operations at the same time. If this is not possible, then they will choose one of the possible operations to perform, and the experimenter will not know which choice was made. For example, if the participants receive the instruction to work quickly and accurately, they may concentrate on accuracy at the expense of speed because both speed and accuracy cannot be achieved simultaneously. This means that the experimenter will not know which component of the instructions contributed most to the dependent variable measure. Similarly, vague instructions (for example, instructions telling the participants to imagine, guess, or visualize something) allow the participants to place their own interpretations on the task. It is best to avoid such instructions whenever possible.

As you can see, instructions should be clear, unambiguous, and specific, but at the same time they should not be too complex because of the possibility of a memory overload (Sutcliffe, 1972). Beginning researchers often think that directions should be extremely terse and succinct. Although this style is good for writing the research report, in writing instructions one runs the risk that the participants will not grasp important points. Instructions should be very simple, down to earth, and at times even redundant. This will provide added assurance that the participants understand all the instructions.

Scheduling of Research Participants

Scheduling research participants in the experiment involves the consideration not only of when the researcher has time available but also of the type of participants being used. With rats, for example, there is the problem of the lighting cycle. As Sidowski and Lockard (1966, p. 10) have noted:

> Rats and other nocturnal animals are most active in the dark phase of the lighting cycle and do most of their eating and drinking then. From the animal's point of view, the light portion of the day is for sleeping and inactivity but may be interrupted by an experimenter who requires him to run or bar-press for food. It is unfortunate that the amount of lighting and the timing of the cycle are usually arranged for the benefit of the caretaker and not the animals or the experimenter.[2]

This problem is most commonly handled by leaving the light on in the animal laboratory twenty-four hours a day. In this way, the animals will not form a schedule based on the light/dark phase of the lighting cycle, and thus the lighting cycle should not represent a source of confounding.

When one is scheduling human participants, there is a completely different set of issues to consider. First, the experiment must be scheduled at a time when the experimenter and the participants are all available. Some participants will undoubtedly fail to show up, so it is often advisable to allow for limited rescheduling. Some participants who do not show up at the designated time will not want to be rescheduled, which creates a problem with the randomization control technique. In such instances, the researcher may want to use replacement participants, in which case more participants must be selected than the experiment calls for and then replacement participants must be scheduled to substitute for those who drop out.

STUDY QUESTION 13.3

- **What purpose do the instructions to participants serve?**
- **What guidelines should be followed in preparing these instructions?**
- **What issues need to be considered in scheduling human and animal research participants?**

[2]From *Experimental Methods and Instrumentation in Psychology* by J. B. Sidowski and R. B. Lockard. Copyright © 1966 by McGraw-Hill, Inc. Used with permission of McGraw-Hill Book Co.

Procedure

After the scheduling of participants has been completed, you must specify the procedure to be used in data collection. The events to take place in the experiment must be arranged so that they flow smoothly. Awareness of what is to take place is not sufficient; the investigator must carefully think through the whole experiment and specify the sequence in which each activity is to take place, laying down the exact procedure to be followed during data collection. For animal research, this means not only specifying the conditions of the laboratory environment and how the animals are going to be handled in the laboratory, but also specifying how they are to be maintained in their maintenance quarters and how they are to be transferred to the laboratory. These are very important considerations because such variables can influence the animals' behavior in the laboratory. For an extended discussion of transient and environmental factors that can influence animals' behavior, see Sidowski and Lockard (1966, pp. 10–14).

With human participants, the researcher must specify what the participants are to do, how they are to be greeted, and the type of nonverbal behavior (looking at the participants, smiling, using a particular tone of voice in reading instructions, etc.) as well as verbal behavior in which the experimenter is to engage. Friedman (1967) has shown the wide variety of ways in which the same experimenter may react to different participants, both verbally and nonverbally. Every effort should be made to eliminate these variations. In a depression study funded by the National Institute of Mental Health, attempts were made to maximize the possibility that the therapists would treat the depressed patients in a consistent manner by having them go through an intensive training session before actually administering therapy to the depressed participants. The therapists were also checked periodically during the study to ensure that they maintained a consistent approach to conducting therapy.

If you are conducting an Internet based study, Birnbaum (2001) recommends including a number of "warmup" trials prior to beginning the study. These are pretest trials that are similar to those the participant would complete in the actual study. They are included to ensure that the research participant understands the instructions and the way they are to respond.

Pilot Study

Pilot study
An experiment that is conducted on a few participants prior to the actual collection of data

Once each of these phases has been specified, the investigator must then conduct a pilot study. A **pilot study** is a run-through of the experiment with a small number of participants. It is in fact a pretest of the experiment and should be conducted as conscientiously as if data were actually being collected. The pilot study can provide a great deal of information. If the instructions are not clear, this will show up either in the debriefing session or by virtue of the fact that the participants do not know what to do after the instructions have been read.

The pilot study can also indicate whether the independent variable manipulation produced the intended effect. Debriefing can help to determine if fear, surprise, or some other state was actually generated. If none of the pilot participants reports the particular emotion under study, then their help can be solicited in assessing why it was not generated, after which changes can be made until the intended state is induced. In a similar manner, the sensitivity of the dependent variable can be checked. Pretesting may suggest that the dependent variable is too crude to reflect the effect of the manipulation and that a change in a certain direction would make it more appropriate.

The pilot study also gives the researcher experience with the procedure. The first time the experimenter runs a research participant, he or she is not yet wholly familiar with the sequence and therefore probably does not make a smooth transition from one part of the study to another. With practice, one develops a fluency in carrying out these steps, which is necessary if constancy is to be maintained in the study. Also, when running pilot participants, the experimenter tests the procedure. Too much time may be allowed for certain parts and not enough for others, the deception (if used) may be inadequate, and so on. If there are problems, the experimenter can identify them before any data are collected, and the procedure can be altered at this time.

If you are conducting an Internet-based study you should complete the online study tasks yourself as well as have a few pilot participants complete the study tasks. Completing the study yourself will allow you to understand how it feels to be a participant and having pilot participants complete the study will allow you to get feedback. Completing a pilot run of your online study will also give you information in terms of whether the study works properly in your browser and if the data is returned to you in a manner that is understandable and arranged in the desired way.

There are many subtle factors that can influence the experiment, and the pilot phase is the time to identify them. Pilot testing involves checking all parts of the experiment to determine if they are working appropriately. If a malfunction is isolated, it can be corrected without any damage to the experiment. If a malfunction is not spotted until after the data have been collected, it *may* have had an influence on the results of the study.

STUDY QUESTION 13.4

- **What procedural issues must be specified prior to actual data collection?**
- **What purpose is served by a pilot study?**

Institutional Approval

After you have designed your study and have decided on such aspects as the nature of the research participants, from where you will obtain the participants, and any instructions they will receive, you must obtain approval from one of two institutional committees before you can actually carry out the study. If you are conducting a study that uses animals as research participants, you must receive approval from the Institutional Animal Care and Use Committee (IACUC). If you are conducting a study that uses humans as research participants, you must receive approval from the Institutional Review Board (IRB). In either case, you must prepare a research proposal that details all aspects of the research design, including the type of participants you propose to use and the procedures that will be employed in conducting the study. An example of such a research proposal was presented in Exhibit 5.4 in Chapter 5. This detail is necessary because these two committees review the research proposal to determine if it is ethically acceptable.

The IACUC reviews studies to determine if animals are used in appropriate ways. Specifically, the IACUC reviews studies to determine such things as whether the procedures employed avoid or minimize pain and discomfort to the animals, whether sedatives or analgesics are used in situations requiring more than momentary or slight pain, whether activities involving surgery include appropriate pre- and postoperative care, and whether methods of euthanasia are in accordance with accepted procedures. If the study procedures conform to acceptable practices, the IACUC will approve the study and you can then proceed with data collection. However, if it does not approve the study, the committee will detail the questionable components and the investigator can revise the study in an attempt to overcome the objections. Of course, the investigator can also refuse to compromise and not conduct the study.

The IRB reviews studies involving human participants to determine if the procedures used are appropriate. The primary concern of the IRB is the welfare of human participants. Specifically, the IRB will review proposals to ensure that participants provide informed consent for participation in the study and that the procedures used in the study do not harm the participants. This committee has particularly difficult decisions to make when a procedure involves the potential for harm. Some procedures, such as administering an experimental drug, have the potential for harming research participants. In such instances the IRB must seriously consider the potential benefits that may accrue from the study relative to the risks to the participants. Thus the IRB frequently faces the ethical questions discussed briefly in Chapter 5. Sometimes the board's decision is that the risks to the human participants are too great to permit the study; in other instances the decision is that the potential benefits are so great that the risks to the human participants are deemed to be acceptable. Unfortunately, the ultimate decision seems to be partially dependent on the composition of the IRB—Kimmel (1991) has revealed that males and research-oriented individuals who worked in basic areas were more likely to approve research proposals than were women and individuals who worked in service-oriented contexts and were employed in applied areas.

Although there may be differences among IRB members with regard to the way ethical questions are resolved, the board's decision is final and the investigator must abide by it. If the IRB refuses to approve the study, the investigator must either redesign the study to overcome the objections of the IRB, supply additional information that will possibly overcome the objections of the IRB, or not conduct the study.

Receiving approval from the IRB or the IACUC is one of the hurdles that investigators must overcome in order to conduct their proposed studies. Conducting research without such approval can cause investigators and their institutions to be severely reprimanded and jeopardize the possibility of receiving Public Health Service funding for future research projects.

Data Collection

Once you have laid out the procedure, obtained institutional approval, tested the various phases of the experimental procedure with the pilot study, and eliminated the bugs, you are ready to use research participants to collect data. The primary rule to follow in this phase of the experiment is to adhere as closely as possible to the procedure that has been laid out. A great deal of work has gone into developing this procedure, and if it is not followed exactly you run the risk of introducing contaminates into the experiment. If this should happen, you will not have the well-controlled study you worked so hard to develop, and you may not attain an answer to your research question.

Consent to Participate

When the research participants arrive at the experimental site, the first task of the experimenter is to obtain their consent to participate in the study—unless, of course, you have received a waiver of the requirement to obtain consent. Most studies require that you obtain the research participant's informed consent to participate in the study. However, as stated in Chapter 5, there are a number of limited circumstances, listed in Table 13.2, in which the IRB will waive this requirement. Remember that it is the IRB that makes the determination as to whether consent to participate can be waived in any study. Therefore, if you think that it would be appropriate to waive consent, you should request such a waiver from the IRB.

If you do not receive a waiver of the requirement to obtain informed consent from research participants, you must inform the research participants of all aspects of the study that may influence their decision to participate. This information, included in the consent to participate form, is typically provided in written form. Ideally, a consent statement should be written in simple, first-person, layperson's language. If a potential participant does not read or speak the language in which the form is written, the terms must be explained in detail. If the research participant is a minor over the age of seven, he or she must give assent. When minors are the research participants, a separate form written to their level of understanding must be provided.

TABLE 13.2

Situations That May Allow the IRB to Waive the Informed Consent Requirement

1. When the identity of the research participant will be completely anonymous and the study involves minimal risk

2. When it is not feasible to obtain informed consent due to the cultural norms of the population being studied and when the study involves minimal risk

3. When signing the consent to participate form would subject the participant to possible legal, social, or economic risk, e.g., revealing the status of an undercover drug enforcement investigator

The consent to participate statement should be prepared so that it includes the following elements.

1. What the study is about, where it will be conducted, the duration of the study, and when the research participant will be expected to participate should be specified.

2. The statement should list what procedures will be followed and whether any of them are experimental. In the description of the procedures, the attendant discomforts and risks should be spelled out.

3. Any benefits to be derived from participation in the study and any alternative procedures that may be beneficial to the participant should be identified.

4. If the research participant will receive any monetary compensation, this should be detailed, including the schedule of payments and the effect (if any) on the payment schedule in the event the participant withdraws from the study. If course credit is to be given, the statement should provide an explanation of how much credit will be received and whether the credit will still be given if the research participant withdraws from the study.

5. If the study involves responding to a questionnaire or survey, participants should be informed that they can refuse to answer, without penalty, any questions that make them uncomfortable.

6. Studies that investigate sensitive topics such as depression, substance abuse, or child abuse should provide information on where assistance for these problems can be obtained, such as from counselors, treatment centers, and hospitals.

7. The participants must be told that they can withdraw from the study at any time without penalty.

8. The participants must be informed as to how the records and data obtained will be kept confidential.

As you can see, the consent to participate statement is quite involved and attempts to provide research participants with complete information about the study so that they can make an intelligent and informed choice as to whether they want to participate. Exhibit 5.4 in Chapter 5 gives an illustration of a consent to participate form prepared for a study investigating beliefs about success, failure, and self-esteem in cognitive tasks. Only after consent has been obtained can you proceed to collect the data necessary for answering the research question.

STUDY QUESTION 13.5

- **What purpose is served by the IACUC and IRB, and what is the primary concern of these committees?**
- **What is the purpose of the consent form, and what information is included in this form?**

Debriefing, or Postexperimental Interview

Once the data have been collected, there is the tendency to think that the job has been completed and the only remaining requirement (other than data analysis) is to thank the participants for their participation and send them on their way. However, the experiment does not—or should not—end with the completion of data collection. In most studies, following data collection there should be a debriefing or **postexperimental interview** with the participants that allows them to comment freely on any part of the experiment. This interview is very important for several reasons. In general, the interview can provide information regarding the participants' thinking or strategies used during the experiment, which can help explain their behavior. Orne (1962) used this interview to assess why participants persisted at a boring, repetitive task for hours. Martin, in the course of conducting learning studies with extremely bright participants, found that these participants could learn a list of nonsense syllables in one trial (C. J. Martin, 1975, personal communication). Upon seeing such a performance, he essentially asked them, "How did you do that?" They relayed a specific strategy for accomplishing this task, which led to another study (Martin, Boersma, and Cox, 1965) investigating strategies of learning.

Postexperimental interview
An interview with the participant following completion of the experiment during which all aspects of the experiment are explained and the participant is allowed to comment on the study

Debriefing Functions

Tesch (1977) has identified three specific functions of debriefing. First, debriefings have an ethical function. In many studies, research participants are deceived about the true purpose of an experiment. Ethics dictate that we must undo such deceptions, and the debriefing session is the place to accomplish this. Other experiments generate some negative affect in the participants or in some other way create physical or emotional stress. (For example, electric shock creates physical pain and failure at a task can create problems with self-esteem.) The researcher must attempt to return the participants to their preexperimental state by eliminating any stress that the experiment has generated. Second, debriefings have an educational function. The typical rationale used to justify requiring the participation of introductory psychology students in experiments is that they learn something about psychology and about psychological research. The third function of debriefing is methodological. Debriefings are frequently used to provide evidence regarding the effectiveness of the independent variable manipulation or of the deception. They are also used to probe the extent and accuracy of participants' suspicions and to give the experimenter an opportunity to convince the participants not to reveal the experiment to others.

Sieber (1983) has added a fourth function. She states that participants should, from their participation in the study, derive a sense of satisfaction from the knowledge that they have contributed to science and to society. This perceived satisfaction should come from the debriefing procedure.

How to Debrief

Given these functions of debriefing, how do we proceed? Two approaches have been used. Some investigators use a questionnaire approach, in which research participants are handed a postexperimental survey form to complete. Others use a face-to-face interview, which seems to be the best approach because it is not as restrictive as the questionnaire.

If you want to probe for any suspicions that the participants may have had about the experiment, this is the first order of business. Aronson and Carlsmith (1968) believe that the researcher should begin by asking the participants if they have any questions. If so, the questions should be answered as completely and truthfully as possible. If not, the experimenter should ask the participants if all phases of the experiment—both the procedure and the purpose—were clear. Next, depending on the study being conducted, it may be appropriate to ask a participant to "comment on how the experiment struck him, why he responded as he did, how he felt at the time, etc. Then he should be asked specifically whether there was any aspect of the procedure that he found odd, confusing, or disturbing" (p. 71).[3]

If the experiment contained a deception and the participants suspected that it did, they are almost certain to have revealed this fact by this time. If no suspicions have been revealed, the researcher can ask the participants if they thought there was more to the experiment than was immediately apparent. Such a question cues the participants that there must have been. Most participants will therefore say yes, so this should be followed with a question about what the participants thought was involved and how this may have affected their behavior. Such questioning will give the investigator additional insight into whether the participants had the experiment figured out and also will provide a perfect point for the experimenter to lead into an explanation of the purpose of the study. The experimenter could continue "the debriefing process by saying something like this: 'You are on the right track, we *were* interested in some problems that we didn't discuss with you in advance. One of our major concerns in this study is . . .'" (Aronson and Carlsmith, 1968, p. 71).[4] The debriefing should then be continued in the manner suggested by Mills (1976). If the study involved deception, the reasons that deception was necessary should be included. The purpose of the study should then be explained in detail, as well as the specific procedures for investigating the research question. This means explaining the independent and dependent variables and how they were manipulated and measured. As you can see, the debriefing requires explaining the entire experiment to the participants.

The last part of the debriefing session should be geared to convincing the participants not to discuss any components of the experiment with others, for obvious reasons. This can be accomplished by asking the participants not to describe the experiment to others until after the date of completion of the data collection, pointing out that communicating the results to others may invalidate the study. If the study were revealed prematurely, the experimenter would not know that the results were invalid and the participants would probably not tell (Altemeyer, 1971), so the experimenter would be reporting inaccurate data to the scientific community. Aronson (1966) has found that we can have reasonable confidence that the participants will not tell others; but Altemeyer (1971) has shown that if participants do find out, they will probably not tell the experimenter.

At this point you might wonder whether this debriefing procedure accomplishes the functions it is supposed to accomplish. The ethical function will be accomplished

---

[3]Reprinted by special permission from "Experimentation in Social Psychology" by E. Aronson and J. M. Carlsmith, in *The Handbook of Social Psychology,* 2nd edition, volume 2, edited by G. Lindzey and E. Aronson, 1968, p. 71. Reading, MA: Addison-Wesley.

[4]Reprinted by special permission from "Experimentation in Social Psychology" by E. Aronson and J. M. Carlsmith, in *The Handbook of Social Psychology,* 2nd edition, volume 2, edited by G. Lindzey and E. Aronson, 1968, p. 71. Reading, MA: Addison-Wesley.

quite well if these procedures are followed. The educational function is fulfilled less completely in debriefing. Most investigators seem to think, or rationalize, that the educational function is served if the participants participate in the experiment and are told of its purpose and procedures during debriefing. Tesch (1977) believes that this function would be better served if the researcher also required the participant to write a laboratory experience report, which would relate the experimental experience to course material. However, data indicate that participants perceive psychological experiments to be most deficient in educational value, although they view debriefing in general to be quite effective (Smith and Richardson, 1983). It is possible that our psychological experiments are not as educational as we hoped and that even a good debriefing procedure cannot adequately enhance their educational value. The methodological function seems to be served quite well because the validity of the experiment is often dependent on it. The investigator sometimes does extensive pilot study work to ensure that, for example, the manipulation checks actually verify the manipulations.

It is also questionable as to whether all the functions of debriefing are fulfilled when conducting an online research study. The most common and direct way of providing debriefing is to post the debriefing at the Web site on which the study is located. This way you can tailor the debriefing to the study you are conducting. It is even possible to make the debriefing material available to those who decide to terminate the study prior to completion by having a "leave the study" link button, or a pop-up window that executes when a person leaves a study. While these techniques will present the debriefing material, online research makes it difficult to engage in the desensitizing component of debriefing because it is difficult to assess the participant's psychological state and determine if an individual has been stressed by the study. It is also difficult to determine if any stress that has been created by the study has been reduced through debriefing because it is difficult to receive feedback from the research participant.

STUDY QUESTION 13.6 | • **What function is served by the postexperimental interview?**
| • **How should you proceed in conducting this interview?**

Summary

Following completion of the study design, the investigator must make a number of additional decisions before beginning to collect data. The investigator must first decide on the type of organism to be used in the study. Although precedent has been the primary determining factor guiding the selection of a particular organism, the research problem should be the main determinant. The organism that is best for investigating the research problem should be used when possible.

Once the question of type of organism has been resolved, the researcher needs to determine where these organisms can be attained. Infrahumans, particularly rats, are available from a number of commercial sources. Most human research participants used in psychological experimentation come from departmental participant pools, which usually consist of introductory psychology students. If the study calls for participants other than those represented in the participant pools, the investigator must locate an available source and make the necessary arrangements. One source that is used with increasing frequency is the Internet.

In addition to identifying the source of research participants, the experimenter needs to determine how many participants should be used. A power analysis is used for determining sample size.

Instructions must also be prepared for studies using human research participants. The instructions should include a clear description of the purpose (or disguised purpose) of the task required of the participants.

Next, the investigator must specify the procedure to be used in data collection—the exact sequence in which all phases of the experiment are to be carried out, from the moment the investigator comes in contact with the research participants until that contact terminates. It is helpful to conduct a pilot study to iron out unforeseen difficulties. Once the procedure has been streamlined, it is necessary to obtain institutional approval before the study can be conducted. After approval is received, data collection can begin.

When the research participant arrives at the experimental site, the first task of the experimenter is to obtain the research participant's consent to participate in the study. This means that the participant must be informed of all aspects of the study that may affect his or her willingness to participate. Only after this information has been conveyed and the participant agrees to participate can the experimenter proceed with the study and collect the data that will answer the research question.

Immediately following data collection, the experimenter must conduct a postexperimental interview, or debriefing session, with the participants. During this interview, the experimenter attempts to detect any suspicions that the participants may have had. In addition, the experimenter explains to the participants the reasons for any deceptions that may have been used, as well as the entire experimental procedure and purpose.

Key Terms and Concepts

Power	Pilot study
Effect size	Postexperimental interview

Related Internet Site

http://opl.apa.org
This site offers a number of classic studies in psychology in which students can participate. After participating in an online experiment, they can analyze the data collected as well as see the results of the data collected.

Practice Test

The answers to these questions can be found in Appendix A.

1. The type of organism that should be used in research studies
   a. Is typically determined by precedent
   b. Should be determined by the research question
   c. Is the type of organism available to the researcher
   d. Should be the type used in prior studies
   e. Is either rats or college students

2. Sample size should be determined by a combination of which of the following factors?

 a. Effect size, alpha level, power
 b. Effect size, alpha level, significance level
 c. Significance level, alpha power, straight power
 d. Alpha level, power, beta level
 e. Beta level effect size, significance level

3. Which of the following journals will be helpful in identifying a specific piece of apparatus or computer program to assist in data collection?

 a. *Journal of Applied Psychology*
 b. *Psychological Methods*
 c. *Psychological Assessment*
 d. *Behavioral Research Methods, Instruments, and Computers*
 e. *Psychological Instrumentation and Computers*

4. If you have pretested your entire procedure on a few participants prior to actually collecting data you have

 a. Sampled your procedure
 b. Conducted a pilot study
 c. Conducted a postexperimental debriefing
 d. Tested the effectiveness of the independent variable manipulation
 e. Wasted participants that could have contributed to the study

5. What function does debriefing serve?

 a. Ethical function
 b. Educational function
 c. Methodological function
 d. Participant satisfaction from contributing to science
 e. All of the above are functions of debriefing.

Challenge Exercise

1. Employment agencies are in the business of finding employment for individuals. One of the difficulties these agencies have is identifying individuals with the necessary skills to keep a job after they are placed. Let's assume that you are aware of this difficulty and you have developed a four-week course designed to teach individuals the skills they need to retain a job. Your four-week course consists of training in dealing with a boss, dealing with other difficult employees, dressing for the job, and other skills such as just ensuring that the worker arrives on time for work. The basic design you want to use is a simple posttest-only randomized design with a treatment and control group. With this as your research problem and experimental design, answer the following questions.

 a. What research participants do you plan to use, and how do you plan to obtain these participants?

b. How many participants should you use? Identify how you would decide on the number of participants to use if you do not have sufficient information to identify the specific number.

c. What factors do you have to take into consideration in presenting the treatment condition and control conditions and how will you implement these factors? What outcome measures will you use to test the effectiveness of the treatment condition?

d. What type of approval is needed to enable you to conduct this study?

e. Prepare a short consent form for this study.

f. Prepare a short debriefing statement for this study.

14 Data Analysis

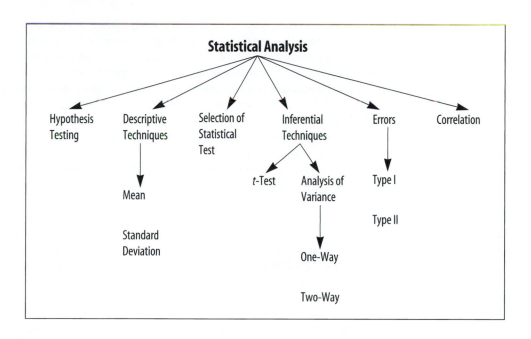

Lenard Hebert, a forty-year-old recovering drug addict, started using drugs during his tour as a Marine in Vietnam in 1967. This began a twenty-five-year history of doing whatever drug was most popular. When he returned home in the 1970s, he "did strictly reefer. A good militant did natural, herbal things. Then I went disco. I snorted cocaine for ten years. It was chic because it was so expensive." When crack appeared on the drug scene, Hebert switched from cocaine and turned his apartment into a crack den. This ultimately led to his downfall. Just before he arrived at the Phoenix House, a residential drug treatment center, he had been sleeping in abandoned cars and shelters for the homeless (Hurley, 1989).

Hebert's story resembles that of thousands of other Americans who, since the early 1960s, have been engaged in a tremendous social experiment with drugs. During the early 1960s, LSD was the most abused drug. Emphasis shifted to marijuana in the mid-1960s, to heroin from 1969 to 1971, and to cocaine in the late 1970s and the 1980s. In the early 1990s a smokable, fast-acting form of methamphetamine, known as ice, became popular. In the latter part of the decade of the '90s, ketamine and gamma-hydroxybutyrate (GHB) became the hot new party drugs. It seems as though the youth of America are constantly experimenting with an ever-increasing range of drugs, many of which can be lethal.

Given the devastating effects of drugs on society, there has been an ongoing attempt to find effective treatments as well as to identify factors that predispose individuals to drug abuse. Although it might seem that everyone would be equally predisposed to drug abuse, there is actually a lot of variability. If the predisposing factors could be identified, extra efforts could be directed toward helping susceptible individuals to overcome their tendency to abuse drugs. The best way to combat drug abuse is through effective prevention.

One researcher who has focused attention on prevention is Susan Schenk. Schenk's efforts in this area began rather serendipitously while she was a graduate student at Concordia University in Montreal. She had designed a drug study that required the use of about forty rats. Because she did not have the funds to purchase the rats, she did what all resourceful graduate students do: She scrounged. Another graduate student had just completed a study on the effects of social interactions on rats from the time of weaning to about nine weeks of age. Because he no longer had any use for the rats, he let Schenk use them in her drug study. Much to her surprise, these rats did not demonstrate the expected drug effect. Schenk speculated that this was because the rats had been provided with an enriched social environment (burrows, tubes, extensive handling by the experimenter, access to other rats, etc.) rather than being housed alone in the typical sterile environment of a rectangular steel cage. She decided to conduct a study investigating the role of environmental factors in drug abuse.

To investigate the role of environment in drug abuse, Schenk, Lacelle, Gorman, and Amit (1987) housed rats either in isolation or four to a cage for a period of six weeks. They then inserted catheters into their jugular veins and trained the rats to press a lever that would give them an infusion of 1.0 mg/kg of cocaine. After the rats had learned to press the lever to get cocaine, both groups were observed on three different occasions to determine the number of times they pressed the lever during a three-hour test period. On one occasion, each lever press delivered a 1.0 mg/kg infusion of cocaine; on another occasion, a 0.5 mg/kg dose; and on the third occasion, a 0.1 mg/kg dose.

After Schenk completed this study, she had data consisting of the number of times the rats in the two housing conditions made lever presses to obtain the various amounts of cocaine. She had to somehow use this data to get an answer to her research question of whether the type of environment in which the rats were reared influenced the extent to which they abused cocaine. The way in which she did this was to statistically analyze her data. The statistical analysis she conducted revealed that rats reared in isolation were more likely to abuse cocaine than were rats reared in an enriched environment.

Chapter Preview

The opening vignette to this chapter reveals that the use of statistical analysis is necessary to reach conclusions regarding the results of the experiment that we have conducted. After conducting any experiment we will have collected outcome data on the dependent variable; this outcome data will typically be a bunch of numbers. From this large group of numbers, we have to reach some conclusion regarding the original research question. Instead of conducting an experiment, we could also have conducted any number of nonexperimental quantitative studies such as those discussed in Chapter 2. When conducting a nonexperimental quantitative study we will have collected outcome data on the variables on which we are interested. This outcome data would be a bunch of numbers similar to that which we would have collected had we conducted an experimental study. This is where statistics comes in. Statistics, for research psychologists, are tools that assist in making decisions in the fact of uncertainty. When faced with all the numbers we collect on the outcome variable or variables in an experimental or nonexperimental quantitative study, we are typically uncertain as to how to interpret them without some way of summarizing them and extracting meaning from them. Statistics gives us the tools that allow us to extract meaning from these numbers. Although many students studying research methods have had a basic statistics course, they usually find it difficult to apply statistical principles to a research study. In this chapter I take a very applied approach, showing how to use statistics to make sense of collected data. I review a number of statistical tools that you probably covered in your basic statistics course and show you how these tools can be applied to the data collected from a research study to reach conclusions regarding the outcome of the study. From this discussion you should see not only why statistical analysis is an essential part of psychological research but also how statistics and research design go hand in hand and that statistical analysis must be considered when a study is designed. This discussion will focus first on an experimental type of study and then on a correlational type of study as these are the two types of studies that are most frequently investigated by psychologists.

Introduction

The question in Schenk's experimental cocaine study was whether environmental conditions predispose an organism to drug abuse. To answer this question, the researchers reared rats in either a sterile or a socially enriched environmental condition and then assessed the extent to which the rats self-administered three different dosages of cocaine. The amount of self-administration was measured by the number of times the rats pressed a lever that infused a measured amount of cocaine into their jugular veins.

Suppose that you hypothesized that rats would increase their abuse of cocaine as their access to it increased. To test this hypothesis, you trained two groups of rats to press a lever that would give them either 0.5 mg/kg (Group 1) or 1.0 mg/kg (Group 2) of cocaine. The hypothetical results of your experiment are displayed in Table 14.1.

TABLE 14.1

Number of Lever Presses Made by Rats Receiving One of Two Cocaine Dosages

Group 1 (0.5 mg/kg dose)	Group 2 (1.0 mg/kg dose)
35	25
25	19
29	22
27	21
24	20
27	21
26	22
25	25
27	29
29	21
26	22
20	20
$\Sigma X_1 = 320$	$\Sigma X_2 = 267$
$\Sigma X_1^2 = 8,672$	$\Sigma X_2^2 = 6,027$
$\Sigma \bar{X}_1 = 26.67$	$\bar{X}_2 = 22.25$
$N = 12$	$N = 12$

Once such data have been collected, they must be statistically analyzed to obtain an answer to the research question and to determine whether the stated hypothesis has been supported. Therefore, whenever you reach this stage in the research process, you are engaged in hypothesis testing.

Testing the Hypothesis

Hypothesis testing is a decision-making process. To conduct an experiment, you formulate a scientific hypothesis or make a prediction of the relationship among the variables being investigated. You then design a study and collect data to test the validity of the stated hypothesis. After the data have been collected, you must examine them to determine whether there is support for the scientific hypothesis. Recall from Chapter 4 that you must actually deal with two hypotheses: the scientific hypothesis and the null hypothesis. The scientific hypothesis is a statement of the predicted relationship among the variables being investigated, and the null hypothesis is a statement of no relationship among the variables being tested. Any time we test a hypothesis statistically, we test the null hypothesis because it is impossible to test the scientific hypothesis directly. Evidence for the existence of the scientific hypothesis is always obtained indirectly through a rejection of the null hypothesis: If you can reject the null hypothesis (that there is no relationship among the variables being investigated), then a relationship must exist among the variables.

As Figure 14.1 illustrates, a test of the null hypothesis actually involves determining whether you are dealing with one or two populations. If you do not reject the null hypothesis, you are stating that only one population of research participants exists. If you reject the null hypothesis, you are stating that two populations exist. The null hypothesis in the cocaine study conducted by Schenk et al. (1987) was that environmental conditions did *not* have any effect on the extent to which the rats abused drugs. As Figure 14.1(*a*) shows, a finding that the two groups of rats did not differ significantly in their tendency to abuse cocaine indicates that both groups came from a common population with a similar tendency to abuse drugs. In this case the null hypothesis would not be rejected, providing no support for the scientific hypothesis. As Figure 14.1(*b*) illustrates, however, a finding that the two groups of rats differed in their tendency to abuse drugs indicates that they came from two different populations. In this case the null hypothesis would be rejected, providing support for the scientific hypothesis.

Once you have collected data on your research participants, you must make a decision to reject or not reject the null hypothesis. Making such a decision requires an analysis of the data collected on the dependent variable. For the cocaine study, you would analyze the number of lever presses made by the two groups of rats because this was the response measure used to determine whether the two groups of rats had a differential tendency to abuse cocaine. One type of analysis might involve computing the mean number of lever presses made by the rats receiving the 0.5 mg/kg cocaine dosage and comparing that to the mean number of lever presses made by the rats receiving the 1.0 mg/kg dosage. Such an analysis would tell you which group of rats self-administered cocaine most frequently.

FIGURE 14.1
Hypothesis testing.

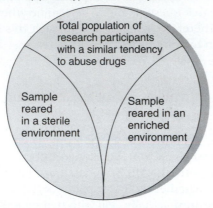

(a) Null hypothesis not rejected

Total population of research participants with a similar tendency to abuse drugs

Sample reared in a sterile environment

Sample reared in an enriched environment

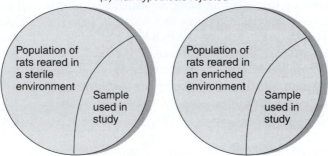

(b) Null hypothesis rejected

Population of rats reared in a sterile environment

Sample used in study

Population of rats reared in an enriched environment

Sample used in study

The Mean

Mean

The arithmetic average of a group of numbers

The **mean** is the arithmetic average of a group of numbers. It is computed by dividing the sum of all the scores by the number of scores in the group:

$$\text{Mean} = \frac{\text{sum of scores}}{\text{number of scores}} \quad \text{or} \quad \bar{X} = \frac{\Sigma X}{N}$$

where

$\bar{X}$ = mean
ΣX = sum of scores
N = number of scores

If we compute the mean number of lever presses for the two groups of rats based on the data in Table 14.1, we have

$$\bar{X}_1 = 26.67 \quad \text{and} \quad \bar{X}_2 = 22.25$$

where Group 1's mean is denoted by $\bar{X}_1$ and Group 2's mean is denoted by $\bar{X}_2$. This clearly shows that the group of rats receiving the 0.5 mg/kg dose pressed the lever more often (and thus self-administered cocaine more often) than did the rats receiving the 1.0 mg/kg dose. Such data seems to indicate that the concentration of the cocaine dose makes a difference, in which case the null hypothesis should be rejected. Remember, however, that the groups' mean scores reflect only the central tendencies of the two groups. We want to determine whether the experimental treatment conditions produced a *real* effect. In other words, we must determine whether the difference between the groups' mean scores is so large that it is unlikely to be due to chance. This is a difficult task because even a large group mean difference could occur by chance. No two groups of research participants are alike, so the rats in the two groups would be expected to respond somewhat differently even if they received the same dose of cocaine. To determine whether the difference between the group mean scores is due to chance or to the independent variable, we need some indication of the variability of the participants' scores in each group.

Standard Deviation

Standard deviation
A measure of the extent to which a group of scores vary about their mean

The two primary and interrelated measures of variability used in psychological research are *variance* and **standard deviation.** They both provide an index of the extent to which the scores in a group vary about their mean. However, variance is the average of the sum of the squared deviations of the scores about their mean, whereas standard deviation is the square root of the average of the sum of squared deviations of the scores about their mean. Consequently, standard deviation is the square root of variance. A small variance or standard deviation indicates that the scores cluster closely about the mean, whereas a large variance or standard deviation indicates that the scores deviate considerably from the mean.

The variance of a group of scores is computed most economically by using the following formula:

$$s^2 = \frac{\Sigma X^2 - \frac{(\Sigma X)^2}{N}}{N - 1}$$

where

s^2 = variance
X = individual scores
N = number of scores in the group

The standard deviation of a group of scores is computed most economically by using the following formula:

$$s = \sqrt{\frac{\Sigma X^2 - \frac{(\Sigma X)^2}{N}}{N - 1}}$$

where

> s = standard deviation
> X = individual scores
> N = number of scores in the group

The formulas for variance and standard deviation show clearly that standard deviation is the square root of variance. The discussion that follows focuses on standard deviation because standard deviation is the measure of variability that is most frequently reported. However, as you will see at a later point in this chapter, variance is the measure that is used in some more elaborate statistical tests.

Using the data presented in Table 14.1, we can compute the standard deviation of the number of lever presses made by the two groups of rats as follows:

$$s_1 = \sqrt{\frac{8{,}672 - \dfrac{(320)^2}{12}}{12 - 1}} = 3.55$$

$$s_2 = \sqrt{\frac{6{,}027 - \dfrac{(267)^2}{12}}{12 - 1}} = 2.80$$

The standard deviation for Group 1 is 3.55, and the standard deviation for Group 2 is 2.80. Thus more variability exists among the lever presses made by the rats receiving the 0.5 mg/kg dose. It is important to note that the standard deviation of the scores in the 0.5 mg/kg group, 3.55, approximates the difference between the means of the two groups, 4.42. The size of the standard deviation is important because it gives us some idea of whether the group mean differences are real (that is, due to manipulation of the independent variable) or are due to chance.

Figure 14.2 presents a graph of the distribution of lever presses made by rats receiving the two cocaine dosages. The two distributions overlap, suggesting that the mean difference between the two cocaine treatment conditions may be due to chance

FIGURE 14.2
Distribution of the number of lever presses made by two groups of rats.

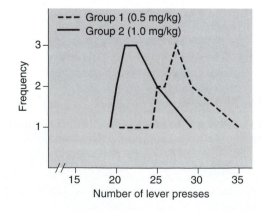

and that the participants may have come from one population with the same tendency to abuse cocaine. It is also possible, however, that the group mean difference represents a real difference due to the experimental treatment condition. The point is that we don't know just by looking at the data—we are still uncertain as to whether to reject the null hypothesis.

How can we assess whether the observed difference associated with the experimental treatment condition is real or just a chance difference due to variability in subject performance? The necessary information could be gained by repeating the experiment with different rats and seeing whether the same results occurred again. This would give evidence of the reliability of the obtained findings. The more often the study was repeated with similar results, the more faith we have that the experimental treatment conditions produced the results because, if the difference were due to chance, it should average out to zero over many replications of the experiment. Sometimes the rats receiving the 0.5 mg/kg dose would press the lever more often than would the rats receiving the 1.0 mg/kg dose, and sometimes the rats receiving the 1.0 mg/kg dose would press the lever more often than would the rats receiving the 0.5 mg/kg dose. The absence of a reliable finding would suggest that a given difference between the two groups of rats was the result of chance.

Although it is possible to determine whether an obtained difference between scores is real by repeating the study many times on different groups of rats, this is not a very economical approach. It is more economical to conduct the experiment on a sample of rats and then use some mechanism to infer from the data obtained whether the observed difference was due to chance or to a real difference—one that mirrored differences in the population. Fortunately there is a mechanism that allows us to make an inference to the population from data collected on a sample of research participants. This mechanism is referred to as inferential statistics.

Inferential statistics is a set of statistical tests that enable us, with some degree of error, to infer the characteristics of a population from a sample. This is accomplished by determining the probability of an event's happening by chance. Through inferential statistical analysis, we can estimate the amount of difference that could be expected between the group mean scores by chance and then compare this value with what was actually found. If the actual difference is much greater than what would be expected by chance, we say that the difference is a real one.

STUDY QUESTION 14.1

- **Discuss the decision-making process used in hypothesis testing.**
- **What role or contribution do the mean and standard deviation play in hypothesis testing?**

Selection of a Statistical Test

At this point in the research process, you must analyze your data statistically to determine whether the difference in the group mean scores is so large that it cannot reasonably be attributed to chance. You must decide which statistical test to use in

FIGURE 14.3
Decision tree for
selecting the appro-
priate statistical test.

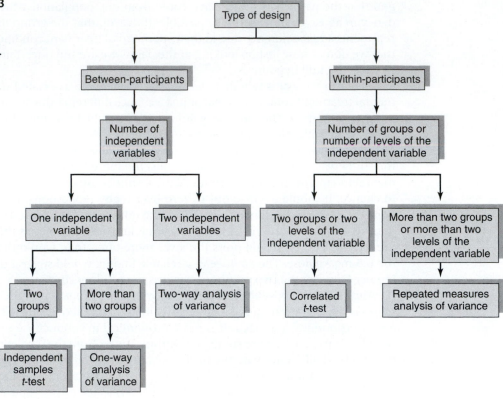

analyzing your data—a decision dictated by the design of your experiment. Figure 14.3 illustrates the intimate relationship between statistics and research design.
Specific statistical tests are best suited to the analysis of data collected using specific
types of designs. This is why you must consider the statistical analysis of your data
while you are designing the study. It is possible to design a study that is not amenable
to any type of statistical analysis or that is amenable only to a type of statistical analysis that does not provide an answer to the research question.

To provide some practical experience in selecting a statistical test, let us use Figure 14.3 to choose the appropriate statistical test for the two-group cocaine study. In
this study rats were administered one of two different cocaine doses, so the study had
a between-participants design. There was one independent variable, with two levels
consisting of the two different concentrations of cocaine. A different group of rats was
administered each cocaine dose, so there were two groups of subjects. Therefore,
according to Figure 14.3, the appropriate statistical test for analyzing the data is an
independent samples *t*-test.

Independent Samples *t*-Test

Independent samples *t*-test

A statistical test for analyzing data collected from a two-group between-participants design

The **independent samples *t*-test** should be familiar to those of you who have had a statistics course. It is a statistical test for analyzing the data obtained from two different groups of participants to determine whether the group mean difference score is so large that it could not reasonably be attributed to chance. The formula for the *t*-test is

$$t = \frac{\bar{X}_1 - \bar{X}_2}{\sqrt{\dfrac{\Sigma X_1^2 - \dfrac{(\Sigma X_1)^2}{N} + \Sigma X_2^2 - \dfrac{(\Sigma X_2)^2}{N}}{N_1 + N_2 - 2}\left(\dfrac{1}{N_1} + \dfrac{1}{N_1}\right)}}$$

Although it is not readily apparent, the *t* value obtained from this formula represents a ratio of the difference between the group mean scores to the average variability of the scores within the two groups:

$$t = \frac{\text{group mean difference}}{\text{average within-group variability}}$$

Therefore, the greater the *t* value, the greater the between-group mean difference compared with the average within-group variability and the greater the probability that the group differences are real and not due to chance. Recall that earlier we computed the mean number of lever presses for the two groups of rats and found that the difference between these mean scores was 4.42. Then we computed the standard deviation of each group's scores and found that the extent of their variation about the mean suggested that the difference between the group means might be due to chance and not to the treatment conditions. However, this assessment was completely impressionistic and not based on any rigorous quantitative assessment. The *t*-test makes a similar assessment in a precise quantitative manner by comparing the difference between the group means to the natural variability that exists between the scores of the individual rats.

If we analyze the lever-press data in Table 14.1 by means of the *t*-test, we obtain the following result.

$$t = \frac{26.67 - 22.25}{\sqrt{\dfrac{8{,}672 - \dfrac{(320)^2}{12} + 6{,}027 - \dfrac{(267)^2}{12}}{12 + 12 - 2}\left(\dfrac{1}{12} + \dfrac{1}{12}\right)}}$$

$$= \frac{4.42}{1.305}$$

$$= 3.39$$

The value of *t* is 3.39, which means that the between-group mean difference is 3.39 times greater than the average within-group variability. Now we must determine whether this difference is large enough for us to say that it is significant, leading to a rejection of the null hypothesis and therefore providing support for the scientific hypothesis.

Significance Level

Is there a guideline that determines how large a difference must be to be considered real? Only rarely can we be absolutely sure that the obtained difference between group means is not due to chance. Even very large differences could occur by chance, although the probability would be very low. Figure 14.4 illustrates the distribution of group mean differences that would be expected to occur by chance. Note that the mean of this distribution is equal to zero, which means that the average difference between such groups, if the null hypothesis is true, is zero. Note also that although the tails of the distribution approach the baseline, they never touch it. The fact that a very large difference *could* occur by chance means that, except in rare cases with a restricted and finite population, we can never be completely sure that a difference is real and not due to chance. We can, however, determine the probability that a given difference is the result of chance. Ninety-five percent of all chance mean difference scores will fall between the dashed lines in Figure 14.4; 99 percent of all chance mean difference scores will fall between the solid lines. If the difference we find between the group mean scores in an experiment is so large that it falls outside the dashed lines, the likelihood that it occurred by chance is only 5 in 100. Similarly, if the group difference obtained in an experiment is so large that it falls outside the solid lines, the likelihood that it occurred by chance is only 1 in 100.

How certain do we have to be before we can say that the obtained difference between groups is real? The most common practice is to state a significance level that must be reached. A **significance level** is a statement of the probability that an observed difference is a chance difference. The most commonly used significance levels are 0.05 and 0.01. If, before calculating your statistical tests, you decide that the

Significance level
The probability that the difference between the mean scores of the experimental and control groups is due to chance

FIGURE 14.4
Sample distribution of mean difference scores due to chance.

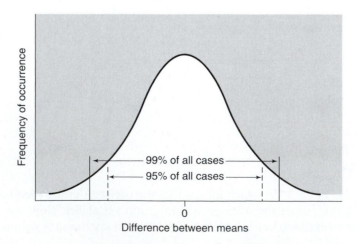

EXHIBIT 14.1

Null Hypothesis Significance Testing Controversy

Null hypothesis significance testing, in general, involves constructing a null hypothesis stating that no difference exists between the treatment conditions or that no association exists between the variables being investigated. A statistical test, such as a *t*-test, is then computed, from which a *p* value is calculated. The *p* value defines the probability of getting the obtained difference in the treatment conditions, given that the null hypothesis is true. When the *p* value is less than some specified criterion, almost always 0.05, the null hypothesis is rejected and the experimenter concludes that a real difference is produced by the various treatment conditions.

Although null hypothesis significance testing is the typical approach used by experimenters, it has been severely criticized (e.g., Cohen, 1990, 1994; Loftus, 1996; Oaks, 1986), even to the point of critics' stating that it should be abandoned. The basic thrust of these criticisms is that null hypothesis significance testing does not tell us what we want to know (Cohen, 1994). This conclusion is reached because null hypothesis significance testing does not tell us anything about the truth of the null hypothesis or anything about the probability that the research or alternate hypothesis is true (Cohen, 1990), both of which are factually correct statements. If we do abandon null hypothesis testing, what type of statistical analysis should be conducted? Cohen (1990, 1994) and others have embraced the idea that measures of effect size and confidence intervals are the appropriate statistical tests to use in data analyses.

This position has been countered by others (e.g., Cortina & Dunlap, 1997; Frick, 1996; Hagen, 1997) who state that null hypothesis testing has a legitimate and valuable role to play in psychological research. The general position of these individuals is that null hypothesis testing, effect size, and confidence intervals all have their place in psychological research because they provide different types of useful information. Frick (1996) has pointed out that research may have either a quantitative and/or ordinal research goal. If we have a

quantitative goal, we are interested in effect size because we are interested in determining the size of the effect of an experimental treatment. If we want to make a claim about the precision of this estimate of effect size, we also calculate and report the confidence interval around the observed effect size. If we have an ordinal goal, then we are interested in determining whether one treatment condition produces more or less of something than another treatment condition. In this case the appropriate statistical analysis is null hypothesis testing because it will establish the order of the treatment conditions that will meet the ordinal goal.

Null hypothesis significance testing has its limitations. However, when the goal of the research is to test an ordinal hypothesis, then null hypothesis significance testing is appropriate. This is a common goal of psychological research. The issue, therefore, does not seem to be one of whether null hypothesis significance testing is appropriate but in what situations is its use appropriate. In the late 1990s, the American Psychological Association's Board of Scientific Affairs set up a task force on statistical inference, which was charged with looking into the state of psychological data analysis, based to a great extent on the criticisms of null hypothesis significance testing. This task force concluded that "researchers often draw conclusions without fully understanding their data or its meaning ..." (Azar, 1997, p. 26). This seems to have been prompted by the proliferation of statistical software enabling researchers to easily compute many statistical analyses without first looking closely at their data. Based on their review, the task force urged better description and analyses of data by not only providing more extensive descriptions including means, standard deviations, and discussions of missing data, but by also providing a better characterization of the data by going beyond reporting *p* values and including both direction and size of effect and confidence intervals. Such a recommendation seems very appropriate because it would allow researchers to meet both the ordinal and quantitative goals.

0.05 significance level is to be used, this means that you will accept as a real difference only one that is so large that it could have occurred by chance only 5 times in 100. If the 0.01 significance level is selected, then the difference can be expected to occur only 1 time in 100 by chance.

Now let us look at the results of the statistical analysis of the data obtained from the cocaine experiment. The t-test provided a t value of 3.39. Assuming that we decided to use the 0.05 significance level, we need to determine whether this t value is so great that it could have occurred by chance only 5 times in 100. To determine whether the obtained t value is large enough to be significant, we must consult a table of critical values of t, using the appropriate number of degrees of freedom for the study.

You may recall from your statistics class that the t-test has $N-2$ degrees of freedom, where N is the total number of scores. The cocaine study has 24 scores, so there are $24 - 2$, or 22, degrees of freedom. The critical values of t are listed in Appendix B. If you look at this table you will see that degrees of freedom (df) are listed on the left-hand column of this table. The six columns to the right represent the critical values of t. To identify the appropriate critical value, you need to establish whether a one- or two-tailed level of significance is to be used prior to conducting the study. Remember from your statistics course that a one-tailed level of significance is used when a directional hypothesis is made and a two-tailed level of significance is used when a nondirectional hypothesis is made. A directional hypothesis was made in the cocaine study because it was hypothesized that abuse of cocaine would increase as access to it increased. This means that you must use a one-tailed test of significance. Using a 0.05 level of significance and a one-tailed test, the critical value of t for the cocaine study is at the intersection of the row depicting 22 df and the column representing the 0.05 level of significance for a one-tailed test. At this intersection you should find the value of 1.717, which is the critical value of t. If a nondirectional hypothesis had been stated, a two-tailed test of significance would be used. In this case the critical value of t, using the 0.05 level of significance, would be 2.074.

The t value computed for the cocaine study is 3.39. This value is greater than the critical value of t required for significance at the 0.05 level regardless of whether a one- or two-tailed level of significance were used. This provides the information needed to make a decision regarding the null hypothesis. Because the obtained value of t is greater than the critical value of t, the likelihood that the difference in the mean scores of the two groups of rats occurred by chance is *less* than 5 in 100. Thus the null hypothesis of no difference between the two groups can be rejected. Although this null hypothesis significance testing approach is the standard approach used by most researchers, it has been the subject of debate, as revealed in Exhibit 14.1.

Now that we have concluded that a difference exists between the two groups in self-administration of cocaine, it is important to identify the dose condition that produced the greatest amount of self-administration. To make this determination, we must look at the mean number of lever presses made by the rats in the two groups. Table 14.1 shows that Group 1 pressed the lever more often and hence demonstrated the greater tendency to self-administer cocaine.

Next let us look at a method for analyzing data from a design that uses more than two groups.

STUDY QUESTION 14.2

- **What determines the statistical test to be used when testing a hypothesis?**
- **How does the *t*-test work in hypothesis testing? Incorporate significance levels in your answer.**

Analysis of Variance

Analysis of variance
A general statistical procedure for analyzing data obtained from a between-participants design with more than two levels of the independent variable and one or more independent variables

Analysis of variance is an extension of the *t*-test. It is a general statistical procedure appropriate for analyzing data generated from a research design that uses more than two levels of one independent variable and/or more than one independent variable.

One-Way Analysis of Variance

One-way analysis of variance
A statistical test for analyzing data collected with a simple randomized design

The simplest form of analysis of variance (ANOVA) is **one-way analysis of variance**. The one-way ANOVA is the statistical test applied to data collected on the basis of a simple randomized participants design. Assume that, based on the results of the two-group experiment just discussed, you hypothesize that rats will increase their rate of self-administration of cocaine as access to cocaine decreases. This hypothesis sounds logical because a rat receiving a 0.5 mg/kg dose for each lever press would have to press the lever twice as often as would a rat receiving a 1.0 mg/kg dose to receive the same amount of cocaine.

To test this scientific hypothesis, you allow three groups of rats to press a lever to receive one of the following doses of cocaine: 0.1 mg/kg (Group 1), 0.5 mg/kg (Group 2), or 1.0 mg/kg (Group 3). Table 14.2 shows the hypothetical data obtained from this study.

Referring to Figure 14.3, you can see which type of analysis is required to analyze the data obtained from this three-group experiment. The data were collected on the basis of a between-participants design because there were three different groups of rats. There was only one independent variable, and it had more than two groups of rats. Therefore, the appropriate statistical analysis is the one-way ANOVA.

Total variation
A measure of the overall variability of the scores obtained from a given experimental design

Analysis of variance is a statistical procedure that allows us to estimate the probability that the observed difference between the means of three groups is the result of chance factors. The process is to partition the total variation in the data into two independent sources of variation. The **total variation** in any data set represents a measure of the overall variation of the scores obtained from all participants within the experiment. This total variation is calculated by summing the squared deviations of all the scores from the mean of all the scores:

$$\text{Total variation} = \Sigma X^2 - \frac{(\Sigma X)^2}{N}$$

where

X = individual scores
N = total number of scores

TABLE 14.2
Number of Lever Presses Made by Rats Receiving One of Three Cocaine Dosages

Group 1 (0.1 mg/kg dose)	Group 2 (0.5 mg/kg dose)	Group 3 (1.0 mg/kg dose)
35	126	67
41	64	40
4	19	32
8	33	10
29	24	45
27	75	22
12	48	41
0	30	20
1	30	24
17	29	40
30	25	16
19	44	15
1	40	21

$\Sigma X_{0.1} = 224$ $\Sigma X_{0.5} = 587$ $\Sigma X_{1.0} = 393$

$\Sigma X_{0.1}^2 = 6{,}252$ $\Sigma X_{0.5}^2 = 36{,}729$ $\Sigma X_{1.0}^2 = 14{,}901$

$\bar{X}_{0.1} = 17.23$ $\bar{X}_{0.5} = 45.15$ $\bar{X}_{1.0} = 30.23$

$N = 13$ $N = 13$ $N = 13$

$\Sigma X_{tot}^2 = 1{,}204$

$\Sigma X_{tot}^2 = 57{,}882$

$N_{tot} = 39$

(Students who are familiar with statistics should recognize this variation as the total sum of squares.) Using this formula to calculate the total variation of the data in Table 14.2, we have

$$\text{Total variation} = \Sigma X^2 - \frac{\Sigma X^2}{N}$$

$$= 57{,}882 - \frac{(1{,}204)^2}{39}$$

$$= 57{,}882 - 37{,}169.64$$

$$= 20{,}712.36$$

This total variation can be divided into two estimates of independent variation: one that reflects the variation *within* the various treatment groups and another that reflects the variation *between* the various treatment groups. The **between-groups**

Between-groups
variation
Variability arising from
the effect of the
independent variable
and chance factors

variation is actually a measure of two different sources of variability in the data. One source is the effect that may be produced by the independent variable. Consider the data from the cocaine study in Table 14.2. In this study, each of the three groups of rats received a different amount of cocaine. Each of the three amounts of cocaine was hypothesized to have a different effect on the rats. In other words, the three groups of rats should have pressed the lever a different number of times depending on their group assignment. Therefore, some of the variation in response among the three different groups could be due to the effect of the independent variable, typically referred to as the treatment effect.

The other source of variation in response between the three different groups is the effect of chance factors. If the independent variable had absolutely no effect on the extent to which the rats pressed the lever, we would still expect the rats in each of the three groups to respond somewhat differently, simply because of chance factors. Thus the between-groups variation is composed of variation arising from the independent variable (the treatment effect) and that arising from chance factors:

Between-groups variation = treatment effect + chance variation

The between-groups variation is calculated as follows:

$$\text{Between-groups variation} = \frac{(\Sigma X_1)^2}{N_1} + \frac{(\Sigma X_2)^2}{N_2} + \cdots + \frac{(\Sigma X_n)^2}{N_n} - \frac{(\Sigma X_{tot})^2}{N_{tot}}$$

where

$(\Sigma X_1)^2$ = sum of the scores in Group 1 squared

$(\Sigma X_2)^2$ = sum of the scores in Group 2 squared

$(\Sigma X_{tot})^2$ = sum of all the scores squared

N_1 = number of scores in Group 1

N_2 = number of scores in Group 2

N_{tot} = number of scores in the entire study

(Students familiar with statistics should recognize the between-groups variation as the between sum of squares.) If this formula is applied to the data in Table 14.2, we have the following:

$$\begin{aligned}
\text{Between-groups variation} &= \frac{(\Sigma X_1)^2}{N_1} + \frac{(\Sigma X_2)^2}{N_2} + \frac{(\Sigma X_3)^2}{N_3} - \frac{(\Sigma X_{tot})^2}{N_{tot}} \\
&= \frac{(224)^2}{13} + \frac{(587)^2}{13} + \frac{(393)^2}{13} - \frac{(1,204)^2}{39} \\
&= 42,245.69 - 37,169.64 \\
&= 5,076.05
\end{aligned}$$

The **within-groups variation** is a measure of the variation of the responses of the research participants within the experimental treatment groups. The within-groups variation is therefore a measure of chance variability because all research participants within each experimental group should be treated the same way or be exposed to the same treatment condition. For example, in the cocaine study the rats in each group were reared under identical environmental conditions and received the same dose of cocaine for each lever press. Therefore, the variation in the response of the rats within each experimental treatment group has to be the result of chance factors:

Within-groups variation = chance variability

The within-groups variation is calculated as follows:

$$\text{Within-groups variation} = \Sigma X^2 - \frac{\Sigma X_{\text{gp}}^2}{N_{\text{gp}}}$$

where

ΣX^2 = sum of all the scores in the study after each score has been squared
ΣX_{gp}^2 = sum of all the scores in the treatment groups after the scores in each treatment group have been totaled and then squared
N_{gp} = number of scores in each group (this assumes an equal number of scores in each group)

(Students familiar with statistics should recognize the within-groups variation as the within sum of squares.) When this formula is applied to the data in Table 14.2, we have the following:

Within-groups variation

$$= (35)^2 + (41)^2 + (4)^2 + \cdots + (15)^2 + (21)^2 - \frac{(224)^2 + (587)^2 + (393)^2}{13}$$

$$= 57{,}882 - 42{,}245.69$$

$$= 15{,}636.31$$

Now that we have computed the between- and within-groups variation, we can see that the total variation of the scores obtained in the experiment is equal to the sum of the between-groups variation and the within-groups variation:

Total variation = between-groups variation + within-groups variation
20,712.36 = 5,076.05 + 15,636.31
20,712.36 = 20,712.36

Once the between- and within-groups variations have been calculated, it is necessary to divide each of these measures by its appropriate degrees of freedom to generate an estimate of between- and within-groups variance. In computing ANOVA this variance is referred to as **mean square** (MS). The number of degrees of freedom for the between-groups measure is the number of groups minus 1, or $3 - 1$ for the cocaine study because three different groups of rats were used. Therefore, the between-groups variance, or mean square, is

$$MS_{bet} = \frac{\text{between-groups variation}}{\text{degrees of freedom}}$$

$$= \frac{5,076.05}{2}$$

$$= 2,538.02$$

The number of degrees of freedom for the within-groups variance is the total number of scores in the experiment minus the number of groups, or $39 - 3 = 36$. Therefore, the within-groups variance, or mean square, is computed as follows:

$$MS_{within} = \frac{\text{within-groups variation}}{\text{degrees of freedom}}$$

$$= \frac{15,636.31}{36}$$

$$= 434.34$$

F-ratio
The ratio of two variance estimates used as a test of the effect of an independent variable

Now that the between- and within-groups mean squares have been calculated, it is possible to compute the one-way analysis of variance. As the name implies, analysis of variance involves the analysis of different variances. This analysis, commonly referred to as the *F*-test, is performed by forming a ratio of the between-groups variance, or mean square, to the within-groups variance, or mean square. This ratio is referred to as the **F-ratio:**

$$F\text{-ratio} = \frac{MS_{bet}}{MS_{within}}$$

Because of the relationship that exists between these two measures of variance, this ratio provides a test of the independent variable. Remember that the between-groups variance is a measure of both the experimental treatment effect and chance variability and that the within-groups variance is a measure of just chance variability. Therefore,

$$\frac{MS_{bet}}{MS_{within}} = \frac{\text{treatment effect} + \text{chance variability}}{\text{chance variability}}$$

Both the numerator and the denominator of the right-hand side of this equation contain a measure of chance variability, and these two measures cancel one another out. Thus only the treatment effect is left. If there is no treatment effect, then both variance measures will be measuring only chance variability and the ratio will be 1.

$$\frac{0 + \text{chance variability}}{\text{chance variability}} = 1$$

As the ratio of between- to within-groups variance gets larger, the probability increases that the difference between the groups is due to the independent variable and not to chance. Similarly, as the ratio approaches 1, the probability increases that chance explains the difference between the groups.

Let us now compute the F-ratio for the data in Table 14.2.

$$F\text{-ratio} = \frac{MS_{bet}}{MS_{within}}$$

$$= \frac{2{,}581.1}{434.34}$$

$$= 5.94$$

The value of the F-ratio is 5.94, indicating that the between-groups variance is six times greater than the within-groups variance. The fact that the F-ratio is much greater than 1 suggests that the between-groups differences were not due to chance.

STUDY QUESTION 14.3

- **One-way ANOVA is used to analyze data collected from which type of research design?**
- **Explain how the F-ratio statistically provides a test of the effect of the independent variable or treatment effect.**

Analysis of Variance Summary Table

The preceding computation of the one-way ANOVA for the experiment on self-administration of cocaine may appear to involve numerous and difficult calculations. Actually, this is the simplest of the ANOVA designs, so more complex designs may appear even more intimidating with all the calculations they require. Fortunately, once you have mastered the basics of ANOVA, there is seldom a need to perform the mathematical calculations by hand. There are many statistical packages that make use of computers to perform the calculations. You need only a summary of the results of these calculations to make a decision regarding the outcome of an experiment. The results of any analysis of variance computations are typically presented in an *analysis of variance summary table,* such as the one in Table 14.3. This table summarizes calculations for the cocaine experiment.

You can see that the summary table not only provides a summary of the ANOVA calculations but also provides a summary of the information relevant to the F-ratio. The table is arranged so that the columns describe the various quantities obtained in the analysis. There are separate columns for the sums of squares (SS), degrees of free-

TABLE 14.3
ANOVA Summary Table for a One-Way Analysis of Variance

Source of Variation	SS	df	MS	F
Between-groups	5,076.05	2	2,538.02	5.94
Within-groups	15,636.31	36	434.34	
Total	20,712.36	38		

dom (df), mean squares (MS), and F-ratio. The rows of the table define the sources of variation in the data: between-groups, within-groups, and total variation. In addition, the table clarifies the relationships among these quantities. From the table it can be seen that the total variation is partitioned into between- and within-groups variation. These two sums *must* add up to the total variation. Similarly, the between and within degrees of freedom, df, must add up to the total df. The table also reveals that the mean square, MS, is obtained by dividing the sums of squares, SS, by the degrees of freedom, df. That is, the between mean square is obtained by dividing the between sums of squares by the between df, and the within mean square is obtained by dividing the within sums of squares by the within df. Finally, Table 14.3 reveals that the F-ratio is obtained by dividing the between mean square by the within mean square; the resulting value appears in the column labeled F.

Interpreting the Results of the Analysis of Variance

Once the F-ratio has been computed, we must determine the actual probability that the group mean differences were due to chance. If we are operating at the 0.05 significance level, we must determine whether the F-ratio is so large that the results could occur by chance only 5 times in 100. To make this assessment, we must, as we did with the results of the t-test, consult a table of critical values of F, using the appropriate degrees of freedom. These degrees of freedom can easily be obtained from an analysis of variance summary table. Table 14.3, for example, reveals that there are 2 degrees of freedom for the between-groups variation and 36 degrees of freedom for the within-groups variation. These are the two values for degrees of freedom that must be used when a table of critical values of F, such as in Appendix C, is consulted to determine the value of the computed F-ratio required for significance. In Appendix C, you can see that this table contains the critical values for the F-distribution required for significance at the 0.05 (lightface type) and 0.01 (boldface type) level. To identify the critical value of F needed for your experiment to reject the null hypothesis, you must make use of the degrees of freedom associated with the between- and within-groups variation. The degrees of freedom associated with MS_{bet} is found across the top row of the table. The degrees of freedom associated with MS_{within} is found on the far left column of the table. The critical value of F is the value found in the body of the table located at the intersection of these two degrees of freedom. In the cocaine experiment, MS_{bet} has 2 df and MS_{within} has 36 df. When you locate 2 df on the top row and 36 df on the far left column of Appendix C, you will find, at the intersection of these two dfs, a value of 3.26 for the 0.05 level of significance and a value of 5.25 for the 0.01 level of significance. A 0.05 probability level was stated at the outset of the experiment as the level required for significance. Therefore, the critical value of 3.26 is compared with the value of 5.94 obtained from the computed F-ratio. Because the F-ratio we computed from the cocaine data exceeds the critical value of F, we reject the null hypothesis and accept the scientific hypothesis that the different cocaine dosages differentially affected the number of lever presses made by the rats in the various groups.

Now that we have concluded that the dosages differentially affected the response rate, we must return to the data and identify the dosage that produced the greatest effect. The *F*-ratio told us only that there was a significant difference among the three groups. It did not tell us which group pressed the lever most frequently and thus had the greatest tendency to abuse cocaine. To obtain such information we must use descriptive statistics, because we want to describe the response rate of each group of rats. The best way to do so is to compute the mean number of lever presses for each group. From Table 14.2 we know that the group receiving the 0.5 mg/kg dose of cocaine had the greatest number of responses (mean = 45.15) and the group receiving the 0.1 mg/kg dose had the smallest number of responses (mean = 17.23). Now we know not only that the groups differed significantly but also which group self-administered, or abused, cocaine the most.

It would be appropriate to conduct another statistical test to determine which of the groups differed significantly from one another. The *F*-test and ANOVA tell us only that there is a significant difference among the three groups, not which groups are significantly different. It may be that the 0.1 mg/kg-dose group produced significantly fewer responses than did the other two groups, but that these two groups did not produce significantly different numbers of responses. Such information is needed to completely interpret the data from such an experiment. Acquiring this information requires knowledge of post hoc tests, however, and they are beyond the scope of this book.

STUDY QUESTION 14.4

- **What is the purpose of an ANOVA summary table?**
- **How would you interpret the results of an *F*-ratio?**

Two-Way Analysis of Variance

Two-way analysis of variance
A statistical test for analyzing data collected with a factorial design

The **two-way ANOVA** is a statistical test that is applied to data collected from a factorial design. You will recall from Chapter 10 that a factorial design is one in which two or more independent variables are studied simultaneously to determine their independent and interactive effects on the dependent variable. The two-way ANOVA is the simplest form of test to apply to a factorial design; it is used to analyze data from studies that investigate the simultaneous and interactive effects of two independent variables. For example, assume that you want to conduct an experiment that investigates whether consuming caffeine at an early age sensitizes individuals to cocaine abuse.

To test this hypothesis you randomly assign one group of young rats to receive a dose of 1 gm of caffeine per 5 kg of body weight in drinking water and another group to receive quinine-laced drinking water each day for a period of two months. Both of these substances are bitter, so the taste of the water should be similar for both groups. This manipulation will create one group of rats that is pre-exposed to caffeine and another that is not. Then you randomly assign the rats in each of these two groups to receive one of the following doses of cocaine: 0.1 mg/kg, 0.5 mg/kg, or 1.0 mg/kg. This provides two independent variables—caffeine pretreatment and cocaine dose—and gives six different groups of subjects, as illustrated in Table 14.4.

Table 14.4 shows hypothetical data on number of lever presses obtained from this study, where each lever press provides the rats with a predetermined 0.1, 0.5, or 1.0 mg/kg dose of cocaine. Figure 14.3 can be used to determine the type of analysis

TABLE 14.4

Number of Lever Presses Made by Rats Receiving One of Three Cocaine Doses and Preexposed or Not Preexposed to Caffeine

	Group 1 (A1) (0.1 mg/kg dose)	Group 2 (A2) (0.5 mg/kg dose)	Group 3 (A3) (1.0 mg/kg dose)	
Caffeine preexposure (B1)	35	64	67	$\Sigma B1 = 763$
	41	19	40	
	14	33	52	$\bar{X}_{B1} = 42.39$
	18	24	60	
	29	75	45	$N_{B1} = 18$
	27	48	72	
Nonexposure to caffeine (B2)	12	30	41	$\Sigma B2 = 433$
	0	30	20	
	1	29	24	$\bar{X}_{B2} = 24.06$
	17	25	40	
	30	44	16	$N_{B2} = 18$
	19	40	15	
	$\Sigma A1B1 = 164$	$\Sigma A2B1 = 263$	$A3B1 = 336$	
	$\Sigma A1B2 = 79$	$\Sigma A2B2 = 198$	$A3B2 = 156$	
	$\Sigma A1 = 243$	$\Sigma A2 = 461$	$\Sigma A3 = 492$	
	$\bar{X}_{A1} = 20.25$	$\bar{X}_{A2} = 38.42$	$\bar{X}_{A3} = 41.00$	
	$N_{A1} = 12$	$N_{A2} = 12$	$N_{A3} = 12$	
	$\Sigma X_{tot} = 1,196$	$\Sigma X_{tot}^2 = 51,884$	$N_{tot} = 36$	

required with the data obtained from this six-group study. The data were collected using a between-participants design because there were six different groups of rats. There were two independent variables, so the appropriate statistical test is a two-way analysis of variance.

Like the one-way analysis of variance, the two-way ANOVA is accomplished by partitioning the total variability in the data into the components that reflect the sources of variation in the experiment. The total variation in the one-way ANOVA was partitioned into between and within variation, where the between variation was the variation that included the effect of the independent variable and the within variation was the measure of chance variability.

For the two-way ANOVA, the total variation is partitioned into four different components.

1. A component that measures the variation for the independent variable of cocaine dose, or factor A

2. A component that measures the variation for the independent variable of caffeine pretreatment, or factor B

3. A component that measures the interaction between factors A and B, or between cocaine dose and caffeine pretreatment

4. A measure of chance variability

The total variation in the data is calculated by summing the squared deviations of all scores from the mean of all scores. The raw score formula is

$$\text{Total variation, or } SS_{tot} = \Sigma X^2 - \frac{(\Sigma X)^2}{N}$$

Using this formula to calculate the total variation of the data in Table 14.4, we have

$$SS_{tot} = \Sigma X^2 - \frac{(\Sigma X)^2}{N}$$
$$= 51,884 - \frac{(1,196)^2}{36}$$
$$= 51,884 - 39,733.78$$
$$= 12,150.22$$

The variation for the independent variable of cocaine dose, factor A, is calculated as follows:

$$\text{Factor A variation, or } SS_A = \frac{(\Sigma X_{A1})^2}{n_{A1}} + \frac{(\Sigma X_{A2})^2}{n_{A2}} + \frac{(\Sigma X_{A3})^2}{n_{A3}} - \frac{(\Sigma X_{tot})^2}{N_{tot}}$$

Using this formula to calculate the variation for factor A, the cocaine dose independent variable, we have

$$SS_{tot} = \frac{(243)^2}{12} + \frac{(461)^2}{12} + \frac{(492)^2}{12} - \frac{(1,196)^2}{36}$$
$$= 42,802 - 39,733.78$$
$$= 3,068.22$$

The variation for the caffeine pretreatment independent variable, factor B, is calculated as follows:

$$\text{Factor B variation, or } SS_B = \frac{(\Sigma X_{B1})^2}{n_{B1}} + \frac{(\Sigma X_{B2})^2}{n_{B2}} - \frac{(\Sigma X_{tot})^2}{N_{tot}}$$

When this formula is applied to the data in Table 14.4, we have the following:

$$SS_B = \frac{(763)^2}{18} + \frac{(433)^2}{18} - \frac{(1,196)^2}{36}$$
$$= 42,758.78 - 39,733.78$$
$$= 3,025$$

The variation for the interaction between the cocaine dose and caffeine pretreatment is calculated as follows:

Interaction effect, or $SS_{A \times B}$

$$= \frac{(\Sigma X_{A1B1})^2}{n_{A1B1}} + \frac{(\Sigma X_{A2B1})^2}{n_{A2B1}} + \frac{(\Sigma X_{A3B1})^2}{n_{A3B1}} + \frac{(\Sigma X_{A1B2})^2}{n_{A1B2}}$$

$$+ \frac{(\Sigma X_{A2B2})^2}{n_{A2B2}} + \frac{(\Sigma X_{A3B2})^2}{n_{A3B2}} - \frac{(\Sigma X_{tot})^2}{n_{tot}} - SS_A - SS_B$$

$$= \frac{(164)^2}{6} + \frac{(263)^2}{6} + \frac{(336)^2}{6} + \frac{(79)^2}{6} + \frac{(198)^2}{6}$$

$$+ \frac{(156)^2}{6} - \frac{(1196)^2}{36} - 3,068.22 - 3,025$$

$$= 46,457.0 - 39,733.78 - 3,068.22 - 3,025$$

$$= 630$$

The chance variation in the data, also known as error, can be calculated using the following formula:

Chance variation, or SS

$$= \Sigma X^2 - \left[\frac{(\Sigma X_{A1B1})^2}{n_{A1B1}} + \frac{(\Sigma X_{A2B1})^2}{n_{A2B1}} + \frac{(\Sigma X_{A3B1})^2}{n_{A3B1}} + \frac{(\Sigma X_{A1B2})^2}{n_{A1B2}} + \frac{(\Sigma X_{A2B2})^2}{n_{A2B2}} + \frac{(\Sigma X_{A3B2})^2}{n_{A3B2}} \right]$$

However, this variation is more commonly calculated by subtraction, as follows:

$$SS_{error} = SS_{tot} - SS_A - SS_B - SS_{A \times B}$$

$$= 12,150.22 - 3,068.22 - 3,025 - 630$$

$$= 5,427$$

The next step in computing the two-way ANOVA is to calculate the mean square for each source of variation. This is accomplished by dividing each source of variation by its appropriate degrees of freedom. The formulas for computing the degrees of freedom, df, for each source of variation are as follows:

$$df_A = A - 1, \quad or \ 3 - 1 = 2$$
$$df_B = B - 1, \quad or \ 2 - 1 = 1$$
$$df_{A \times B} = (A - 1)(B - 1) = (3 - 1)(2 - 1) = 2$$
$$df_{error} = N - AB, \quad or \ 36 - (3)(2) = 30$$

Once the degrees of freedom have been calculated, you can compute the mean square for each effect, as follows:

$$MS_A = \frac{SS_A}{df_A} = \frac{3,068.22}{2} = 1,534.11$$

$$MS_B = \frac{SS_B}{df_B} = \frac{3,025}{1} = 3,025$$

$$MS_{A \times B} = \frac{SS_{A \times B}}{df_{A \times B}} = \frac{630}{2} = 315$$

$$MS_{error} = \frac{SS_{error}}{df_{error}} = \frac{5,427}{30} = 180.9$$

After the mean square values have been computed, it is possible to compute the F-ratio for each of the three effects of interest: the two main effects of cocaine dose and caffeine pretreatment and the interaction of these two effects. These F-ratios are computed by dividing the mean square of each effect by the MS_{error}. The F-ratio for the cocaine main effect is

$$F = \frac{MS_A}{MS_{error}} = \frac{1,534.11}{180.9} = 8.48$$

The F-ratio for the caffeine pretreatment main effect is

$$F = \frac{MS_B}{MS_{error}} = \frac{3,025}{180.9} = 16.72$$

The F-ratio for the interaction effect is

$$F = \frac{MS_{A \times B}}{MS_{error}} = \frac{315}{180.9} = 1.74$$

Table 14.5 is an ANOVA summary table for these analyses. To determine whether the main effects and the interaction effect are significant you must compare the computed F-value with the critical value of F found in Appendix C. Remember that you must enter this table using the degrees of freedom corresponding to the mean square values in the numerator and denominator of the F-ratio. For example, the F-ratio for the cocaine main effect is obtained by computing the ratio of the cocaine mean square to the error mean square. There are 2 degrees of freedom for the cocaine mean square and 30 degrees of freedom for the error mean square. This means that you must enter Appendix C with 2 and 30 degrees of freedom. Using these df reveals that an F-ratio of 3.32 is needed for the cocaine main effect to be considered significant, an F-ratio of 4.17 is needed for the caffeine pretreatment to be considered significant, and an F-ratio of 2.42 is needed for the interaction effect to be considered significant at the 0.05 level. When these critical values are compared with the F-ratios shown in the ANOVA summary in Table 14.5, it can be seen that the F-ratios for the cocaine and caffeine main effects exceed the critical values, but the F-ratio for the interaction effect does not. This means that you should reject the null hypothesis for the cocaine and caffeine main effects but fail to reject the null hypothesis for the interaction effect. Therefore, you conclude that both cocaine and caffeine differentially affect lever pressing but that caffeine pretreatment does not differentially influence the effect of cocaine (the interaction).

To determine how cocaine dose and caffeine pretreatment affect the self-administration of cocaine, as measured by lever pressing, it is necessary to look at the mean

TABLE 14.5
ANOVA Summary Table for a Two-Way Analysis of Variance

Source of Variation	SS	df	MS	F
Cocaine	3,068.22	2	1,534.11	8.48
Caffeine pretreatment	3,025.00	1	3,025.00	16.72
Cocaine × caffeine pretreatment	630.00	2	315.00	1.74
Total	12,150.22	30		

scores for each treatment group. The mean scores for the three cocaine dose groups reveal that the 0.1 mg/kg dose group had the lowest number of lever presses (mean = 20.25), whereas the 1.0 mg/kg group had the greatest number of lever presses (mean = 41), indicating that lever pressing increases as cocaine dose increases. The group that was pretreated with caffeine had the greatest number of lever presses (mean = 42.39), whereas the nonpretreated group had fewer responses (mean = 24.06). The experiment, therefore, reveals that as cocaine dose increases, the extent to which rats self-administer, or abuse, cocaine also increases. It also reveals that if rats are pretreated with caffeine they will increase lever pressing, or that caffeine increases the extent to which rats self-administer cocaine.

STUDY QUESTION 14.5

- **When would you use a two-way ANOVA?**
- **What advantage is derived from a study using a two-way ANOVA over a one-way ANOVA?**
- **How would you interpret the results obtained from a two-way ANOVA?**

Rejecting versus Failing to Reject the Null Hypothesis

The foregoing should give you some appreciation of the necessity of performing statistical tests on the data. If the statistical tests reveal that a significant difference (one that has reached the specified significance level) exists between the scores of the various groups, then the null hypothesis is rejected and the scientific hypothesis is accepted as real. If the obtained difference does not reach the specified significance level, then the experimenter *fails* to reject the null hypothesis. The expression *fails to reject* is used because it is very difficult to obtain evidence supportive of a null or no-difference conclusion. At first glance, it seems that if the null hypothesis cannot be rejected, it should logically be accepted. To see why the null hypothesis cannot be accepted if the significance level is not attained, consider the following experiment. Nation, Bourgeois, Clark, and Hare (1983) studied the effects of chronic cobalt exposure on the behavior of adult rats. The experimental group of rats was fed laboratory chow laced with cobalt chloride, and their lever-pressing speed was compared with that of a control group of rats who were fed standard laboratory chow. The results of one component of this study revealed that there was not a significant difference between the lever-pressing responses of the control and experimental groups at the 0.05 significance level. Consequently, the null hypothesis could not be rejected. However, although the experimental and control groups did not differ in lever-pressing response rates at the 0.05 level, a difference in response rates did exist. In order to accept the null hypothesis, we must be able to state that the observed variance represents a chance difference, and to assume that any observed difference is entirely due to chance is very hazardous. In the Nation et al. experiment, it is possible that the cobalt did have an effect but that the effect was too weak to be detected at the 0.05 significance level. In such a situation, some of the observed difference in response would be due to the treatment condition, which means that it would be inappropriate to accept a no-difference or null conclusion. Thus the expression *fails to reject* is used in place of *accept*.

Although it is logically impossible to accept the null hypothesis of no difference, "practical concerns demand that we sometimes have to provisionally act as though the null hypothesis were true" (Cook, Gruder, Hennigan, and Flay, 1979). As Greenwald (1975) has pointed out, there is a pervasive anti–null-hypothesis prejudice, which can lead to a variety of behavioral symptoms, such as "continuing research on a problem when results have been close to rejection of the null hypothesis ('near significant'), while abandoning the problem if rejection of the null hypothesis is not close" (Greenwald, 1975, p. 3). Such undesirable behavioral manifestations have led Greenwald to conclude that we should do research in which any outcome, including a null hypothesis outcome, is possible. This means, however, that the research must be conducted in such a manner as to allow for the tentative acceptance of the null hypothesis.

Harcum (1990) takes a similar position. While recognizing that it is very risky to consider accepting the null hypothesis or even making a null prediction, Harcum also recognizes the useful role for null predictions. Null predictions can help establish the boundary conditions for a phenomenon. For example, a null hypothesis is useful in determining when a drug dose is so low that it has no demonstrable effect. Null predictions can also help in deciding which variables are not worth further study.

Although null hypothesis predictions can be valuable in scientific research, they should be approached with caution. It is easy to support a null prediction just by using a weak research design that does not eliminate confounding variables or one that does not present a strong independent variable. In an attempt to avoid such problems, Harcum (1990) has proposed several criteria that must be met to reach a null conclusion. These are as follows:

1. No data that present a problem for the null conclusion may exist. In other words, there may be no studies that refute the null conclusion. For example, the results of studies regarding the effect of carbohydrates on mood of normal individuals are contradictory. Some studies (e.g., Spring, Chiodo, Harden, Bourgeois, & Lutherer, 1989) have demonstrated a mood-altering effect of carbohydrates, whereas other studies (e.g., Christensen & Redig, 1993) have not. In such an instance it would be inappropriate for Christensen and Redig to reach a null hypothesis conclusion that carbohydrates did not affect mood. Rather than reaching a null conclusion,

these investigators concluded that the effect of carbohydrates on mood was ephemeral and that a strong design with a large number of subjects was required to demonstrate a mood-altering effect of carbohydrates.

2. The probability of the null hypothesis's being false must be large. In other words, if the statistical test you used to analyze the data indicated a significance level of 0.06, you would be on very shaky ground in attempting to reach a null conclusion. However, a significance level of, say, 0.45 would provide more assurance of a null conclusion's being correct.

3. The research design must be sufficiently powerful. This is a key element in the ability to predict and reach a null conclusion. If the research design does not control for the influence of rival hypotheses or confounding variables or is conducted inappropriately, then a null result will occur, not because of the absence of an effect, but because of a lack of precision in the research design. However, a null result gains credence if confounding variables are controlled and the research is conducted appropriately.

Even when criteria such as these are met, the acceptance of a null result must be approached with caution. Additional guidelines for research that may lead to support for the tentative acceptance of the null hypothesis may be found in Greenwald (1975) and Cook et al. (1979).

STUDY QUESTION 14.6

- **Why do we use the expression *fail to reject the null hypothesis* versus *accept the null hypothesis?***
- **What criteria must be met to consider drawing a null conclusion?**

Potential Errors in the Statistical Decision-Making Process

In the preceding section, primary concern was given to determining when one should accept a difference as being significant. The commonly accepted significance levels of 0.05 and 0.01 mean that a wrong decision will occur only 5 times or 1 time in 100, respectively. In setting this stringent level, we are being very conservative, making sure that the odds of being correct are definitely in our favor. It is somewhat like going to a horse race with the intention of maximizing the possibility of winning—you increase your chances of winning if you bet on a horse that has only a 5 percent chance of losing rather than on one that has a 50 percent chance of losing. In like manner, scientists have set the odds so that they are quite sure of making the correct decision. Note, however, that even with this stringent significance level, scientists will be wrong a given percentage of the time: 5 percent of the time if they operate at the 0.05 significance level, and 1 percent of the time if they operate at the 0.01 significance level. In other words, if we conduct the same experiment one hundred times, we can expect that five of these times we will, by chance alone, obtain a mean difference large enough to allow us to reject the null hypothesis at the 0.05 significance level. This means that we could be wrong when we reject the null hypothesis, whether we are operating at the 0.05 or the 0.01 significance level.

TABLE 14.6
Possible Outcomes in Hypothesis Testing

		True Situation	
		Null Hypothesis True	**Null Hypothesis False**
Decision	Do not reject null hypothesis	Decision correct	Type II error
	Reject null hypothesis	Type I error	Decision correct

Type I error
False rejection of the null hypothesis

Type II error
Failure to reject the null hypothesis when it is false

When we falsely reject the null hypothesis, we commit a **Type I error**. Type I error is controlled by the significance level that is set. If the 0.05 significance level is set, the probability of being wrong and committing a Type I error is 5 in 100. It may appear that there is an easy solution to this type of problem: simply set a more stringent significance level, such as 0.0001. There are two difficulties with this approach. First, it is not possible to eliminate Type I error, because, by definition, there will always be some possibility of obtaining a chance finding as large as the observed difference. Second, and more important, another type of error tends to be inversely related to Type I error. As the probability of falsely rejecting the null hypothesis (Type I error) decreases, the probability of failing to reject the null hypothesis when it is false, called **Type II error**, tends to increase. Note the phrase *tends to increase*—there is no *direct* relationship between Type I and Type II errors. However, the risk of committing a Type I error generally increases as the risk of committing a Type II error decreases, and the risk of committing a Type II error generally increases as the risk of committing a Type I error decreases. Therefore, we face a dilemma. We must make a decision based on the results of our experiment, but we always run the risk of making an error. Table 14.6 illustrates this dilemma. If you do not reject the null hypothesis and it is true, you have made a correct decision; if it is false, you have committed a Type II error. If you reject the null hypothesis and it is false, you have made a correct decision; if it is true, you have committed a Type I error.

As scientists, we must weigh the hazards of committing each of the two types of errors and determine which mistake would be more detrimental. In most instances, it is assumed that a Type I error is worse, which is why the rather stringent 0.05 or 0.01 significance level is used as the decision point for rejection of the null hypothesis. However, there are times when committing a Type II error would be very detrimental. For example, if a drug were needed to combat a deadly epidemic, it would be important to make sure that an effective drug was identified. Avoiding a Type II error in such an instance would be considered more important, so the significance level would be raised to, say, the 0.15 level, to maximize the chances of identifying a drug that would combat the disease.

STUDY QUESTION 14.7 | **Discuss the relationship between Type I and Type II errors as they relate to hypothesis testing.**

Correlation

I am sure that you have heard many stories, bits of folk wisdom, and old wives' tales about the relationship between different variables. For example, haven't you heard people state that blonds have more fun, that a person with red hair has a fiery temper, that more murders are committed during a full moon, or that aching joints indicate that rain is coming? All of these are relationships, beliefs, or associations. Psychologists frequently are interested in determining if there is any validity to such presumed beliefs and associations. We ask questions about associations between violence and temperature to determine if violence increases as ambient temperature rises. Others have attempted to determine if there is any relationship between schizophrenia of parents and children assuming that if parents have schizophrenia that their children are at increased risk for schizophrenia. The only way to identify the truth or falsity of such presumed associations is to conduct a quantitative study that actually measures the extent of the relationship.

When you conduct such a study you are seeking to determine if the presumed relationship between the variables actually exist. The way in which you identify the degree of relationship that exists is to compute a correlation coefficient. For example, several years ago a graduate student of mine and I (Christensen & Pettijohn, 2001) were interested in finding out if carbohydrate cravings were related to emotional distress. To answer this question we collected data on the extent to which individuals experience emotional distress and carbohydrate cravings. Part of this study involved asking a large group of individuals to rate the extent of their carbohydrate cravings and to complete the Beck Depression Inventory. The data for ten of these research participants are presented in Table 14.7. Once such data has been collected, they must be statistically analyzed to identify the exact degree of relationship which exists between ratings of carbohydrate craving and depression. The appropriate statistical analysis to identify this degree of relationship is a correlation.

Computation of Correlation

Pearson Product-Moment Correlation Coefficient
The most commonly used statistical measure of degree of relationship between two variables

The statistical test that is most frequently used to measure the degree of association that exists between two variables is the **Pearson Product-Moment Correlation Coefficient**, which is designated by the letter r. Although there are several formulas that could be used to calculate r, the simplest is the raw score formula which takes the following form:

$$r = \frac{\Sigma XY - \dfrac{(\Sigma X)(\Sigma Y)}{N}}{\sqrt{\left[\Sigma X^2 - \dfrac{(\Sigma X)^2}{N}\right]\left[\Sigma Y^2 - \dfrac{(\Sigma Y)^2}{N}\right]}}$$

where
r = correlation coefficient
X = raw scores for one variable (e.g., carbohydrate crave rating)

TABLE 14.7
Ratings of Carbohydrate Craving and Beck Depression Scores

Participant	Crave Rating (X)	Depression Score (Y)	XY
1	2	8	16
2	3	14	42
3	6	4	24
4	5	12	60
6	1	10	10
7	3	15	45
8	5	5	25
9	2	10	20
10	4	16	8
	$\Sigma X = 31$	$\Sigma Y = 94$	$\Sigma XY = 326$
	$\Sigma X^2 = 129$	$\Sigma Y^2 = 1126$	

Y = raw scores for the second variable (e.g., depression score)
ΣXY = sum of the cross products of X and Y; to obtain the sum of cross products you multiply each person's X and Y score and then sum these products
N = number of participants

If we computed the correlation between the crave ratings and the depression scores using this formula, we would have the following:

$$r = \frac{326 - \dfrac{(31)(94)}{10}}{\sqrt{\left[129 - \dfrac{961}{10}\right]\left[1126 - \dfrac{8836}{10}\right]}}$$

$$= \frac{326 - 291.4}{\sqrt{[32.9][242.4]}}$$

$$= \frac{34.6}{89.3}$$

$= 0.387$ which is rounded to 0.39

The correlation coefficient that was calculated from the data in Table 14.7 is 0.39 or r = 0.39. Once you have calculated the correlation coefficient that exists between a set of variables, you must then interpret it. In other words, what does the correlation coefficient of 0.39 mean?

Interpretation of Correlation

The first bit of information you must have when interpreting a correlation coefficient is its direction. A correlation coefficient can be either positive or negative. A **positive correlation** indicates that, as the values of one variable increase so do the values in the other variable. If a positive correlation existed between crave ratings and depression, then as crave ratings increased so would the depression scores. A **negative correlation** indicates that, as the values of one variable increase the values of the other variable decrease. If a negative correlation existed between the crave ratings and depression, then as crave ratings increased, depression scores would decrease, or as depression scores decreased the crave ratings would increase.

Positive correlation
When an increase in one variable corresponds to an increase in the other variable

The second bit of information you need when interpreting a correlation coefficient is the magnitude or strength of the correlation. Correlation coefficients range from -1.00 through 0.00 to $+1.00$. A correlation coefficient of -1.00 or a $+1.00$ is the strongest relationship that can exist between two variables because it indicates that a change in one variable corresponds to an exact change in the other variable. Note that the magnitude or strength of the relationship doesn't depend on whether the correlation is positive or negative, only the size of the correlation. The closer it is to $+$ or -1.00 the stronger it is. A correlation of 0.00 indicates no relationship between the variables. Therefore, a correlation of $+0.67$ reveals that a stronger relationship exists than does a correlation of $+0.35$. Similarly, a correlation of -0.78 reflects a stronger relationship than does a correlation of -0.48. Also, a correlation of -0.78 reflects a stronger relationship than does a correlation of $+0.67$.

Negative correlation
When an increase in one variable corresponds to a decrease in the other variable

Now let us take a look at the correlation coefficient of 0.39 that was computed between the crave ratings and depression scores. In looking at this correlation coefficient we immediately see that it is a positive correlation so that means that an increase in one of these variables corresponds to an increase in the other variable. However, the correlation coefficient was 0.39 which is much less than 1.00 so we also know that the relationship between these two variables is not very strong.

So just what does a correlation of 0.39 mean? Just what does the number 0.39 indicate? To fully interpret our correlation of 0.39 we must square it to obtain a squared correlation, $(0.39)^2$, which is 0.15. Once we square the correlation coefficient we have a number that tells us the proportion of variation in one of the variables that is accounted for by the other variable. For our study on carbohydrate cravings and depression, the squared correlation of 0.15 tells us that 15 percent of the variation in craving scores is accounted for by a person's feelings of depression as represented by their depression scores.

To make this concept a little clearer, look at the craving scores in Table 14.7. You can easily see that the crave ratings ranged from 1 to 6. In other words, some people indicated that they had rather severe cravings, a rating of 6, and others said they did not crave carbohydrates, a rating of 1. Others indicated some degree of cravings indicated by ratings of 2 to 5. These differences in crave ratings represent the variation in different people's perceived carbohydrate cravings. One question you might ask is what accounts for these differences in the extent to which people say they crave carbohydrates, as indicated by their crave rating? The correlation that exists between carbohydrate crave ratings and depression scores tells us that these two variables are related and that depression can account for some of the variation that exists in the extent to which people say they crave carbohydrates. How much of the variation in crave ratings can depression account for, 15 percent or the correlation coefficient of 0.39 squared?

Knowing this, we can say that depression accounts for 15 percent of the variation in ratings of carbohydrate cravings. We also know that depression accounts for only a small portion of this variation. This means that there are other things that contribute to carbohydrate cravings. This study identified one of the contributors, although it was very small. If we want a complete understanding of why people crave carbohydrates we have to conduct other studies to identify other contributors to carbohydrate crave ratings.

From this discussion, you should be able to see that you need at least three items of information to interpret a correlation coefficient. First you need to identify the direction of the relationship, designated by the sign of the correlation. Next you need to identify its magnitude, indicated by the size of the correlation. Finally, you need to square the correlation coefficient to identify the proportion of variation accounted for. With these three bits of information you can make a reasonable interpretation of any correlation coefficient.

STUDY QUESTION 14.8

- **What is the difference between a positive and a negative correlation?**
- **What is the strongest correlation and what is the weakest correlation?**
- **What has to be done to extract meaning from a correlation coefficient?**
- **If I squared the correlation coefficient of 0.40 I would get the quantity of 0.16. What does this quantity of 0.16 mean?**

Summary

Following the collection of the data, the investigator must make a decision as to whether to reject the null hypothesis. If the mean response has been computed for each group of research participants, we know which group made the greatest number of responses. However, some differences in the mean responses of groups are to be expected on the basis of chance variability in responding. Computing the variance or standard deviation of the responses in each group provides an index of variability of the data and establishes some basis for assessing whether group mean differences are due to chance or are real differences resulting from manipulation of the independent variable. However, if we rely solely on a measure of variability, our decisions will lack precision and will be based primarily on judgment.

The most appropriate procedure for testing the null hypothesis is to analyze the data using one of the available statistical tests. The statistical test appropriate for analyzing the data collected is dictated by the design of the study. Every experimental study involves one or more independent variables, several levels of which are administered either to a single group of participants or to different groups of participants. These factors dictate the type of statistical analysis to be applied to the data. If two levels of one independent variable are used in a study and each level of the independent variable is administered to a different group of research participants, then an independent samples t-test is the appropriate statistical test. If more than two levels of one independent variable are used in a study and each level of the independent variable is administered to a different group of research participants, then a one-way analysis of variance is the appropriate statistical test.

No matter which statistical test is selected, the results must be used to make a decision as to whether the obtained group difference is large enough to be considered real or is more likely to be due to chance factors. This decision is based on the significance level set; the significance levels typically used in psychological research are 0.05 and 0.01. If the results of the statistical test reveal that the group mean differences are so large that they could occur by chance only 5 times or less in 100, then, if we accepted the 0.05 significance level, we would reject the null hypothesis and accept the scientific hypothesis.

Note, however, that there will still be an error either 1 percent or 5 percent of the time. This is referred to as a Type I error—the probability of accepting a hypothesis that is false. The Type I error could be decreased by setting a more stringent level for acceptance of the hypothesis, but then the probability of rejecting the hypothesis when in fact it is true—a Type II error—tends to increase. There needs to be a balance between these two types of error, and the typical balance is obtained by using the 0.05 and 0.01 significance levels.

In some studies the purpose is to identify the degree of relationship that exists between two variables. When this is the goal of the study you must compute a correlation coefficient. Once the correlation coefficient has been computed it must be interpreted. To interpret a correlation coefficient you must first look at its direction and magnitude. A correlation coefficient can be either positive or negative and its magnitude can range from −1.00 through 0.00 to +1.00 with the strongest correlation coefficient being either a −1.00 or a +1.00. After looking at the direction and magnitude of the correlation coefficient, you must square it. The squared correlation coefficient tells you the proportion of variation in one of the variables that is accounted for by the other variable.

Key Terms and Concepts

Mean	Mean square
Standard deviation	F-ratio
Independent samples t-test	Two-way analysis of variance
Significance level	Type I error
Analysis of variance	Type II error
One-way analysis of variance	Pearson Product-Movement
Total variation	Correlation Coefficient
Between-groups variation	Positive Correlation
Within-groups variation	Negative Correlation

Related Internet Sites

www.stat.sc.edu/rsrch/gasp/
This site provides the basic data analysis procedures needed to analyze data collected from most psychological studies. This site includes the *t*-test, regression, and one-way ANOVA, as well as other descriptive statistical procedures. Nine educational procedures are also included to assist in teaching statistics online.

www.sportsci.org/resource/stats/errors.html
This Internet site gives a discussion of Type I and Type II errors.

www.sportsci.org/resource/stats/pvalues.html
This site provides a discussion of statistical significance.

Practice Test

The answers to these questions can be found in Appendix A.

1. If you have conducted an experiment that hypothesizes that people who are depressed increase their intake of simple carbohydrates over nondepressed individuals and this hypothesis is confirmed, then you are

   a. Stating that simple carbohydrates cause depression
   b. Stating a null hypothesis
   c. Stating a scientific hypothesis
   d. Stating that there are two populations with regard to consumption of carbohydrates
   e. Stating that there is one population and it is composed of depressed people who eat carbohydrates and nondepressed people who eat fewer carbohydrates.

2. If you conducted a study in which you randomly assigned people to two groups and tested them on a measure of attention, which statistical test would you use to determine whether the two groups differed on the measure of attention?

   a. Two-way analysis of variance
   b. One-way analysis of variance
   c. *t*-test
   d. Standard deviation
   e. Mean

3. If you conducted a study in which there were twenty-five people randomly assigned to each of two groups, how many degrees of freedom would you have if you analyzed this data with a *t*-test?

   a. 50
   b. 48
   c. 25
   d. 24
   e. 23

4. When conducting a one-way analysis of variance, the within and between variation should equal

    a. The total variation
    b. The mean square total
    c. The *F*-ratio
    d. The combined chance and treatment variation
    e. The total sum of squared variation

5. If you have conducted your statistical analysis and the results state that you can reject the null hypothesis but this, in fact, is incorrect, you have

    a. Made a Type I error
    b. Made a calculation error
    c. Made a Type II error
    d. Used the wrong statistical test
    e. Stated the wrong hypothesis

6. If you wanted to measure the degree of relationship that existed between two variables you would conduct a(n)

    a. *t*-test
    b. correlation coefficient
    c. *F*-test
    d. repeated measures analysis
    e. median test

Challenge Exercises

1. Assume that you conducted an experiment to determine whether novice or expert karate students were better at recalling new karate moves. Your hypothesis was that expert karate students would show better recall for the new moves than would novice students and that males would be more accurate than females. To test this hypothesis, you recruit ten female and ten male expert students and ten female and ten male novice students. Experts were defined as students with a first-degree black belt or at least 3.5 years of experience in a particular karate style. Novices were students with fewer than 1.5 years of training. The procedure you followed was to instruct all students to observe a person performing a kata (a series of karate moves). After seeing the instructor perform the kata, each person made a judgment of the frequency with which each technique, such as a downward block, occurred. After collecting this information, you computed the number of errors made by each person in his or her judgment of the frequency of occurrence of each technique. For example, if five kicks were performed and a person stated that seven were made and if four arm blocks were made and the person stated that three were made, this would total three errors in judgment. Assume that the following data were collected from these participants. Using these data, answer the questions.

Novice	Males	Females	Errors	Expert	Male	Female	Errors
1	Y		8	1		Y	4
2	Y		12	2	Y		1
3		Y	9	3	Y		5
4	Y		14	4	Y		4
5		Y	11	5		Y	8
6	Y		20	6		Y	10
7		Y	10	7	Y		6
8		Y	5	8	Y		0
9		Y	6	9		Y	12
10	Y		8	10	Y		2
11		Y	19	11		Y	8
12	Y		15	12		Y	6
13	Y		11	13	Y		2
14		Y	9	14	Y		5
15	Y		16	15		Y	10
16	Y		18	16	Y		4
17		Y	7	17	Y		1
18		Y	7	18		Y	12
19		Y	12	19		Y	7
20	Y		12	20		Y	15

a. What is the design of this study?
b. What statistical analysis should be used to answer the research question?
c. What effects are significant? This requires you to analyze these data using the statistical analysis you selected in b.
d. What do the data tell you about your research question? In other words, interpret the results of the study and present the data either in the form of a table or a graph.

2. Assume that the superintendent of a high school wanted to find out if there was any relationship between the grades that parents made when they were attending high school and the grades that their children are making in high school. To answer this question the superintendent identified the grades of ten parents and one of their children. These grades are as follows:

Parent	Parent's Grade	Child	Child's grade
1	3.4	1	2.16
2	1.75	2	2.64
3	2.95	3	3.04
4	3.1	4	2.73
5	3.9	5	1.86
6	2.26	6	3.21
7	1.43	7	2.79
8	0.87	8	2.96
9	2.34	9	0.48
10	3.27	10	2.65

a. What statistical analysis should be used to identify the relationship between parents and children's grades?
b. Conduct the appropriate statistical analysis and then interpret the obtained result.

15

The Research Report

The Research Report

- APA Format
- Preparation of the Research Report
  - Writing Style
    - Language
- Editorial Style
  - Italics
  - Abbreviations
  - Headings
  - Quotations
  - Numbers
  - Physical Measurements
  - Presentations of Statistical Results
  - Tables
  - Figures
  - Figure Captions
  - Reference Citations
  - Reference List
  - Typing
  - Ordering of Manuscript Pages
- Submission of the Research Report
  - Acceptance of the Manuscript
- Presenting Research Results at Professional Conferences
  - Oral Presentation
  - Poster Presentation

Introduction

Throughout this book, I have presented the various steps involved in the research process and discussed in detail the intricacies of each. A thorough presentation was made to enable you to conduct a sound scientific study. As a scientist, however, you have a responsibility not only to conduct a well-designed and well-executed study but also to communicate the results of the study to the rest of the scientific community. Your study may have answered a very significant research question, but the results are of no value unless they are made public. The primary mechanism for communicating results is through professional journals. Within the field of psychology, the American Psychological Society publishes four journals, and the American Psychological Association publishes thirty journals and a magazine. As Table 15.1 illustrates, these periodicals cover a wide variety of areas and provide an outlet for studies conducted within just about any field of interest. There are other journals that also publish the results of psychological studies. In order to facilitate the clear communication of research results, the APA has published a manual (American Psychological Association, 2001) that gives a standardized format for authors to follow when preparing research reports. Because many periodicals instruct their authors to prepare their manuscripts according to the style specified in the APA manual, this is the format I present here for writing a research report.

Prior to preparing a report on a study that you have completed, you must ask yourself if the study is important enough to justify publication. Would others be interested in it, and, more important, would it influence their work? As a general rule, you should never conduct a study you don't think is publishable. If you think the study is significant, you must decide whether it is free from flaws that would preclude drawing any causal relation between the independent and the dependent variables. For example, you must ask yourself whether you have built in the controls needed to eliminate the influence of rival hypotheses. If you can satisfy yourself with regard to these two questions, then you are justified in proceeding with the preparation of the research report.

TABLE 15.1

Journals Published by the American Psychological Association and the American Psychological Society

Name of Journal	Area Covered
American Psychological Association Journals	
American Psychologist	Contains archival documents and articles focusing on current issues in psychology, issues relating to the science and practice of psychology, and the contribution psychology makes to public policy
Behavioral Neuroscience	Contains original studies in anatomy, chemistry, endocrinology, genetics, pharmacology, and physiology as they relate to behavioral neuroscience
Clinician's Research Digest: Briefings in Behavioral Science	Provides monthly reviews and highlights of the most relevant articles of over 100 journals
Developmental Psychology	Publishes articles relating to human development across the life span
Emotion	Publishes articles on all aspects of emotional processes
Experimental and Clinical Psychopharmacology	Publishes research integrating pharmacology and behavior
Health Psychology	Devoted to furthering an understanding of the relationship between behavioral principles and physical health or illness
Journal of Abnormal Psychology	Publishes articles relating to the determinants, theories, and correlates of abnormal behavior
Journal of Applied Psychology	Publishes articles that contribute to our understanding of any applied area of psychology except clinical psychology
Journal of Comparative Psychology	Contains behavioral studies that relate to evolution, development, ecology, control, and functional significance of various species
Journal of Consulting and Clinical Psychology	Contains research investigations pertaining to development, validity, and use of various techniques for diagnosing and treating disturbed behavior in all populations
Journal of Counseling Psychology	Contains articles pertaining to evaluation, application, and theoretical issues surrounding counseling
Journal of Educational Psychology	Publishes studies and theoretical papers concerned with all levels of instruction such as learning and cognition
Journal of Experimental Psychology: Animal Behavior Processes	Publishes experimental and theoretical studies on animal behavior
Journal of Experimental Psychology: Applied	Focuses on studies that bridge practically oriented problems and psychological theory
Journal of Experimental Psychology: General	Publishes integrative articles of interest to all experimental psychologists

American Psychological Association Journals (continued)

Journal of Experimental Psychology: Human Perception and Performance	Focuses on perception, planning and control of physical actions and related cognitive processes
Journal of Experimental Psychology: Learning, Memory, and Cognition	Contains original studies on all cognitive processes
Journal of Family Psychology	Focuses on the study of family systems and processes and on problems such as marital and family abuse
Journal of Personality and Social Psychology	Contains articles on all areas of personality and social psychology
Neuropsychology	Publishes articles on the relation between the brain and human cognitive, emotional, and behavioral function
Professional Psychology: Research and Practice	Focuses on the application of psychology
Psychological Assessment	Publishes articles on assessment techniques
Psychological Bulletin	Publishes evaluative and integrative reviews of substantive issues in scientific psychology
Psychological Methods	Devoted to the development and dissemination of methods for collecting, analyzing, understanding, and interpreting psychological data
Psychological Review	Publishes articles that make a theoretical contribution to psychology
Psychology and Aging	Publishes articles on the physiological and behavioral aspects of aging
Psychology of Addictive Behaviors	Publishes articles on alcoholism, drug use and misuse, eating disorders, tobacco and nicotine addiction and other compulsive behaviors
Psychology, Public Policy, and Law	Focuses on the link between psychology as a science and public policy and /or law
Rehabilitation Psychology	Publishes theoretical and empirical research, demonstration projects, and policy issues on topics related to chronic illness and physical, mental, and emotional disability

American Psychological Society Journals

Psychological Science	The flagship research journal of APS–publishes articles of interest across all areas of psychology
Current Directions in Psychological Science	Contains reviews spanning all areas of psychology and its applications
Psychological Science in the Public Interest	Publishes definitive assessments of topics in which psychological science may have the potential to inform and improve the well-being of society
Perspectives on Psychological Science	Publishes theoretical statements, literature reviews, viewpoints or opinions, research presentations, and scholarship

The APA Format

The structure of the research report is very simple and tends to follow the steps one takes in conducting a research study. To illustrate the format of the research report, an article that was published in the *Journal of Consulting and Clinical Psychology* is reproduced on the following pages, using the format required when an article is submitted for publication.[1] Adjacent to each section of the research report is an explanation of the material that should be included in that section. This explanation may include some recommendations that are not illustrated in the research report because each study will not include all the elements listed in the publication manual (American Psychological Association, 2001).

When reading through each section of the research report and then when writing your own report, you should keep its purpose in mind. The primary goal is to report as precisely as possible what you did, including a statement of the problem investigated, the methods used to investigate the problem, the results of your investigation, and any conclusions you may have reached. Is there any criterion you can use to determine whether you have clearly and explicitly reported your study? The criterion of replication is probably the most important. If another investigator can read your research report and precisely replicate your study, then chances are good that you have written a clear and complete report.

The following sample research report was prepared according to the guidelines specified in the APA publication manual. This type of research report could be submitted to a journal such as the *Journal of Abnormal Psychology* or *Behavior Therapy*.

[1]"Virtual Reality Exposure Therapy for the Treatment of Fear of Flying: A Controlled Investigation" by N. Maltby, I. Kirsch, M. Mayers, and G. Allen, 2002, *Journal of Consulting and Clinical Psychology, 70,* 1112–1118. Copyright 2002 by the American Psychological Association. Reprinted with permission.

Running head

The running head is an abbreviated title typed flush left at the top of the first (title) page but below the manuscript page header. It is typed in all uppercase letters. It is an abbreviated title of not more than fifty characters in length, counting letters, punctuation, and spaces between words.

Title

The title should be centered on the upper half of the first page of the manuscript and typed in upper- and lowercase letters. It should state the main topic of the study and concisely identify the variables or theoretical issues under investigation. A typical title length is ten to twelve words.

Authors' names and institutional affiliations

The names of the authors in the order of their contribution to the study appear immediately below the title typed in upper- and lowercase letters and centered on the page. The preferred form is to list first name, middle initial, and last name, with titles and degrees omitted. The institutional affiliation where the study was conducted is centered under the author's name on the next double-spaced line. Affiliations outside the United States should include the city, state or province, and country. Authors from different institutions should be typed on separate lines.

Virtual 1

Running head: VIRTUAL REALITY

Virtual Reality Exposure Therapy for the Treatment of

Fear of Flying: A Controlled Investigation

Nicholas Maltby

The Institute of Living

Irving Kirsch, Michael Mayers,

and George J. Allen

University of Connecticut

Page number and header
The page number as well as a shortened title, header should appear in the upper right-hand corner of all manuscript pages except those containing figures. The header should consist of the first one to three words of the title above or five spaces to the left of the page number. This will allow for identification of the page of the manuscript if the pages are separated during the review process. All pages should be numbered consecutively, beginning with the title page.

Abstract
The abstract is a one-paragraph comprehensive summary of the contents of the research report of no more than 120 words in length. It is typed on a separate page, with the word *Abstract* centered at the top of the page in upper- and lowercase letters and no paragraph indentation for the first paragraph. The abstract of an empirical study should include a brief statement of the problem, a summary of the method used (including a description of the participants, instruments, or apparatus), the procedure, the results (including statistical significance levels), and any conclusions and implications.

Abstract

Forty-five participants who refused to fly during a screening test and who also met *Diagnostic and Statistical Manual of Mental Disorders* criteria for specific phobia, agoraphobia, or panic disorder with agoraphobia were randomly assigned to 5 sessions of either virtual reality exposure (VRE) or attention-placebo group treatment (GT). At posttreatment, 65% of VRE participants and 57% of GT participants flew during a test flight. Both groups showed significant improvement following treatment on standardized self-report measures of flight anxiety, with a better outcome for the VRE group on 4 of 5 of these measures. At 6-month follow-up, however, most group differences had disappeared; VRE resulted in a better outcome on only 1 of 5 standardized flight anxiety measures.

Introduction

The text of the research report begins on a new page with the title of the paper typed at the top center of the page. The introductory text is not labeled because of its position in the paper. The introduction is funnel shaped in the sense that it is broad at the beginning and narrow at the end. It should begin with a very general introduction to the problem area and then start to narrow by citing the results of prior works that have been conducted in the area and that bear on the specific issue that you are investigating, leading into a statement of the variables to be investigated. In citing prior research, do not attempt to make an exhaustive review of the literature. Cite only those studies that are directly pertinent, and avoid tangential references. This pertinent literature should lead directly into your study and thereby show the continuity between what you are investigating and prior research. You should then state the purpose of your study and your hypothesis. The introduction should give the reader the rationale for the given investigation, explaining how it fits in with, and is a logical extension of, prior research.

Virtual Reality Exposure Therapy for the

Treatment of Fear of Flying: A Controlled Investigation

Virtual reality exposure (VRE) therapy is a potential alternative to traditional behavioral interventions for anxiety disorders. As in conventional behavioral treatments for anxiety disorders, the central component of VRE is exposure to the feared stimulus situation. The main difference between VRE and other exposure-based treatments is that VRE involves exposure to a computer generated rather than an actual or imagined feared stimulus. Stimuli are presented as part of a virtual environment that is interactive and allows patients to become immersed enough that they react to virtual scenarios as though they were real (Nash, Edwards, Thompson, & Barfield, 2000; Regenbrecht, Schubert, & Friedmann, 1998).

In theory, VRE offers a number of advantages over in vivo or imaginal exposure (Rothbaum, Hodges, Smith, Lee, & Price, 2000). Because VRE can be administered in traditional therapeutic settings, it may be more convenient, controlled, and cost-effective than in vivo exposure. It can also isolate focal concerns more efficiently than in vivo exposure. For instance, in treating fear of flying, if takeoff is the most anxiety-producing component of flight, takeoffs can be repeated quickly and as often as necessary without having to wait for the airplane to land. Finally, VRE may provide a more concrete exposure stimulus that is more involving emotionally than imaginal exposure. This could facilitate more efficient extinction of the fear response.

In controlled and single-case studies, VRE has been found to reliably elicit fear and effectively treat acrophobia (Emmelkamp et al., in press), claustrophobia (Botella et al., 1998), arachnophobia (Carlin, Hoffman, & Weghorst, 1997), and posttraumatic stress disorder among Vietnam veterans (Rothbaum et al., 1999).

To date, one randomized, controlled study of VRE for fear of flying has been conducted. Rothbaum et al. (2000) compared VRE with standard exposure therapy (SE) to a wait-list control. Both experimental conditions consisted of four sessions of anxiety management followed by either four sessions of exposure to a virtual flight environment (VRE), or four sessions of a hybrid in vivo–imaginal exposure paradigm consisting of in vivo exposure to an airport and static aircraft and imaginal exposure to flying conducted while sitting in the static aircraft (SE). At posttreatment, 53% of the VRE group, 67% of the SE group, and 7% of the wait-list control group took a test flight. Average in-flight anxiety ratings were nearly identical for the two treatment groups: 33.19 ($SD = 15.6$) for VRE and 33.88 ($SD = 16.3$) for SE. On standardized questionnaires, VRE led to average effect size improvements of 1.27 standard deviation units, and SE, to improvements of 1.58 standard deviation units, a difference which was not significant. At 6-month follow-up, treatment gains on self-report measures were maintained or improved on for both treatment groups. In addition, 79% of VRE participants and 69% of SE participants reportedly had flown spontaneously since the posttreatment test flight.

In comparison to previous interventions for fear of flying, the Rothbaum et al. (2000) study yielded posttreatment rates of flying that are consistent with systematic desensitization (82%; Howard,

Murphy, & Clarke, 1983), systematic desensitization where exposure was delivered by video (65%; Denholtz & Mann, 1975; 70%; Solyom, Shugar, Bryntwick, & Solyom, 1973), stress inoculation training (82%; Beckham, Vrana, May, Gustafson, & Smith, 1990), and imaginal–in vivo exposure hybrid treatments (91%; Haug et al., 1987).

The fear-of-flying outcome studies reported above have been criticized by Öst, Brandberg, and Alm (1997) for not including both pre- and posttreatment test flights. Öst et al. argued that, as the majority of flight phobics can already fly, studies without a pretreatment test flight would overestimate treatment effectiveness by not excluding participants who would have flown without treatment.

This literature also varies widely on inclusion of comparison control conditions. Wait-list or no-treatment control conditions were most commonly used (e.g., Beckham et al., 1990; Howard et al., 1983; Rothbaum et al., 2000), although several investigations (Denholtz & Mann, 1975; Haug et al., 1987; Öst et al., 1997) did not use control groups. One investigation (Solyom et al., 1973) compared behavioral interventions with group therapy as a placebo control. Use of such placebo interventions may help attenuate overestimation of treatment effectiveness by providing a comparison that capitalizes upon motivational factors (e.g., loyalty to the therapist) to increase the likelihood of flying.

The present study compared five sessions of VRE for fear of flying to an attention-placebo group therapy treatment (GT) designed to control for nonspecific treatment effects. GT was selected to be a plausible treatment yet be devoid of behavioral elements. To address

Method

The purpose of the method section is to tell the reader exactly how the study was conducted. This is the part of the research report that must directly satisfy the criterion of replication. If another investigator could read the method section and replicate the study you conducted, then you have adequately described it. Stating exactly how you conducted the study is necessary so that the reader can evaluate the adequacy of the research and the reliability and validity of the results. In order to facilitate communication, the method section is typically divided into subsections: participants; apparatus or materials; and procedure. Deviation from this format may be necessary if the experiment is complex or a detailed description of the stimuli is called for. In such instances, additional subsections, as in the sample article, may be required to help readers find specific information.

criticisms of previous studies, the present study included a screening flight to exclude participants who could fly and a posttreatment test flight. Self-report data were collected before and after treatment and at 6-month follow-up. It was hypothesized that (a) a significantly greater percentage of VRE recipients would successfully fly following treatment, (b) VRE recipients would report significantly less anxiety during the post-treatment flight, and (c) gains favoring VRE would be maintained at a 6-month follow-up.

Method

Participants

Participants were recruited through advertisements placed in local newspapers offering free treatment to people who were unable to fly because of their fear of flying. Seventy potential participants responded to the advertisements and were evaluated for the follow- ing criteria: (a) meeting *Diagnostic and Statistical Manual of Mental Disorders* (4th ed.; *DSM-IV* American Psychiatric Association, 1994) criteria for specific phobia, situational type; agoraphobia; or panic disorder with agoraphobia, where flying is the primary feared stimu- lus, and (b) refusing to fly during a pretreatment screening test. Forty-five participants meeting these criteria were randomly assigned to VRE therapy or an attention-placebo GT.

Demographic and pretreatment characteristics of the sample were consistent with those reported in other studies (Rothbaum et al., 2000; Wilhelm & Roth, 1997b). Participants ranged in age from 20 to 72 years, with a mean of 45.34 years. They were relatively wealthy and well educated, with a median income of $80,000 and a

Participants

The participants subsection should tell the reader who the research participants were, how many there were, their characteristics (age, sex), and how they were selected and assigned. Any other pertinent information regarding the participants should also be included, such as the numbers assigned to each experimental condition, the number of participants that were selected for the study but did not complete it (and why), and any inducements that were given to encourage participation. If animals were used, their genus, species, strain number, and supplier should be specified, in addition to their gender, age, weight, and physiological condition.

mean level of education of 16 years. The majority were women (79%, $n = 34$), Caucasian (95%, $n = 41$), and married (72%, $n = 31$).

On average, they had been scared of flying for 18.6 years and had not flown for 4.9 years. Participants averaged 18.8 lifetime roundtrip flights and 7.2 roundtrip flights since their fear of flying began. Seven percent ($n = 3$) had never flown because of their fear. A total of 65% ($n = 28$) were diagnosed with specific phobia, situational type, 12% ($n = 5$) with agoraphobia without panic disorder, and 23% ($n = 10$) with panic disorder with agoraphobia. Twenty-eight percent ($n = 12$) had previously received treatment for fear of flying.

Multiple analyses of variance (age, years of education, income, years scared of flying, total flights, total flights since fear of flying began, years since last flight, self-reported motion sickness, and scores on standardized questionnaires) and chi-square analyses (gender, marital status, diagnosis, and past treatment for fear of flying) yielded only one significant group difference on demographic and pretreatment variables. VRE participants reported a longer history of fear of flying ($M = 22.8$ years, $SD = 12.6$ years) than GT participants ($M = 15.0$ years, $SD = 9.5$ years). This variable was not used as a covariate in later analyses because it did not correlate with any outcome measures. Two participants in the VRE condition withdrew from the study, one because she experienced motion sickness while in the virtual environment and the other because of persistent scheduling conflicts. No participants dropped out from group treatment.

Apparatus, materials, measures, and instruments
In this subsection, the reader can learn what apparatus or materials were used. Sufficient detail should be used to enable the reader to obtain comparable equipment. In addition, the reader should be told why the equipment was used. Any mention of commercially marketed equipment should be accompanied by the firm's name and the model number or, in the case of a measuring instrument such as an anxiety scale, a reference that will enable the reader to obtain the same scale. Custom-made equipment should be described; in the case of complex equipment, a diagram or photograph may need to be included.

Apparatus

VRE was conducted using an Integraph TDZ 2000 computer with a 330mhz PII multiprocessor with 128 MB of RAM and a Realism GL2 video card. A Virtual Research V6 head mounted display with stereo earphones was paired with this system to transmit the VR image and accompanying sound.

Therapists

Two male graduate students with 2 and 4 years of clinical experience administered the treatments. Both were experienced in treating phobias and were supervised by a licensed clinical psychologist with over 25 years of experience.

VRE Therapy

VRE was conducted by the graduate student therapists and consisted of five individual treatment sessions spaced over 3 weeks. Session 1 lasted 90 min and consisted of an orientation to the rationale for VRE, anxiety management skills, and an introduction to the virtual reality equipment. Participants also were given an educational handout on the safety and mechanics of flight. They were encouraged to read it but received no didactic instruction on these topics. Anxiety management consisted of imaginal relaxation/progressive muscle relaxation and the development and use of rational responses to counter anxiety-producing thoughts and images about flying. Specifically, participants were taught relaxation skills for 20 min and were asked to practice relaxation twice a day during the study. They were then guided by the therapist to list anxiety-producing thoughts they typically had about flying and to develop rational responses to use during flight. To aid immersion during the exposure phase of treatment, patients ended the session with a brief introduction to the virtual environment.

Sessions 2 through 5 lasted approximately 50 min each and were devoted to graded exposure to flying in the virtual environment. The virtual flying environment consisted of 10 hierarchical levels: an empty hallway devoid of flight-related cues, the airport terminal, walking to a small general aviation airplane, entering the airplane, engine start, taxing to the runway, takeoff, cruise, landing, and taxing back to the airport. Levels were seamlessly connected and participants could navigate through them using a joystick. In addition, three levels of intensity, *smooth, turbulent,* and *stormy,* could be selected by the therapist to provide exposure to more anxiety-producing scenarios.

Participants began in the hallway of the airport on the smooth intensity level. They then used the joystick to walk at their own pace through the terminal and out to the airplane. Once in the airplane they could no longer move using the joystick. Engine start, taxi, takeoff, cruise, landing, and taxing back to the terminal were then accomplished in order and at each participant's pace and discretion. Participants were encouraged to tolerate high or rising anxiety in a scene and to move on only when they felt a decrease in anxiety. On successful completion of all scenes, intensity level was increased and the 10 scenes repeated. When all levels of intensity were completed, treatment focused on any remaining problem areas, such as takeoff or cruise flight.

Group Treatment

Developing a credible but inert treatment is one of the major obstacles to using attention-placebo interventions. Although not an optimal control because it differed from VRE in mode of use (individual vs. group), nonspecific group treatment was selected because a body of evidence supports both its credibility and its ineffectiveness at reducing fear of flying (Greco, 1989; Solyom et al., 1973; Walder, McCracken, James, & Brewitt, 1987).

GT was designed to control for nonspecific treatment effects. It consisted of education about the safety and mechanics of flight and elicitation of each participant's flying history and fears about flying. Participants were encouraged to comment on each other's stories and otherwise engage in group process. No behavioral techniques were used and the therapists made no references to exposure or anxiety management skills. GT was matched to VRE for number and length of treatment sessions. Groups consisted of 4–6 members. The treatment rationale given to participants was that learning the facts about flying, sharing one's fears among understanding peers, and the interpersonal process inherent to group therapies helps to alleviate anxiety.

Measures

Flight Anxiety Situations Questionnaire (FAS). The FAS (Van Gerwen, Spinhoven, Van Dyck, & Diekstra, 1999) is a 32-item self-report questionnaire assessing on 5-point Likert scales the degree of anxiety experienced in different flying-related situations. Three subscales are derived from the FAS: (a) Anticipatory Flight Anxiety, measuring anxiety in anticipation of flying; (b) In-Flight Anxiety, assessing anxiety experienced during a flight; and (c) Generalized Flight Anxiety, assessing generalized fear about flying when no flight is planned. Examples of generalized anxiety include fearful reactions to hearing airplanes fly overhead or seeing an airplane on television when the person has no intent to fly. The FAS, including the In-Flight Anxiety Scale, was not administered during flight. Internal consistency and reliability for all scales have been found to be adequate with Cronbach's alphas ranging from .88 to .97 and test–retest reliability ranging from .90 to .92. The FAS also has been found to be sensitive to treatment changes and to have adequate convergent and divergent validity.

Flight Anxiety Modality Questionnaire (FAM). The FAM (Van Gerwen et al., 1999) is an 18-item self-report questionnaire assessing the symptoms by which flying-related anxiety is expressed. Two scales measuring somatic and cognitive anxiety are derived from the FAM. The Somatic Anxiety Scale assesses the physical symptoms of flight anxiety and the Cognitive Anxiety Scale assesses common maladaptive thoughts and fears about flying. Internal consistency and temporal stability for both scales is good. Cronbach's alpha for both scales was .89 and test–retest reliability ranged from .79 to .84. Van Gerwen et al. (1999) report that the FAM also has been found to be sensitive to change and has adequate convergent and divergent validity.

Flying History Form. The Flying History Form is a 4-item self-report questionnaire assessing flying activities and fear of flying during the follow-up period. Items asked whether the participant flew since the end of treatment, the number of flights, if any, anxiety levels during any flights, and treatment-seeking behavior.

DSM-IV diagnostic status across the three domains associated with fear of flying, specific phobia, situational type; agoraphobia without panic disorder, and panic disorder with agoraphobia, was assessed with an unstructured interview conducted by Nicholas Maltby. The latter two diagnoses led to inclusion in the study only if flying was the primary feared stimulus.

Test flights. Test flights assessed avoidance of flying and anxiety during flight. They were conducted in small, general aviation aircraft (four-seat Piper Warrior 11s) and were provided free of charge to each participant. Each flight was broken down into seven steps: walking to the aircraft, entering the aircraft, engine start, taxi, take-off, cruise, and landing. At each step, participants had control over whether to continue to the next step or stop. If they chose to fly, the test flight lasted approximately 10 to 15 min. Participants were flown one at a time and were accompanied by the pilot and the therapist not assigned to treat them. Refusing any step prior to takeoff was the primary inclusion criterion for participation in the study. During feedback, participants reported that the small airplane was at least as fear producing as if they had to fly commercially. Small aircraft have been used previously to assess outcome (Beckham et al., 1990; Wilhelm & Roth, 1997a) and to conduct in vivo exposure (Greco, 1989).

Subjective units of discomfort (SUDS). SUDS ratings were assessed during the posttreatment test flight. SUDS were made on

Virtual   13

a 101-point scale ranging from 0 (*no anxiety*) to 100 (*maximum anxiety*). Procedurally, SUDS levels were obtained by prompts from the accompanying therapist at three points during the flight: climb-out, level flight, and approach to landing.

Procedure

At initial contact, potential participants were interviewed over the phone for possible inclusion and the project was explained to them in detail. Those meeting preliminary criteria were mailed informed consent and pretreatment questionnaires and were asked to participate in a test flight that was explained to them in detail. On arrival at the airport for the pretreatment test flight, both the informed consent and test flight rationales were reviewed and pretreatment questionnaires, previously completed at home, were collected.

Nicholas Maltby then conducted an unstructured interview to assess *DSM-IV* diagnostic status across the three domains associated with fear of flying: specific phobia, situational type; agoraphobia without panic disorder; and panic disorder with agoraphobia. Evidence for the latter two diagnoses led to exclusion from the study, unless flying was the primary feared stimulus.

During the test flight procedure, no one was forced or coerced to fly. Up until actual takeoff, participants were asked whether they wanted to advance to the next step, thus maintaining control over whether to continue to the next step or stop. If they chose to fly, the test flight lasted approximately 10 to 15 min. Participants were flown singly, accompanied by the pilot and the therapist not assigned to treat them.

Procedure

In the procedure subsection, the reader is told exactly how the study was executed, from the moment the participant and the experimenter came into contact to the moment their contact was terminated. Consequently, this subsection represents a step-by-step account of what both the experimenter and the participant did during the study. This section should include any instructions or stimulus conditions presented to the participants and the responses that were required of them, as well as any control techniques used (such as randomization or counterbalancing). In other words, you are to tell the reader exactly what both you and the participants did and how you did it.

Results

The purpose of the results section is to tell the reader exactly what data were collected, how they were analyzed, and what the outcome of the data analysis was. This section should tell what statistical tests were used. Before reporting specific results, state the alpha level used or specify the alpha level when reporting each result. Significant values of any inferential tests (e.g., *t*-tests, *F*-tests, and chi-square measures) should be accompanied by the magnitude of the obtained value of the test, along with the accompanying degrees of freedom, probability level, and direction of the effect. The exact probability (*p* value) should be reported. Sufficient descriptive statistics (e.g., means, standard deviation) should be included to ensure the understanding of the effect being reported. In illustrating the direction of a significant effect (nonsignificant effects are not elaborated on for obvious reasons), you need to decide on the medium that will most clearly and economically serve your purpose. If a main effect consisting of three groups is significant, your best approach is probably to incorporate the mean scores

Refusing any step prior to takeoff was the primary inclusion criterion for participation in the study. Six potential participants flew during the test flight. After flying, these 6 were debriefed and offered an alternative opportunity to receive treatment. No further assessment was conducted with this population. Potential participants meeting criteria were then randomly assigned to treatment condition and scheduled for the initial treatment session.

Both five-session treatments were conducted at a University of Connecticut-based psychology services clinic. At the end of the fifth session, participants completed posttreatment questionnaires and were scheduled for the posttreatment test flight. The posttreatment test flight was conducted according to the procedure noted above. Participants flew singly and were accompanied by the researcher not assigned to treat them.

Follow-up assessment was conducted 6 months after treatment. Participants were mailed standardized questionnaires and a brief follow-up to assess flying activities and fear of flying during the intervening 6 months. Flying during the follow-up up period was assessed by self-report rather than by a test flight.

Results

Evaluation of Treatment Effects

A series of 2 (treatment group) $\times$ 2 (time: pretreatment, posttreatment) repeated measures analyses of variance were conducted on self-report measures. Wherever interactions were significant, test of simple effects were computed. Two measures of effect size, *d* and η^2, were also computed to express between-groups and pre-for each of these groups into the text of the report. If the significant effect is a complex interaction, the best approach is to summarize your data by means of a figure or a table, which is placed on a separate page at the end of the research report. If you do use a figure or table (a decision that you must make), be sure to tell the reader, in the text of the report, what data it depicts. Then give a sufficient explanation of the presented data to make sure that the reader interprets them correctly. When means are reported always include an associated measure of variability, such as standard deviation or mean square error. In writing the results section, there are several things you should not include. Individual data are not included unless a single-case study is conducted. Statistical formulas are not included unless the statistical test is new, unique, or in some other way not standard or commonly used.

posttreatment effects in terms of standard deviation units and the proportion of variability accounted for by the treatment conditions, respectively (Dunlop, Cortina, Vaslow, & Burke, 1996). In addition, multiple 2 (treatment group) $\times$ 2 (time: pretreatment, 6-month follow-up) repeated measures analyses of variance were conducted to determine the extent to which treatment effects were maintained. Table 1 presents pretreatment, posttreatment, and 6-month follow-up descriptive statistics and interaction effects for self-report dependent measures.

The clinical significance of changes on the FAS and FAM were determined with a procedure defined by Jacobson, Roberts, Bems, and McGlinchey (1999) for use when norms for a functional group are not available. Accordingly, an improvement of two standard deviations from the population mean was used to functionally define a score as falling outside the range of fearful fliers and thus represent clinically significant change.

In-Flight Anxiety Scale

Pre–posttreatment analysis of the In-Flight Anxiety Scale of the FAS yielded a significant Treatment Group $\times$ Time interaction, $F(1, 37) = 14.85$, $p < .01$, $\eta^2 = .29$. Tests of simple effects indicated that at posttreatment both groups reported significantly reduced in-flight anxiety, but VRE therapy led to significantly greater reductions with a within-group effect size of 2.43 standard deviation units compared with 0.72 standard deviation units for GT. The between-groups effect size was 0.79 standard deviation units. Clinically significant change in in-flight anxiety was achieved by 70% of VRE participants and 22% of GT participants, a difference that was statistically significant, $\chi^2(1) = 10.54$, $p < .01$. At 6-month follow-up both groups maintained their treatment gains but VRE no longer yielded significantly lower scores than GT. This resulted in 50% of VRE participants and 32% of GT participants meeting criteria for clinically significant change, a difference that was not significant.

Anticipatory Flight Anxiety Scale

Pre–posttreatment analysis of the Anticipatory Flight Anxiety Scale of the FAS yielded a significant Treatment Group × Time interaction, $F(1, 38) = 5.94$, $p < .05$, $\eta^2 = .14$. Tests of simple effects indicated that at posttreatment both groups reported significantly reduced anticipatory flight anxiety, but VRE therapy led to significantly greater reductions with an effect size of 1.35 standard deviation units compared with 0.62 standard deviation units for GT. The between-groups effect size was 0.88 standard deviation units. Clinically significant change in anticipatory flight anxiety was achieved by 35% of VRE participants and 9% of GT participants, a difference that was statistically significant, $\chi^2(1) = 5.03$, $p < .05$. At 6-month follow-up both groups maintained their treatment gains but VRE no longer yielded significantly lower scores than GT. Thirty-nine percent of VRE participants and 32% of GT participants met criteria for clinically significant change, a difference that was not significant.

Generalized Flight Anxiety Scale

Pre–posttreatment analysis of the Generalized Flight Anxiety Scale of the FAS yielded only a significant main effect for time, $F(1, 39) = 12.21$, $p < .01$, $\eta^2 = .24$. At posttreatment, both groups reported significantly reduced generalized flight anxiety with effect sizes of 0.71 standard deviation units for VRE and 0.38 standard deviation units for GT. The between-groups effect size was 0.25 standard deviation units. Clinically significant change could not be computed for this scale because the population mean was within 2.0 standard deviations of zero. At 6-month follow-up, both groups maintained their respective treatment gains.

Somatic Anxiety Scale

Pre–posttreatment analysis of the Somatic Anxiety Scale of the FAM yielded a significant Treatment Group × Time interaction, $F(1, 37) = 9.23$, $p < .01$, $\eta^2 = .20$. Tests of simple effects found that at posttreatment VRE therapy resulted in significant reductions in somatic anxiety with an effect size of 1.29 standard deviation units, whereas GT was unchanged with an effect size of 0.02 standard deviation units. The between-groups effect size was 1.17 standard deviation units. Clinically significant change could not be computed for this scale because the population mean was within 2.0 standard deviations of zero. Repeated measures analysis of pretreatment and 6-month follow-up scores yielded a significant main effect only for time, $F(1, 37) = 21.36$, $p < .01$, $\eta^2 = .37$. Both groups were significantly improved from pre-treatment and VRE no longer yielded significantly lower scores than GT.

Cognitive Anxiety Scale

Pre–posttreatment analysis of the Cognitive Anxiety Scale of the FAM yielded a significant Treatment Group × Time interaction, $F(1, 37) = 12.91$, $p < .01$, $\eta^2 = .26$. Tests of simple effects indicated that at posttreatment both groups reported significant reductions in cognitive anxiety, but VRE led to significantly greater reductions with an effect size of 1.78 standard deviation units compared with 0.38 standard deviation units for GT. The between-groups effect size was 0.76 standard deviation units. Clinically significant change was achieved by 35% of VRE participants and 17% of GT participants, a difference that was not significant. Repeated measures analysis of pretreatment and 6-month follow-up scores yielded a significant Treatment Group $\times$ Time interaction, $F(1, 37) = 5.55$, $p < .05$, $\eta^2 = .13$. Both groups maintained their treatment gains and VRE continued to yield significantly lower scores than GT. The pre-posttreatment effect size was 1.72 standard deviation units compared with 0.58 standard deviation units for GT. The between-groups effect size was 0.62 standard deviation units. Forty-four percent of VRE and 32% of GT participants met criteria for clinically significant change, a difference that was not significant.

Posttreatment Test Flight

A total of 13 of 20 VRE participants (65%) and 13 of 23 GT participants (57%) flew during the posttreatment test flight, a difference that was not significant. SUDS ratings during flight did not differ for participants receiving VRE or GT. Average in-flight SUDS were 51.7 ($SD = 27.1$) for VRE participants and 63.2 ($SD = 21.3$) for GT participants with a between-group effect size of 0.47 standard deviation units.

At 6-month follow-up, 9 of 19 VRE participants (47%) and 8 of 22 GT participants (36%) reported having flown spontaneously

in the 6 months since treatment ended, a difference that was
not significant. Retrospective SUDS ratings during these flights
were 32.3 (*SD* = 15.8) for VRE participants and 48.8 (*SD* = 29.1)
for GT participants, a difference that was not significant.
The between-groups effect size was 0.62 standard deviation
units.

Relationships Between Flying and Indices of Subjective Distress

Table 2 presents product–moment intercorrelations among the
standardized measures of flight anxiety collected following treatment and point–biserial correlations between these five standardized
measures and successfully flying at postintervention, separately for
the VRE and GT groups. The anxiety measures were substantially
intercorrelated, suggesting some overlap in the previously described
analyses of means.

For VRE participants only, lower self-reported anxiety on three of
the five measures was associated significantly with the likelihood of
flying after treatment, specifically on the Generalized (−.48), Anticipatory (−.55), and Somatic flight anxiety scales (−.74). For GT participants, self-reported anxiety was unrelated to the decision to fly
on all five dependent measures. Pairwise comparison of these correlations indicated that the biggest difference was found for the
Somatic flight anxiety subscale (−.74 for VRE vs. .03 for GT participants), with this being the only significant difference between the
respective coefficients, *z* = 2.90, *p* < .01.

Discussion

The purpose of the discussion section of the research report is to interpret and evaluate the results obtained, giving primary emphasis to the relationships between the results and the hypotheses of the study. Begin the discussion by stating whether the hypothesis of the study was or was not supported. Following this statement, you should interpret the results, telling the reader what you think they mean. In doing so, you should attempt to integrate your research findings with the results of prior research. Note that this is the only place in the research report where you are given any latitude for stating your own opinion, and even then you are limited to stating your interpretation of the results and what you think the major shortcomings of the study are. In general, the discussion should answer the questions, (a) what does the study contribute, (b) how has it helped solve the study problem, and (c) what conclusions and theoretical implications can be drawn from the study.

Discussion

The present study compared VRE therapy to an attention-placebo GT designed to control for nonspecific treatment effects. At posttreatment, both conditions yielded similar rates of flying on a test flight and significant improvements on standardized measures of flight anxiety. VRE, however, yielded significantly greater improvement on four of five standardized measures of flight anxiety. The average effect size improvement on these measures was 1.51 standard deviation units for VRE and 0.42 standard deviation units for GT, corresponding to large and medium effect sizes, respectively (Cohen, 1988). On the three scales for which clinically significant change could be computed, an average of 46% of VRE participants and 16% of GT participants met criteria for clinically meaningful change.

By 6-month follow-up, however, most group differences had disappeared or attenuated. VRE was superior to GT on only one of five standardized measures of flight anxiety and 45% of VRE, and 32% of GT participants met criteria for clinically meaningful change.

Results are consistent with those of Rothbaum et al. (2000) and provide additional support for the efficacy of virtual reality treatments for fear of flying. Both studies yielded similar rates of flying after treatment and similar effect size changes on self-report measures of flight anxiety. Considering both investigations, VRE appears to yield rates of flying equivalent to hybrid or imaginal exposure-based treatments but somewhat less than in vivo exposure. Direct comparisons, however, are limited by the lack of either a pretreatment test flight or a control group in most of the previous studies.

When discussing the shortcomings, you should mention only the flaws that may have had a significant influence on the results obtained. You should accept a negative finding as such rather than attempting to explain it as being due to some methodological flaw (unless, as may occasionally occur, there is a very good and documented reason why a flaw did cause the negative finding).

One unexpected finding of the present study is the relatively good outcome for those receiving the attention-placebo GT. More than half flew after treatment, and they were significantly improved on four of five standardized measures of flight anxiety at posttreatment and five of five measures at 6-month follow-up. Educational and nonspecific factors seem to have a relatively large impact on flying behavior and fear of flying. Nonetheless, for GT participants only, degree of anxiety reported at posttreatment was unrelated to the ability to fly successfully. In contrast, reduced scores on measures of flight anxiety for VRE participants was significantly associated with successfully flying. This differential outcome suggests that VRE participants at least believed that they would fly with greater comfort, whereas GT participants might have been influenced by other less-specific factors such as loyalty to the therapist, intervention, hope, and self-disclosure (Forsyth & Corazzini, 2000).

Studies that report only average anxiety levels during test flights do not discriminate successful flyers from unsuccessful ones. To better make this discrimination, future studies should include pretreatment test flights to provide baseline data from which to measure treatment success. In addition, use of various end-state assessments (Brown & Barlow, 1995) could provide meaningful information about the phenomenological experiences of sufferers during flights. Finally, the collection of norms for nonfearful fliers on measures such as the FAS and FAM would increase our ability to determine clinically significant change on these measures.

One limitation of the present study is that test flights were conducted in small, general aviation planes rather than large, commercial aircraft. Although small aircraft have been used to assess treatment outcome (Beckham et al., 1990; Wilhelm & Roth, 1997a), most people usually fly in larger planes. This difference may well weaken the generalizability of the present findings. In addition, our decision to select participants on the basis of their refusal to fly, although simplifying interpretation of the outcomes, also yielded a more restricted sample that may not be representative of typically fearful fliers.

VRE, in its present iteration, presents several barriers to treatment including expense of hardware and software components and the occasional experience of motion sickness in virtual environments. The price of systems has come down dramatically in the past and, if trends continue, much more affordable systems should be available in the near future. Motion sickness is experienced by some patients and, although it usually passes with time, it may lead patients to drop out of treatment (Nichols, Haldane, & Wilson, 2000). One patient in the present study dropped out because of motion sickness. The effects of motion sickness on the quality of presence and on treatment outcome are unknown but remain a potential source of error variance. Finally, because VRE is computerized, it is limited to its protocol. If people request an element not included in the program, it cannot easily be provided. In this study, several participants commented that the lack of physical motion to simulate turbulence limited their sense of presence. Adding this feature is not reasonably done during the course of treatment. As normative knowledge increases, treatment protocols should become more comprehensive, provide a more robust menu of features, and lead to improved outcomes.

The emerging nature of virtual reality technology suggests that much of its potential is of yet unrealized. For instance, achieving a sense of presence (i.e., treating the virtual world as if it were real) may be critical to treatment success, but presence and how to best manipulate treatment components to maximize it are only rudimentarily understood (Nichols et al., 2000; Regenbrecht et al., 1998). Perhaps the greatest potential gain is in developing virtual reality applications that focus on the unique strengths of this technology.

References

The purpose of the reference section, as you might expect, is to provide an accurate and complete list of all the references cited in the text of the report. All the listed references in the text must be cited and presented in alphabetical order using a hanging indent format. This means the first line of each reference is set flush left and subsequent lines are indented.

References

American Psychiatric Association. (1994). *Diagnostic and statistical manual of mental disorders* (4th ed.). Washington, DC: Author.

Beckham, J. C., Vrana, S. R., May, J. G., Gustafson, D. J., & Smith, G. R. (1990). Emotional processing and fear measurement synchrony as indicators of treatment outcome in fear of flying. *Journal of Behavior Therapy & Experimental Psychiatry, 21,* 153–162.

Botella, C., Banos, R. M., Perpina, C., Villa, H., Alcaniz, M., & Rey, A. (1998). Virtual reality treatment of claustrophobia: A case report. *Behaviour Research & Therapy, 36,* 239–246.

Brown, T. A., & Barlow, D. H. (1995). Long-term outcome in cognitive-behavioral treatment of panic disorder: Clinical predictors and alternative strategies for assessment. *Journal of Consulting and Clinical Psychology, 63,* 754–765.

Carlin, A. S., Hoffman, H. G., & Weghorst, S. (1997). Virtual reality and tactile augmentation in the treatment of spider phobia: a case study. *Behaviour Research & Therapy, 35,* 153–158.

Cohen, J. (1988). *Statistical power analysis for the behavioral sciences.* Hillsdale, NJ: Erlbaum.

Denholtz, M. S., & Mann, E. T. (1975). An automated audiovisual treatment of phobias administered by non-professionals. *Journal of Behavior Therapy & Experimental Psychiatry, 6,* 111–115.

Dunlop, W. P., Cortina, J. M., Vaslow, J. B., & Burke, M. J. (1996). Meta-analysis of experiments with matched groups or repeated measures designs. *Psychological Methods, 1,* 170–177.

Emmelkamp, P. M. G., Krijn, M., Hulsbosch, L., de Vries, S., Schuemie, M. J., & van der Mast, C. A. P. G. (in press). Virtual reality treatment versus exposure in vivo: A comparative evaluation in acrophobia. *Behaviour Research & Therapy.*

Forsyth, D. R., & Corazzini, J. G. (2000). Groups as change agents. In C. R. Snyder & R. E. Ingram (Eds.), *Handbook of psychological*

Virtual 25

change: Psychotherapy processes and practices for the 21st century (pp. 309–336). New York: Wiley.

Greco, T. S. (1989). A cognitive-behavioral approach to fear of flying: A practitioner's guide. *Phobia Practice & Research Journal, 2,* 3–15.

Haug, T., Brenne, L., Johnsen, B. H., Berntzen, D., Gotestam, K., & Hugdahl, K. (1987). A three-systems analysis of fear of flying: A comparison of a consonant vs. a non-consonant treatment method. *Behaviour Research & Therapy, 25,* 187–194.

Howard, W. A., Murphy, S. M., & Clarke, J. C. (1983). The nature and treatment of fear of flying: A controlled investigation. *Behavior Therapy, 14,* 557–567.

Jacobson, N. S., Roberts, L. J., Berns, S. B., & McGlinchey, J. B. (1999). Methods for defining and determining the clinical significance of treatment effects: Description, application, and alternatives. *Journal of Consulting and Clinical Psychology, 67,* 300–307.

Nash, E. B., Edwards, G. W., Thompson, J. A., & Barfield, W. (2000). A review of presence and performance in virtual environments. *International Journal of Human-Computer Interaction, 12,* 1–41.

Nichols, S., Haldane, C., & Wilson, J. R. (2000). Measurement of presence and its consequences in virtual environments. *International Journal of Human-Computer Studies, 52,* 471–491.

Öst, L. G., Brundberg, M., & Alm, T. (1997). One versus five sessions of exposure in the treatment of flying phobia. *Behaviour Research & Therapy, 35,* 987–996.

Regenbrecht, H. T., Schubert, T. W., & Friedmann, F. (1998). Measuring the sense of presence and its relations to fear of heights in virtual environments. *International Journal of Human-Computer Interaction, 10,* 233–249.

Rothbaum, B. O., Hodges, L., Alarcon, R., Ready, D., Shahar, F., Graap, K., et al. (1999). Virtual reality exposure therapy for PTSD

Vietnam veterans: A case study. *Journal of Traumatic Stress, 12,* 263–271.

Rothbaum, B. O., Hodges, L., Smith, S., Lee, J. H., & Price, L. (2000). A controlled study of virtual reality exposure therapy for fear of flying. *Journal of Consulting and Clinical Psychology, 68,* 1020–1026.

Solyom, L., Shugar, R., Bryntwick, S., & Solyom, C. (1973). Treatment of fear of flying. *American Journal of Psychiatry, 130,* 423–427.

Van Gerwen, L. J., Spinhoven, P., Van Dyck, R., & Diekstra, R. F. (1999). Construction and psychometric characteristics of two self-report questionnaires for the assessment of fear of flying. *Psychological Assessment, 11,* 146–158.

Walder, C. P., McCracken, M. H., James, P. T., & Brewitt, N. (1987). Psychological intervention in civilian flying phobia: Evaluation and three-year follow-up. *British Journal of Psychiatry, 151,* 494–498.

Wilhelm, F. H., & Roth, W. T. (1997a). Acute and delayed effects of alprazolam on flight phobics during exposure. *Behaviour Research & Therapy, 35,* 831–841.

Wilhelm, F. H., & Roth, W. T. (1997b). Clinical characteristics of flight phobia. *Journal of Anxiety Disorders, 11,* 241–261.

Virtual   27

Author Note

Nicholas Maltby, Anxiety Disorders Center, The Institute of Living, Hartford, Connecticut; Irving Kirsch, Michael Mayers, and George J. Allen, Department of Psychology, University of Connecticut.

Disclosure statement: Research funding for this project was provided by ArgusVR, Inc., which is developing products related to the research described in this article. In addition, Irving Kirsch and Nicholas Maltby serve as consultants to ArgusVR, Inc.

Correspondence concerning this article should be addressed to Irving Kirsch, Department of Psychology, University of Connecticut, 406 Babbidge Road, U-1020, Storrs, Connecticut 06269. E-mail: irving.kirsch@uconn.edu

Author note

Author identification notes appear with each printed article and are for the purpose of acknowledging the basis of a study (such as a grant or a dissertation), acknowledging assistance in the conduct of the study or preparation of the manuscript, specifying the institutional affiliation of the author, and designating the address of the author to whom reprint requests should be sent. These notes are typed on a separate page, with the words *Author Note* centered at the top of the page in upper- and lowercase letters. Each note should start with a paragraph indentation. The order is authors' names and departmental affiliations, then any special circumstances (e.g., dissertation) and acknowledgments, and finally the author's address for correspondence. These notes are not numbered or cited in the text and appear on the title page if the report is to be blind-reviewed, or reviewed in the absence of any information that would identify the author.

Footnotes

Footnotes are numbered consecutively, with a superscript arabic numeral, in the order in which they appear in the text of the report. Most footnotes are content footnotes, containing material needed to supplement the information provided in the text. Such footnotes are typed on a separate page, with the word *Footnotes* centered in upper- and lowercase letters. The first line of each footnote is indented five to seven spaces or one-half inch, and the superscript numeral of the footnote should appear in the space just preceding the beginning of the footnote. Footnotes are typed in the order in which they are mentioned in the text.

Virtual   28

Footnotes

There were no footnotes in this manuscript, but if there were they would be presented on this page.

Table 1

Descriptive Statistics, ANOVA Interaction Effects, and Effect Sizes at Pretreatment, Posttreatment, and 6-Month Follow-Up on Fear of Flying Measures

Variable	VRE (n = 20)		GT (n = 23)		ANOVA		Simple
	M	*SD*	*M*	*SD*	$F(1, 37)$	η^2	effects
In-Flight Anxiety Scale							
Pretreatment	37.94	4.62	36.63	9.05			
Posttreatment	20.50	9.05	28.92	12.02	14.85**	.29	VRE < GT
6-month follow-up	24.31	12.08	29.14	12.76	3.12	.08	
Anticipatory Flight Anxiety Scale							
Pretreatment	44.45	11.72	45.72	8.48			
Posttreatment	28.00	12.64	39.11	12.48	5.94*	.14	VRE < GT
6-month follow-up	29.00	13.84	35.76	14.76	1.41	.04	
Generalized Flight Anxiety Scale							
Pretreatment	10.70	5.66	10.43	6.04			
Posttreatment	7.00	4.74	8.26	5.51	0.83	.02	VRE < GT
6-month follow-up	5.89	4.61	7.81	5.67	2.91	.07	
Somatic Anxiety Scale							
Pretreatment	14.16	8.24	15.45	8.15			
Posttreatment	5.74	4.19	15.25	10.74	9.23**	.22	VRE < GT
6-month follow-up	4.53	6.23	10.95	8.92	1.70	.04	
Cognitive Anxiety Scale							
Pretreatment	23.05	5.35	21.60	6.73			
Posttreatment	12.92	6.02	18.65	8.79	12.91**	.26	VRE < GT
6-month follow-up	12.18	7.13	17.10	8.72	5.55*	.13	VRE < GT
Subjective units of discomfort[a]							
Posttreatment	51.7	27.1	63.2	21.3	1.46	.04	
6-month follow-up	32.3	15.8	48.8	29.1	2.19	.05	

Note. ANOVA = analysis of variance; VRE = virtual reality exposure; GT = attention-placebo group treatment.

[a]*F* values reported for subjective units of discomfort ratings are between-groups comparisons.

* $p < .05$.   ** $p < .01$.

Table 2

Intercorrelations Between Subscales and Flying for Each Treatment Group

Variable	1	2	3	4	5	6
			VRE (*n* = 20)			
1. Flew	—	−.41	−.55*	−.48*	−.74**	−.22
2. In-flight		—	.83**	.70**	.63**	.72**
3. Anticipatory			—	.81**	.81**	.68**
4. Generalized				—	.68**	.69**
5. Somatic					—	.42
6. Cognitive						—
			GT (*n* = 21)			
1. Flew	—	−.19	−.38	−.39	.03	−.39
2. In-flight		—	.65**	.67**	.45*	.71**
3. Anticipatory			—	.76**	.51*	.77**
4. Generalized				—	.52*	.89**
5. Somatic					—	.67**
6. Cognitive						—

Note. VRE = virtual reality exposure; GT = attention-placebo group treatment.

* *p* < .05. ** *p* < .01.

Preparation of the Research Report

In the preceding section you saw an example of the way a research report must be prepared in order to be submitted for possible publication in a psychological journal. Although the essence of the report was discussed in the marginal notes, there are still many style rules that must be considered.

The APA *Publication Manual* presents the stylistic requirement authors must adhere to in the preparation of manuscripts submitted for possible publication in APA journals as well as many non-APA journals. These explicit stylistic requirements have gone through a number of changes to reflect the maturing nature of the language of psychology. As such, they have evolved along with psychology. The first set of requirements was published as a seven-page writer's guide in the February 1929 issue of the *Psychological Bulletin*. This document was succeeded in 1944 by a thirty-two-page document. In 1952, the 1944 document was expanded to sixty pages and carried the title *Publication Manual*. New revisions followed in 1957, 1967, 1974, 1983 and 1994. The current 2001 revision reflects updated information on manuscript preparation and the policies of the various APA journals.

Since the publication of the 1994 edition of the *Publication Manual*, many changes have been made in the publishing world and in the technology used by authors, editors, and publishers. The current 2001 revision updates and clarifies many of the issues relating to the technological world in which we live and the impact it has had on the publishing world. This fifth edition updates the formats for electronic and legal references and provides instructions for manuscripts that are prepared with the nearly universal use of sophisticated word processors. Some of the other changes include the return to the hanging indent and that authors can use italicized and bold-faced entries as they will appear in the published article.

In the following pages I summarize the stylistic requirements that are most frequently used in preparing the research report. Space does not permit the presentation of all stylistic requirements and the *Publication Manual* should be consulted for those requirements that are not presented here. Those presented should allow you to prepare a research report for class.

Writing Style

If you have decided that the study you have conducted is important enough to prepare a research report, you must prepare that research report in a manner that clearly communicates to the reader. Good writing is a craft and an art that requires thoughtful concern for the presentation and language used. Good writing is usually a developmental process that is acquired over time and instructing in its mastery is beyond the scope of the material presented in this book.

However, for the student who has difficulty writing, I recommend an excellent book by W. Strunk, Jr., and E. B. White, *The Elements of Style*. This book is a classic and has the virtue of being short. For assistance in reasoning and writing clearly, I recommend J. T. Gage's *The Shape of Reason*, and for additional assistance in preparing your research, R. L. Rosnow and M. Rosnow's *Writing Papers in Psychology* is excellent. C. A. Hult's book, *Researching and Writing in the Social Sciences*, is also an excellent reference.

Finally, some years ago H. F. Harlow published a very humorous commentary on the content and style of a research report in the *Journal of Comparative and Physiological Psychology.* (See the References for bibliographic data on all these titles.) What I give you are some general principles elaborated on in more detail in the APA *Publication Manual* (2001).

To clearly communicate the essence of a research report, you must have an orderly presentation of ideas. There must be a continuity of words, concepts, and thematic development from the beginning to the end of the report. This continuity can be achieved by the use of punctuation marks to show the relationship between ideas and by the use of transitional words, such as *then, next, therefore,* and *however.* However, some transitional words (for example, *while* and *since*) create confusion and should be used cautiously. *Since* is often incorrectly used in place of *because.* Scientific writing requires precision and use of these transitional terms should be limited and correct.

The preparation of the research report requires a smoothness and economy of expression. Smoothness of expression is achieved by avoiding ambiguity and the insertion of the unexpected, shifting topics, tense, or person, all of which add to the confusion of the reader. For example, an unnecessary shift in verb tense may create an abruptness that precludes smooth expression. By being consistent with verb tenses, smooth expression is enhanced. Economy of expression is achieved by being frugal with words. This means eliminating redundancy, wordiness, jargon, evasiveness, overuse of the passive voice, circumlocution, and clumsy prose as well as overly detailed descriptions of any part of the research report such as participants or procedures.

With respect to writing, there are a number of points I want to make that may assist you. Some people have trouble getting started. They sit down at a computer or with a pencil and pad of paper, and the words or ideas just do not develop. In such instances you can use one of two approaches. Rosnow and Rosnow (1992) suggest that you begin with the section you feel will be easiest to write. For example, this may be the method section because you should already know details such as the characteristics of the research participants you tested and the procedure followed in testing them. Once you have begun writing this section, you may find that other sections such as the introduction are easier to write. The other technique is to force yourself to begin writing a section even if you don't like what you are saying. This technique has the advantage of getting something down on paper and giving you something to work with and revise. It also forces you to move beyond the beginning point, which may cause the ideas to begin flowing. To use this technique you must accept the fact that your first draft is just that. Seldom if ever should you consider the first draft the final product. Rather, you should produce the first draft and then revise it. This process should continue until you are satisfied with the final product.

When you have completed the final product, you should let it rest for several days and then reread it. This rereading several days later should result in additional revisions because the time lapse should allow you to approach the paper more objectively and identify sections that need work.

In preparing the research report, make sure that you avoid plagiarism. *Plagiarism* means that you are kidnapping another person's ideas or efforts and passing them off as your own. In several sections of the research report, particularly the introduction, you must make use of others' work. When you do so, make sure that you give them credit.

Language

The language used to communicate the results of research should be free of demeaning attitudes and biased assumptions in addition to being accurate and clear. The APA *Publication Manual* provides a set of three guidelines—specificity, sensitivity to labels, and acknowledging participation—that should be followed to achieve the goal of unbiased communication.

Specificity   When referring to a person or people, you should choose accurate and clear words that are free from bias. When in doubt, err in the direction of being more rather than less specific. For example, if you are describing age groups it is better to provide a specific age range (for example, *ages eight to twelve*) instead of a broad category (for example, *under twelve*). *People at risk* is too broad. It is preferable to identify the risk and the people involved (for example, *children at risk for sexual abuse*). Similarly, *gender* is preferred when referring to men and women as a social group rather than *sex* because *sex* can be confused with sexual behavior.

Labels   The preferences of the participants in any study must be respected and they should be called what they prefer to be called. This means avoiding labels when possible, or, as has been common in science, broadly categorizing participants as objects (e.g., *the elderly*) or equating participants with their conditions (*depressives* or *stroke victims*). One way to avoid such labels is to use adjectival forms such as *gay men* or *stroke patients*. Another option is to place the person first followed by a descriptive phrase (for example, *individuals with a diagnosis of major depression*). Similarly, sensitivity should be given to any suggestion that one group is better than or is the standard against which another is to be judged. For example, it would be inappropriate to contrast *depressed individuals* with *normal individuals,* thus stigmatizing the depressed people. A more appropriate contrast would be between *depressed* and *nondepressed* individuals.

Participation   Writing about the research participants should be done in such a way that acknowledges their participation. Many research reports use the term *subjects*. This impersonal term should be replaced with a more descriptive term, such as *participant, college students, older people,* or *children*. Making use of the passive voice (for example, *the students were administered*) should be replaced with the active voice (*the students completed*). In general, tell what the research participants did and do so in a way that acknowledges this participation.

Specific Issues   These are the three guidelines that should be followed to avoid writing in a way that reflects demeaning attitudes and biased assumptions. Keeping these in mind, specific attention should be given to the following issues.

Gender. Participants should be described in such a way that avoids ambiguity in sex identity or sex role. This means that you should avoid using *he* to refer to both sexes or *man* or *mankind* to refer to people in general. The words *people, individuals,* or *persons* can be substituted without losing meaning or clarity of expression.

Sexual Orientation. Sexual orientation should not be equated with sexual preference. To avoid labeling and the possible accompanying offensive tone, the use of sexual orientation is preferred unless the implication of choice is intentional. This means that such terms as *homosexual* should be replaced with terms such as *gay men, lesbians,* and *bisexual women or men.* Sexual behavior described with terms such as *same gender, male-male, female-female,* and *male-female* is appropriate because these terms communicate specific instances of sexual behavior regardless of sexual orientation.

Racial and Ethnic Identity. When referring to racial and ethnic groups, it is important to remember that designations can become dated and sometimes negative. The APA *Publication Manual* (2001) encourages authors to ask their participants about their preferred designation. If you designate a racial and ethnic group by proper nouns, such as *Black,* make sure that they are capitalized.

Disabilities. When describing individuals with disabilities, it is important to maintain their integrity as human beings. This means that you should avoid language that equates them with their condition, such as describing participants as *stroke victims* or *depressives.* Again, the principle of specificity is important in describing these individuals. For example, describe a participant as a *person who has a stroke* rather than a *stroke victim.*

Age. The general rule to follow regarding age is to be specific in describing the age of participants and avoid open-ended definitions, such as *over 65.* People of high school age and younger can be referred to as *boys* and *girls.* Call people eighteen and older *men* and *women. Older person* is preferred to *elderly.*

The issues discussed in this section focus on ensuring that biased communication does not enter the research report. In writing this research report you have to also decide whether to use a first- or third-person writing style. Some individuals prefer a first-person writing style; others believe the research report should be impersonal and written in the third person. Polyson, Levinson, and Miller (1982) found that journal editors do not agree on which type of writing style should be used. Similarly, the *Publication Manual* does not take a specific position on this issue. Rather, the emphasis is on clarity and precision in word choice. In the final analysis, it seems as though the writing style chosen should be the one that will facilitate communication of the research study.

Editorial Style

Editorial style refers to the rules or guidelines used by a publisher to ensure a clear, consistent presentation of published material. These rules specify the construction of many of the elements included in a research report such as tables and figures as well as the uniform use of punctuation and abbreviations. Here I list and discuss some of these rules. The *Publication Manual* lists many other rules and guidelines and should be consulted if you have questions about any other style issue not presented here.

Italics   As a general rule, use italics infrequently. Underline any words that are to appear in italics if you are using a typewriter. Otherwise use the italics function of your computer.

Abbreviations   Use abbreviations sparingly. Generally speaking, abbreviate only when the abbreviations are conventional and likely to be familiar to the reader (such as IQ) or if you can save considerable space and avoid cumbersome repetition. In all instances, the Latin abbreviations *cf.* (compare), *e.g.* (for example), *etc.* (and so forth), *i.e.* (that is), *viz.* (namely), and *vs.* (versus, against) are to be used only in parenthetical material. The exception to this rule is the Latin abbreviation *et al.,* which can be used in the text of the manuscript. The unit of time *second* is abbreviated *s* rather than *sec.* Periods are omitted with nonmetric measurements such as *ft* and *lb*. The only exception is *inch,* which is abbreviated *in.* with the period. Units of time such as *day, week, month,* and *year* are never abbreviated. There are many other abbreviations that can be used in a research report. For many other abbreviations you should consult the *Publication Manual* (2001).

Headings   Headings serve to outline the manuscript and to indicate the importance of each topic. There are five different levels of headings that can be used in a manuscript. They have the following top-down progression: (level 1) centered main heading in upper- and lowercase letters; (level 2) centered main heading, italicized, in upper- and lowercase letters; (level 3) flush side heading, italicized, in upper- and lowercase letters; (level 4) indented, italicized, in lowercase paragraph heading ending with a period; and (level 5) centered main heading in uppercase letters. However, all headings are not used in every manuscript, and the specific level of headings are not necessarily consecutive.

If only one level of heading is needed in an article, use only the level 1 heading or a heading that is centered in uppercase and lowercase letters. If two levels are needed use level 1 and level 3 as follows:

Method

Procedure

If three levels of heading are needed, use level 1, level 3, and level 4 as follows:

Method

Procedure

   Meal composition

If four levels of headings are needed, use level 1, level 2, level 3, and level 4 as follows:

Experiment 1

Method

Procedure

Mode of stimulus presentation

If all five levels of heading are needed in an article, the level 5 heading appears first and this heading is followed by the other four.

Quotations   A quotation of fewer than forty words should be inserted into the text and enclosed with double quotation marks. Quotations of forty or more words should be displayed in a freestanding block of lines without quotation marks. The author, year, and specific page from which the quotation is taken should always be included.

Numbers   The general rule about expressing numbers in the text is to use words to express any number that begins a sentence as well as any number below ten. Use figures to express all other numbers. There are several exceptions to this rule, and the APA *Publication Manual* should be consulted for these exceptions. A second rule to follow in stating numbers is to use arabic and not roman numerals.

Physical Measurements   All physical measurements are to be stated in metric units. If a measurement is expressed in nonmetric units, it must be accompanied, in parentheses, by its metric equivalent.

Presentation of Statistical Results   When presenting the results of statistical tests in the text, provide enough information to allow the reader to corroborate the results. Although what counts as sufficient information depends on the statistical test and analysis selected, in general it means including information about the magnitude or value of the test, the degrees of freedom, the probability level, and the direction of the effect. For example, a *t*- and *F*-test could be reported as follows:

$t(36) = 4.52, p = .04$

$F(3,52) = 17.35, p = .02$

When reporting a chi-square value, you should report the degrees of freedom and the sample size in parentheses as follows:

$X^2 (6, N = 68) = 12.64, p = .03$

Such common statistical tests as *t*- and *F*-tests are not referenced, and the formulas are not included in the text. Referencing and formulas are included only when the statistical test is new, rare, or essential to the manuscript, as when the article concerns a given statistical test.

After the results of a statistical test are reported, descriptive statistical data such as means and standard deviations must be included to clarify the meaning of a significant effect and to indicate the direction of the effect.

Tables   Tables are expensive to publish and therefore should be used only when they can convey and summarize data more economically and clearly than can a lengthy discussion. Tables should be viewed as informative supplements to the text. Although each table should be intelligible by itself, it should also be an integral part of the text. As a supplement, only the table's highlights should be discussed. If you decide to use tables, number them with arabic numerals in the order in which they are mentioned in the text.

In preparing the table, you can use the tables presented in the sample article as guides. Each table should have a brief title that clearly explains the data it contains. This title and the word *Table* and its number are typed flush with the left margin and at the top of the table. Each column and row of data within the table should be given a label that identifies, as briefly as possible, the data contained in that row or column. Columns within the table should be at least three spaces apart. The *Publication Manual* lists the various types of headings that can be used in tables. When placing data in the rows and columns, carry each data point out to the same number of decimal places, and place a dash to indicate an absence of data.

If you report the results of ANOVA statistics in a table, make sure that you include degrees of freedom, and *F*-ratios for each source and mean square errors. Mean square errors are enclosed in parentheses and explained in a general note to the table. The *Publication Manual* discusses the specifics for other tables, such as regression tables and path and LISREL tables. These statistical analyses and accompanying tables require more advanced knowledge than usually exists among students taking an undergraduate methods course and are not discussed.

When writing the manuscript, you should refer to the table somewhere in the text. This reference should tell what data are presented in the table and briefly discuss the data. When referring to a table, identify it by name, as in *the data in Table 3*. Do not use a reference such as *the above table* or *the table on page 12*.

After you have constructed a table, use to following checklist to ensure that you have constructed it according to the specifications listed in the *Publication Manual.*

- Is the table necessary?
- Is the table double-spaced throughout?
- Have all tables been similarly constructed?
- Does the title briefly explain the contents of the table?
- Does every column have a heading?
- Are all abbreviations, dashes, and symbols explained?
- Are the probability level values correctly identified and are table entry asterisks defined?
- Have you sequenced any notes by placing general notes first, then specific notes, and finally probability notes?
- Have you eliminated all vertical lines?
- Will the table fit on a journal page?
- Have you referred to the table in the text?

Figures   Figures are any illustration other than a table and may be a chart, graph, photograph, drawing, or any other depiction. Although tables are preferred for the presentation of quantitative information, figures give an overall view of the pattern of results but require the reader to estimate values. There are, however, times when figures can convey a concept more effectively than a table can, such as when an interaction is described. If you are considering using a figure, ask yourself the following questions:

- Do I need a figure to most accurately convey the idea?
- Will a figure most efficiently present the information?
- What type of figure will most efficiently convey the information?

If you decide that a figure is needed, you can have the figure mechanically produced or computer generated. Most figures are computer generated and a glossy or high-quality laser print of a figure is acceptable. When generating a figure with a computer, do not use special effects such as three-dimensional effects. When printing a computer-generated figure, use a high-quality, bright white paper, make sure that the printer has a resolution of at least 300 dots per inch, and make sure that the final print has smooth curves and crisp lines showing no jagged areas.

Once the figures have been prepared, number them consecutively with arabic numerals in the order in which they are used in the manuscript. Write the number of the figure lightly with a pencil on the top right edge and outside the area of the figure. If the figure takes up the entire page, write the number on the back of the figure. Also on the back, write the article's short title in pencil and the word *top* to designate the top of the figure.

Figure Captions   Each figure has a caption that provides a brief description of the contents and serves as a title. However, these captions are not placed on the figure but are typed on a separate page with the words *Figure Captions* centered and typed in upper- and lowercase letters at the top of the page. Flush with the left margin of the page, each caption should begin with the word *Figure* and the number of the figure followed by a period, all in italics. The caption is typed on the remainder of the line. If more than one line is needed, each subsequent line also begins flush left.

Reference Citations   In the text of the research report, particularly in the introductory section, you must reference other works you have cited. The APA format is to use the author–date citation method, which involves inserting the author's surname and the publication date at the appropriate point, as follows:

Doe (1999) investigated the . . .

or

It has been demonstrated (Doe, 2002) . . .

With this information, the reader can turn to the reference list and locate complete information regarding the source. Multiple citations involving the same author are arranged in chronological order:

Doe (1997, 1979, 2001, 2002)

Multiple citations involving different authors are arranged alphabetically, as follows:

Several studies (Doe, 2003; Kelly, 2002; Mills, 2002) have revealed . . .

If a citation includes more than two but fewer than six authors, all authors should be cited the first time the reference is used. Subsequent citations include only the name of the first author, followed by the words *et al.* and the year the article was published. If six or more authors are associated with a citation, only the surname of the first author followed by *et al.* is used for all citations.

You should consult the APA *Publication Manual* if you encounter references from other sources, such as works with no author, authors with the same surname, or personal communications.

Reference List   All citations in the text of the research report must be accurately and completely cited in the reference list so that it is possible for readers to locate the works. This means that each entry should include the name of the author, year of publication, title, publishing data, and any other information necessary to identify the reference. All references are to appear in alphabetical order, typed double-spaced with a hanging indent on a separate page with the word *References* centered at the top of the page in upper- and lowercase letters.

The general form of a reference is as follows for a periodical, book, and book chapter:

Canned, I. B., & Rad, U. B. (2002). Moderating violence in a peaceful society. *Journal of Violence and Peace Making, 32,* 231–234.

Wind, C. (2001). *Why children hurt.* New York: Academic Publishers.

Good, I. M. (2003). Moral development in violent children. In A. Writer and N. Author (Eds.), *The anatomy of violent children* (pp. 134–187). Washington, DC: Killer Books.

If you have cited information obtained from the Internet you must cite the reference to this material in the reference list. In citing Internet sources you should, when possible, reference specific documents, and not home pages or menu pages, and provide Internet addresses that work. An example follows of a reference for an article published in a journal appearing only on the Internet and for a document appearing on the Internet.

Van Camp, R., & Roth, C. (2002). Role of parental discipline on classroom behavior. *Journal of Child and Adolescent Behavior, 21,* 121–132. Retrieved September, 24, 2002, from http://jcab.org/articles.html

Task force on teen pregnancy in the Southeastern Region. *Methods for reducing teen pregnancy.* Retrieved November, 12, 2002, from http://www.reduceteenpregnancy.org

There are many other items that could be included in a reference list such as book chapters, brochures, monographs, magazine articles, and many types of information retrieved from the Internet. If you have included a source not mentioned here or if you have a variation of a source mentioned here and are not sure how it should be presented, you should consult the APA *Publication Manual*.

Serif
A typeface in which each character has small strokes at the ends of the lines that form it

Typing In typing the manuscript, double-space all material and select a **serif** typeface. The preferred typefaces are 12-pt Times Roman and 12-pt Courier. There should be one inch (2.54 cm) at the top, bottom, left, and right of every page. You should use the italic and bold functions on your word processor as well as other special fonts or styles of type as specified in the APA *Publication Manual*. Each page should contain no more than twenty-seven lines of text.

Ordering of Manuscript Pages The pages of the manuscript should be arranged as follows:

1. *Title page*. This is a separate page (numbered page 1) and includes the title, author's name, institutional affiliation, and running head.
2. *Abstract*. This is a separate page, numbered page 2.
3. *Text of the manuscript*. The text begins on page 3 and continues on consecutive pages through the completion of the discussion section.
4. *References*. References begin on a separate page.
5. *Author notes*. These notes begin on a new page.
6. *Footnotes*. Footnotes also begin on a new page.

Submission of the Research Report for Publication

If you have conducted an independent research project and have completed the preparation of a research report (aside from the laboratory reports that you may have prepared in this class), you must now decide whether to submit it to a journal for possible publication. Earlier in this chapter I stated that no study should be undertaken if you do not believe it is potentially worthy of publication. But even if at the outset you believe that the study you are conducting is worthy of publication, you may change your mind once the study is completed and you have prepared the research report. Therefore, at this stage you must make a final decision whether to submit the manuscript to a journal. This final decision should be based on your judgment of the significance of the study and the extent to which rival hypotheses were controlled in the study. Frequently it is valuable to have a colleague read and provide a critique of the article before you submit it for possible publication. A colleague presents a new perspective and can evaluate the worth of the article and its potential problems more critically and objectively.

If both you, as the author, and a colleague agree that the manuscript should be submitted for publication, you must then select the journal to which you are going to submit the article. Journals vary both in the percentage of submitted manuscripts they accept and in the types of articles that they will publish. From Table 15.1 you can see that each journal focuses on a different subject area. You must select a journal that publishes articles on subjects similar to yours. In making this selection, you must also decide whether your manuscript makes a contribution significant enough to warrant possible publication in one of the most prestigious journals. In the field of psychology, the APA and APS journals are generally considered the most prestigious, as well as some of the most difficult to get into. Many of these journals accept only about 15 percent of the manuscripts submitted to them.

Once you have selected the appropriate journal, send the required number of copies of the manuscript to the journal editor, with a cover letter stating that you are submitting the manuscript for possible publication in that journal. The cover letter should give the journal editor information regarding (a) whether the manuscript has been presented at a scientific meeting, (b) if other closely related manuscripts have been published or submitted to other journals, (c) the title, length, and number of tables and figures, and (d) a statement verifying that the treatment of animal or human participants was in accordance with APA ethical standards. If you desire a masked review, you should request this in the cover letter and transfer any identifying material that would normally appear on the Author Notes page to the title page. Finally, you should include your telephone number, fax number, e-mail address, and address for future correspondence. Once the journal editor receives the manuscript either electronically or by first-class mail, he or she assigns it a number and, usually within forty-eight hours, sends an acknowledgment of receipt to the author.

At this point the control of the manuscript is out of your hands and in the hands of the journal editor. The journal editor typically sends the manuscript to several individuals who are knowleddegable regarding the topic of your study, and they review the manuscript and reach a decision about its acceptability. Their comments are returned to the journal editor, who makes the final decision. This decision can be a rejection, an acceptance, or an acceptance pending approval of recommended revisions. This last is the most typical mode of acceptance. The whole process typically takes two to three months.

If you get an outright acceptance—a very rare occurrence—you can celebrate. If you get a provisional acceptance—acceptance pending approval of recommended revisions—you can evaluate the recommendations and attempt to conform to them. Once the revisions have been made, you must resubmit the manuscript, which is then reevaluated by the journal editor. The editor may elect to accept the manuscript at this point, send it out for another review, or request additional revisions. If you get a rejection, try to evaluate the reviewers' comments regarding their reasons for rejecting the manuscript. If you agree with the reviewers' comments, you may reevaluate the manuscript and decide that it really was not worthy of publication. Alternatively, you may disagree with the reviewers' comments and believe that the manuscript still warrants publication. In this case, you should find another journal that focuses on the subject matter of your study and then start the process over. As you can see, the process of getting an article published is time consuming, involves a lot of work, and is subject to the approval and recommendation of your peers. Many studies are never published. Although the procedure just outlined has its flaws, it is probably the best that can be established to ensure that only high-quality research is published.

Acceptance of the Manuscript

After an article has been accepted for publication, the journal editor sends the corresponding authors two forms: a copyright transfer form that transfers the copyright of the published article to the APA and an author certification form with which authors accept responsibility for the contents of the published article and indicate agreement on the order of authorship.

If you have used a computer in preparing your manuscript, the APA and many other publishers will request that you provide, on disk or by e-mail, an electronic word-processing file of the manuscript for editing and production. This eliminates the cost and potential for creating errors of the process of rekeying the article from the paper manuscript. If electronic copies of figures are requested, TIFF is the preferred file format.

The final version of the accepted manuscript will be edited by both the journal editor and a copy editor to correct any errors, to ensure conformation to APA stylistic requirements, or to clarify expression. After the manuscript is copyedited, it is sent back to the author for review. The author must review any changes to ensure that the meaning or content of the manuscript has not been altered. Typically, the author is requested to have the copyedited manuscript returned within forty-eight hours. If you have submitted an electronic version of the manuscript, you will receive a printout of text showing the editing changes and another copy with the changes incorporated. You will also receive queries from the copy editor to which you must respond.

After you have returned the copyedited version of the manuscript, it is set in type. The typesetter then sends you the manuscript and two sets of typeset proofs. You are to read these proofs and make sure that they correspond to the copyedited version of the manuscript. At this stage you cannot make any changes in the content of the manuscript. Any changes are limited to production errors and to updates of references, citations, or addresses. The original proofs and the manuscript are to be sent back to the Production Editor within forty-eight hours. Once you have sent the proofs back, you have completed your role in the publication process. The only thing you have to do is wait and see the manuscript in print, which typically takes about four to six months.

Presenting Research Results at Professional Conferences

The ultimate goal of a research study is to communicate the results by having the written report of the study published in a scholarly journal. However, many times the results of a research study are presented at one of the numerous conferences that are held each year prior to being published in a scholarly journal. The conferences at which these presentations are made include the national meetings of the American Psychological Association and the American Psychological Society, the regional meetings of various psychological associations (e.g., the Southeastern Psychological Association, SEPA), and various international meetings. Also, a number of colleges and universities host conferences that are geared toward undergraduate research. The common thread running through all these conferences is that their primary activity is the presentation of research conducted by psychologists. Typically these associations put out a call for submissions of research studies. Researchers who wish to present their findings submit a written report or an abstract of a report of their research study to a designated individual, who in turn sends the submissions out for review. The selected reviewers review the submissions and recommend the acceptance or rejection of the submission. If the submission is accepted, it is placed on the program for the meeting and the researcher who sent in the submission is obligated to attend the meeting and present the results of his or her research study. This presentation can take the form of an oral presentation or a poster presentation.

Oral Presentation

If you are scheduled to make an oral presentation of your research at a profession conference, make sure that you read and follow the guidelines that you will receive because there are a number of restrictions that dictate what can be done during the oral presentation. Typically, the oral presentations by individuals conducting research on similar topical areas are grouped together for a session that usually lasts one hour. Each person has fifteen minutes to make his or her presentation and answer any questions. Because time has to be allowed for questions, you should make sure that your presentation does not exceed twelve minutes and, because you have only twelve minutes to present the results of your research, the preparation for the presentation differs from a written report that you would prepare for publication. Here are some recommendations for the preparation of an oral presentation.

- Concentrate on only one or two points. Keep reminding the audience of the central theme by relating each section to that theme. In other words, tell the audience what you are going to say, and then say it.

- Omit most of the specifics of the research design because this will probably be too much detail for the listener to follow.

- Focus on the following points
  1. State what you studied
  2. State why you studied it
  3. State how you studied it—give a general description of your research design
  4. State what you found
  5. State the implications of your results

- Do not read your presentation because this tends to be boring. Instead, talk to the audience as if you were having a conversation with them. This means that you must know your topic well and have the presentation rehearsed. It is better to have notes from which you can talk in a conversational tone than to read from a prepared document

- If you include audio–visual presentations, make sure they are readable and comprehensible from a distance.
- Practice giving the presentation to others to ensure that you stay within your time limit and that everything flows smoothly.

Being prepared will make your presentation most informative to your audience and will allow you to feel most confident, especially if this is your first presentation.

Poster Presentation

If you are scheduled to make a poster presentation of your research at a professional conference, you should read the directions that you will receive carefully because different associations have specific requirements, such as the number of pages that are permitted to be visually displayed. A poster presentation consists of presenting your research as a poster at a specific session on that topic or theme along with many other individuals at the same time. This means that you need to prepare a visual presentation of your research and present it as a poster that anyone can see and read. After you have placed the visual presentation of your research on the poster, you are to remain by the poster for the duration of the poster session, which is typically one hour. It is important that you bring a number of written copies of your research report to give to interested individuals. The advantage of this procedure is that you can discuss your research with interested individuals who walk by and read your poster, and they can get a copy of your research that they can take home with them. In this way, you increase your chances of finding other individuals with similar interests. As a result of these conversations, you may develop new research ideas and may even meet individuals with whom you will collaborate on subsequent research projects.

Here are some tips that you can use in preparing your poster.

- The layout of the poster is important and should flow naturally from the introduction to the results and conclusion. Figure 15.1 presents one possible layout.
- When preparing the poster, use a typeface that is easy to read such as Times New Roman. Do not try to get fancy because this will generally reduce readability.
- Use a font size that is large enough to read from a distance of about ten feet. A font size of 24-pt. or greater should be sufficient.
- Make your points with as few words as possible.
- If you can present the various pages of your poster on one large poster board, this is desirable. If not, then mount each page of your poster on a backing using an attractive color. Make sure that you bring pins to mount your poster to the bulletin board that will be available.

After you have mounted your poster to the available bulleting board, relax and enjoy the conversations that you will have with individuals who wish to discuss your research. Remember that you conducted the research, so you will have the most knowledge about it and will be the expert on this research study.

FIGURE 15.1
Template for a poster
presentation.

Summary

After a research study is completed it is the author's responsibility to communicate the results of the study to the rest of the scientific community. The primary mechanism of communication is through professional journals. To facilitate clear communication of research results the APA has published a manual that gives a standardized format for authors to follow when preparing their research reports. This manual specifies the specific sections of the research report and gives directions and suggestions for the type of material that is to be included in each section. The main sections of the research report are the title; abstract; introduction; method section, which includes a description of the participants, any materials or apparatus, and the procedure followed in collecting the data; results section; discussion section; references; and author note.

In preparing the research report there are a number of stylistic requirements that should be adhered to. The writing style should clearly communicate the essence of the research report. In general, this means that there must be a smoothness and economy of expression. The language used should be free of bias, which means that the words chosen must be specific and generally free of labels. Any communication about the research participants should be done in a way that acknowledges their participation. The writing should avoid demeaning attitudes and biased assumptions that can creep in when describing a person's sex identity, sexual orientation, racial or ethnic identity, disability, or age.

The APA *Publication Manual* specifies an editorial style, a set of rules or guidelines to ensure a clear, consistent presentation of published material. There are rules for when to use italics and abbreviations; how to list headings of various topics; how to present numbers, physical measurements, and statistical results; when to use quotations, tables, and figures; how to construct the tables and figures; and how to reference other works cited in the report. In general, there are rules and guidelines specifying the entire construction of the research report.

In addition to reporting the results of research studies in professional journals, results are often reported at professional conferences. These reports are either oral or poster presentations. Oral presentations are short and should be focused on a few points so that the audience does not get overwhelmed with the specifics of the design or statistical analysis. Poster presentations should be prepared so that they are easily read from some distance and the layout of the poster should naturally flow from the introduction to the conclusion.

Key Terms and Concepts

Running head
Title
Authors' names and institutional affiliations
Page number and header
Abstract
Introduction
Method
Participants

Apparatus, materials, measures, and instruments
Procedure
Results
Discussion
References
Author note
Footnotes
Serif

Related Internet Sites

www.psychology.org
This site provides links to other sites that should assist students in writing papers using the APA format. To find the sites relating to APA style, use this site to search for the related links by doing an *APA style* search.

www.apastyle.org
This is the site maintained by the American Psychological Association and contains information about the *Publication Manual.* It also has links to Style Tips, What's New in the publication manual, and answers to some frequently asked questions.

www.vanguard.edu/faculty/ddegelman/index.cfm?doc_id=796
This Web site provides a list of the core elements of APA style that can be used as a guide in writing or checking a written research report.

Appendixes

APPENDIX A
Answers to Practice Tests

Chapter 1   Introduction to Scientific Research
1. a   2. e   3. b   4. b   5. c

Chapter 2   Nonexperimental Research Approaches
1. a   2. e   3. c   4. b   5. d

Chapter 3   The Experimental Research Approach
1. a   2. d   3. b   4. c

Chapter 4   Problem Identification and Hypothesis Formation
1. a   2. e   3. d   4. e   5. b

Chapter 5   Ethics
1. b   2. a   3. c   4. e   5. e

Chapter 6   Variables Used in Experimentation
1. d   2. b   3. d   4. b   5. a

Chapter 7   Reliability and Validity in Experimental Research
1. c   2. b   3. c   4. e   5. d   6. b

Chapter 8   Construct and External Validity in Experimental Research
1. b   2. e   3. b   4. a   5. b   6. b

Chapter 9   Control Techniques
1. a   2. d   3. c   4. e   5. c

Chapter 10   Experimental Research Design
1. b   2. e   3. d   4. a   5. e

Chapter 11   Quasi-Experimental Designs
1. c   2. b   3. d   4. d   5. b

Chapter 12   Single-Case Research Designs
1. a   2. d   3. b   4. c   5. d

Chapter 13   Data Collection
1. b   2. a   3. d   4. b   5. e

Chapter 14   Data Analysis
1. d   2. c   3. b   4. a   5. a   6. b

APPENDIX B
Critical Values of *t*

	Level of Significance for One-Tailed Test					
	0.10	0.05	0.025	0.01	0.005	0.0005
	Level of Significance for Two-Tailed Test					
df	0.20	0.10	0.05	0.02	0.01	0.001
1	3.078	6.314	12.706	31.821	63.657	636.619
2	1.886	2.920	4.303	6.965	9.925	31.598
3	1.638	2.353	3.182	4.541	5.841	12.941
4	1.533	2.132	2.776	3.747	4.604	8.610
5	1.476	2.015	2.571	3.365	4.032	6.859
6	1.440	1.943	2.447	3.143	3.707	5.959
7	1.415	1.895	2.365	2.998	3.449	5.405
8	1.397	1.860	2.306	2.896	3.355	5.041
9	1.383	1.833	2.262	2.821	3.250	4.781
10	1.372	1.812	2.228	2.764	3.169	4.587
11	1.363	1.796	2.201	2.718	3.106	4.437
12	1.356	1.782	2.179	2.681	3.055	4.318
13	1.350	1.771	2.160	2.650	3.012	4.221
14	1.345	1.761	2.145	2.624	2.977	4.140
15	1.341	1.753	2.131	2.602	2.947	4.073
16	1.337	1.746	2.120	2.583	2.921	4.015
17	1.333	1.740	2.110	2.567	2.898	3.965
18	1.330	1.734	2.101	2.552	2.878	3.922
19	1.328	1.729	2.093	2.539	2.861	3.883
20	1.325	1.725	2.086	2.528	2.845	3.850
21	1.323	1.721	2.080	2.518	2.831	3.819
22	1.321	1.717	2.074	2.508	2.819	3.792
23	1.319	1.714	2.069	2.500	2.807	3.766
24	1.318	1.711	2.064	2.492	2.797	3.745
25	1.316	1.708	2.060	2.485	2.787	3.725
26	1.315	1.706	2.056	2.479	2.779	3.707
27	1.314	1.703	2.052	2.473	2.771	3.690
28	1.313	1.701	2.048	2.467	2.763	3.674
29	1.311	1.699	2.045	2.462	2.756	3.659
30	1.310	1.697	2.042	2.457	2.750	3.646
40	1.303	1.684	2.021	2.423	2.704	3.551
60	1.296	1.671	2.000	2.390	2.660	3.460
120	1.289	1.658	1.980	2.358	2.617	3.373
∞	1.282	1.645	1.960	2.326	2.576	3.291

Source: Appendix B is taken from Table III of Fisher & Yates (1974): *Statistical Tables for Biological, Agricultural and Medical Research,* published by Longman Group Ltd. London (previously published by Oliver and Boyd Ltd. Edinburgh) and by permission of the authors and publishers.

APPENDIX C

The 5 Percent (Lightface Type) and 1 Percent (Boldface Type) Values for the F-Distribution

n_1 Degrees of Freedom (for greater mean square)

n_2	1	2	3	4	5	6	7	8	9	10	11	12	14	16	20	24	30	40	50	75	100	200	500	∞
1	161	200	216	225	230	234	237	239	241	242	243	244	245	246	248	249	250	251	252	253	253	254	254	254
	4,052	**4,999**	**5,403**	**5,625**	**5,764**	**5,859**	**5,928**	**5,981**	**6,022**	**6,056**	**6,082**	**6,106**	**6,142**	**6,169**	**6,208**	**6,234**	**6,258**	**6,286**	**6,302**	**6,323**	**6,334**	**6,352**	**6,361**	**6,366**
2	18.51	19.00	19.16	19.25	19.30	19.33	19.36	19.37	19.38	19.39	19.40	19.41	19.42	19.43	19.44	19.45	19.46	19.47	19.47	19.48	19.49	19.49	19.50	19.50
	98.49	**99.00**	**99.17**	**99.25**	**99.30**	**99.33**	**99.34**	**99.36**	**99.38**	**99.40**	**99.41**	**99.42**	**99.43**	**99.44**	**99.45**	**99.46**	**99.47**	**99.48**	**99.48**	**99.49**	**99.49**	**99.49**	**99.50**	**99.50**
3	10.13	9.55	9.28	9.12	9.01	8.94	8.88	8.84	8.81	8.78	8.76	8.74	8.71	8.69	8.66	8.64	8.62	8.60	8.58	8.57	8.56	8.54	8.54	8.53
	34.12	**30.82**	**29.46**	**28.71**	**28.24**	**27.91**	**27.67**	**27.49**	**27.34**	**27.23**	**27.13**	**27.05**	**26.92**	**26.83**	**26.69**	**26.60**	**26.50**	**26.41**	**26.35**	**26.27**	**26.23**	**26.19**	**26.14**	**26.12**
4	7.71	6.94	6.59	6.39	6.26	6.16	6.09	6.04	6.00	5.96	5.93	5.91	5.87	5.84	5.80	5.77	5.74	5.71	5.70	5.68	5.66	5.65	5.64	5.63
	21.20	**18.00**	**16.69**	**15.98**	**15.52**	**15.21**	**14.98**	**14.80**	**14.66**	**14.54**	**14.45**	**14.37**	**14.24**	**14.15**	**14.02**	**13.93**	**13.83**	**13.74**	**13.69**	**13.61**	**13.57**	**13.52**	**13.48**	**13.46**
5	6.61	5.79	5.41	5.19	5.05	4.95	4.88	4.82	4.78	4.74	4.70	4.68	4.64	4.60	4.56	4.53	4.50	4.46	4.44	4.42	4.40	4.38	4.37	4.36
	16.26	**13.27**	**12.06**	**11.39**	**10.97**	**10.67**	**10.45**	**10.27**	**10.15**	**10.05**	**9.96**	**9.89**	**9.77**	**9.68**	**9.55**	**9.47**	**9.38**	**9.29**	**9.24**	**9.17**	**9.13**	**9.07**	**9.04**	**9.02**
6	5.99	5.14	4.76	4.53	4.39	4.28	4.21	4.15	4.10	4.06	4.03	4.00	3.96	3.92	3.87	3.84	3.81	3.77	3.75	3.72	3.71	3.69	3.68	3.67
	13.74	**10.92**	**9.78**	**9.15**	**8.75**	**8.47**	**8.26**	**8.10**	**7.98**	**7.87**	**7.79**	**7.72**	**7.60**	**7.52**	**7.39**	**7.31**	**7.23**	**7.14**	**7.09**	**7.02**	**6.99**	**6.94**	**6.90**	**6.88**
7	5.59	4.74	4.35	4.12	3.97	3.87	3.79	3.73	3.68	3.63	3.60	3.57	3.52	3.49	3.44	3.41	3.38	3.34	3.32	3.29	3.28	3.25	3.24	3.23
	12.25	**9.55**	**8.45**	**7.85**	**7.46**	**7.19**	**7.00**	**6.84**	**6.71**	**6.62**	**6.54**	**6.47**	**6.35**	**6.27**	**6.15**	**6.07**	**5.98**	**5.90**	**5.85**	**5.78**	**5.75**	**5.70**	**5.67**	**5.65**
8	5.32	4.46	4.07	3.84	3.69	3.58	3.50	3.44	3.39	3.34	3.31	3.28	3.23	3.20	3.15	3.12	3.08	3.05	3.03	3.00	2.98	2.96	2.94	2.93
	11.26	**8.65**	**7.59**	**7.01**	**6.63**	**6.37**	**6.19**	**6.03**	**5.91**	**5.82**	**5.74**	**5.67**	**5.56**	**5.48**	**5.36**	**5.28**	**5.20**	**5.11**	**5.06**	**5.00**	**4.96**	**4.91**	**4.88**	**4.86**
9	5.12	4.26	3.86	3.63	3.48	3.37	3.29	3.23	3.18	3.13	3.10	3.07	3.02	2.98	2.93	2.90	2.86	2.82	2.80	2.77	2.76	2.73	2.72	2.71
	10.56	**8.02**	**6.99**	**6.42**	**6.06**	**5.80**	**5.62**	**5.47**	**5.35**	**5.26**	**5.18**	**5.11**	**5.00**	**4.92**	**4.80**	**4.73**	**4.64**	**4.56**	**4.51**	**4.45**	**4.41**	**4.36**	**4.33**	**4.31**
10	4.96	4.10	3.71	3.48	3.33	3.22	3.14	3.07	3.02	2.97	2.94	2.91	2.86	2.82	2.77	2.74	2.70	2.67	2.64	2.61	2.59	2.56	2.55	2.54
	10.04	**7.56**	**6.55**	**5.99**	**5.64**	**5.39**	**5.21**	**5.06**	**4.95**	**4.85**	**4.78**	**4.71**	**4.60**	**4.52**	**4.41**	**4.33**	**4.25**	**4.17**	**4.12**	**4.05**	**4.01**	**3.96**	**3.93**	**3.91**
11	4.84	3.98	3.59	3.36	3.20	3.09	3.01	2.95	2.90	2.86	2.82	2.79	2.74	2.70	2.65	2.61	2.57	2.53	2.50	2.47	2.45	2.42	2.41	2.40
	9.65	**7.20**	**6.22**	**5.67**	**5.32**	**5.07**	**4.88**	**4.74**	**4.63**	**4.54**	**4.46**	**4.40**	**4.29**	**4.21**	**4.10**	**4.02**	**3.94**	**3.86**	**3.80**	**3.74**	**3.70**	**3.66**	**3.62**	**3.60**
12	4.75	3.88	3.49	3.26	3.11	3.00	2.92	2.85	2.80	2.76	2.72	2.69	2.64	2.60	2.54	2.50	2.46	2.42	2.40	2.36	2.35	2.32	2.31	2.30
	9.33	**6.93**	**5.95**	**5.41**	**5.06**	**4.82**	**4.65**	**4.50**	**4.39**	**4.30**	**4.22**	**4.16**	**4.05**	**3.98**	**3.86**	**3.78**	**3.70**	**3.61**	**3.56**	**3.49**	**3.46**	**3.41**	**3.38**	**3.36**
13	4.67	3.80	3.41	3.18	3.02	2.92	2.84	2.77	2.72	2.67	2.63	2.60	2.55	2.51	2.46	2.42	2.38	2.34	2.32	2.28	2.26	2.24	2.22	2.21
	9.07	**6.70**	**5.74**	**5.20**	**4.86**	**4.62**	**4.44**	**4.30**	**4.19**	**4.10**	**4.02**	**3.96**	**3.85**	**3.78**	**3.67**	**3.59**	**3.51**	**3.42**	**3.37**	**3.30**	**3.27**	**3.21**	**3.18**	**3.16**
14	4.60	3.74	3.34	3.11	2.96	2.85	2.77	2.70	2.65	2.60	2.56	2.53	2.48	2.44	2.39	2.35	2.31	2.27	2.24	2.21	2.19	2.16	2.14	2.13
	8.86	**6.51**	**5.56**	**5.03**	**4.69**	**4.46**	**4.28**	**4.14**	**4.03**	**3.94**	**3.86**	**3.80**	**3.70**	**3.62**	**3.51**	**3.43**	**3.34**	**3.26**	**3.21**	**3.14**	**3.11**	**3.06**	**3.02**	**3.00**
15	4.54	3.68	3.29	3.06	2.90	2.79	2.70	2.64	2.59	2.55	2.51	2.48	2.43	2.39	2.33	2.29	2.25	2.21	2.18	2.15	2.12	2.10	2.08	2.07
	8.68	**6.36**	**5.42**	**4.89**	**4.56**	**4.32**	**4.14**	**4.00**	**3.89**	**3.80**	**3.73**	**3.67**	**3.56**	**3.48**	**3.36**	**3.29**	**3.20**	**3.12**	**3.07**	**3.00**	**2.97**	**2.92**	**2.89**	**2.87**
16	4.49	3.63	3.24	3.01	2.85	2.74	2.66	2.59	2.54	2.49	2.45	2.42	2.37	2.33	2.28	2.24	2.20	2.16	2.13	2.09	2.07	2.04	2.02	2.01
	8.53	**6.23**	**5.29**	**4.77**	**4.44**	**4.20**	**4.03**	**3.89**	**3.78**	**3.69**	**3.61**	**3.55**	**3.45**	**3.37**	**3.25**	**3.18**	**3.10**	**3.01**	**2.96**	**2.89**	**2.86**	**2.80**	**2.77**	**2.75**
17	4.45	3.59	3.20	2.96	2.81	2.70	2.62	2.55	2.50	2.45	2.41	2.38	2.33	2.29	2.23	2.19	2.15	2.11	2.08	2.04	2.02	1.99	1.97	1.96
	8.40	**6.11**	**5.18**	**4.67**	**4.34**	**4.10**	**3.93**	**3.79**	**3.68**	**3.59**	**3.52**	**3.45**	**3.35**	**3.27**	**3.16**	**3.08**	**3.00**	**2.92**	**2.86**	**2.79**	**2.76**	**2.70**	**2.67**	**2.65**

(continued)

n_1 Degrees of Freedom (for greater mean square)

n_2	1	2	3	4	5	6	7	8	9	10	11	12	14	16	20	24	30	40	50	75	100	200	500	∞
18	4.41 8.28	3.55 6.01	3.16 5.09	2.93 4.58	2.77 4.25	2.66 4.01	2.58 3.85	2.51 3.71	2.46 3.60	2.41 3.51	2.37 3.44	2.34 3.37	2.29 3.27	2.25 3.19	2.19 3.07	2.15 3.00	2.11 2.91	2.07 2.83	2.04 2.76	2.00 2.71	1.98 2.68	1.95 2.63	1.93 2.59	1.92 2.57
19	4.38 8.18	3.52 5.93	3.13 5.01	2.90 4.50	2.74 4.17	2.63 3.94	2.55 3.77	2.48 3.63	2.43 3.52	2.38 3.43	2.34 3.36	2.31 3.30	2.26 3.19	2.21 3.12	2.15 3.00	2.11 7.92	2.07 2.84	2.02 2.76	2.00 2.70	1.96 2.63	1.94 2.60	1.91 2.54	1.90 2.51	1.88 2.49
20	4.35 8.10	3.49 5.85	3.10 4.94	2.87 4.43	2.71 4.10	2.60 3.87	2.52 3.71	2.45 3.56	2.40 3.45	2.35 3.37	2.31 3.30	2.28 3.23	2.23 3.13	2.18 3.05	2.12 2.94	2.08 2.86	2.04 2.77	1.99 2.69	1.96 2.63	1.92 2.56	1.90 2.53	1.87 2.47	1.85 2.44	1.84 2.42
21	4.32 8.02	3.47 5.78	3.07 4.87	2.84 4.37	2.68 4.04	2.57 3.81	2.49 3.65	2.42 3.51	2.37 3.40	2.32 3.31	2.28 3.24	2.25 3.17	2.20 3.07	2.15 2.99	2.09 2.88	2.05 2.80	2.00 2.72	1.96 2.63	1.93 2.58	1.89 2.51	1.87 2.47	1.84 2.42	1.82 2.38	1.81 2.36
22	4.30 7.94	3.44 5.72	3.05 4.82	2.82 4.31	2.66 3.99	2.55 3.76	2.47 3.59	2.40 3.45	2.35 3.35	2.30 3.26	2.26 3.18	2.23 3.12	2.18 3.02	2.13 2.94	2.07 2.83	2.03 2.75	1.98 2.67	1.93 2.58	1.91 2.53	1.87 2.46	1.84 2.42	1.81 2.37	1.80 2.33	1.78 2.31
23	4.28 7.88	3.42 5.66	3.03 4.76	2.80 4.26	2.64 3.94	2.53 3.71	2.45 3.54	2.38 3.41	2.32 3.30	2.28 3.21	2.24 3.14	2.20 3.07	2.14 2.97	2.10 2.89	2.04 2.78	2.00 2.70	1.96 2.62	1.91 2.53	1.88 2.48	1.84 2.41	1.82 2.37	1.79 2.32	1.77 2.28	1.76 2.26
24	4.26 7.82	3.40 5.61	3.01 4.72	2.78 4.22	2.62 3.90	2.51 3.67	2.43 3.50	2.36 3.36	2.30 3.25	2.26 3.17	2.22 3.09	2.18 3.03	2.13 2.93	2.09 2.85	2.02 2.74	1.98 2.66	1.94 2.58	1.89 2.49	1.86 2.44	1.82 2.36	1.80 2.33	1.76 2.27	1.74 2.23	1.73 2.21
25	4.24 7.77	3.38 5.57	2.99 4.68	2.76 4.18	2.60 3.86	2.49 3.63	2.41 3.46	2.34 3.32	2.28 3.21	2.24 3.13	2.20 3.05	2.16 2.99	2.11 2.89	2.06 2.81	2.00 2.70	1.96 2.62	1.92 2.54	1.87 2.45	1.84 2.40	1.80 2.32	1.77 2.29	1.74 2.23	1.72 2.19	1.71 2.17
26	4.22 7.72	3.37 5.53	2.98 4.64	2.74 4.14	2.59 3.82	2.47 3.59	2.39 3.42	2.32 3.29	2.27 3.17	2.22 3.09	2.18 3.02	2.15 2.96	2.10 2.86	2.05 2.77	1.99 2.66	1.95 2.58	1.90 2.50	1.85 2.41	1.82 2.36	1.78 2.28	1.76 2.25	1.72 2.19	1.70 2.15	1.69 2.13
27	4.21 7.68	3.35 5.49	2.96 4.60	2.73 4.11	2.57 3.79	2.46 3.56	2.37 3.39	2.30 3.26	2.25 3.14	2.20 3.06	2.16 2.98	2.13 2.93	2.08 2.83	2.03 2.74	1.97 2.63	1.93 2.55	1.88 2.47	1.84 2.38	1.80 2.33	1.76 2.25	1.74 2.21	1.71 2.16	1.68 2.12	1.67 2.10
28	4.20 7.64	3.34 5.45	2.95 4.57	2.71 4.07	2.56 3.76	2.44 3.53	2.36 3.36	2.29 3.23	2.24 3.11	2.19 3.03	2.15 2.95	2.12 2.90	2.06 2.80	2.02 2.71	1.96 2.60	1.91 2.52	1.87 2.44	1.81 2.35	1.78 2.30	1.75 2.22	1.72 2.18	1.69 2.13	1.67 2.09	1.65 2.06
29	4.18 7.60	3.33 5.42	2.93 4.54	2.70 4.04	2.54 3.73	2.43 3.50	2.35 3.33	2.28 3.20	2.22 3.08	2.18 3.00	2.14 2.92	2.10 2.87	2.05 2.77	2.00 2.68	1.94 2.57	1.90 2.49	1.85 2.41	1.80 2.32	1.77 2.27	1.73 2.19	1.71 2.15	1.68 2.10	1.65 2.06	1.64 2.03
30	4.17 7.56	3.32 5.39	2.92 4.51	2.69 4.02	2.53 3.70	2.42 3.47	2.34 3.40	2.27 3.17	2.21 3.06	2.16 2.98	2.12 2.90	2.09 2.84	2.04 2.74	1.99 2.66	1.93 2.55	1.89 2.47	1.84 2.38	1.79 2.29	1.76 2.24	1.72 2.16	1.69 2.13	1.66 2.07	1.64 2.03	1.62 2.01
32	4.15 7.50	3.30 5.34	2.90 4.46	2.67 3.97	2.51 3.66	2.40 3.42	2.32 3.25	2.25 3.12	2.19 3.01	2.14 2.94	2.10 2.86	2.07 2.80	2.02 2.70	1.97 2.62	1.91 2.51	1.86 2.42	1.82 2.34	1.76 2.25	1.74 2.20	1.69 2.12	1.67 2.08	1.64 2.02	1.61 1.98	1.59 1.96
34	4.13 7.44	3.28 5.29	2.88 4.42	2.65 3.93	2.49 3.61	2.38 3.38	2.30 3.21	2.23 3.08	2.17 2.97	2.12 2.89	2.08 2.82	2.05 2.76	2.00 2.66	1.95 2.58	1.89 2.47	1.84 2.38	1.80 2.30	1.74 2.21	1.71 2.15	1.67 2.08	1.64 2.04	1.61 1.98	1.59 1.94	1.57 1.91
36	4.11 7.39	3.26 5.25	2.86 4.38	2.63 3.89	2.48 3.58	2.36 3.35	2.28 3.18	2.21 3.04	2.15 2.94	2.10 2.86	2.06 2.78	2.03 2.72	1.98 2.62	1.93 2.54	1.87 2.43	1.82 2.35	1.78 2.26	1.72 2.17	1.69 2.12	1.65 2.04	1.62 2.00	1.59 1.94	1.56 1.90	1.55 1.87
38	4.10 7.35	3.25 5.21	2.85 4.34	2.62 3.86	2.46 3.54	2.35 3.32	2.26 3.15	2.19 3.02	2.14 2.91	2.09 2.82	2.05 2.75	2.02 2.69	1.96 2.59	1.92 2.51	1.85 2.40	1.80 2.32	1.76 2.22	1.71 2.14	1.67 2.08	1.63 2.00	1.60 1.97	1.57 1.90	1.54 1.86	1.53 1.84
40	4.08 7.31	3.23 5.18	2.84 4.31	2.61 3.83	2.45 3.51	2.34 3.29	2.25 3.12	2.18 2.99	2.12 2.88	2.07 2.80	2.04 2.73	2.00 2.66	1.95 2.56	1.90 2.49	1.84 2.37	1.79 2.29	1.74 2.20	1.69 2.11	1.66 2.05	1.61 1.97	1.59 1.94	1.55 1.88	1.53 1.84	1.51 1.81
42	4.07 7.27	3.22 5.15	2.83 4.29	2.59 3.80	2.44 3.49	2.32 3.26	2.24 3.10	2.17 2.96	2.11 2.86	2.06 2.77	2.02 2.70	1.99 2.64	1.94 2.54	1.89 2.46	1.82 2.35	1.78 2.26	1.73 2.17	1.68 2.08	1.64 2.02	1.60 1.94	1.57 1.91	1.54 1.85	1.51 1.80	1.49 1.78

APPENDIX C (continued)

n_1 Degrees of Freedom (for greater mean square)

n_2	1	2	3	4	5	6	7	8	9	10	11	12	14	16	20	24	30	40	50	75	100	200	500	∞
44	4.06	3.21	2.82	2.58	2.43	2.31	2.23	2.16	2.10	2.05	2.01	1.98	1.92	1.88	1.81	1.76	1.72	1.66	1.63	1.58	1.56	1.52	1.50	1.48
	7.24	5.12	4.26	3.78	3.46	3.24	3.07	2.94	2.84	2.75	2.68	2.62	2.52	2.44	2.32	2.24	2.15	2.06	2.00	1.92	1.88	1.82	1.78	1.75
46	4.05	3.20	2.81	2.57	2.42	2.30	2.22	2.14	2.09	2.04	2.00	1.97	1.91	1.87	1.80	1.75	1.71	1.65	1.62	1.57	1.54	1.51	1.48	1.46
	7.21	5.10	4.24	3.76	3.44	3.22	3.05	2.92	2.82	2.73	2.66	2.60	2.50	2.42	2.30	2.22	2.13	2.04	1.98	1.90	1.86	1.80	1.76	1.72
48	4.04	3.19	2.80	2.56	2.41	2.30	2.21	2.14	2.08	2.03	1.99	1.96	1.90	1.86	1.79	1.74	1.70	1.64	1.61	1.56	1.53	1.50	1.47	1.45
	7.19	5.08	4.22	3.74	3.42	3.20	3.04	2.90	2.80	2.71	2.64	2.58	2.48	2.40	2.28	2.20	2.11	2.02	1.96	1.88	1.84	1.78	1.73	1.70
50	4.03	3.18	2.79	2.56	2.40	2.29	2.20	2.13	2.07	2.02	1.98	1.95	1.90	1.85	1.78	1.74	1.69	1.63	1.60	1.55	1.52	1.48	1.46	1.44
	7.17	5.06	4.20	3.72	3.41	3.18	3.02	2.88	2.78	2.70	2.62	2.56	2.46	2.39	2.26	2.18	2.10	2.00	1.94	1.86	1.82	1.76	1.71	1.68
55	4.02	3.17	2.78	2.54	2.38	2.27	2.18	2.11	2.05	2.00	1.97	1.93	1.88	1.83	1.76	1.72	1.67	1.61	1.58	1.52	1.50	1.46	1.43	1.41
	7.12	5.01	4.16	3.68	3.37	3.15	2.98	2.85	2.75	2.66	2.59	2.53	2.43	2.35	2.23	2.15	2.06	1.96	1.90	1.82	1.78	1.71	1.66	1.64
60	4.00	3.15	2.76	2.52	2.37	2.25	2.17	2.10	2.04	1.99	1.95	1.92	1.86	1.81	1.75	1.70	1.65	1.59	1.56	1.50	1.48	1.44	1.41	1.39
	7.08	4.98	4.13	3.65	3.34	3.12	2.95	2.82	2.72	2.63	2.56	2.50	2.40	2.32	2.20	2.12	2.03	1.93	1.87	1.79	1.74	1.68	1.63	1.60
65	3.99	3.14	2.75	2.51	2.36	2.24	2.15	2.08	2.02	1.98	1.94	1.90	1.85	1.80	1.73	1.68	1.63	1.57	1.54	1.49	1.46	1.42	1.39	1.37
	7.04	4.95	4.10	3.62	3.31	3.09	2.93	2.79	2.70	2.61	2.54	2.47	2.37	2.30	2.18	2.09	2.00	1.90	1.84	1.76	1.71	1.64	1.60	1.56
70	3.98	3.13	2.74	2.50	2.35	2.23	2.14	2.07	2.01	1.97	1.93	1.89	1.84	1.79	1.72	1.67	1.62	1.56	1.53	1.47	1.45	1.40	1.37	1.35
	7.01	4.92	4.08	3.60	3.29	3.07	2.91	2.77	2.67	2.59	2.51	2.45	2.35	2.28	2.15	2.07	1.98	1.88	1.82	1.74	1.69	1.62	1.56	1.55
80	3.96	3.11	2.72	2.48	2.33	2.21	2.12	2.05	1.99	1.95	1.91	1.88	1.82	1.77	1.70	1.65	1.60	1.54	1.51	1.45	1.42	1.38	1.35	1.32
	6.96	4.88	4.04	3.56	3.25	3.04	2.87	2.74	2.64	2.55	2.48	2.41	2.32	2.24	2.11	2.03	1.94	1.84	1.78	1.70	1.65	1.57	1.52	1.49
100	3.94	3.09	2.70	2.46	2.30	2.19	2.10	2.03	1.97	1.92	1.88	1.85	1.79	1.75	1.68	1.63	1.57	1.51	1.48	1.42	1.39	1.34	1.30	1.28
	6.90	4.82	3.98	3.51	3.20	2.99	2.82	2.69	2.59	2.51	2.43	2.36	2.26	2.19	2.06	1.98	1.89	1.79	1.73	1.64	1.59	1.51	1.46	1.43
125	3.92	3.07	2.68	2.44	2.29	2.17	2.08	2.01	1.95	1.90	1.86	1.83	1.77	1.72	1.65	1.60	1.55	1.49	1.45	1.39	1.36	1.31	1.27	1.25
	6.84	4.78	3.94	3.47	3.17	2.95	2.79	2.65	2.56	2.47	2.40	2.33	2.23	2.15	2.03	1.94	1.85	1.75	1.68	1.59	1.54	1.46	1.40	1.37
150	3.91	3.06	2.67	2.43	2.27	2.16	2.07	2.00	1.94	1.89	1.85	1.82	1.76	1.71	1.64	1.59	1.54	1.47	1.44	1.37	1.34	1.29	1.25	1.22
	6.81	4.75	3.91	3.44	3.14	2.92	2.76	2.62	2.53	2.44	2.37	2.30	2.20	2.12	2.00	1.91	1.83	1.72	1.66	1.56	1.51	1.43	1.37	1.33
200	3.89	3.04	2.65	2.41	2.26	2.14	2.05	1.98	1.92	1.87	1.83	1.80	1.74	1.69	1.62	1.57	1.52	1.45	1.42	1.35	1.32	1.26	1.22	1.19
	6.76	4.71	3.88	3.41	3.11	2.90	2.73	2.60	2.50	2.41	2.34	2.28	2.17	2.09	1.97	1.88	1.79	1.69	1.62	1.53	1.48	1.39	1.33	1.28
400	3.86	3.02	2.62	2.39	2.23	2.12	2.03	1.96	1.90	1.85	1.81	1.78	1.72	1.67	1.60	1.54	1.49	1.42	1.38	1.32	1.28	1.22	1.16	1.13
	6.70	4.66	3.83	3.36	3.06	2.85	2.69	2.55	2.46	2.37	2.29	2.23	2.12	2.04	1.92	1.84	1.74	1.64	1.57	1.47	1.42	1.32	1.24	1.19
10000	3.85	3.00	2.61	2.39	2.22	2.10	2.02	1.95	1.89	1.84	1.80	1.76	1.70	1.65	1.58	1.53	1.47	1.41	1.36	1.30	1.26	1.19	1.13	1.08
	6.66	4.62	3.80	3.34	3.04	2.82	2.66	2.53	2.43	2.34	2.26	2.20	2.09	2.01	1.89	1.81	1.71	1.61	1.54	1.44	1.38	1.28	1.19	1.11
∞	3.84	2.99	2.60	2.37	2.21	2.09	2.01	1.94	1.88	1.83	1.79	1.75	1.69	1.64	1.57	1.52	1.46	1.40	1.35	1.28	1.24	1.17	1.11	1.00
	6.64	4.60	3.78	3.32	3.02	2.80	2.64	2.51	2.41	2.32	2.24	2.18	2.07	1.99	1.87	1.79	1.69	1.59	1.52	1.41	1.36	1.25	1.15	1.00

Source: Reproduced from Snedecor and Cochran (1989): Statistical Methods, Iowa State University Press, Ames, Iowa, by permission of the author and publisher.

APPENDIX D

Table of Random Numbers

Row/Col.	(1)	(2)	(3)	(4)	(5)	(6)	(7)	(8)	(9)	(10)	(11)	(12)	(13)	(14)
1	10480	15011	01536	02011	81647	91646	69179	14194	62590	36207	20969	99570	91291	90700
2	22368	46573	25595	85393	30995	89198	27982	53402	93965	34095	52666	19174	39615	99505
3	24130	48360	22527	97256	76393	64809	15179	24830	49340	32081	30680	19655	63348	58629
4	42167	93093	96243	61680	07856	16376	39440	53537	71341	57004	00849	74917	97758	16379
5	37570	39975	81837	16656	06121	91782	60468	81305	49684	60672	14110	06927	01263	54613
6	77921	06907	11008	42751	27756	53498	18602	70659	90655	15053	21916	81825	44394	42880
7	99562	72905	56420	69994	98872	31016	71194	18738	44013	48840	63213	21069	10634	12952
8	96301	91977	05463	07972	18876	20922	94595	56869	69014	60045	18425	84903	42508	32307
9	89579	14342	63661	10281	17453	18103	57740	84378	25331	12566	58678	44947	05585	56941
10	85475	36857	53342	53988	53060	59533	38867	62300	18158	17983	16439	11458	18593	64952
11	28918	69578	88231	33276	70997	79936	56865	05859	90106	31595	01547	85590	91610	78188
12	63553	40961	48235	03427	49626	69445	18663	72695	52180	20847	12234	90511	33703	90322
13	09429	93969	52636	92737	88974	33488	36320	17617	30015	08272	84115	27156	30613	74952
14	10365	61129	87529	85689	48237	52267	67689	93394	01511	26358	85104	20285	29975	89868
15	07119	97336	71048	08178	77233	13916	47564	81056	97735	85977	29372	74461	28551	90707
16	51085	12765	51821	51259	77452	16308	60756	92144	49442	53900	70960	63990	75601	40719
17	02368	21382	52404	60268	89368	19885	55322	44819	01188	65255	64835	44919	05944	55157
18	01011	54092	33362	94904	31273	04146	18594	29852	71585	85030	51132	01915	92747	64951
19	52162	53916	46369	58586	23216	14513	83149	98736	23495	64350	94738	17752	35156	35749
20	07056	97628	33787	09998	42698	06691	76988	13602	51851	46104	88916	19509	25625	58104
21	48663	91245	85828	14346	09172	30168	90229	04734	59193	22178	30421	61666	99904	32812
22	54164	58492	22421	74103	47070	25306	76468	26384	58151	06646	21524	15227	96909	44592
23	32639	32363	05597	24200	13363	38005	94342	28728	35806	06912	17012	64161	18296	22851
24	29334	27001	87637	87308	58731	00256	45834	15398	46557	41135	10367	07684	36188	18510
25	02488	33062	28834	07351	19731	92420	60952	61280	50001	67658	32586	86679	50720	94953
26	81525	72295	04839	96423	24878	82651	66566	14778	76797	14780	13300	87074	79666	95725
27	29676	20591	68086	26432	46901	20849	89768	81536	86645	12659	92259	57102	80428	25280
28	00742	57392	39064	66432	84673	40027	32832	61362	98947	96067	64760	64584	96096	98253
29	05366	04213	25669	26422	44407	44048	37937	63904	45766	66134	75470	66520	34693	90449
30	91921	26418	64117	94305	26766	25940	39972	22209	71500	64568	91402	42416	07844	69618

References

Ackermann, R. J. (1989). "The new experimentalism." *British Journal for the Philosophy of Science, 40,* 185–90.

Adair, J. G. (1973). *The human subject.* Boston: Little, Brown.

Adair, J. G. (1978). Open peer commentary. *Behavioral and Brain Sciences, 3,* 386–387.

Adair, J. G., Dushenko, T. W., & Lindsay, R. C. L. (1985). Ethical regulations and their impact on research practice. *American Psychologist, 40,* 59–72.

Adair, J. G., & Spinner, B. (1981). Subjects' access to cognitive processes: Demand characteristics and verbal report. *Journal for the Theory of Social Behavior, 11,* 31–52.

Allen, K. E., Hart, B., Buell, J. S., Harris, F. R., & Wolf, M. M. (1964). Effects of social reinforcement on isolate behavior of a nursery school child. *Child Development, 35,* 511–518.

Altemeyer, R. A. (1971). Subject pool pollution and the postexperimental interview. *Journal of Experimental Research in Personality, 5,* 79–84.

American Psychological Association. (1953). *Ethical standards of psychologists.* Washington, DC: Author.

American Psychological Association. (1982). *Ethical principles in the conduct of research with human participants.* Washington, DC: Author.

American Psychological Association. (2001). *Publication Manual of the American Psychological Association* (5th ed.). Washington, DC: Author.

American Psychological Association. (2002). *Ethical principles of psychologists and code of conduct.* Washington, DC: Author.

Anderson, E. R. (1993). Analyzing change in short-term longitudinal research using cohort-sequential designs. *Journal of Consulting and Clinical Psychology, 61,* 929–940.

Anderson, R. E., Franckowiak, S., Christmas, C., Wal-

ston, J., & Crespo, C. (2001). Obesity and reports of no leisure time activity among older Americans: Results from the third national health and nutrition examination survey. *Educational Gerontology, 27,* 297–306.

Anderson, T., & Kanuka, H. (2003). *E-research: Methods, strategies, and issues.* Boston: Houghton Mifflin.

Aronson, E. (1961). The effect of effort on the attractiveness of rewarded and unrewarded stimuli. *Journal of Abnormal and Social Psychology, 63,* 375–380.

Aronson, E. (1966). Avoidance of inter-subject communication. *Psychological Reports, 19,* 238.

Aronson, E., & Carlsmith, J. M. (1968). Experimentation in social psychology. In G. Lindzey & E. Aronson (Eds.), *The handbook of social psychology* (2nd ed.). Reading, MA: Addison-Wesley.

Aronson, E., & Cope, V. (1968). My enemy's enemy is my friend. *Journal of Personality and Social Psychology, 8,* 8–12.

Aronson, E., & Mills, J. (1959). The effect of severity of initiation on liking for a group. *Journal of Abnormal and Social Psychology, 59,* 177–181.

Asch, S. (1952). *Social psychology.* Englewood Cliffs, NJ: Prentice Hall.

Atkeson, B. M., Calhoun, K. S., Resick, P. A., & Ellis, E. M. (1982). Victims of rape: Repeated assessment of depressive symptoms. *Journal of Consulting and Clinical Psychology, 50,* 96–102.

Azar, B. (1997). APA task force urges a harder look at data. *Monitor, 28,* 3, 26.

Babbie, E. R. (1990). *Survey research methods* (2nd ed.). Belmont, CA: Wadsworth.

Baldwin, E. (1993). The case for animal research in psychology. *Journal of Social Issues, 49,* 121–131.

Baltes, P. B., Reese, H. W., & Nesselroade, J. R. (1977).

Life-span developmental psychology: Introduction to research. Monterey, CA: Wadsworth Publishing Co.

Bannister, D. (1966). Psychology as an exercise in paradox. *Bulletin of British Psychological Society, 19,* 21–26.

Barber, T. X. (1976). *Pitfalls in human research: Ten pivotal points*. New York: Pergamon Press.

Barber, T. X., & Silver, M. J. (1968). Fact, fiction, and the experimenter bias effect. *Psychological Bulletin Monograph, 70,* 1–29.

Barlow, D. H., Sakheim, D. K., & Beck, J. G. (1983). Anxiety increases sexual arousal. *Journal of Abnormal Psychology, 92,* 49–54.

Beach, F. A. (1950). The snark was a boojum. *American Psychologist, 5,* 115–124.

Beach, F. A. (1960). Experimental investigations of species specific behavior. *American Psychologist, 15,* 1–8.

Beck, A. T., Ward, C. H., Mendelson, M., Mock, J., & Erbaugh, J. (1961). An inventory for measuring depression. *Archives of General Psychiatry, 4,* 561–571.

Becker, L. J., Rabinowitz, V. C., & Seligman, C. (1980). Evaluating the impact of utility company billing plans on residential energy consumption. *Evaluation and Program Planning, 3,* 159–164.

Beckman, L., & Bishop, B. R. (1970). Deception in psychological research: A reply to Seeman. *American Psychologist, 25,* 878–880.

Beecher, H. K. (1966). Pain: One mystery solved. *Science, 151,* 840–841.

Benbow, C., & Stanley, J. C. (1980). Sex differences in mathematical ability: Fact or artifact? *Science, 210,* 1262–1264.

Berg, B. L. (1998). *Qualitative research methods for the social sciences*. Boston: Allyn & Bacon.

Bergin, A. E. (1966). Some implications of psychotherapy research for therapeutic practice. *Journal of Abnormal Psychology, 71,* 235–246.

Bergin, A. E., & Strupp, H. H. (1970). New directions in psychotherapy research. *Journal of Abnormal Psychology, 76,* 13–26.

Bergin, A. E., & Strupp, H. H. (1972). *Changing frontiers in the science of psychotherapy*. New York: Aldine-Atherton.

Berkowitz, L., & LePage, A. (1967). Weapons or aggression-eliciting stimuli. *Journal of Personality and Social Psychology, 7,* 202–207.

Berkun, M., Bialek, H. M., Kern, P. R., & Yagi, K. (1962). Experimental studies of psychological stress in man.

Psychological Monographs: General and Applied, 76(15), 1–39.

Berscheid, E., Baron, R. S., Dermer, M., & Libman, M. (1973). Anticipating informed consent: An empirical approach. *American Psychologist, 28,* 913–925.

Bijou, S. W., Peterson, R. F., Harris, F. R., Allen, K. E., & Johnston, M. S. (1969). Methodology for experimental studies of young children in natural settings. *Psychological Record, 19,* 177–210.

Billewicz, W. Z. (1965). The efficiency of matched samples: An empirical investigation. *Biometrics, 21,* 623–644.

Birnbaum, M. H. (2001). *Introduction to behavioral research in the Internet*. Upper Saddle River, NJ: Prentice Hall.

Blascovich, J., Spencer, S. J., Quinn, D., & Steele, C. (2001). Africian Americans and high blood pressure: The role of stereotype threat. *Psychological Science, 12,* 225–229.

Boice, R. (1973). Domestication. *Psychological Bulletin, 80,* 215–230.

Bolger, H. (1965). The case study method. In B. B. Wolman (Ed.), *Handbook of Clinical Psychology* (pp. 28–39). New York: McGraw-Hill.

Boring, E. G. (1954). The nature and history of experimental control. *American Journal of Psychology, 67,* 573–589.

Boris, M., & Mandel, F. S. (1994). Foods and additives are common causes of the attention deficit hyperactive disorder in children. *Annals of Allergy, 72,* 462–468.

Box, G. E. P., & Jenkins, G. M. (1970). *Time-series analysis: Forecasting and control*. San Francisco: Holden-Day.

Box, G. E. P., & Tiao, G. L. (1965). A change in level of a non-stationary time series. *Biometrics, 52,* 181–192.

Bracht, G. H., & Glass, G. V. (1968). The external validity of experiments. *American Educational Research Journal, 5,* 437–474.

Braden, J. P., & Bryant, T. J. (1990). Regression discontinuity designs: Applications for school psychologists. *School Psychology Review, 19,* 232, 239.

Bradley, A. W. (1978). Self-serving bias in the attribution process: A reexamination of the fact or fiction question. *Journal of Personality and Social Psychology, 36,* 56–71.

Brady, J. V. (1958). Ulcers in "executive monkeys." *Scientific American, 199,* 95–100.

Brainard, J. (2000, Dec. 8). As U.S. releases new rules on

scientific fraud, scholars debate how much and why it occurs. *The Chronicle of Higher Education*, p. A26.

Brand, M. (1976). *The nature of causation*. Urbana, IL: University of Illinois Press.

Bridgman, P. W. (1927). *The logic of modern physics*. New York: Macmillan.

Britton, B. K. (1979). Ethical and educational aspects of participation as a subject in psychology experiments. *Teaching of Psychology, 6*, 195–198.

Broden, M., Bruce, M., Mitchell, M., Carter, V., & Hall, R. V. (1970). Effects of teacher attention on attending behavior of two boys at adjacent desks. *Journal of Applied Behavior Analysis, 3*, 199–203.

Brown, W. F., Wehe, N. O., Zunker, V. G., & Haslam, W. L. (1971). Effectiveness of student-to-student counseling on the academic adjustment of potential dropouts. *Journal of Educational Psychology, 62*, 285–289.

Bunge, M. (1967). *Scientific research*. New York: Springer.

Campbell, D. (1957). Factors relative to the validity of experiments in social settings. *Psychological Bulletin, 54*, 297–312.

Campbell, D. T. (1969). Prospective: Artifact and control. In R. Rosenthal & R. L. Rosnow (Eds.), *Artifact in behavioral research*. New York: Academic Press.

Campbell, D. T. (1988). Definitional versus multiple operationalism. In E. S. Overman (Ed.), *Methodology and Epistemology for social science: Selected papers*. Chicago: University of Chicago Press.

Campbell, D. T., & Boruch, R. F. (1975). Making the case for randomized assignments to treatments by considering the alternatives: Six ways in which quasi-experimental evaluations in compensatory education tend to underestimate effects. In C. A. Bennett & A. A. Lumsdaine (Eds.), *Evaluation and experiment: Some critical issues in assessing social programs*. New York: Academic Press.

Campbell, D. T., & Erlebacher, A. (1970). How regression artifacts in quasi-experimental evaluations can mistakenly make compensatory education look harmful. In J. Hellmuth (Ed.), *Compensatory education: A national debate:* Vol. 3. *Disadvantaged child*. New York: Brunner/Mazel.

Campbell, D. T., & Stanley, J. C. (1963). *Experimental and quasi-experimental designs for research*. Chicago: Rand McNally.

Campbell, K. E., & Jackson, T. T. (1979). The role of and

need for replication research in social psychology. *Replications in Social Psychology, 1*, 3–14.

Caporaso, T. A., & Ross, L. L., Jr. (1973). *Quasi-experimental approaches: Testing theory and evaluating policy*. Evanston: Northwestern University Press.

Carlopia, J., Adair, J. G., Lindsay, R. C. L., & Spinner, B. (1983). Avoiding artifact in the search for bias: The importance of assessing subjects' perceptions of the experiment. *Journal of Personality and Social Psychology, 44*, 693–701.

Carlsmith, J. M., Collins, B. E., & Helmreich, R. L. (1966). Studies in forced compliance: I. The effect of pressure for compliance on attitude change produced by face-to-face role playing and anonymous essay writing. *Journal of Personality and Social Psychology, 4*, 1–3.

Carlson, R. (1971). Where is the person in personality research? *Psychological Bulletin, 75*, 203–219.

Carlston, D. E., & Cohen, J. L. (1980). A closer examination of subject roles. *Journal of Personality and Social Psychology, 38*, 857–870.

Centers for Disease Control and Prevention. (2001). *Helicobacter pylori and peptic ulcer disease* [Online]. Retrieved December 4, 2001, from http://www.cdc.gov/ulcer/history.htm

Chalmers, A. F. (1999). *What is this thing called science?* (3d ed.). Indianapolis, IN: Hackett.

Christensen, L. (1968). Intrarater reliability. *The Southern Journal of Educational Research, 2*, 175–182.

Christensen, L. (1977). The negative subject: Myth, reality or a prior experimental experience effect. *Journal of Personality and Social Psychology, 35*, 392–400.

Christensen, L. (1981). Positive self-presentation: A parsimonious explanation of subject motives. *The Psychological Record, 31*, 553–571.

Christensen, L. (1988). Deception in psychological research: When is its use justified? *Personality and Social Psychology Bulletin, 14*, 664–675.

Christensen, L., & Brooks, A. (in press). Changing food preference as a function of mood. *The Journal of Psychology*.

Christensen, L., Krietsch, K., White, B., & Stagner, B. (1985). The impact of diet on mood disturbance. *Journal of Abnormal Psychology, 94*, 565–579.

Christensen, L., & Pettijohn, L. (2001). Mood and carbohydrate cravings. *Appetite, 36*, 137–145.

Christensen, L., & Redig, C. (1993). The effect of meal

composition on mood. *Behavioral Neuroscience, 107,* 346–353.

Cialdini, R. B., Cacioppo, J. T., Bassett, R., & Miller, J. A. (1978). Low-ball procedure for producing compliance: Commitment then cost. *Journal of Personality and Social Psychology, 36,* 463–467.

Clay, R. A. (1999). Coping with the high risks of breast cancer. *Monitor, 30*(6), 27.

Cochran, W. G., & Cox, G. M. (1957). *Experimental designs.* New York: Wiley.

Cohen, J. (1988). *Statistical power analysis for the behavioral sciences.* Hillsdale, NJ: Lawrence Erlbaum Associates.

Cohen, J. (1990). Things I have learned (so far). *American Psychologist, 45,* 1304–1312.

Cohen, J. (1994). The earth is round ($p < .05$). *American Psychologist, 49,* 997–1003.

Conover, M. R. (1985). Alleviating nuisance Canada goose problems through methiocarb-induced aversive conditions. *Journal of Wildlife Management, 49,* 631–636.

Conrad, H. S., & Jones, H. E. (1940). A second study of familial resemblances in intelligence. *39th yearbook of the National Society for the Study of Education* (pp. 97–141). Chicago: University of Chicago Press.

Conroy, R. T., & Mills, J. N. (1970). *Human circadian rhythms.* London: J. & A. Church.

Converse, P., & Traugott, M. (1986). Assessing the accuracy of polls and surveys. *Science, 234,* 1094–1098.

Cook, T. D., & Campbell, D. T. (1976). Experiments in field settings. In M. Dunnette (Ed.), *Handbook of industrial and organizational research.* Chicago: Rand McNally.

Cook, T. D., Gruder, C. L., Hennigan, K. M., & Flay, B. R. (1979). The history of the sleeper effect: Some logical pitfalls in accepting the null hypothesis. *Psychological Bulletin, 86,* 662–679.

Cooper, H., & Hazelrigg, P. (1988). Personality moderators of interpersonal expectance effects: An integrative research review. *Journal of Personality and Social Psychology, 55,* 937–949.

Cortina, J. M., & Dunlap, W. P. (1997). On the logic and purpose of significance testing. *Psychological Methods, 2,* 161–172.

Cowley, G. (2002, Sept. 16). The science of happiness. *Newsweek,* pp. 46–48.

Creswell, J. W. (1998). *Qualitative inquiry and research design.* Thousand Oaks, CA: Sage.

Cronbach, L., & Furby, L. (1970). "How should we measure change"—or should we? *Psychological Bulletin, 74,* 68–80.

Crosbie, J. (1993). Interrupted time-series analysis with brief single-subject data. *Journal of Consulting and Clinical Psychology, 61,* 966–974.

D'Amato, M. R. (1970). *Experimental psychology methodology: Psychophysics and learning.* New York: McGraw-Hill.

Darley, J. M., & Latané, B. (1968). Bystander intervention in emergencies: Diffusion of responsibility. *Journal of Personality and Social Psychology, 8,* 377–383.

Davidson, R. (1986). Source of funding and outcome of clinical trials. *Journal of General Internal Medicine, 1,* 155–158.

Davis, H., & Memmott, J. (1983). Autocontingencies: Rats count to three to predict safety from shock. *Animal Learning and Behavior, 11,* 95–100.

De Waal, F. B. M. (1999). Animal behaviour: Cultural primatology comes of age. *Nature, 399,* 635.

DeAngelis, T. (2005). Cosmetic surgery's dark side. *Monitor on Psychology, 36* No. 10, 41.

Deese, J. (1972). *Psychology as science and art.* New York: Harcourt Brace Jovanovich.

Denzin, N. K., & Lincoln, Y. S. (Eds.). (1994). *Handbook of qualitative research.* Thousand Oaks, CA: Sage.

DePaulo, B. M., Dull, W. R., Greenberg, J. M., & Swaim, G. W. (1989). Are shy people reluctant to ask for help? *Journal of Personality and Social Psychology, 56,* 834–844.

Dewsbury, D. A. (1990). Early interactions between animal psychologists and animal activists and the founding of the APA committee on precautions in animal experimentation. *American Psychologist, 45,* 315–327.

Diener, E., & Crandall, R. (1978). *Ethics in social and behavioral research.* Chicago: University of Chicago Press.

Dipboye, R. L., & Flanagan, M. F. (1979). Research settings in industrial and organizational psychology. Are findings in the field more generalizable than in the laboratory? *American Psychologist, 34,* 141–150.

Dittmann, M. (2005). Plastic surgery: Beauty or beast? *Monitor on Psychology, 36* No. 8, 30–32.

Dorfman, D. D. (1978). The Cyril Burt question: New findings. *Science, 201,* 1177–1186.

Dority, B. (1999). The columbine tragedy: Countering the hysteria. *The Humanist, 59* (4), 7.

Dukes, W. F. (1965). N = 1. *Psychological Bulletin, 64,* 74–79.

Ebbinghaus, H. (1913). *Memory, a contribution to experimental psychology.* 1885. Translated by H. A. Ruger and C. E. Bussenius. New York: Teachers College, Columbia University.

Ellen, R. F. (1984). *Ethnographic research.* New York: Academic Press.

Ellickson, P. L. (1989). *Limiting nonresponse in longitudinal research: Three strategies for school-based studies* (Rand Note N-2912-CHF). Santa Monica, CA: Rand Corporation.

Ellickson, P. L., & Hawes, J. A. (1989). An assessment of active versus passive methods for obtaining parental consent. *Evaluation Review, 13,* 45–55.

Ellsworth, P. C. (1977). From abstract ideas to concrete instances: Some guidelines for choosing natural research settings. *American Psychologist, 33,* 604–615.

Ellsworth, P. C. (1978). Open peer commentary. *The Behavioral and Brain Sciences, 3,* 386–387.

Ellsworth, P. C., Carlsmith, J. A., & Henson, A. (1972). The stare as a stimulus to flight in human subjects. *Journal of Personality and Social Psychology, 21,* 302–311.

Epstein, S. (1979). The stability of behavior: I. On predicting most of the people much of the time. *Journal of Personality and Social Psychology, 37,* 1097–1126.

Epstein, S. (1981). The stability of behavior: II. Implications for psychological research. *American Psychologist, 35,* 790–806.

Epstein, T. M., Suedfeld, P., & Silverstein, S. J. (1973). The experimental contact: Subject's expectations of and reactions to some behavior of experimenters. *American Psychologist, 28,* 212–221.

Ericsson, K. A., & Simon, H. A. (1980). Verbal reports as data. *Psychological Review, 87,* 215–251.

Ericsson, K. A., & Simon, H. A. (1993). *Protocol analysis: Verbal reports as data* (Rev. ed.). Cambridge, MA: MIT Press.

Eysenck, H. J. (1952). The effects of psychotherapy: An evaluation. *Journal of Consulting Psychology, 16,* 319–324.

Eysenck, H. J. (1967). *The biological basis of personality.* Springfield, IL: Charles C. Thomas.

Feingold, B. (1975). *Why is your child hyperactive?* New York: Random House.

Ferguson, G. A. (1966). *Statistical analysis in psychology and education.* New York: McGraw-Hill.

Ferster, C. B., & Skinner, B. F. (1957). *Schedules of reinforcement.* New York: Appleton-Century-Crofts.

Festinger, G. L., & Carlsmith, J. M. (1959). Cognitive consequences of forced compliance. *Journal of Abnormal and Social Psychology, 58,* 203–211.

Festinger, L. (1957). *A theory of cognitive dissonance.* Evanston, IL: Row, Peterson.

Feyerabend, P. K. (1975). *Against method: Outline of an anarchistic theory of knowledge.* London: New Left Books.

Fillenbaum, S. (1966). Prior deception and subsequent experimental performance: The faithful subject. *Journal of Personality and Social Psychology, 4,* 532–537.

Fisher, C. B., & Fyrberg, D. (1994). Participant partners: College students with the costs and benefits of deception research. *American Psychologist, 49,* 417–427.

Fisher, R. A. (1935). *The design of experiments* (1st ed.). London: Oliver and Boyd.

Fisher, R. A., & Yates, F. (1974). *Statistical tables for biological, agricultural and medical research.* London: Longman.

Flaherty, C. F., & Checke, S. (1982). Anticipation of incentive gain. *Animal Learning and Behavior, 10,* 177–182.

Folkman, S. (2000). Privacy and confidentiality. In B. D. Sales & S. Folkman (Eds.). *Ethics in Research with Human Participants.* Washington: American Psychological Association.

Fouts, R. S. (1973). Acquisition and testing of gestural signs in four young chimpanzees. *Science, 180,* 978–979.

Frick, R. W. (1996). The appropriate use of null hypothesis testing. *Psychological Methods, 1,* 379–390.

Friedman, N. (1967). *The social nature of psychological research.* New York: Basic Books.

Fuller, R. L., Luck, S. J., McMahon, R. P., & Gold, J. M. (2005). Working memory consolidation is abnormally slow in schizophrenia. *Journal of Abnormal Psychology, 114,* 279–290.

Gadlin, H., & Ingle, G. (1975). Through the one-way mirror: The limits of experimental self-reflection. *American Psychologist, 30,* 1003–1009.

Gage, J. T. 1991. *The shape of reason* (2nd ed.). New York: Macmillan.

Gage, N. L., & Cronbach, L. J. (1955). Conceptual and methodological problems in interpersonal perception. *Psychological Review, 62,* 411–422.

Gallup, G. G., & Suarez, S. D. (1985). Alternatives to the use of animals in psychological research. *American Psychologist, 40,* 1104–1111.

Garcia, J. (1981). Tilting at the paper mills of academe. *American Psychologist, 36,* 149–158.

Gardner, G. T. (1978). Effects of federal human subjects regulations on data obtained in environmental stressor research. *Journal of Personality and Social Psychology, 36,* 628–634.

Gathercole, S. E., & Willis, C. S. (1992). Phonological memory and vocabulary development during the early school years: A longitudinal study. *Developmental Psychology, 28,* 887–898.

Gazzaniga, M. S., Ivry, R. B., & Mangun, G. R. (2002). *Cognitive neuroscience: The biology of the mind* (2nd ed.). New York: W. W. Norton & Co.

Gelfand, D., & Hartmann, D. (1968). Behavior therapy with children: A review and evaluation of research methodology. *Psychological Bulletin, 69,* 204–215.

Geller, E. S., Russ, N. W., & Altomari, M. G. (1986). Naturalistic observation of beer drinking among college students. *Journal of Applied Behavior Analysis, 19,* 391–396.

Gholson, B., & Barker, P. (1985). Kuhn, Lakatos, and Laudan: Applications in the history of physics and psychology. *American Psychologist, 7,* 755–769.

Gilgun, J. F., Daly, K., & Handel, G. (Eds.). (1992). *Qualitative methods in family research.* Thousand Oaks, CA: Sage.

Gilovich, T. (1991). *How we know what isn't so: The fallibility of human reason in everyday life.* New York: Free Press.

Glass, G. (1976). Primary, secondary and meta-analysis of research. *Educational Research, 5,* 3–8.

Glass, G. V., Tiao, G. C., & Maguire, T. O. (1971). The 1900 revision of German divorce laws. *Law and Society Review, 5,* 539–562.

Glass, G. V., Willson, V. L., & Gottman, J. M. (1975). *Design and analysis of time series.* Boulder, CO: Laboratory of Educational Research Press.

Gottman, J. M., & Glass, G. V. (1978). Analysis of interrupted time-series experiments. In T. R. Kratochwill (Ed.), *Single subject research: Strategies for evaluating change.* New York: Academic Press.

Gottman, J. M., & McFall, R. M. (1972). Self-monitoring effects in a program for potential high school dropouts: A time-series analysis. *Journal of Consulting and Clinical Psychology, 39,* 273–281.

Gottman, J. M., McFall, R. M., & Barnett, J. T. (1969). Design and analysis of research using time series. *Psychological Bulletin, 72,* 299–306.

Greenough, W. T. (1991, May/June). The animal rights assertions: A researcher's perspective. *Psychological Science Agenda,* pp. 10–12.

Greenwald, A. G. (1975). Consequences of prejudice against the null hypothesis. *Psychological Bulletin, 82,* 1–20.

Groves, R. M., & Kahn, R. L. (1979). *Surveys by telephone: A national comparison with personal interviews.* New York: Academic Press.

Gubrium, J. F., & Sankar, A. (Eds.). (1993). *Qualitative methods in aging research.* Thousand Oaks, CA: Sage.

Gunsalus, C. K. (1993). Institutional structure to ensure research integrity. *Academic Medicine, 68* (Sept. Suppl.), 533–538.

Haber, E. (1996). Industry and the university. *Nature Biotechnology, 14,* 441–442.

Hagen, R. L. (1997). In praise of the null hypothesis statistical test. *American Psychologist, 52,* 15–24.

Hainer, C. (1999, Feb. 17). Face it: Your features reveal inner truths. *USA Today,* p. 9D.

Hall, R. V., & Fox, R. W. (1977). Changing-criterion designs: An alternative applied behavior analysis procedure. In C. C. Etzel, G. M. LeBlanc, & D. M. Baer (Eds.), *New developments in behavioral research: Theory, method, and application* (in honor of Sidney W. Bijou). Hillsdale, NJ: Lawrence Erlbaum Associates.

Harcum, E. R. (1990). Methodological versus empirical literature: Two views on causal acceptance of the null hypothesis. *American Psychologist, 45,* 404–405.

Hare-Mustin, R. T., & Marecek, J. (Eds.). (1990). *Making a difference: Psychology and the construction of gender.* New Haven: Yale University Press.

Harlow, H. F. (1976). Fundamental principles for preparing psychology journal articles. *Journal of Comparative and Physiological Psychology, 55,* 893–896.

Hartmann, D. P., & Hall, R. V. (1976). A discussion of the

changing criterion design. *Journal of Applied Behavior Analysis, 9,* 527–532.

Hashtroudi, S., Parker, E. S., DeLisi, L. E., & Wyatt, R. J. (1983). On elaboration and alcohol. *Journal of Verbal Learning and Verbal Behavior, 22,* 164–173.

Haslerud, G., & Meyers, S. (1958). The transfer value of given and individually derived principles. *Journal of Educational Psychology, 49,* 293–298.

Hauri, P., & Ohmstead, E. (1983). What is the moment of sleep onset for insomniacs? *Sleep, 6,* 10–15.

Hazelrigg, P. J., Cooper, H., & Strathman, A. J. (1991). Personality moderators of the experimenter expectancy effect: A reexamination of five hypotheses. *Personality and Social Psychology Bulletin, 17,* 569–579.

Heinsman, D. T., & Shadish, W. R. (1996). Assignment methods in experimentation: When do nonrandomized experiments approximate answers from randomized experiments. *Psychological Methods, 1,* 154–169.

Helmstadter, G. C. (1970). *Research concepts in human behavior.* New York: Appleton-Century-Crofts.

Hersen, M., & Barlow, D. H. (1976). *Single case experimental designs: Strategies for studying behavioral change.* New York: Pergamon Press.

Hersen, M., Gullick, E. L., Matherne, P. M., & Harbert, T. L. (1972). Instructions and reinforcement in the modification of a conversion reaction. *Psychological Reports, 31,* 719–722.

Herzog, H. A. (1995). Has public interest in animal rights peaked? *American Psychologist, 50,* 945–947.

Hetherington, E. M., Clingempeel, W. G., Anderson, E. R., Deal, J. E., Stanley Hagan, M., Hollier, E. A., & Lindner, M. S. (1992). Coping with marital transitions: A family systems perspective. *Monographs of the Society for Research in Child Development, 57*(2–3, Serial No. 227).

Hewett, F. M., Taylor, F. D., & Artuso, A. A. (1969). The Santa Monica project: Evaluation of an engineered classroom design with emotionally disturbed children. *Exceptional Children, 35,* 523–529.

Hilgartner, S. (1990). Research fraud, misconduct, and the IRB. *IRB: A Review of Human Subjects Research, 12,* 1–4.

Hippocrates. (1931). Aphorisms. In *Hippocrates,* translated by W.H.S. Jones (pp. 128–129). Cambridge, MA: Harvard University Press.

Holden, C. (1987). NIMH finds a case of "serious misconduct." *Science, 235,* 1566–1567.

Holder, A. R. (1993). Research records and subpoenas: A continuing issue. *IRB: A Review of Human Subjects Research, 15,* 6–7.

Holmes, D. S. (1973). Effectiveness of debriefing after a stress-producing deception. *Journal of Research in Personality, 7,* 127–138.

Holmes, D. S. (1976a). Debriefing after psychological experiments: I. Effectiveness of postdeception dehoaxing. *American Psychologist, 31,* 858–867.

Holmes, D. S. (1976b). Debriefing after psychological experiments: II. Effectiveness of postexperimental desensitizing. *American Psychologist, 31,* 868–875.

Holmes, D. S., & Bennett, D. H. (1974). Experiments to answer questions raised by the use of deception in psychological research: I. Role playing as an alternative to deception; II. Effectiveness of debriefing after a deception; III. Effect of informed consent on deception. *Journal of Personality and Social Psychology, 29,* 358–367.

Hult, C. A. (1996). *Researching and writing in the social sciences.* Boston: Allyn & Bacon.

Humphreys, L. (1970). *Tearoom trade.* Chicago: Aldine.

Hurley, D. (1989, July/August). Cycles of craving. *Psychology Today.* 54–58.

Hyman, R., & Berger, L. (1966). Discussion. In H. J. Eysenck (Ed.), *The effects of psychotherapy* (pp. 81–86). New York: International Science Press.

Institute of Laboratory Animal Research, Commission on Life Sciences, National Research Council. (1996). *Guide for the care and use of laboratory animals.* Washington, DC: The National Academy Press.

Jason, L. A., McCoy, K., Blanco, D., & Zolik, E. S. (1981). Decreasing dog litter: Behavioral consultation to help a community group. In H. E. Freeman & M. A. Solomon (Eds.), *Evaluation studies review annual* (Vol. 6, pp. 660–674). Thousand Oaks, CA: Sage.

Jasper, J. M., & Nelkin, D. (1992). *The animal rights crusade: The growth of a moral protest.* New York: The Free Press.

Johnson, D. (1990). Animal rights and human lives: Time for scientists to right the balance. *American Psychological Society, 1,* 213–214.

Johnson, R. F. Q. (1976). The experimenter attributes effect: A methodological analysis. *Psychological Record, 26,* 67–78.

Jones, J. H. (1981). *Bad blood: The Tuskegee syphilis experiment.* New York: Free Press.

Karhan, J. R. (1973). *A behavioral and written measure of the effects of guilt and anticipated guilt on compliance for Machiavellians.* Unpublished master's thesis, Texas A&M University.

Kassin, S. M., & Kiechel, K. L. (1996). The social psychology of false confessions: Compliance, internalization, and confabulation. *Psychological Science, 7*(3), 125–128.

Katz, J. (1992). Psychophysiological contributions to phantom limbs. *Canadian Journal of Psychiatry, 37,* 282–298.

Kavale, K. A., & Forness, S. R. (1983). Hyperactivity and diet treatment: A meta-analysis of the Feingold hypothesis. *Journal of Learning Disabilities, 16,* 324–340.

Kavanau, J. L. (1964). Behavior: Confinement, adaptation, and compulsory regimes in laboratory studies. *Science, 143,* 490.

Kavanau, J. L. (1967). Behavior of captive whitefooted mice. *Science, 155,* 1623–1639.

Kaye, B. K., & Johnson, T. J. (1999). Research methodology: Taming the cyber frontier. *Social Science Computer Review, 17,* 323–337.

Kazdin, A. E. (1973). The role of instructions and reinforcement in behavior changes in token reinforcement programs. *Journal of Educational Psychology, 64,* 63–71.

Kazdin, A. E. (1978). Methodological and interpretive problems of single-case experimental designs. *Journal of Consulting and Clinical Psychology, 46,* 629–642.

Kazdin, A. E. (1980). *Research design in clinical psychology.* New York: Harper & Row.

Kazdin, A. E. (1992). *Methodological issues and strategies in clinical research.* Washington, DC: American Psychological Association.

Kazdin, A. E., & Kopel, S. A. (1975). On resolving ambiguities of the multiple-baseline design: Problems and recommendations. *Behavior Therapy, 6,* 601–608.

Keller, E. F. (1984). Feminism and science. In S. Harding & J. F. O'Barr (Eds.), *Sex and scientific inquiry.* Chicago: University of Chicago Press.

Kelman, H. C. (1967). Human use of human subjects. *Psychological Bulletin, 67,* 1–11.

Kelman, H. C. (1968). *A time to speak.* San Francisco: Jossey-Bass.

Kelman, H. C. (1972). The rights of the subject in social research: An analysis in terms of relative power and legitimacy. *American Psychologist, 27,* 989–1016.

Kendler, T. S., Kendler, H. H., & Learnard, B. (1962). Mediated responses to size and brightness as a function of age. *American Journal of Psychology, 75,* 571–586.

Kennedy, J. L., & Uphoff, H. F. (1939). Experiments on the nature of extrasensory perception: III. The recording error criticism of extra-chance scores. *Journal of Parapsychology, 3,* 226–245.

Kerlinger, F. N. (1973). *Foundations of behavioral research.* New York: Holt, Rinehart and Winston.

Kerlinger, F. N., & Pedhazur, E. J. (1973). *Multiple regression in behavioral research.* New York: Holt, Rinehart and Winston.

Key, B. W. (1980). *The clam-plate orgy and other subliminal techniques for manipulating your behavior.* Englewood Cliffs, NJ: Prentice-Hall.

Kihlstrom, J. F. (1995). On the validity of psychology experiments. *APS Observer, (9),* 10–11.

Kimmel, A. J. (1991). Predictable biases in the ethical decision making of American psychologists. *American Psychologist, 46,* 786–788.

Kimmel, A. J. (1996). *Ethical issues in behavioral research.* Cambridge, MA: Blackwell Publishers.

Kimmel, A. J. (1998). In defense of deception. *American Psychologists, 53,* 803–805.

Kirsch, I., & Sapirstein, G. (1998). Listening to Prozac but hearing placebo: A meta-analysis of antidepressant medication. *Prevention & Treatment, 1,* Article 0002a [Online]. Retrieved September 10, 2002, from http://www.journals.apa.org/prevention/volume1/pre0010002a.html

Knight, J. A. (1984). Exploring the compromise of ethical principles in science. *Perspectives in Biology and Medicine, 27,* 432–441.

Krantz, J. H., Ballard, J., & Scher, J. (1997). Comparing the results of laboratory and World-Wide Web samples on the determinants of female attractiveness. *Behavioral Research Methods, Instruments, & Computers, 29,* 264–269.

Kratochwill, T. R. (1978). Foundations of time-series research. In T. R. Kratochwill (Ed.), *Single subject research: Strategies for evaluating change.* New York: Academic Press.

Kraut, R., Mukopadhyay, T., Szczypula, J., Kiesler, S., & Scherlis, W. (1998). Communication in information: Alternative uses of the Internet in households. In

Proceedings of the CHI 98 (pp. 368–383). New York: ACM.

Kraut, R., Patterson, M., Lundmark, V., Kiesler, S., Mukopadhyay, T., & Scherlis, W. (1998). A social technology that reduces social involvement and psychological well-being? *American Psychologist, 53*, 1017–1031.

Kruglanski, A. W. (1976). On the paradigmatic objections to experimental psychology: A reply to Gadlin and Ingle. *American Psychologist, 31*, 655–663.

Kuhn, T. S. (1962). *The structure of scientific revolutions.* Cambridge, MA: Harvard University Press.

Kusche, C. A., & Greenberg, M. T. (1983). Evaluative understanding and role-taking ability: A comparison of deaf and hearing children. *Child Development, 54*, 141–147.

Lakatos, I. (1970). Falsification and the methodology of scientific research programs. In I. Lakatos & A. Musgrave (Eds.) *Criticism and the growth of knowledge* (pp. 91–196). Cambridge, England: Cambridge University Press.

Lana, R. (1959). Pretest-treatment interaction effects in longitudinal studies. *Psychological Bulletin, 56*, 293–300.

Lana, R. E. (1969). Pretest sensitization. In R. Rosenthal and R. L. Rosnow (Eds.), *Artifact in behavioral research.* New York: Academic Press.

Latané, B. (1981). The psychology of social impact. *American Psychologist, 36*, 343–356.

Laudan, L. (1977). *Progress and its problems.* Berkeley: University of California Press.

Lawler, E. E., III, & Hackman, J. R. (1969). Impact of employee participation in the development of pay incentive plans: A field experiment. *Journal of Applied Psychology, 53*, 467–471.

Leak, G. K. (1981). Student perception of coercion and value from participation in psychological research. *Teaching of Psychology, 8*, 147–149.

Leavitt, F. (2001). *Evaluating scientific research: Separating fact from fiction.* New Jersey: Prentice-Hall.

Lefkowitz, M., Blake, R. R., & Mouton, J. S. (1955). Status factors in pedestrian violation of traffic signals. *Journal of Abnormal and Social Psychology, 51*, 704–705.

Leikin, S. (1993). Minors' assent, consent, or dissent to medical research. *IRB: A review of human subjects research, 15*, 1–7.

Leitenberg, H. (1973). The use of single-case methodology in psychotherapy research. *Journal of Abnormal Psychology, 82*, 87–101.

Leitenberg, H., Agras, W. S., Allen, R., Butz, R., & Edwards, J. (1975). Feedback and therapist praise during treatment of phobia. *Journal of Consulting and Clinical Psychology, 43*, 396–404.

Leitenberg, H., Agras, W. S., Thompson, L., & Wright, D. E. (1968). Feedback in behavior modification: An experimental analysis in two phobic cases. *Journal of Applied Behavior Analysis, 1*, 131–137.

Levenson, H., Gray, M., & Ingram, A. (1976). Current research methods in personality: Five years after Carlston's survey. *Personality and Social Psychology Bulletin, 2*, 158–161.

Levine, J. M. (2000). Groups: Group processes. In A. Kazdin (Ed.), *Encyclopedia of psychology.* Washington, DC & New York: American Psychological Association and Oxford University Press.

Liddle, G., & Long, D. (1958). Experimental room for slow learners. *Elementary School Journal, 59*, 143–149.

Lilienfeld, S. O. (1998). Pseudoscience in contemporary clinical psychology: What it is and what we can do about it. *The Clinical Psychologist, 51*, 3–9.

Lilienfeld, S. O., Lohr, J. M., & Morier, D. (2001). The teaching of courses in the science and pseudoscience of psychology: Useful resources. *Teaching of Psychology, 28*, 182–191.

Lilienfeld, S. O., Lynn, S. J., & Lohr, J. M. (2003). Science and pseudoscience in clinical psychology. In S. O. Lilienfeld, Lynn, S. J., & Lohr, J. M. (Eds.), *Science and pseudoscience in clinical psychology* (pp. 1–14). New York: Guilford Press.

Llieva, J., Baron, S., & Healey, N. M. (2002). Online surveys in marketing research: Pros and cons. *International Journal of Marketing Research, 44*, 361–375.

Lockard, R. B. (1968). The albino rat: A defensible choice or a bad habit? *American Psychologist, 23*, 734–742.

Loftus, G. R. (1996). Psychology will be a better science when we change the way we analyze data. *Current Directions in Psychological Science, 5*, 161–171.

Logue, A. W., & Anderson, Y. D. (2001). Higher-education administrators: When the future does not make a difference. *Psychological Science, 12*, 276–281.

Lord, F. M. (1969). Statistical adjustments when comparing preexisting groups. *Psychological Bulletin, 72*, 336–337.

Lyons, J. (1964). On the psychology of the psychological experiment. In C. Schurer (Ed.), *Cognition-theory, research, promise.* New York: Harper.

Maier, N. R. F. (1949). *Frustration: The study of behavior without a goal.* New York: McGraw-Hill.

Maier, N. R. F. (1973). Experimentally produced neurotic behavior in the rat. In M. H. Marx & W. A. Hillix (Eds.), *Systems and theories in psychology* (p. 13). New York: McGraw-Hill. (Original paper presented 1938)

Maltby, N., Kirsch, I., Mayers, M., & Allen, G. (2002). Virtual reality exposure therapy for the treatment of fear of flying: A controlled investigation. *Journal of Consulting and Clinical Psychology, 70,* 1112–1118.

Marks-Kaufman, R., & Lipeles, B. J. (1982). Patterns of nutrient selection in rats orally self-administering morphine. *Nutrition and Behavior, 1,* 33–46.

Marquart, J. W. (1983). *Cooptation of the kept: Maintaining control in a southern penitentiary.* Unpublished doctoral dissertation, Texas A&M University.

Marques, J. F. (1998). Raiders of the lost reference: Helping your students do a literature search. *APS Observer, 11,* 30–35.

Marshall, B.J. (2002). The discovery that helicobacter pylori, a spiral bacterium, caused peptic ulcer disease. In B. J. Marshall (Ed.) *Helicobacter Pioneers: First hand accounts from scientists who discovered helicobacters 1892–1982.* Boston: Blackwell Scientific.

Martin, C. J., Boersma, F. J., & Cox, D. L. (1965). A classification of associative strategies in paired-associate learning. *Psychonomic Science, 3,* 455–456.

Martinson, B. C., Anderson, M. S., & de Vries, R. (2005). Scientists behaving badly. *Nature, 420,* 739–740.

Marx, M. H. (1963). *Theories in contemporary psychology.* New York: Macmillan.

Marx, M. H., & Hillix, W. A. (1973). *Systems and theories in psychology.* New York: McGraw-Hill.

Masling, J. (1966). Role-related behavior of the subject and psychologist and its effects upon psychological data. *Nebraska Symposium on Motivation, 14,* 67–103.

Matlin, M. W. (1993). *The psychology of women.* New York: Harcourt Brace Jovanovich.

McCabe, K. (1986, August). Who will live, who will die? *The Washingtonian,* p. 112.

McClelland, D. C. (1953). *The achievement motive.* New York: Appleton-Century-Crofts.

McCullough, J. P., Cornell, J. E., McDaniel, M. H., &

Mueller, R. K. (1974). Utilization of the simultaneous treatment design to improve student behavior in a first-grade classroom. *Journal of Consulting and Clinical Psychology, 42,* 288–292.

McFall, R. M. (1970). Effects of self-monitoring on normal smoking behavior. *Journal of Consulting and Clinical Psychology, 35,* 135–142.

McGuigan, F. J. (1963). The experimenter: A neglected stimulus object. *Psychological Bulletin, 60,* 421–428.

McLoughlin, J. A., & Nall, M. (1988). Teacher opinion of the role of food allergy on school behavior and achievement. *Annals of Allergy, 61,* 89–91.

Mees, C. E. K. (1934). Scientific thought and social reconstruction. *Sigma Xi Quarterly, 22,* 13–24.

Melinder, M. R. D., Barch, D. M., Heydebrand, G., & Csernansky, J. G. (2005). Easier tasks can have better discriminating power: The case of verbal fluency. *Journal of Abnormal Psychology, 114,* 385–391.

Mellgren, R. L., Nation, J. R., & Wrather, D. M. (1975). Magnitude of negative reinforcement and resistance to extinction. *Learning and Motivation, 6,* 253–263.

Mellgren, R. L., Seybert, J. A., & Dyck, D. G. (1978). The order of continuous, partial and nonreward trials and resistance to extinction. *Learning and Motivation, 9,* 359–371.

Menges, R. J. (1973). Openness and honesty versus coercion and deception in psychological research. *American Psychologist, 28,* 1030–1034.

Messick, S. (1995). Validity of psychological assessment: Validation of inferences from persons' responses and performances as scientific inquiry into score meaning. *American Psychologist, 50,* 741–749.

Meyer, R. G., & Osborne, Y. V. H. (1982). *Case studies in abnormal behavior.* Boston: Allyn and Bacon.

Middlemist, R. D., Knowles, E. S., & Matter, C. F. (1976). Personal space invasions in the lavatory: Suggestive evidence for arousal. *Journal of Personality and Social Psychology, 33,* 541–546.

Milgram, S. (1964a). Group pressure and action against a person. *Journal of Personality and Social Psychology, 69,* 137–143.

Milgram, S. (1964b). Issues in the study of obedience: A reply to Baumrind. *American Psychologist, 19,* 848–852.

Mill, J. S. (1874). *A system of logic.* New York: Harper.

Miller, A. G. (1972). Role playing: An alternative to

deception? A review of the evidence. *American Psychologist, 27,* 623–636.

Miller, E. (1999). Positivism and clinical psychology. *Clinical Psychology and Psychotherapy, 6,* 1–6.

Miller, N. E. (1957). Objective techniques for studying motivational effects of drugs on animals. In S. Garettini & V. Ghetti (Eds.), *Psychotropic drugs.* Amsterdam: Elsevier.

Mills, J. (1976). A procedure for explaining experiments involving deception. *Personality and Social Psychology Bulletin, 2,* 3–13.

Monster experiment. (2001, June 11). *Mobile Register,* p. 2A.

Mook, D. G. (1983). In defense of external invalidity. *American Psychologist, 38,* 379–387.

Morgan, C. T., & Morgan, J. D. (1939). Auditory induction of abnormal pattern of behavior in rats. *Journal of Comparative Psychology, 27,* 505–508.

Morison, R. S. (1960). "Gradualness, gradualness, gradualness" (I. P. Pavlov). *American Psychologist, 15,* 187–198.

Moskowitz, J. T., & Wrubel, J. (2005). Coping with HIV as a chronic illness: A longitudinal analysis of illness appraisals. *Psychology & Health, 20,* 509–531.

Musch, J., & Reips, U. (2000). A brief history of Web experimenting. In M. H. Birnbaum (ed.). *Psychology experiments on the Internet.* New York: Academic Press.

Nation, J. R., Bourgeois, A. E., Clark, D. E., & Hare, M. F. (1983). The effects of chronic cobalt exposure on behaviors and metallothionein levels in the adult rat. *Neurobehavioral Toxicology and Teratology, 9,* 9–15.

Nederhof, A. J. (1985). A comparison of European and North American response patterns in mail surveys. *Journal of the Market Research Society, 27,* 55–63.

Neergaard, L. (1999, May 16). Sex and medicine: Prescribing drugs based on gender. *Mobile Register,* pp. 6A–7A.

Newburger, C. (2001). Home computers and Internet use in the United States: August 2000. *Current Population Reports* [Online], U.S. Census Bureau, U.S. Department of Commerce. Retrieved November 23, 2002, from www.census.gov/prod/2001pubs/p23-207.pdf

Nezu, A. M. (1986). Efficacy of a social problem-solving therapy approach for unipolar depression. *Journal of Consulting and Clinical Psychology, 54,* 196–202.

Nicks, S. D., Korn, J. H., & Mainieri, T. (1997). The rise and fall of deception in social psychology and personality research, 1921–1994. *Ethics & Behavior, 7,* 69–77.

Nosek, B. A. & Banaji, M. R. (2002). E-research: Ethics, security, design, and control in psychological research on the Internet. *Journal of Social Issues, 58,* 161–176.

Oakes, W. (1972). External validity and the use of real people as subjects. *American Psychologist, 27,* 959–962.

Oaks, M. (1986). *Statistical inference: A commentary for the social and behavioral sciences.* New York: Wiley.

Office for Protection from Research Risks, Protection of Human Subjects, National Commission for the Protection of Human Subjects of Biomedical and Behavioral Research. (1979). *The Belmont Report: Ethical principles and guidelines for the protection of human subjects of research* (GPO 887-809). Washington, DC: U.S. Government Printing Office.

Office for Protection from Research Risks. (2001, December 13). Protection of Human Subjects: Title 45, Code of federal regulations 45 (Part 46). Washington, DC: U.S. Government Printing Office.

Oliver, R. L., & Berger, P. K. (1980). Advisability of pretest designs in psychological research. *Perceptual and Motor Skills, 51,* 463–471.

Orlebeke, J. F., Knol, D. L., & Verhulst, F. C. (1999). Child behavior problems increased by maternal smoking during pregnancy. *Archives of Environmental Health, 54,* 15–19.

Orne, M. T. (1962). On the social psychology of the psychological experiment: With particular reference to demand characteristics and their implications. *American Psychologist, 17,* 776–783.

Orne, M. T. (1973). Communication by the total experimental situations: Why it is important, how is it evaluated, and its significance for the ecological validity of findings. In P. Pliner, L. Kramer, & T. Alloway (Eds.), *Communication and affect.* New York: Academic Press.

Ortmann, A., & Hertwig, R. (1997). Is deception acceptable? *American Psychologist, 52,* 746–747.

Ossip-Klein, D. J., Epstein, L. H., Winter, M. K., Stiller, R., Russell, P., & Dickson, B. (1983). Does switching to low tar/nicotine/carbon monoxide–yield cigarettes decrease alveolar carbon monoxide measures? A randomized trial. *Journal of Consulting and Clinical Psychology, 51,* 234–241.

OSTP (2005). *Federal Policy on Research Misconduct.* Retrieved September 2005 from www.ostp .gov/html/ 001207_3.html

Page, S., & Yates, E. (1973). Attitudes of psychologists toward experimenter controls in research. *The Canadian Psychologist, 14,* 202–207.

Pappworth, M. H. (1967). *Human guinea pigs: Experimentation on man.* Boston: Beacon Press.

Pardes, H., West, A., & Pincus, H. A. (1991). Physicians and the animal-rights movement. *The New England Journal of Medicine, 324,* 1640–1643.

Pasternak, D., & Cary, P. (1995, Sept. 18). Tales from the crypt: Medical horror stories from a trove of secret cold-war documents. *U.S. News & World Report,* pp. 70, 77.

Patton, M. Q. (1990). *Qualitative evaluation and research methods.* Thousand Oaks, CA: Sage.

Paul, G. L. (1969). Behavior modification research: Design and tactics. In C. M. Franks (Ed.), *Behavior therapy appraisal and status.* New York: McGraw-Hill.

Pavlov, I. P. (1928). *Lecture on conditioned reflexes.* Translated by W. H. Gantt. New York: International.

Payne, J. W. (1994). Thinking aloud: Insights into information processing. *Psychological Science, 5,* 245–248.

Pfungst, O. (1965). *Clever Hans (the horse of Mr. Von Osten): A contribution to experimental, animal, and human psychology.* Translated by C. L. Rahn. New York: Holt, Rinehart and Winston. (Originally published 1911)

Picou, J. S. (1996). Compelled disclosure of scholarly research: Some comments on high stakes litigation. *Law and Contemporary Problems, 59,* 149–157.

Pihl, R. D., Zacchia, C., & Zeichner, A. (1981). Follow-up analysis of the use of deception and aversive contingencies in psychological experiments. *Psychological Reports, 48,* 927–930.

Plutchik, R. (1974). *Foundations of experimental research.* New York: Harper.

Polanyi, M. (1963). The potential theory of absorption. *Science, 141,* 1010–1013.

Polyson, J., Levinson, M., & Miller, H. (1982). Writing styles: A survey of psychology journal editors. *American Psychologist, 37,* 335–338.

Popper, K. R. (1968). *The logic of scientific discovery.* London: Hutchinson and Co.

Posner, M. I., & Raichle, M. E. (1994). *Images of the mind.* New York: W. H. Freeman & Co.

Potera, C. (1998). Trapped in the web. *Psychology Today, 31,* 66–72.

Povinelli, D. J., & Bering, J. M. (2002). The mentality of apes revisited. *Current Directions in Psychological Science, 11,* 115–119.

Pribram, K. H. (1971). *Languages of the brain: Experimental paradoxes and principles in neuropsychology.* Englewood Cliffs, NJ: Prentice-Hall.

Proctor, R. W., & Capaldi, E. J. (2001). Improving the science education of psychology students: Better teaching of methodology. *Teaching of Psychology, 28,* 173–181.

Provine, R. R. (2005). Yawning. *American Scientist, 93,* 532–539.

Quattrochi-Tubin, S., & Jason, L. A. (1980). Enhancing social interactions and activity among the elderly through stimulus control. *Journal of Applied Behavior Analysis, 13,* 159–163.

Regan, P. C., & Llamas, V. (2002). Customer service as a function of shopper's attire. *Psychological Reports, 90,* 203–204.

Regan, T. (1983). *The case for animal rights.* Berkeley: University of California.

Reips, U. (2000). The Web experiment method: Advantages, disadvantages, and solutions. In M. H. Birnbaum (Ed.). *Psychology experiments on the Internet.* New York: Academic Press.

Resnick, J. H., & Schwartz, T. (1973). Ethical standards as an independent variable in psychological research. *American Psychologicst, 28,* 134–139.

Rich, C. L. (1977). Is random digit dialing really necessary? *Journal of Marketing Research, 14,* 300–305.

Richard, D. (1999). The literature review: A resource for beginning researchrs. *APS Observer, 12,* 28.

Richter, C. P. (1959). Rats, man, and the welfare state. *American Psychologist, 14,* 18–28.

Riemen, D. J. (1986). The essential structure of a caring interaction: Doing phenomenology. In P. M. Munhall & C. J. Oiler (Eds.), *Nursing research: A qualitative perspective.* Norwalk, CT: Appleton Century Crofts.

Rind, B., & Bordia, P. (1996). Effect on restaurant tipping of male and female servers drawing a happy, smiling face on the backs of customers' checks. *Journal of Applied Social Psychology, 26,* 218–225.

Ring, K., Wallston, K., & Corey, M. (1970). Mode of debriefing as a factor affecting reaction to a Milgram-type obedience experiment: An ethical inquiry. *Representative Research in Social Psychology, 1,* 67–88.

Risley, T. R., & Wolf, M. M. (1972). Strategies for analyzing behavioral change over time. In J. R. Nesselroade & H. W. Reese (Eds.), *Life-span developmental psychology: Methodological issues*. New York: Academic Press.

Ritchie, E., & Phares, E. J. (1969). Attitude change as a function of internal-external control and communicator status. *Journal of Personality, 37,* 429–443.

Roberson, M. T., & Sundstrom, E. (1990). Questionnaire design, return rates, and response favorableness in an employee attitude questionnaire. *Journal of Applied Psychology, 75,* 354–357.

Roccatagliata, G. (1986). *A history of ancient psychiatry.* Westport, CT: Greenwood Press.

Rogers, T. F. (1976). Interviews by telephone and in person: Quality of responses and field performance. *Public Opinion Quarterly, 40,* 51–65.

Rosenberg, M. J. (1969). The conditions and consequences of evaluation apprehension. In R. Rosenthal and R. L. Rosnow (Eds.), *Artifact in behavioral research.* New York: Academic Press.

Rosenberg, M. J. (1980). Experimenter expectancy, evaluation apprehension, and the diffusion of methodological angst. *The Behavioral and Brain Sciences, 3,* 472–474.

Rosenthal, R. (1966). *Experimenter effects in behavioral research.* New York: Appleton-Century-Crofts.

Rosenthal, R. (1969). Interpersonal expectations: Effects of the experimenter's hypothesis. In R. Rosenthal and R. L. Rosnow (Eds.), *Artifact in behavioral research.* New York: Academic Press.

Rosenthal, R. (1976). *Experimenter effects in behavioral research* (2nd ed.). New York: Irvington.

Rosenthal, R. (1978). How often are our numbers wrong? *American Psychologist, 33,* 1005–1007.

Rosenthal, R. (1980). Replicability and experimenter influence: Experimenter effects in behavioral research. *Parapsychology Review, 11,* 5–11.

Rosenthal, R., & Fode, K. L. (1963). The effect of experimenter bias on the performance of the albino rat. *Behavioral Science, 8,* 183–189.

Rosenthal, R., Persinger, G. W., Vikan-Kline, L., & Mulry, R. C. (1963). The role of the research assistant in the mediation of experimenter bias. *Journal of Personality, 31,* 313–335.

Rosenthal, R., & Rosnow, R. L. (1975). *The volunteer subject.* New York: Wiley.

Rosenthal, R., & Rubin, D. B. (1978). Interpersonal

expectancy effects: The first 345 studies. *The Behavioral and Brain Sciences, 3,* 377–415.

Rosnow, R. L. (1997). Hedgehogs, foxes and the evolving social contract in science: Ethical challenges and methodological opportunities. *Psychological Methods, 3,* 345–356.

Rosnow, R. L., & Rosenthal, R. (1998). *Beginning behavioral research.* Upper Saddle River, NJ: Prentice-Hall, Inc.

Rosnow, R. L., & Rosnow, M. (1992). *Writing papers in psychology* (2nd ed.). New York: Wiley.

Rotton, J., & Kelly, I. W. (1985). Much ado about the full moon: A meta-analysis of lunar–lunacy research. *Psychological Bulletin, 97,* 286–306.

Rugg, E. A. (1975). *Ethical judgments of social research involving experimental deception.* Unpublished doctoral dissertation, George Peabody College for Teachers, Nashville, TN.

Russ, N. W., & Geller, E. S. (1987). Training bar personnel to prevent drunken driving: A field evaluation. *American Journal of Public Health, 77,* 952–954.

Ryan, J. P., & Isaacson, R. L. (1983). Intraaccumbens injections of ACTH induce excessive grooming in rats. *Physiological Psychology, 11,* 54–58.

Saigh, P. A. (1986). In vitro flooding in the treatment of a 6-year-old boy's posttraumatic stress disorder. *Behaviour Research and Therapy, 24,* 685–688.

Sales, B. D., & Folkman, S. (2000). *Ethics in research with human participants.* Washington, DC: American Psychological Association.

Sanders, G. S., & Simmons, W. L. (1983). Use of hypnosis to enhance eyewitness accuracy: Does it work? *Journal of Applied Psychology, 68,* 70–77.

Saxe, L. (1991). Thoughts of an applied social psychologist. *American Psychologist, 46,* 409–415.

Schachter, S., & Singer, J. E. (1962). Cognitive, social and physiological determinants of emotional state. *Psychological Review, 69,* 379–399.

Schenk, S., Lacelle, G., Gorman, K., & Amit, Z. (1987). Cocaine self-administration in rats influenced by environmental conditions: Implications for the etiology of drug abuse. *Neuroscience Letters, 81,* 227–231.

Schoenthaler, S. J. (1983). The Los Angeles probation department diet–behavior program: An empirical analysis of six institutional settings. *International Journal of Biosocial Research, 5,* 88–98.

Scholtz, J. A. (1973). Defense styles in suicide attempters. *Journal of Consulting and Clinical Psychology, 41,* 70–73.

Schouten, J. W., & McAlexander, J. H. (1995). Subcultures of consumption: An ethnography of the new bikers. *Journal of Consumer Research, 22,* 43–61.

Sears, R. R., Whiting, J. W. M., Nowlis, V., & Sears, P. S. (1953). Some child-rearing antecedents of aggression and dependence in young children. *Genetic Psychology Monographs, 47,* 135–234.

Seeman, J. (1969). Deception in psychological research. *American Psychologist, 24,* 1025–1028.

Seligman, M. E. P. (2002). *Authentic happiness: Using the new positive psychology to realize your potential for lasting fulfillment.* New York: Free Press.

Selltiz, C., Jahoda, M., Deutsch, M., & Cook, S. W. (1959). *Research methods in social relations.* New York: Holt.

Severson, H. H., and Ary, D. V. (1983). Sampling bias due to consent procedures with adolescents. *Addictive Behaviors, 8,* 433–437.

Shadish, W. R., Cook, T. D., & Campbell, D. T. (2002). *Experimental and quasi-experimental designs for generalized causal inference.* New York: Houghton Mifflin.

Shadish, W. R., & Reis, J. (1984). A review of studies of the effectiveness of programs to improve pregnancy outcome. *Evaluation Review, 8,* 747–776.

Shannon, D. M., Johnson, T. E., Searcy, S., and Lott, A. (2002). Using electronic surveys: Advice from survey professionals. *Practical Assessment, Research and Evaluation, 8* [Online]. Retrieved September 10, 2002, from http://ericae.net/pare/getvn.asp?v=8&n=1

Shapiro, F. (1995). *Eye movement desensitization and reprocessing: Basic principles, protocols, and procedures.* New York: Guilford Press.

Sharpe, D., Adair, J. G., & Roese, N. J. (1992). Twenty years of deception research: A decline in subjects' trust? *Personality and Social Psychology Bulletin, 18,* 585–590.

Shermer, M. (1999). *USA Today* survey shows belief in weird things is on the rise. *Skeptics, 6*(2), 18.

Shi, R., & Werker, J. F. (2001) Six-month-old infants' preference for lexical words. *Psychological Science, 12,* 70–75.

Shuell, T. J. (1981). Distribution of practice and retroactive inhibition in free-recall learning. *Psychological Record, 31,* 589–598.

Sidman, M. (1960). *Tactics of scientific research.* New York: Basic Books.

Sidowski, J. B., & Lockard, R. B. (1966). Some preliminary considerations in research. In J. B. Sidowski (Ed.), *Experimental methods and instrumentation in psychology.* New York: McGraw-Hill.

Sieber, J. E. (1982). Deception in social research: I. Kinds of deception and the wrongs they may involve. *IRB: A Review of Human Subjects Research, 4*(9), 1–5.

Sieber, J. E. (1983). Deception in social research: III. The nature and limits of debriefing. *IRB: A Review of Human Subjects Research, 5*(3), 1–4.

Sieber, J. E., Iannuzzo, R., & Rodriguez, B. (1995). Deception methods in psychology: Have they changed in 23 years? *Ethics and Behavior, 5,* 67–85.

Sieber, J. E., & Stanley, B. (1988). Ethical and professional dimensions of socially sensitive research. *American Psychologist, 43,* 49–55.

Sigall, H., Aronson, E., & Van Hoose, T. (1970). The cooperative subject: Myth or reality. *Journal of Experimental Social Psychology, 6,* 1–10.

Silverman, D. (1993). *Interpreting qualitative data: Methods for analyzing talk, text, and interaction.* Thousand Oaks, CA: Sage.

Silverman, I. (1974). The experimenter: A (still) neglected stimulus object. *The Canadian Psychologist, 15,* 258–270.

Singer, P. (1975). *Animal liberation.* New York: Avon.

Skinner, B. F. (1953). *Science and human behavior.* New York: Macmillan.

Skinner, B. F. (1956). A case history in scientific method. *American Psychologist, 11,* 221–223.

Smith, R. E. (1969). The other side of the coin. *Contemporary Psychology, 14,* 628–630.

Smith, S. S., & Richardson, D. (1983). Amelioration of deception and harm in psychological research: The important role of debriefing. *Journal of Personality and Social Psychology, 44,* 1075–1082.

Smith, T. E., Sells, S. P., & Clevenger, T. (1994). Ethnographic content analysis of couple and therapist perceptions in a reflecting team setting. *Journal of Marital and Family Therapy, 20,* 267–286.

Smucker, B., S., Earleywine, M., & Gordis, E. B. (2005). Alcohol consumption moderates the link between cannabis use and cannabis dependence in an Internet survey. *Psychology of Addictive Behaviors, 19,* 212–216.

Snedecor, G. W., & Cochran, W. G. (1989). *Statistical methods*. Ames, Iowa: Iowa State University Press.

Society for Research in Child Development. (2003). *Ethical standards for research with children* [Online]. Retrieved March 12, 2003, from http://www.sred.org/about.html#standards

Soliday, E., & Stanton, A. L. (1995). Deceived versus non-deceived participants' perceptions of scientific and applied psychology. *Ethics & Behavior, 5*, 87–104.

Solomon, D. J. (2001). Conducting Web-based surveys. *Practical Assessment, Research and Evaluation, 7*(19) [Online]. Retrieved September 10, 2002, from http://ericae.net/pare/getvn .asp?v=7&n=19

Solomon, R. (1949). An extension of control group design. *Psychological Bulletin, 44*, 137–150.

Southwick, R. (2000, Oct. 27). Animal-rights groups gain ground with subtler approaches, worrying researchers. *The Chronicle of Higher Education*, pp. A31–A32.

Southwick, R. (2002, June 28). Researchers face more federal scrutiny on animal experimentation. *The Chronicle of Higher Education*, pp. A23–A24.

Spring, B., Chiodo, J., Harden, M., Bourgeois, M. J., & Lutherer, L. (1989). Psychobiological effects of carbohydrates. *Journal of Clinical Psychiatry, 50* (Suppl.), 27–33.

Stake, R. E. (1995). *The art of case study research*. Thousand Oaks, CA: Sage.

Steele, C. M., & Southwick, L. (1985). Alcohol and social behavior: I. The psychology of drunken excess. *Journal of Personality and Social Psychology, 48*, 18–34.

Steinberg, J. A. (2002). Misconduct of others: Prevention techniques for researchers. *Observer, 15*, 11, 40.

Stevens, S. S. (1939). Psychology and the science of science. *Psychological Bulletin, 36*, 221–263.

Stratton, G. M. (1897). Vision without inversion of the retinal image. *Psychological Review, 4*, 341–360, 463–481.

Strunk, W., Jr., & White, E. B. (1979). *The elements of style* (3rd ed.). New York: Macmillan.

Suddendorf, T., & Whiten, A. (2001). Mental evolution and development: Evidence for secondary representation in children, great apes and other animals. *Psychological Bulletin, 127*, 629–650.

Sudman, S., & Bradburn, N. M. (1982). *Asking questions: A practical guide to questionnaire design*. San Francisco: Jossey Bass.

Sulik, K. K., Johnston, M. C., & Webb, M. A. (1981). Fetal alcohol syndrome: Embryogenesis in a mouse model. *Science, 214*, 936–938.

Sullivan, D. (2004). Major search engines and directories. Retrieved September 2005 from http://searchenginewatch.com/links/article.php/2156221

Sutcliffe, J. P. (1972). On the role of "instructions to the subject" in psychological experiments. *American Psychologist, 27*, 755–758.

Swann, W. B., Jr., Wenzlaff, R. M., Krull, D. S., & Pelham, B. W. (1992). Allure of negative feedback: Self-verification strivings among depressed persons. *Journal of Abnormal Psychology, 101*, 293–306.

Taffel, C. (1955). Anxiety and the conditioning of verbal behavior. *Journal of Abnormal and Social Psychology, 51*, 496–501.

Tedeschi, J. T., Schlenker, B. R., & Bonoma, T. V. (1971). Cognitive dissonance: Private ratiocination or public spectacle. *American Psychologist, 26*, 685–695.

Terror at rush hour. (2005, July 18). *Newsweek*, p. 29–36.

Tesch, F. E. (1977). Debriefing research participants: Though this be method there is madness to it. *Journal of Personality and Social Psychology, 35*, 217–224.

Thayer, H. S. (Ed.). (1953). *Newton's philosophy of nature: Selections from his writings*. New York: Hafner.

Thorne, S. B., & Himelstein, P. (1984). The role of suggestion in the perception of satanic messages in rock-and-roll recordings. *Journal of Psychology, 116*, 245–248.

Tinbergen, E. A., & Tinbergen, N. (1972). *Early childhood autism: An ethological approach*. Berlin: Paul Parey.

Tryon, W. W. (1982). A simplified time-series analysis for evaluating treatment interventions. *Journal of Applied Behavior Analysis, 15*, 423–429.

Tunnell, G. B. (1977). Three dimensions of naturalness: An expanded definition of field research. *Psychological Bulletin, 84*, 426–437.

Turner, L. H., & Solomon, R. L. (1962). Human traumatic avoidance learning: Theory and experiments on the operant–respondent distinction of failures to learn. *Psychological Monographs, 76*(Whole No. 559), 1–32.

Underwood, B. J. (1959). Verbal learning in the educative process. *Harvard Educational Review, 29*, 107–117.

Unger, R., & Crawford, M. (1992). *Women and gender*. New York: McGraw-Hill.

U.S. Department of Agriculture. (1989, August 21). Animal welfare: Final rules. *Federal register.*

U.S. Department of Agriculture. (1990, July 16). Animal welfare: Guinea pigs, hamsters and rabbits. *Federal Register.*

U.S. Department of Agriculture. (1991, February 15). Animal welfare: Standards; final rule. *Federal Register.*

Velten, E., Jr. (1968). A laboratory task for induction of mood states. *Behavioral Research & Theory, 6,* 473–482.

Vernon, H. M., Bedford, T., & Wyatt, S. (1924). *Two studies of rest pauses in industry* (Medical Research Council, Industrial Fatigue Research Board Report No. 25.) London: His Majesty's Stationery Office.

Veroff, J., Douvan, E., & Kulka, R. A. (1981). *The inner American.* New York: Basic Books.

Vokey, J. R., & Read, D. (1985). Subliminal messages: Between the devil and the media. *American Psychologist, 40,* 1231–1239.

Wade, E. A., & Blier, M. J. (1974). Learning and retention of verbal lists: Serial anticipation and serial discrimination. *Journal of Experimental Psychology, 103,* 732–739.

Wagner, R. K., Torgesen, J. K., Laughon, P., Simmons, K., & Rashotte, C. A. (1993). Development of young readers' phonological processing abilities. *Journal of Educational Psychology, 85,* 83–103.

Walker, D. (2005, September 14). PETA halts campaign after complaints of racism. *Mobile Register,* p. 7B.

Walker, H. M., & Buckley, N. K. (1968). The use of positive reinforcement in conditioning attending behavior. *Journal of Applied Behavior Analysis, 1,* 245–250.

Walster, E. (1964). The temporal sequence of post-decision processes. In L. Festinger (Ed.), *Conflict, decision, and dissonance.* Stanford: Stanford University Press.

Webb, E. J., Campbell, D. T., Schwartz, R. D., & Sechrest, L. (1966). *Unobstructive measures: Nonreactive research in the social sciences.* Chicago: Rand McNally.

Webb, J. F., Khazen R. S., Hanley, W. B., Partington, M. S., Percy, W. J. L., & Rathbun, J. C. (1973). PKU screening: Is it worth it? *Canadian Medical Association Journal, 108,* 328–329.

Whewell, W. (1967). *The philosophy of the inductive sciences* (Vol. 2). New York: Johnson Reprint. (Original work published 1847).

White, P. A. (1990). Ideas about causation in philosophy and psychology. *Psychological Bulletin, 108,* 3–18.

Williams, R. J. (1959). *Alcoholism: The nutritional approach.* Austin: University of Texas Press.

Wilson, T. D. (1994). The proper protocol: Validity and completeness of verbal reports. *American Psychological Society, 5,* 249–252.

Wilson, V. L. (1981). Time and the external validity of experiments. *Evaluation and Program Planning, 4,* 229–238.

Winerman, L. (2005). A congressional attack on peer-reviewed behavioral research. *Monitor on Psychology, 36,* 22–23.

Woods, S. P., Rippeth, J. D., Frol, A. B., Levy, J. K., Ryan, E., Soukup, V. M., et al. (2004). Interrater reliability of clinical ratings and neurocognitive diagnosis in HIV. *Journal of Clinical and Experimental Neuropsychology, 26,* 759–778.

Woodworth, R. S., & Sheehan, M. R. (1964). *Contemporary schools of psychology* (3rd ed.). New York: Ronald Press.

Wundt, W. (1902). *Outlines of psychology* (Trans., 2nd ed.). Oxford: Engelmann.

Wyer, R. S., Jr., Dion, K. L., & Ellsworth, P. C. (1978). An editorial. *Journal of Experimental Social Psychology, 14,* 141–147.

Young, K. S. (1996). Psychology of computer use: XL. Addictive use of the Internet: A case that breaks the stereotype. *Psychological Reports, 79,* 899–902.

Zaidel, D., & Sperry, R. W. (1974). Memory impairment after commissurotomy in man. *Brain, 97,* 263–272.

Zimney, G. H. (1961). *Method in experimental psychology.* New York: Ronald Press.

Index

AAALAC (American Association for the Accreditation of Laboratory Animal Care), 385
ABAB design, 361, 363
ABA design
  examples of, 358–61
  problems with, 361–2
  reversal design, 362–3
  withdrawal, 362–3
ABBA technique, 279–81
abbreviations, in research report, 483
absenteeism rates, for work groups, 342–3
abstract, in research report, 450
acceptance, of manuscript for publication, 489, 490
accuracy, of web page, 114
ACTH, excessive grooming in rats and, 186–7
active consent, 153
active deception, 155
additive and interactive effects, 224–5
ad hoc hypotheses, 16
age, of participants, 482
age-cohort effect, 46–7
aggression, 193
AIDS research, 129
ALDF (Animal Legal Defense Fund), 168–9
ALF (Animal Liberation Front), 168–9
American Association for the Accreditation of Laboratory Animal Care (AAALAC), 385
American Psychological Association (APA)
  ethical standards for research, 145–8
    animal studies and, 172
    code of ethics, 145, 151–2, 163
    ethical guidelines, development of, 140–1
  as information source, 116
  journals of, 445, 446–7
  PsycINFO, 106

Publication Manual, 479
  research report format (*See* research report, APA format)
American Psychological Society, 116
  journals of, 446–7
  web site, 387
analysis, in ethnography, 65
analysis of variance (ANOVA)
  definition of, 419
  one-way, 419–24
  results, interpretation of, 425–6
  summary table, 424–5
  two-way, 426–31
anarchists theory of science, 13
androgens, 232
anecdotal evidence, in science *vs.* pseudoscience, 17–18
Animal Legal Defense Fund (ALDF), 168–9
Animal Liberation Front (ALF), 168–9
animal research
  acquisition of animals for, 173
  alternative procedures, 170–1
  caring/housing of animals, 172–3
  cobalt exposure, behavioral effects of, 431–2
  educational use of animals, 174
  ethical considerations for, 127
  ethics in, 168–71
  experimental procedures for, 173–4
  field, 174
  guidelines for, 171–4
  justification of, 172
  mediation of experimenter expectancies, 246
  personnel, 172
  rats, obtaining, 385
  safeguards for, 171
animal rights, 168–70, 172
animal welfare, 171–2
Animal Welfare Act, 170
Annual Review of Psychology, 105
anomia, 354

anonymity, 162–3
ANOVA. *See* analysis of variance
antidepressant medications, placebo effect, 52
APA. *See* American Psychological Association
apparatus
  for data collection, 390–2
  in research report method section, 456
artificiality, of experimental approach, 85–6
assent, 152
assessment
  of construct validity, 234–5
  of reliability, 213–15
assuming causation, fallacy of, 43
astrology, belief in, 15
Attention deficit hyperactivity disorder, 262
attitude formation, 5–6
attrition, 223–4
attrition bias, in nonequivalent comparison group design, 335
author, of research report, 166
  identification note, 475
  institutional affiliation, 449
authority
  knowledge acquisition and, 7
  prejudice and, 19
  web page, 114
autistic children, naturalistic observational study of, 49
autocastration, 67
automation, 291
autonomy, 141–2

BAAB sequences, 281
baseline
  definition of, 359
  for single-case designs, 373–4
Beck Depression Inventory, 208–9, 435, 436